RECKONING

RECKONING

The Ends of War in Guatemala

DIANE M. NELSON

DUKE UNIVERSITY PRESS *Durham & London 2009*

© 2009 Duke University Press
All rights reserved
Printed in the United States of America
on acid-free paper ∞

Designed by Jennifer Hill
Typeset in Chaparral Pro by Tseng Information Systems, Inc.

Library of Congress Cataloging-in-Publication Data
appear on the last printed page of this book.

To Marcie and Sonya
For honoring the past and inspiring the future

dupe *n.* [OFr. *duppe* <L., *upupa*, hoopoe, stupid bird] a person easily tricked or fooled.

reckoning *vt* [OE *recenian* akin to count< IE. base *reg-*, to direct, whence RIGHT L. *regere*, to rule]
1. the act of one who reckons (to count, figure up);
2. a measuring of possibilities for the future;
3. *a)* a bill, account; *b)* the settlement of rewards or penalties for any action.

To speak when everyone else is silent, to see when everyone else keeps their eyes covered, to listen when everyone else prefers to hide in the swelling multitudes whose shouts drown out the cries of the victims; this is the greatest challenge to those of us, women and men, living in difficult times. Myrna confronted these challenges with her work, she saw and listened and decided to speak. She was the voice of those without voice in a moment when you paid with your life for being intelligent and daring to speak . . . she gave her life in the hopes of economic, political, and social changes in our country. She bet on the future. Rigoberta Menchú Tum

What happens in critique to fascination, where danger and promise are imbricated? . . . If enlightenment is not just one thing—if in some cases knowledge itself can be deployed for deception—then perhaps we need to construct the possibility that "deception," too, is not one thing and that there might even be special cases where we can know and act only through the detour of the "false" or the meretricious. Ackbar Abbas

I beg you, learn to see "bad" films; they are sometimes sublime. Ado Kyrou

CHEAT SHEET ON ASSUMPTIONS

"What happens when you assume? You make an ass out of you and me"

Assumption One that which is taken for granted, the unconscious, unexamined prerequisite for those identities that appear self-evident, default mode

Assumption Two false pretenses, an assumed identity is one that is not true, taken on for nefarious purposes. Its exposé brings the glee of truth telling, of being the non-duped

Assumption Three to take on an identity, to become, as in the ecstatic Virgin Mary's assumption to heaven, ensconced in her true, eternal identity. Judith Butler says, "Subjection is . . . a power *assumed by* the subject, an assumption that constitutes the instrument of that subject's becoming"

❖ Contents ❖

LITTLE DID I KNOW

What happens when you assume? You make an ass
out of u and me. Old saw

In the battle between good and evil we are winning.
Button bought at a gas station outside Camp Lejeune
U.S. Marine Corps base, North Carolina, May 2003

Guatemala is our big success story!
Attaché to the U.S. Embassy in Caracas, Venezuela

To treat Arendt's statement . . . that revolutionaries
. . . "were fooled by history, and they have become the
fools of history" . . . as an axiom of the new world order
. . . is to willfully confuse the triumph of the forces that
militated against Third World revolution with the idea
that this triumph was just or inevitable. At the limit,
it is to argue that anyone who believed in or fought for
a revolutionary utopia is morally responsible for the
often dystopian result of the failure of this project: the
Revolutionary here is not just a fool, but a criminal,
whose own undoing was his crime. Carlota McAllister

KNOWING AND BEING BETWEEN POSTWAR GUATEMALA AND AT-WAR UNITED STATES

This is a book about reckoning: how it is troubled by suspicions of duping
and foolishness, and how it is saturated by loss and hope. People make war
to achieve certain ends, aka what is desired or hoped for, and when war ends,
when it is over, they continue to struggle, if by other means. Through these
experiences they assume different identifications. In other words, if people
make war, war also makes people. Such assumed identities — which can look
two-faced or false — destabilize assumptions, what we think we know. Perhaps this is why many Guatemalans talk about *engaño* (duplicity) and *babosadas* (foolish things) to describe their experience of civil war and its end/s.

In December 1996 the Guatemalan government and the guerrillas of the Guatemalan National Revolutionary Unity (URNG) signed a peace treaty ending a war that began in 1962. In 2005 the UN peacekeeping force, MINUGUA, pulled out, ending the peace-processing period. "Now we're just another third world country," said a Guatemalan friend of mine. This book is about the in-between, about an end (the postwar) that is not quite a beginning (of peace) and about the essential but highly fraught process of reckoning. Reckoning can mean to count, figure up; to measure possibilities for the future; and to settle rewards or penalties for any action. It promises clarity, an accounting or balancing out. However, the specific ways in which the Guatemalan war was carried out, through the counterinsurgency's targeting of hearts and minds, the embodiment of horror, and multiple forms of *forcivoluntaria* collaboration in the violence, destabilize this promise. While these special effects of war are particularly acute in Guatemala, I hope that exploring this case will shed light on more general experiences of the insecurity of knowing the assumptions of identity.

Working in Guatemala in the postwar period, I've found many people questioning their assumptions, what they thought they knew. This leads many to question who they were and are. They are pondering what to make of the individual and collective experiences of consciousness raising, of organizing, and of opting for or against projects—like land reform and transforming a government rooted in ethnic and class exclusion—that seemed to promise liberation from exploitation, immiseration, racism, and injustice. For many this was the end, or goal, of their activism. But they are also reckoning with the devastation caused by the military state's scorched-earth counterinsurgency campaigns that killed and wounded hundreds of thousands and swept up millions of people as victims *and* as perpetrators. Depending on one's perspective, this violence ended either the threat of or hopes for radical change. To measure possibilities for the future people ask: What was it all about? what kind of person was I? am I? What kinds of people surround me? Is resistance futile? What exactly do we resist? Of course, Guatemalans are not the only ones to ask such questions.

In Guatemala, in nonviolent social movements and in armed combat, both with and against the state, people experienced intense sociality, their lives placed in the hands of others. In many cases this trust was well placed. In others, people strove to be trustworthy but were acted on—sometimes by an interest in reward or improvement, at other times by threats and violence, or by even less tangible forces that now lead them to speak of possession and exorcism. Some couldn't help themselves when they *delataron*, turned someone in, or inflicted harm themselves. But others wholeheartedly meted out death, sometimes because they thought they were defending their own and others' lives. A clear divide between armed combatants and civilian casualties, between one's own beliefs and army or neoliberal propaganda, between the State and the Population, especially as close to a million men became active state agents through the Civil Patrols, became blurred and shape shifted. Very few Guatemalans escaped some sort of collaboration in the violence and its aftermath. Responsibility becomes difficult to assume.

Time passes. War has ended. Even the postwar draws to a close. There's a new generation. For some, the balance sheet has been drawn up, the winners and losers declared. The book should be closed. Yet the simultaneous personal and political struggle remains. And that is where this book opens. How do you trust others, yourself, what you know (or thought you did) for sure? How do you work on new and shifting terrain? How do you reckon in order to act? Are there shared values among humans? Or is there an essential divide among kinds (*genos*) of people—indigenous, nonindigenous, oligarch, peasant, intellectual, man, woman? Are they (we) always duping and duped—corrupt, co-opted, deceitful, bought, and sold? Is there hope for a more just future, for some improvement in the lot of the struggling majorities? Or is to hope simply to *meterse en babosadas*, to get involved in foolish things? These suspicions are simultaneously everyday, enmeshed in the smallest calculations of lived sociality, and horrifyingly existential, constantly threatening to engulf one in the dark night of the soul.

And not only in Guatemala do discourses of *engaño*, *babosadas*, and *manipulación* (duping, foolishness, manipulation) circulate as commonsense assumptions about how the world works. In El Salvador (Binford 1999, Zilberg 2007), Peru (de Gregori 1989, Yezer 2007), Argentina (Gordillo 2004, Valenzuela 1983), Colombia (Taussig 1992), postsocialist Europe (Borneman 1997), Cambodia (Hinton 2002, 2005), Rwanda (Mamdani 2001), South Africa (Comaroff and Comaroff 1999), the United States (Jackson 2005, Kick 2001, Rajiva 2005, Ricks 2006), and elsewhere, duplicity—the sense that the world available to our senses hides another face behind it—is a site of intense affective and hermeneutic investment in the aftermaths and ongoing experiences of war and violence. Simultaneously, notions of reckoning, transparency, accountability, and audit circulate with the promise of fixing singular identifications, like victim or perpetrator. But uncertainty about assumptions in the epistemic sense—what you can take for granted that you know—is lashed to nervousness about assumed identities—what you can take for granted about who you or others are.

In the highland Guatemalan town of Joyabaj, Quiché, a former civil patroller remembers the training he received from the army "as a campaign of penetration . . . until it was engraved in our heads . . . 'a guerilla seen is a guerilla dead' and 'for the guerrilla neither bread nor tortilla'" (Remijnse 2002:128). In nearby San Bartolomé Jocotenango patrollers were drilled with phrases like "A los que se metieron en babosadas los engañaron [those who got involved in foolishness were duped]; those who were organized brought the problems; they are the pure thieves" (González 2002:432). In 2005 Dr. Héctor Nuilá, a former guerrilla and secretary general of the URNG political party, said, "We are really seeing the effects of the army's slogan 'muera la inteligencia!' [death to thinking!].[1] They killed anyone who thought, our best minds. People ask why Guatemala has no Nelson Mandela, and I have to remind them that there were no political prisoners here. They killed everyone, and now it's almost the reverse of Descartes: I don't think, therefore I am." "Is it normal?" asks an anguished urban activist. "Is it normal for people to turn on each other? People who know you, who you've worked with for years, to suddenly accuse you of corruption? Is it normal to betray each other?"

In turn, the anthropologist might ask, *cui bono*? Who benefits from distrust? from the belief that "the Revolutionary is not just a fool, but a criminal, whose own undoing was his crime" (McAllister 2003:366)? Who benefits? A vital query, but just as vital is to question the question itself, to ask what it assumes about power—i.e., there is someone behind the scenes, pulling the strings. We'll see that addressing "two faces" often means asking more than one question.

"Subjection is . . . a power *assumed by* the subject, an assumption that constitutes the instrument of that subject's becoming," says Judith Butler (1997:10). Subjectivization through our names, sex, gender, ethnicity, nationality, or class is deep seated. These are identifications assumed in the sense of taken on, inhabited. In hindsight they may come to feel false (an assumed identity), but even if we blame them on great and powerful forces like Patriarchy, Capitalism, or History, it's hard to name individuals hiding behind the curtain and pulling our strings, benefiting from our manipulation. We assumed them our selves. Indeed, where would we be without them? But some identifications *are* the result of plans and networks, the end-goals of actual people. "Economics are the method," Margaret Thatcher said, "but the object is to change the soul" (in Harvey 2005:23). "They've had a bad cassette put in their heads. Our job is to change the cassette," a Guatemalan army colonel told me in 1985. "The Guatemalan army did enormous physical and material harm to Maya Guatemalans and their way of life, it also and equally deliberately, destroyed certain Maya capacities for political action" (McAllister 2003:370).[2] So, how do we know when our knowledge, soul, hearts, minds, and capacities for action are precisely the target of well-funded and mass-marketed counterinsurgency? These identifications are also assumed, incorporated. They come to feel perfectly real. Can we tell which is which? What is the we that might tell? Is self-possession — the etymological root of authenticity, defined as that which really is what it is represented to be — possible? A lot hangs in the balance.

These are very large questions, dazzling, even paralyzing. Trying to avoid such a fate, I approach them sideways, through the ways in which people in postwar Guatemala and the United States deploy stories (*contar* in Spanish) about *engaño*, doubleness, fooling, and duplicity. Perhaps this is similar to Walter Benjamin seeking a method to confront the phantasmagoria of the commodity spectacle which he chose to examine *through* the small, discarded object, *via* the arcade as a marginal site of amusement, *by* traversals (2001; see also Abbas 1999, Taussig 1999). How are Guatemalans reckoning with similarly huge and freakish entities like the state or the postcolonial racism condensed into the stereotype of the two-faced Indian? How are they accounting for horror, anger, guilt, disillusionment, sadness, history, memory, as well as hope and the process of assuming or taking on (*asumir*) responsibility and new identifications? I'll suggest it is through traversing the relations between knowing and being and the simultaneous transformations in both. This is a path that the form and content of this book seek to duplicate, so please don't expect a big unveiling of the Truth or that I'll get to the crux of the matter for more than a moment before moving on. That's in part because the word "crux," or the essential point, is two-faced, simultaneously meaning "a puzzling thing." And in part because there is an unstable, unreachable variable at the heart of the object of study — be it victim, perpetrator, Mayan, indigenous, nonindigenous, the war itself, or interests and the nature of power — that shape-shifts just as it seems legible.

An important moment for knowing and being in the end or closure of Guatemala's war was the accounting rendered in 1999 by the UN's Commission of Historical Clarification (CEH), which not only quantified victims and blame, finding state forces responsible for 93 percent of the violence studied, but qualified the military state's end-goal as genocide against the Mayan people. While such claims were advanced in the early 1980s and dismissed as *babosadas*, or conspiracy theories, by the state, this was a special form of knowing, of things going *with* saying. The CEH lashed together international law with the rule of UN-warranted experts with *testimonio* (the storytelling, or *contar*, of those who lived it) to make powerful knowledge. The report became a new actor in the trials of strength (Latour 1987) over the meaning of the war, and it changed what could be assumed about ethnicity, race, and class. In conjunction with many other actors and actants it continues to influence postwar assumptions of identity. While contextualized within twelve volumes of history, statistics, analysis, and quotations, the genocide ruling has given weight to particular claims about victims and perpetrators and impacted understandings of what the end of war will entail. For example, it has allowed activists to swerve around the army's self-granted amnesty, which cannot cover crimes against humanity, to bring charges in national and international courts, and it has revivified struggles for reparations, individual and collective. Some felt vindicated that the special trauma of racism was finally highlighted, while others fear it has emphasized race war when the end-goal of many who were struggling, indigenous and nonindigenous, was political economic restructuring. It is hotly contested whether people were killed because they were Maya or because they challenged the structures controlling land and labor. Given this book's interest in two faces, it will often answer questions posed as either/or with both/and.

My end-goal is not to produce horror that there may be little solidity in knowing or in subjectivity; I do argue, however, that horror is a productive experience. Instead I invoke the Virgin of the Assumption, patron of both Guatemala City and Joyabaj, the small town where I have learned so much about reckoning, to accompany us through this book. Also known as the Virgen de Tránsito, Our Lady of Contingency and Constant Transformation, in loose translation, she helps us explore how—in our specific locations and in our loci of relations—we reckon and act. This is no time for paralysis!

This time it's personal.

I was pushed to write this book on reckoning with duplicity/*engaño* by hearing the term over and over again in postwar Guatemala, and also by my own experiences of transformation via duplicity. Upon reflection I see it was incubated both in twenty-plus years of fieldwork and by a long series of discoveries that I myself had been conned, hornswoggled, and bamboozled by a whole set of assumptions—things I, as a middle-class, white, midwestern North American had taken at face value. (You might call my little *Bildüng* "Gullible's Travels.") Heteronormative monogamy; a sunny suburban sense that all was right with the world; race, and class privilege . . . as I grew up and put away childish things this standard packaging took on a different, more propagandistic look.

Perhaps my biggest discovery was finding out I was a *gringa*—a North American outside the United States (Adams 1999, Nelson 1999). This was occasioned by the U.S. invasion of Grenada while I was studying in Spain. At first I couldn't figure out why the United States would be taking over a small city in Andalusia (Granada). Confusing Grenada and Granada sounds like a stupid joke, but, pathetically, I truly and sincerely did. Living in Spain in the early years of the flamboyant filmmaker Pedro Almodóvar, where news, lectures, and opinions about U.S. policy in Latin America were powerfully articulated (especially horror at U.S. support of the anti-Sandinista *contras* in Nicaragua and of murderous regimes in El Salvador and Guatemala), was a classic consciousness-raising experience. Why, after all my years of schooling, didn't I know that in 1954 the Central Intelligence Agency (CIA) had overthrown Colonel Jacobo Arbenz, Guatemala's democratically elected president?[3] Why didn't I know that over a quarter of a million people had been killed or "disappeared"[4] since then and more than a million displaced, in a country of eight million? I'd been swallowing whole what the Jesuit Ignacio Martín-Baró, murdered in San Salvador by U.S.-trained troops, called "official lies" (1989).

As my assumptions about my national identity began to change, I realized I wasn't the girl I used to be—I was assuming, or taking on, a new identity. Acknowledging how personal the political is can be most unpleasant. Like Neo in *The Matrix*, confronting a countertruth to his existence, I shuddered and tried to turn away as my deeply held sense of self, of being on the right side in battles between good and evil, revealed an uncanny double, as I realized the face in the mirror might look very different to a Guatemalan peasant or an Iraqi national. How to reconcile these two faces? How to acknowledge power, responsibility, and guilt without assuming those are the only faces? How to avoid being duped into believing that resistance is futile,[5] and keep hope alive that economic, political, and social change is possible? And how to resist such a fluid power—one that acts through us without our knowing it? How to refuse to fix a singular enemy—because, as Donna Haraway says, one is not enough but two is too many (1991)?

And even later, when I felt I was in the know about how official stories had made me believe that U.S. foreign policy was disinterested, undertaken for the good of the world, I was still not immune from duping (little did I know!). As I became a fieldworker in Guatemala, an author, activist, teacher, and finally a professional anthropologist, I always thought I was expressing my true identity, although, granted, it wasn't the same identity as the girl who rode horses with 4H and was president of the high school Thespian Club. So it was a bit of a shock when one of my brothers put me on to *Class* (1983) by Paul Fussell, whose persnickety prose I read with glee, recognizing all manner of other people's unconscious expressions of class. The delight drained away on page 90, however, where there is a picture of *my* TV set and a precise definition of *my* intentions: "drained of some of its nastiness by Parody Display—indicating that you're not taking the TV at all seriously by using the top as a shelf for ridiculous objects like hideous statuettes, absurd souvenirs, and the like." When *I* put the grotesque ceramic hula girl (already an ironic present from my anthropologist sister) on my TV, I thought I was expressing my own creativity and refusal to be duped by the culture industry's outpost in my home. Duped again!

This book is a rumination on this unhappy feeling of finding that what seemed to be an expression of the inside may actually express something coming from the outside. Exploring assumptions of identity raises the unsettling sense that we know not what we do. Why, after all, do drug trials have to be *double* blind? As Freud suggested in his theory of screen memories, not only are there malevolent forces out there keeping me from being in the know, but I'm even fooling my self.

The very notion of duplicity suggests the possibility of and inspires the desire for singularity, unveiling the real face so two become one, or a balance, where two cancel each other out into zero. The massive death and widespread destruction of the war in Guatemala make this desire into far more than a theoretical quandary. The need to account for what happened, for those responsible to *asumir responsabilidad* for their actions, for acknowledgment and reparations is a constant undercurrent in the news and conversation—even as gang activity, political corruption, and *fútbol* make the headlines. Behind the apparent normalcy that makes the U.S. embassy claim Guatemala as a success story[6]—economic and military sanctions lifted, a succession of elected politicians taking office, some of whom were avowed revolutionaries, public protests and scathing critiques of the government filling streets and newspaper columns, growth in productivity—is another face. For many it is never-ending pain, fear, and the certainty that the horror could return again at any moment. For others it is remorse, guilt at what they've done and/or fear of retribution via the courts or supernatural entities.[7] Many also see *poderes ocultos*, hidden or occult powers, behind the civilian front of the government. While my focus is Guatemala, I would suggest that the difficulties of reckoning amidst seemingly ubiquitous duplicity and under the threat of bodily harm may be the conditions of possibility for political action and knowledge in our age. Remember that the singular word "knowledge" in English is a double entendre in Romance languages: *conocimiento* and *sabiduría* in Spanish, *connaissance* and *savoir* in French. Michel Foucault says,

> It's a question, then, of understanding once more the formation of a knowledge [*connaissance*], that is, of a relation between a determinate subject and a determinate field of objects, and of grasping it in its historical origin, in that "movement of knowledge" [*savoir*] that renders it pos-

sible. Everything that I have occupied myself with up till now essentially regards the way in which people in Western societies have had experiences that were used in the process of knowing a determinate, objective set of things while at the same time constituting themselves as subjects under fixed and determinate conditions. (1991:70)

This book explores the "ethnographic fact" that many Guatemalans use duplicity as an act of interpretation when they talk about the war—saying they were duped or that they duped others. But it also stems from when I myself sort of knowingly collaborated in duplicity. I began working in Guatemala in 1985 as a researcher on other people's projects.[8] In a way I was a prosthetic, extending the reach of people, both North American and Guatemalans in exile, who could not themselves go to Guatemala for fear of their lives. I think my naïveté was good for the job. Twenty-two years old, Caucasian, just out of college, long-haired, wearing tourist clothes, I would walk up to army bases with my traveling companion and innocently ask to speak to the commander. But both in the highlands, where people would stop talking if a child came by to stare at the gringas—for fear the kid was a spy—and in Mexico City, where Guatemalan exiles could still be disappeared, I began to learn about the bodily discipline that living clandestinely demands and the deep fog it creates around attempts to be in the know (and not only for gringas). Counterinsurgency violence and the counterstrategies developed to survive it implanted terror at very deep levels.[9] Guatemalans knew from experience that a careless word, especially one uttered near an outsider, someone who hadn't learned the techniques of secrecy in her very body, could mean death or, even worse, torture for them and others. It came home to me again how deeply assumed clandestinity was when I interviewed a former guerrilla member in 2001, five years into the postwar. We had a great conversation about election plans and other work the new URNG party was doing, but when we started talking about his past he started coughing till it got so bad we couldn't continue. He told me his body itself would not let him speak about the time he spent underground.

These silences, interrupted sentences, and cultivated secret keeping are hallmarks of the clandestine life. Is this the duplicity of the less powerful, a weapon of the weak (Scott 1987)? Do the very swerves and evasions that sidestep a suicidal direct engagement contribute to the stereo (double)-type of the subaltern as two-faced, untrustworthy? Do the reverbs of this stereotype in turn help produce the colonial ambivalence, epistemic murk, paranoia beyond reason that is greater than the sum of its parts, irreducible to a cost-benefit analysis, and that may explode into the excessive violence

"Never Again: The Mechanisms of Horror." Cover of the report of the Guatemalan Archbishop's Office of Human Rights on the Recuperation of Historical Memory, Volume 2 (REMHI). The wings of the angel are the bones of a body exhumed from a massacre site in 1997. Photograph by Daniel Hernández-Salazar. Used with kind permission.

of genocide? In a sort of dialectics of deception, does state power produce clandestinity and also reproduce itself through these fantasmatics of threat? In turn, must these effects be hidden away via the "mechanisms of horror" (REMHI 1998) of paramilitary death squads, secret detention centers, clandestine cemeteries, murdered witnesses, and "plausible deniability"?[10] And aren't the lives of those who "man" these parastatal sites similarly marked by silences, interrupted sentences, and cultivated secret keeping? In turn, what networks of accountability might magically transform the face of state impunity into one of vulnerability—as a dead body that was proof of one thing (we can kill whomever we want) morphs into evidence at a war crimes trial?

These were not questions I was grappling with in 1987, when I was both acted on and acted with these weapons of concealment, secrecy, and masquerade. As I increasingly assumed the identity of gringa-in-relation-with-Guatemala by becoming a researcher, that is, a medium through which others did their work, I was more and more positioned in-between—where I remain to this day. As a gringa, and like any anthropologist, I live, feel, and work between field site and home, between Guatemala and the United States. This book might be described as similarly suspended between two faces: the terror and fascination of conspiracy theory and the hopefulness and perhaps naïveté of optimism of the will. I tell the following story, at the risk of being dubbed an enemy combatant, because it further explains my stakes in the fraught questions of knowledge and its relation to self and to action.

Owing to the culture of secrecy engendered by the ongoing war and to my role as a relative newcomer to the Guatemala scene, I was unaware in 1986, on my second trip to Guatemala to research the army's counterinsurgency resettlement areas, that there had been an acrimonious split in the Guatemalan left and that I was working with people identified with one side of the divide. I also didn't know that because of my association with them my next research job fell through. I only knew that I'd rushed to finish a project on the Development Poles (published anonymously by CEIDEC in 1988), quit my secretarial job, and was ready to go back to Guatemala when word came that my services would no longer be required. No further explanation was forthcoming. So I cried a lot, then went back to temp jobs and solidarity work, saved my money, and landed a freelance journalism gig to return on my own. In Mexico City a Guatemalan friend cryptically told me that I might be able to repair the damage, and he'd try to set me up.

I had invested a great deal in my assumed identity as a medium — a good researcher and trustworthy ally — so I jumped at the chance to go back to Guatemala with my links to Guatemalans reestablished. The job that came through, however, was a team project consisting of two Mexican women and two gringas overseen by Guatemalan exiles to research alternative development strategies in Mexico for a consortium of European NGOs (nongovernmental agencies). I longed to be in Guatemala, but this was my assignment, and I was living and working with Guatemalans, commuting between Chiapas and Mexico City, so I could hardly complain. I was also learning lessons I would not appreciate till later about the day-to-day effects of clandestinity as, even in our shared house and in the relative security of living in exile in Mexico, its rules held firm. Four months after we began sharing our lives, I ventured to ask my two roommates in the privacy of our kitchen how they'd gotten involved. The conversation came to a sudden halt. They looked at me in shock and said, "You should know never to ask about that!" Our relationship cooled for a while afterward, and I never broached the subject again. Many accounts of wartime and postwar Guatemala stress the double silencing of government cover-up and opposition clandestinity, but I want to stress here, for readers unfamiliar with how it feels and also for those of us who have begun to relax and forget, how very difficult it was to be in the know.

In the meantime, our team grew increasingly frustrated at the lack of resources provided for the project. Only much later did we realize the bulk of them had been filtered through us to Guatemala for activities that could not be openly funded. I'm pretty sure some of the Europeans were aware that our project was a rather elaborate front. But our team was not. Did our very ignorance, our sincere belief, make the project "work"?[11] So there I was, two-faced, both duped and duper. And, just as I sincerely believed then, there's no guarantee that I'm not equally duped now. And perhaps duping you?

Another warning. This book is a sequel to earlier work on Quincentennial Guatemala (Nelson 1999) that focused on 1992 and the commemoration of the five hundred years since Columbus—although I find, to my surprise, that the past weighs more heavily now than it did then. Here I follow the torquing of identifications that emerged out of the event of 1992, with the rise of the Mayan movement and peace treaty negotiations. *Caveat Emptor.* The schlock horror film *Scream II* warns that one of the rules of horror films (like "Don't say, 'I'll be right back' 'cause you'll be dead for sure!") is that there's always a sequel, but that sequels always suck.

After writing my dissertation and getting an academic job, I returned to Guatemala in 1998 to find stories of duplicity running rampant, especially about the Maya, a term first applied to cultural rights activists but now far more generalized. Unsympathetic ladinos, aka nonindigenous,[12] *and* indigenous people (not an isomorphic category with Maya; see note 2) claimed that the Mayan activists were duping themselves with make-believe—a pathetic amalgam of new age exotica, ritual recipes culled from old anthropology texts, and a sad desire for real identity. They were deracinated urban people with no ties to the authentic indigenous of the rural highlands and therefore two-faced. However, many commentators claimed that no real "Indians" existed there either, what with the effects of five hundred years of colonialism, the ethnocide of the war, the recent massive penetration of Protestant sects,[13] and so many people going to the United States and coming back gringoized, if they returned at all. Not only were the Maya duped, according to these widespread commentaries, but they were also duplicitous. They were tricking their naïve supporters—especially the gringos, but also the poor benighted indigenous people who were being talked into curricular and legal reforms that would set them back decades, even centuries.

I wanted to explore these charges and the struggles over authenticity, but I was also interested in the many ways people were talking about the past as a site of duplicity—enacted by the left and the military state, among others—*and* about the new postwar state as itself two-faced—a democratic mask hiding the ongoing power of the military and economic elites. As I was exploring duplicity in postwar Guatemala, my "own" country went to war, after falling prey to nepotistic election fraud, called by some a coup d'état, that has led to an increasingly secretive and repressive government, self-censorship in the press and academia, the disappearance of suspected subversives, torture-murder of detainees by soldiers and private contractors who were "just following orders," and a far too literal "war of the cross"— openly called a crusade by the selected leader waging it but not paying the price. Little did I know I'd be telling the story of the Guatemalanization of my homeland's insecurity.

Wondering if the planet can survive this transformation makes me quite personally invested in reckoning how the assumptions of identity can articulate with political action and the possibilities for justice and reconciliation, despite not being in the know. There are those who attribute the current disarray in the Euro-American left, unable to staunch the right-wing *Anschluss*, to the very set of theories I will draw on here. There is a call for stronger convictions to match those of the right and the free market in their march to victory. It is a pressing project, in Guatemala and elsewhere, to reckon with a certain failure, to account for what happened and what is happening. This entails exploring what induces some people to stay home, keep their heads down, stay out of *babosadas*, even as their interests seem clearly at stake, or, alternatively, what leads others to step out of the everyday rhythms of their daily lifeworlds and risk trying to change their milieu—whether it's heading for the hills to engage in guerrilla struggle or just going to a demonstration. By what means is one possessed to act and, post (f)acto, how do we account for them?

A small, local example points to some of the complexities of this query. I used to teach at a small college in Portland, Oregon, where a number of students worked to mobilize participation in the anti–World Trade Organization (WTO) protests planned for Seattle in November 1999. There were teach-ins at which experts laid out careful arguments for the democracy-destroying and ecology-devastating effects of WTO policies and debates in which pro and con arguments were aired. Articles were published in the school newspaper, attractive fliers and pamphlets were distributed, and testimonials from charismatic victims of these policies were proffered. As interest grew on campus it had a snowball effect. It started to feel like going to Seattle was *the* cool thing to do. Plus it was made ridiculously simple. Rides, places to stay, and food were all arranged; all you had to do was show up. Even so, I wasn't planning on going until my students en masse informed me that class was canceled and I'd better accompany them.

Now, I was utterly convinced intellectually of the evil inherent in the

WTO and could rattle off any number of documented cases of its perfidious effects. As a veteran of many protests I didn't have to be convinced of the strategy or of the need for taking political action in general. Yet my attendance, like that of many of the students, was undertaken, if not in a fit of absentmindedness, then at least rather serendipitously and at the last minute. But the action itself, despite the cold and the wet and the lack of sleep, the clouds of tear gas, the storm trooper police tactics, and the fright turning to thrill of successfully facing down a bulldozer sent to dislodge us, was one of the more remarkable experiences I've had of human solidarity and the embodi/meant[14] of "THIS is what democracy looks like!" For many of us it was transformative, morphing a somewhat casual attention to globalization into a site of committed and passionate attachments. Boy, did those losers who stayed home feel bad when we returned, armed with our amazing tales, which thus continued the contagious effects of the experience. Who knew at the time that it would become the touchstone of the worldwide anti–corporate globalization movement and spawn books, movies, and later reverential comments like, "Wow! You were in SEATTLE?" Of course, this mobilization lasted only a few days outside our usual schedules. It did not involve the threat of being expelled from school or of losing our jobs or our lives, and it achieved its ends/goals of shutting down the WTO and garnering global media coverage. Best of all, no one was seriously hurt. If it had gone badly would some of us who went because we believed, but mostly because our friends were going, recall it as something we were duped into doing? Would we blame those friends rather than the cops for things going awry? Would it be their fault for not foreseeing the risk? This raises Pascal's old puzzle—do I do something because I believe? Or do I believe because I do it?

And what happens when you stop believing? How is the doing commemorated? In turn, what if it is power's fondest hope that you stop believing? What if hopelessness is counterinsurgency's most powerful weapon? In addressing these questions, this book, I hope, provides some clues for theory and action, but it is only one of many accounts and is not the truth of Guatemala or of the United States. That is constantly being assumed and produced by all of us.

A last confession about my own faces of duped, nonduped, and duper and about how this book is tied to my interest in keeping my job. It germinated in the preparation of my tenure case and the demand for a second project that at least looked to be well under way. "You wouldn't actually have to write it," said my kindly mentor, "but isn't there something you could say you were working on?" Reviewing my writing, I found, to my surprise, that while I seemed to be addressing various issues—the popularity of horror films, the Rigoberta Menchú "scandal," the state at its margins, and malaria, which I considered my real next project—what I was "really" concerned with was duping. Aha!, I thought, I will write a duplicitous book proposal about duping. Little did I know. The longer I took on this assumed identity (in the sense of a false one), the more it came to seem real. I sincerely wanted to write it, making assumed identities both the how and the what of this book.

To introduce my methods, what I know is, of course, also limited by the conditions of production, including increasing institutional demands, work speedup, the temporal vampirizing of e-mail, and family responsibilities that made it impossible to do long-term, all-at-once fieldwork. I have visited the highland majority-indigenous town of Joyabaj, which forms the setting for part of this book, annually since 1999, but I have not lived there full-time, nor can I speak or understand Maya-K'iche'. I learned a great deal, but this is not an in-depth ethnographic study of the town. That has already been written by Simone Remijnse as *Memories of Violence: Civil Patrols and the Legacy of Conflict in Joyabaj, Guatemala* (2002), and the REMHI and CEH reports also describe events in the area. I would also direct the reader to important in-depth works on nearby towns by Carlota McAllister, Matilde González, Charles Hale, and Abigail Adams and to recent studies of the war and postwar by Richard Adams, Santiago Bastos, Manuela Camus, Ricardo Falla, Susanne Jonas, Beatriz Manz, Juan Hernández Pico, Luis Solano, and Arturo Taracena, among others.

This book is about milieu, what is in-between or what circulates, like Guatemala's patron saint, the Virgen de Tránsito, aka the Virgin of the Assumption, under whose sign I write. It is less about a place than about the deployment and assumption (taking on) of modes of understanding such as to reckon, or *asumir responsabilidad*; *engaño*; ends; the postwar; to settle accounts, or *cobrar facturas*. It is also about assumptions in terms of the taken for granteds that structure our lifeworlds, what Lacanian psychoanalysis calls the *nom du père*, or name of the father, emphasizing the patriarchal undergirding—to which colonial racism must be added—of the supposed normal. These include progress, transparency, risk and insurance, race improvement, and audit culture. *Nom du père* is a multifaced pun that can also mean the no of the father, that is, the apparati that repress us, that resist change—from without and within, and also *les non-dupes errant*, the non-duped err. Slavoj Žižek says that those in the know are lost precisely because "as one 'in the know,' he [*sic*] is caught in transference" (1989:42). It is a call to humility.

Chapter 1 begins with festival in Joyabaj, a space and time in which it's easy to get lost in the crowd, presided over by the Virgin of Assumption/s. It is peopled by masked beings mimicking a powerful colonial stereotype, The Two-Faced Indian, a figure that will accompany us through the first half of the book. In *bailes*, dances that simultaneously commemorate the past and may foretell the future, these masked men are doubled over yet also rebel. We'll also meet a man who assumes the identity of two-faced from working simultaneously with the church and with the army during the war. Now he labors for development and Mayan rights. Here we begin in earnest our traversing of the assumptions of identity. Chapter 2 more fully describes the context or milieu of postwar Guatemala and explores some of the identities assumed there. We will navigate the dual forms of counterinsurgency I gloss as the wars of the sword and of the cross and look at specific cases of reckoning—settling penalties for actions—in the struggles of people like Helen Mack, Jennifer Harbury, and Esperanza León for justice in the deaths of their family members. I am also interested in the decisions people make about the appropriate sites of struggle at this time. Chapter 3 asks why so many postwar Guatemalans like to go to horror movies. Are they dupes of the global culture industry? Maybe. But I'll also argue that there is something about horror films, full as they are of embodiment, of beings that are not what they appear (heroes morph into victims, victims transform into killers, girls act like boys and vice versa), and their resistance to ends (a sequel always lurks) that might shed light on commemoration and collaboration, reckoning and duplicity in Guatemala.

Chapter 4 explores charges leveled by the U.S. anthropologist David Stoll that Nobel laureate Rigoberta Menchú Tum, Guatemala's most famous citizen and a spokeswoman for the dispossessed, is duplicitous: a liar and con artist, an Indian giver. Why did Stoll's accusations create such a scandal, even though he does not dispute many aspects of her story? Why were some people around the globe so quick to assume they'd been duped? Accusations of duplicity position the accuser as nonduped, a position, I'll admit, I find attractive. But do the nonduped err? If we do, then what? Chapter 5 returns us to the carnival atmosphere of *fiesta*, where we began with the *bailes*, to wander through a variety of sideshow exhibits of stereotyped (stereo as double, not mono) Indians. Here I look in most detail at how people are defining authenticity, postwar indigeneity on the ground, and the workings of the assumptions of that figure of myth and legend, The Two-Faced Indian.

The second half of the book turns to duplicitous states and sovereign power as two-faced—hiding behind a curtain, it can be revealed as actual people with a plan to control us, yet it is also bigger than that, magical, a great and powerful traumatic excess. It is a State and simultaneously ecstasis. I begin chapter 6 exploring a familiar stereotype bouncing off the indigenous and sticking to the state, which is also two-faced. We'll traverse a range of suspicions about what lies behind the front of the postwar state and the modes by which Guatemalans and others try to unveil them. Chapter 7 explores the state's other face, how power may work "behind the backs of or against the wills of even the most powerful actors" (Ferguson 1994:18) by comparing the state's role in two wars—one to counter the insurgency of popular and revolutionary uprising, and the other to wipe out the plasmodium that causes malaria. Here the state appears Janus-faced with its simultaneous right of death and power over life. As I do throughout the text, here I focus on the assumptions of identity as both producing and produced by milieu and interests, both of which mean "that which lies between." In the last chapters I swerve back on these accounts to explore the notion of reckoning more generally—the memory work, the disavowal of assumed identities, the post facto readings that lead to charges of duplicity or claims of being nonduped, and the ludicrous task of the anthropologist, who attempts to "settle accounts, to determine [at least textually] the rewards or penalties for any action." I engage how reckoning itself arises from another double. The "modern fact" that accounts can be balanced derives from the practices of double entry bookkeeping, but Mary Poovey (1998) suggests this practice may be a con, duping us in the very act of performing transparency. Reckoning also arouses millennial hopes of justice and of aligning the faces into a singular identification of a truly postwar Guatemala, fed by fervent desires for peace. Hoping, always, to veer away from dead reckoning, I'll sum up these attempts at historical clarification through "audit culture." This will entail attending to both the apparent balance promised by zero and to its horror: the null, the void, the end of genocide. Despite everything, that project has come to naught, and Guatemalans of many kinds are collaborating to end it as a possibility, reckoning with war and terror to learn "the secrets of [their] termination" (E. V. Walter in Sluka 2000:16).

In writing this book I am experimenting with what might be called a Pink Freud methodology. By this I mean I concatenate attention to political economy (pinko) with Freud, Lacan, and the film and gender theory they have influenced, mixing in a strong dose of cultural studies, particularly the focus on popular culture—thus the reference to rock stars Pink Floyd—all combined with a sensitivity to the queer (more pink), aka gender, sexuality, desire, fantasy, and perversion, which etymologically means swerving, troping, or trans/acting. I take rumor and conspiracy seriously as ways of being in the know as well as "high" theory, "low" culture, and much that is in-between.

There's a lot to be reckoned with in this not-yet-postwar planet, and great danger of possession by the evil twins, gloom and hopelessness.[15] The jokes and movie analyses are invitations to consider and engage with the in-human—both what is in us, yet what most horrifies us (Feldman 1995:245)—but via a contemplation (muse) that also amuses (to pleasantly distract), so we can keep going. Some might think the only appropriate mien before the horror of what has occurred in Guatemala is shock and awe. These are justified and important emotions and form one of the faces of this book. I feel them, and I will probably evoke them in this account. However, they are certainly not the only face Guatemalans turn to their experiences.[16] I also fear that a demand for such a singular, unmoving response may swerve into self-righteousness and pessimistic functionalism while proffering the enjoyments of vicarious martyrdom. In any case, such a face is too static for my purposes. I'm not sure it can reckon with how things work close to thirty years after the worst of the genocide. And shock and awe, no matter where deployed, is a form of counterinsurgency. It is meant to freeze you, incapacitate you, convince you there is no alternative. As Mikhail Bakhtin said, "Things are tested and reevaluated in the dimensions of laughter, which has defeated fear and all gloomy seriousness . . . [objects are liberated] from the snares of false seriousness, from illusions and sublimations inspired by fear" (1984:376). If pain is one way the state acts on the body, then finding pleasure where we can is a form of resistance. In turn, pleasure's embodi/meant is a serious way to be in the know. It is a counter-counterinsurgency hermeneutic. In the twenty-first century's "war of the worlds" (Latour 2002) we need many arrows in our quivers, including both shudders of horror and gales of laughter.

Because this book is interested in the in-between and in playing with clear-cut divisions between content and form and one chapter and another, readerly traversings swerve through short intertexts that read films and novels to elaborate on the conceptual milieu.[17] Each intertext lays out the theoretical questions I will explore in the following chapter, and the first, "Those Who Are Transformed," is the most overt conceptual guide. One reason I chose this form is to focus on the ambiguity of accounting. I try to account, in the sense of reckon, with identification in postwar Guatemala, but to do so I rely on many different accounts or narratives, stories, and image repertoires that articulate, if momentarily, understandings for Guatemalans, myself, and hopefully you. Žižek warns of a danger in playing on the resonance between high and mass culture: "How to elude the notion of some common *Zeitgeist* as its interpretive device," positing some level that will be revealed—like resolving two faces into one? I will try to follow his Lévi-Straussian suggestion of playing them against each other "to interpret alternately one with the help of the other" (1992:113), a method also known as dialectical montage. This helps us remember that neither high nor low culture may be quite so powerful or so powerless as they first appear. Whether or not it's the message, pop culture media (media: an intervening thing through which a force acts or an effect is produced) are important modes for the assumptions of identity—even in apparently isolated hamlets of highland Guatemala. Juan, the eighteen-year-old son of Esperanza León, a war widow, gently mocked me when I said I feared for him crossing the U.S. border. He told me he wasn't worried about his upcoming trip. Pointing to the image on his black T-shirt he said, "I am the son of Bruce Lee!" And, perhaps possessed by this spirit, he did indeed make it across safely.[18] This is my wish for all of us traversing the end/s of war.

❖ AcKNOWLEDGEmeants ❖

This book contemplates attempts to reckon, or to be in the know. Despite working in Guatemala since 1985, I have to admit that little did I know, and thus this book owes its existence to the support, challenges, and fluidarity of those below, and many others. While I explore claims of authenticity, the dictionary defines that as "one who does things herself," making this artifact you hold deeply inauthentic.

First, and most important, I want to thank all the people in Guatemala who have given so generously of their time, experience, and analyses, especially all the Xoye of Joyabaj and its hamlets. Anastasia Mejía and her family have been enormously helpful—a true intellectual companion, also Maestro Andrés and Maestra Santos and their family; Guillermo, Irma, and their family; Alfonso García and his family. Doña Cae and her kin have offered a second home. In Patzulá I am deeply grateful to the teachers who shared their room and much else, and to Esperanza León and her family. Also, José de la Cruz, his family, and the young men who graciously and often thrillingly recounted their experiences of *tránsito* (journeying), and everyone else in that beautiful place with its enormous sky, who answered questions, shared a soft drink on the steep mountain paths, told ghost stories in the firelight, went on carnival rides, and watched movies with me.

While not technically Xoye, I am deeply indebted to Liz Oglesby and Simone Remijnse. Without Liz I would never have gone to Joyabaj or written this book, and she constantly inspires me by her example of a *geógrafa comprometida* (committed geographer). Simone biked up to meet us on our first blustery night in Joyabaj with fresh bread under her arm and since then has generously shared her insightful understandings of the town's complexities. I have also been blessed with *compañeras y compañeros imprescindibles* at AVANCSO (Association for the Advancement of the Social Sciences in Guatemala). It is the living and *combatiente* legacy of Myrna Mack Chang. Special thanks go to Clara Arenas, Rodolfo Kepfer, Matilde González, Rubén Nájera, the hermanos Caballero, Juan Vandeveire, and all the team members. The quality and complexity of their written work and their practice of shared intellectual life in the midst of constant danger are exemplary. Thanks to the people of CIRMA (Center for Mesoamerican Research), especially Tani Adams and Arturo Taracena, and of Grupo de Mujeres Mayas Kaqla', especially Emma Delfina Chirix García, Hermelinda Magzul, Francisca Alvarez, and Adela Delgado Pop. Special thanks to my fellow anthropologist Carmen Victoria Alvarez, whose spunk and intellect I have admired since we danced to Madonna music in 1985. Domingo Hernández Ixcoy has also been a friend and helpmeet since then. Being in the know in and out of Guatemala means reading the astute analyses of Inforpress while sipping fair trade Café Transparencia, made possible by Matt Creelman, a great joke teller, and Gladis Pappa. Oscar Maldonado, and Daniel Hernández-Salazar, like José Manuel Chacón, are brave interlocutors with their milieu/*ambiente*— insisting that beauty, artistry, and laughter accompany the "mechanisms of horror." Dr. Gehlert-Mata of SNEM and the busy but generous staff of the Vectors Program in the Public Health Ministry were extremely helpful, and I wouldn't have even embarked on the malaria business without Jorge Mario Aguilar Velásquez (and Amitav Ghosh). Thanks as well to everyone at the Instancia Nacional de Salud for their struggle for life, especially to Lucrecia Hernández Mack.

I also want to thank the many Guatemalans and gringos who have watched and discussed horror films and shared jokes and other forms of dialectical montage with me, but most especially José Fernando, aka Pepe, Lara, who has been a true friend as well as fellow cinephile. I am so sad he could not see this book to fruition, having cultivated it for so long. Marcie Mersky has generously offered very incisive critique and warm refuge for over twenty years as well as an example of living with integrity. Santiago Bastos and Manuela Camus are wonderful for everything, and I deeply value their companionship. To Concha Deras, woman of the theater, acerbic commentator, and tenacious survivor, I owe much of my understanding. José Fernando García Noval has been an often puzzled but always generous interlocutor and an image of lived ethics, as has Kully Singh.

Traversings between Guatemala and the global north are woven tightly through identi-ties. Special thanks for sharing many of the greatest delights of my life to my compadres Paula Worby and Luis Solano and my beloved *ahijada* Sonya Solano Worby, *la más loca*. Abigail Adams, Greg Grandin, who was responsible for the archive effect and many other improvements, Ramón González Ponciano, Sarah Hill, David Holiday, Paul Kobrak, Carlota McAllister, Amy Ross, Rachel Seider, Ron Strochlic, and Irma Alicia Velasquez Nimatuj have all shared those difficult and terribly productive in-between places. Marcial Godoy-Anativía, graceful traverser, kept me worrying these ideas, and I have benefited greatly from the critiques and support of Charlie Hale, Jean Jackson, Beatriz Manz, Carol Smith, Kay Warren, and other members of the Guatemala Scholars Network, with special thanks to Maury Hutcheson and to the researchers at NISGUA (Network in Solidarity with the People of Guatemala) and the Guatemala Human Rights Commission–USA.

I must account for the enormous influence of Bill Maurer's work and person in these pages, always irreducible to zero. Bob Goldman gently reminds me that there's no escape from ideology, but you still have to keep struggling, and Deborah Heath turned me on to F for Fake and always inspires me with her anthropological acumen. Many, many thanks to Donald Moore for fixed and fluidary attention and for feverishly supporting this project for so many years. Ranji Khanna (who went to the Fair), Srinivas Aravamudan (get a Clue), and Jackie Orr (keeping company at Coney Island and Camp Lejeune) all keep me sensitive to the planetary costs of war without sacrificing enjoy/meant. Without Orin Starn and Anne Allison this tome would not exist. Wahneema Lubiano's laser eyes keep me sharp, and her wisdom, engagement, and 6-foot four-inch frame are always and never a DRAG. Thanks are also due to John Jackson, Fernando Coronil, Lee Baker, Tom Boellstorf, Jon Hunt (anti-helot), Marcia Klotz, Rob Latham, Fernando Luera, Alejandro Lugo, Lee Medovoi, Scott Mobley, Eric Worby, and Tomiko Yoda, and I am still ruminating on all I've learned from Akhil Gupta, George Collier, and Carol Delaney. Peter Redfield and Silvia Tomásková's skills in the uses of discipline *and* pleasure often moved me forward, and Zoe explained the workings of Oz and other spaces of girl rebellion. I wish I were better at copying Stefan Helmreich and that I responded more often in kind. Cathy Davidson, Leon Dunkley, Esther Gabara, John French, Andrew Janiak, Negar Mottahedeh, Joli Olcott, Charlie Piot, and Rebecca Stein let me try out ideas on them in the Durham heat. I also number Joe Dumit, Ron Eglash, and Randy Martin among my important investors. Duke University has provided a rich humus for growing ideas, and my thinking has been greatly helped by the following study groups: Oceans Connect–Atlantic Cultures, Feminism, Transnationalism, and the International, especially Robyn Wiegman and Ranji Khanna, Marxism and Society, Comparative Imperialisms, especially Alberto Moreiras, and the Critical Cosmopolitan working group, especially Walter Mignolo, Rom Coles, Ebrahim Moosa, and Nelson Maldonado-Torres. Rashmi Varma, Karen Booth, and especially Elyse Crystal have been extraordinary and Pro/F/Ne. Members of the Sweet Bay Ladies Drinking and Subversion Society have been wonderful companions, with special thanks to Ann Ragland for making me realize that North Carolina, whose motto is To be and not to seem, was the best place to write this book and to Emily Adams for helping me go fast even when things felt very slow indeed.

My students at Lewis and Clark College and Duke University have been sounding boards for many of these ideas and helped flesh them out as well as pay my salary. Members of the 2003 grad theory seminar Anthropology of the "Facts" of "Life" and Anthropology of Numbers have been especially sharp goads. I am more grateful than I can say for the extraordinary friendship, intellectual companionship, and inspirations of Georgia Lawrence and Netta van Vliet, who have morphed from students to teachers. In addition to her constant and unwavering insistence that I write this book, Netta has been an exemplary *esclava* and most excellent research assistant. Rocio Trinidad, Tara Walker, and Lorien Olive also provided invaluable research assistance, and Erika Nelson was essential in the final push to make this make sense.

Chapter 1 was helped by presentation at the "Deprivation, Violence, and Identities" conference at Ohio State University, organized by Craig Jenkins and Esther Gottlieb. Chapter 3 was much improved by input from members of the Witnessing conference at Princeton University, organized by Michelle Cohen and Chris Garces. An earlier version of chapter 4 appeared as "Indian Giver or Nobel Savage: Duping, Assumptions of Identity and Other Double Entendres in Rigoberta Menchú Tum's Stoll/en Past," in *American Ethnologist* 28 (May 2001): 303–31. Chapters 5 and 6 germinated in the wonderful School for American Research seminar "The State at its Margins," with special thanks to Veena Das and Deborah Poole, and parts are reprinted by permission from *Anthropology in the Margins of the State*, edited by Veena Das and Deborah Poole, copyright © 2004 by the School for Advanced Research, Santa Fe, New Mexico. A version of chapter 7 appeared as "Life During Wartime: Guatemala, Vitality, Conspiracy, Milieu," in *The Anthropology of Modernity*, edited by Jonathan Xavier Inda, Blackwell Press, 2005. I have also greatly benefited from editorial suggestions by Rob Albro, Jeff Himpele, Jonathan Xavier Inda, and three anonymous reviewers for *American Ethnologist*. Greg Grandin, an anonymous reviewer, and especially Carlota McAllister contributed enormously to improving this book. I am very grateful to the artists whose work adds so much to these pages: José Manuel Chacón, Daniel Hernández-Salazar, Julio César Castillo Carpio, Dick Smith, Pepe Lara, Felipe Natareno, and Netta van Vliet, and to Enrique Recinos from the Myrna Mack Foundation for his many forms of gracious assistance.

My fieldwork was funded by the National Science Foundation, Lewis and Clark College, and Duke University Title VI and Mellon grants, the Arts and Sciences Research Fund, and a generous faculty research stipend. Special thanks to Natalie Hartman and Holly Francis for heroic accounting, to Pat Bodager for making my DUS duties light, and to Bonnie McManus and Jenny Snead Williams. Thanks to all the participants in the John Hope Franklin

Humanities Center seminar and the fellowship that gave me time and companionship. Ken Wissoker showed great enthusiasm for this project long before it deserved it, and with the horror and with delights has been a wonderful friend and interlocutor. Thanks as well to Courtney Berger, Mandy Earley, Lawrence Kenney, Mark Mastromarino, and Duke University Press.

At the heart of the biopolitics of this project lie my kin and kind. Thank you so much to Lois, who taught me to read; to Donald the philatelist; Erika, hula girl donor among many other gifts; Brian, guide in economic, computer, military, and Venezuela matters; Philip Nelson; and to my extended networks: Judi Nelson (whose girlhood stamp collecting in the Amazon recirculates here); Gene *père*, whom we lost before this was completed; Chris, Quinn, Gene, Donna, and Ryan Driscoll; Nancy, Larry, John Paul and Luke Manning; Joan and Jenny Hosmer and K; and, newer to the mix, Natalia Vergara. I owe a special debt to Mark Driscoll for just about every kind of exchange (with an emphasis on kind), with special thanks for his assumption smashing. He's the one who left *Discipline and Punish* on my doorstep. He is my First and Final Girl, the central relationship of my milieu.

Chapter One

UNDER THE SIGN OF THE VIRGEN DE TRÁNSITO

One is too few, but two are too many. Donna Haraway

I have two faces. Mayan catechist

There is at the head of this great continent a very
powerful country, very rich, very warlike and capable
of anything. The U.S. seems destined to plague and
torment the continent in the name of freedom.
Simón Bolívar

MASKS AND DISPOSSESSION

A drum is playing and the thin reedy song of the oboelike *chirimia*. The sun is very hot for the mid-August titular festival in the highland town of Joyabaj. The streets are jammed with people, as everyone—even Evangelical Christians disdainful of the *fiesta*'s paganism and depravity—comes down from the hamlets to sell or buy in the bustling market, to try the carnival rides and games, to watch a video, or to fulfill ritual obligations through dancing or hosting. At any one time there may be five or more dances going on, sometimes all at once, in the square in front of the church, whose facade was one of the few things left standing after the devastating earthquake of 1976.[1] Buses are busy bringing people back from work on the South Coast and from the capital, and children home from boarding school. Some Joyabatecos return from as far away as the United States, where a sizeable number now live for a few months, years, or a lifetime. Mindful of luring workers to cut cane in the upcoming harvest, sugar plantations sponsor banners congratulating the town on its fiesta. Periodically a group of men dressed as angels and *monos* (monkeys) and often rather inebriated, approach the huge pole, fashioned from a single tree trunk, erected in the central square. Both climb up, and the angels hook their feet into stirrups on ropes wound around the top, and jump—the trunk turns, and they go twirling, circling, and slowly descending to earth.[2] All this is to honor the patron of Joyabaj, the Virgin of the Assumption, known colloquially as La Virgen de Tránsito (transition, transformation, or journey).[3]

Virgen de Tránsito, Our Lady of
Assumption, ensconced in her
magnificent frame, exits the
Joyabaj church to take a turn
about the town. August 15, 2003.
Author photograph.

Baile del Palo Volador. In the central square of Joyabaj dancers repeatedly leap from
the pole and circle slowly, descending to earth, while other dances are performed below.
Author photograph.

Down a side street, dancers dressed in heavy costumes and thick wooden
masks trace the back-and-forth steps of the Baile de la Culebra (Dance of the
Snake). Unlike the Baile del Venado, in which humans are disguised as deer,
or the Baile de los Monos, in which humans take the part of monkeys, in
this the snakes the dancers handle are real and poisonous. In brown masks
drawn from old Spanish images of "the Moors," dancers repeat the yearly
rituals of being contracted to work as *mozos* (laborers) on the sugarcane
and coffee plantations on the fever-ridden Pacific coast. In the masquerade
an indigenous man also assumes the role of a ladino, or nonindigenous, by

(cross)-dressing as a Spaniard, in blonde wooden curls. The agent of national and transnational capital in its local form, he bends one dancer over to use his back as a table to mark down the men's names in a book, recording how much they owe for the drink he just bought them or for the cash advance they received when their child fell ill. It is an act I've seen repeated out of costume, that is, in real life, in the main square.[4] While in that life it is quite difficult to escape the combined forces of debt collectors and the iron law of wages, in the dance the names provided for the notebook are "generally nonsense names, or puns, or malapropisms. . . . The dancers have a lot of fun with each other and the specific exchanges are highly improvisational . . . humorous non-sequiturs that turn on the miscommunications so common between ladinos and Maya" (Maury Hutcheson, pers. comm. 2004). However, experience on the *fincas* (plantations) is anything but fun. It is described as hateful, abhorrent *sufrimiento* (suffering) rather than work (McAllister 2003:85). It is a place where one goes to work without earning anything, where one contracts malaria.

Meanwhile, the *contratista's* (contractor) two companions, his "wife," a man (cross)-dressed in the *huipil*[5] of the department capital, and his shaman, or *Maxe*, in the traditional dress of nearby Chichicastenango, seem to be dallying behind his back. In the slow rhythms of the dance the workers plan a revolt. Rituals are performed, including passing the snakes among the dancers so that each gets a solo with one around his neck, and as the master is sleeping they creep up and put the snake under his clothes. After much struggle he dies, and the workers rejoice. But their joy is short-lived, as the shaman performs powerful necromantic spells that bring him back to life. Things seem to go back to the way they were.

When I saw the dance in 2000 and 2002, amidst gales of laughter and shrieks when the snakes came too close, the audience yelled out, "Maxe necio!" (naughty Maxe), among other things. Maxe is a nickname for people from neighboring Chichicastenango, where everyone is reputed to be a shaman. People in Joyabaj call themselves Xoye. Both speak the K'iche' language. As in the Dance of the Conquest—a Spanish dance commemorating the expulsion of the Moors in 1492, reworked as Pedro Alvarado beating the K'iche' hero Tekum Umán, which is sometimes performed amid great cacophony right next to the dance I've just described—in the Baile de la Culebra the people united are defeated.

These are dances about loss and dispossession. They enact many of the tensions that interest me: tensions around remembering, forgetting, and actively covering up; identity and pain; fascination and danger; the rational-

Baile de la Culebra, Dance of the Serpent. In the right foreground the figure in the straw hat is the Maxe from Chichicastenango who has doubled over the worker in front of him to use his back as a table for noting down his debts. Photograph by Felipe Natareno. Used with kind permission.

ization of everyday life (the debt notebook) and its magic. They are about embodi/meant (the corporeal) and enjoy/meant (in both the sense of pleasure and, more fiercely, *jouissance*). They conjure unexpected allies, like the snake, not all of them human, and sudden, deadly reversals. The dances and this book are about relations between the highlands and the rest of Guatemala and with other parts of the planet. They are also about class, ethnicity, and gender, which are not things but relations—relations that accumulate capital. David Harvey, drawing on Rosa Luxemburg, calls them two-faced. One face consists of the everyday economic processes like those depicted in the *baile*, in factories or agricultural estates and mediated by transactions between capitalist and laborer. The other face is the rapacious and brutal "accumulation by dispossession" between capitalist and noncapitalist modes of production mediated via colonial policy, the international loan system, and war (2003:137). The dances are ways to co-memorate, or remember together, the experiences of dispossession and collective action. They contemplate the failure of that action to reach its immediate goal, all in the midst of ongoing exploitation and danger. They play with masks, truth, and power, and in that spirit I'll situate the end of war (its conclusion) by telling a story about some ends (or goals) of people who participated in a rebellion similar to that of the *mozos* against their *patrón* (boss). They were struggling for possession of land, labor, capital, dignity, and power, a struggle that has not ended.

THE ENDS OF WAR: STRUGGLES FOR POSSESSION

It is difficult to define the postwar because the stains of five hundred years of accumulation by dispossession have kept war in people's veins (Williams 1991). Ritual processes—like the dances performed in indigenous communities, the National University's annual *Huelga de Dolores*, and Catholic masses for their martyrs—monuments, family storytelling, books, cassette tapes, videos, and DVDs co-memorate and motivate organizing, taking up arms, reform, democratization, coups, nationwide mobilizations, counterinsurgency terror, survival, and rebuilding. To tell part of that story, I'll go back to 1978, when a goodly number of Guatemalans were actively involved in trying to create massive social change at every level, from the individual out through the family, community, church, local economies, regional politics, and on up to the nation-state—with many hoping, in turn, to transform Guatemala's relations with the world. They were addressing both of Harvey's faces of capital accumulation, which meant intervening locally, nationally, and transnationally, with Rigoberta Menchú Tum's *testimonio* being the most incisive intervention in the latter. The status quo—a somewhat stabilized relation of subordination, always dependent on a great deal of violence—could no longer hold, as it became increasingly understood as an unnatural domination.

Activism took many forms, from holding Bible study groups to conducting electoral campaigns; from colonizing jungle areas inspired by utopian visions of dignified human communities and unalienated production to reconceptualizing the alphabets of Mayan languages; from unionizing workers across ethnic and linguistic identities to engaging in massive strikes for better wages and working conditions; from teaching in shantytowns to joining one of the guerrilla movements. Accounts from that time, and people's current memories, evoke enormous hope, enthusiasm, effort, and learning. The names people chose for their organizations and the words they use today to describe these experiences suggest unstoppable forces and telluric entities—volcanoes, fire, streams flowing into rivers. People use terms like "euforia insurreccional" and "calor del momento revolucionario" (the heat of the revolutionary moment) (Bastos and Camus 2003:57), "acceleration," or remember being "swept up in this dynamic," this "vortex" (McAllister 2003:268).

Those who did take up arms also took on a second name, or *nom de guerre*—a name that inspired them to become another person, to assume a different identity than they had before. Likewise, naming guerrilla fronts after international symbols of resistance to violent imperialism like Augusto Sandino and Ho Chi Minh worked like a GPS, or Global (south) Positioning System, to call, via the sympathetic magic of the name, such resistance into being via the individual bodies of recruits. The groundwork for this effervescence was laid by decades of organizing around a host of issues. Also essential were the consciousness raising and practical experience gained through people's lived activities in institutions like the school, the church, the town hall, the cooperative store, the military, the health clinic, the land registry, the courts, and the multicultural barracks on the South Coast plantations, where families of *mozos*, migrant workers from all over the highlands—including indigenous and ladino poor people—lived together chockablock. All these coalesced with memories of hopes raised, shattered, and raised again through national experiences like the social and land reforms of the Guatemalan Spring of 1944–54 and the subsequent repression and insurgency—and with a moment of global crisis encompassing tenacious and ultimately successful anticolonial movements in Asia, Africa, and parts of Latin America, the Cuban Revolution, the nonaligned movement, the Tricontinental projects, and the worldwide May '68s.[6]

In Guatemala these mobilizations involved an enormous amount of talking and thinking, reading and more talking, and practical experimentation. How do you organize a cooperative store? What crops grow in cleared jungle soil? How does a village respond to thieves? What do you do when your husband reacts badly when you tell him you've gone to a meeting? How do you organize a political action with someone who doesn't speak your language? How do you take care of a gun? Do you use *Usted*, *Tu*, or *Vos* (formal or informal "you") with compañeros of a different ethnicity? And then more talking. The mobilizations were laboratories, sites for trying things out and experimenting, then contemplating the outcomes. The talking and acting, aka *crítica /auto-crítica*, aka praxis, took place in USAID-sponsored bilingual education workshops, in kitchens, on sugarcane plantations during a strike, on the campus of the National University, in high schools and on elementary school playgrounds, on the production lines of factories, between rows of corn or banana trees. A ladina lawyer remembers going, in the mid-1970s, to the eastern highlands where the Arbenz land reforms had been most developed and, in the late 1950s, were most brutally overturned, to offer legal advice and consciousness raising to indigenous peasants. To her surprise, she says, they were way ahead of her. "'The time for that is past,' they said. "Where are the guns?'" No more than the anti-British struggles in India, were these actions undertaken in a fit of absentmindedness (Guha 1983:9).[7]

Increasingly, as the decade progressed, some people gave their whole lives over to these processes, living full time in guerrilla camps, aka "revolutionary schools for new men [sic]" (Andersen 1983, see also Hale 2006, Harbury 1994) or visiting and even residing among insurrectionaries in countries like El Salvador, Mexico, Nicaragua, Cuba, Vietnam, and Morocco. "Really," said an urban psychologist, remembering his student days, "you didn't know from one day to the next if you were going to up and head for the mountains. It seemed like every day someone else from our circle had gone to join the guerrilla." The Mayan leader Rigoberto Quemé recalled those times: "In the 80s there were three possibilities for the people in [the highland city of] Quetzaltenango working for social change: join the rebels, go into exile or stay in Quetzaltenango. The last option was, for many, a death sentence" (in Grandin 2000a:236).

People mobilized into a wide range of activities (only some of them armed) and for a number of different reasons, or ends. Projects that had been coalescing for decades became articulated—connected—in the late 1970s. It was a multiple-front process, and people changed their strategies as the terrain of struggle changed—as when peaceful protest was met by a hail of army bullets in the Panzós massacre of 1978 (Grandin 2004). The great majority of tactics were nonviolent, although by the early 1980s the counterinsurgency had pushed more and more people to take up arms, what few they could get their hands on. A turning point for many was the peaceful occupation in 1980 of the Spanish embassy by students and peasants involved with the Campesino (Peasant) Unity Committee (CUC), which was the culmination of a number of unsuccessful efforts to raise awareness about land usurpations and army murders in the mostly indigenous highlands. The army surrounded the embassy, it caught on fire, and almost everyone inside was killed, leading many to believe that unarmed resistance was futile.

However, the very breadth of the mobilization above- and underground in the legal, religious, educational, military, and productive realms gave rise to classic counterinsurgency prose (Guha 1988) denouncing it as two-faced. The military state insisted that legal protests and human rights work were nothing but a front for the lawless guerrillas, designed to dupe the government, international observers, and maybe even the activists themselves. In this view, although they *thought* they sincerely believed in economic and political justice, they were really doubled over, puppeting Communist propaganda, mindlessly repeating the "Havana line."[8]

In colonial discourse or counterinsurgency prose we will see again and again this deployment of duplicity as double. Resistors are two-faced, both above ground and clandestine, and therefore dupers. But they themselves are duped. Rebellion is clearly a *babosada* (idiotic act), so anyone who tries it must have been tricked or possessed. When the army offered people the choice between death and amnesty if they confessed to being tricked by the insurgency, or when David Stoll suggests that Rigoberta Menchú needs to find herself as a Maya and not as a leftist, rather than both, they are rehearsing one formula of the assumption of identities. The confession of having been duped (Assumption Two) opens the way to transformation (Assumption Three) into the nonduped—two faces are "fixed" into one.

The Guatemalan revolution challenged a system grounded in one of the most unequal distributions of productive resources in Latin America, condensed into the Baile's image of dispossession in which an indigenous person is doubled over, contracting himself for labor in the export production system. It was met by an articulation of interests and counterinsurgency practices that also spanned class, ethnic, and national identifications, not unlike the Baile's *contratista*, allied to lowland plantation owners, police, transnational accounting procedures, sugar consumers in the overdeveloped world, and his *Maxe* magician. Guatemalan elites, deeply sensitive to the fates of their Cuban and Nicaraguan brethren, were terrified of losing their access to land and cheap labor. Many also read it as the long-prophesied "race war," the fulfillment of deep-seated fantasmatic fears of savages pouring down from the hills to murder, rape, and pillage. Elsewhere I analyze the voluptuous qualities of these oft-repeated tales. Like many horror scenarios and stereotypes, they stand constantly at the ready for revivification (Nelson 1999a, see also González Ponciano 1991, 1997). These "race"-based fears mobilized some poor ladinos to side with the military government against what might appear to be their class interests. But so did a number of poor indigenous people who felt themselves threatened by, in part, the modernizing and secularizing aspects of the insurgency.[9]

Tiny Guatemala, laboratory for emergent Cold War policies, was made a "showcase for the Americas" after the coup of 1954. It was "the first instance in history where a Communist government has been replaced by a free one," as then–Vice President Nixon said (in NACLA 1974:74), and it would certainly not be left to its own devices to settle these affairs. The United States was strongly, though often unofficially, involved in the "anti-Communist" counterinsurgency. The Guatemalan military also received aid from countries that included Israel, Taiwan, and Argentina. In other words, in refusing popular demands for a more just distribution of wealth, more than one father uttered the *non du père*, the No! of the father. The result was scorched-earth war that decimated the popular movement and the guerrilla forces and their bases. It destroyed a generation of incipient rural and urban leaders. It shattered the public university system and killed or exiled almost the entire progressive intelligentsia. But the war also sharply challenged traditional economic and political organization, forcing plantation elites to scramble to survive, and it articulated different class and financial relations from those that once held.

We now live in a different time, a time when, despite Seattle and Porto Alegre, first home of the World Social Forum, the idea that collective action could effectively improve the world for the dispossessed has been made to seem ludicrous, a *babosada*, a dupe.[10] We find the very words we might use to describe our fondest hopes have been hollowed out and parasitically inhabited by their polar opposites, so that freedom is on the march to the tune of Predator drones and depleted uranium devices, and "Democracy at Gunpoint" is a nonironic newspaper headline. It seems that we can no longer express ourselves without appearing to collaborate; the actions taken just to survive shame us into passivity.[11] This book reckons these genealogies of the present via duplicity, one mode of accounting, in the sense of narration or storytelling, for war and its end/s. I explore how accounts of duplicity articulate experiences of collaboration and of assuming identities that in turn trouble struggles over responsibility, impunity, settling accounts, and reckoning with who is winning that supposed war between good and evil.

Struggles for possession of land, labor, capital, dignity, and power continue to be hard fought in postwar Guatemala and increasingly turn on possession of new identifications like "Mayanness" and victim status. Because they are struggles over identity and authenticity, charges of duplicity become powerful weapons—their power drawing from a postcolonial paradox. While the term "identity" comes from a Latin root meaning "essence," in Guatemala, five hundred years after the invasion, fifty years after the Cold War Arbenz coup, and forty years after the start of civil war, the sense of self-possession we associate with the word "identity" seems contingent on tenuous articulations among shifting sites of power and struggle. I call these identi-ties. How self-possessed is the person doubled over so his or her back can be used as a table to annotate debt? They and their families and communities with them are tied into vast and long-standing networks of global exchange as well as to other connections among people that, for example, keep the Dance of the Snake going year after year. It is through identi-ties that identification is assumed, but it is always haunted by the suspicion of Assumption Two, inauthenticity. In the dance these very exchanges are simultaneously commemorated and made ludicrous, as is the colonial stereotype of the Two-Faced Indian.

But that is only one two-faced figure haunting postwar Guatemala, waiting to be unmasked. Another is the war perpetrator, who committed dastardly deeds and then, seemingly acknowledging their badness, covered them up by "disappearances" and clandestine cemeteries, and by hiding ill-gotten gains off the books. And duplicity doubles back again through the complex ways in which actions — of indigenous people, perpetrators, *mozos*, bosses, et al. — are also effects of being acted on by systems of great power, bigger than those humbugs who can be unmasked and named, that take our hearts and minds as a battleground. Sometimes we have what I call the hula girl moment, when our most sincerely held beliefs, most deeply cherished desires, and most carefully considered home decorating decisions stand revealed as not, after all, an expression of one's self, but the effect of our possession by class, gender, ethnic, or national positions within historically specific relations of power.

Passing through such a *nacer de conciencia* (consciousness raising), people may begin to assume an identity that challenges these structures. This is a risky identification that often calls for swerves and evasions to sidestep a suicidal direct engagement with power's powerfulness, doubling us back to the stereotype of the less powerful as two faced, as "Indian Givers." Clandestinity is produced dialectically through engagement with the force of power's counterinsurgency and may produce this stereotype of the subaltern as untrustworthy, duplicitous. But power not only accuses its enemies of duping it (you say you are a war orphan, but you are really a dangerous guerrilla!). It also struggles to convince them that they are duped—by the very idea that another world is possible. It wants us to believe that resistance is futile. There is a strong current of fear and even despair in postwar Guatemala that the peace accords have duped people into thinking change was possible while behind the scenes *los meros jefes*, the ones really in charge, have consolidated their power. Yet the same people who seem so hopeless may take a different tack in the next breath, engaging a stubborn hope that recalls the powerful also suffering setbacks and unexpected reversals.

So I will address duping as multiple, acknowledging the many struggles to name names and to pull back the curtain on perpetrators, but also the more existential stakes in what Ackbar Abbas suggests is "the possibility that 'deception,' too, is not one thing and that there might even be special cases where we can know and act only through the detour of the "false" or the meretricious" (1999:352). Laboring under the sign of the Vírgen de Tránsito, I try to show how reckoning is also, always, on the move. In this I follow Akhil Gupta's take on the complex relations among duping, individual interests, and those powers no one really controls. He says:

> I neither presume an identity between statements and interests nor do I assume that discourses are epiphenomenal to "real" interests. Both these positions are reductionist. It seems to be perfectly sensible that interested parties would employ discourses strategically so as to conceal, misstate, or otherwise modify the public "face" of their interests; at the same time, interests have to be articulated to be held, changed, and disputed or to persuade others to support them. Discourses, therefore, are the medium in which interests are articulated; representations of interests in discourses always have a strategic dimension. But that means that we have to pay attention to the manner in which discourses give shape and meaning to interests rather than assume that they are the hollow form occupied by ontologically prior, well-shaped interests. (1998:370)

ENGAÑO/DUPING

When postwar Guatemalans explain the war as the result of *engaño* (being deluded, beguiled, or duped), sometimes it is other people who were fooled— by the army, the government, the guerrilla, the nongovernmental organizations (NGOs), or by the person telling the story. Others attribute their survival to the ability to dupe others, to live with two faces. But often people explained their own actions as being based on *engaño*, a result less of their own will than of someone else's will working on them.

Žižek says, "An ideology really succeeds when even the facts which at first sight contradict it start to function as arguments in its favour." He recalls the anti-Semitic stereotype that "hiding one's real nature, duplicity, is the basic feature of the Jewish nature" (1989:49) and how it is impervious to reality-based arguments. Some Guatemalans appear to assign this same "basic feature" to indigenous people (see chapter 5), but it is also rubbery, bouncing all over, affixing among both Maya and nonindigenous thinking to the opposite, the ladinos. Carlota McAllister worked in Chupol, Chichicastenango, an almost entirely indigenous town not far from Joyabaj. She says Chupolenses consider ladinos *"tramposos, mentirosos y engañadores* (cheaters, liars, and deceivers)" (2003:224). Diego Molina, who was a well-known ladino photographer, said of his people, "The ladinos are liars, traitors, charlatans, thieves, hypocrites, cowards, co-opted, sold out, and always taken advantage of." For a brilliant genealogy of these two-faced stereotypes, see the Guatemalan historian Severo Martínez Pelaez's *Patria del Criollo* (1990).

Similarly, in an interview with the indigenous mayor of Joyabaj (*alcalde indí-gena*) about the situation of *mozos* (agricultural laborers), he quite matter-of-factly began talking about the *patrón* (owner or boss), Julio Herrera, as a volcano; Herrera's family holds vast tracts of land around the township, as well as sugar plantations that stretch all the way to the sea. I had to interrupt him several times because I didn't understand. "Yes, yes," he said, "he is a man, and also a volcano." He meant, drawing on older notions of the accumulation of power (Hill 1992, Vogt 1990), that while Herrera might look ordinary when he comes to town on philanthropic visits, he has another face, a connection to the in-human. No ordinary person could amass such power. North Americans and other foreigners do not escape the sticky stereotype of having two faces, as we are suspected of being *robaniños* (child snatchers) or Satanists rather than friendly tourists or anthropologists. McAllister at first was denied access to Chupol because, people said, they "had experienced much deceit [*engaño*] so people didn't believe" her when she said she wanted to work there and help them (2003:45).

Perhaps people really *are* duped by some beguiling, insidious power, as I myself have been, but I am more curious as to why stories of two faces and *engaño* explain such a variety of things to so many different people now. I am also intrigued by how these stories double the uncanny sense in the Baile de la Culebra of being bent to the will of another.

To be duped is different from claiming ignorance, although that is also a way of remembering the war in Guatemala, as in many postwars.[12] It is also different from being forced to do something. Duping suggests you went willingly but under false pretenses. What you assumed to be true was not. What you took for granted was wrong. Perhaps you ended up doing something or being someone you did not intend to be. Claiming to be duped is a way to admit you did something but to avoid full responsibility. It occurred, but it's not your fault. If you've been duped, the deflation felt when the con is revealed can be laughing bewilderment or red-faced embarrassment about being taken in. You assumed, and it made an ass out of u and me. You're a sucker, a rube.

But duping can also be world shattering. Trust is deceived, betrayed. You've been double-crossed. Not only is confidence in the other shaken, but so is faith in one's own judgment. At the moment of becoming conscious of the duplicity the self splits into the pre-self that didn't know and the new self that is in the know. A familiar narrative is shattered, and the pieces fall together in a new configuration. The very I that thinks—and therefore is—becomes uncertain. If confidence can be defined as self-possession, its loss raises the question of who then possesses the self? And how does one continue to act in the world after such revelations?

But the person claiming to have been duped could just be dissimulating, evading responsibility.[13] How would you know?

DOUBLING OVER

In Joyabaj the violence of the civil war arrived on a motorcycle in July 1980, just as the festival preparations got under way. Two masked men roared up to the church, shot the Spanish priest, Padre Villanueva, and drove away. Not long afterward the army occupied the town, and several *cofrades*, members of the brotherhoods that customarily sponsor the dances, were disappeared.[14] Then the army began massacring people in the surrounding hamlets, where many of the more traditional indigenous people live. With the violence, dislocation, and ensuing economic disaster, no one had the monetary resources or the temerity to put on the dances. This did not change until 1983, when the occupying military ordered the dances to be performed, following a rumor that the guerrillas had forbidden them: "People who refused to participate were ordered to appear at the military base, after which they were only too eager to comply" (Remijnse 2002:134).

If dispossession is partly the content of the Baile de la Culebra, during the war it thus became its form, as engaging in one's own culture became the sign of collaboration. The dance's performance of the worker acted on by the will of the contractor, doubling him over to act as a table, accepting the debt and plantation labor it entailed, is doubled by the dancers themselves, acted on by an occupying force. It seems less an expression of free will than an act of auto-minstrelsy.

A month before I first saw the Baile de la Culebra I was sitting on a dirt floor covered with pine needles in a schoolroom in Patzulá, an outlying hamlet of Joyabaj. It was the first day in a week of mission work connected to the Vatican's Jubilee Year (July 2000). A catechist was in his second hour of speaking in Maya-K'iche' about martyrs. He linked the martyrdom of the biblical Israelis with Jesus Christ, then with the assassination of the local priest in 1980, and finally with the recent state-sponsored genocide of the "Mayan people."[15] He is a corn farmer who also migrates to pick coffee and, unlike most men his age, wears *traje* (traditional clothing). Genocide was not part of the standardized lesson plan distributed by the church. It was, however, the major finding of the UN's CEH report, presented in February 1999. Several days after I heard his talk the catechist told me he had been the Civil

Patrol leader in the hamlet, the army-run militias responsible for atrocities during the war. "I have two faces," he said. "One I show to the army, the other I show to my people."

War survivors frequently use this term of self-dispossession when talking to ethnographers in postwar Guatemala (González 2002, Green 1999, McAllister 2003, Zur 1998) to explain how they lived through the government's counterinsurgency campaigns. The Civil Patrol system, or Patrulla de Auto-Defensa Civil (PAC), was instituted in 1981 and was quite diabolical, inducing community members to surveil, incriminate, and punish each other. This allowed the military state to keep some distance from these crimes, which in turn warped and undermined community solidarity.[16] Throughout much of the country but especially in indigenous communities every man from age fourteen to sixty was incorporated into the patrols. Some leaders were former soldiers or military commissioners whose face already pointed toward the state; sometimes, however, these same people used their military experience to train local youth for the guerrilla. In many cases, however, the army laid this onerous task on respected local leaders, often catechists, cooperative members, or schoolteachers. Compared to other Latin American countries that had dirty wars, Guatemala was exceptional for the almost total incorporation of its civilians into the counterinsurgency. In addition to cover-ups, official denials, and even the murder of critics of the patrols, the density of collaboration achieved by these policies makes questions of both individual and aggregate responsibility difficult to assess (Montejo 1993a, Warren 2000). Attempts to blame the PAC for violence against civilians are made difficult by the fact that the patrols pretty much *were* the civilian population.

Primarily men patrolled, but because missing duty could result in fines or corporal punishment, women sometimes took the place of male kin. Women also had to collaborate in various ways: by picking up the labor men could not perform because of their patrol duties and exhaustion, by cooking special meals for patrollers, and by performing usually unpaid services for the occupying military, including cooking and laundry. In addition to performing sex work for soldiers, which was nominally compensated, in the highlands women were also kept in rape houses, sometimes for months at a time (González 2002), where they were forced to be available to both soldiers and patrollers. No one was exempt.

The role of the PAC, which the CEH found responsible for 12 percent of the state-backed atrocities in the war, makes reckoning especially fraught in Joyabaj. That is in part because the CEH based the ruling of genocide on four case studies. One was the township of Zacualpa, Joyabaj's neighbor, and in many cases it was the men of Joyabaj who committed the atrocities that led to the ruling. They are still remembered by people in Zacualpa as *"fuerte, enojados, bravos* (strong, angry, out of control)" (see intertext 2). In the same way individuals like the catechist were split between two faces, hamlets and the town of Joyabaj itself were also deeply divided, and terrible things were done by Xoye to Xoye as well, as I examine in more detail below.

In 1993 Leonel Ogáldez, the ladino leader of the Joyabaj patrols, was charged with the murder of Tomás Lares Ciprian, an indigenous Joyabaj man who was working to abolish the patrols. Ogáldez simply denied involvement and was freed (Remijnse 2001:466). In July 2000, eight people were lynched in a hamlet of neighboring Chichicastenango by former patrollers after initiating a legal proceeding for crimes committed by the patrols. No one was ever tried. But not all enjoy impunity. Xoyes closely followed the three trials of Cándido Noriega, a patrol leader in nearby Chiché who, in the midst of threats and violence, was acquitted twice but eventually found guilty of multiple murders and sentenced to 220 years in prison (Alianza contra la impunidad 2001; see also Paul and Demarest 1988). Xoye also tell stories of other kinds of justice: how the patrol leader of the Xeabaj hamlet, renowned for his brutality and arrogance, was flayed alive and left to die in agony. In a sort of unaccountable moral reckoning, it was not clear in the various tellings I heard if the agents of retribution were human or not.

Much of this book is concerned with the difficulty, but not the impossibility, of separating the two faces of victim and perpetrator. I find duping discourses intriguing because they explore what is in-between and because powerful people also complain of being duped. In postwar Guatemala the Civil Patrols, who have been loudly proclaiming their victim status since 2000, have become a central site for struggle over these faces. Later I address in more detail attempts to *account* for the patrols in the senses of (1) how people endure(d) them as a "mechanism of horror" that produced collaboration in acts of violence; (2) how to tell a story about them; and (3) how, as both patrollers and their victims demand reparations, to financially balance debits and credits and under what form of "audit culture." The patrols were not the only forms of self-dispossession of life during wartime. Most of the soldiers carrying out the genocide were also indigenous kids, many of them forcibly recruited (America's Watch 1986, Kobrak 1997, Manz 1988, Schirmer 1998).

Another site of struggle over two faces and naming names emerged in 1999, when the U.S.-based National Security Archive obtained and released a Guatemalan army dossier of disappeared people (NSA 1999). It revealed what had been assiduously covered up, and it terrifyingly suggested being doubled over as well as proving that the left's insistence on clandestinity was not so paranoid. A document of the bureaucracy of death, it consists of page after page of names, photos, affiliations, activities, and fates.[17] For many, it was the first official acknowledgment of what became of their loved ones. It caused a huge sensation as photocopies and CD-ROM versions were feverishly produced and distributed hand to hand. A Guatemalan psychologist who treats survivors of the violence said he and his colleagues were overrun with former patients who were suddenly and horrifically reliving those times. He said he himself was almost overwhelmed with flashbacks, as if it were those days again: "I felt exactly the same."

One of the more terrifying aspects of the dossier was the instances in which a name was followed by the name of someone from the same cell. Clearly people were tortured and forced to *delatar* (betray or denounce), leading to the capture, torture, and often murder of their comrades. It also turned out that the army had released some of those who had "confessed," making them work as spies.[18] After the dossier appeared, several of the people who appeared in it contacted the newspapers to explain their experiences and offer tear-filled apologies to the families of their former compañeros. "I couldn't help myself," said one (Rosales O. 1999). An activist told me that during the war, immediately upon hearing that anyone from their cell had been arrested, everyone in the group tried to get out of the country. "We knew we had less than forty-eight hours. We told each other, try to hold out at least that long so we can save ourselves, but we knew that no one, no matter how strong, could withstand the torture any longer than that."

A young university student who feels she was "untouched" by the violence told me the following story in 2000: "I was in class and we were asked to talk about our experience of the war and everyone realized how we are all *hijos de la guerra* [children of the war]. We've been marked by it—even the people who didn't suffer as much. It made me remember when I was little, a friend came into my house one day yelling, 'Hay un muerto! hay un muerto!' [someone's dead!]. We all went running to see, about two blocks from our house. I remember it so clearly. But I didn't think much about it then. Later I met a boy who lived around there, and it turned out that it was his father who was the dead man. Then, just recently, it turned out that his father's name was in the dossier! *Ay dios!* It was so emotional, so terrible—I just cried and cried! I saw him at the University and asked him if he'd seen the list. . . . I wasn't sure he'd want to. He said he hadn't, and I said I had a copy, was he sure he wanted to see it? He said yes, so we went off campus, to a little corner and I showed it to him and he just broke down. All I could do was hold him and try to make him feel better. What can we do? It makes me

5. MYNOR ELVIDIO GIRON CABRERA
   (s) ALEJANDRO
   Miembro del M.R.P.   ,
   12-09-83: Capturado en la Aduana Central

   22-09-83: Entregado a la D.I.

θ-5

6. RODRIGO MORALES LEMUS
   (s) ROCKY ó MANUEL
   2do. en Interferencias radiales del F.U.
   de la ORPA.
   Viajó a Cuba
   21-09-83: Capturado en la Colonia Belén,
   Zona 7 de Mixco.
      O AVE. 3-48 ZONA 7, COL. BELENCITO
   Quedó libre para contactos.

W-6

7. CESAR AUGUSTO OVALLE VILLATORO
   (s) ALEJANDRO ó PANCHO
   Estudiante de Leyes y conocimientos de --
   electrónica.
   Miembro de Interferencias de la ORPA.
   21-09-83: Capturado en la Escuela Tipo -
   Federación, Zona 12.

   04-01-84: Se lo llevó PANCHO.

W-7

8. MIRIAM ELIZABETH DOMINGUEZ HERRERA
   (s) TANIA ó REGINA
   Nombre falso: VILMA ARACELY RODAS MOLINA
   Miembro de la ORPA., dijo estar desconec-
   tada.
   22-09-83: Capturada en una casa cerca --
   del INCA.
   Servía de pantalla a (s) ERNESTO ó MANUEL

   Enviada a Coatepeque.

W-8

9. JOSE MIGUEL GUDIEL ALVAREZ
   (s) ERNESTO ó MANUEL
   Nombre falso: RIGOBERTO ALVAREZ TOBAR
   Estudiante y reportero.
   Estuvo en el Frente Guerrillero No. 6 de
   donde se desertó.
   22-09-83: Capturado en el Parque Isabel
   La Católica.
   ?'
   Enviado a Coatepeque.

W-9

-2-

Death squad dossier. The dates of capture, ranging from the twelfth (12–09–83) to the twenty-second of September 1983, suggest they *delataron*, or revealed enough information for their companions to be captured. "Se lo llevó Pancho," or "Pancho took him," is code for death in captivity; note that this was not until January 1984. "Quedó libre para contactos" suggests he was released to be used as a spy. From the National Security Archives. Used with kind permission.

so sad." "And so angry," said her friend, who was also listening to this story. "Yes, enraged! I'm so angry about it! But I also feel sort of guilty, that I was not killed. The exiles make me feel that way too. Why didn't I have to go? What was I doing then? Going to parties? Why wasn't I doing something to improve things? Why wasn't I involved?"

"Did you know," said an elderly friend, "that the Jesuits found out how brainwashing works? After the Pellecer case they had to study the techniques, the special ones developed here in Guatemala, developed with help from the gringos, of course. The *chafas* [disrespectful term for the military] had lots of people to work on, to experiment with. Many didn't work. They turned into zombies so they would kill them or sometimes just let them go. But Pellecer, they brainwashed him. I remember seeing him on TV, his eyes, his face. It was him but not him."

The Jesuit priest Luis Eduardo Pellecer Faena was disappeared in early June 1981, and in late September he appeared on national television denouncing his former colleagues, saying he had been inculcated in the guerrilla struggle by the Church. My friend told me the story much as one would tell a ghost story, her voice lowered, pulling me close to her. The terror, for many progressives, that this would justify and intensify violence against the Church was matched by that of seeing a companion so doubled over. The spectacle itself was a mechanism of horror leading to "paranoia within reason" (Marcus 1999). People speculate. How did they do it? How would I react? What possessed him?

STRUGGLES AGAINST POSSESSION

Possession has been called nine-tenths of the law and has, since at least the 1600s in the global north, been the sign of full humanity, the seat of rights. In the postcolony, those who once were their own king are now dispossessed by the "sword and the cross," by the armies of soldiers, priests, merchants, and other camp followers mobilized under the banners of property and propriety. Indigenous people, nonindigenous people, and everyone in-between, including the anthropologists who study them, are involved in complex articulations of what possessing identity means and what role it might play in struggles over repossession: of material goods, disappeared family members, tradition and modernity, community bonds, progress, a sense of moral worth, and the complex emotions surrounding collaboration in violence, even if this meant being uninvolved.

In Guatemala these struggles are waged in the context of geno- and ethnocide, syncretism, ladinization, exclusion, militarization, and a myriad of centuries-old divide-and-conquer strategies. While indigenous people are the majority in Guatemala, they comprise more than twenty ethnolinguistic groups (K'iche' being the largest) with extremely strong community identifications like Maxe and Xoye further fractioning this nonhomogeneous category. In turn, the idea that identity is singular, as in the word "individual," meaning not able to be divided, is not shared by all residents of Guatemalan territory.

In Mayan cosmologies identification may be understood as double or even more multiple. For example, the soul, a misnomer when rendered in Christian English, is in pieces, and parts of it can be dislodged as in *susto* or fright illnesses, or by witchcraft, or move about on their own. In turn, everyone, even gringos, has a companion spirit, often associated with an animal, whose personality and fate affect the human. The world itself is animated — telluric entities, ancestors, time, and other forces deeply influence human affairs (Cook 2000, B. Tedlock 1992, D. Tedlock 1993, Vogt 1990, Wilson 1995). Creatures like the *rajav a'a* may look and act human, but they peel off their flesh at night to roam about in another form (Warren 1993).[19] One is acted on by internal forces, sometimes described as having certain blood types or humoral tendencies (sanguine, bilious). Or external forces may make one ill as a sign that she or he has been called to take up a responsibility (*cargo*) as a healer or because they neglected *costumbre* while undertaking service to a saint.

Abigail Adams describes how, even in a community in which people had converted to Protestant Christianity several generations ago, it was understood that a man's deadly fall while working on the new church was the building itself killing him for neglecting the proper rituals. In this same community several women began speaking in the voice of the *Tzuultaq'a*, or mountain owners, giving instructions on proper relations to the world (Adams 1998). Similarly, I know a young woman who had been born and bred into a family heavily involved in the church group Catholic Action and its projects to "purify" the church of "pagan" elements (more on this in chapters 2 and 5). She held no truck with such traditions and had been further secularized by her participation in the revolutionary movement and the experience of exile. She fell ill not long after she returned to Guatemala with a mysterious malady for which doctor after doctor offered remedies, but nothing worked. Friends even pitched in to send her to the United States for treatment, to no avail. She finally consulted a Mayan priest and was told it was the call to take up training as a healer herself. She emphatically resisted. Her political activities and NGO job plus her family took up all her time, and she didn't really believe the priest's diagnosis anyway. Several months later, in increasing pain, she began the traditional training, and her health immediately began to improve.

In the western highland town of Momostenango, K'iche' men working with Garrett Cook included a number of activities in what they call *costumbre*, activities like praying correctly at the right time and place, sexual abstinence, and attitude. "When someone is not focused entirely on the enterprise, when they have second thoughts about the burden they have agreed to carry, when they are resentful of the expenses of service, then they are of two hearts (*quieb ru c'ux*). This can lead to insanity or death and is one of the greatest dangers of service" (Cook 2000:27). Further on we'll see that *costumbristas* are not the only ones concerned about the heart's relation to actions, especially its wholeness or lack thereof.

This is a world in which, just as one may be acted on, one may also, unconsciously even, act on others. Understandings of *mal de ojo*, or "evil eye," hold that simply admiring something like a newborn may unleash, through the force of one's desire toward this precious thing, unintended danger. "It's never *a propósito* [on purpose]," said a Maya-Kaqchiquel friend. "You can harm without meaning to. You should touch the baby and then it will be okay. People should express these feelings." In other cases of unintentional harm, drunks and foreigners are seen as being hot, their simple presence endangering the vulnerable. Some Maya-K'iche' call the human ability to differentiate good from bad and to act on that understanding *conciencia* (McAllister 2003). Being able to do this oneself and to determine if others have conciencia is a fraught but essential hermeneutic project at all times. Like these other understandings of self in the world, however, it is different from enlightenment assumptions that value a one-to-one relation between face and true self.

For those who share these understandings, at the best of times this is a world full of risk: It is *muy delicado* (powerful, painful, dangerous).[20] Those who practice *costumbre* take great care in hedging themselves with proper practices to mitigate the force of these powers. They see these practices as part of their responsibility for the common good, for protecting their communities. Other villagers, however, began to develop more secular understandings of risk. They saw it as emanating from a system of unequal land tenure, exploitative labor relations, racialized hierarchy, and state-backed violence, and they began to work to ensure their own futures and those of their communities in other ways—through organizing to challenge these structures. Domingo Hernández Ixcoy, one of the founders of the Campesino Unity Committee (CUC) near Santa Cruz del Quiché, about an hour's bus ride from Joyabaj, said, "There was always activism, people fighting and seeking ways to develop. There were the cooperatives and trying to get fertilizer, but each offered only part of a solution. People would be blocked for a little while, and then they would become more active." As the world became more *delicado* and uncertainty grew about whom one could trust, people developed other protective mechanisms. In 2006 a member of the unarmed wing of the Guatemalan Workers Party (PGT) said, "With clandestinity, the main thing is that you are never ever ever direct about anything. You go around [she motioned with her hands]. Round and round about. You take the back ways. And that's not just in the everyday world, how you get from one place to another, but in how you talk, how you relate to people. And it's still strong." A priest who was sitting with us nodded in emphatic agreement. "It's part of every relation, every decision," he said. They take great care in hedging themselves with proper practices to mitigate the force of these powers.

People may begin to feel possessed by this fear that they never know whom to trust, as suspicion comes to mediate every relation. In turn, when an activist was arrested, disappeared, or killed, friends and family who had been kept in the dark, often to protect them, frequently felt betrayed at not being in the know, at being distrusted—especially if they agreed with the cause. "Why couldn't she tell me?" For many, finding out that someone they love lived a double life shattered their un/shared past and threw it into new, uncanny patterns. Guatemalans have a reputation in Central America for being *enconchados*, *encerrados*, closed off or turned inward like a snail in its shell. When asked about the effects of the war, many say it only increased these tendencies. "People, families, they shut down. They don't talk about things. There's a generation gap because young people don't know what happened in their families, if people were involved," said a young ladina woman who had recently joined the URNG political party.

In the course of the first postwar, the emerging indigenous rights movement became another way to reckon with sources of risk. For some it has come to be seen as emanating from the revolutionary left. This movement is assuming a relatively new identity—"the Maya"—one forged in struggle, both with and outside of the popular movement, both with and outside of the state. And it is dependent upon internal divisions like gender, whereby Mayan women maintain the link to traditional culture so that some Mayan men can modernize, in order to demand rights without losing their identity (Alvarez 1996, Delgado Pop et al. 2000, Chirix García 2003, Nelson 1996, 2001a, Stoltz Chinchilla 1998). It is community-bound, both tied to and heading toward an always receding horizon, rather than always already existing (Nelson 1999a). This makes it hard to assume much of anything about these identifications.

But I have already deployed a translation that seems to define it, at least through its other. I did this by calling ladinos nonindigenous and associating them with the economic and political elite. Perhaps it's misleading to imply that indigenous men may dress up like them for festival dances but that everyone knows very well that ladinos are not Maya. Ladino means mestizo or nonindigenous but also not white, and the term is marked as much by class, culture, and clothing as by race. As a Guatemalan joke puts it "What is a ladino? An Indian with money." It may be taken as an insult, depending on the context, and decomposes into myriad terms that mark class, distinction, color, and history.[21] The word comes from the Roman Empire, where it described colonized people who spoke Latin, giving the category its own frisson of two languages, perhaps two faces.

In turn, by suggesting the Maya work with and outside the state, I am assuming some border between inside and out when what I'm actually interested in is what lies between. So here, despite the linguistic cunning, I am caught in the prison house of language. Despite efforts to prove that gender or race or nationality or other identifications are assumed, aka false, that the personal is not separate from the political, or the state from civil society, once those linguistic divisions are made, we make believe that there *are* such things. I am acted on by these inescapable forms that distort my meaning. Even as I strive to convince you that these are, despite their real effects, false binaries, I am possessed by a force outside myself, yet without it I could not communicate at all.[22]

Identity terms *do* describe things. State power and economic control *are* disproportionately held by people who would vehemently deny having any "Indian blood" (Casaus Arzú 1992). Indigenous people *do* tend to be the most dispossessed in Guatemala. Every time I go to Guatemala I *am* identified by Guatemalans of every station as a gringa, a representative of the great, rich, ambivalent power that Bolívar named. I am reminded over and over again by the Xoye in Joyabaj that I possess that great modern value of U.S. citizenship—an identity that means I won't die trying to illegally cross the border into Guatemala in order to earn my living. I will argue, however, that even these are not singular descriptions, but instead two-faced. That's because these are more sites and stakes of struggle than unproblematic possessions (Althusser 1971:147).

That may be why the stereotype of being duplicitous bounces back and forth between Mayan and ladino and also between the state and its people. Not only does government counterinsurgency seek to unmask clandestine rebels, to fix two faces into one, but a counter-counterinsurgency herme- neutics reads the state itself as two-faced. When it claims to represent all the people, that is simply a cover for its docile service to a small class segment (most of whom have very pasty skin tones)—just as Bolívar unmasked the powerful as acting "in the name of freedom" when they actually plague and torment.[23] Here, the name (of freedom) is supposed to identify and fix, but it is just rhetoric, a false identity hiding true intentions. Words may hide reality, but if we work hard enough we can see through to the truths: of torture not justice, exploitation not freedom. Charges of duplicity may be an analytic talisman, a way to resist the lure of being acted on in the name of something that does not really have your best interests at heart. But just as I cannot escape the language I argue in (making it hard to talk about what's between state and people, between ladino and indigenous), perhaps we should not be too quick to deny the power of the name.

The state may also seem to have two faces because it is the carrier of both suffering and benefits. Both perpetrator and succor, it dispenses death *and* life. The scorched-earth counterinsurgency of the early 1980s, called Cenizas 81 (Ashes), that killed so many Xoye in Joyabaj was enacted by the govern- ment of General Romeo Lucas García, who was replaced in 1982 in a coup d'état by General Efraín Ríos Montt. The new government unleashed a two- pronged strategy of "Security and Development" through a campaign called *Frijoles y Fusiles* (beans and bullets). The army pulled back in urban areas and offered food and other desperately needed support to those willing to submit to total army control, while an even fiercer attack was unleashed on those who remained in rebellion. Ríos Montt's later return to power under allegedly democratic rule—serving both as a congressman and leader of the governing party in the late 1990s as well as making a strong bid for the presidency in 2003—hinged on interpretations of this strategy. Did it really improve things in Guatemala or was it two-faced: claiming to help but really more deadly than any government before or since? Currently the latter read- ing is winning. "El General" is now facing murder charges and a class-action genocide case.

Yet at the same time the military state seemed Janus-faced, omnipo- tent and all-seeing, it was also read as dupable, as the two-faced catechist suggested. He could show one face to the army and one to his people. In a larger frame, not only the traditionally subaltern struggle over the posses- sion of identity. Decades of military dictatorship, civil war, international

"WANTED for Crimes Against Humanity and War Crimes: Ríos Montt and his military high command of 1982." The names listed are "victim communities" and the dates of massacres. Poster published and distributed anonymously.

opprobrium, and structural adjustment mean even Guatemala's apparently powerful—like national state actors and economic elites—seem dispossessed, illegitimate, acted on by outside forces like Cold War politics, trade agreements, NGOs, and debt refinancing packages.

So, this book is also about that other meaning of possession: as with the tortured Father Pellecer transformed into a zombie or the kind Adams (2000) describes, in which the *Tzuultaq'a* mountain deities speak through a woman's mouth. This is the kind of possession portrayed in U.S. horror films like *The Exorcist*: the magical sense that one has been taken over, acted on by an outside force, bent to act to another, alien will. This is both a horrifying and a fascinating possibility, leading, perhaps, to the popularity of horror films, which make possession and two faces a central concern. These two faces—terrible and fine—swerve through different valencies of what it means to assume an identity.

ASSUMING IDENTITIES

Some people assume an identity for pleasure. The Baile de la Culebra is a form of hybrid comedy grouped under the name *Tz'ul*, referring to "foulmouthed tricksters, fools, or contrary persons" (Cook in Hutcheson 2003:79) and relying on "spontaneity, acrobatic horseplay, verbal improvisations, and perverse or contrary behavior that irreverently pokes fun at the norms of daily life" (Hutcheson:81, see also Clendinnen 1991, Bricker 1973, García Escobar 1998, Tedlock 1992). In Momostenango Cook says the *Tzulab* open the way for the resurrected Jesucristo, "as rain prepares the earth for planting and opens the germinating seed" (2000:172), and it is full of explicit ribald sexuality, corporal punishment, live snakes with their whiff of danger and associations with ancient powers like plumed serpents, and connections to twinned mythic figures.[24] Little historical documentation of these dances exists, and Hutcheson suggests this is because "the disruptive jesting of the players continually subverts attempts at explanation" (77)—a more general problem for anthropologists. And in Joyabaj the audience members were doubled up with laughter at the jokes, most of which I could not understand.

Masquerades, like the *baile* and many other narrative genres, play with the pleasures of assumptions that turn out to be wrong, although these forms tend to be judged as popular or low entertainment rather than great art or social science. Many jokes are based on double entendres. Suspense, mystery, and horror all turn on keeping the audience guessing about guilt and innocence, about the epistemic status of the data proffered. The good caper film provides a trick ending, a "gotcha," its quality evaluated on what it gives away and when—if it's too soon it spoils the fun. Unless some yahoo has ruined it, the final surprise reveals you've been duped, negating everything that went before and forcing a re-viewing with the new knowledge. It creates an entirely different story as the audience puts the same pieces back together again in a new configuration. In other words, there's a con in the text—and that's part of the fun.

You are reading a text and perhaps wondering if it deserves your confidence, especially given Bronislaw Malinowski's warning about the ludicrous position of the anthropologist (1961). He was referring to attempts to seize hold of something at the very moment it was supposedly melting away. But ludicrous can mean variously "laughably absurd," "to play," and "to rebuke." Much anthropology styles itself as a rebuke—to ethnocentrism, orientalism, heteronormativity, racism, and neocolonial violence[25]—by providing context, that is, by explaining history, economics, politics, kinship relations, and spiritual understandings. And we often borrow suspense genre tropes: first, an apparently unfathomable behavior is described, such as sailing long distances to exchange greasy pieces of shell, believing a witch made a granary fall on you, or enjoying guilt-free sex as a woman. Then the behavior is contextualized and shown to be perfectly rational within the "cultural whole" in which it occurs. I've started to do that here by showing how fantastic creatures like Two-Faced Indians and duplicitous states, both murderous and legitimate, can exist and even make sense—and make believe. However, anthropology itself has been rebuked for a range of crimes and misdemeanors, including being duped by its own good intentions and, knowingly or not, collaborating with the very structures of power it claims to resist. "Unthinking" racism, heteronormativity, Eurocentrism, and self-righteousness is a lot easier as an adjective than a verb. They are deep assumptions in the social sciences of the global north (Asad, 1973, Said 1978, Starn, 2004, Trinh 1989).

CONTEXT AND CONS IN THE TEXT

So, is there a con in this text? Indubitably. The anthropologist is in a ludicrous position, armed with theories of suspicion honed to see through deception, yet haunted by fears that the nonduped err. She is trained to turn the image in the camera obscura head over heels. But doing so may dispel the very beguiling luminosity that attracted her in the first place. You may be confident that interesting stories will be told and audacious theoretical insights proffered, but I would be a charlatan to suggest this book will be the last word on any of these matters. As Žižek warns, "those in the know are lost" (1989:42).

For one thing, I claim to explore postwar Guatemala, but perhaps there is no such clearly defined, freestanding thing. Writing about the postwar means accounting for the war, but its end/s—temporally or its objectives—are ludicrously unclear. Guatemala itself may appear to be a demarcated place, yet not only do at least one-eighth of its population live in Mexico and the United States, but also its history, politics, economics, tastes, and possibilities for the future are defined at least as much in relation to other places, especially but not only the United States, as they are essential to some imaginary geographic entity. I find it much more adequate to explore postwar Guatemala as a network as much as a thing, one which has effects in the world as an organized political and geographic unit, yet one strung together through popular culture, coups, arms markets, revolutionary examples, solidarity activism, remittances, ideas about eugenics and other theories of development, movies, organizational models like bookkeeping, and consciousness.[26] While power is unequally distributed through and via this network, it is not a site for solely unilateral action by any one part on any other. Each node is a multiconductor. Influence goes in multiple directions. Even the United States is affected by this relation. These *relational* identifications may make the one face of postwar Guatemala seem two-faced.

There are other cons in this text—ones I'll explore at two levels, and the first is precisely the metaphor of two levels: the power of the idea of a double reality, of duplicity, with its implicit promise of a transformation into singularity and transparency. This is one of the most powerful theoretical tools in Western metaphysics. It undergirds Plato's cave, Marx's camera obscura, Freud's unconscious, Du Bois's double consciousness, and the many projects grouped under the proper names of structuralism and poststructuralism. Marie Langer, the liberation psychologist and founder of the Argentine Psychoanalytic Association, said, "Behind what appears to us as reality, Freud and Marx both discovered the actual forces that govern us: Freud, the unconscious; and Marx, class struggle" (in Hollander 1997:48). It lies deeply ensconced in anthropology's cherished methods of interview, observation, and participation, which assume you can't really trust what the "natives" say or what they show you. Instead, you have to embody it yourself to be in the know. It animates current anticorruption campaigns like Transparency International and "audit cultures" more generally (Power 1997, Strathern 2000). And to what else do we owe the frantic polling, surveillance, biometrics, and mainstream justifications for torture if not to the state's and the corporation's deep anxieties that the supposed one-to-one relation of representational democracy is actually a dupe, that the populace, the immigrant, the teen, the housewife are all hiding other identities: desperation, plans for disruption, subversive intent? Assuming there are two faces is part of many progressive projects, and my aim is neither to do away with this potential, nor to delegitimate those moments of insight when one realizes that her or his privilege, or lack of it, is not natural. Such a move would simply reinstall the double relation between error and truth, duped and nonduped.

Assumed identities can be fun, but they also, rightly, raise suspicion. That's because it may be done to advance one's interests, in the sense of increasing compensation or creating an advantage. Taking off or, now, putting on traje can make it easier to get a job. A democratic election can enhance a country's credit rating, regardless of how national decisions are made. The famous "aka," shorthand for "also known as," on FBI wanted posters points to the nefarious sense that suspected criminals are hiding their real identities to rip you off, escape justice, or take *your* identity.[27]

On what I hope is the other hand, anthropology's participant observation could be seen as one long assumption of identity, like any development or training. One is not born a Ph.D., farmer, bureaucrat, punk musician, or woman. But as long as one works hard and goes through the proper channels, rituals, and accreditation, we tend to take it for granted that these new identities can be assumed. Anthropologists may repeat this ritual numerous times, apprenticing to other people's culture in order to "speak for" them. We may be compensated for our troubles, if we're lucky, through book contracts, speaking engagements, and teaching gigs—aka authority. But because it's assumed, this identity is open to question, both through the discipline's well-known self-reflexivity and the Oedipal and Oresteian gestures exposing famous anthropologists as both duped and duping.

Is this why U.S. anthropologists are so often read as being two-faced? Not the eager students we claim to be, but CIA agents, spies, child robbers, blood and fat suckers like vampires and *pishtacos*, or, alternatively, as Communists or otherwise threatening (Adams 1997, Metcalf 2002, Price 2004, Rabinow 1999, Weismantel 2001)? Does the in-betweenness that is supposed to help us make the strange familiar and the familiar strange, that makes us feel at home in several places, also make us uncanny, *unheimlich*? Does the interestedness of our work, the fact that we gain something from it in the other world we live in, make us seem two-faced?

In the film *The Wizard of Oz*, a tale chock-full of two faces, the Wizard tells the wanderers that they are each missing something that would make their identities real. To Scarecrow he says, "Where I come from we have universities. Seats of great learning where men go to become great thinkers. And when they come out they think deep thoughts and with no more brains than you have. *But* they have one thing that you haven't got—a diploma," and he hands him a "degree in thinkology." The Scarecrow immediately begins rattling off mathematical formulas. "Oh Joy, Rapture, I've got a brain!" For the Tin Woodsman it's a testimonial, and for the Lion it's a medal. Each of these things is a warrant, a guarantee, of the credibility or authenticity of an assumed identity. But at the very moment such accreditations seem to fix, they simultaneously unsettle. Wasn't the Scarecrow already smart, the Woodsman already kind, the Lion already brave? Didn't their actions prove this? Why do they need these trinkets, and what is the authority that thinks it can grant them?[28] This inconsistency at the crux of authentification raises a doubt: is there ever a process so pure that it lies beyond the suspicion of impropriety?

I want to reiterate the pleasure, even ecstasy, of our playful assumptions of identity—think of theater and film, Halloween, role-playing games (RPGs), carnival, drag and transvestism, and all the everyday formations of fantasy that enliven our workaday worlds. If you're good at it, you may make a little money, but usually no one gets hurt, no great interests are at stake, and while a bit uncanny, it is rarely denounced as deception or betrayal (Schwartz 1996). Sometimes, as with art forgery, it's because such a denunciation would threaten the entire system, while delighting all those

who chafe at the rule of experts. But many relations across identity boundaries *are* haunted by suspicions of two-facedness. Is interest in someone
else's culture, as in, say, classic and modern-day minstrelsy, a sincere form
of flattery? Or is it outright appropriation, aka stealing? As bell hooks asks,
when Madonna metaphorically "blackfaces" her show is she a soul sister or
a plantation mistress (1992)? Charges of being a wannabe, a waspafarian, a
jafaikan, a wigger, and so forth are both jokes and carry a stinging accusation of fakery. How can the more powerful engage with difference without
simply appropriating it? How can the less powerful acknowledge being recognized and the political or financial support, it may bring, while remaining
the inappropriate(d) other (Trinh 1986)?

On the other hand, some people must assume identities in desperate attempts to survive when their own identity becomes a target. Regardless of
what you truly believed, if, in Guatemala in the 1980s the army assumed you
were subversive, it meant death. For example, because *traje* is site specific,
during the war you could be disappeared simply for wearing clothing from
an area known to be a guerrilla stronghold. To survive, many Guatemalans
assumed another identity: indigenous people began wearing Western clothing and many people changed their names, their addresses, or their work.
"I hid in the private sector," one activist told me. They developed two faces
and by doing so hoped to escape the singular identity of victim. But the horrifying thing about the Guatemalan genocide is that it was often neighbors,
friends, even family who carried out the dispossession. It was often victims
who assumed the identity of perpetrators. One of the most important sites
of postwar politics has been the struggle against impunity for crimes committed during and after the war. Yet how is responsibility to be justly reckoned in the face of two faces?

Then there are the nefarious cons, the plots, as in the apparently disinterested broker who really robs you blind, and conscious, well-planned cover-
ups of economic and political malfeasance: the Allende coup, Iran-contra,
the Panama deception, Enron, weapons of mass destruction (WMDs), and
so on. The interested parties may assume the mantle of freedom fighters,
innocent bystanders, or victims of duplicity themselves, but they stand to
gain enormously in financial, political, and cultural capital. *These* assumed
identities can have terrible consequences: as the bumper sticker says, "He
lied, They died."

So, is asking *cui bono*, who benefits, the recipe for discovering truth behind the mask? Do we just need to follow the money? Would this dissolve
two into one?

Given that in Guatemala the slightest hint or most unfounded rumor that one had ties to the revolutionary movement was an automatic death sentence, clandestinity, read as duplicity, was actually *produced* by state policy. Given popular demands that the state live up to its rhetoric to be of, by, and for the people, cover-ups of violence and corruption may be produced by democracy. In other words, could both sorts of duplicity be part of a single productive network? Or does that lose the vital critical insights of Marx, Freud, and other masters of suspicion? If there *are* two faces, what happens to our analysis when we focus on what lies between them—on milieu, interesse? In turn, what if the con is in the very promise of being in the know, of being nonduped, of adequately accounting for, of reckoning? If so, can we still struggle for justice?

I started with a traditional dance that, like Bruce Lee, a schlocky martial arts star, and a range of actants I'll explore throughout—including a war memorial, the testimonial of a young indigenous woman, a cartoon, a twelve-volume UN report, a court decision, an accountant's ledger, a water pump, a U.S. horror movie, this book itself—is a media representation deployed in and through postwar Guatemala. All are about make-believe as they struggle to say something that, if the struggle works, can begin to go without saying, that is, become an assumption. Yet, in the end I hope this book works like a good caper story in which the conclusion, rather than shutting down possibilities, opens the narrative up to active reconfiguration. I'll try to make you believe that being in the know is an ongoing process, a horizon, not a fixed state. It is a continuous, contradictory assumption of identity.

This text reckons with great horror, terrible pain, and dispossession, but I began with dances performed in Joyabaj, a place that suffered and perpetrated genocidal violence, because people also laugh and transform. Ecstasy/ *ec-stasis* means coming out of stillness. The identities I examine throughout—indigenous, ladino, gringo, anthropologist, accountant, victim, perpetrator, survivor, heroine, or healthy—are not one (Irigaray 1985). They cannot be fixed or bound to singularity or stasis but are mobile. Their patroness is the Virgen de Tránsito. Donna Haraway says that one is not enough to contain these identifications, these uncanny possessions. But two—as in clear-cut divisions between unconnected entities—is too many. Later she revises herself to say two is only one possibility (1991). There are always alternatives to singular visions, but to keep from making asses of ourselves we need to carefully interrogate our assumptions and our selves.

THOSE WHO ARE TRANSFORMED

Farce [Fr., stuffing; used to fill interludes between acts] 1. an exaggerated comedy based on broadly humorous, highly unlikely situations; 2. something absurd or ridiculous, as an obvious pretense
Crux *n.* [L., CROSS] 1. a cross; 2. a difficult problem, puzzling thing; 3. the essential or deciding point
Account [OFR<*aconter*< to tell < *computer*: to determine (a number) by reckoning] to consider or judge to be; value—*vi* 1. to furnish a reckoning (*to* someone) of money received and paid out; 2. to make satisfactory amends; 3. to give satisfactory reasons or an explanation; 4. to do away with as by killing

DOUBLE AND TRIPLE WORDPLAY

This book explores possession, duplicity, and hopes of being in the know as ways people live in postwar Guatemala and elsewhere by looking at assumption as a process and as a triple wordplay. The *Baile de la Culebra* is a form of dance called *Tz'ul* or *Patzkarin*, meaning "those who are transformed" (Hutcheson 2003:77), and I mimic this meaning to elaborate on assumptions of identity as a series of traversals rather than a state or essence. But there's that pesky language game again—setting up one thing rather than another, in this case a divide between being and becoming.

Now, notions of ontology or being have been under assault for centuries in the Western tradition by thinkers far more sophisticated than I. But identity has a stubborn habit, in common sense and elsewhere, of preserving the sense of essence, stasis, authenticity (Jackson 2006). In everyday relations with people we struggle to uncover what they are really like.[1] In our mundane political actions we seek the hidden meanings behind the spin, the submerged interests that drive policy, regardless of whose name it's in, by following the money to the other, truer world lurking behind this one.

As I said earlier, I am curious about this image of the world as two-faced and the accompanying promise of a nonduped, transparent access to truth. In turn, I wonder about the sense that it is nobler in the mind to suffer a constant becoming and somehow a little pathetic to believe sincerely in being. I want to hold on to the experience of identity and the inequalities it gives rise to. I believe there are lies and lying liars who tell them, that we are subjected to weapons of mass distraction, and that some representations are more accurate than others. But one — whether it be either or or — is not enough to think. Two, as if absolute difference existed between, is both too many *and* only one possibility (Haraway 1991). To paraphrase F. Scott Fitzgerald, the test of a first-rate word is the ability to hold two opposed ideas at the same time and still retain the ability to function. Such words will be signposts in this book's efforts to think simultaneously, without overvaluing any One, to hold, however loosely, certain convictions without losing sight of constant transformation. "Cleave" is such a word, meaning simultaneously to separate and bring together. So is "fact." Mary Poovey calls this term "epistemologically peculiar" (1998:xxv) because it seems to separate description from interpretation, induction from deduction, and "credible" from "interested," but it's really two-faced. Another first-rate word is "crux," for when we look for it — that deciding point where two or more valences intersect — we often find a puzzle.

Similarly, the word "identity" suggests an essence, but when we assume an identity we are entertaining at least three quite contrary ideas. I suggest that identification is simultaneously a traversal through and a hunkering down into these senses. In the first, an assumption is taken for granted. It is the unconscious, unexamined prerequisite for those identities that appear self-evident. It is a "given."[2] Second, assumption suggests false pretenses — an assumed identity is one that is not true, perhaps taken on for nefarious purposes: it dupes. But the assumption of an identity is also the real deal — as in the Virgin of the Assumption, who is taken up into her true identity, her body and soul ascending into heaven. It is "an assumption that constitutes the instrument of that subject's becoming" (Butler 1997:10). Linked to Foucault's elaborations on *savoir* it is "a process through which the subject finds himself [sic] modified by what he knows or rather by the labor performed in order to know. It is what permits the modification of the subject and the construction of the object" (1991:69–70).

This triple wordplay mimics Raymond Williams's classic work on ideology. He glosses it as follows: "(i) a system of beliefs characteristic of a particular class or group; (ii) a system of illusory beliefs — false ideas or false consciousness — which can be contrasted with true or scientific knowledge;

(iii) the general process of the production of meanings and ideas" (1977:55). It means simultaneously that which is most true *and* most false.

This slipperiness of double, even triple meanings confounds clear-cut reckonings or coming to terms with Guatemala's war. This is unnerving because the word "reckoning" promises a fixed position, from which to decide. But it also has several definitions: (i) to count, figure up; (ii) to measure possibilities for the future; (iii) to settle rewards or penalties, as in Day of Reckoning. Like accounting, it carries a promise of transparency, settlement, restitution, healing, and the end to war, and, as Bill Maurer argues (2002b), "accounting" in turn means simultaneously audit, narration, and religico-cosmopolitical judgment. The Spanish *contar* conjures both to count or number *and* to tell or reckon. The CEH was set the task of clarifying (*esclarecer*) history, basically to audit it, but this was also a heavy cosmic task and a political struggle to avoid a merely cosmetic relation to the past. Not surprisingly, participants say that in both their fieldwork and the writing-up it was a constant challenge to balance the different powers of numbers and counting (the modern fact, the general) and the narratives of individuals' testimony (the particular). Does one clarify while the other obscures? Perhaps because of this both/and relation, both are open to charges of duplicity.

Following Maurer, the multiple meanings and senti/meants of accounting line up surprisingly well with the One, Two, and Threes of assumption and ideology. (i) "perhaps one could ... define a society as a 'group of people who subscribe to a common accounting theory'"; (ii) the numeric and narrative forms of accounts keeping are in constant tension, as both promise yet also betray the hopes that they can fully account for the world; (iii) "accounting theory *is* the culture, at least in the anthropological sense" (2002b:6). For those of us who have trouble balancing our checkbooks or filling out IRS forms, accounting may seem far removed from our daily lives, hardly our culture! However, Maurer suggests that it is a deep-seated assumption that produces meanings, understandings of justice, and definitions of truth for accountants, lion tamers, and activists as much as for anthropologists and war victims struggling for accountability.[3] Accounting practices arise from the transactions of buying and selling, in which, today, we cannot help but engage, so deeply, perhaps, that in English "to buy" something means to believe it. Maurer and Poovey trace how these practices come to be a given as forms of double-entry bookkeeping, in which credits and debits supposedly always balance into zero, increasingly regulate and guarantee global commerce. In the chapters that follow I explore how forms of duplicity — such as collaboration, the gift, and the Indian giver, the X-tra value that accrues through circulation (interest), and how preserved possibilities that imagine improvement through generations — all trouble such givens. But while such fixing may be a fixion, it is also inescapable.

SWORD AND CROSS / FORCE AND IDEOLOGY / DOMINIO AND EGEMONIA / DEATH AND LIFE

It has become standard to gloss the invasion and occupation of the Americas (Mayan activists refuse the term "conquest") as occurring through the sword and the cross. These are metaphors for the two faces of a power that seeks to bend others to its will. The sword works through physical force: obedience at pain of death. *Chafarote* is Spanish for "cutlass" or "sword" and is a disrespectful term, sometimes shortened to *chafa*, for the army in Guatemala (*chafar* means to flatten, crush, or silence). The cross does a more subtle job on "hearts and minds": through church conversion, social organization like the *cofradías* (brotherhoods), and subjection to the priestly Spanish father. It also works through the assumptions of, in the sense of taking on, structures of feeling like guilt, the glorification of the abnegating virgin mother, internalized racism, homophobia, and so forth. "Colonization by the cross" is a way to talk about inducing someone, without the explicit use of force, to do something that is not necessarily in their interests and yet feels as if it were. It attempts to name, in a singular fashion, what often goes without saying. The promise of proselytizing religions like Christianity — that anyone can be saved if only they believe — instantiates at its very crux the same radical insecurity of any assumption of identity. The Assumption promises true identity but always carries the threat of Assumption Two, of falsity — that the converted indigenous people are duping the priests with their "idols behind altars." Irene Silverblatt situates the very foundations of European modernity in the Spanish Inquisition's tools and techniques to ferret out the truths of these constitutively unstable identifications (2004). The modern self germinates in this milieu of suspicion, and in the torture chambers that call on the body to fix these elusive assumptions. But fears of *engaño* stick not only to the tortured but also to the torturers. While probably etymologically unrelated,[4] in Guatemalan slang *chafa* means something false, sold as if it were quality when in fact it is useless, similar to the common phrase *dar gato por liebre* (give a cat for a hare). Many Guatemalans associate *chafa* with both the military and a cheat.

The war of the cross might also be called power, culture, hegemony, tradition, habitus, society, the procession of the simulacra, the black box, Capital, the Veil, the State, God, Empire, the Phallus, the Force, the Matrix, and so on. All of these notions have deeply influenced this book.[5] Some I'll draw on specifically, others will remain implicit, while I'll also suggest that these are all paradigms that are "not one."

This is because I'm interested in how often these singular terms take on a double sense. For one thing, many of them seem to exist out there as well as in here—both in the world and in the person. The familiar, who we really are, is thus also unfamiliar, uncanny, like Durkheim's weird quote: "There is something impersonal in us because there is something social in us" (1995:447). How does something foreign come to be lodged so deeply in one's body? What is the process of internalization?

These may seem like esoteric questions, but ivory tower academics aren't the only ones who care about them. In fact, Second and Third Christian Millennium U.S. popular culture is constantly throwing up contemplations of interpellation—Louis Althusser's term for how the subject comes to be "hailed," or called into being, and called to account, as before a court (1971). Indeed, many blockbuster movies seem almost obsessed with the issue and offer some quite creative and productive ponderings of the assumptions of identity.[6]

HAILED BY THE SCREEN

A screen both hides and reveals. To screen something off is to put a barrier between it and us, to conceal something or protect it. One of its roots is (s)ker—to cut, and to screen out is to separate and exclude. It can aid duplicity, as in a smoke screen. But movies are projected onto screens that catch the light, thus revealing an image that would otherwise disperse into nothingness. I draw on films and a novel in these intertexts because their content helps work through philosophical concepts and because their form mirrors the very procedures I am trying to understand—and also because I'm influenced by Žižek to torque everything you wanted to know about subjectivity but were afraid to ask the Warchowski brothers. Here I'll briefly address John Carpenter's *They Live*, Joss Whedon's and Fran Rubel Kuzui's *Buffy the Vampire Slayer*, the Warchowski brothers' *Matrix* cycle, and *The Wizard of Oz*.

In the first, our hero is a homeless construction worker named Nada, waiting for his luck to change. He comes upon a pair of glasses that, when he puts them on, reveal an entirely different world all around him. Splashy billboards, newspapers, and magazines are replaced with stark black and white messages: CONSUME; MARRY AND REPRODUCE; STAY ASLEEP; DO

NOT QUESTION AUTHORITY; and on the dollar bill, THIS IS YOUR GOD. Loudspeakers whisper the same messages, and the beings driving BMWs and wearing business suits turn out to be aliens. Everything he took for granted about the world, that he should work hard and play fair and it'll all work out, turns out to be false.[7] Nada must struggle to convince his buddy to put on the glasses, and struggle they do—the stars are World Wrestling Federation luminaries—in an amazing and hilarious send-up of the homoeroticism of the fisticuffs tradition. Then they must resist the aliens' lure of cooptation by becoming yuppies too, and in so doing they assume the new identity of heroic defenders of independent thought against Reagan-era bromides and the rapacious greed that undergirds them.

Apparently inhabiting a quite different world, Buffy Summers is a contented cheerleader in a normal suburban high school when she is "hailed" by the Watcher. He tells her that she is the Chosen, the incarnation of the Slayer, and must assume the mantle by killing the vampires that threaten her hometown. Buffy first scoffs at, then actively resists this identity. But to her surprise she seems to have a knack for bumping off hell fiends. Even her menstrual cramps turn out to be an early warning system of the presence of bloodsuckers. It begins to seem that she was always already the Slayer, even as the initial imposition of the name felt like a total and unwelcome surprise. And she saves her hometown. A lot.

In *The Matrix* our hero, Mr. Anderson, aka Neo, already suspicious that there's more to life than his dead-end cubicle job, is similarly called out. Morpheus gives him a choice: "Take the blue pill and the story ends. You wake up in your bed and believe whatever you want to believe. If you take the red pill you stay in Wonderland and I show you how deep the rabbit hole goes." Taking the red pill, Neo discovers that everything, including his experience of his own body, is a computer simulation, designed to turn him and all other humans into a Coppertop battery—aka a producer of surplus value. Neo resists this vision: "No, no! It can't be true! I don't believe it!" he cries, turning, horrified, from the loss of his assumptions. He is soon asked to assume the identity of the One, the savior of the other world he has found hiding behind the surface mask of existence (in which, unlike in the fantasy where everyone wears form-fitting latex, all you get is scratchy burlap). But it feels fake. He can't leap over tall buildings and, worse, the Oracle confirms he's not the One. But the very process by which Neo is duped into thinking he's a fraud is what makes possible the assumption of his true identity, which in turn saves Zion (Driscoll 2003, Irwin 2002). He also gets a lot of help from people of color and women.[8]

While Alice is overtly referenced as Neo's Girl Guide, Dorothy Gale's experiences in Oz are similar—her assumptions about the real world are shown to be illusory, and she is assumed to be a killer of witches, a false identity she vehemently denies. But her traversal of Oz to get home is a dupe, because she had that power all the time, and instead it makes her what she really is, even as it feels like a by-product and an accident when she kills another witch.

Turning from fantasy to the "desert of the real," we find that some people grow up suspicious of assumptions and some people study anthropology, finding the "tight chemise" of life looking very different through its "spyglass" (Hurston 1990:1).[9] Some, in turn, have suspicion thrust upon them. Rigoberta Menchú Tum, like many Guatemalan activists, talks about a "birth of consciousness" (*Así me nació la conciencia* is the subtitle of her original Spanish testimonial), when normal, everyday, codified, and accepted forms of physical and psychic violence are suddenly experienced as unbearable domination that demands action (Menchú Tum 1985). For the Maya-K'iche' of Chupol, *conciencia* is theory and practice, encompassing the human ability to tell good from evil and a cosmic demand to act on that knowledge (McAllister 2003).

In all these examples this realization of Durkheim's "something impersonal in us" is experienced post facto, through consciousness raising. What had been familiar becomes strange, what had felt personally true, just how the world works (Assumption One) becomes a false identity (Assumption Two) that in turn gives way to what feels like a truer sense of the self (Three) that may be the condition of possibility for political action. If this newly assumed identity feels sure enough of itself it can withstand the defense systems of the entrenched interests that benefit from people staying asleep, accepting the Coppertop status quo, unaware of the vampires in their midst. The formerly unquestioned powerful will undoubtedly accuse these assumed identities of being false and duped by silly conspiracy theories and other *babosadas*. If that doesn't work they may concede on some points, appealing to the immediate material interests of the rebels—offering beer and sausages or a nice virtual steak. And if that doesn't work it will show its other face: the sword. As Marx, Rosa Luxemburg, and others have argued, the process of facing these challenges is precisely the mechanism by which assumed identities become grounded, taken on as truly one's own, which in turn can transform the whole milieu (Laclau and Mouffe 1985). Identification and politics may be a continuous dancing of the Tz'ul. We are all transformed.

But what if the movement cannot withstand the loss of life, the ebbing of confidence, the exhaustion of the willingness to sacrifice, the constant repetition of the counterinsurgency hermeneutic that "*A los que se metieron en babosadas los engañaron* (those who got involved in foolishness were duped); Those who were organized brought the problems"? What happens when there's no professional wrestler, vampire slayer, Neo, or witch killer to save the day, no Guatemalan Nelson Mandela because everyone was killed, no pure heroes or heroines because everyone collaborated? What happens to assumptions and identity when the war is lost? And what defines loss? Are the two faces of winning versus losing, the "war between good and evil" too many for thinking about postwar Guatemala? Can we account for the current moment, adding and subtracting the different accounts (stories), separating means and ends till we get a balanced rendition, a reckoning?

Chapter Two

THE POSTWAR MILIEU: MEANS, ENDS, AND IDENTI-TIES

La paz firmado pero no firme. / Peace is formalized but not yet firmalized. Filóchofo

Do you know how to make *moronga* [blood sausage], Diana? Well, you take a mess of blood and boil it and boil it and boil it until it hardens into sausage. That's what's happened to Guatemalans. All the suffering, the blood spilled in the violence and then the boiling and boiling of the decades of war, the counterinsurgency, we have a hard time thinking new thoughts because our brains have become hard like *moronga*. Guatemalan ladino

Mean 1. to have in mind, intend; 2. to be used to express, signify, or indicate; 3. between extremes, in an intermediate position as to place, time, quantity, quality, kind, value, etc.; 4. vicious, contemptibly selfish, malicious.[1]
End 1. point of beginning or stopping; 2. the last part, completion; 3. what is desired or hoped for.

THE WAR OF THE SWORD AND THE CROSS IN THE MIDST OF THE INFORMATION AGE

On December 29, 1996, when the Guatemalan government and the URNG signed the "Acuerdo de Paz Firme y Duradera," or Firm and Lasting Peace Accord, there was a really big party on Sexta Avenida in the main square of Guatemala City.[2] In a scenario impossible for thirty-five years, guerrilla commanders stood next to army officers in a public space inside the nation. Exiles returned from all over the world, and young people came down from the hills to rejoin their families. Under the rubric of treaty implementation, a whole series of structural transformations was envisioned, with generous funding promised from the international community (Aldana et al. 1996, Armon et al. 1998, Inforpress 1996, Sieder 1998). It was a sincerely euphoric time, although few believed that Guatemala's entrenched problems would immediately disappear: the army had, after all, given itself a generous amnesty. In one of his editorial cartoons, for example, the Guatemalan philosopher and trickster Filóchofo, aka José Manuel Chacón, punned on the verb "signed" (*firmado*) and in/firm to point out the contradictions in this historic moment.

In fact, a processing period was built in to the peace accords to allow for disarmament of fighters and their reintegration into civilian life; refugee return; constitutional reforms; institutionalization of Mayan demands; and an official accounting of the violence through the CEH Commission of Historical Clarification. These were the means to an end of the war, the in-between or milieu. The UN Mission for Guatemala (MINUGUA) had already been installed to oversee the end of negotiations and the implementation of these processes and to produce frequent updates on their progress. MINUGUA's exit from Guatemala was postponed several times but finally occurred in early spring 2005. If the signing of the accord was the official end of the war, the closing of the MINUGUA offices would seem to signal the end of the postwar. Would such an end provide what is desired or hoped for? Will it yield peace—finally firm and not just *firmado*? Or is this all war by other means?

When Is the Postwar?

Most agree that the war started in 1962 with the outbreak of guerrilla struggle. The first guerrillas were nationalist army officers horrified that, among other things, the CIA was training Cuban mercenaries for the Bay of Pigs invasion on Guatemalan soil.[3] Or maybe it started in 1954 with the overthrow of Arbenz and the ensuing slaughter of activists and rollback of basic social and economic reforms (fifty years ago to the day as I write this).[4] Or maybe it started in the late nineteenth century as liberalism attacked the basis of highland indigenous survival in the interests of export plantation production. Or maybe it started even earlier, as Bolívar suggests, with growing U.S. interest in its "backyard." Or maybe it started in 1524 with the invasion by the Spanish and their Mexica allies, the opening salvo in the five-centuries-long war on indigenous people (who weren't exactly peaceful pre-Columbus). As the CEH report *Guatemala: Memory of Silence* notes, these were all factors in the civil war.

The postwar, like most posts,[5] is likewise rather difficult to pin down. The war itself waxed in the late 1960s and again in the late 1970s and early 1980s and waned over its thirty-five years, flaring in different places at different times and with different faces. Popular memory, outside observers, and the

"La Firma de la Paz." "Signing the Peace Accords should not only silence the guns: health, education, work, social justice . . . and above all access to the basic goods needed to sustain life . . . must also be democratized, otherwise . . ." On the sidebar: "Today peace is signed . . . Today begins the struggle to defend the signed accords 29/12/96." At the bottom: "Today at 15:00 in front of the memorial plaque for Oliverio Castañeda de León—with a red carnation—all lovers of peace." Castañeda de León was a student leader assassinated on Sexta Avenida, one block from the National Palace. Filóchofo. Used with kind permission.

CEH report, however, mark the period of 1978 to 1983 as the worst years, the army killing, disappearing, and massacring tens of thousands of people during that period,[6] leading the CEH to define the scorched-earth campaigns in four areas as genocide under international law.

After 1984 the fighting continued, and thousands of people were killed, tortured, and threatened. But Guatemalans began to look back on what was often called, simply, *La Violencia* or *el ochenta* (the eighties), as something that had ended but could always return. By then the army had undoubtedly won the military war, even as critics denounced it as the peace of the graveyard. The sword—machetes, guns, fire, aerial bombing—had done its work, but the war of the cross—over hearts and minds, the *meaning* of the war—was only just beginning. Of course, it had begun in 1982 with the coup by Efraín Ríos Montt and the installation of the army's Plan of Action in

Areas of Conflict (PAAC). This included the two-faced *Frijoles y Fusiles* (beans and bullets), the later *Techo, Trabajo, y Tortilla* (shelter, work, food), and the Development Pole policies (Government of Guatemala 1985, CEIDEC 1988, Schirmer 1998), all of which provided some shelter, food, potable water, and even psychological counseling for people who were captured or voluntarily turned themselves in to the army (see army P.R. images and chapter 7).

Post-1983 was the time of the classic Clausewitzian inversion: politics as war by mostly other means, as presiding General Hector Gramajo said (1995:441).[7] A new constitution was drafted, replacing that of 1965, which had legitimized military control of the state, and thirty years of military governments ended when a civilian was elected president in 1985, and another was elected in 1990, although he left power in disgrace in 1993. His successor was named by the elected National Congress, and power has turned over peacefully to elected wealthy ladino men four more times.

By "the cross" I mean ideology, that many-faced thing, which, according to Louis Althusser, works through a series of "ideological state apparatuses" (ISA), including the church, the home, the school, the law, communications, bookkeeping, politics, and culture, defined as literature, art, and sports (1971:143). Rosa Luxemburg focuses on the commodity market and the place where surplus value is produced but where accumulation appears to be a purely economic process: "Peace, property and equality prevail and the keen dialectics of scientific analysis were required to reveal . . . how commodity exchange turns into exploitation and how equality becomes class rule" (in Harvey 137). You could say these ISAs are the means to an end. They are how something—like interpellation or assuming an identity—gets done. Below I trace how the war by other means was waged on all these sites.

The war of the cross is a war over meaning, significance, and also over intent. It struggles to convert you but is always suspicious that it's being duped. It often hinges on a notion of two faces, the question of what lies behind a particular statement or action. From the state's point of view a woman asking for the return of her disappeared husband or child may say she only wants her loved one back, but her real intent is subversive—to make the government look bad. From an antigovernment point of view the state may say the war is over and democracy is flowering, but its real intent is to maintain the unequal status quo. These are struggles over make-believe—both to decipher the meaning or intent of the other and to translate one's own hopes into a desired end. Between 1983 and December 1996 Guatemala's government tried to prove that its assumed identity as human rights pariah was false and that its true identity was a good investment climate and upstand-

Giving water to the people. The caption reads, "Another source of water in Acul. If potable water used to be a distant dream, today it is no longer new but available everyday, to improve the standards of living and production (Army Public Relations)." Government of Guatemala, 1985.

The caption reads, "Potable water, electric light, new and comfortable houses, these are the works of the government helping the residents of Acul, who were previously dispersed, now they are resettled after undergoing the uprooting and suffering inflicted by the subversion (Public Relations of the State Command)." Government of Guatemala, 1985.

A grandmother in front of the former military academy shows photographs of her grandchildren who disappeared during the armed conflict. Photograph by Daniel Hernández-Salazar. Used with kind permission.

ing member of the international community. Networks of Guatemalans and solidarity activists throughout the global north, in turn, struggled to raise consciousness about past and ongoing violence and thereby influence governmental and UN/International Monetary Fund (IMF)/World Bank policies toward Guatemala. We pushed hard against military aid and for concrete reforms, not just rhetoric, justice for the perpetrators of war crimes, and a peace treaty. In fact, Guatemalan military personnel frequently complained that despite the army's battlefield successes the guerrilla were, with the help of their allegedly duped supporters, winning the global propaganda war.

Meanwhile, Guatemala was becoming ground zero for another form of political struggle — over ethnic-national identifications in the context of the Columbus Quincentennial of 1992. The Mayan movement that began making global headlines was the culmination of decades of local, hemispheric, and global organizing of indigenous peoples, some of it in collaboration with nonindigenous people and organizations like the UN. In Guatemala this process was marked by the specific roles indigenous people played in the civil war—as guerrillas, soldiers, victims, patrollers, peasants, survivors, and increasingly human rights activists, teachers, lawyers, and international celebrities.[8] Rigoberta Menchú Tum, a Maya-K'iche' woman, was awarded the Nobel Peace Prize (the youngest person ever so honored) and named UN Goodwill Ambassador.

Perhaps this period, from 1983 to 1996, was the first postwar.

Reckoning the Postwar

This book primarily focuses on the period from December 1996, which marked the end of overt hostilities and the official beginning of the postwar, to 2005, when, after a protracted process, the UN mission closed. It's not easy to reckon the end/s of the war/s, either temporally or in terms of achievements. If anything, the situation of poverty, insecurity, and human rights may be worse for many people now than in 1996. As with the assumptions of identity, when I try to get at the crux of the matter, to draw the fine line between war and peace, I am seeking the deciding point. But a crux (cross) is "a puzzling thing" — as if the very idea of truly figuring things out were a con.[9] So I'll swerve, following Judith Butler, who posits a power "relentlessly marked by a figure of turning" (1987:3), into context, which might also be called the *ambiente* (environment or setting). In this I am inspired by Filóchofo, the nom de plume of a well-known Guatemalan cartoonist and passionate *ambientalista*. By this I mean he is an environmentalist, interested in limiting destructive oil exploration, saving the rain forest, cleaning up toxic waste, and protecting endangered species. And for Filóchofo these include not only jaguars and quetzals but also fellow *chapines* (slang for Guatemalan). As a good "Green" he knows this does not mean simply saving individual creatures, but the entire ecology that sustains them. In pursuit of this end he has employed various means: he is an important interventionist in Guatemala's social and political environment through his books, ecoactivism with the organization Madre Selva (Mother Jungle), and especially his popular op-ed cartoons. These not only skewer corrupt politicians by revealing the hypocrisy hiding behind the rhetoric, but also network people through the sidebars that denounce particular abuses or announce demonstrations, benefit concerts, and so forth. In this he's rather more effective than the government's official ombudsperson. And precisely because of this he has been increasingly censored.

Laclau and Mouffe (1985) connect the several senses of "articulate" — meaning both to connect and to speak well or put into words — to political practice. Like "cleave," it means simultaneously to be separated into joints and connected by them. Filóchofo is articulate — often finding the perfect symbol or turn of phrase to condense the personalities of the powerful, for example, Ríos Montt as a deathless, blood-loving vampire. He is also both a remarker on and active participant in his surroundings or milieu. He articulates or lashes together ideas, people, and place. For him, as for Laclau and Mouffe, articulation is recombinant, a relationship that changes what it relates. Satire is defined as "irony, derision, or caustic wit used to attack or expose human folly, vice, or stupidity," and it can be alchemical. Jokes are a swerving means to reckon with meanness or cruelty, a way to expose unexpected connections via the laughter linking teller and recipient.

I would connect this to Bruno Latour's discussion of science-in-action, the construction of facts through the lashing or tying together of actants. Appropriately enough, his patron is the two-faced Janus. Latour describes laboratories as highly social, their science is strong, real, only if they can mobilize the highest number of associations, linkages, resources, and allies. "The construction of facts . . . is a collective process" (1987:104). He coins the term "technoscience" to emphasize the networking involved ("technic" from Gr. *technikos* < *techne*, an art, artifice < IE. base *tekth-* to weave, build, join) in the process of discerning, of actively *making* sense and meaning. Science-in-action means looking at what labs do, which is to lash or tie actants—human and nonhuman—together into networks. They translate what lies in-between them (*inter-esse*) so they can begin to act together.

One of many examples he uses is a windmill. A tool is a single element held directly in the hand. A machine severs the link between tool and body and ties them to one another: "The pestle is a tool in the woman's hand; she is stronger with it than with her hands alone, for now she is able to grind corn. However, if you tie the grinder to a wooden frame and if this frame is tied to the sails of a mill that profits from the wind, this is a machine, a windmill, that puts into the miller's hands an assembly of forces no human could ever match." This entails negotiations with the wind, the farmers, and the nuts and bolts. The miller "has to tailor a machine that can stay open to the wind and still be immune to its deleterious effects. Severing the association between the sail mechanism and the tower on which the mill is built will do the trick. The top of the mill now revolves. Of course, there is a price to pay, for now you need more cranks and a complicated system of wheels, but the wind has been made into a valuable ally." People too become interested in the mill: "No matter how good they were at handling the pestle, they now have to pass through the mill. Thus they are kept in line just as much as the wind is" (1987:129). Laboratories are a similar form of machine, elements simultaneously separated out and lashed together. They seek to hold on to borrowed forces and keep them in check so that none can fly apart from the group. They struggle to become an "obligatory passage point" (1987:129).

But Latour also suggests that even as each element tied together becomes a conductor or transmitter, it is a multiconductor as well, and an unpredictable one at that. Each element may act in multifarious ways, modifying, appropriating, ignoring, mutating, incorporating into it new elements, and incorporating it into new contexts. Latour says that laboratories become "powerful enough to define reality" but "reality, as the Latin word res indicates, is what resists. What does it resist? Trials of strength" (1987:93).

I borrow from Filóchofo, Laclau, Mouffe, and Latour to explore the articulations, networks, or means of what we might call the postwar in action. This may be less a period with a definite end (temporal *or* outcome) than a laboratory where different interests — the former insurgency, the counterinsurgency, the state, the army, the elites, indigenous people, the popular movement, the Maya, transnational actors — struggle to hold on to borrowed forces and to create "obligatory passage points." Perhaps this is what gives the impression of multiple faces.

While these articulations are structured by dominance and inequality, they are also sites and stakes of struggle, often highly unpredictable. These borrowings, through the recombinant action of articulation, become assumptions of identity. The very connection of, say, being related to a victim of state violence, *may* lead to interpellation, being hailed, like Buffy, Nada, Neo, and Dorothy, to take on a new identity of, say, widow, then activist. I emphasize the word "may," however, because this is an unpredictable process, each element acting in multifarious ways, owing, in part, to its other connections. So identity may be less an end than a means, less a thing than a set of relations like Butler's "passionate attachments" (Butler 1997:6), identities.

Here I explore several trials of strength that, like the CEH, produced reality in the postwar *ambiente*. I focus on the mobility of identi-ties and on what lies between, aka interest or mean: between war and its end/s, between the accords and implementation, between action and reckoning, and the struggles over what can be assumed, or made to go without saying. What are the assumptions of identity produced in this lab?

AN END AND A BEGINNING: JANUARY 1997–ON

The CEH concludes that agents of the State of Guatemala,
within the framework of counterinsurgency operations
carried out between 1981 and 1983, committed acts of genocide
against groups of Mayan people. . . . This conclusion is based
on the evidence that, in light of Article II of the Convention on
the Prevention and Punishment of the Crime of Genocide, the

> killing of members of Mayan groups occurred; serious bodily
> or mental harm was inflicted; and the group was deliberately
> subjected to living conditions calculated to bring about its
> physical destruction in whole or in part. UN Commission for
> Historical Clarification (CEH)

Enormous energy and enthusiasm were poured into implementing the various accords that make up the final peace treaty. Refugees were resettled both in their original communities and on new plots provided by the government, usually bought at exorbitant prices from opportunistic landowners (Manz 2004, Taylor 1998, Velásquez Nimatuj 2005, Worby 2002a, 2002b). The Mayan cultural rights movement gained in organization, sophistication, and institutionalization, especially in education and law. The popular movement, including students, unions, peasants, and indigenous organizing, came above ground and, despite threats and the assassinations of a number of members, has made important headway in land, labor, and other rights. In June 2004 and March 2005 they shut down the entire country to protect access to land and to protest the Central America Free Trade Agreement (CAFTA). Civic committees and progressive political parties have emerged and won congressional seats and mayorships. Women, both ladinas and Maya, have become increasingly well organized, in part, like many of these constituencies, through the very process of negotiating and implementing the peace accords. Organizations of gay, lesbian, and transgender people have emerged, and Guatemala City saw its first Pride march in 2000.[10] Once impossible, academic and applied research by Guatemalans is flourishing through the universities and a number of investigation centers. NGOs devoted to all manner of projects are working, although some people complain of the *tallerización* of civil society, constant workshops that never accomplish anything, and, thanks to audit culture, that many activists must spend most of June and July scrambling to finish their annual reports to international funders.

These accomplishments are truly heroic, especially given the devastation the war visited on these sectors. All of these gains were achieved in the face of passionate divisions, debilitating splits, and debates over means, ends, and interests. The latter were often couched in the language of corruption—are you really here to advance the cause or only to get rich or pursue a personal agenda? Actual stealing and fraud may be widespread as witnessed by the leap in class strata made by many public servants, but unfounded rumors of malfeasance can also have devastating effects. Losing the faith of an international donor has doomed more than one postwar project. Accounting as an auditing procedure—those increasingly ubiquitous funders' reports—promises to ensure that personal enrichment, at least, will not occur. But charges of corruption, or duplicity, with their accompanying promise of accountability, the rendering of a single, transparent face, also traffic in far more "religico-cosmopolitical judgments" (Maurer 2002b:6).

Postwar reckoning also butts up against the deep-seated material interests of social blocs that were willing to commit genocide to maintain their positions. The accords concerning the role of the military in peacetime and the socioeconomic structure were the most contentiously debated (popular rejection of the latter almost derailed the negotiations in 1996) and remain the hardest to implement, even in their watered-down form. This is because they address the crux of the war—its ends (transformation in the relations of production vs. maintenance of plantation-based and now maquila export–led development) and its means (multicultural social democracy installed by armed resistance or militarized pigmentocracy). It could be argued that the war of the sword was most ferocious when these issues were truly at risk, in 1981–82, when it looked like the guerrillas could take power. When that threat was eliminated the government could turn its soft face, that is, the cross, for the mop-up operations. This is true (and pessimism of the intellect at its best). But it does not account for how much transformation has occurred in these sites—if far more slowly than the popular movement hoped for. Throughout I'll explore the means and ends of development and suggest that the economy of the supposedly autonomous free market (one that is not enough) is not separate from the social and political. The accountant's pen and ledger are intimately connected to the sword (*non du père*) and the cross (*nom du père*).

On another down side to implementation, the peace accords were meant to be popularly legitimated after their signing. In the torturous means to reach this end, everything negotiated for almost a decade was condensed into four questions[11] on which Guatemalans were to vote simply yes or no (Bastos and Camus 2003, Saqb'ichil/COPMAGUA 2000, Jonas 2000, Hernández Pico 2005, Warren and Jackson 2002). There was incredible grassroots organizing by referendum supporters throughout the country. However, the often racist claims of opponents that it would force ladinos to learn all twenty-plus Mayan languages; that it would give indigenous people the right to claim whatever land they wanted—like your swimming pool—by saying it was a sacred area; and that it would encourage indigenous men to have sex with ladina women, as well as widespread confusion about the process, led to the defeat of the reforms at the ballot box, despite an overwhelming

"¡SI, estamos con las reformas!" "To take power away from the army; to make health care free; to improve the justice system; to respect the Mayan Peoples; to improve the wages of state workers; and for the 200,000 victims of the war . . . YES, We are with the reforms!" Filóchofo. Used with kind permission.

"Areas where the YES won." Voting on the Popular Consultation divided the country between the majority indigenous north (yes) and the mostly ladino south (no). Filóchofo. Used with kind permission.

majority for the yes in rural and indigenous areas. Struggles continue on various sites for these stakes, but it was a terrible blow to the implementation of the peace accords.

Perhaps the greatest success of this period was in rendering accounts of what occurred through the two so-called truth commissions. REMHI (Recuperation of Historical Memory) was organized by the Catholic Church's Human Rights Office of the Archbishop and published as the four-volume *Guatemala Nunca Más!* (Never Again!) (REMHI 1998). But the success came at a terrible price. Just days after its public presentation Monseñor Juan Gerardi, the bishop overseeing the investigation, was brutally murdered.[12] Things have changed dramatically since the 1980s and even more since the treaty was signed. Before 1996 most people would not even utter the name of a guerrilla organization out loud, and now they are a political party. But fear of a horrifying death hangs over every attempt to reckon with what occurred. All of the networking and struggle I address entails constant fear, long nights worrying if your children will be okay, wondering if every phone call or footfall heard passing by your home brings a threat. Since 1997 activists have been killed while walking to their fields, while driving in their cars down busy urban streets, while eating lunch in a small restaurant. Even

"Never Again: Impacts of the Violence." Cover of the report of the Guatemalan Archbishop's Office of Human Rights on the Recuperation of Historical Memory, Volume 1 (REMHI). Photograph by Daniel Hernández-Salazar. Used with kind permission.

such well-known actors as Menchú Tum do not feel safe in Guatemala, as she resumed a semi-exile in Mexico City in the early 2000s. Being a multi-conductor requires enormous courage.

The second truth commission, the UN's CEH, opened offices throughout the country and interviewed thousands of people to create its twelve-volume report entitled *Guatemala: Memory of Silence*. On February 25, 1999, the findings were presented in the National Theater on Sexta Avenida in downtown Guatemala City, where all two thousand seats were packed and hundreds of people watched the proceedings on screens outside. The audience visibly reacted to the power of the conclusions, especially that of genocide. Unlike its counterpart in South Africa, the CEH was empowered neither to identify or punish individual perpetrators nor to provide any sort of reparations to the victims, but the findings and recommendations were meant to be taken into account in government policies (although making this happen is an ongoing struggle). Both reports were published in condensed form in newspapers, on-line, on CD-ROM, and in popular formats—meaning easily accessible, in simpler language—in newspaper and illustrated comic book form. Despite their limitations, they opened a public and national-level reckoning, both a figuring up—and out—and a measuring of possibilities for the future.

"¡Eso no es cierto!" "The government has lowered the profile of the CEH report because 'the army continues to exercise the real power'" (Aldo Morales, CONADEHGUA [a human rights organization]). "THAT'S NOT TRUE!" says President Alvaro Arzú (in his conquistador helmet). Filóchofo. Used with kind permission.

Denial Is Not Just a River in Egypt

As so many of the reckonings of the war make clear in their titles—Memory of Silence, Refugees of a Hidden War, Silence on the Mountain, There is Nothing Hidden that Will Not Be Discovered—secrecy, cover-up, and denial were widespread. Silence allowed certain assumptions—for example, that the state holds the monopoly on the legitimate use of force—to go unchallenged. As Gerardi's assassination made clear, being in the know is a site and stake of struggle. "Muera la inteligencia!" But knowing alone may not be enough. "Everyone" may know something very well without its becoming a fact, without its creating a new consciousness which would entail people assuming it in the third sense, of its becoming a true identity.

The CEH's intricately argued finding of genocide was perhaps the biggest surprise of the report's presentation. Because genocide is a special class of crime, the finding opened the door to trying army officers. It created a new reality, and in its wake global legal structures lash with highland indigenous peasants, forensic anthropologists, and organizations like the Menchú Foundation and the Centro de Asistencia Legal y de Derechos Humanos (CALDH, Center for Legal Defense and Human Rights), to bring military men to court. However, the United States has used the current government's responses to the report as justification to renew military aid. As Bill Maurer suggests, "Audit cultures" link accounting as narration with numeric record keeping into "new regimes of management, organization and control" that promise balance and clarity (Maurer 2002b:3). Symptomatically, in their joint news conference on March 24, 2005, announcing the lifting of the ban, President Oscar Berger of Guatemala and U.S. Secretary of Defense Donald Rumsfeld both spoke of transparency. Rumsfeld said, "I've been impressed by the reforms that have been undertaken in the armed forces. I know it is a difficult thing to do but it's been done with professionalism and transparency." Berger said, "The shadow that was above our army has disappeared. . . . Today we have a transparent army with half the personnel" (Thompson 2005:A7). But critics question the accounting. They insist that the vaunted transparency, anticorruption measures, and troop reductions are a ruse. The army has cooked the books by privatizing, or parastating, continuing human rights violations and its drug and weapons running into what activists call "clandestine apparatuses." They are demanding, as I explore in chapter 6, a fuller accounting.

Below I explore several trials of strength that untied the realities of denial and impunity and produced new facts and new assumptions of identity. While acknowledging that it is a puzzle as much as a deciding point, the crux of the postwar is a war of the cross—a struggle over ideas, belief, information, denial, assumptions, ideology, which means, as I said, both what is most false and most true, knowledge, and acknowledgment.

In two cases these new facts took the form of apologies. In April 2004 the Guatemalan government officially recognized and apologized for its role in the assassination of the Guatemalan anthropologist Myrna Mack Chang. "In the name of the state, I ask for the forgiveness of the Mack family and of the people of Guatemala for the murder of this young anthropologist," said the newly installed President Berger, accompanied by the heads of Congress and the Supreme Court (Associated Press 2004). This public act of recognition was ordered by the CIDH (Interamerican Court of Human Rights), as was payment of some $780,000 of indemnization. The government was also ordered to take specific steps to counter impunity. Given that for over a decade the state and parastatal actors had denied its role, protected the perpetrators, and threatened and even killed people who might expose or confirm this very information, it was a historic event.[13]

It was also historic when, in July 1999, President Bill Clinton went to Guatemala and offered an apology for the role of the United States in the war. He asked forgiveness for the mistake made by the United States in supporting a repressive, right-wing government and said that "for the United States it is important that I state clearly that support for military forces and intelligence units which engaged in violence and widespread repression was wrong, and the United States must not repeat this mistake" (Broder 1999:A1).

Suspicion as to the sincerity of the apologies may be justified. Are they just words, only symbolic? Cynical reason might mimic Bolívar's worries that apologies are, like "the name of freedom," a cover-up; or, worse, represent a nefarious new role assumed by the state/s, Guatemalan and United—a more cunning form of governmentality, aka war by other means. As Althusser reminds us, states reduced to violently imposing power are actually weaker than those in which "the vast majority of (good) subjects work all right 'all by themselves,' i.e. by ideology" (1971:181). Are the apologies meant to bamboozle? To co-opt? The Berger government managed to convince two of the most powerful symbols of the popular movement, Nobel laureate Menchú Tum and CALDH lawyer Frank LaRue, to act in its name.[14]

On the other hand, while Berger and Clinton were saying what almost everyone already knew, the enunciation was still important. What is at stake in naming responsibility, in acknowledge/meant? Taking articulation seriously means attending to what is spoken and the power of the name. And understanding the postwar in action means paying strict attention to interest, while keeping in mind Gupta's warning that "discourses give shape and meaning to interests rather than assume that they are the hollow form occupied by ontologically prior, well-shaped interests" (1998:370). This means cultivating a cynical or conspiratorial sense of what is desired by such actions, and how we may be possessed or doubled over to be used for others' interests because power does deny and lie, trying to show a smiling face to cover horrific violence. But it also means, simultaneously, paying attention to *inter-esse* as what lies in-between. Between, for example, the face that denies and the face that acknowledges, aka the struggle, the lashing, the making believe. Our patroness, the Virgen de Tránsito, keeps us tuned to mobility and to each node in these networks as an unpredictable multi-conductor. If men make war and war makes men, then exploring the assumptions of identity may help us understand how the postwar is made by people (in what follows I happen to focus on women) and how those people are made.

DÓNDE ESTÁ EL FUTURO / WHERE IS THE FUTURE? SOME ASSUMPTIONS OF IDENTI-TIES

[Myrna Mack] gave her life in the hopes of economic, political, and social changes in our country. She bet on the future.
Rigoberta Menchú Tum

We cannot reduce the action of the microbe to a sociological explanation, since the action of the microbe redefined not only society but also nature and the whole caboodle. Bruno Latour

When we lose certain people, or when we are dispossessed from a place, or a community, we may simply feel that we are

> undergoing something temporary, that mourning will be over
> and some restoration of a prior order will be achieved. But
> maybe when we undergo what we do, something about who we
> are is revealed, something that delineates the ties we have to
> others, that shows us that these ties constitute what we are,
> ties or bonds that compose us. Judith Butler

Myrna Mack was assassinated on September 11, 1990.[15] She was stabbed twenty-seven times as she was leaving the AVANCSO office, the research institute she helped found. From the start, many suspected that the official story—that her murder was a common crime—was false. In fact, it was a classic public secret that the government at the time, the first that was democratically elected and civilian in twenty years, was mostly a mask for the still-regnant military.

But while an official, internationally recognized seal of approval for postwar democratization bestowed after fair enough elections often does mask deeply undemocratic structures, I'm arguing that the process itself is a site and stake of struggle. Mack's murder, like Bishop Gerardi's in 1998, shows that war is not really two-faced because sword and cross always work together. Two is too many (a mask versus a real face), but one (it's all the same) is not enough. In this sense 1990 was part of the first postwar. Things *were* different from the early 1980s.

In this section I explore the milieu of Myrna Mack's work, her murder, and finally the actions that led to President Berger's apology for it. Along the way I'll situate President Clinton's apology, which was also the effect of great struggle and extraordinarily welcome, although it was quite literally the least he could do. I'll reckon with the importance of U.S. collaboration in Guatemala's agony but don't want to reinscribe gringo narcissism by making it the prime or only actant. This would drain Guatemalans of agency and responsibility for the war and the postwar and be more a great powers version of history than the more mobile, tenuous assumption of identity version I'm trying to articulate. To do so, I'll map out a network that focuses on a league of extraordinary gentlewomen and their assumptions of identity, using Mack's trajectory to quilt these identi-ties.

Historically in Guatemala it has been assumed that gender, ethnic, national, and other identifications hinge on a series of apparent binaries like public/private, knowledge/secrecy, state/civil society, political/personal, dictatorship/democracy, urban/rural, ladino/indigenous, man/woman, Christian/pagan, owner/worker. You will note that these are not simple binaries but power inequalities. The end or goal of the Guatemalan popular and revolutionary projects was to transform—to untie and relink these sites in new ways, to redistribute power, with some members focusing more or less on particular binaries. And this movement was actually quite successful in creating collaborations. It often managed to bridge the gaps among identifications, relating ladinos with indigenous peoples and indigenous peoples among themselves as well as lashing in transnational actors from both the global north and south, including radicalized Spanish priests, revolutionaries from Cuba, El Salvador, Nicaragua, and elsewhere, NGO financial support, and solidarity from a range of actors, including academics, the UN, international indigenous organizations, labor, and members of rural U.S. Protestant churches, among others. Possessing such new identities as the means to an end was often a recombinant process that redefined both means and ends. People in the United States lashed in, via Menchú's testimonial, for example, to feel concern for the murder of innocent indigenous people and might find themselves questioning U.S. foreign and domestic policy more generally, thereby becoming *gringos*—a North American in relation to Guatemala. Indigenous people who joined the Campesino Unity Committee (CUC) for access to better wages and land began to understand their situation as being about both class oppression and racism (becoming Maya). People in these movements carefully theorized these processes through Liberation Theology and/or Marx and/or Che Guevara and the idea of the New Man [sic], in which the milieu dialectically produces people; a revolution makes different kinds of humans than godless capitalism does. These new people in turn transform the milieu. Thus the end is also a means. In turn, the transformation results from both structural changes and active intent, like criticism/self-criticism sessions and other techniques of the self, a process McAllister describes in detail for the *conciencia* of people in the liberated zone of Chupol. These assumptions of identity sublate—they simultaneously carry along power inequalities and they redefine the "whole caboodle."

To return to a personal example of these politics, Myrna Mack and her siblings grew up on the privileged side of these divisions. Their parents fled mainland China and became wealthy plantation owners in Guatemala. Myrna was raised with the children of the elite, riding fine horses, studying ballet, and receiving the best education private Catholic institutions could offer. These institutions, however, were being unlashed from the traditional church (the ultraconservative archbishop Mario Casariego served from 1964 to 1983 and actively supported the military governments, even blessing army vehicles) and connecting to a new cross, of "the preferential option for the poor." Unlike her siblings, who went into lucrative careers in business, Myrna became involved at school with a group of Jesuits, including Father Pellecer, who was later tortured and turned against the popular movement, and Father Ricardo Falla, an anthropologist, activist, and author (1980, 1984, 1988, 1992), and with community members of both the urban slums and the indigenous highlands, many of whom were active in Catholic Action. Myrna studied anthropology, and that, in turn, indirectly connected her with a woman I'll call Esperanza León.

León lives in a small compound in Patzulá, a tiny hamlet of Joyabaj with her two daughters and a granddaughter. Her son, the one who likes Bruce Lee, has gone to the United States to work. She's not sure where he is, but he still sends a little money now and then. Unlike Myrna, she received no formal education. She, like her daughters, speaks K'iche' but very little Spanish and cannot read or write. She and her husband were very involved in Catholic Action as lay church workers.

Formed in 1905 and gaining strength through the 1930s, Catholic Action was a church revitalization movement to purge "pagan" elements. In the mid-1950s it was enlisted by the post-Arbenz counterinsurgency state to purge Communism from the countryside. However, the sword and cross of the Cold War assault on Guatemala's rural area created unexpected networks with unintended consequences (Falla 1978, González 2002, McAllister 2003). Catholic Action became a powerful local tool to challenge the gerontocracy—a way to make meaningful the huge changes in production and the increasing influence of the (trans)national on local organization (Brintnall 1979, Cook 2000, Warren 1989). By exorcising *costumbre* from the Church and instilling more Weberian attitudes toward saving money and resisting excessive drinking, Catholic Action seemed to offer progressive possibilities. Thus, through a series of unexpected articulations, in some places it shed its anti-Communist face and linked to Liberation Theology and to the popular, then to the revolutionary movement; some priests even became guerrillas, as did many catechists. Service as a catechist linked people to wider-ranging power networks, and many now-prominent indigenous people, including Menchú Tum and Rosalina Tuyuc, tied in. It was through Catholic Action that many Guatemalans articulated Liberation Theology with already well-defined goals of social justice and land reform. Catholic Action connected with the Ligas Campesinas (Peasant Leagues) and incubated the CUC and the Christian Democrat (DC) party. In 1974 the DC presidential candidate, Ríos Montt, won but was not allowed to take office.[16] In 1978 the DC mayoral candidate won in Joyabaj, becoming the first mayor ever to identify as indigenous, but he was forced to flee for his life several years later.

In Joyabaj, as elsewhere, Catholic Action and the CUC organized production and consumption cooperatives, local land reform initiatives, strikes for better wages on the plantations, and, when these actions met violent reactions from local and national elites, protests of human rights abuses. In January 1980 members of CUC and student activists occupied the Spanish embassy in Guatemala City to draw attention to the violence occurring in the highlands, including the murder of Menchú Tum's little brother. The Guatemalan army stormed the embassy, killing almost everyone inside by fire, including Vicente Menchú, Rigoberta's father. The single survivor was disappeared from his hospital bed, his body later dumped at the National University. The embassy massacre was a turning point, convincing many people, ladino, indigenous, and international, that peaceful change was impossible. Inspired in part by the recent Sandinista victory in Nicaragua, thousands took up arms against economic exploitation, racist exclusion, and brutal repression.

The army and elites had also learned from Nicaragua and had no desire to "wash dishes in Miami" as one colonel told me. As I mentioned earlier, state violence hit Joyabaj in fiesta season when the parish priest, although not considered particularly political, was assassinated on July 10, 1980, and the military occupied the town. Priests, nuns, and catechists were murdered throughout the highlands, leading the Catholic Church to completely shut the Quiché diocese in protest. Army massacres began in the Joyabaj hamlets in February 1981, the Cenizas 81 offensive. In scenes out of a bad horror film, bodies were mutilated and decapitated, and families were barred from burying the dead. "They were eaten by dogs . . . until they got fat. . . . If someone tried to [bury them] he would die just like the corpses," a survivor recalls (REMHI testimony 00945 in Remijnse 2002:117). Esperanza's husband was killed, and she and her children, like tens of thousands of other rural Guatemalans, spent months living "like animals" in the surrounding hills and ravines, eating what they could find, terrified the army would find them and kill them.

Many people in remote areas of the departments of Quiché, Peten, and the Verapaces remained in hiding from the army but within Guatemalan territory, forming the Communities of Population in Resistance (CPR).[17] The existence of the CPR was the topic of excited rumor among some and of intense denial by the military state, because if it were lashed together in a particular formation with international laws of war, they could constitute a liberated territory which would redefine the whole caboodle. Of course, for much of the war, the military denied the existence of guerrillas as well. Father Falla accompanied the CPR for several years (described in Falla 1992, 1998), and Myrna was researching their situation when she was murdered.

Her study, *Dónde Está el Futuro? Procesos de reintegración en comunidades de retornados* (Where Is the Future? Processes of Reintegration in Returnee Communities) (AVANCSO 1992), was heroically completed by Myrna's grieving research team, who themselves feared for their lives. Unlike the CPR, but like many people in southern Quiché, Esperanza and other survivors moved back to her hamlet and tried to rebuild a life.

One reason the CEH found that genocide occurred is that government counterinsurgency tended to be selective among ladinos, singling out leaders, members of organizations, or people who stuck out, like priests, nuns, or researchers like Mack. Violence against the indigenous people in certain areas, however, was massive, indiscriminate, and terribly lethal, destroying whole villages at a time, displacing at least a million people — some for months, like Esperanza, some for years or even decades.

In the early 1980s the army seemed caught between two faces. On the one hand they wanted to publicize the threat of subversion to fit neatly into anti-Communist sentiment and funding opportunities in the United States under Ronald Reagan and to show their success in combating it. But on the other they consistently denied they were doing much of anything, much less that they were purposefully targeting indigenous people.[18] They also made it practically impossible for Guatemalans or gringos to go to the highlands to either confirm or deny the stories that leaked out of the refugee camps or from the few who made it into exile.[19]

Another form of denial practiced in the highlands but particularly affecting urban ladinos was disappearance. While it is said that "to disappear" became a verb in Guatemala, it is a staple of counterinsurgency practices throughout Latin America, and now, in the post–9/11 United States also, under the euphemism extraordinary rendition). It means an unacknowledged kidnapping: family members do not know where their loved one is, what is happening to them, or whether they are still alive (Figueroa Ibarra 1991). It removes the possibility of mourning or healing because the fate of the disappeared remains unclear. It is linked to plausible deniability and official stories that are hard to disprove: the missing person has gone off to join the guerrillas, they have run off with another woman, they have tried to emigrate to the United States but didn't make it, and so on. It is a mechanism of horror.

Nineth García de Montenegro lost her husband to this practice in the early 1980s and went on to found the Mutual Support Group for Families of the Disappeared (GAM), and later became an outstanding human rights activist and congresswoman. While receiving constant death threats, she was named Guatemala's Woman of the Year in 2004. In the mid-1980s two organizations, first GAM and later the Guatemala National Widows' Committee (CONAVIGUA), a primarily indigenous organization, began to connect family members of victims of disappearance and other state violence. They demanded, and still demand, information as to the whereabouts of their loved ones, their return, and justice for those responsible. "¡Vivos Los Llevaron, Vivos Los Queremos!" (Alive You Took Them, Alive We Want Them Back!) is their slogan. The response was repressive in the word's double entendre—neither information nor their loved ones were forthcoming, and leaders like Hector Gómez Calito and Rosario Godoy de Cuevas and her son and brother, like other members of GAM, were murdered.

The state called these deaths accidents or common crime or denounced the activists as duplicitous. Really fronts for guerrilla organizations (*babosadas*), they were responsible for their own deaths, their own undoing was proof of their crime. Of course, masquerade is the ruse of the oppressed, and some of the participants in GAM, CONAVIGUA, and other popular mobilizations were already politicized before their loved ones were disappeared (Velásquez Nimatuj 2005:121). They *were* consciously strategizing ways to change the power equation in the country, within a terribly circumscribed terrain. But many others assumed this identity of political actor through these very experiences of dispossession or went clandestine because of state strategies of violence.

Resettled in her hamlet, Esperanza León was already active as a catechist in the slow revival of Catholic Action, although this was a face clearly identified by the army as dangerous. According to the CEH, in the Joyabaj area "the repression affected religious, political and development leaders. The principal victims . . . were members of Catholic Action, the Mayan priests, members of CUC, and members of the improvement committees and Cooperatives" (CEH 5.3:380). Nonetheless, León also became an early member of CONAVIGUA, which was started by Tuyuc and other indigenous women, many of whom had also been active in Catholic Action and had also lost their husbands, sons, and/or fathers. Identifying with CONAVIGUA meant that Esperanza had to trek several hours back and forth from Patzulá to Joyabaj for meetings and confronted not only the terrifying suspicions of the powerful that "meetings are suspect and subversive," but also the ugly suggestions of other indigenous women that members were "indecent and improper women," neglecting their housework and walking around the place instead (Remijnse 2002:184). In 2002 one of their members, Manuel García de la Cruz, was tortured and murdered. In 2003 Esperanza helped organize the exhumation of a clandestine cemetery in Patzulá.

Sites and Stakes of Struggle

For Esperanza and other members of GAM, CONAVIGUA, and Catholic Action as well as victims of dirty wars throughout Latin America, the notion of the home, family, and church as external to state functioning was brutally traversed by counterinsurgency practices that targeted precisely these sites (see Bouvard 1994, Bunster-Burotto 1986, CEH 1999, Franco 1999). In turn these sites pivot, as conduction points, becoming unexpected loci of articulation and resistance in ongoing tests of strength.

Articulation is both connection—Esperanza walking about the highlands, linking via meetings and activism with larger organizations like the Church, other widows, forensic anthropologists, and gringas like me—and putting into words. Knowledge is not only power, but also information. The way facts are linked together to make sense was and is a site and stake of struggle, a matter of life or death. With the macabre humor I've found common in Guatemala, Myrna Mack would joke, "In the United States, you say 'publish or perish.' Here, we say 'if we publish, we perish'" (in Oglesby 1995:255). Like the GAM leaders and more recently murdered activists, she was killed over information, specifically her research with refugees and the internally displaced. However, it was not only this information gathering that was read as threatening to the plausible deniability and sanctioned ignorance that smoothes state functioning. It was her active meaning-*making*, the way she connected the dots, and by doing so articulated or lashed together relations—both analytic and human.

Mack's murder was an act of terrorism: "premeditated, politically motivated violence perpetrated against noncombatant targets by subnational groups or clandestine agents, usually intended to influence an audience" (US Code Title 22 Section 2656f[d]). Terror seems simultaneously aimed at destroying sense and at sending a clear-cut message. In Guatemala City on September 11, 1990 and in New York City on September 11, 2001, as well as in Kabul on October 7, 2001, and Baghdad on March 19, 2003, bodies are used to send a message. In Guatemala the militarized state assumed (took for granted) that the meaning made through Myrna's public murder, as through disappearances and the clandestine graves of massacre victims, was that resistance is futile, there is no alternative. But the body, like the family, home, church, school, and law is an ambivalent tool, like the cross, deployed to conquer and to resist. Living and dead, it is less a thing than a relation of power.

Through struggle Myrna's body assumed (took on as a true identity) a rather different meaning than the state had intended. As with members of

GAM and CONAVIGUA, Myrna's family relations were the pivot point that transformed her death from one of hundreds of thousands where the authors got away with murder into an international cause célebre, resulting in the historic state apology. In relation with other struggles preceding and surrounding it, Myrna's sister Helen Mack helped generate this change.

Before the assassination, Helen Mack was pretty distant from Myrna's work. A successful businesswoman, she enjoyed close ties to the highest ranks of the government and to one of the most conservative expressions of the cross, the Catholic order of Opus Dei.[20] Helen, like many privileged Guatemalans, believed that anyone who was killed must have had it coming for *metiendose en babosadas*. In retrospect she says that when Myrna was assassinated she realized that people she considered good friends must have been involved. In response, Helen trained herself in the law and became a tireless campaigner for legal redress of the crime.

On the first anniversary of Myrna's death, September 11, 1991, it became clear that her body remained connected to the very networks the army had hoped to disarticulate. For one of the first times in over a decade the streets of Guatemala City were full of marchers demanding an end to impunity. The National Cathedral was bursting with people commemorating Myrna's assassination. It was her and her family's privilege that made her death, unlike those of so many others, remarkable. However, many who gathered there that day and continue to gather on each anniversary since, were, by relation, mourning the hundreds of thousands of lives lost to government counterinsurgency.[21]

As an anthropologist, Myrna's relation to the poor, indigenous, displaced survivors transformed a political situation into a personal one through participant observation. This linked her to her "blood" relation, Helen, who made a political act of assassination personal by dedicating her life to legally prosecuting the murderers. Helen also made a personal loss political by rejecting the story that Myrna deserved to die because she'd gotten involved in foolishness. Helen linked to people in already existing networks like AVANCSO, GAM, CONAVIGUA, CALDH, and also to unexpected others, like members of the military, and after she won the Right Livelihood award, an international human rights prize, she founded a new networking node, the Myrna Mack Foundation.

No more than the family, school, or church does the law exist outside these linkages of power. Terror can be made legal by the states that carry it out, and perfectly legal systems can enact serious terrorism, as on the U.S. African American community. But the law can also be lashed in to other ends, as power is recrafted from sources invariably impure.[22] All these actors

Demandan justicia en asesinato de Myrna Mack

La Premio Nobel Rigoberta Menchú se solidariza con la activista de DDHH Helen Mack, quien llora durante una protesta frente a la Corte Suprema de Justicia, dolida por la impunidad que rodea a la demanda contra tres militares acusados de la autoría intelectual del asesinato de su hermana, la antropóloga Myrna Mack. Catorce organizaciones protestaron por la suspensión del juicio contra Edgar Godoy, Juan Valencia y Juan Oliva ► **Pág. 2**

Headline on front page of *Prensa Libre*: "They demand justice for the murder of Myrna Mack." The text reads, "Nobel Laureate Rigoberta Menchú comforts human rights activist Helen Mack, who cried during a protest in front of the Supreme Court, mourning the impunity that surrounds the demands against three military officers accused of being the intellectual authors of the assassination of her sister, the anthropologist Myrna Mack. Fourteen organizations protested the suspension of the case against Edgar Godoy, Juan Valencia, and Juan Oliva." October 11, 2001. Photograph by Daniel Herrera. Used with kind permission.

and actants were tied in, via Helen's node, to the machine that—despite the murder in broad daylight of a military commander aiding in the investigation, despite continuing threats and harassment, and despite more than a dozen judges withdrawing from the case because they were terrorized—led to the trial and conviction of Noél de Jesús Beteta, the Guatemalan army specialist who actually killed Myrna. Through these linkages Helen articulated a compelling story in a court of law that has made it possible for others to bet on the future. She did not stop there, continuing to press for the trial of the "intellectual authors" of the crime, the military higher-ups (evidence suggests it went all the way to the president) who ordered the assassination.

Meanwhile Guatemala and the United States were encountering another relational tie that was recrafting a missing loved one into a site of resistance, one that also forced a reckoning of actions formerly immune. In October 1994 Jennifer Harbury began her second hunger strike in Guatemala City (the first was for a week in September 1993). She would endure for thirty-two days. As she made clear, she was just like the women of GAM and CONAVIGUA because she wanted to know what had happened to her husband, the Guatemalan guerrilla commander Everardo aka Efraín Bámaca

Velásquez. Unlike them, she had U.S. citizenship and a Harvard law degree. But like other loved ones of the disappeared she had heard emphatic denials that the military was holding him after he was wounded in combat. Like them, she inquired through proper channels, then went public, making her grieving body a spectacle during her first, weeklong hunger strike on Avenida la Reforma in Guatemala City, in front of the central military base. In 1994 she spent over a month in the Central Park in front of the national palace and, four months later, ten days in the United States in front of the White House. She articulated her body and her starvation to similar losses in Guatemala, to the physical hunger her husband had endured his entire life as an indigenous *mozo* in the plantation system (the very reason for his armed struggle) and to the hunger for justice and reckoning that linked her to Guatemala. She also articulated her gringa activist body, both separate from and connected, with Guatemalan elites and U.S. foreign policy (Harbury 1994, 2000).

Harbury first became connected to Guatemala through her work as a public interest attorney on the Texas border. She went to Guatemala in 1985 to research background material for asylum claims and began to help members of the popular movement get out of the country and to accompany members of GAM in the hopes that a gringa presence would dissuade acts of violence. Several years later she returned to Guatemala to write a book about the guerrillas and met Bámaca, a Maya-Kiche' combatant in the Revolutionary Organization of the People in Arms (ORPA), one of the member groups of the URNG. Reader, she married him. When he went missing she believed he was killed in combat, until escaped prisoners claimed to have seen him alive, although terribly tortured, in army custody. After exhausting every other channel she undertook the hunger strikes, insisting that "alive he was taken, alive she wanted him back." She was not granted this devout wish, but her struggle did lash in a number of allies, from Guatemalan activists and other gringo victims of violence in Guatemala to U.S. congresspeople and celebrities like Bianca Jagger and Susan Sarandon.

These articulations and trials of strength resulted in a confession by U.S. and Guatemalan officials that they had knowingly lied to her when they told her they had no knowledge of Bámaca's whereabouts. The case also led to an unprecedented investigation of CIA actions in Guatemala by the U.S. congressional Intelligence Oversight Board (IOB) (Harbury 2000, IOB 1996). This report unveiled what many already knew but which had never before been officially acknowledged: the role of the CIA in military counterinsurgency in Guatemala.[23] Despite walls of lies, evasions, and cover-ups, the investigation disclosed, among other things, that a CIA "asset," Colonel Julio

Alpírez, had not only participated in the torture and murder of Bámaca and in a number of other human rights abuses, but also had ordered the assassination of the U.S. citizen Michael Devine, apparently because Devine knew too much about the colonel's drug running operations. Two-faced, Alpírez was the very person U.S. intelligence was supporting to control drug trafficking.[24] The report in turn led to new facts via the reorganization of CIA practices—now involved in new trials of strength with the post–9/11 Bush administration and the revival of military aid to Guatemala, which had been suspended in the wake of the IOB report.[25] It also led, perhaps unsurprisingly, to charges that Harbury was a fraud, that she had never actually married Bámaca—that a white, Harvard-educated lawyer would desire an indigenous man seemed especially hard for some Guatemalan commentators to stomach—and that the whole thing was a duplicitous effort to sabotage Guatemala and the United States (Adams 1997).

These facts of the IOB report were lashed together with the REMHI and CEH findings, the National Security Archives publication of the "dossier of death," long-term solidarity struggles in the United States which heavily pressured President Clinton on the eve of his trip of July 1999, and surely with other accounting procedures like U.S. attempts to win hearts and minds to support the creation of a Latin America free trade zone. Less an expression of the essential goodness of his heart, the apology came about because President Clinton was *obliged* to pass through this point by these ties and trials of strength.

The apology, in turn, was articulated to both Helen Mack's and Jennifer Harbury's ongoing court cases against those who ordered the murders of Myrna Mack and Bámaca. Harbury took her case to the U.S. Supreme Court, and Helen managed to bring cases against General Augusto Godoy Gaitán, Colonel Juan Valencia Osorio, and Colonel Juan Guillermo Oliva Carrera before the Guatemalan courts. Then, because she was able to prove that the case could not be fairly heard in Guatemala, it went to the Inter-American Court in Costa Rica. The ruling there against the Guatemalan state was part of what made the apology in 2004 a fact.

The war may be over, but in the postwar in action terror tactics dog those involved in these cases. In Washington, D.C., the car of Harbury's lawyer, José Pertierra, was firebombed in the driveway of his house, and Harbury's home was shot at. Helen Mack receives almost constant death threats and has had to leave Guatemala on numerous occasions. Harassment of AVANCSO, Myrna's research center, has been fairly constant. This is due both to the court cases and to the courageous way they maintain her legacy of making meaning through research, writing, and other identi-ties. Members of AVANCSO have suffered death threats, including the direct intimidation of Director Clara Arenas and investigators like Matilde González, the beating of the cleaning woman to send a message, and frequent *allanamientos*, or break-ins, dismissed by the authorities as common crime, in which work areas are dismantled and information is stolen but valuables like money and radios are left untouched.

Harbury lost her case in the U.S. Supreme Court but won in the Inter-American Court of Human Rights and continues to articulate ideas and people through her book *Searching for Everardo*, the film about her struggle, *Dirty Secrets: Jennifer, Everardo and the CIA in Guatemala* (Goudvis 1998), and her work with torture victims through Coalition Missing. In January 2003 the Guatemalan government acknowledged responsibility for Bámaca's death and complied with the order of the Inter-American Commission on Human Rights to pay $498,000 to his survivors. As I was first writing this section on June 25, 2004, the *New York Times* editorial page ran a paid advertisement titled "STOP our Children from Becoming Torturers." Signed by Jennifer Harbury for the Unitarian Universalist Service Committee, it articulates (tells the story, as it connects) the torture-murder of Efraín Bámaca and so many other Central Americans with the U.S. policy of torturing detainees and hiding their existence at the Guantánamo, Abu Ghraib, and other prisons.

The Mack case was both lost and won and continues to be a tenacious, ongoing trial of strength over fifteen years after Myrna's murder. While the Guatemalan court appeared to accept the argument that higher-ups were responsible by finding Colonel Valencia Osorio guilty, it acquitted the other two, and later Valencia Osorio was freed on appeal.

Helen's enormous efforts—tied together with other actants like GAM, CONAVIGUA, AVANCSO, Jennifer Harbury, Esperanza León, the Swedish Parliament, sympathetic journalists, judges hearing the case despite death threats, solidarity supporters all over the world, and so many others—have made Myrna's murder a central test case for the rule of law against terror in Guatemala. As Elizabeth Oglesby writes, "Myrna Mack's assassination produced results that were in many ways the opposite of what her killers intended. Helen Mack's battle against military impunity attracted the attention of Guatemalan society, and as Guatemalans learned more about Myrna and her research, public concern for the victims of the war grew. Ironically, Myrna's death led to more concrete assistance for the displaced communities, a goal that had frustrated her during her fieldwork" (1995:256, see also Fundación Myrna Mack 2000). Her work set the stage for one of the most successful refugee returns in history. The AVANCSO study and the Mack legal case became essential parts of the REMHI and CEH reports, which in turn are being used as evidence in court cases brought against those responsible for the Guatemalan genocide. These articulations are both ends and means.

I've been telling stories about how the cruelties of war, its meanness, *make* people, as they swerve through the ideological apparatuses of the family, the church, the law, the school, accounting, and communications. In turn the meanings of war are made by those people. Myrna and Helen Mack, Esperanza León, and Jennifer Harbury were all transformed through the process I've described as interpellation, or the assumption of an identity that at first may have felt false and certainly looked that way—like *babosadas*—to their untransformed friends and family, but then became their true identity. Assuming new identifications called into question what they had taken for granted, and they were themselves called into question, accused of duplicity. They made passionate attachments to other people and other meanings and by doing so transformed the postwar milieu. They forced power to shed its denying face and grudgingly *asumir* (acknowledge) its responsibility. They changed the whole caboodle, and now it more easily goes without saying that the army's victims were not involved in stupid things, that they did not deserve to die, and that state professions of innocence are a cover-up.

This is the postwar in action. It crosscuts intended meanings and transforms bodies: the dead, both those hidden away and those spectacularly displayed; and the living, now marching in the streets, filling the churches, and appearing in the Congress, first as protestors, then as witnesses, then as congresswomen, testifying in court, conducting exhumations, researching, writing, making meaning, articulating.

I am obviously rather passionately attached to these women myself, but I don't want to con you into thinking that this is the only direction these unpredictable multiconductors can go. Through my articulations with Guatemala via personal, professional, and political links and through telling stories about it like this book I assumed the identity of a partial anthropologist and gringa in fluidarity (Nelson 1999a). I also assumed that most poor and/or indigenous Guatemalans would be interested in changing the unjust power relations that consigned them to brutal underpaid labor and their children to malnutrition, illiteracy, and a lifetime of fearing the swift death of repression and the slow death of disease and hunger. That so many had risen up time and again against impossible odds suggested some safety in the assumption that "it is better to die on your feet than live forever on your knees." This resonates with the other face of double consciousness: that those who are out of luck are in the know. But G. W. F. Hegel and W. E. B. Du Bois both insist that this is never a given, that possession of consciousness comes from labor, struggle, facing death, and from relations with others—as well as from the uncanny sense that we may be possessed.

Now, the end of preventable deaths is probably desired by most people in Guatemala, but the means—what lies in-between—are sites and stakes of furious struggle. What is a good life? What is progress or development? What is the person desiring it? Are all indigenous people the same? all poor people? as Myrna and Helen Mack prove, even rich people aren't all the same but are produced through their articulations. Remembering what assuming does (making an ass) and the ludicrous task of anthropology, what does it mean to be in the know? The counterinsurgency, too, was adept at creating relations, at traversing apparent boundaries between state and people, in translating interests, and lashing together identi-ties.

With Us or Against Us?

The confession of the Mayan catechist and patrol leader that he was two-faced is both singular, his own unique experience, and also fits right into long-standing colonial stereotypes. Homi Bhabha writes that the stereotype is always double. In the Americas stereotyping has articulated indigenous people into the two-faced figure of the wild Indian and the Noble Savage. The duplicitous native is revivified every time an English-speaker says, "Indian giver," someone who offers a gift only to take it back, or "Indian summer," a tantalizingly brief period of warm weather after the first chill of fall.

In the next three chapters I'll try to untangle some of the stereotypes and identi-ties assumed about and among mostly indigenous people in the war and postwar. But the discourse of duplicity is mobile and can be applied to indigenous people, ladinos, *and* gringos. Anyone, really, can be accused of being a front, of assuming an identity, or experience the uncanny doubling over of being acted on. Among some ladinos in Guatemala there is a saying, "Me salió lo indio" (the Indian came out of me) to refer to acting rudely or like a brute, suggesting that the assumption of ladino identity may be disrupted by its second face, the Indian. Matt Creelman reports that this saying has become more politically correct on the *fútbol* fields he frequents, as now people say, "Me salió lo maya." Another Guatemalan friend reports a driving companion exploding with rage at the traffic disruption caused by the blocking of a boulevard on Sundays for pedestrians. After venting about the *chusma* (low-class people) this attracted, he said a bit shamefacedly, "Me salió la Yaqui." Yaqui, she explained to me, is the heroine of a very popular satirical radio show. She is the ultimate spoiled nouveau riche, Papí's girl. He is a progressive activist but finds himself acted on by this contagious personality.

Edgar Gutiérrez was a young star of the struggling aboveground left when I met him in 1985. An amazingly insightful journalist and writer, he is powerfully articulate—whether weaving together facts and conjecture to create a fascinating analysis of the inner workings of power or metaphor and feeling to create a beautiful poem. Seductive and charming, he was enormously helpful to non-Guatemalan researchers, becoming through the late eighties and early nineties something of an obligatory passage point for anyone trying to understand the conjuncture. He was also an important part of the Guatemala City activist and social scene and a *compañero* to a wide range of people. He was one of the cofounders, with Myrna Mack and others, of AVANCSO, headed the REMHI research team, and later held an important position at the Myrna Mack Foundation. He was thus an important node in accounting for—producing the facts about—the extent of the violence in the early 1980s, especially under General Ríos Montt's regime and in the trials of strength trying to bring Mack's killers from the first postwar civilian government to justice. Thus, when he accepted a job offer from President Alfonso Portillo in the Guatemalan Republican Front (FRG) government, General Ríos Montt's new party, many of his colleagues were aghast.

The Guatemalan Constitution explicitly denies the presidency to anyone who has taken power illegally, as in a coup d'état. Ríos Montt tried for years to get on the ballot and when that failed ran a two-faced campaign, with the general in the foreground running for Congress and Portillo as the presidential face. Ríos Montt did run in 2003 but lost in the first round. In the 1990s the FRG's Janus-face, Ríos Montt and Portillo, formed an interesting couple: the old genocider who offered a firm hand to a nation tired of crime and corruption and a younger hotshot who openly claimed to have ties to the guerrillas and spoke in a deeply populist idiom.[26] Ríos Montt on his own plays a double role pretty well. There's actually a morbid joke about him that goes, "Did you know Ríos Montt has a twin? Unfortunately he was born dead with signs of torture." He consistently claims that *he* ended the war with the beans and bullets projects, and he is remembered for easing counterinsurgency in the cities while intensifying scorched earth in the highlands. He critiques the elites in ways that resonate with people's knowledge of his humble beginnings as a poor, rural child from remote Huehuetenango who made his way up through the ranks of the army.[27] He cultivates an image of moral piety as a Protestant minister and claims to eschew corruption, although nepotism seems to be okay—his brother was named bishop, his son has risen precipitously through the army's ranks, and his daughter serves in the Guatemalan Congress, is married to a U.S. Republican congressman, and is being groomed for a presidential run. Unlike almost any other government, Ríos Montt's has created roles for indigenous people. In 1982 he set up the State Councils with indigenous representation, and Portillo named the first Mayan ambassadors in Guatemalan history. But for those in the know about Ríos Montt's other, genocidal face, he and his party seem like excellent bamboozlers, and anyone buying into these phony fronts and *babosadas* was either a pathetic dupe or a self-interested, amoral sellout.

Which was Edgar Gutiérrez when he agreed to join the FRG government and take over the intelligence offices? Neither, he would laugh. He was being given a historic opportunity to really make a difference in the new government by cleaning up the infamous Security Section and creating an entirely new, clean, democratic way to gather information and make use of it. It would be similar to the work he had been doing, only now with access to state resources and some real power to make the reckonings stick, exactly what REMHI and the CEH lacked. Transforming the security apparatus was a primary part of the peace accords that he and everyone else had been assiduously pursuing for so many years. He had also been assured by Portillo, a boyhood friend and former drinking buddy, that he would be given a free hand. Some of his colleagues from the early days admired his decision to work on the inside. They would call him when they received threats and felt they had an important ally in high places. But others wondered if he'd just been duped. They pointed to his attempts to clean up the spy center as barely making a dent in the apparatus and worried that his presence there, and later as foreign minister where he skillfully negotiated aid packages,[28] actually lent a façade of legitimacy to a government otherwise sorely lacking it. Why would he use his intellect and connections in support of the very powers that murdered his friends and colleagues Myrna Mack and Bishop Juan Gerardi and against whom he used to throw all his many talents— when he seemed to get so little in return? What possessed him?

These questions led some to see something more nefarious at work— that he is not duped but a duper, an active collaborator. Some even wonder if his face has really changed or if the one they thought they knew was the deception. Perhaps he had always been an infiltrator, always a spy. Perhaps he bamboozled them as they worked together in the most intimate sites of politics and passion because his true face was turned toward the enemy. Some wonder, is that why/how they killed some of the people closest to him? They rethink past years, seeing a history all broken and cobbled back together in light of the suspicions that he was an informer rather than an ally. His current position transforms the whole caboodle of their shared histories. Whom *can* you count on?

Like Gutiérrez, many members of the popular movement and the guer-

Poster commemorating the first anniversary of the assassination of Myrna Mack, titled "Breaking the Wall of Impunity, Myrna Mack." The names on the bricks are of individuals murdered or disappeared by the army. Panzós and Santiago Atitlán are communities where massacres occurred. Myrna Mack Foundation. Used with kind permission.

rilla have made their peace with the FRG or with the state more generally. One high-ranking member of the URNG directorate who was a central architect of the peace accords told me, just before he accepted a position in the Portillo/Ríos Montt government, that he had had to "exorcise a number of demons" in order to do it. He said he had to let go of the way the past possessed him. Those who are lashing in to these state-related identi-ties are challenging their own assumptions about the world and power. They are assuming identifications that challenge the old divide of the war years between the good popular movement and the enemy state. They claim power is more porous now, they can continue to pursue the ends of the war by other means. Yes, they have families and need a steady job, but it's also a more effective way to work than an NGO, an underfunded research center, or, heaven forbid, the collapsing University. These are the unpredictable linkages of populism that Laclau describes, arising from "an ambiguous *demos* which is, on the one hand, a section within the community (an underdog) and, on the other hand, an agent presenting itself, in an antagonistic way, as *the whole* community" (nd:13). If power is everywhere, as Foucault argues, does it matter which site you choose for struggling? Isn't this just another form of articulation, which changes the people and the structures they link to, the assumption of new identities in the milieu of the postwar in action?

Why, in turn, is duplicity, the sense there's something hiding behind the neat summing up, such a powerful means of making sense of these end/s of the war? I'll close with these horror film–like scenarios of possession and exorcism, struggles over the role of the past in reckoning possibilities for the future, and one more scary image, this one from the poster commemorating the first anniversary of Myrna's murder, September 11, 1991. At the top against a background of bricks, it said, "We are breaking down the wall of impunity." In the midst of the bricks is a space, smashed open, and through it we see blue skies and Myrna, smiling, her hand reaching out to us. The names of people killed and tortured and communities that were massacred by the army are on the surrounding bricks. But as we look again, our perspective slips, and we see that there is a body, a man's suit, black shoes, a knife in one hand, and we see that we are the head of this body, looking down at the cobblestones of the sidewalk where she was murdered. We are placed in the position of the victimizer.

CO-MEMORATION AND CO-LABORATION:
SCREENING AND SCREAMING

The [Peace] Accord emphasizes the need to remember
and dignify the victims of the fratricidal confrontation
among Guatemalans. The CEH considers historic memory,
individual and collective, to be the foundation of national
identity. The memory of the victims is a fundamental
aspect of historic memory and allows us to valorize the
struggles for human dignity. CEH

What is living, present, conscious, here, is only so
because there's an infinity of little deaths, little accidents,
little breaks, little cuts in the sound track, as William
Burroughs would say, in the sound track and the visual
track of what's lived. And I think that's very interesting
for the analysis of the social, the city, politics. Our vision
is that of a montage, a montage of temporalities which
are the product not only of the powers that be, but of
the technologies that organize time. . . . It's no accident
that religious thought instituted all sorts of prohibitions,
holidays—the sabbath, etc. . . . They regulated time, they
were aware of the necessity of stopping for there to be a
religious politics. Paul Virilio

CUTTING THROUGH AND CUTTING ACROSS

Laying two unlikely things like two faces beside each other is the methodology of dialectical montage. Pioneered in the global north by Russian revolutionary filmmakers like Sergei Eisenstein and Dziga Vertov, it was slammed
into people's faces by the Surrealists and later Situationists, and eulogized
by Walter Benjamin and Michael Taussig. In montage the cut is the lively
rendering space between the images. The cut calls on the viewers' active participation in making meaning. In turn, cutting is the central formal technique of filmmaking more generally—a vital tool in make-believe.

In film, cutting from one image to another allows for the shot-reverse-
shot that establishes point of view (p.o.v.). This is the entry point for the

viewer's assumption of identification, aka suture (Silverman 1983). For example, we see a shadowy figure *cut* we see a woman looking *cut* we see (now knowing it's through her eyes) the figure a bit closer *cut* the ground rises to meet us *cut* we see the scary figure from below *cut* we see the street begin to pass us, we are running with her, we begin to feel with her *cut.* We have sutured or been sewn in to her position.

Cuts show time passing and are also what make special effects work. Close-up on woman's face, eyes wide in terror, mouth open to scream *cut* knife falling *cut* red liquid splatters on the ground *cut.* We don't actually see her get stabbed yet we know she has been hurt. Perhaps we have sutured so much that we jump as if to escape the knife ourselves or feel sadness or horror that she is dead. It's a con, of course. We are accustomed to mix our enjoy/meant with the orientation of the expert, since we know she is an actress, the blood is fake, and the effect is produced by cutting between scenes. But we came to the cinema for precisely this duping, this double experience of knowing very well and yet . . .

The cuts, those little dark spaces between these filmic events, seem extraneous to the narrative and yet are essential to how film works. Through them we actively co-laborate, flooding these openings with our own meanings. These include acknowledge/meant: our keen minds recognize genre conventions, intellectually preparing us for spaceships, romance, or comic relief; senti/meant: we feel with and for particular characters so that their pain is ours and identify against others so that their pain instead causes cheers or laughter; and embodi/meant: our bodies themselves respond, often in ways we cannot predict, twitching, laughing, screaming, crying. Or *are* they our own meanings? Are we not responding like well-tuned instruments to the button pushing of the filmmakers, possessed by an external force doubling us over?

Cuts, like blows (*coups*) are central mechanisms of the make-believe demanded by the sword and the cross as they act on us. I have described cuts in human flesh, in family relations, in identi-ties, in communi-ties, in consciousness, and in time. I suggested that cuts act on bodies, hearts, and minds, and they certainly do bend us, but not always in the intended directions.[1] The very opening that a cut enacts can break assumptions—what goes without saying—and become an opportunity for different links to be formed, different identifications to be assumed. Like cleavage, it is simultaneously a separation and a coming together, a break and a movement.

No single cut began or ended the war. Instead there are unending struggles to flood these openings with meaning, to seize hold of them and turn them to different ends. Perhaps they did not, on their own, bring perpetrators to justice, redress victims' losses, or transform the material conditions of oppression that fueled the war. But the REMHI and CEH reports cut to the bone of the silence and denial that had surrounded the violence of the war. They transformed the milieu.

Those who labored on the reports know very well that the dead are not safe, which is why the first recommendation of the CEH report, coming after four volumes that detail the economic, social, and political structures that gave rise to the war and its brutal, horrifying effects, is "Means to Preserve the Memory of the Victims." It calls on the government and the guerrilla to take full public responsibility for the acts they committed and for the state and society to "commemorate the victims through 1. a nationally recognized, annual day of remembrance 2. construction of monuments and public parks throughout the country 3. assigning names of victims to schools, public buildings and roads 4. acknowledging the multicultural character of the nation by raising monuments and creating communal cemeteries in accord with the collective memory of the Maya" (1999:5:61–62). Other recommendations include reparations for victims, trials of perpetrators, the establishment of a commission to investigate the role of the armed forces and purify them of criminal elements, exhumation of clandestine cemeteries, and clarification of the whereabouts of the disappeared.

Of course, the Guatemalan landscape is littered with signs of these occurrences, and everyone who lost someone remembers, although it may be with shame and guilt rather than the respect and co-memoration the CEH calls for. Churches, NGOs, the civilian government, and human and indigenous rights groups have been grappling with how to fix these memories and make them public in a seemly way. In the next chapter I compare these courageous, beautiful efforts with less official, more inchoate ways of remembering. I hope to explore how popular memory is rendered and the tensions over the end/s of war—between history and memory, and within memorializing itself. In this intertext I describe commemorations of the victims, while in chapters 3 and 8 I am particularly interested in struggles to address the horrific way government counterinsurgency implicated everyone.

THE NEED TO REMEMBER AND
DIGNIFY THE VICTIMS

In the Central Park on Sexta Avenida, the main thoroughfare of Guatemala City, in front of the National Palace and among the clowns, proselytizers, homeless, and sparking couples, a glass box on a pedestal held an "eternal flame" to commemorate the December 1996 signing of the peace accords.

Column in front of the National Cathedral in downtown Guatemala City with the names of disappeared victims from Quiché province. Other columns carry the names of murdered individuals and massacred villages, all documented in the REMHI report.

The box has now been moved inside the Palace, which has been transformed into a Museum of Culture. The flame periodically went out and was easy to miss if you didn't know where to look, but lots of people got their snapshots taken beside it by the itinerant Polaroid handlers who troll the square. As part of a larger project to reclaim the Centro Histórico, a group of cultural activists organized all the churches in the area to ring their bells on New Year's eve at midnight to commemorate the treaty, and for several years people gathered near the little box to listen to the tintinnabulation.

Nearby, the creamy columns that hold the fence sealing off the Cathedral from busy Seventh Avenue have been inscribed with the names of people killed during the war and of villages where massacres occurred. It's an awe-full experience to read the long lines of tiny letters covering the towering columns from top to bottom. Unfortunately, the letters are invisible unless you're right next to them, and you have to cross a busy street and navigate the fence to see them. The Cathedral has been the site of numerous masses to honor the war's dead, including annual services for Myrna Mack Chang, and for the survivors, including a glorious high service honoring Rigoberta Menchú Tum's Nobel Peace Prize.

Farther down Sexta Avenida, about four blocks from the National Palace and the army base that until recently housed the Presidential Guard—

implicated in a number of high-profile murders — is the San Sebastián church and parochial house where Bishop Gerardi lived and died when his head was smashed with a brick. In the small park in front, where schoolchildren play and homeless men wash cars for a living, is a monument to Gerardi. An undulating stone wall, about six feet high and surrounded by water and flowers, it shows an open book with the REMHI title: "*Guatemala: Nunca Más* [Never Again]." A manacled hand with a broken chain rises above it, and beside that is an image of Gerardi's face. Commemorative meetings are held there, and masses are celebrated in the church. Right across the street are the new AVANCSO offices with a brass plaque commemorating Myrna Mack, provided under court orders by the government, and unveiled on September 11, 2005. It reads, "Aspiramos a ser consecuentes con las semillas que nos heredó [We aspire to do worthy work with the seeds we have inherited]."

In Joyabaj, Gerardi's murder was commemorated along with that of their assassinated priest, Padre Villanueva, in July 1998. For the first time, people came to mass with small crucifixes to commemorate each family member lost in the war. Simone Remijnse says, "Some people carried only one or two, but I saw people carrying as many as nine or ten. For many people this was the first time they had openly shown that they had lost family members" (2002:263). However, Gerardi's murder was terrifying for many people, especially those who had participated in REMHI, often against their family's wishes. They fully expected to be murdered too.[2]

On the night before the first anniversary of Gerardi's death the artist Daniel Hernández-Salazar and his collaborators wheat-pasted giant images of his photographed "angel" from the REMHI covers all over Guatemala City, on highway underpasses, on the Cathedral walls, on the bulwarks supporting the National Theater. But rather than the "see no evil" angel from the second volume, this one's eyes and ears are open, along with its mouth, crying aloud. Urban Guatemalans woke up to find the image everywhere, and although many of the posters were at least partially scraped away within a month, for over a year parts of the angel were visible around the city (Maldonado 2007).

In Zacualpa, Quiché, as elsewhere, the church was taken over by the army during the war and used for torture and executions. There, one room has been left as it was found when the army decamped, and the Italian priest was happy to take Simone Remijnse and me through it in June 2001. There were ropes hanging from the beams, and the army had made a drainage hole in the floor for the blood. Although the church washed that up, there was still dried blood on the walls and what looked like claw marks in the adobe. A figure of a kneeling Virgin is in one corner. She has distinctly Mayan fea-

"Para que todos lo sepan," For all to know: In memory of Monsignor Juan Gerardi. This photograph graced the cover of volume 4 of the REMHI report and has appeared throughout Guatemala and at other sites to commemorate human rights violations, including Hiroshima, Japan, and near the offices of the Mothers of the Plaza de Mayo in Buenos Aires. Photograph by Daniel Hernández-Salazar. Used with kind permission.

tures and is dressed in the local purple and red *traje*. Apparently some ladino parishioners felt that this reflection of Mayan parishioners went too far, so she was consigned here. The priests had also moved the image of Christ on the cross, which the army had hacked up, from the sanctuary into the room, and there were pictures of some of the people killed. "There is a catechist here," said the priest, "who was tortured in this room." He gestured to his side. "He has wounds, scars all along here, almost exactly like this statue. We think there were one thousand people killed here and dumped behind the church. The church is trying to buy that land where the bodies are so we can have an exhumation. . . . We have a Commission on Martyrs and they are planning what to do with these spaces. We want to build walkways with niches and names. . . . The army brought patrollers from Joyabaj, Quiché. The people there are different. They are *fuerte, enojados, bravos* [strong, angry]. They came and killed the people of Zacualpa."

While Joyabaj is infamous throughout southern Quiché for having *bravo* civil patrollers, Xoye were also victims. The crucifixes Reminjse mentions were made from popsicle sticks, each inscribed with the name of someone

Torture room in Zacualpa parish. The sign says "And they shed their blood for Guatemala"; the photographs are of priests from the diocese who were murdered. The kneeling figure of the Virgin is clothed in local Maya dress.

killed in Joyabaj and deposited in a small room off the main sanctuary in the church, where Father Villanueva is now buried. They line the walls, cascading from the little piles where they were laid, hundreds and hundreds and hundreds of them.

June 30 is Army Day in Guatemala, a day when Sexta Avenida fills with marching infantry, camouflaged sharpshooters, dread Kaibiles (the elite fighting forces whose name is appropriated from the Mayan *Popol Wuj*) trained attack dogs, tanks, floats, and road-building equipment; the air quivers with helicopters and jet flyovers. In the early 1990s GAM and other human rights groups began to intervene in the soldiers' parade, carrying pictures of the disappeared and calling for their reappearance. Accompanied at times by allies from throughout the Americas, like the Argentine Madres de la Plaza de Mayo, they held vigil by the stand where the president, generals, and foreign dignitaries review the marching troops. In 2000 a group called HIJOS (sons and daughters) held signs and papier-mâché skulls inscribed with the names of massacred villages. That year the Guatemalan performance artist Aníbal Lopez covered an entire block of Sexta's parade route in ashes, recalling both the burned villages and the colorful sawdust carpets that line the streets during Easter week. Much of the ash was swept up by the time the soldiers marched through, and few of the spectators noticed it—but visitors to the Venice Biennial in 2001 could see documentation of the event, which won a prize. The military parade was suspended after that, but, perhaps as a sign of the end of the postwar, in 2006 it was revived. The official newspaper-size pamphlet distributed by the government at the new parade had photos of laughing and mostly indigenous-looking soldiers and military police, half men and half women, and said, "Ten years after signing the Peace, we are exporting it." This is because now, rather than receiving, Guatemala is providing UN peacekeepers, mainly to Congo and Haiti. Human rights groups, in turn, papered the city with posters proclaiming "250,000 heroes and martyrs, 250,000 voices claiming justice. We do not forget. We do not forgive. We are not reconciled. Justice and Punishment for the Geno-ciders." The words were surrounded by rows of ID photos that recalled the dossier of death. The posters also advertised a forum called "Memory: An At-tack on Imperialism" and a counterdemonstration ("Gran Marcha Nacional de la Memoria").

These and many other monuments and commemorations through-out Guatemala (Flores 2004) are brave co- and counter-memorations and clearly respond to the CEH recommendation to "Preserve Memory." They are mostly public and clearly very important, doing vital memorializing work. Monuments, including the reports, seek to co-memorate, to create a pub-lic, shared, and fixed rendering of the mass experience of violence. But you don't see people jostling, crowding in to see them or willing to pay for the privilege or even paying much attention at all. In fact, many people involved in creating the REMHI and CEH reports are frustrated that they have not had more resonance (Oglesby 2004). One reason is that most people's ener-gies are devoted to barely surviving and, especially to many young people, massacres from twenty years ago seem less pressing than their romantic lives or schemes for getting to the United States. Another reason may be that the monuments that aren't ephemeral take a certain determination to experience. That experience, in turn, is rather pacified, contemplative, fixed. Except for the Army Day protests there is not much opportunity for inter-action, for embodiment, for active rendering.

These monuments are one face of co-memoration. They are powerful means for preserving the memory of the victims. They cut through as-sumptions that the past is over, the dead are buried. Through them and the struggles of relations, kin, the past is reanimated. This is, of course, a central trope in bad horror movies and, continuing my dialectical montage, I cut to another face that contemplates the mechanisms of horror: film—source of my metaphor of cutting and its relation to the assumptions of identity.

Guatemala itself has almost no filmmaking tradition, although there are

Recuerdan masacres atribuidas al Ejército

Front page of *Prensa Libre*, headlined, "They Remember the Massacres Attributed to the Army." The caption reads, "Yesterday human right activists shouted 'murderers' at the participants in the Army Day parade as they passed the National Palace. They held skulls made of papier-mâché on which were written the names of places where the army carried out massacres during the internal war. They demanded that the day be renamed "Day of the Martyrs." July 1, 2000. Photograph by Antonio Jiménez. Used with kind permission.

now several video-production studios. One exception is Rafael Lanuza Martínez, who, beginning in the 1970s, mainly made horror films. Lanuza Martínez's first feature film was *Superzán y el Niño del Espacio* (Superzán and the Boy from Space) (1971), which was distributed throughout Latin America. It was followed by *El Castillo de las Momias de Guanajuato* (The Castle of the Guanajuato Mummies), *Leyendas Macabras de la Colonia* (Macabre Legends of the Neighborhood), *La Mansión de las Siete Momias* (The Mansion of the Seven Mummies), and his greatest hit, *Terremoto en Guatemala* (Earthquake in Guatemala), which is considered a national treasure (*Revue* 1999). It was a huge success in Guatemala when it was released, although some of the actors are Mexican, and is still shown. Made in 1976, *Terremoto* is a schmaltzy love story full of everyday scenes like *sexteando*, shopping and strolling along Sexta, and horror film effects, as the honeymoon suite of our protagonist couple falls in, trapping the blonde, postcoital bride. The distraught groom runs stumbling through the real-life horrors of the demolished city, as actual documentary footage is spliced into the narrative. He desperately seeks help, but everything is a shambles, everyone has lost someone. The woman dies, unable to fulfill the fantasy sequences we see of the happy nuclear family, but he is inspired by her sacrifice and goes out to help reclaim the city.

The earthquake of 1976 itself was a massive cut into Guatemala's physical, social, and political milieu. It cracked open the earth and smashed much of the physical infrastructure of the central highlands, leaving vast regions in ruins and killing some twenty thousand people. But it also smashed assumptions about the organization of everyday life, racism, and the roles of state and local institutions. A joke that immediately began to circulate went, "'How is the earthquake like a Western movie?' 'Only Indians die.'" The joke was later updated to the *war* being like a Hollywood Western. Both versions suggest what I argue in the next chapter, that movies (note word) are good to think with. Many activists recall that the quake mobilized vast sectors of the population to help out, as it exposed not only the insufficiency of the military government, but also its corruption. Ladino and indigenous people worked side by side, and many people remember a feeling of enormous solidarity and unity. As an NGO coordinator told Remijnse in Joyabaj, "The earthquake also created new patterns of association and organization in the rural areas. Nearly every community organized a reconstruction or a betterment committee. They were not just spaces to talk about potable water, school or housing reconstruction. They were spaces to talk about *la realidad nacional* (the national reality)" (2002:84). As the subject of Guatemala's only successful feature film, *Terremoto* continues to preserve the memory of the victims and to contemplate horror.

The more recent horror is also being commemorated in short films by video collectives like *Comunicarte/Arte y Communicación* and *Luciérnaga* (firefly). Several document exhumations of clandestine cemeteries mixed with interviews with survivors. *Semblanza de una Profeta* (Portrait of a Prophet) is the story of Bishop Juan Gerardi, his life, the REMHI report, and his assassination. It opens with a fast montage of cuts—the murder scene, a pool of blood, the stained brick, the covered body, the sheet dappled in red—set to the screams of a guitar, before giving way to more traditional documentary footage of talking heads and archive photos. The extraordinary *No hay cosa oculta que no venga a descubrirse: la tragedia de Santa María Tzejá* (There is Nothing Hidden That Will Not Be Discovered) began as a play devised by returned refugee children and their North American *compañero* Randall Shea in Santa María Tzejá in the far north of Quiché province. The children interviewed their parents about their experiences of the war and then used the material to create a play in which they reenact torture, murder, grief, and displacement. The anthropologist Beatriz Manz, who has accompanied the people of Santa María since the 1970s, says the play created angst, disagreements, and fears of army reprisals. It "spurred intense discussions and caused heartbreak, tears, and trauma, but also, most important, accelerated the process of coping with what took place" (2004:233). The young people have performed the play all over Guatemala, literally embodying both victims and perpetrators. It was later filmed and supplemented with interviews with survivors and material from the REMHI and CEH reports.[3] It has had contagious effects as people elsewhere, like schoolchildren and community members who survived the brutal massacre in Plan de Sánchez, have also re-created their experiences. As one said, "These are not theatrical plays. They are the stories of our families, so that [history] will never repeat itself and we will never forget them" (Brown 2005:10).

Guatemalans construct dialectical montage with the materials at hand. I follow their lead by laying other media for contemplating horror side by side with these preservations of memory (media: "intervening thing through which an effect is produced"). Specifically, schlock horror films, which I had assiduously avoided my entire life until living in Guatemala during my dissertation fieldwork in 1993.

I had never seen a horror film, except for high culture ones like *Psycho*, until some friends dragged me to see *Candyman*. To my shock, the film was smarter than I was—dealing with anthropology, racism, history, the violent haunting of memory, and complicity. It concerns Helen, a young white woman struggling to finish her dissertation (an obvious suture point for me) on urban legends while her professor-lover is stealing her stuff and getting it on with undergrads. Needing a special angle to impress her committee, she travels from her upscale apartment complex near the university to the infamous Chicago "project" of Cabrini Green to investigate sightings of Candyman, a terrifying killer with a hook instead of a hand. He appears when his name is uttered five times before a bathroom mirror. Our intrepid heroine has to endure many assumed identities—suspicion from Cabrini Green's inhabitants, who think she's a cop, and from the authorities, who can't understand why any white person would go there, and an attack from a drug dealer styling himself as Candyman. Just when she thinks she's unmasked him, however, the "real" Candyman begins to appear to her, usually slaughtering someone, for which she is blamed—at one point she is locked up as criminally insane. It turns out Candyman is the ghost of an artist and former slave who, in Reconstruction times, fell in love with a white woman. The woman's father organized a lynch mob that first cut off Candyman's hand, the one he painted with, and stuck a hook into the bloody stump, before torture-murdering him, all this on the original Cabrini Green. Accused of stealing the child of one of her informants, Helen herself ends up dying on the Green while wresting the child from the fiery grasp of Candyman. In the final shock of the film she herself appears when summoned five times before the bathroom mirror to wreck havoc on her two-timing advisor. She assumes an identity, is interpellated, much as Buffy and Neo were. But because it's a horror film and not action adventure or camp, for Helen the cuts are real. They don't heal by the next scene, and her consciousness raising about class and race privilege exacts a heavy price. The large theater on Sexta Avenida where I saw it was full.

Now, I know that

> when people claim to not like horror, this is not simply a neutral claim. Often it also involves other, more implicit claims: that horror is moronic, sick and worrying; that any person who derives pleasure from the genre is moronic, sick and potentially dangerous; that the person who is making the claim is reasonable and healthy; and that they are therefore in a position to define what, in Andrew Ross's terms, needs to be "governed and policed as illegitimate or inadequate or even deviant" (1989:61). . . . Horror films have been attacked as violent and misogynist in ways that imply that a taste for horror is itself deeply problematic. (Jancovich 2002:18)

Or, as Noël Carroll suggests,

> There appears to be something paradoxical about the horror genre. It obviously attracts consumers, but it seems to do so by means of the expressly repulsive. Furthermore, the horror genre gives every evidence of being pleasurable to its audience, but it does so by means of trafficking in the very sorts of things that cause disquiet, distress, and displeasure. So . . . "Why are horror audiences attracted by what, typically (in everyday life) should (and would) repel them?" or "How can horror audiences find pleasure in what by nature is distressful and unpleasant?" (2002:33)

Commemorations of earthquakes and genocide in postwar Guatemala also traffic in things that cause distress, and there are many Guatemalans who feel that returning to this past is sick and potentially dangerous. Sometimes these reactions come from those explicitly interested in screening off, in the sense of hiding, the past. But at times the victims themselves differ sharply in their understandings of the best way to lay these histories to rest. Carlota McAllister (pers. comm.) recalls one villager's macabre response to the exhumation of a mass grave, saying to her neighbors, "What are you going to do with those bones? Make a soup?" The popularity of films that make dis-memberment and re-membering their theme points to the assumptions and puzzles at the heart of postwar Guatemala. Why the enjoy/meant?

I know it may not be what the CEH had in mind when it emphasized the need to remember and dignify the victims, but I follow Candyman's lead in addressing the "mechanisms of horror" (REMHI 1999) via embodiment, memory, racism, and collaboration. I am especially interested in the spaces opened up by these co-memorations of apparently clear-*cut* differences between victim and victimizer. This is simultaneously an absolutely vital task and one rent with tension and slippages, especially given the way counterinsurgency worked in Guatemala. How is memory to be preserved of those, documented in the dossier of death, who *delataron*, who broke under pressure and turned in their compañeros? What of those *enojados* from Joyabaj who committed murder in neighboring Zacualpa? What is an appropriate and dignified way to witness and remember the war's brutal attacks on the flesh? How is meaning made of such embodiments? And perhaps most difficult, from what sense of self does one remember when one has been acted on from outside? When you can't help yourself? When you have taken on the double (or more) roles of victim, perpetrator, witness, survivor?

Chapter Three

HORROR'S SPECIAL EFFECTS

PROLOGUE

> How then can one not see to what extent horror becomes
> fascinating, and how it alone is brutal enough to break
> everything that stifles? Georges Bataille

One year after the World Trade Center towers fell a small controversy erupted in New York City around a statue meant to commemorate those who died. Called "Tumbling Woman," she was naked and upside down, in the act of jumping/falling. Placed near the skating rink at Rockefeller Center, the statue inspired revulsion in some, leading to a call-in and newspaper campaign to have it removed. It was called "not appropriate to be thrust on your face," "sick," "shameful," and "brutal" (Peyser 2002:7). Many did not want to look at it. For awhile it was hidden behind a screen and surrounded by guards, and then it disappeared. The artist, Eric Fischl, said, "It was a sincere expression of deepest sympathy for the vulnerability of the human condition. Both specifically toward the victims of Sept. 11 and toward humanity in general." But Jim Burke, who works in the complex, said, "This is just like opening up wounds that are not yet healed" (7).

Commemoration of the events at the World Trade Center has been ongoing since 9/11/01 and has taken many forms. Why was this one so controversial? Perhaps addressing human vulnerability upset viewers enmeshed in simultaneously gearing down from the war in Afghanistan and gearing up for the attack on Iraq? Perhaps the specificity of her embodiment, as opposed to luminous towers of light, was too much to bear? Perhaps it was the mobility of the form, its unfixedness? Besides the question of *which* victims of world trade are commemorated, these issues of *how* to remember haunt every scene of death.

"MEANS TO PRESERVE THE MEMORY
OF THE VICTIMS"

I would turn our gaze from the past. It is dangerous, frankly,
to keep looking over our shoulders. George Tenet, former
director U.S. Central Intelligence Agency

I don't know how to describe it, there was blood everywhere,
like someone had dumped buckets of blood on her. There
was so much it looked fake. It was like . . . it was like a horror
movie. Description by a friend of the deceased of the police
photographs of the assassination of Myrna Mack Chang on
September 11, 1990

This chapter reckons with various postwar assumptions of identity reflected
and enacted through efforts to co-memorate the war. The memorializing
is at least two-faced: there is the public, aggregate aspect, like memorials
or the oft-cited numbers—200,000 dead, 626 massacres—and then there
is the individual experience, how each person in his or her context lived
and relives what happened. I suggest that popular memory is rendered and
multifaceted, and I explore the tensions between history and memory and
within memorializing itself. I am particularly interested in struggles to address what the REMHI report called "the mechanisms of horror"—the ways
government counterinsurgency implicated everyone, especially in the indigenous highlands, where victims are two-faced because they are also perpetrators, where no one survived who did not participate in some atrocity,
at the very least by having to stay silent (González 2002, Warren 2000). To
paraphrase Lévi-Strauss, I'll argue that horror films are good to think with.

Real and Reel Horror

I beg you, learn to see "bad" films; they are sometimes
sublime. Ado Kyrou

I know this is a dangerous claim. If there should not be poetry after Ausch-
witz, what is at stake in talking about bad horror movies after scorched-
earth massacres? Allan Feldman suggests this is always a tension for anthropologists dealing with violence:

Terror and violence expand the definition of the anthropological by engaging the *in-human*, which is beyond yet intrinsic. This is why ethnographers and others who write about violence from within particularity,

who explore the coherence of its non-sense, are frequently accused of dehumanizing their subjects. . . . It is suggested we generate a form of pornography . . . , practice sensationalism, or are simply amoral and perhaps morbid. . . . These insinuations frequently culminate in high-minded appeals to the anchor of a commonsensical universal humanity. (1995:245)

These are the same critiques and assumptions that horror fans face, as did the 9/11 sculpture, and it is this very "commonsense" anchor that horror, and horror films, destabilize. Horror movies are popular in Guatemala, in the sense that lots of people watch them. And I will argue that they may supplement the preservation of memory by making certain forms of the popular, or collective—both bodily experience and collaboration—central to their form and content. In Guatemala, where the war is officially over but peace is still a process, where you're never sure which innocent-looking face hides a serial murderer, where survival is never assured, and violent sequels constantly threaten, horror films, along with the reports, monuments, altars, and art works I've mentioned, may serve as tools—or weapons.

I'll start in two places to try to convince you that horror films are good to think with. One is a small hotel in Zone One, Guatemala City, that catered to international solidarity travelers and was run by CONAVIGUA, one of the most daring challengers of military impunity. The young people who cooked for and cleaned up after the foreigners were all in the guerrilla forces and had been demobilized in 1997. Some of them had been "in the mountains" since they were twelve or thirteen and now (1998), at nineteen or twenty-two, were struggling to complete primary school while working long hours at the hotel and trying to continue their radical politics.

The anthropologist was hanging out with them in the common room one evening as they watched television. A horror movie with really gruesome special effects was on. The squeamish anthropologist begged to change the channel, and during a commercial break they surfed through the Mexican comedies, dubbed U.S. sitcoms, music videos, and news programs available, but nothing else interested the young people, and they returned to the horror film. They watched it with relish and several sutured intensely and kinesthetically, crying out when a character was killed, jumping in their seats when something unexpected happened. The anthropologist wondered, as the film's body count rose, what was going on. She knew these young people had lost members of their family to army violence and had probably seen or enacted very similar things during the war. She sat in agony, hating the film, disgusted at the cheap and obvious special effects, assuming she'd stir up painful old memories if she enquired but too puzzled to stay quiet. She finally blurted out, "How can you watch this?!" One of the young men replied, "This is what happened in our country. We have to watch this so we don't forget."[1]

Horror films are also popular on Sexta Avenida. This is the main drag of downtown Guatemala City, the Sexta Avenida that is once again the site of the Army Day parade and of demonstrations by human rights groups. It is also the Sexta where Mayan organizations protested the Columbus Quincentennial on October 12, 1992, the same Sexta that opens on to the National Palace, Cathedral, and Bank of the Army, where so much violence, resistance, and now memorialization has occurred. This is also where, on New Year's Eve 1997, the beginning of the postwar was celebrated. Sexta also leads to the National Archives, where history, which is not quite the same as memory, is catalogued and stored. And palimpsested with all this is the Sexta Avenida that is the home of *Cannibal Holocaust*, *Texas Chainsaw Massacre*, *Thrill Killers*, *Evil Dead*, *Hell Night*, *The Haunting*, and *Scream* (parts I, II, and III) among many, many others. It is the site of sticky-floored movie houses, Kyrou's "bad, sublime" cinema, and SRO matinee crowds. In 1985, when I first went to Guatemala, there were at least ten movie theaters with a total of twenty-seven screens in a three-by-eight-block area centered on Sexta Avenida. While there are fewer theaters now, but still about twenty screens in this same area, and free trade has brought many more first-run Hollywood films to Sexta, there are two theaters that always show horror on at least one screen and often soft-core pornography on another. A truly enormous selection of pirated DVDs is also available from the informal vendors on Sexta, who say that after children's movies *películas de terror* are their highest sellers.

Horror and maybe a giggling fascination is what I and most of my friends, gringo and Guatemalan, expressed when we passed by these titles and movie posters as we went *sexteando*, making our slow way through the informal sector that crowds the avenue. In the eighties this main thoroughfare was lined with movie theaters showing primarily B and lower-grade films of violence, gore, and soft-core sex. Monsters, psycho killers, nightmares, dismemberment, spewing guts, prisons, schlock action with plenty of gory special effects and loads of fake blood remain standard fare at the remaining cinemas downtown. Such films fill the video stores in the department capitals, much to the dismay of the internationalists living in the highlands to implement the postwar. Along with action films, they are staples of the "salons" that flourish on the weekends in many highland towns like Joyabaj, which consist basically of a TV, VCR, or DVD player and benches in someone's front room. Such movies are also the stock of traveling video shows that set up in town squares throughout the highlands for festivals and feast days. Many people shudder at these low-culture tastes of the masses. "How can that trash be so popular?" "How can they watch that stuff with all the *real* violence around them?"

In the mid-1980s, when I first went to Guatemala, I was a "kill your TV" hippy, unexposed to critical thinking on popular culture. So, as we walked up and down Sexta to interview people, eat, and shop, or hung out in the central squares of highland towns during the fiestas, I could only feel nausea at the prominently displayed posters. I suffered nightmares from having to watch the previews when I'd gone to a more "wholesome" film. I was shocked at their popularity, especially given what I was learning about the real violence that had killed or maimed so many—leaving barely a single family untouched. How, then, could the theaters be flooded with people paying to watch this reel violence?

Of course, this is the general reaction of elites to horror films everywhere. Mark Jancovich says,

> "A theoretical question about horror" frequently arises that does not arise in the same way "with respect to other popular genres" . . . "how can we explain its very existence, for why would anyone *want* to be horrified?" (Carroll 2002:33) While people may not actually like specific genres, many consider the appeal of horror films a problem in itself. A taste for westerns may be strange, but a taste for horror films is often seen as somehow "sick." (2002:22)

In fact, this may be how the upper crust reacts to the popular more generally. Ernesto Laclau (2004) traces how elites, including scholars, dismiss populism as intellectually empty, cynically manipulated, mystifying, parasitic, seductive rather than reasonable, cultic, contagious, vague, and imprecise, all of which are horror film tropes. He quotes Le Bon's precise expression of these fears: "Ideas, sentiments, emotions and beliefs possess in crowds a contagious power as intense as that of microbes. This phenomenon is very natural, since it is observed even in animals when they are together in number. . . . In the case of men collected in a crowd all emotions are very rapidly contagious" (2004:22).

It's one thing to try to figure out why privileged teenagers in the global north love the films: they've been analyzed as reflecting the kids' burgeoning sexuality, as symptoms of late capitalist alienation, or as showing the cluelessness of authority figures.[2] But why would someone who had lived through such things, like the young people at the hotel, feel that a schlocky

U.S. feature driven by obvious special effects is good to remember with? Are horror films proof of the army's fear that the popular classes are persons easily tricked or fooled, even as they seem to rely on such malleability when they seek to "change the cassette," or reeducate them?

The Popular and the Reel

> At no point in time, no matter how utopian, will anyone win the masses over to a higher art; they can be won over only to one nearer to them. And the difficulty consists precisely in finding a form for art such that, with the best conscience in the world, one could hold that it is a higher art. This will never happen with most of what is propagated by the avant-garde of the bourgeoisie. Walter Benjamin

The easiest answer for a critic from the global north, as well as for Guatemalans distinguishing themselves from these questionable popular delights, is to follow Theodor Adorno's sour view of the culture industry as duping the audience. I've been reminded at public presentations of these ideas, that people are easily manipulated by popular culture and that the force of U.S. media has great power over weak minds. The easy cultural studies response is that it's always more complicated—and that the disdain for the popular may itself be a double-cross, creating a self-constituting other for the more discriminating critic. But the popular, like Ríos Montt's populism, is a two- (or even more) faced thing. Rigoberta Menchú Tum seems duplicitous when she is "uncovered" as a political actor and not the transparent representative of the people (see chapter 4). Picturesque indigenous people lynch suspected thieves, Satanists, and baby-snatchers and call it popular justice (Mendoza and Torres-Rivas 2003).[3] Popular is what politicians of all persuasions want to be, that is, everyone's favorite, and what they claim to represent, both speaking for and making an image of.[4] Stuart Hall says,

> Popular culture always has its base in the experiences, the pleasures, the memories, the traditions of the people. It has connections with local hopes and local aspirations, local tragedies and local scenarios that are the everyday practices and the everyday experiences of ordinary folks. Hence, it links with . . . the informal, the underside, the grotesque. . . . Counterposed to elite or high culture, and . . . thus a site of alternative traditions . . . that is why the dominant tradition has always been deeply suspicious of it, quite rightly. (1992:25)[5]

In fact, those hoping to channel, mold, or represent popular sentiment for liberatory or other projects often seem like researchers from the SETI project, in search of extra-terrestrial intelligence, an elusive, contradictory entity. On the one hand the popular feels, well, common, its tastes vulgar, low. Many of the social scientists and progressive activists who claim to describe, act on behalf of, or even speak for the popular classes wouldn't be caught dead paying $8 (or 15 quetzales) to see *Saw* (*Motosierra*). They are like me, before I lost my horror film virginity with *Candyman*. Once inside, we often don't know the etiquette for watching them. Instead of jumping, cowering, screaming along, and yelling back at the screen, we try to shush people or make a point of moving in a huff, trying to find a quiet space for contemplation. Cultural studies has changed some of the attitudes I'm caricaturing, although I once held them quite sincerely. The history of forms of viewing is very much about assumptions of class distinction and raciology, sometimes pointedly remarked upon in the lower registers (Bourdieu 1987, hooks 1992). For example, in Keenan Ivory Wayans's *Scary Movie* the upright, proper white folks trying to enjoy *Shakespeare in Love* lynch an African American woman for talking too much. She was treating high culture like a horror film. Similarly, the comfortable mirroring I experienced at the beginning of *Candyman* in the heroine as anthropology grad student morphed quickly. While at first the filmic Helen personified self-possession, a favored affect of my class that let her chuckle at the urban legends and boldly go into her field site, she is soon affecting fear, a less pleasing emotion to suture into but perhaps enjoyable from a counterposed p.o.v. Unlike in more mainstream, allegedly higher art forms, *Candyman* portrays her race and class privilege as dangerous to herself and others. In turn, her terrorizer, the ghost of a black man lynched by a white mob, is two-faced, also a terrorized victim. As I explore below, such fluxions may be popular in part because they reflect ordinary folks' experiences of the world. They might also play to the ordinary misogyny that enjoys seeing damsels in distress.

On the other, more traditionally political hand, in Guatemala both the revolution and the army sometimes found that their national or universalist goals (Hale 2006) articulated well with the popular, "local hopes and local aspirations." But both were also tripped up as "local tragedies and local scenarios" doubled them over to settle personal scores or showed only one of its faces. For the left in the late 1970s, mass public action, as when villages joined the guerrilla en masse, seemed a vindication. But the same mass action could also betray assumptions, as the people, some wholeheartedly, participate in the Civil Patrols or later vote for monsters like Ríos Montt emerging from a past that had seemed vanquished. Here, or in highland lynchings, the heroic popular seems more a mob than a people. No longer autonomous individuals but an other being—the paranoid crowd, stupidly panicked by silly rumors (Welles 1973, Orr 2005).

If the popular is so fluid, what is popular memory? What would be adequate to the "collective historic memorialization" posited by the CEH as vital to national identity? What, in turn, is "the nation," as a Maya-K'ekchi' man asked during a presentation of the CEH findings? Guatemalans and gringos may experience the same event first- or secondhand, but how does it become part of public consciousness, of popular common sense, assumed in the sense of being taken for granted, in such contradictory ways? How is it that for some Ríos Montt is a war criminal and for others he has proved himself worthy of ruling the country; for some the Japanese tourist lynched in Todos Santos was an innocent victim and for others he was a Satanist threatening their children? (See chapter 6.)

Borrowing a horror film scenario from *Texas Chainsaw Massacre*, I suggest that popular memory, like all assumptions of identity, is rendered. In a rendering plant bodies are torn up and made useful, as when dead animals are made into glue, dog chow, or Jell-O. Similarly, it takes work or labor to dis- and re-member, to fix—in the sense of creating a particular meaning— dead and injured bodies. In Latourian language this is memory-in-action. In turn, the struggles to rend meaning from the cuts of violence and trauma are always inspired by the hope of fixing, in the sense of repairing. But the desire to fix and hold still sits uneasily with rendering's mobility and slipperiness. It is in constant flux, a fixion rather than a fix. This raises a tension between the face of the popular as the most true expression of a people or folk and the sneaking suspicion that it's all been rendered, that they are the most duped: Can't they see it's all fake? Don't they remember what Ríos Montt did?

In Guatemala the term "popular movement" refers to the combined political organizing of workers, students, peasants, indigenous people, Christians, slum dwellers, families of crime victims, anticorruption activists, and returned refugees and exiles, among others. It often stands in for the authentic, the real. However, I am arguing that the identity posited by the term is a mobile series of assumptions rather than an ever-fixed mark. In the postwar-in-action *el pueblo* is not always *unido*. This processed identity may be as adequately represented in schlock horror films—with their filmic special effects, kinesthetic affect, and shifting identifications among victim and perpetrator—as in some other forms of co-memoration.

Embodi/meant

The cinema shows us what our consciousness is. Our
consciousness is an effect of montage. Paul Virilio

Excess is marked by recourse not to the coded articulations of
language but to inarticulate cries—laughing, screaming—both
onscreen and in the audience. Joan Hawkins

Laura Kipnis (1993) has discussed how disgust at pornography, like at the
F/X (special effects) of horror films, and the sense that it is low, correspond
to a Cartesian corporeal-moral mapping in which high is about the head
or the mind, while going down or dealing explicitly with the body is cor-
respondingly less valuable, less legitimate, low class. Horror films concern
themselves graphically with corpo-reality and spend a great deal of time and
effort contemplating the body and how it functions, what it can bear, at
which point it betrays.[6] Soldiers, interrogators, and torturers, that is, those
seeking domination without hegemony, are also concerned with the corporeal. They act directly *on* the body, as we know from testimonials of survivors,
declassified CIA handbooks (Weiner 1997), and Abu Ghraib photos leaked to
the *New Yorker* (Hersh 2004). This raises another tension in my conceit that
horror films are good to think with, since thinking is often concerned with
the head (the cross) while horror and the rendering of submission deploy
their special effects on and through the body.[7]

Horror films may feel low because they merge form and content. Not
only are they about the body, but watching them tends to *be* very embodied.
Unlike the catharsis of supposed higher forms, where a few discrete tears
may fall as the heterosexual couple is thwarted—as Juliet stabs herself,
as Leonardo DiCaprio sinks into the icy North Atlantic—horror films are
grossly kinesthetic. Most people respond to them in very physical ways. In
fact, we can't help ourselves. We recoil, shake, cover our faces, cry out, groan,
grab the person next to us, duck, cover, laugh, scream.[8] But who screams
when "I can't help myself"? Who is co-laborating?

Before I saw *Candyman* I would have sided with one respondent to this
chapter who said, "U.S. pop culture is only about making money. Rich executives make these movies, what could they know?" After seeing it, I had
to revise my self-righteous assumptions about the popular. I began to watch
these bad, low films as often as I could and experienced the intense kinesthesia and corpo-reelity they offer.

In Wes Craven's aptly titled film *Scream* (1996) there is a scene in which teenagers are watching John Carpenter's *Halloween*. They move simultaneously, jerking back, yelling out, screaming, and laughing. I went to see *Scream 3* on Sexta Avenida with a former guerrilla, someone who had seen many compañeros fall. Together we gasped, screamed, laughed, and cringed, and by the end of the film my arm was bruised and red where he had grabbed it so roughly and so often. In the highland village of Joyabaj I sat on a rustic bench shoulder to shoulder, hip to hip, with about twenty-five Maya K'iche' men, a few ladinos, and about ten women in *traje*. We were watching a forgettable, subtitled U.S. horror film on a television in a small room opening up onto the main drag on a rainy market day. We had each paid one quetzal, fifteen cents or about one-tenth of a day laborer's wage, to get in.[9] Every space on the benches was taken, and several people were standing at the rear, while the doorway was crowded with boys straining to catch a free glimpse of the screen. Because our bodies pressed so tightly together I was deeply aware of how we all moved together, startling, shaking, laughing. At a particularly gruesome dismemberment scene we all jumped and cried out. I looked around and saw many in the audience sheepishly peering about to see if anyone had noticed their outburst. Horror films are good for thinking about the lower registers, the body.

During the civil war, the Guatemalan government's "mechanisms of horror" were deeply concerned with embodi/meant. They sought to fix particular forms of popular understandings (the war was aimed at the whole population) via the body and visceral experiences. This assault on the popular, the body politic, is, of course, experienced through the individual bodies of both victims and victimizers. As Scarry (1985) tells us, this translation from the general to the particular is slippery, never clear-cut, and even more so is the reverse, when individuals attempt to render the meanings of embodied experience back to a larger public.

This is further complicated in Guatemala by the war's mixing of the public theater of cruelty with the enforced privatization of pain and guilt. The massive repression—leaving whole villages, along with those who didn't flee, in smoking ruins and dumping tortured bodies in public spaces like roadsides and Zone One city sidewalks—taught private repression. Keep the secrets, never speak out. It made every witness a collaborator, especially when they could do nothing to save the victim. Guilt and horror paralyzingly combine. McAllister describes mothers' guilt for what happened to their children, and children's guilt for what happened to their parents: "One man told of going back after an army patrol passed to find his aged mother, who had fallen behind. All he found were her clothes lying on the path, her skirt neatly tied at the waist, her blouse tucked into it, and even her shoes below it, but with no body inside. He is tortured by this uncanny image and asked me if I thought that the soldiers had eaten her" (2003:286).

Many others embodied the violence more directly, not only surviving attacks on their own bodies and within their own families, but they themselves co-laborating, they themselves inflicting the harm. Pablo Policzer, a Chilean political scientist, said that what most surprised him about the counterinsurgency in Guatemala was that "the army managed to incorporate *everyone*. In Chile," he said, "they never accomplished anything like that" (pers. comm.). González describes the collective rape of women in San Bartolomé Jocotenango by soldiers and local men as a "spectacle of shame" through which the entire community became accomplices in war crimes. The army sought to "dirty everyone, *mancharlos de vergüenza*, stain them all with shame, this way no one was free, no one had the moral solvency to judge, much less denounce what had happened" (2002:415). She also emphasizes the horrific intimacy of collaboration: "The women who were kept in the rape houses had to cook every day for the very men who were raping them" (pers. comm.). While the CEH seeks to untie these links between silence and hiding, horror continues to actively render co-memoration via this slipping and stuttering between what everyone knows and everyone did but few can say, the "public secret" (Taussig 1999).

Forms of forcing collaboration were often ingenious and always gruesome. For example, a long-distance bus driver in northern Huehuetenango told me that at 4 am on a high mountain road in 1982 the bus had suddenly started shaking. When he got out to see what was wrong he found that the army had laid fifteen indigenous men, bound and gagged, in the road and that his bus had just killed them. The truth commission reports and recent ethnographies overflow with instances of such co-laboration. A woman who took testimony for the CEH recalled a man who couldn't speak because of what he'd done. "Usually," she said, "once they got started it would just flow out of people. But this guy came really late, after we'd been in the village for several weeks, and we had to leave the next day. He came at 12:30 at night to give the testimony of how he had killed his own son. It was so hard, his whole body, his throat, the *vergüenza*, *the culpa* (the shame, the guilt) [she was speaking in English but said these words in Spanish]. It really hurt me to watch. It was maybe the hardest testimony I took in all that time. The next day he came to us as we were leaving with his hands held out for us to tie him up and take him to jail. He felt he belonged there because of what he'd done. . . . The CEH opened up these areas for people. I wonder if perhaps that was the worst part of it? There has been no follow-up. What has happened to these people?" Is even co-memoration a form of collaboration?

A major vehicle of incorporation into the mechanisms of horror was the army-imposed Civil Patrol system, which forced every man in the rural areas to participate in twenty-four-hour guard duty, perform frequent patrols to hunt down refugees or confront the guerilla, spy on neighbors, and carry out massacres, usually with the weapons to hand, like farming tools. Having to report for duty meant, of course, that you yourself were always being spied on. In Joyabaj in 1982 the army called together all the men of the town and various outlying hamlets and made them walk through the night to a distant hamlet. There they were treated to drink and food and praised for their efforts on behalf of the nation. A few weeks later when they were called again to walk through the night to the hamlet of Xeabaj, most expected a similar experience. Instead they were forced to kill the residents with their machetes.

"Awful things happened there," said Alfonso García, who thanked God he had been out of town that day. "My brother had to go. There were bodies, blood, the whole square was full. He couldn't stand it. He went and hid in the woods for a long time." Doña Miguela, an older K'iche' woman from the town, said, "*Ay dios! Ay dios!* It was so horrible! So horrible! They killed babies," and she acted it out in her kitchen, as if she were lifting up an infant and smashing its head on her oven, "children, women, old people. My husband had to go. Everyone had to go. We had to cook but when they came back they couldn't eat. Their mouths were so bitter with all they had seen. All they had done. Terrible! Terrible! *Ay dios!*"

Remijnse says there is still no accurate accounting for this day. Estimates of those murdered range from fifty to two hundred. "A river of blood ran down the mountain," a witness told her (2001:463).[10] In 1981 and 1982 there was a wave of army-ordered patrol massacres in the Joyabaj/Zacualpa region, which then gave way to more "privatized" violence, "used more and more by individual patrol commanders for their own purposes—to improve their own economic position in the village by confiscating land and cattle from disappeared or fleeing neighbors. 'That way lots of land changed owners. They saw that there was a good piece of land . . . and they took it'" a Xoye told Remijnse (2001:458). A prewar grudge between two ladino hamlets was settled by patrol members in southern Joyabaj during the fiesta: "While the marimba played they were killing the PAC of Boquerón" (in Remijnse 2001:459). Twenty men died that day.

Like the other hundreds of massacres, what happened in Xeabaj was a very public staging of what could happen to a people who were judged to be subversive and a display of what one could be forced to do. Even twenty years later very few people who were involved are willing to talk about Xeabaj, although everyone knows that everyone participated (Remijnse 2002).

What is meant when one embodies terror? For boys forcibly conscripted into the army? For villagers turned into civil patrollers macheteing their neighbors, repeating the daily actions of cutting foliage but on human flesh? For women, performing the engrained daily labor of hand-grinding corn, but to feed the bodies of those who violate them and murder their kinfolk? For everyone remaining silent, complicit, thereby betraying their neighbors, family members, even their relation to the dead? What is an appropriate mechanism for co-memorating this popular (in the sense of common) experience of co-laborating, of living with blood on your hands?

In 2006 an indigenous Xoye told me he had been sick for the whole year since I last visited. He had suffered attacks and been hospitalized and treated for depression, but nothing, not even the exercise regime and anti-anxiety drugs he'd been prescribed, seemed to help. "It's because of the war. We lived *entre miedo* [in fear] and it was so long!! 1979 to 1985," and he began to count on his fingers. Twice through he counted, "79, 80, 81, 82, 83, 84, 85 . . . seven years! All that time we were always afraid! Always! You just don't recover from this! I saw such horrible things, the army, the patrol. I saw people killed. I saw people tortured. And I couldn't do anything. I was afraid, so afraid! And I couldn't do any of the work I love. I couldn't support development. I couldn't help people. Because I didn't know," he paused, "you didn't know if what you were doing might get you killed. Me decepcionó el ejército [the army deceived me]. I saw the terrible things they did." On the table between us was a pirated DVD of *La Profecía* (The Omen) that his kids, studying in the capital, had bought him on Sexta Avenida. They said they thought he'd like it.

I don't know if those children, who I know are very worried about their father, saw this gift as mere distraction or something else. They'd watched it together the night before and hoped to see it again before they returned to Guatemala City. And I can't honestly say Doña Miguela's husband, who walked through the night to Xeabaj, gets any "therapeutic" benefit from watching horror films. I know he goes to those little crowded rooms, and he drinks a lot. We have jumped and cried out together, even though the family has a television that shows many films of the same genre, and he could have watched at home. I'm not a psychologist and I'm certainly not arguing that there is a one-to-one correspondence between the films and the war or between watching them and feeling "better." I'm making a more modest argument—that they're good to think with about people's engagement with the war in the postwar moment. I find the films' extravagant relation to embodi/meant particularly evocative.

I am emboldened to make this claim by parallel efforts of the Mayan women's organization Kaq'la' to address the body and emotions as sites and stakes of struggle over the postwar and assumptions of identity. After finding that more standard talk-based forms of working with women survivors were not as effective as they'd hoped, in their current research and activism the women of Kaq'la' are experimenting with more corporeal and affective methods of co-memorating. For the past few years they have held workshops in which testifying, listening to lectures, theorizing, and holding small group discussions are combined with body work like yoga, massage therapy, dance, breathing and meditation, acting out experiences, energy conservation, and traditional Mayan practices like pulsing, *limpieza*, and *sanamiento* (cleaning, healing) of spaces and bodies, and attention to eating hot or cold foods (Grupo de Mujeres Mayas Kaqla 2004). The returned exile who had been unwillingly called by illness to take up a *cargo*, or burden, by training as a healer is a now a leader of the group. As one participant said, "We are doing lots of body work in the sessions and paying a lot of attention to emotions. Some of it is very intense [*chocante*], and many of us were very resistant, but now we meet all the time. It is very powerful." After I gave a lecture to the group as part of a two-day series of events, they let me read the women's evaluations. The strongly expressed consensus was that the talk was okay, but what the women really appreciated was work with the body![11]

What these people seem to know, like viewers of horror films, is that embodi/meant and returning to such events in the company of others may be an affective and effective form of rendering co-memoration. Perhaps horror, in its brutality (as Bataille suggests), may do supplementary work to other, more official memory projects.

Too, I'm uncomfortable assuming that the young people at the hotel were duped into thinking the horror film was about "what happened in our country." They may have meant that, among the other forms of making sense of the civil war and of the ongoing violence that undergirds everyday life, global popular culture like horror films is good to think and feel with—offering unexpected metaphors and shared experience, even small pleasures. Carlota McAllister relates that she accompanied the indigenous family she lived with in Chupol on an excursion to the capital, where they saw the Mel Gibson film *The Patriot*, which is about the American Revolutionary War. Partway through she began to regret it because the film is about brutal counterinsurgency in which the British, just like the Guatemalan army in the 1980s, herd an entire town into their church and burn them alive. She kept checking to see if her friends were all right, if they wanted to leave, but they seemed bound to the screen and kept shushing her. At the end they were enthusiastic, especially because the good guys (the revolutionary guerrilla fighters) won!

In another montage of media and meaning-making, the anthropologist Linda Green writes, "One young man told me that when the army grabbed him for military service, he managed to escape by throwing himself from a truck using a Ramboesque stunt" (1999:255). A young man who is very active in the urban Mayan scene "came out" to me as a former guerrilla combatant when we walked by a video store in Zone One that had a poster of Sylvester Stallone in the window. "You know Rambo? What he does?" Here he acted out shooting off machine gun rounds with both hands. "We did that. Not against the Vietnamese, of course! Against the soldiers." Another merging of the real and reel was in the way so many described September 11, 2001, as "just like a movie."

The Way We Were: "Like a Movie," or Reverberation Between Events?

> Things "happen" in the history of the individual but memory resides in the reverberations between events. Trauma has no real existence as such but is a function of representation ... "deferred action" is a working over, through time, of the implications of one event as its reading feels the impact of other events. Mary Anne Doane

There is a tension in many recent works on trauma around the definition of memory (Antze and Lambeck 1996, Boyarin 1994, Leys 2000, Remijnse 2002, Schacter 1995). One theory corresponds to a scene in the (bad? sublime?) film *Donald Duck in Math-magicland*. In it we are privileged to enter Donald's head, which is a real mess! Half-open cabinets with files all astray, partially read books left open, and unorganized paper lying everywhere. The paternalist narrator remonstrates the duck for the disorder, which is magically cleared up, allowing Donald to more easily remember things like his multiplication tables. Here, memory is like a movie—the images laid on the film just sit there until you fire up the VCR, exactly like they were when the movie was made.[12] And for Donald it's all contained, in his head, with no messy embodiment.

In more psychoanalytic understandings, however, memory always occurs *aprés coup*, or after the blow. This means that memory is always retroactive, constructed, worked over, elaborated (with emphasis on the labor) after the event. In Guatemala, when a literal coup or blow—a massacre, a disappearance, a murder, an attack, or a coup d'état—occurs, everything is chaotic, fear and horror take over, people feel without fully comprehending. It is only later that we realize that we saw it coming, that the clues were everywhere, that a chain of command made decisions, that our lives were shattered for a reason. We render it. In this sense, memory is less mechanical and more recombinant, articulatory. Each new experience causes reverberations that kaleidoscope memory, making its pieces fall together in new and different ways. This is methodologically messy for anthropologists trying to make sense of horrifying things they have not experienced or witnessed first-hand. Horror as lived and the acts, milieu, and ecology that sustain it are not always public. We depend on moments when it is publicized, like testimonials or the kinesthesia of watching horror films in Joyabaj, so that we can work on it (e/co-laborate).

Memory may work in both ways, caught on film to be relived and constantly reworked. When I told Doña Miguela that I'd walked up to Xeabaj she seemed to make a tiger's leap into the past, to remember almost exactly how it was when her husband came home, with his mouth too bitter to eat the food she had prepared. "*Ay dios!*" she exclaimed. She acted out a kinesthetically powerful moment she had only heard about, not experienced. Judith Zur found similar relivings among K'iche' widows and their children: "Martín's memories are particularly distressing: as an under-age fourteen year old patroller he had been on duty that day and had been involved in rounding up its victims and roping them together. He had seen his father beaten almost to death from close quarters, although he did not see his death and burial. The exhumation caused him to relive the trauma which he describes in terms of experiencing a 'video' which has been 'engraved in his head' ever since. Martín told me he has never mentioned this to his family because of the overwhelming sadness of it all; the 'video' still plays in his head and continues to disturb him" (1998:295).[13]

But memory also changes things, reflecting more how it is seized hold of in a dangerous present than how things "actually happened." In criticizing Menchú's testimonial by contrasting it with other people's versions of events, collected ten years later, David Stoll (1999) tends to downplay this aspect of memory: that what it means to be willing to die or to kill will change through time depending on whether the goal of that death was achieved, whether you won or not (this is why counterinsurgency is so interested in it). McAllister says, "Understanding Chupol's revolutionary violence and what it subsequently wrought is . . . a task it is neither desirable nor feasible to perform objectively. . . . The defeat of Chupol's revolutionary project was not inevitable, but once it failed, the desires that gave rise to it could not be retrieved in their original form" (2003:253). Postwar elaboration, working through an event after the fact, is necessary to stay sane and is always political, an effect of struggle, an assumption of identity. As Freud says, "The material present in the shape of memory-traces is from time to time subjected to a rearrangement in accordance with fresh circumstances . . . memory is present not once but several times over . . . it is registered in various species of 'signs'" (in Doane 1991:89).

What is the sense of *el nacer de conciencia* — of consciousness raising — except as the construction of a new narrative that makes sense of past blows, the unforeseeable swerves veering out of the opening of the cut? Whereas the old consciousness, the old self, has one narrative for making sense of things, the new consciousness rearranges events into a new story; it feels different reverberations between events and may feel conned by its earlier assumptions. An old consciousness may understand the disappearance of a loved one as a defensible state action against a dangerous subversive, while the new consciousness understands that it is a deep injustice and must be resisted tooth and nail. An old consciousness may read the Columbus Quincentennial as a celebration of the civilization of barbarians or the mixing of two cultures, while an emerging Mayan consciousness will make sense of it as five hundred years of trauma which must be addressed if a healthy body politic is ever to emerge (Adams and Bastos 2003, Cojtí Cuxil 1990, 1994, Filóchofo 1999). All three forms of assumption are hard at work here.

SUBJECT FORMATION IN THE MIDST OF VIOLENT BOUNDARY TRANSGRESSIONS

The vision of a pacified world achieved through the scientific arrangement of society and the domination of nature, and crowned in a museum is one we will encounter again.
Paul Rabinow

Drenched in taboo and encroaching vigorously on the pornographic . . . the world of horror is one that knows very well that men and women are profoundly different but one that at the same time repeatedly contemplates mutations and slidings whereby women begin to look a lot like men. Carol Clover

Perhaps because of its self-reflexivity, the film *Scream* is particularly good to think with. I've seen all three *Screams* with capacity crowds on Sexta Avenida, and the original, translated as *Máscara del terror* (Mask of terror), was *still* showing there in August 2003, seven years after its release! In the movie a bunch of clean-cut, white, middle-American high school students are terrorized by a monster killer in black robes and Edvard Munch's *Scream* face. One joke of the movie is its postmodern irony; that the kids are all well versed in the genre of horror film. The killer demands answers to horror trivia questions as he terrorizes his victims. As they are picked off one by one they discuss the monster's next move in the horror aisle of the local video store and analyze horror's rules: don't ever say I'll be right back, cause then you'll be dead for sure, only virgins survive, etc. In one scene the film geek pauses the horror movie they're watching (making his friends moan at this cut in their suture) to explain, "Break the rules and you end up dead."

In fact, the killers turn out to be *produced by* the horror canon: they "watched a few films and took a few notes" in order to follow the rules of the genre. Sidney, our heroine, covered in blood, all her friends dead, and her lover revealed as one of the psycho-killers, cries, "Why? Why?" They only chuckle at her desire for a motive and agree that the very lack of one increases the terror they seek to sow. Here is precisely that tension between the fixed rules—as long as you obey you'll survive—and rendering—the only rule is, there are no rules; between memory as a movie and as always open to reinterpretation.

In Guatemala the "mechanisms of horror" laid out in the truth commission reports practically form a genre. As Luisa Valenzuela says in *Lizard's Tail*, her magic realist novel about Argentina's dirty war, "Tyrannies are not what they used to be. Now they have replaceable parts. One president falls and another is ready to take over. There's no shortage of generals" (1983:280). Counterinsurgency terror is a commodity in Latin America—one with training manuals, imported experts, and diploma-granting institutions (Armony 1999, Cullather 1999, *Death Squadrons* 2003, Grandin 2006, *Hidden in Plain Sight* 2002, Weiner 1997) where military personnel studying at the "School of the Americas," recently renamed the Western Hemisphere Institute for Security Cooperation (WHISC),[14] mimic the way the psycho-killers in *Scream* watch horror films.

The victims, struggling to survive, are very aware of the rules, but those rules keep changing. The peace treaty was supposed to open the door for democracy, but one day those trying to exercise democratic rights are lauded and the next they are killed. If you obeyed the state when it told you to kill, it wouldn't kill you, but now some low-level, mostly indigenous soldiers and patrollers are facing the death penalty for their roles in atrocities. With coup attempts, death squad activity, and murder coming in waves, like a movie sequel, horror feels both new and numbingly familiar. Militarism, anti-Communism, and counterterror, like the monsters of the movies, keep coming back, no matter how many times you think you've vanquished them (Ríos Montt, portrayed by Filóchofo as a deathless vampire; Gulf War II: "Son of . . .").

Just as Sidney seeks a motive, we too might query: Why? (a question I pursue in chapter 6). Are the army, elites, and supportive foreign powers simply pursuing clear-cut political economic interests? This would correspond to one of Harvey's faces of everyday surplus extraction—maintaining a docile workforce, ensuring unimpeded access to natural resources, and making money off defense contracts. But how do we account for the scale of violence, the overwhelming horror of it, its "special effects"? What rules *do* they follow? (Certainly not the Geneva Convention!) The ruling of genocide in Guatemala and explorations of racist and misogynist terror (Bunster-Burrotto 1986) seek to acknowledge the "extra"-vagance of the violence. Purely rational motives may exist but don't entirely fix anything. If cause and effect were calculated in a ledger book the way debt and labor are in the *Baile de la Culebra*, they would never balance out. But is it enough to say this is just Harvey's and Luxemburg's "second face" of rapacious and brutal "accumulation by dispossession"?

As the war grinds down in Guatemala and the postwar peters out, the struggle continues to re-member the nation, to make sense of the past. Horror haunts these attempts to re-present the civil war, as it does the thousands of patrons of Sexta Avenida's schlock movie theaters, my friend the former guerrilla, the young people at that hotel, and those K'iche' and ladino men and women and the gringa crowded onto those benches in Joyabaj, jumping and yelping in unison. What spine-tingling pleasures do horror films afford that make so many return time and again to this well-worn, even hackneyed terrain like teenagers inexorably drawn to the umpteenth reincarnation of Jason at the multiplex? Despite the many attempts by the government and popular movements to fix (repair) the national body politic by fixing and holding still particular co-memorations, this past is not really over, it's not even past. It can suddenly return, a zombie unexpectedly appearing on television denouncing his friends, a human bone in freshly turned soil, a memory of death reenacted in a kitchen. Like a psycho leaping out of a closet, this past slashes through attempts to contain it.

Popular struggles over commemoration are like horror films because they are about assumptions of identity, about subject formation in the midst of violent boundary transgressions. In horror films some traumatic founding act of violence (like slavery and the lynching in *Candyman*) and the resulting familial and communal dysfunction, gender blur, sexual and racial confusion, and bodily mutation produce the psycho killer: think of Norman Bates in *Psycho*, possessed by his mother. This is like the founding acts of invasion, the resulting dispossession of exploitative power structures, and the race, class, and identity confusion of colonialism, imperialism, anti-Communism, and the horrors of civil war.

Too bad the monsters in *Scream* hadn't read Carol Clover's *Men, Women and Chainsaws*, because then they would have known an important rule that does seem to hold: our heroine, the killer's main target throughout the film, turns the tables. In *Scream*, as in most modern horror films, this "Final Girl," as Clover calls her, is smart, wary of sex, and resistant to the killer's games because she sees through the horror genre ("it's always some mama's boy") even as she's a part of it (she wants to keep her relationship with her boyfriend "PG-17"). This is central. While she is victimized, she is not only a victim. She is also a perpetrator. The Final Girl runs, she flinches, she falls, she screams, she cries, she bleeds, she runs some more. But in the final showdown she takes away the monster's weapons: in *Scream* this includes the horror film genre itself in the form of a television playing John Carpenter's *Halloween*, in *The Wizard of Oz* it's via homely items like a house or water that accidentally kill. She wears the mask, stabs with the knife, destroys with the chainsaw, turning them back on the monster or killers and saving herself, at least till the sequel. She co-laborates.

Horror films may be popular in Guatemala, where lots of people go to see them, because they evoke popular experience, what many Guatemalans lived. In addition to the kinesthetic rather than the purely rational experience of one's body being acted on by an outside force such as the film or the army, Clover's list of the movies' generic mechanisms corresponds almost point for point to Guatemala's "mechanisms of horror." (1) There is always a killer or monster, the product of repressed trauma, often someone familiar. (2) The victim(s). (3) The Terrible Place, home of the terrible family—in Guatemala, churches, schools, and homes were often sites of torture and death. (4) The weapons, which, Clover emphasizes, are always tactile and short-range like knives, ice picks, hooks, and chainsaws; they require intimate interaction and getting your hands dirty. (5) The Final Girl, who shrieks, runs, sustains injury, and finally fights back and wins with the monster's own weapons. Often close to a third of the generic horror film will be given over to her struggle, and expert fans will often judge a film by its quality. In these films, as in Guatemala, the boundaries among victim, victimizer, survivor, and victor are terribly porous.

Those struggling over memory and history in Guatemala may be like Clover's Final Girl—simultaneously caught up in a past of horror and memory; suspicious, seeking to render it meaningful; and noninnocent participants in brutal attempts to survive. Horror films may offer momentary embodi/meant of these co-memorations and co-laborations.

Horror Mutations

> The exploration of violence must address the blood on people's hands. It must consider the utter devastation of families and communities in a world where community members denounced their neighbors as subversives to the army because of interfamilial feuding and where widows saw their husbands killed or disappeared by an army in which their own sons served as soldiers. It must acknowledge the horror of living side by side with the person responsible for the murder of your father, or of remaining silent and fearful in the face of the half secrets of who did what to whom. Linda Green

"How can they watch that stuff?" How is this past to be commemorated? What means are adequate to preserve the memory of the people who were massacred in Xeabaj, of the people in neighboring Zacualpa, murdered by the patrollers of Joyabaj? Does accounting for them as purely victims remember their other faces, perhaps as "good people" precisely insomuch as they were consciously and willfully resisting political and economic domination (McAllister 2002)? And how are those forced to carry out the massacres to live in the world, much less be commemorated? With what sort of hazmat suit are people supposed to handle this toxic past? Many soldiers believed they were killing to defend the nation against subversion, others were interpellated through internalized racism and misogyny, while still others were simply trying to survive themselves (Wilson 1995). Many have suicided or lose themselves to alcohol or other fixes. In turn, many in the guerrilla killed in the belief they were defending themselves and the nation against rapacious elites and the vampiric transnational capitalism that sucks out the country's lifeblood, leaving it weak, unable to defend itself. Each side paints itself as the hero/victim and the other as the victimizer. The CEH finding that the army was responsible for 93 percent of the abuses they investigated bolsters the claims of the popular movement. But, again, who comprises that army? Who are these victimizers?

In turn, the Mayan movement is raising a longer past, of five hundred years of colonial murder and dispossession, which more profoundly incriminates many of those struggling for a more just future. Here another horror trope may help us think. The main cause of the haunted houses that so afflict Euro-Americans in horror films is that they were built on Indian burial grounds. In *Poltergeist*, *The Shining*, *Amityville Horror*, and a host of others, the historical past of genocide and dispossession always returns. While a nice Caucasian family may settle innocently into the upscale home or hotel, just trying to improve their lot in life, they cannot escape their collaboration in such crimes. In Guatemala, nice ladinos in the mainstream and in the popular movement, struggling against already horrific odds, find the history of five hundred years of murder, despoliation, exploitation, and racist exclusion returning to haunt the landscape and destabilize popular or supposedly shared identifications.

Mayan cultural rights activists are also like Final Girls, struggling with the responses of nonindigenous sectors to their claims to represent the Mayan past and to fight for the Mayan future. The CEH report calls for "acknowledging the multicultural character of the nation by raising monuments and creating communal cemeteries in accord with the collective memory of the Maya." In the context of the peace treaty, including the Accord on Indigenous Rights and Identity, and the ratification of the International Labor Organization's Convention 169, which contain a number of rights available only to indigenous people, the stakes are high for Mayan identity claims. Those claims are partly based on memory, and the debates over the content and ownership of that memory, of making sense of or re-membering a violent past after the blow, are passionate. Some ladinos claim that the Maya care *only* for memory and thereby have no claim on the national future. A well-known newspaper columnist wrote, "They all want to live in *Mayassic Park*" (Morales 1992). This is an intriguing reference to *Jurassic Park*, a big budget, rather than B-grade, horror film in which the past, in the form of female dinosaurs, resurfaces; it troubles, it turns the present's feeling of being "at home" into an illusion. Others claim there is no such thing as a specifically Mayan memory, that Guatemala is a mestizo nation and must be re-membered as that, now that the war is ended. Similarly, the recent past is hotly contested. The popular movement's claims to have fought for and with the indigenous majority conflict with some Mayan memories of racism and exclusion on the left: was it race war or class war? With memories of the ancient and recent past so contested, how will it be clarified?

Horror films know, as did Freud, that the past is inescapable. In the struggles to make sense of the multiple blows of Guatemala's past, organizations like the Sectors Arising from the Violence, the forensic anthropology teams, the Historic Memory projects, and the Mayan rights movements also know that "the past is aggressive, it returns, it haunts, it sometimes dominates the present" (Doane 1991:91). Just like in schlock horror films, attempts to repress memory always result in the monster returning, more psycho and more violent than ever. Those who have not learned this lesson of horror are parodied in the films: the disbelieving sheriff or politician who pooh-poohs the Final Girl's suspicions. "She's crazy," "It's her own fault," are their dubious explanations of strange violences and unusual phenomena. Similarly in Guatemala, Mayan attempts to deal with the racist past and exclusionary present are often faulted for *creating* the problem, "their undoing is their crime." Indigenous activists are denounced as two-faced—claiming to be victims when they are actually the cause of the problems—while they in turn see the ladino as involved in a cover-up. The Mayan activist Antonio Pop Caal, tragically assassinated in 2002 in a crime yet to be clarified, said, "The ladino tries to erase and put a veil over the problem, not because he is convinced that discrimination does not exist, but because he is afraid that putting a finger in the national wound will stir up conflicts between both groups" (in Bastos and Camus 1993:27).

The standard reaction to this aggressive past of memory and the horror of unsettled identities is screening, veiling. Horror films and Mayan organizers, like rights activists, might agree that "past and present are fully imbricated, locked in a struggle in which forgetting is no longer a simple accident but a defensive weapon aimed against the past" (Doane 1991:91). Those who resist memory are trying to write what psychoanalysis calls "history": they want to "effect a clean break between the past and the present, to put the past in museums and archives, to neutralize it and sanitize its psychic impact" (91).

What survivors of genocide, who may also be perpetrators, and viewers of horror film know, unlike the Mayassic Park pundit, who is bitten by his own metaphor, is that a horror film theory of memory—one which acknowledges the body and the role of the past—is more effective than attempting to cut off the past from the present through "history." The horror film may be so popular in the Terrible Place of the wounded Guatemalan nation because it mimics the working out and creation of a narrative to contain the reverberations of memory, of the sliding of past and present, victim and victimizer. How can wounds be fixed/healed, memory be fixed/held still, when identifications are so two-faced, so unfixed—or fixional? When they are still in the process of being rendered?

Horror, the War, and Slippery Identities

> The distinguishing mark of modern horror is the problematization of identity. Carol Clover

Is this unfixity how Guatemalans can watch those reel horrors when so much real horror surrounds them? Is this why a schlocky film helps kids in the hotel remember what happened in their country? Is this the attraction of the overcrowded video salons in Joyabaj? The short-term fix may be the films' corpo-ree(a)lity and (thinking in Clover's categories) that they emphasize the sliding of identifications. The films echo how—in both official co-memorations of traumatic events like monuments, reports, and ethnographies—and in daily life's odd, unexpected moments, the past aggressively returns to haunt and sometimes dominate the present.

Both horror films and postwar Guatemala must grapple with Feldman's "in-human." Official works of preserving memory are indispensable, but they often take refuge in a "commonsensical universal humanity" which relies on fixing binary oppositions of hero/villain, winner/loser, victim/victimizer. Did anyone really win Guatemala's civil war? Or does it remain unfixed, full of unpredictable multiconductors transforming the whole caboodle? Certainly there were many, many victims, heroes, and heroines, but survival in many cases meant getting blood on your hands. The CEH is absolutely correct: it is vitally important "to remember and dignify the victims of the fratricidal confrontation among Guatemalans." But such re-membering can render out the complexity of identifications and the agency of those killed and wounded. It can silence their active participation in movements for radical social change or the way state-backed violence was deployed in complex and very local ways (González 2002, Kobrak 1997, Paul and Demarest 1988). Are forcibly recruited indigenous boys killed in battle victims or victimizers? What about a thirteen-year-old who becomes a guerrilla to avenge her family's murder by the army? What about someone forced to *delatar*, who says, "I couldn't help myself"? In turn, do the Maya who accuse ladinos of race war have clean hands themselves? To paraphrase Clover, the world of horror is one that knows very well that victims and perpetrators are profoundly different, but one that at the same time repeatedly contemplates mutations and slidings whereby one begins to look a lot like the other.

Both the horror film genre and emerging ways of understanding the civil war are deeply imbricated with the fluidity of identity. Early horror presented one monster and one victim, as in Hitchcock's *Psycho* or Dracula's attentions to Mina Harker. In these films the hero function is played by the boyfriend, often in cahoots with a scientist and a law enforcer: think of the shrink explaining Norman Bates in the police station or Jonathan Harker, Dr. Van Helsing, and the triple boyfriend cohort of cowboy, aristocrat, and psychologist in *Dracula*. Similarly, one narrative for remembering the war is as a Manichean relation between the military state and *el pueblo*, or the popular movement. Here, depending on which side you are on, the hero is posited as the state or as the national liberation movement. Both claim to link passion, science, and the law to save the victimized people, for some, from the Communist subversives, for others, from the psychotic genocidal state.

Especially at the height of the war, such differentiations were important for legitimizing the violence to both participants and outsiders. The popular movement was very popular, enlisting hundreds of thousands of people from all walks of life, the majority of them indigenous. They came very close to winning the war in the early 1980s. But the military, after forty years in power, had consolidated a political economic bloc and foreign support. These fixed positions mask the deep divisions within both sides—the state marked by three coups between 1974 and 1983, the guerrilla struggling to unite four different organizations, in addition to splits over strategy and over the relation between class struggle and race war.

After 1983, as scorched-earth policies gave way to a putative democratization and an initial accounting of the war, Guatemala began to look more like later slasher films, in which the single monster produces multiple victims, like the van- or house-load of murdered kids in *Texas Chainsaw Massacre* or *Halloween*. Just as the civil war opened up bodies and blurred physical boundaries, the war and the peace process—including the expanding Mayan rights movement—have problematized identities. Government counterinsurgency shocked many ladinos because it treated them like "Indians"—expendable, worthless, bereft of civil and human rights.[15] Likewise, the Mayan movement, insisting on the presence of the Mayan past, is problematizing Guatemalan national *and* ladino/mestizo/criollo/shumo ethnic identities. But even as the CEH calls for acknowledging multicultural reality and Mayan collective memory, Mayan identity is also unstable and mobile. Indigenous people in the popular movement question whether "the Maya" represent them, and Mayan women have in turn challenged their exclusion from leadership positions. Some rural indigenous people find that Mayan claims resonate with them, while others have never heard of the movement. Similarly, the claims of women have fragmented the unitary identity of *el pueblo*. The gendered dimensions of the colonized victim as the nation in distress saved by the heroic boyfriend of national liberation begins to be explored, and the hero function in general begins to raise doubts.

Clover argues that in the 1970s a mode of horror film emerged that unified victim, monster, and hero in the same person, as in *Carrie*. This further unsettled clear-cut identifications and increasingly opened up sites for multiple cross-identifications as U.S. boy audiences identified with girls in fear and pain *and* with girls picking up the monster's weapons and using them, via intimate contact. Guatemalan counterinsurgency horrifically popularized co-laboration in the violence. Via civil patrolling, soldiering, rape, and silencing and in the violence deployed by the guerrillas, most everyone had to live in intimate contact with killing. Thus, in Guatemala's civil war, the monster's identity is fluid. The "killer" as well as the victims is fissured and multiple, more than two-faced.

Clover also argues that for horror film audiences identification is mobile. For example, in the post-*Carrie* horror film, both gender and audience identification constantly mutate and slide. We first see through the camera eye of the killer, often cheering his dastardly deeds or at least enthusiastically groaning at their grossness. But then we slip into screaming for the victim and warning, "Don't go in there!" Even later we urge on the Final Girl's heroics, "we can't help ourselves." Film theory suggests that in narrative cinema audiences undergo a condensed reenactment of subject formation (Silverman 1983). We relive the movement from traumas of childlike incapacity and fear to an adultlike control of our worlds. In turn, feminist film criticism has shown how Hollywood positions the male as subject and the female as object of his gaze. However, Clover suggests that, unlike standard cinema, horror allows for multiple gender identifications, inducing masochistic identification, not only sadistic control. This instability may also help explain the repetition compulsion in horror and the popularity of Sexta Avenida's movie houses and highland video rooms.

In the winter of 2000 there was a landslide behind the convent in Joyabaj. A number of human remains were exposed, forcing the town authorities to call in an exhumation team.[16] As they did throughout the highlands, the army lived in the Joyabaj church compound and used the convent as a prison and torture chamber, dumping bodies in the ravine right behind it. In the mid-1990s the army moved its barracks to the outskirts of town. By the time I visited in June 2000 the forensic team had come and gone but everyone wanted to talk about the exhumation. Doña Miguela's grown daughter, Adela, recounted, "They found some bodies and then more and more. More than twenty-five. The people came, two gringos working so hard, sweating, in the heat, and no one would help them. No one would help! La gente tiene miedo — tiene miedo!, the people are afraid. The army was still here. Maybe if they had been gone by then, it would have been different, but the people are afraid, they didn't help. Many, many people came down from the villages to see, to see if they were their family. But it was very hard to tell. So many were naked, naked. They are all complete, complete skeletons. One of them, the whole side of his face," she gestures "was destroyed, mashed in. Others were strangled, with the ropes still there! Some were all jumbled together. There were three bodies all very close. They must have been buried still partly alive because in their agony they got all tangled up. One head here, another here, their legs all bunched together" [this was very graphic, she was acting it all out] "in such a tiny place. They were still alive! And there was a dog, a little dog. They took the dog with its master and they are buried there together.

"Every time my mother sent me to get something in the market I would buy it as quickly as I could and then run and look. They got to know me there, I tried to go every day. One day they found a soccer player. He must have been taken right off the field. He still had his shoes on, his uniform, all complete. His jersey, his socks. Just like they found him on the field, that's how they left him! The *forenses* were so careful, so patient! I wanted them to just open it right up, get them out, I wanted to see it, but the way they did it, they would put a little dust in the sifter, a little more dust in the sifter, I wanted to scream, just get them out! They say there's a lot more — a hole down below with many bodies. But the team went away. They took the bodies, and we don't know what happened to them."

Then, for the first time, after I had known her and her family for several years, she told me her older brother was forcibly conscripted in the army: "He was sent to Zacualpa in 1983, and he saw really horrible things there! Holes full of bodies. He talks about it a little, but he says he doesn't know about what happened here. Not many people who served here have been willing to talk about it. But my brother has a friend who knows someone in Chichicastenango who says he was here, a soldier in the war, and he killed lots of people. He brags about it! He says he liked it. He said, 'They made me kill but then I realized me goce matar, I enjoy killing.' He brags about strangling them, hanging them, doing all these terrible things. He says there are LOTS more bodies around, but that no one will ever find them, that they can't find the holes." Then she told me her uncle was disappeared by the army when it was stationed in Joyabaj, and they were hoping they would find his body in the exhumation but nothing suggested any of the remains belonged to him.

Adela's complex and kinesthetic responses were echoed by a number of people I talked to that summer. She recounted, in much more detail than I'm recounting here, with enormous energy and vigorous gestures her mix of horror and fascination at the homely (the dog, the soccer jersey) and grotesquely uncanny things uncovered in the landslide and subsequent exhumation. What are we to make of the "reverberations between events"—between the violence of the early 1980s and its sequel in 2000, between the real images and the reel ones? What might it mean that these experiences are, like the police photographs of Myrna Mack's murder, "like a horror film"? What does it mean that Adela's description of going every chance she could mimics horror movie fans, who know what they'll find but go back again and again? In her immediate family there were both victims and perpetrators. She has had children with, but never married, one of the soldiers stationed there but rarely speaks of him. He lives elsewhere now.

AUDIENCE PARTICIPATION

I beg you, learn to see bad films. They are good to think with about possession—the experience of one's body being acted on by an external force and sometimes finding you like it, "me goce"—and about the shifting positions involved in living simultaneously as victim, victimizer, witness, and survivor in the aftermath of civil war. They capture, in form and content, the embodi/ meant of co-laboration. Perhaps horror films, combined with other forms of memorialization, help e/laborate these ongoing, still-being-rendered, lived experiences.

The "you" Kyrou and I address may not be you, dear reader, but let's face it, this book's lectors are less likely to represent the amorphous popular and more likely to shudder at popular fare like *Candyman* and *Scream*—and to wonder, How can they watch that stuff? Perhaps one should not ask this rhetorically, because we already know that it's gross, sick, brutal, and inhuman and that those who watch them are duped. Better, maybe, to enquire sincerely into what Clover calls the attraction of the Terrible Place, home of the "terrible family," where murder, incest, and cannibalism prevail.

In Guatemala there *are* victims and victimizers. Struggles against the impunity of the latter are essential. But alone they cannot fix Guatemala, or any other place. Horror audiences, fascinated with blood, willingly return to the same story told over and over—although the rules do change—and enact the tension between fixing and rendering. The truth commissions, exhumations, court cases over war crimes, the efforts of Final Girls like Helen Mack, Jennifer Harbury, Esperanza León, and others (boys included), and maybe even anthropological accounts like this one, are returns to the civil war *and* the past five hundred years, investigating the haunting of Indian burial grounds, the serial returns of psycho-killers, revolting natives, and global collaboration. Because identity is never stable, it must be constantly reiterated: thus the sense of fix as a drug filling a need. But the fix is only tentative, a fixion—we know rendering will continue with the sequel. Following the crowds to experience the bad sublime of horror, which breaks everything that stifles, reminds us that the popular is movement, it must be rendered via the postwar in action.

In telling you how Guatemalans taught me to think through horror's special effects I am partly engaging in the old anthropological project of showing the rational kernel in apparent irrationality, dispersing the con in the text via context. Certain forms of global mass culture, like horror films, experienced publicly on Sexta and in those close-packed video rooms on Joyabaj market days and festivals, might co-memorate certain popularly lived experiences, ones that periodic unfixing (rendering) may best fix or heal. But I want to be careful not to suggest that such rendering can somehow cancel out the causes or effects of the mechanisms of horror. There is an extra there not amenable to the balancing acts of such double-entry bookkeeping. Horror films are good to think with about the painful tendency of identities to mutate and slide in Guatemala's peace process, where Mayan activists and former rebels are now state officials, the once-powerful popular movement is painfully split over charges of exclusion and corruption, struggles rage over *quién es más Maya?* (who is more Maya?), terrible poverty stalks city slums and highland villages, and mudslides reveal public secrets. Here, horror films are metaphors *and* appropriated tools.[17]

Finally, horror films may be good to think with, but they point beyond thinking—to labor, co-laboration, and embodi/meant. As McAllister says, "To heal the effects of past violence it is not enough simply to establish the nature of the past: rather, the possibility of arguing over the past must be kept alive . . . a subjective loss cannot be recognized by objective means" (2003:369–70). The extravagance of horror's special effects breaks through the containments of the rational, gesturing toward Feldman's in-human, simultaneously not us, yet "in" us. It cuts the ship loose from the anchor of a commonsensical universal humanity and leaves us grasping instead for any weapon at our disposal—a coat hanger, a television set, a bucket of water, an assumed identity. A horror film theory of memory reminds us that Final Girls and Boys are both vulnerable and embodied, acted on by forces outside their control (screaming, flinching), and they are also armed. But with weapons that require intimate intercourse with monsters.

CONFIDENCE GAMES

Art is a lie. A lie that makes us realize the truth.
Pablo Picasso (according to Orson Welles)

CHARLATANS AND MAGIC TRICKS

F for Fake is not a horror movie, unless you're an art collector with big investments in the market. Made in 1973, it's a whimsical little film by Orson Welles
about forgery, trickery, art, and reality. It's kind of a lark. Welles exposits
on the similarities among actors, magicians, and other notorious swindlers
while he tucks into mouthwatering repasts under murals by, we assume,
famous artists and ruminates in a cutting room, where he runs pieces from
someone else's documentary film about Elmyr de Hory, a man with many assumed identities. Elmyr is an art forger, and his biographer, Clifford Irving,
ended up in a lucrative hoax of his own, the Howard Hughes papers scandal
in the 1970s, and recently got a movie of his own. It's a delightful film and
hard to describe, cutting from Welles performing magic tricks on a foggy
train siding to roaming the sunny streets of Ibiza to re-creating a femme
fatale's seduction and reproduction of Picasso. Like any number of films, it
reminds us that both cons and films work via weapons of mass distraction,
among other special F/X.

Welles patches together the story of Elmyr, who claims his work hangs
in many of the great museums and private art collections. Unable to sell his
own work under his own name, he says a buyer once misrecognized one of
his sketches as a Lautrec, and Elmyr, hungry and desperate, did nothing to
dissuade him. Soon he was producing drawings and paintings in a number of
artists' styles and claiming to have smuggled them out of Hungarian collections to sell in the West. We see him, with utter confidence and in practically
a single fluid line, create a work that looks exactly like a Matisse. He laughs
and says he could get eight to ten thousand dollars for it, then throws it in
the fire. Even knowing it's a fake, it is beautiful, and we are shocked to see it
go up in flames.

But what makes it beautiful? How can it be both worth thousands of dollars and worthless? What is the power of the name that its simple appear-

ance under a squiggle on a canvas means the canvas can go at auction for millions? And if the hand of a man named Elmyr rather than Picasso writes that name, assumes that identity, is the picture less pretty, the rose less sweet? If it is by his works you shall know him, then what of the story Welles recounts of Picasso dismissing several fake Picassos? When someone says "But I watched you paint this with my own eyes," Picasso said, "I can paint false Picassos as well as anyone." On the other hand, when Kees van Dongen was shown an Elmyr in his style he swore that he himself had painted it, even that he remembered doing so (bringing us back to the mysterious labors of memory).

Mixed in with the saga of Elmyr, Welles regales us with (tall?) tales of his own start as a faker. After failing as a painter, he convinced a theater owner in Ireland that he was a star in the United States and thereby got his first acting gig. It was an assumed identity, but he did well enough to get more work. In fact, he assumed the identity so well that he is now considered one of the great artists of our time. Pretty good for a charlatan. Welles became famous in the 1930s for his fake radio transmission of *War of the Worlds*, another Wells (H. G.) work. So many people bought the story that the United States was under attack from Martians that it became the first modern panic (Orr 2005). What makes people believe? Why do they run out of their houses and hide in the hills—from Martians or to fight the Guatemalan army? Why do they shell out huge sums of money for some paint on a canvas or some promise from a politician or a broker?

There are a couple of mysteries here. One is the magical power of the name to endow a work with aura. Is it a condensation point that channels the ancient sacred power of an icon via the new, modern god—the individual great (white) man? Is there something essential and powerful about the person making the art that is transferred to the thing via the signature, thereby warranting its value? Walter Benjamin, of course, was thrilled that mechanical reproduction was cutting this link between the work and its maker, although he warned of the compensatory star cult that would emerge from its demise (1969).

There's also the mystery of something as immaterial as a belief actually creating reality (the crux of the war of the cross). Elmyr was really famished, but his work was not really a Lautrec. However, when the collector believed it was, or believed he could get someone else to believe it was, Elmyr received real money. This connects to a puzzle Welles poses via a Rudyard Kipling verse: "When first the flush of the newborn sun fell on the green and gold / Our father Adam sat under the tree and scratched with a stick in the mold / The first rude sketch that the world had seen was joy to his mighty heart / Till the devil whispered from behind the leaves / It's pretty but is it Art?"

What changes an enjoyment-inducing doodle to Art? Is there something essential in a work or a person that makes it worthy? Or does transformation occur when it is shown to someone who likes it, believes in it, buys it? Through what alchemy does it go from creating enjoy/meant for its maker or senti/meant for someone who receives it as a gift, to being judged worthy of real money? What, in turn, about the hearty suspicions of those living outside the world of cognoscenti that their child could drip or scrawl something just as good? What makes their disbelief powerless against the mysterious forces that will determine its price? Who issues the Scarecrow's diploma so that only with it does he feel smart, even as he really helped figure the way out of each scrape on the yellow brick road?

This is where the expert comes in. As I write this I recognize how clunkily I transition compared to Welles's deftness. I'm not really capturing the montage effect of his little film, full of cuts, quips, puzzles, lies, and jokes as I transform his lighthearted caper to fit, farcically, between my chapters. I do it to draw on Welles's authority to explicate a theoretical point. But he laughs at the expert: pompous, and pretentious folks claiming to be in the know, ludicrously making their living off seeing through assumptions of identity and adjudicating value. Welles says, "Hanky panky men have always been with us. What's new are the experts. They are the new oracles. . . . They speak to us with the absolute authority of the computer and we bow down before them. They're God's own gift to the faker."

In the next chapter I explore an anthropological expert's claim that something considered valuable is actually a fraud. I'm perhaps less interested in whether there's a true face or a just price than I am in the mysteries Welles lays out. Just as important insights into language were gained through work on its limits in aphasia, and neurophysiologists learned about the body image through the phantom limb afflicting wounded bodies, perhaps we may learn about larger systems of reckoning value through what appears to be value's greatest threat—the fake.

Elmyr was caught and then reformed. Only through this process do we even know of his existence, as most forgers live deep in the shadows of anonymity and clandestinity: their survival depends on it. But not only *their* survival. Irving asks Elmyr why there was no full-scale investigation of his forgeries. Elmyr pauses. "They didn't want to know," he says, and laughs. Why didn't they? What might happen to that warrant, the name we assume fixes identity and thereby worth? Would revealing Elmyrs all over the art world prove that the nonduped erred? Or, more systemically, that the fix is in: The outcome was dishonestly arranged beforehand? Does Elmyr threaten the whole caboodle? Or just show how it really works?

Value, as I've been arguing about identification more generally, may emanate less from an essential, one-to-one identification between artist and work than from its double life. It also reflects the faces of the receivers, who in turn invest it with attributes, including a price. They assume (take for granted) that it is good or bad and thereby both it and they assume an identity: owners of valuable art or discerning experts who reject crap. In discussing assumptions of identity, I've focused on the sense of possession, of being doubled over by an alien will that we sometimes assume as our own identity. As I suggested about articulation, however, this is a two-way street. We are interpellated and we invest. To invest, in turn, is a double entendre. In one sense it means to clothe, in ways that show a transformation in identity, or to surround, relating it to milieu. It also means to put money into something for the purpose of attaining a profit, relating it to interest. Who is invested in revealing a fraud? Who profits from covering it up? Is the problem *in* Elmyr and his duplicity or, as the etymology of "invest" suggests, should we look to what surrounds it, what lies in-between, inter-esse?

PLANS AND MOTLEYS

Partway through the film, in the midst of playing with these puzzles and undermining any fixed identification, Welles made me cry. I couldn't help myself. He cuts from the furious struggles over the name on a painting and the plethora of interests invested in it to contemplate an unsigned work, Chartres cathedral. In the darkening of eventide he intones

> a celebration to God's glory and to the dignity of man. All that's left most artists seem to feel these days is man. Naked, poor, forked radish. There aren't any celebrations. Ours, the scientists keep telling us, is a universe which is disposable. You know, it might be just this one anonymous glory, of all things, this rich stone forest, this epic chant, this gaiety, this grand enquiring shout of affirmation which we choose when all our cities are dust, to stand intact to mark where we've been, to testify to what we had in us to accomplish. Our works, in stone, in paint, in print, are spared, some of them, for a few decades or a millennium or two, but everything must finally fall in war or wear away into the ultimate and universal ash. The triumphs and the frauds, the treasures and the fakes, a fact of life.

We're going to die. Be of good heart cry the dead artists out of the living past. Our songs will all be silenced. But what of it? Go on singing. Maybe a man's name doesn't matter all that much.

Now, no more than many of my Guatemalan friends does Welles wax melancholic for long. But for both, on the lower frequencies, the works and people fallen in war resonate continuously. Both contemplate ends — simultaneously the reasons why we struggle, work, risk, and create, and the destruction of those works, the constant possibility that they will come to naught. But here, at least, Welles defeats fear and all gloomy seriousness with a mysterious optimism of the will, a belief in inquiry and affirmation that might also carry the rest of us through.

For David Turnbull, a sociologist of technoscience, Chartres is also an important example. In his case, of knowledge production and what lies between. He calls Chartres (as he does malaria, see chapter 7) a motley, an assemblage of heterogeneous components, interactive and contingent, "sustained and created by social labour" (2000:4). He is interested in the apparent mystery that Chartres was built entirely without a plan or even shared understandings of measurement, much less structural theory. He follows the physicist R. R. Wilson to suggest that cathedrals are comparable to laboratories in three ways. First, their construction was a series of full-scale experiments — for example, drying mortar allowed detection of stress so buttresses could be added as needed; second, "local, tacit and messy knowledge practices of groups of practitioners are transformed through collective work into coherent tradition"; and third, they absorb and concentrate "resources, skills and labour" (2000:67). He is interested in how the local knowledges of masons, craftspeople, clerics, and patrons were translated and lashed together, without any overarching plan — that great sign of modernity and of conspiracy theory. He begins by arguing that the basis of knowledge is less empirical verification than trust. He quotes Steven Shapin: "'Trust is, quite literally, the great civility. Mundane reason is the space across which trust plays. It provides a set of presuppositions about self, others, and the world which embed trust and which permit both consensus and civil dissensus to occur'" (2000:20).

Such a position shakes our notions of the experimental method, throwing us back into some old debates about rhetoric — the ability to convince someone with words (Poovey 1998, a point I'll return to in chapter 8). How *do* we know? Turnbull goes on:

> I suggest that it is having the capacity for movement that enables local knowledge to constitute part of a knowable system. This mobility re-

quires devices and strategies that enable connectivity and equivalence, that is the linking of disparate or new knowledge and the rendering of knowledge and context sufficiently similar as to make the knowledge applicable. Connectivity and equivalence are prerequisites of a knowledge system but are not characteristics of knowledge itself. They are produced by collective work and facilitated by technical devices and social strategies. (2000:20)

Via talk, templates, and tradition these knowledges acquire a taken-for-granted air, and, somehow, Chartres stands eight hundred years later.

You may wonder why Chartres pops up here between horror films and the testimony of a Guatemalan survivor. In part, it's because cathedrals were a major pop culture of their time and place, full of special effects and images of bodies in pain. It also helps me keep the two faces of the cross in view. One is its glorious beauty and its promise of transcendence, as Welles intones, and like the Virgin's Assumption. But churches are also terrible places, playing a central role in the violence of the Inquisition, historically mobilizing hatreds in the service of slavery, nationalism, misogyny, and homophobia, and, in the 1980s, they were sites of agony as the army tried to re-mark the progressive church by torturing people in its sanctuaries. Cathedrals and the cross they materialize are two-faced, simultaneously documents of civilization and of barbarism.

I will trace questions of trust and the mobility of knowledge and identifications through the next few chapters. I am also intrigued by the question of a plan. Many accusations of duplicity turn on the suspicion that a fake identity (Assumption Two) is planned—that there is devious intention, usually to advance one interest at the expense of another. This leads to the conspiracy theorists' motto, "Follow the money" or *cui bono?* Discovering who benefits from an action that might otherwise seem irrational can be quite epistemically and politically productive.[1] I want to both use and interrogate Turnbull's and Shapin's understanding of the role of trust to explore the shock and dismay expressed at its "betrayal" by those who bought Stoll's allegations of Rigoberta Menchú Tum's duplicity. He argued, in claims that made the front pages of global media, that she lied about what happened to her family and about why the guerrilla were fighting, and that the whole thing was planned by Menchú's leftist ladino advisors to win international sympathy for their cause.

Investigating this case will lash us back into questions of how to understand people who think they have erred (or had a *nacer de consciencia*), who find they have been bamboozled by deeply held assumptions about, say, market economies or promises of development and thereby assumed new identities. What experiences, in turn, might make those identities seem false? And what then? How do we reckon with the demands to *asumir responsabilidad*, which often assume there was a plan when there might not have been? Perhaps, instead, contingent translations of different interests, of unpredictable multiconductors, of duping itself, can result in an amazing and mysterious effect—a cathedral, exchange value, an assumed identity that feels absolutely real. What happens to confidence, to assumptions, and the taken-for-granted if this is "really" the case? What if the nonduped can't help but err?

Elmyr claims he was surprised when an expert bought his work, and Welles wonders, if there were no experts would there be fakes? Certainly neither Myrna Mack's family nor her murderers planned on the changes Oglesby describes as effects of her martyrdom: "ironically, Myrna's death led to more concrete assistance for the displaced communities, a goal that had frustrated her during her fieldwork." Neither Helen Mack nor Jennifer Harbury could have planned that what were at first quite lonely crusades would end up tying in so many interests that they would rock the foundations of power in their respective countries. While Menchú Tum's book is about consciousness, many of the incidents that led to hers being born were contingent—even the decision to write the book with Elisabeth Burgos-Debray was only one of many such efforts made by different people, ladino and indigenous, to connect personal narratives to the larger issues in Guatemala and then to the international community. Many of the people involved in creating the book, including Menchú Tum herself, say they were taken totally by surprise at the effect it has had. They could not foretell the way it would lash in to other ongoing struggles in Europe and the United States over multiculturalism, third world feminism, curricular reform, foreign policy, etc., and in Latin America and elsewhere over the role and future of indigenous peoples.

Now a cynic or a conspiracy theorist might say that Menchú Tum's "handlers" tell tales of contingency as a smokescreen to cover up their duplicitous plans to bend Menchú Tum to their will, to deploy her assumed identity of victim for their own benefit. Stoll disputes several issues in Menchú's testimonial, which I address in greater detail in the next chapter. First, he says she was not as poor or as uneducated as she claims—her family had access to land, and she was studying at a Catholic boarding school. Second, she did not actually witness the brutal torture-murder of her brother in the town square, a scene movingly recounted in the book, because she was away at school, and he was really killed outside the town. Third, according to Stoll, the famous Spanish embassy fire in 1980 that killed her father, Vincente Menchú, and many others was not an army massacre of unarmed peasants and students in a diplomatically immune space but a revolutionary mass suicide. Finally, his larger argument is that neither Vicente's nor Rigoberta's "consciousness was born" in the connectivity, equivalences, and collective work of knowledge production that created and was created by the popular and revolutionary movements. Instead, they were duped by the guerrillas, doubled over and used—victimized, in fact, by the left, not by the Guatemalan army. Incipient attempts to overcome racism and connect poor people, ladino and indigenous, and other allies were just bamboozling because the indigenous people were really caught "between two armies" (Stoll 1993).

These claims have spawned a massive literature. My remarks address only a small corner of the debates, which have been skillfully limned elsewhere, especially in *The Rigoberta Menchú Controversy* (Arias 2001), with essays that systematically address each of these claims as well as the historical context, the genre issues surrounding *testimonio*, and the philosophical questions of specific vis-à-vis more general truths (see also Grandin and Goldman 1999, Grandin 1995). In Menchú's reactions to Stoll, she explains many of the differences between her versions of events and Stoll's as necessary to protect those who witnessed what she reports or those who sheltered her. She also suggests how agonizing the experience has been for her: "In reality, the intention is to destroy the myth of Rigoberta Menchú. But he doesn't realize that this myth called Rigoberta Menchú has blood in her veins, believes in the world, believes in humanity, believes in her people. This myth is not carved out of stone, but is a living, breathing person" (in Burt and Rosen 1999:10). But the agony is even greater because "it humiliates the victims. It's not enough to kill the dead. It's not enough that my mother, my father, my brothers, were killed, but now they are trying to use the dead for their own purposes [se quiere polemizar con los muertos]" (Aznárez 1999:x). Menchú Tum also expresses shock that this story received so much press when the REMHI and CEH reports abundantly document all of her denunciations.

The "between two armies" description of a population during civil war has been widely deployed in Latin America, aka "between two fires," "between the sword and the wall," or "the sandwich," between two slices of bread, as McAllister (2003) and Oglesby (2004) have explored. These metaphors may acknowledge that history can enter one's life as an unexpected blow/*coup* or as a sudden detour that defines the self, but it also renders peoples' engagements with such forces as primarily passive.

Guatemala's postwar milieu is troubled not only by the question of how can they watch that? but also of how to reckon with ends, or the reasons why people did things. Why did people kill? Why did they die? At the root of his complex argument Stoll suggests the answer is *engaño*. Highland indigenous people were hoodwinked by an urban ladino left, who took "expert advantage" (Stoll 1999:173) of them. Stoll argues that, in turn, leftists themselves were duped by utopian dreams, possessed by the figure of the "New Man"—an identity they hoped to assume—and fanaticized by the loss of comrades. They were all doubled over, acted on by a force coming from outside them. Using U.S. Cold War slang for Communists, this would be Pink(o) Fraud.

There are those who wonder if Stoll himself is duped (and/or a duper). However, he *is* representing an emerging articulation concerning the means, both the methods and the cruelty, of the war. His argument is both a studied intervention that seeks to influence the war's end/s, *and* one that is voiced by some highland peasants and urban experts in Guatemala. I have heard similar stories, perhaps most forcefully from Otilia Lux Cotí, a Maya-K'iche' woman and one of the three CEH commissioners, who later served as culture minister in the FRG government.[2] At the Maya studies conference in Guatemala City in 1999, not long after Stoll's book was published, she said, "We were between two armies. This war was not ours. Ninety-nine percent of the violence was brought on us by ladinos, those who benefit from national racism. Maya people were killed by both the left and the right, but both were ladino." Then she warned, "Es la hora de cobrar facturas" (it is time to settle accounts).

Since at least the nominal transfer of state power to civilians in 1986, stories told about the civil war have been in flux. In my interviews, in the genocide findings of the CEH report, in public statements, and in media coverage, for some, race increasingly explains what the war was about. In broad strokes, what in the 1980s was a class war with an ethnic component—left versus right, society versus the state, poor versus rich, with most indigenous people being poor—is, for some people in the 2000s, conceptualized as a race war. Rather than suffering as peasants, subversives, or rebels with a cause, Maya were repressed for being indigenous. This is, of course, partly true. However, it seems more in the action film genre than a horror film version of the past, with relatively one-faced villains and victims. I will address these readings through the next four chapters and consider what "cobrando facturas" might entail. As always, is one face (race *or* class) enough? Returning to the ledger book on the doubled-over back of the dancer in the *Baile de la Culebra*, what would paying off these debts entail?

And what other sorts of self-making might be going on? Stoll casts doubt on the class-conscious indigenous self expressed in Menchú Tum's testimony, suggesting it's an assumed identity in the sense of a false one. But does he in turn assume an identity in the third sense, as he really becomes the empiricist expert, the nonduped? Or is the expert, as Welles might ask, always haunted by that second sense of assumed identity? If there is no double-cross in the single truth of the expert, then why do Stoll's charges against Menchú Tum so perfectly duplicate centuries-old stereotypes of indigenous people as duplicitous, two-faced? And why does he seem to be shouldering a familiar burden in which all the ladinos are racist, the state and all the left are ladino, but he will speak for the authentic Maya?[3]

While there was little interest in investigating the full extent of Elmyr's forgeries, what about asking who benefits from denouncing Menchú Tum as a fraud? Although Elmyr made money that might have gone to a real artist, or more likely to a dealer/expert (and isn't Elmyr real? flesh, blood, producer of beautiful things?), his duplicity reinforces the larger structures of art evaluation. Menchú Tum has certainly benefited from her global celebrity and lives better than the majority of Guatemalans — many jokes circulate to this effect. But her story undermined trust in the structures undergirding wartime Guatemala. Stoll's allegations, with their attendant assumptions that everything was going fine until the guerrilla showed up, help legitimize, in some hearts and minds, the counterinsurgency. Not only were they extremely hurtful to Menchú personally, but they had almost immediate disarticulatory effects on the many networks in which she is a node and which are struggling to intervene in the postwar-in-action. International donations to her foundation fell off precipitously, which severely curtailed its initiatives in anti-impunity struggles, voter registration, health care, indigenous rights, and education. These effects have led many to suspect that such deleterious ends were planned by Stoll. There are even rumors that he is part of a CIA conspiracy. To rephrase Kipling, what interests might some devil have in whispering, "It's powerful storytelling but is it True?" Now, while I don't think Lee Harvey Oswald worked alone, I also don't buy the notion of Stoll as a double agent. Technically I have no idea if he has ties to intelligence agencies, but over the next few chapters I will explore the more complex processes of interpellation, investment, and the stakes of believing sincerely in both conspiratorial plans and in their unveiling — processes in which many of us collaborate.

By introducing the next chapter on accusations of duplicity lodged against Nobel laureate Menchú Tum with this intertextual rumination on an art forger I may be giving you the false impression that Menchú lied. She did not. It's All True.[4] Every family member she says was killed *was* killed and by the people she says were responsible — the Guatemalan army. Her descriptions of child death by malnutrition, parasite infection, and pesticide

Rigoberta Menchú Tum dancing, with other Mayan activists.
Photograph by José Fernando Lara.

poisoning in the hardscrabble highlands or on the South Coast export plantations are all accurate, and their incidence remains widespread. Her claims of suffering racism and exclusion can be verified by even the most inexpert witness via quite short-term investigations. But more epistemologically, while "no one expects the Spanish Inquisition" as Monty Python jokes, Stoll works the same crux of insecurity and suspicion that surrounds all modern conversions (Silverblatt 2004). How do you know if an assumption of identity, a consciousness raising, is ever assumed in the third sense (true) rather than the second? I hope that my exploring of these uncertainties will clue us in, like the phantom limb, to otherwise less visible circuits.

Menchú Tum is simultaneously a flesh and blood human woman, an icon, and a Final Girl. She has to fight with monsters and use their tools, and she is transformed in the process even as she transforms her milieu. She has suffered more than most of us could ever bear, but somehow she goes on singing, sending out "a grand enquiring shout of affirmation." As she once said about Myrna Mack (see the book's epigraphs), she herself bets on the future. And through as much horror as she has endured, she also dances, laughs, and is an expert in telling Rigoberta Menchú jokes.

Chapter Four

INDIAN GIVER OR NOBEL SAVAGE?: RIGOBERTA MENCHÚ TUM'S STOLL/EN PAST

That a valuable symbol can also be misleading is the paradox that obliged me to write this book. The problem does not exist simply on the level of what did and did not happen in one corner of Guatemala. It also extends into the international apparatus for reporting human rights violations, reacting to them, and interpreting their implications for the future—the world of human rights activism, journalism, and scholarship. In a world swayed by the mass media, in which nations or people live or die by their ability to catch international attention, how do the gatekeepers of communication deal with the mixture of truth and falsehood in any movement's portrayal of itself, including those we feel morally obliged to support? Must we resign ourselves to be apologists for one side or the other? David Stoll

We aren't only ignorant as Mr. Stoll says, but Communism and Liberation Theology manipulated our brains, and created us and made us into a myth, and me especially, they made me into a cruel, barbaric myth, a mysterious fantasm. . . . Some people think I have a hidden agenda, a hidden truth, and they must reveal that truth. Today I can say all this because no one will be assassinated tomorrow. Rigoberta Menchú Tum

LIES

On December 15, 1998, the *New York Times* ran a front-page story entitled "Nobel Winner Finds Her Story Challenged" (Rohter A1). The paper of record had sent a reporter to the Guatemalan highlands to investigate the claims of the anthropologist David Stoll that Rigoberta Menchú Tum had stretched the truth in her autobiographical *I, Rigoberta Menchú.*

In the book, Menchú Tum recounts her childhood in the highland village of Chimel, where her family eked out a living as farmers and migrated to work on the plantations of the South Coast (where malnutrition and pesticides, she wrote, killed her younger brother). She also describes their indigenous culture, her parents' struggles for land, and the family's involvement in Catholic Action. She tells how her brother was killed in the Chajul town square, how her father died in the Spanish embassy massacre in January 1980, and how her mother was torture-murdered, all at the hands of the Guatemalan army. The book ends with her younger sister joining the guerrilla and Menchú going into exile in Mexico (1983). Menchú Tum was not awarded the Nobel Prize because she saw her brother killed by the Guatemalan army or because her father sued someone over land or because she is completely self-taught, claims that Stoll questions. She did not win because she was very poor or because her mother, father, and brother were killed by the Guatemalan army—facts not disputed by Stoll. She is acknowledged because she experienced these things, and they did not break her. Instead, they made her a political activist struggling on college campuses, in refugee camps, in the United Nations, and in the battered justice system of Guatemala for human and indigenous peoples' rights. She also won because of her symbolic power, as an articulate indigenous woman in the quincentennial year.

Nonetheless, the *Times* coverage and the subsequent publication of Stoll's book *Rigoberta Menchú and the Story of All Poor Guatemalans* unleashed a scandal in the United States, one marked by heavy coverage in both academic and popular media. The search for "The Truth About Rigoberta Menchú" (Canby 1999) included front-page stories in *Newsweek*, the *Chronicle of Higher Education*, and the *New York Review of Books* and coverage in the *Wall Street Journal*, most local and regional papers, radio programs, the progressive press, college newspapers, plenary panels at national meetings, and extensive discussion on the Internet (in Intertext 3 I lay out the charges). There were passionate defenses of both sides as well as scholarly disquisitions on everything from the genre of testimonial to the dangers of celebrity. Nine months after the first revelations, the Sunday pundit television show McLaughlin Group was still flogging the issue, introducing its segment with the superimposition of the word "LIES!" over images of Menchú Tum and headlines about the case (August 22, 1999). While Stoll's claims excited interest in Guatemala, especially among conservative op-ed writers—Greg Grandin suggests that most oligarch families probably own a copy of the book—the February 1999 CEH report and the release of the death squad dossier pushed it from the headlines. However, the recent opening of an international legal case brought by Menchú Tum for the Spanish embassy massacre has led to renewed interest in some quarters.

In the United States, out of the blue, most Guatemalanists were deluged with requests for interviews and talks. Reactions from friends, colleagues, and cocktail party acquaintances were saturated with emotion and kinesthesia. People said they felt "kicked in the stomach," "betrayed," "How could she lie to us? Why doesn't she apologize?" "Can I still teach the book?" "I'm taking down my poster!" "What was she thinking? Doesn't she know she only hurts her cause by falsifying data?" "She should have known this would happen. She deserves to have the Nobel taken away." Alums wrote to their schools outraged that they'd been taught something that was not true and determined that the next generation would not be so duped. Some students felt shocked and sad, while others inundated their campus papers with boilerplate letters denouncing the deception perpetrated by teaching the testimonial. One such letter starts, "A fraud lurks in Academia: There is a sickness fast spreading through the halls of academia . . . it is from the scholarly elite that are teaching [us]" (Whetstone 1999).[1] In March 1999, David Horowitz targeted scholars who defended Menchú Tum by buying advertisements in their campus newspapers that called Menchú a "Marxist Terrorist Liar" (Chronicle 1999:A10). By the time of this writing, this is what many students "know" about Rigoberta Menchú—that she lied. Fraud, duping, a con, an assumed identity now exposed—these are images that haunt the debates close to a decade later.[2]

I don't so much want to dismiss or exonerate either side (because two is too many) as to refract these discourses of deception through the assumptions of identity. As I explore below, Stoll suggests that Menchú Tum became an icon because of various gift exchanges that circulate around her— specifically, that she offers redemption to her followers. In fact, Menchú Tum figures as a gift giver in a Guatemalan Christmas card from 1993, which shows a Mayan Adoration of the Magi, with an indigenous Mother and Child accepting gifts, including the Nobel Prize from the laureate. However, Stoll's revelations situate Menchú Tum as an Indian giver, an old racist stereotype of someone who proffers a gift, then wants it back. The colloquialism foregrounds an ethnic charge to the always-ambivalent exchange of the gift, but in addition to being Maya-K'iche' Menchú Tum is a woman and a Guatemalan, and gender and national boundaries also come into play through other exchanges like jokes, the politics of naming, and the circulation of stereotypes—sites through which global identifications detour and are assumed. Menchú Tum is a nodal point for many emotional, political, and intellectual investments. She uses her position like a modern-day Caliban: you taught me celebrity, and my profit on't is to raise global consciousness about the war in Guatemala and indigenous rights. In turn, she may be used for (possessed by) a variety of projects that flow through gendered and ethnically hierarchical relations of power. I want to explore this sense of being used or duped as part of the enormous senti/meant generated through the debates over Menchú's "Stoll/en" past.

At a talk I gave at an East Coast campus a young woman first asked if the problems in the story weren't the fault of Elisabeth Burgos-Debray, Menchú Tum's amanuensis. She then very powerfully described how betrayed she felt by Rigoberta (first name only) and then burst into tears.[3] In academic circles I have encountered shock that there is so much investment in Menchú Tum's story and a sense that only the extremely naïve — Doris Sommer calls them Rigoberta's "sentimental readers" (1996:132) — would take it so seriously as to feel duped when the *testimonio* turns out to be political as well as personal. But it is precisely Menchú Tum's uncanny power that intrigues me. What is her hold on those in solidarity with her struggles, on those whose own heritage feels reflected in her story, on those who gleefully denounce her as a LIAR, and on Stoll, who is thereby in the know and uses her to argue about peasants, revolution, and the gift Menchú Tum gives to gringos? I take seriously both Stoll's text and the context, that is, news coverage and popular reactions in both the United States and Guatemala — especially the discourse of duplicity — because they are components in the postwar-in-action.

In doing so, I draw on Donna Haraway's Latour-inspired explorations of the trans/actions of technoscience, the "dense nodes of human and non-human actors that are brought into alliance by the material, social, and semiotic technologies through which what will count . . . as matters of fact get constituted for — and by — many millions of people" (1997:50). Haraway shows how transuranic elements and transgenic organisms "simultaneously fit into well-established taxonomic and evolutionary discourses and also blast widely understood senses of natural limit" (56) (a bit like Final Girls). I argue that the trans/actions of Menchú Tum's "Indian Gift" suggest a similar simultaneity, like the strangely comfortable fit of the stereotype or the blast of assumptions that makes jokes funny.

I explore how the debate in the United States over this indigenous woman's testimonial is what Diana Fuss calls a "detour through the other that defines the self" (1995:3). I assumed my identity as a gringa through a detour through Guatemala and am surprised and gratified by the attention to, and fascinated by the depth and intensity of investments in, Menchú, given that Guatemala's thirty-five years of U.S.-backed coups, revolution, and genocidal counterinsurgency violence have often felt like a hidden war for those in the United States. Menchú Tum's testimonial, read mainly by solidarity activists before it was incorporated into the emerging multicultural university canon, and her constant touring of the globe to tell her story of personal loss and struggle, revealed that war. In Guatemala she condenses a number of ambivalences about national, ethnic, and gender identity and about Guatemala's role in the global system. As a Mayan woman from a poor family, an exile, and someone involved in Catholic Action, CUC, and other movements for radical social change (i.e., she's a revolting peasant),[4] Menchú Tum condenses many points of identification and ambivalence for non-Guatemalans as well. These coalesce into her iconic status, which was both acknowledged and added to by the Nobel Prize. It is her position as icon that attracted Stoll to write his exposé (Warren 1999).

My assumptions about Menchú Tum's story were first shaken when I ran into David Stoll in the highland Guatemalan town of Nebaj, Quiché, in the early 1990s. He had been hearing stories about the Menchú family from people in the region that contradicted the testimonial.[5] My first reaction was holy dread. With the war still on and continuing counterinsurgency violence it seemed blasphemous to contradict her story and thus easy to dismiss his claims. Reading Haraway on the importance of blasphemy suggests dismissal is not the most productive reaction ("Blasphemy has always seemed to require taking things very seriously" [1991:149]). I am as suspicious as anyone of the ways in which race, gender, and transnational privilege overdetermine Menchú's Stoll/en past. Stoll, a Caucasian, Stanford-educated male, takes on the white man's empiricist burden to prove a brown woman with a sixth-grade education is an Indian giver, thus reinscribing the patriarchal etymology of "testimony"—you need to have testicles to be taken seriously. Oddly enough, a number of jokes told about Menchú Tum in Guatemala suggest that she *has* testicles, carries missiles under her skirts, or in other ways is hiding something. For example, "Why won't Rigoberta wear patent leather shoes? Because they reflect her balls." These jokes curiously mirror Stoll's argument that she is duplicitous.

Slavoj Žižek asks, "How does an empirical, positively given object become an object of desire; how does it begin to contain some X, some unknown quality, something which is 'in it more than it' and makes it worthy of our desire" (1989:119)? In Guatemala and the United States a buzz surrounds Menchú Tum wherever she goes, even post-Stoll. Rooms change when she walks in; important people and state officials maneuver to get near her. Having on occasion served as her translator, I have seen hundreds of people

stand in line for a chance to see her in the interstices of her public appearances, hoping for a bit of personal contact (which may have cost a bundle
at fundraising dinners), an autograph, a smile like the one on the poster
they bring to be signed but is real. This mysterious quality, this x that some
people desire, reminds me less of patent leather shoes than of ruby slippers,
and there are times Menchú Tum seems as baffled as Dorothy Gale in *The
Wizard of Oz* by what people want from her. Like Dorothy, Menchú Tum
has deployed this gift in struggles to create a home that is both familiar
and strange—which for Menchú Tum would be a Guatemala safe for Maya,
women, refugees, and political activists. Is that x Menchú Tum contains
related to the ways in which she is both strange and familiar?[6] Is it because
she's hiding something, like balls under her skirt, or the truth? Is it specific
to her gender (woman as masquerade) or the ethnostalgia that surrounds
the Maya (Nelson 1999)?

   While much can be and has been written about authenticity, the subaltern
speaking, and the truth and falsity of Stoll's and Menchú Tum's different
stories, I want to step back a bit from these double entendres of he said, she
said. Instead, I want to explore this x, the intense investments in Menchú
Tum and her story—in Guatemala but primarily in the United States. I am
intrigued by the attendant sense of personal betrayal—the sense of having
been duped. Stoll, in turn, offers the reassuring promise of being nonduped.
So, how did this icon become an "eye-con" (Schwartz 1996:17)? How did this
noble sufferer become a Nobel savage? Why is Menchú Tum now positioned
as an Indian giver, someone who gave us something precious but has now
taken it away? What is the gift, and what might this tell us about reckoning
the ends of war and the assumptions of identity?

ASSUMPTIONS ONE, TWO, THREE

Textually, David Stoll's book about Rigoberta Menchú Tum focuses on all
three kinds of assumptions although (con)textually the second—Menchú
Tum's false, assumed identity—has received the most attention. First, he
argues that North American researchers, solidarity and human rights activists, and Guatemalan ladinos have for too long assumed certain things about
peasants, indigenous people, poverty, and revolution. These assumptions,
supported by Menchú Tum's testimonial—which tells the story of entire
immiserated indigenous villages rising up to support guerrilla struggle—
have, he asserts, misrepresented the desires and actions of men like Vicente
Menchú. When urban ladinos aflame with Che Guevara–inspired romantic

fantasies create the revolutionary Guerrilla Army of the Poor (EGP) and assume they'll easily find recruits in rural indigenous villages, these assumptions carry deadly consequences. Stoll states, "If anyone ignited political violence in Ixil country, it was the EGP. Only then had the security forces militarized the area and turned it into a killing ground" (Stoll 1999a:9).[7]

Stoll tells this story about the URNG: in the 1970s "guerrillas infiltrated popular organizations, robbed banks, and machine-gunned police stations. They also kidnapped oligarchs and ambassadors to exchange them for political prisoners and ransom. This last innovation was disastrous because the ultra right and the army responded in kind and far more effectively, with death squads. The urban cells went down with guns blazing. . . . Interpreting their mandate liberally, the security forces murdered anyone who might be involved" (49). (Hernández Pico [2005] says the first kidnapping for ransom was military.) Here Stoll seems to echo the old minstrel skit (see Intertext 4) in which not-so-bright ne'er-do-wells are caught in the henhouse by the rifle-bearing owner of the chickens, who asks, "Who's there?" When they reply, "Ain't nobody here but us chickens" the audience is asked to laugh at such a ludicrous tactic (chickens can't talk!) and to assume that the farmer has every right to start shooting. The wise farmer, well versed in the stereotypes about blacks and poultry (Williams-Forson 2006), will certainly not be fooled by the attempt of humans to pass as chickens. No more will the Guatemalan military government be persuaded by immature attempts to take over its possessions, that is, the state apparatus, by adventurous ne'er-do-wells trying to pass themselves off as a legitimate resistance movement. "Ain't nobody here but us exploited peasants." Like the farmer who immediately grabs his gun, state forces will easily outgun the opposition. Getting rid of the thieves justifies the risks of losing a few chickens—whose deaths, in this scenario, are the fault of the infiltrators. Stoll goes on:

> Some readers may be disturbed by my approach because it is not the usual one to political violence in Guatemala. . . . Not wanting to blame victims and dilute responsibility, human rights activists argue that the most important issue is who killed whom, not what led up to that outcome. Exonerating the guerrillas may be necessary for solidarity work. Ignoring them may focus human rights campaigns on government abuses. But neither solidarity nor human rights approaches should be confused with sociohistorical analysis. The reason is that the first two require dichotomizing participants into victims and victimizers. On one side is the army and its local allies, on the other hapless victims. Conveniently for the guerrillas, they remain at the margin, along with issues such as how they

tried to recruit peasants, how men like Vicente Menchú responded to them, and how survivors assess the blame for what happened. Failing to ask such questions protects the left's assumptions from scrutiny. (61)

He argues that the map fashioned by Menchú Tum's story precedes the territory for North American researchers and activists and for Guatemalan and other leftists, blinding them to the fact that many highland Maya did not support the guerrilla and may in fact have actively collaborated with the counterinsurgency (which is true). In turn, he suggests, North American researchers and leftist ladinos dismiss any indigenous person who says that she or he supports the army because the person is assumed to be either duped (*engañado*) by reeducation or too afraid to speak the truth.

Stoll's argument occasioned moral outrage. Stoll in turn seems to feel morally righteous because he is resurrecting subjugated knowledges and the disqualified accounts that, because they jar assumptions about revolting peasants, have not been represented. The sense that *he* is speaking for the voiceless motivates his argument about the second sense of assumption— that Menchú Tum is assuming an identity, speaking under false pretenses, inaccurately representing "all poor Guatemalans" and thereby duping her readers. The false identity he claims she assumes is a desperately poor, illiterate, monolingual Indian girl whose family was forced to migrate to lowland plantations for seasonal labor (as in the *Baile de la Culebra*) and was engaged in brutal struggles over land against local ladinos, their violent thugs, and racist state agencies. Stoll paints a picture of a duplicate Rigoberta, an uncanny double, whose family and town were doing very well, thank you, with the support of the Peace Corps, U.S. Christian missionaries and their health center, and the national land registry (INTA), which, just a few days prior to Vicente's death, had deeded over two thousand hectares to him and a group of other families. Menchú Tum was not present when the violence picked up in her hometown of Chimel—and thus unable to witness the public murder of her brother she so eloquently describes in her testimonio—because she was a promising student at a Catholic boarding school in a town many hours away. In Stoll's narrative, any problems the family had were based in her father's almost fanatical litigiousness against his own in-laws, with whom he struggled for decades over a hundred hectares of land, (and, *perhaps*, by his reception of EGP guerrillas). In turn, her father was not politicized through a class struggle overlaid with ethnic issues—poor Indians versus rich ladinos—to help found the CUC as an organic, grassroots representation of peasant interests. Instead, Stoll claims, this was an identity assumed for him by his daughter several years after his death.

Aporias flourish in his text as Stoll tries to recount what really occurred before Vicente's death in the embassy fire. He generally argues that Menchú and other peasants went to the capital, spent some time at the National University with the "immature and self-destructive" (Stoll 1999: 84) radical left, whose members trotted them around town to demonstrations, and then carried Molotov cocktails into the Spanish embassy. Stoll suggests that given that torture was inevitable if they were captured and that they were "fanaticized by the sacrifice of so many of their comrades" (120), the fire could have been a revolutionary suicide. Vicente's reception of the EGP is another unresolved opening in his text. Stoll writes that he does not know what happened when (or even if) the EGP went through Chimel. But he later papers over this uncertainty to say, "I can only speculate as to what Vicente Menchú hoped to accomplish by cooperating with the guerrillas" (277). He argues that the guerrillas took "expert advantage" (173) of unsuspecting peasants and that the peasants participated in their own demise because "welcoming the guerrillas was fatal" (122).[8] Stoll claims that Vicente's assumed identity of a "martyr whose death presaged victory" (1999a:72) obscures the fact that he may have been as much a victim of the ladino left as of the ladino right—cannon fodder in someone else's war.[9]

Stoll thus makes two related but seemingly contradictory arguments. The first is that resistance is futile because you're always outgunned, and they'll kill you no matter what. The second is that resistance is unnecessary because the system works via market forces, and there's no sense in trying to force the invisible hand. With class consciousness thus debunked the Menchú family can claim their true identity as "raced," but with caution, since ladinos can never understand them quite the way an anthropological expert can.

Stoll addresses the third sense of assumption in his investigation of Rigoberta's allure, her almost hypnotic power, and suggests they are the gifts gringos receive from her. First, he argues, she appeals to Western expectations about native people: "However weary Rigoberta has become of stereotypes, her 1982 story was quite a contribution to them, by appealing to a notion of authenticity revolving around monolingualism, illiteracy, and rejection of Western technology" (1999a:232). Second, she gives us the simplified "identification with victims, dissidents, and opposition movements" that allows for solidarity and human rights activism without "much ambiguity, such as a contest between equally sordid factions." Third, we get the "imagery of sacrifice and social redemption" so popular on the Christian left (Stoll 1999a:235, 237). However, her most precious gift to us, as gringos, he suggests, is ourselves. This valuable thing is carefully hidden: "Certainly Rigoberta was a representative of her people, but hiding behind that was a more partisan role, as a representative of the revolutionary movement, and hiding behind that was an even more unsettling possibility: that she represented the audiences whose assumptions about *indígenas* she mirrored so effectively" (1999a:246). Stoll argues that Menchú Tum "provides rebels in far-off places, into whom careerists can project their fantasies of rebellion" (1999a:247). Thus, Menchú Tum allows us to assume an identification: the x, the more that is in her is actually us.[10]

An Indian giver offers something but also threatens. In letters to the *Chronicle of Higher Education* Brian D. Haley and John Watanabe capture this vacillation. Haley is concerned with "the easy seduction of scholars by certain themes and symbols, how and why scholars privilege some indigenous voices over others" (1999:B11). Watanabe writes, "I ceased teaching the book a number of years ago, precisely because I found it rang true for students for all the wrong reasons, by playing on their romanticized stereotypes of egalitarian — and oppressed — Indians who spontaneously rise up against their oppressors, just as we would like to imagine we would do in their place . . . her story had the power to erase an entire term's discussion of the more-complex ways in which such communities could be both cooperative and divisive, nasty and nice to themselves and others" (1999:B10). Here the gifts are seduction and an image we hope mirrors ourselves. The threat is the fear of somehow being made to act against our will, to be doubled over, to forget what we already know. The fear that Menchú Tum is duped, carrying around a left-wing cassette, or that highland villagers have been *engañados*, or fooled, by the ladino left or army reeducation mirrors our own fear that we are the fooled ones. If the story rings true for the wrong reasons, then we have been duped, made to act against our better judgment by a force outside us.[11]

Stoll's exposé makes good on the threat of the Indian giver. This gift, our ideal ego, "our sense of moral worth or our identity as intellectual rebels" (Stoll 1999a:247) is the fraud. We are really silly dupes, hopeless romantics, *metidos en babosadas* (enmeshed in foolishness), which is certainly how I felt. Empiricism has struck back, and we can no longer pin our hopes on Vicente Menchú as the Che Guevaran New Man because he is really the post-NAFTA neoliberal man.

As a bit of recompense, Stoll offers the alternative of being nonduped: face the facts, penetrate the veil of Menchú Tum as a symbol, and blast off the hallucinatory qualities of ethnic, revolutionary, or gender romance. Being nonduped may not be as pleasurable, but, Stoll suggests, it offers its own form of salvation — for Menchú Tum and for gringos. For example, Stoll quotes a UN consultant saying, "They got her very young, and now she's growing up. But now she is a huge public symbol who can no longer be herself because she can no longer get out from behind the 'we' that she was forced to assume and which still keeps her trapped. I suspect that Rigoberta reacts not as a person but as a symbol for a movement, that she's afraid of revealing herself as a person" (Stoll 1999a:299). By forcing her hand with his book, Stoll may hope to allow her this revelation. Indeed, by the end of his narrative she "leaves the guerrilla movement" and is redeemed, speaking now for Maya and victims, rather than for the "Latin American left and its foreign supporters" (Stoll 1999a:282). For the nonduped it's about race, not class. Similarly, in the United States Stoll hopes the "casualties of this debate are literal interpretations and threadbare assumptions that no one in academia admits to holding anyway" (1999b:7).

While not averse to being saved, I am intrigued by the transactions at play here among the entendres of assumption and fascinated by the anxieties about being *engañado*, acted on by an external force, whether it be Menchú Tum "got" too young or gringos so easily seduced. Does being nonduped save us from the power of that X inside Menchú Tum? Does it excuse us from the circuits of exchange with this Indian giver?

Now, I am precisely the subject hailed by Stoll's critique, having assumed the identity of a gringa in solidarity, a border crosser. As such, as Stoll is suggesting, gringo is a category produced through interactions, in a detour through the other. Assuming such an identification through reading Menchú Tum's book or listening to her speak relies on a complex play of double entendres. We both take certain things for granted and experience a momentary false identification as we project ourselves into her text, kinesthetically suture into her experience, cry with her as she loses beloved family members, fantasize about rebellion, receive her gifts. These involvements are ek-static in the sense that gringos go outside themselves and can be ecstatic in the sense of pleasurable.[12]

Now that I've ventriloquized some of the assumptions of the debate, I want to push on the third sense of the assumption of identity—the part of Stoll's argument I think is most important and least addressed. We need to account not just for how gringo assumptions of identity involve a going outside the self, whether it's projecting *our* fantasies of Indians and rebels or unwittingly playing the dupes to *Menchú Tum's* projection of her uncanny seductive power. We need to understand how these transactions are ecstatic and pleasurable, and we need to explore how that pleasure vacillates with threat, the familiar with the strange, and duping with the assumption of identity. I am suggesting that the vacillation itself, the movement, the gift exchange, like the mobile identifications of horror films, is essential. I begin by examining the way in which the debates about Menchú Tum duplicate the form and content of jokes about women and stereotypes about "Indians." In turn, I suggest that Stoll's alternative, being nonduped, doubles the promise of the name, the icon, the signature on the work of art. This is the promise of empiricism and expertise, that the modern fact will hold the target still, stop the procession of simulacra, fully account for the world. However, naming, at least for women, for the Maya, and for rebels, is a transaction rather than a stasis. Likewise, the alternative to being duped may not be salvation.

JOKES AND STEREOTYPES

Jokes, like the embodi/meant of horror, work through an excess of enjoy/ meant that makes us double up with laughter. We are acted on by something coming from outside ourselves, like the something Xtra at stake in Menchú's Stoll/en past.[13] Jokes are a vital way that Guatemalans deal with ambivalence — toward racism and the war and toward Menchú Tum and her Nobel prize. Jokes about Menchú Tum circulating in Guatemala are partly about the ways she blasts assumptions about indigenous women, and they frequently play with the notion that she is assuming an identity. Transactions of gender, ethnicity, and nation are central. A rather complicated joke plays on the way the Mayan woman's traditional skirt (*corte*) is worn wrapped around (*envuelta*) the body. "Why did Rigoberta really win the Nobel Prize? Because she's an *indita desenvuelta* [an unwrapped little Indian]." The joke suggests that she has unwrapped her skirt, taken it off, and is thus sexually available to the men on the Nobel Committee, winning the prize for lascivious reasons, not because she speaks for "all poor Guatemalans." A second assumption that motivates this joke is the importance of the *corte* and *traje* that Mayan women weave and wear as a marker of ethnic identity (Hendrickson 1995, Otzoy 1996). Women who do not wear it are assumed to be ladina, and so being *desenvuelta* suggests that Menchú Tum is not really an Indian and therefore cannot speak for the Maya, but a ladina in disguise. In a triple entendre *desenvuelta* also means to be articulate, to speak well. Thus it seems to mark anxiety about one of the important borders that Menchú Tum crosses: that which marks off women in traje as a silent ground on which national, ethnic, transnational, academic, and other identifications can be formed (I examine this joke at greater length elsewhere [Nelson 1999]).

Guatemalans laugh at this joke, as do gringos once we get it, in part because the slip between the assumed meaning and its entendres releases a *frisson* — a giggle or a groan. Like horror films, it acts on our bodies. The slip is like Freud's famous analysis of the joke that goes, "A man says, 'I sat beside

Salomon Rothschild and he treated me quite as his equal, quite famillio-nairely'" (Freud 1963:16). The joke plays on the similarities between familiar and millionaire, but the humor lies in the fact that the terms are precisely not the same—they emphasize the enormous class differences between the two. These articulations between similar and different were an essential part of the assumptions of identity of Jennifer Harbury and Myrna and Helen Mack. The condensation in jokes mirrors my attempts to get at the conden-sations in assumption—that identification traverses an assumed identity or a false front.

The content of jokes (like hiding something under a skirt) mirrors that mysterious moment of getting the joke, or seeing the second, simultaneous meaning hidden by the first. We feel acted on against our will, doubled over like the dancers, as when the body responds with laughter, shudders, or groans to a stupid or offensive joke, when I feel that I can't help myself. Jokes, like "bad, sublime" films and popular art like the *Tzul bailes* are coded low, in part because it is shameful and ecstatic to be moved by something coming from outside me. Freud said, "Strictly speaking, we do not know what we are laughing at" (1963:102). Is it our projection? Is it the x in Menchú Tum that is us? Or is that frisson actually in the transaction, the telling of the joke?

As the patent leather shoe joke suggests, gender is central to the trans-actions of the joke's content and its form. Telling a joke, Freud argues, espe-cially smut, produces relationships between men through the exclusion of a woman. Lévi-Strauss also explores this special affect but reminds us that even at that quintessential site of men forming a relation with each other through the exchange of women, her double nature brings something X-tra to the trans/action: "Even in a man's world she is still a person, and in so far as she is defined as a sign she must be recognized as a generator of signs. . . . This explains why the relations between the sexes have preserved that affective richness, ardour, and mystery" (1969:496). Is this why the story of *les bijoux indiscrets* (the indiscreet jewels) that tells of a magical ring that can force "the sex which is not one" (women's genitalia) to speak a singular truth, is reanimated through the years to position woman as the sign of both yearning for a fix and its constant, exciting, frustration (Foucault 1980a)? But Menchú Tum is not only a woman exchanged between men. She is also an indigenous person exchanged among the nonindigenous, the ladinos and gringos, which brings us back to the stereotype.

Shivers of Delight in—or Fear of—Novelty

Stereotypes are simultaneously familiar, for example, the romantic or threatening Indian, and carry a built-in difference, one supposed to stabilize identifications. Like gifts, jokes, and horror films, however, stereotypes are simultaneously full of enjoyment and full of threat, shot through with the paradoxical workings of colonial discourse as described by Homi Bhabha. The "dependency on the concept of 'fixity' in the ideological construction of otherness" is paradoxically, ambivalently linked to "shivers of delight in—or fear of—novelty" (1994:66, 73, citing Said 1978:59). In the debates over Menchú's Stoll/en past this sudden swing from icon to Nobel savage suggests the continuing power of those opposite yet twinned figures of the premodern—the wild man and the noble savage.[14] There is some X in these stereotypes which leads Bhabha to suggest that we cannot displace them with the real. This does not engage their effectivity (1994:67). Empiricism, like the attempts to fix memory through monuments that do not offer the strange attractions and horrible special effects of shifting identifications, is vitally important, but it may not be enough. Poovey makes a similar argument about double-entry bookkeeping whose balance, she argues, is the result of a flimflam, of false numbers that can't really represent the surplus being produced through exchange (see chapter 8).

Despite this, as R. Ruth Linder stated in a letter to the *Chronicle of Higher Education*, the "unmasking of the story behind Rigoberta Menchú's story [is] being constructed by the media as a moral and epistemological coup" (1999:B12). Menchú Tum operates under an assumed identity as her Stoll/en past overtakes her with an uncanny double. "Coup" seems an appropriate term given the violence that overdetermines Menchú Tum's testimonial and the experiences of assuming ethnic, gender, and national identifications in Guatemala. A coup is a blow. Like the real, a fix, or naming, it is meant to cut through chaos, to hold things still. But the coup of unmasking seems hardpressed to contain its own swerves, i.e., the ways, in Guatemala and in the United States, in which identity itself is often understood as dis/simulation. Famillionairely, these are the "*same old* stories . . . told (compulsively) again and afresh and are differently gratifying and terrifying each time" (Bhabha 1994:77).

Violence and the Name

Rigoberta Menchú se casó con un francés de appellido Fas. Ahora se llama Menchú Fas. (Rigoberta Menchú married a Frenchman with the last name of Fas, so now she is Menchufas) (*me enchufas*, meaning "you rape me" or "you assault me").

Naming—to identify enemies and form blacklists—is central to coups d'état and to counterinsurgency blows against individuals and organizations. Part of a culture of terror is forcing victims to act against their will by naming names, transacting their own relief from pain for someone else's life. Stoll's allegations about Menchú Tum were pushed out of the press in Guatemala by the CEH report detailing such counterinsurgency strategies and by the release of the death squad dossier that revealed how people were doubled over, made to *delatar*, or name, members of their cell.

Clandestinity, hiding behind different faces and names, became a vital counterstrategy to counterinsurgency practices of disappearing bodies and erasing names through mass, unmarked cemeteries. But the lists of names in Ricardo Falla's essential book *Masacres de la Selva* (Massacres in the Jungle) (1992), in the REMHI report, and on the columns of the National Cathedral in downtown Guatemala City are also important as a praxis of resistance. As Victor Montejo says, "The remembering of victims and protagonists by name becomes a powerful reply to the hopelessness of torture victims who were routinely forced to name 'accomplices'" (in Warren 1998:126).[15]

Judith Butler says that "the name, as part of a social pact and, indeed, a social system of signs, overrides the tenuousness of imaginary identification and confers on it a social durability and legitimacy. . . . It is [the] function of the name to secure the identity of the subject over time" (1993:152–53). Yet this "pact" operates differently for women, for indigenous people under colonialism, and for revolting people. For them, naming may feel "positively hostile and cruel" (Freud's description of a woman's experience of smut). The hostile joke that situates Menchú Tum as asking to be attacked, "me enchufas," is, like many others, intrigued with her changing matronym, Tum. Butler says that such a change is

> a social pact based on the Law of the Father [*nom du père*], a patrilineal organization that implies that it is *patronymic* names that endure over time. . . . Enduring and viable identity is thus purchased through subjection to and subjectivation by the patronym. But because this patronymic line can only be secured through the ritual exchange of women, there is required for woman a certain shifting of patronymic alliance and, hence, a change in name. For women, then, propriety is achieved through having a changeable name. (1993:153)

In Latin American naming practices a woman traditionally retains her birth patronym through marriage but drops her second last name, the mother's patronym. Her child carries her patronym, at least until she marries, but her grandchild does not. Names for the Maya are similarly ambivalent.

Racist stereotypes of indigenous people as sly and duplicitous intertwine with the assumption that they are acting under assumed identities. At the most basic level of naming, this is actually true. Many highland Maya carry at least two names: most bearers of a Christian Hispanicized name, the one used for official business with the ideological state apparatuses of church, land registry, army, school, are also known as someone quite different depending on local naming practices or, more uncannily, are not known to outsiders. On top of this, as Kay Warren describes, it has become conventional for pan-Mayanists to "readopt a Mayan name—drawn from sacred texts or from day names in the Mayan calendar—to displace at least situationally their given names in Spanish" (1998:157).[16]

These naming practices also swerve through pseudonyms—whether the standard anthropological practice to protect the communities and individuals, or writing under assumed names for fear of violent reprisals. Most people active in the Guatemalan left chose to live under *noms de guerre*, like Harbury's husband, Comandante Everardo, aka Efraín Bámaca Velásquez.[17] Many took the names of comrades killed by security forces as a way to keep history alive, and they talk now of feeling almost possessed by their dead, able to do things and take risks in their name that alone they would never have had the courage to do. Many activists also played with passing. As one friend said, "Most of the ladinos from the city would choose names like Baltazar, stuff like that. They wanted to sound as *campesino*, peasant as possible. The indigenous *compañeros* tended to choose names that sounded as foreign as possible—Harvey, etc. I chose different names for different operations. It's a different self. It inspires you to try harder." Rodrigo Asturias, commander of the URNG member organization ORPA, used the nom de guerre Gaspar Ilom from his Nobel laureate father's novel *Men of Corn*. He told Peter Canby, as he handed him his business card, "I've legalized Gaspar Ilom. Now I have two names" (Canby 1999:30).

Unstable Selves

Worries about the instability of naming and the stereotype of indigenous people assuming a false identity, with its attendant desire for unmasking, animate postcolonial discourses in Guatemala. Often condensed as "idols behind altars," the sense that indigenous people look like one thing—baptized Christians—but are really another—stealthy pagans—inspired the inquisitions, Diego de Landa's murderous rages four hundred years ago (Clendinnen 1987) and ongoing waves of purifying movements like Catholic Action. I think similar assumptions also inspired the murderous rages of the counterinsurgency war and current debates over the postwar and its meanings, including the senti/meant surrounding Menchú's Stoll/en past.

These stereotypes inform the joke: "What blood type is Rigoberta Menchú? URNG-positive," i.e., she is a guerrilla and her peace prize is in fact a dupe (I return to the question of blood and biopolitics later).

As the *desenvuelta* joke suggests (without corte she's no longer indigenous), discomfort about passing abounds in discussions of ethnic identity in Guatemala, especially in the ambivalence surrounding the emerging pan-Maya movement. As analyses of *mestizaje* discourses reveal, ladino and Maya identities are "unstable selves," formed through context, language use, clothing, self-identification, etc. (Casaus Arzú 1992, Hale 1996, 2006, C. Smith 1996). To be ladino, that is, nonindigenous, is, like being gringo, a relational identity. As is Maya. While many Guatemalans claim they can always tell a ladino from a Maya (since a lot of privilege is at stake), jokes suggest one can't always take this for granted. To repeat, with a difference, "What is an Indian? A ladino with no money."

Animosity toward Mayan intellectuals who speak Spanish articulately, i.e., they are *desenvuelta*, wear business suits if they're men, and hold positions of power, is often expressed as the fear that they are duplicitously assuming Mayan identity when they are really ladinos. They are imposters and have no right to speak for the collective rights demanded by the movement.[18]

The war has produced other forms of passing, like the catechist and former Civil Patrol leader with two faces and the forcibly recruited Mayan kids "subjected" by the army to the training that made them able to carry out the massacres of the early 1980s. They returned almost unrecognizable to their communities to impose army control, first as soldiers and later as militarized civilians, uncanny doubles of the boys who were taken and drilled into look-alike soldiers (see Schwartz 1996).

This doubles the terrifying returns of the few disappeared who survived torture at the army's hands, perhaps, like Father Pellecer, by confessing, naming names. A friend in Guatemala City says, "The most horrifying moment for me of all those years of horror was when I saw a friend, who I thought had been disappeared, on a bus. I wasn't sure how to react. I felt so happy to see him, but if I greeted him in public, would I be suspect too? I decided to try to get closer to him in the crowd and see if he recognized me. As I pushed through the people and finally stood right next to him, I suddenly couldn't breathe. Because it was him, but it wasn't. My God! What had they done to him? He looked right at me and didn't recognize me. I just stared at him for the whole ride. As I turned to go he asked me for some money, but as if he didn't know me, and you know, I didn't have a cent on me! I couldn't even do that for this wreck of the person I had known! I didn't leave the house for a month after that."

Cassettes and Double Agents

While some ladinos fear being manipulated by duplicitous Maya in business suits, many fear being manipulated, made into someone they are not, by people in camouflage fatigues. The reeducation phases of the army's counterinsurgency, which followed the scorched-earth campaigns of the late 1960s and early 1980s, assumed a different sort of manipulation: that indigenous peasants were "sacks of potatoes" easily moved around. They had been duped by the guerrillas and their promises of a chicken in every pot. Those who survived the army massacres needed to be taught a lesson, as they were several times a day, starting at 6 a.m., in the army-controlled re-settlement camps known as model villages (CEIDEC 1988, Wilson 1995). To repeat what an army colonel in Nebaj told me in 1985, "They've had a bad cassette put in their heads. Our job is to change the cassette."

While Stoll is actually quite careful to note the ambiguities in how and why Menchú Tum's testimonial dissimulates rather than being perfectly similar to her lived experience, at times he gives credence to the notion that she is being manipulated, that she is puppeting a line, playing a "bad cassette." Describing her reaction to President Serrano's "auto-coup" in 1993 he says, "According to the country's main newsweekly, her courage made her 'the leader that she had not yet become.' Then something went wrong. Along with the URNG-aligned popular organizations, Rigoberta went off in a direction that seemed laid down by the *comandantes* in Mexico. . . . Making a mistake, Rigoberta decided that the INC [committee of civic elites] was too compromising to join. Instead, she echoed the URNG position" (1999a:223). He quotes Lionel Toriello, an INC founder, scathingly describing a "meeting with Rigoberta and her advisers as they apparently received instructions over the telephone from Mexico" (306).

Similarly, Peter Canby, fact checker for the *New Yorker*, writes in the *New York Review of Books*, "Seated behind Rigoberta as she spoke was a tall man with a dark beard, a dark suit, and a dark blue shirt. This was Gustavo Meoño, a former Christian radical, former head of the 'mass organizations' for the EGP . . . and now head of the Rigoberta Menchú Foundation. As Rigoberta responded to queries and sometimes got the details wrong, the intense looking Meoño would quietly correct her. . . . Rigoberta cheerfully explained that . . . reporters should speak to Meoño about the details [of their inquiry into Stoll's allegations]" (Canby 1999:32). Is Menchú Tum simply a ventriloquist's dummy for the left? Canby makes this reading almost explicit. Writing of a press conference at the UN, he states, "She is so small that when she sat in a chair her feet barely touched the ground. The combined effect of her very large head and the traditional costume she wore was to make her look disconcertingly like a doll" (32).

Writing about the "culture of the copy" and our anxieties about discernment and agency, doubles and being doubled over, Hillel Schwartz discusses how puppets fit into the "western discourse that associates diminutiveness with subordination, deceit" (1996:131). He describes how ventriloquists' dummies signal in vacillating ways both "subjection and resistance: our fears of being manipulated . . . or of being possessed by the foreign voices of advertisement or propaganda; our dreams of defiance, of talking and acting from the gut" (136). Menchú Tum knows that these are some of her uncanny doubles. Along with ethnic passing and hiding balls under her corte she is suspected of being possessed by propaganda. Stoll quotes her as saying,

> There's a challenge for those who studied the *indios* and made of this their profession, their career, their money and their life. Now at a moment that *indígenas* are speaking for themselves, this affects their career. I know that there are a lot of people who are never going to like us, who are never going to accept that *indígenas* speak, because to the extent that they speak, comes Spanish and they're no longer *indios*, so they say. This is a bit of what many who lack respect have said about me lately. . . . I know many anthropologists . . . and I am not against their profession, [but] they said that I was manipulated by the left because I'd been indoctrinated and was carrying around a left-wing cassette. (Stoll 1999a: 225–26)

Here are repeating images, of an assumed identity, a ventriloquist's dummy, a puppet camouflaging a conspirator, an automaton that plays any cassette placed inside it.

The indoctrination of revolutionary discourse Menchú Tum says she's accused of parroting in the wartime propaganda of her *testimonio* would be the very cassette the army hoped to change through the various intricate forms of counterinsurgency. It is the same indoctrination Father Pellecer denounced in his horrifying television appearance in 1981, and, as with the kidnapped Jesuit, the army seems terribly successful with its own indoctrination. During my fieldwork in the 1980s and early 1990s I often took testimony that strikingly doubled what I had heard elsewhere, in other villages — often word for word: "*Nos engañaron.*" Stoll heard this same refrain, and he asks why many researchers (like me) assume, when Mayan peasants repeat it, that "nos engañan" / *we* are being fooled—by them? Why do we assume that there must be another, truer story, one of rebellion, on that recording device playing the army's cassette?[19] Stoll argues that it's the uncanny power of Menchú Tum's *desenvuelta* testimony (the something in her more than her) that makes us believe that everyone else, lacking that something special, is simply a camoufleur puppeting the army's line. Solidarity, anthropological and/or activist, needs a binary story of victims and perpetrators in order to act. This is the very gift Menchú Tum gives and Stoll spoils.

Indian Giver and Solidarity

The *Oxford English Dictionary* cites a definition of "Indian gift" dating from 1764 in the Massachusetts Bay colony: a gift for which an equivalent return is expected (see also Parry 1986). This understanding, doubled with the more general sense I've been using of a gift reclaimed, points to the work of testimonials like Menchú Tum's and the complex systems of reciprocity that undergird solidarity and may make anthropology so ludicrous. Menchú Tum gives gringos the gift of being made the object of her appeal, the addressee of testimonial, of having a Nobel laureate repeat her story on your college campus with the object of winning over your identification. As Stoll argues, being hailed, or called out, in this way can function like a seal of approval, a space of innocence for the gringa, a site cleansed by good intentions and activist politics from which we can still speak unproblematically of the Other—what Stoll calls redemption. Stoll's politics of the nonduped names this story *engaño* and insists that we give these pleasures back.

But can we become the nonduped by simply refusing to project ourselves into Menchú Tum or other similarly romantic stories? Does such a strategy address the exchange of Menchú Tum as a woman, a Maya, and a Guatemalan in the jokes, debates, and stereotypes? Does being nonduped get at the x that gives the gift its value? Or explain the investments that make the U.S. reactions to Stoll's claims so emotional? I'm not sure disinvestment is possible in a globalizing world, in part because Menchú Tum *is* an Indian giver, asking for something in return for these treasures. Once you've become a gringo, i.e., participated in the transnational exchange of self and other, you've already signed the IOU.

Part of what Menchú Tum wants in return is solidarity, a complex praxis that attempts to see the connections that make a threat to one a threat to all. As such, it is a global phenomenon. The gifts gringo solidarity activists are supposed to give back include creating awareness of U.S. complicity in the militarization that led to Menchú Tum's loss of family and homeland and to continuing violations of human and cultural rights. Receiving the story, we became familiar with Guatemala. Yet we gringos are targeted for reciprocity, lashed into this global network as multiconductors, precisely because we are not the same as Menchú Tum; because, comparatively, we are millionaires, at least in quetzals, the Guatemalan currency. We are asked to deploy the difference that makes a difference—human rights denunciations, installation of UN special rapporteurs, changes in trade policy and credit ratings, the cutoff of military assistance and CIA asset payments, etc. This is very like the articulations that lashed members of the elite like Ricardo Falla and Myrna and Helen Mack together with poor indigenous activists like Esperanza León as a *Guatemalan* popular movement (because two—ladino or Maya; rich or poor—was too many). Like Indian gifts, these articulations were recombinant, demanding reciprocity. And, like the articulations between Menchú Tum and activists in the United States, these connections assumed (took for granted *and* produced) national and global identifications. But one (nation or globe) is not enough. Menchú Tum wants to be treated famillionairely. She, like many Guatemalans, including business executives and state representatives, expends enormous energy on international work—work that is directed at those who are different. This energy goes into writing books, newspaper articles, email communiqués, traveling abroad to argue her case before various global audiences, and donating exorbitant amounts of time to foreign representatives when they go to Guatemala—gifts I have received in good measure—and in 2006 running for president of Guatemala. This orientation toward the exterior has everything to do with Guatemala's global position and the always already-ness of transnational famillionairety. These include the Cold War struggles that led to U.S. military, CIA, Peace Corps, Christian missionary, and anthropological intervention; the transnational debt relations that make Guatemala vulnerable to structural adjustment packages imposed from outside; and the deepening of finance capitalist relationality leading in 1996 to Guatemala's first-ever offering of bonds to the global market and the current "peace bonds" meant to finance reparations and balance the accounts.

The Spanish version of Menchú Tum's testimonial *Me llamo Rigoberta Menchú* is subtitled *Así me nació la conciencia* (this is how my consciousness was born) to mark how external factors like poverty and state violence acted *on* her, made her who she is. Her orientation is similarly aimed at occidental consciousness. She writes, "It has hurt me to repeat and relive [my] story again and again in public. But that's what people listened to. Personal testimony is something which must be shared with moral courage and dignity by those who have been victims. It is a right and also a responsibility" (Menchú Tum 1993:x). Thus her sense of consciousness seems very close to how Mc-

Allister describes *conciencia* for the people of Chupol—meaning both knowing right from wrong and acting on it. Many people in the United States became gringos via knowing Menchú Tum's testimonial, and many of us in turn became activists in response to the way she acted on us from outside. This often entailed a change of consciousness regarding the famillionairety of global relations. Under the sign of genocidal civil war and U.S. complicity—acknowledged by President Clinton's apology—we are asked to imagine *and work for* a different future. For readers and incipient activists this is a process of identification that acknowledges that not only our mutual fund and tax dollars but also our identifications detour through Guatemala accompanied by our soldiers, M-16s, and counterinsurgency know-how. And this is a continuing process, as Slavoj Žižek notes. Just as those dollars need to be exchanged, identity is not some intimate, purely mental state. It "is always *materialized* in our effective social activity" (Žižek 1989:36). But like Turnbull's description of Chartres cathedral, it's more a motley than a plan.

Like Stoll, I am a gringo who took a detour through Menchú Tum's testimonial. But in these tales of process and consciousness is yet another unstable self—what does it mean to say in Spanish that consciousness is born inside us? Where, then, does it come from? and how does it get inside? In English we tend to say our consciousness is raised, suggesting it was always already inside but quiescent, inadequately low, awaiting assumption—as in the Virgin rising. Without going into a history of consciousness, false or otherwise, I am recalled to uncanny doubles, detouring back to the assumptions of identity. We assume, take for granted, that we *are* our consciousness. So, was I always already a solidarity activist before I encountered Menchú Tum's testimony? Was I only passing as a liberal hippy? Or am I passing now, ventriloquating poststructural theories as if they were my own?

These double entendres of the assumptions of identity make Stoll vacillate between two understandings of the consciousness effects of Menchú Tum's testimonial. One is the sense that she is acting *on* well-intentioned but hapless, easily seduced gringos. We are playing her cassette and are thereby blinded to the sordidness of her faction or at least to the complexities of EGP infiltration and of internecine disputes in indigenous villages. Second is the sense that we are acting on her, projecting our desires for rebellion: "the unsettling possibility: that she represented the audiences whose assumptions about *indígenas* she mirrored so effectively" (Stoll 1999a:246). What I like about Stoll's book is this acknowledgment that identification is mobile, formed in relation, X-static or outside stillness. But his analysis seems unable to deal with how identification is ecstatic, shot through with the surplus enjoyment of jokes and the sudden reversals of the stereotype from love to hostility. Why do uncanny doubles pervade jokes in Guatemala, the debates in the United States over Menchú Tum, but in her absence, *and* Stoll's text? Is Stoll's solution, to be the nonduped, the most adequate way to work through these global mysteries?

POSSESSION

I have recounted these various double entendres, the simultaneous and vacillating understandings of passing, simulation, consciousness raising, and the play of mimesis and alterity not simply to suggest that Stoll is unoriginal in depicting Menchú Tum as operating under an assumed identity. Instead, I ask why, even as he represents himself as the nonduped, he seems to be speaking this same old story? Why is it deployed by contestants on various sides of the debates, including myself?

All these entendres of selves—named and nicknamed, passing as Maya or ladinos, hiding things under *cortes*, forced by torture to name names, doubled over, *engañado* them"selves" and therefore duping others—carry the sense of being acted on by an external force. It may be Marxist propaganda, the army's counterinsurgency cassette, the *contratista*, or the seductive charms of Menchú Tum's testimonial. Diana Fuss suggests that there are many historic models for explaining these powerful effects of the other on the self: "demonic or ecstatic possession, contagious passion, animal magnetism, mesmerism, hypnosis" (1995:4). Fuss suggests, in turn, that what is magical or ecstatic about these effects is the very process of self-making: "The astonishing capacity of identifications to reverse and disguise themselves, to multiply and contravene one another, to disappear and reappear years later renders identity profoundly unstable and perpetually open to radical change" (1995:2–3). Both Stoll's attention to Menchú Tum's iconic power and the reactions in the United States to Menchú's Stoll/en past suggest a groping toward this magical-seeming effect. The historic saliency of all these doubles, from idols behind altars to Menchú Tum's cassettes, may lie in the simple (and extraordinarily complex) acknowledgement of how identification is assumed. Bhabha writes that such uncanny doubles are part of the always-ambivalent process of colonial identification (1994:76–77). In turn, Butler insists that the ex-stasis of the assumption of identity is not only colonial, but always gendered *and* the condition of possibility for all identification (Butler 1993:180).

Stoll gets that there is a narcissistic projection of an ideal ego from western selves on to a Mayan female other. He unmasks the famillionarety, the simultaneous acknowledgment of similarity and the disavowal of privilege and guilt at U.S. intervention. These are the emotions, Bhabha argues, that also mark the stereotype. I think Stoll feels he has been the object of aggression because he disrupts these projections and all their assumptions with the heterogeneity of another position, that of Mayan villagers who did not support Menchú Tum and the guerrilla. But he seems stuck in several different ways in terms of the ambivalence of identification.

First, while he critiques solidarity and human rights activists for leaning on clear-cut divisions between victim and victimizer, Stoll retains a very similar fundamental divide. The grid of intelligibility for solidarity and partial anthropology rests on "the internal fission of society into binary oppositions, a means of creating 'biologized' internal enemies, against whom society must defend itself" (Stoler 1995:59). In assuming these two sides, we gringos get a solid ground to stand on in our struggles against and for these self-constituting others. But it is this grid of intelligibility that may lead the nonduped to err. I wish Stoll had pushed further in his quest to counter the solidifying processes of sacralizing Menchú Tum as an icon. Instead, I think he becomes mired once again in the solid categories of a fundamental divide—now between ladinos, left and right, and the apolitical Maya who lack only some Peace Corps support to do just fine.

Second, he seems more single-minded than double-entendred in his understanding of duping. He describes Menchú Tum as traumatized, lost, and empty, and then the left offered a narrative to make sense of her obscene, horrific losses. (Lux Cotí, the CEH commissioner who described the war as ladinos, both army and guerrilla, killing Maya, similarly dismisses the many indigenous people who sided with both left and right in the war.) In turn, the millions of Menchú Tum's supporters around the globe—students, activists, UN officials, Nobel committee members, global indigenous leaders, even Stoll himself, as he readily admits—live empty, bourgeois, postmodern lives, and Menchú Tum fills that space as a mirror that reflects us back as we would like to be seen.

Stoll's mirror of U.S. solidarity as maudlin and easily led astray is not comfortable to behold. Neither is his, to me, strawperson view of the Guatemalan left as ladino, solid, powerful, and clearly aware of the dangers it was creating for the Maya and themselves. While never undertaken in a fit of absentmindedness (as "counterinsurgency prose" would have it [Guha 1988]), the popular movement and the guerilla were always a motley—making stuff up as they went along, shocked and awestruck by the historically unprecedented level of violence unleashed upon them. Stoll also ignores the global conjuncture of the late 1970s, when ongoing African decolonization and the overthrow of U.S.-backed regimes in Vietnam, Iran, and Nicaragua made it feasible to dream of alternative futures. While there is also a certain seat-of-the pants quality to state-backed counterinsurgency (like the utterly inadequate "hillbilly armor" devised by unprotected U.S. soldiers in Iraq), the human, financial, technical, scientific, and globally networked resources that coagulate in that node mean that there often is a plan, a counterinsurgency hermeneutic, and the wherewithal to carry it out. This is why human rights groups are not simply apologists for one side when demanding that states *asumir responsabilidad*.

But Stoll's arguments are sticky because there are indeed simplistic stories undergirding U.S. activism and strong verticalist tendencies in the Guatemalan left. However, Stoll does not acknowledge the dialectic of identification, its constant fluxion. (Or perhaps simplification is one phase in an ongoing process. One might ask if verticalism is an essential identity or one produced through engagement with genocidal counterinsurgency?) Positing a one-way projection—that of Menchú Tum's articulate, *desenvuelta* story on us, or that of our romantic desires for a revolting peasant on her—does not get at the ambi-valence of identification. I simultaneously love, I hate, I require. Is the something, the x, that is in Menchú Tum that is more than her *only* us? Or is it this movement, this fluid, magical, ambivalent exchange? Identi-ties?

I argued in chapter 2 that the postwar-in-action is about networks of assumed identities, and in chapter 3 that the mobility of identification in schlock horror films, as in the *Tzul* dances, may make them popular for rendering popular memory and postwar identifications. Here I've argued that the Menchú jokes are about the points of ambivalent identification, her uncanny doubling of revolutionary, ethnic, gender, sexual, nominal, national, and global identifications. And I've also suggested that their form, the exchange of jokes, like the horror film, like the lashing in of the postwar-in-action, is, in miniature, the very process of identification, the detour through the other that defines the self. The burst of laughter or grimace of pain is a sign of the magical Xtra of ambivalence, the special F/X, the surplus enjoyment, the more that is in Menchú Tum that Stoll can't really account for without a more *mobile* model.

Trans/actions and Traversing: The Nonduped Err

Although there are many ways to describe this x, I'd like to turn back to the Wizard of Oz. Responding to Dorothy's accusations that he lied, the Wizard says, "How can I help being a humbug when all these people make me do things that everybody knows can't be done?" (Baum in Schwartz 1996:116). Now everybody knows that you can't buy the future or make someone else pay for risks that you take. Everybody knows you can't give someone a simple piece of paper and expect to get a box of M-16s in return. But we do these things, and it's easier when certain *noms du père*—a name like United States of America—are on the paper, when NASDAQ tells you how much the future costs, when the John Hancock Insurance Company tallies the price of risk, or when the painting says Picasso and not Elmyr. Drawing on Marx Gayatri Spivak says that, like identification, the value of money is not internal to it. It is materialized in our effective social activity: "Cut off from all relation to (circulation) [money] would not be money, but merely a simple natural object" (Spivak 1988b:163). Similarly, everybody knows a poor *indita* can't win a Nobel Prize and that you can't overthrow a government kept in place by the sword of transnationally supported repressive apparatuses. But these things have been done. Perhaps Menchú Tum is an Indian giver, a bamboozler, precisely because she (and her networks) does them.

Of course, the consciousness necessary to do these things is not internal or only simply projected from one to the other. It arises famillionairely through social activity, from the circulation of identifications. Menchú Tum detours through the EGP, through exile in Mexico, through political activism in Geneva and in Spanish courts, through thousands of lectures and interviews around the world. The URNG detours through indigenous villages and transnational solidarity movements. Edgar Gutierrez detours through REMHI, the Mack Foundation, and the Ríos Montt government. Similarly, gringos, Stoll and myself included, detour through Guatemala, interviewing, reading, and writing about indigenous people, to define our selves. This seems to discomfit Stoll's empiricism, which appears aimed at "cutting Menchú (and gringos) off from all relation to circulation" so she is not Rigoberta "but merely a simple natural" Indian.

Assuming identity is not a thought experiment, it is materialized through *living*. Dorothy could have been told that the Ruby Slippers would take her right back home from Munchkinland, but she had to traverse Oz in order for them to work. Becoming gringo or identifying as an activist is a similar traversing. So was the revolutionary mobilization in Guatemala in the 1970s and 1980s. So are the current struggles over the postwar-in-action, including the debates over cannon (and canon) fodder in Guatemala and the United States, over race vs. class war, and the general attempts to account for and reckon with means and ends. As when following the Yellow Brick Road, there is no shortcut. Žižek says, "If we want to spare ourselves the painful roundabout route through the misrecognition, we miss the Truth itself: only the 'working through' of the misrecognition allows us to accede to the true nature of the other and at the same time to overcome our own deficiency" (1989:60).[20] To overcome the deliberate destruction of capacities for political action, McAllister says, "argument, not fact-finding, is the only means of recuperation" (2003:370).

Perhaps what is recuperable about Menchú's Stoll/en past is that it opens us to just such a working through, an opportunity for gringos and Guatemalans to overcome their own deficiencies. But as long as we remain with the "fundamental divide" of Stoll's ladinos versus Maya, of duped and non-duped, we will miss the Truth of the assumption of identity—its mobility, its fluidity, its embodi/meant, its action. Like horror movies and jokes, identification achieves its effects only through exchange, transference, the multiple entendres of assumption, through effective social activity.

I also think Stoll is doubling Eduard Bernstein's fear of seizing power too soon, before the Maya were a true revolutionary subject, aka this is a struggle over means and end/s. I would ventriloquize Rosa Luxemburg's answer, via Žižek's cassette, that "the 'appropriate moment' cannot arrive without the subjective conditions of the maturity of the revolutionary force (subject) being fulfilled—that is, it can arrive only after a series of 'premature,' failed attempts" (Žižek 1989:59).

The understanding of revolution or counterinsurgency as a duping, a simple manipulation of the populace, neglects the productivity and mobility of the assumptions of identity—its extravagance. As Žižek writes, "The revolutionary subject does not 'conduct,' 'direct' this process from an objective distance, he [sic] is constituted through this process, and because of this—because the temporality of the revolution passes through subjectivity—we cannot 'make the revolution at the right moment' without the previous 'premature' failed attempts" (Žižek 1989:59–60).

I'm not in any way suggesting that Guatemalans should now be ready and eager to pick up arms again. But, first, I do not see Stoll or his supporters acknowledging how understandings of the revolution as a failure are in flux (the postwar is in action). Second, current conditions in Guatemala, depressing as they are under the sign of neoliberalism, are a direct effect of the identifications assumed through the processes of war and peace, including the vibrant Mayan cultural rights movement, women's activism, state support for infrastructure projects, etc. Third, this is why *les non-dupes errant*.

In returning to this Lacanian pun, meaning "the non-duped are wrong," and the no and the name of the father, I'm trying to suggest that, no more than the revolutionary subject, does the partial and always ludicrous anthropologist like Stoll or myself "conduct or direct this process from an objective distance." The grid of intelligibility of a fundamental divide, which leaves anthropologists resigned "to be apologists for one side or the other," easily vacillates to the divide between duped and nonduped. But it is still a divide, not a dialectic. Two is too many. The nonduped err to think they are outside of the assumption of identity formed-in-relation, through exchange. Those in the know are lost precisely because "as one 'in the know,' he [sic] is caught in transference" (Žižek 1989:42).

Thus they err to think that they are not transferring or ventriloquizing the nom du père, that they are not formed in relation to particular discourses of power like empiricism, the Indian gift, or risk calculation.[21] This is another way of saying that "identification names the entry of history and culture into the subject" (Fuss 1995:3). Stoll—and the popular coverage of his claims—is speaking the Name of the Father every time he describes the father, Vicente Menchú, as a Neo (liberal) Man, and every time he unquestioningly deploys the notions of what Mary Poovey calls "the modern fact" (1998), aka "rigorous ethnography," "sociohistorical analysis," or transparent access to a Truth with no double entendres or skirting of the issues. He also does it every time he uncannily doubles colonial discourses of indigenous dissimulation and Indian Givers. Jonathan Parry's work on the "Indian gift" reviews the debates over the ideology of the "pure gift" versus the maximizing gift giver (aka capitalist man), and the gift's relation to salvation in the same "Christian world which developed the theory of pure utility" (1986:468). Paralleling my argument about the nom du père as what goes without saying, he suggests these understandings of gifting have a "particularly close historical association with market trade . . . and belong to a discourse peculiar to a certain kind of society" (1986:469).

Another deep assumption in Stoll's attack on the Guatemalan left is that they and Menchú Tum as their front should have known what their enemy would do and should have taken adequate precautions to ensure against this risk. The assumption undergirding this "taken for granted" is another discourse peculiar to our certain kind of "risk society" and its "insurance rationality." François Ewald traces two competing faces of justice, responsibility, and accountability developed in Europe since the eighteenth century. Both claim totality and operate via specific, mutually exclusive categories, regimes, and economies. "Fault," the way Ewald defines the legal or juridical understanding of responsibility, holds that damage is the result of an individual acting in a certain way. Thus "judicial decisions on accident compensation had to be linked to investigation of the cause of injury." Was it "due to natural causes, or to some person who should bear its cost" (Ewald 1991:206)? The court cases discussed in chapter 2 operate on this logic, as particular persons (and entities writ large as the Guatemalan or United state/s) must apologize and in some cases pay compensation. "Risk," on the other hand, is characteristic of the insurance regime, "a certain type of objectivity, giving certain familiar events a kind of reality which alters their nature" (200). Armed with "the statistical table which establishes the regularity of certain events, and the calculus of probabilities applied to that statistic, which yields an evaluation of the chances of that class of event actually occurring" (202), insurance assumes that all risk is calculable. This means, first, that "even in misfortune one retains responsibility for one's affairs" (207). Second, insurance, taking out policies against unemployment, illness, even death via the new instruments that collectivize such risks, disciplines the future and promises to eradicate poverty and working-class insecurity. Ewald says, "Insurance is a moral technology. . . . To conduct one's life in the manner of an enterprise indeed begins in the eighteenth century to be a definition of a morality whose cardinal virtue is providence" (207). (While they would sorely like to be so moral, there have been so many threats against Guatemalan judges, especially those involved with cases against the military or Ex-PAC, that most have been denied health and life insurance.) Insurance logic may explain some of the more repugnant aspects of Stoll's thesis, such as blaming the victims and appearing uninterested in the good or ill will of those carrying out the genocide. His and his supporters' imperturbability when confronted with questions of justice may have less to do with them being cads and more to do with their deep imbrication in this other rationality, in these assumptions of insurance and calculable risk.

Thus Stoll can't be easily dismissed as a conspirator or as dumb, insincere, or lying. Neither is he simply a dupe of "the modern fact," "pure utility," or the insurance forms of market ideology. That is because those assumptions may be the condition of possibility for him to speak at all. Žižek says, "The externality of the symbolic machine ('automaton') is therefore not simply external: it is at the same time the place where the fate of our internal, most 'sincere' and 'intimate' beliefs is in advance staged and decided" (Žižek 1989:43).

Within patriarchal technoscientific capitalism, sincere and intimate beliefs in empiricism and the market aren't usually something you look back on and say, retroactively, *Así me nació la conciencia* (that's how my consciousness was born). They were always already waiting for you, just like your patronym was when you *nació*. Perhaps this is why, in the end, Stoll's book so weirdly recalls the Borg refrain from *Star Trek*: "Resistance is futile." The Borg in turn resemble the procession of similar stories about the inevitability of globalization, the unlimited money to be made in emerging markets, the self-fulfilling bullishness of the stock market. These aren't lies in the sense that Asian contagions or the meltdowns of Argentina, Brazil, Thailand, Russia, Long Term Capital Management, Enron, Lehman Brothers, Bear Stearns (or reading *Capital*) will make us chuckle at our little foibles, burn our cash, and pull out of our retirement funds—if we're lucky enough to have them. In the same sense, Rigoberta Menchú Tum was not lying so that, now that we know the truth of her Stoll/en past, we can disinvest and no longer care about her. On the contrary, the scandal has generated enormous emotion and copious copy. No more is Stoll lying when he unwittingly portrays her as an Indian giver or tries to fix her into a single essential identity as Maya. This is because the duping is not in the stock market, in Menchú Tum, or in Stoll to be dispelled through interpretation or blasting through to the truth, any more than Art is in Elmyr's paintings. It is in the working of the nom du père as it traverses us. It is in our duped erring, in our exchange of gifts and jokes; in our effective social activity; in our ambivalent famillionairety with the globalizing world. Interest—inter/esse—is what lies between.

But this is also why we don't always have to obey the Borg or the Wicked Witch of the West, who commands, "Surrender, Dorothy." This activity is continuous, in constant detours. One (race *or* class war) is not enough; two (as if race and class were separable from each other or from gender, sexuality, history, culture, or a myriad other detours) is too many. This "name of the father" is not what Spivak calls a "unification church" (1988b:168). The world system is too wracked with crisis and has spawned too many millionaires to be so familiar. Instead, these transactions point to the ambivalent, impossible requirement of politics despite and through the assumptions of identity. There really *is* no place like home because identification is always X-static.

WELCOME TO BAMBOOZLED!
A MODERN-DAY MINSTREL SHOW

Bamboozle (cant form 1700 origin obscure) to deceive
or cheat by trickery, dupe; to confuse or puzzle

Satire (from dish of various fruits) — 1. a literary work
in which human vice or folly is ridiculed or attacked
scornfully, 2. irony, derision, or caustic wit used to attack
or expose human folly, vice, or stupidity. Pierre Delacroix

Bamboozled is Spike Lee's terrifically dense film about minstrelsy, desire, race,[1] gender, class, and ec-static identification. Its somewhat enigmatic title left me wondering who is bamboozled and by whom? Like the Mack poster that closed chapter 2, and contemplations of the *nom du père*, it raises unease about who, exactly, is a perpetrator. The film is a pointed satire, with the opening voiceover defining the word (just after a Stevie Wonder song situates us in a world transformed by 1492) as a warning that human folly will be ridiculed, our ludicrous projects lambasted. It tells the story of an African American television producer who has taken the name Pierre Delacroix, although most of his homies just call him Dela. Like the other crosses (crux/*croix*) I've explored, Delacroix is a passage point. Like indigenous people, slaves, the colonized, women, and the black nationalist hip-hoppers in the film (and maybe everyone), his name comes from elsewhere, outside him.

So does his charge. Ordered by his white boss, who claims to be blacker than he is, to create a real black show for the network, he decides to yes'm to death by creating the blatantly racist *Mantan: The New Millennium Minstrel Show*. To his simultaneous horror and delight it is a huge hit. It spawns a gigantic fan base of African-, European-, and other heritage people who wear blackface, huge painted lips, and Afro fright wigs and who, during the audience warm-ups, proclaim proudly that they are n**gaz.

Like the *Tzul* dances, Rigoberta jokes, and the excessive special effects of horror films, *Bamboozled* is fascinated with possession and other transformations of identity. *Mantan* is a minstrel show, an old practice in which blacks and whites, those supposedly fixed and discrete races, donned another face, just as Stoll accuses Menchú of doing. In a film with a hero named Dela, meaning, like "media," from, through, and beyond, Lee networks modern television to its historic womb of vaudeville and sideshows and contemplates the raciological icons, fixed or conventional images, and eye/cons it simultaneously overcomes and carries along.[2] Avital Ronell also genealogizes the mysterious powers of modern tele-devices through these peripheral sites to explore their horror, their fascination, and the uncanny effects of being acted on by forces coming from outside oneself:

> As with most early technologies and mind sciences, vaudeville was the research center for communication systems. . . . The *mise-en-scène* of the telephone in particular borrowed its concept from the showing and telling of vaudeville, or more accurately still, it was produced along with aberrant structures of technological promise raised by the horror or freak show. The staging of a miraculous thing that contorts, condenses, or somehow usurps partial powers of immortality in profound complicity with the supernatural—this staging includes the unrepresentable presentation even of psychoanalysis as a discipline. The concept of "mind reading," the electrical paradigms of Freud . . . the question of mental telegraphy, unconscious transmission, noncontact hermeneutic stunts, or even Charcot's staging of the hysterical body, all belong to the encyclopedics of nineteenth-century vaudeville. (1989:365–66)

The "shivers of delight in—or fear of—novelty" may be evoked through the stereo/type of minstrelsy's content and the experience of its transmission. A "miraculous thing that contorts," minstrelsy, like sideshows, film with its cuts and screens, and *testimonio* as the story of many in one, is aberrant—full of jokes and enjoy/meant. It is a side attraction but perhaps—replete as it is with mimicry, two faces, and fakery—may also be a central modality in the networks of the assumptions of identity. It is thus like Žižek's symbolic machine: not simply external but also where our internal, most "sincere" and "intimate" beliefs are staged. In the next chapters I continue to explore mediations of identification and entertain/meants by dialectically montaging the apparently immobile state (as of being) and the State with people's relations to movement/s, Mayan, popular, revolutionary, troop, labor. In *Bamboozled*, as in Guatemala, the past aggressively returns to haunt the not-so-settled present. Dela increasingly senses he is being acted on by forces that may not make physical contact but possess him nonetheless.

But Dela's boss thinks he's swell, and Dela can keep up his mortgage payments on a spectacular crib. His parents are shamed, remonstrating him for acting the "coon." His assistant, Sloane, is utterly ambivalent. As a black woman, she wants to succeed in a difficult but prestigious career position, which, like Menchú Tum in the *desenvuelta* joke, the men around her assume she got by sleeping around. But she is also deeply, painfully aware that the conditions of success in a racist image culture are shuckin', jivin', and assuming, as a doubling/troubling, false/true identity, the stereotype. Her contingent response is to insist on total authenticity via detailed attention to the history and technic of minstrelsy. She schools the stars of the show, who are plucked from tap dancing on the streets to a plush television studio, from living in a squat to deluxe apartments in the sky, in the ways of their predecessors and employs genuine burnt cork for the blackface.

Sloane's anguished relation to the show's forebears in minstrelsy mimics the vexed reckonings of all colonized peoples with their appropriated pasts. How does one fit appropriately, that is, make a living, in a world structured in dominance while struggling to be (in)appropriate(d) (Trinh 1986)? It recalls Mesoamerican women and men grappling with the legacy of La Malinche, translator and betrayer, an indigenous woman raped by the colonizer. She is a two-faced, forked-tongue ancestress who still possesses those who claim to speak for the dispossessed. She is reincarnated in Guatemala in a version of the *Culebra* dance in the Maya-K'iche' town of Momostenango. There, as Garrett Cook (2000) describes it, Malinche is the "contractor's wife" (played by a man)—a force of unchecked sexuality who is both a danger and a necessity for the yearly renewal of the world. Like Sloane, those born to a long line of *vendidas*, those who have been sold (Moraga 1983), must sorrowfully ask, what choice do slaves have? (Alarcón 1989). These daughters and sons feel simultaneously trapped in yet enlivened by the stereotype's ongoing double bind-in-action.

In *Bamboozled* Sloane struggles for authenticity, meaning to be trustworthy and believable. But "authenticity" is a word rooted in "self-achieving," and how to accomplish that when one is acted on so strongly by a force from outside? As the new millennium *Mantan* takes off, congratulatory (admonitory?) gifts of "race collectibles" pour in, in the form of old everyday household items in the shape of caricatured African Americans: banks, cookie jars, "lawn jockeys," and ashtrays. As the contradictions in Dela's situation multiply, one of them, a bank in the form of a grinning man who feeds himself coins with the flick of a lever, begins to act on its own account. What moves this automaton? And what does it *mean* to co-memorate with such memorabilia, especially when what it remembers is still in action?

Partway through the movie, Lee inserts a scene from his film *Malcolm X* in which Denzel Washington acts like Malcolm, who had shed the name Detroit Red but not yet assumed his new identity as El Hajj Malik El-Shabazz, to warn folks about being bamboozled. *Bamboozled* leaves it wide open for us to ponder who is the subject of bamboozlement—and who the object? Is this a state of being or an X-stasis—from, by, through, beyond . . . ?

The figure of the gullible black, who is so dumb he thinks everyone else is just as stupid as he is, was a central conceit in minstrel shows and is mercilessly satirized in *Bamboozled* in which the characters Mantan and Sleep 'n' Eat perform the "classic" skit "Ain't nobody here but us chickens" (see chapter 4). The farmer, like the audience, remains nonduped. He shoots, they laugh, as the skit reanimates those recurrent stereotypes of dumb natives—from the white settler stories of fabulous real estate deals and of beautiful maidens falling head over heels for white studs to the founding Guatemalan myth that K'iche' hero Tekúm Umán couldn't tell the horse from the rider and died after spearing the animal rather than the conquistador.[3]

Of course, this is not a one-way street. In the *Tz'ul* dances, Br'er Rabbit and other trickster forms often masquerading as children's stories, and in old wives' tales and other chick lit, the *patrón*, the colonizer, the white, the man is the one bamboozled. In turn, these very targets dismiss such forms of reckoning as folk, schlock, lowbrow, minor literatures but may also take them as proof of the conspiracy against them. Two-facedly, those in power also portray subalterns as being particularly dangerous because of their inscrutability: they seem so dumb yet are really quite sly. Remember Žižek's suggestion that "an ideology really succeeds when even the facts which at first sight contradict it start to function as arguments in its favour." For example, he says, arguing with a racist, one might say, Look at Mr. Stern, your "neighbour: a good man to chat with in the evenings, whose children play with [yours]. . . . [But] his answer would be to turn this gap, this discrepancy itself, into an argument for anti-Semitism: 'You see how dangerous they really are? . . . It is exactly this hiding of one's real nature, this duplicity, that is a basic feature of the Jewish nature'" (1989:49). Mobile, this "basic feature" slips easily from Jewish to Communist to African American to indigenous to woman . . . and even to white men, members of the Chambers of Commerce and elected officials.

Through Delacroix (of and via the [stations of the] cross), who ends up being shot by Sloane, Lee is exploring the process of these assumptions of identity. And not only for Pierre, but also for the white producer who thinks he's black, the light-skinned hip-hopper who can't get the cops to shoot him, and the multihued audiences of *Mantan*. Perhaps they (and we) are all de la—from, for, by, and through. Bamboozled, the film and the experience, opens queries into the "construction of the inner eye." How does one see? How does one know? How does one become? How does one come to function perfectly well by one's self yet also sometimes feel possessed? Could the racist be right that the basic feature of identity is "De la:" a series of trans/actions and mobile assumptions—but for Jews *and* Gentiles, blacks *and* whites, Maya *and* ladino, women *and* men?

I don't mean this in the sense of a prolonged adolescence of constantly morphing and playful performativity, so often satirized as postmodern. Nor in the sense that now that we know we're all essentially duplicitous, can't we all "just get along?" These are deeply staked—even as they are constantly mutable—claims emerging from centuries of dispossession with racism at its crux. Getting along will take a lot of co-memoration and co-laboration. Two may be too many (thus the *and*s), but one is not enough. The famillionairety of identification ensures that even as there are certainly blacks in the film (and indigenous people in Guatemala), there is no unified identity or singular reaction, even to the *Mantan* show (or to the state or to revolution in Guatemala), much less to the histories that have so intensively shaped African-heritage or indigenous identifications throughout the Américas.

For example, one of the young men whom Dela and Sloane have plucked from rags to riches to star in the show begins to recalibrate his investments. "New Millennium, huh? It's the same bullshit, just done over." With a pass of his hand over his face he transforms his frightened and troubled visage into the wide grin of the "happy darkie," "Y'assuh, ah, what you want with me massuh. I sang for ya, I tap dance for ya, I cooned for ya, anything. Just to make you laugh massuh, yassuh." He accuses his longtime companion of getting stuck in the grin, even as he becomes increasingly mean, while for him the gap between the faces has become an unbearable abyss. He quits the show. The film's radical hip-hoppers are less sanguine and more sanguinary in their judgment of *Mantan*'s star. Claiming he has sold out his kind, they force him to mimic the extraordinary dancing he does on the show, but this time with flying bullets providing the rhythm and killing him. It is a horrific enactment of the mainstream news cliché of black-on-black violence. Lee, not entirely a mainstream filmmaker, undercuts the cliché with the even more brutal scene of cops massacring the crew.

People in Guatemala—ladino, indigenous, Maya, and none of the above— are struggling to figure out what it means to have survived violence, including indigenous-on-indigenous, to live in a state called the postwar. They try to reckon with the absolute brutality that met claims for progress and development, ideas that had been instilled by the very nation-state that carried out the massacres. Michael Taussig writes of colonialism's two faces: healing and terror; promises of progress and absolute, unprecedented violence. Like Lee, he cautions against believing we can penetrate the veil of duplicity without losing its hallucinatory, bamboozling quality (1987:10). To metaphorize transformations of victims into perpetrators, humans into debts, sanguinary histories into shamanistic ritual, he evokes the hall of mirrors. This carnival metaphor suggests the way in which the rationality of the ledger book, with its double entries of debt and payment, is laid on the back of the dancer in Joyabaj. It, like Dela's mortgage, transforms magically into an eerie possession, a doubling over that ensnares, if differently, colonizer and colonized.

Halls of mirrors, minstrelsy, modern media, and two faces are hallmarks of the modern Fair, the carnival of colonialism, concatenating capitalist accumulation, raciological fantasy, technological imaginaries, and exotic/erotic appeal. Boardwalks, carnivals, sideshows, midways, these are marginal things, geographically, temporally, morally, and categorically. Like the "low, sublime" horror films, they are mobile, circulating through the countryside. And, instead of sitting still as we do during much of our entertainment, we actively traverse them, moving from one alluring site to the next. Carneys call out promises of fascinating things, lights blink, multiple musics overlap, posters map out dazzling possibilities. Freaks, gender benders, minstrelsy, and hybrid symptoms of the colonies await us in cages, on stages, moldering in formaldehyde tanks. Our bodies get flung about ecstatically on jerky rides. We consume strange delicacies like cotton candy and deep-fried Twinkies®. We try our hands at games of luck,[4] watch magic shows, and giggle at the preposterousness of the whole thing, yet we are somehow eager, desirous of bamboozlement. There is an x there, something in it more than it.

The sideshow, like minstrelsy, like assumptions, crisscrosses the apparent boundaries between and among state and people, center and periphery, ethical and criminal, city and country, up-to-date and old-fashioned, white, brown, and black. While often associated with the modern metropolis—Coney Island in New York, the Santa Monica boardwalk in Los Angeles, the Emerald City—carnivals also travel through the countryside following county fairs, setting up in highland Guatemalan villages for the titular fiesta. It is as a traveling showman that the Wizard of Oz first appears to Dorothy Gale. Midways are clearly aimed at slowly picking your pocket, at seducing you into circulating your money as you yourself are put into circulation. In fact, much of the marginality of the sideshow may lie in its suspicious merging of legitimate entertainment and stealing. As I explore in the next chapters, this merging calls to mind the state, whose legitimacy is so often felt to be a mask for corruption and the personal enrichment of those who embody it. But sideshows are also popular, cheap entertainment. Everyone I knew in Joyabaj went to the carnival when it came to town, if only to gawk. And the state, too, can seem accessible to the popular classes via public services of education, transportation, communication, and health. I'm hoping the sense of moving through the sideshow will help address the concatenations of desire and identification, belief and subjectivity, awfulness and the everyday, the states of fantasy and states of injury (Rose 1996, Brown 1995) that imbue the postwar-in-action.

The signature of any self-respecting amusement park or traveling carnival (or fading imperial power with millennial pretensions) is the Ferris wheel. The device was specially invented for the World's Columbian Exposition in Chicago in 1892, celebrating Columbus's quatricentennial and the progress of civilization, references that, satirically, open *Bamboozled*. In Spanish it is still called *La Rueda de Chicago*, the Chicago Wheel. The original Ferris wheel crowned an emerging colossus trembling on the verge of becoming a colonizing power: "very rich, very warlike and capable of anything," appearing live on the carney's stage. A central attraction at the Chicago Fair was the Smithsonian's sideshow dedicated to "the evolution of man." Here one could traverse "live exhibits of the Teutonic and Celtic peoples, then pass the Asians and Arabs, and finally 'descend to the savage races': the Africans and Indians. 'What an opportunity,' the *Chicago Tribune* would later write, 'was here afforded to the scientific mind to descend the spiral of evolution, tracing humanity in its highest phases down almost to its animalistic origins'" (Wilkinson 2002:193). Before or after this contemplation one could also enjoy its embodi/meant, rising and falling on the Ferris wheel and getting one's head measured to see where you fell on the scale—not unlike the fans of *Mantan*, detouring through their assumed identities.

Compared to the main events of the Guatemalan peace process—the signing of the accords, the REMHI and CEH reports, blockbuster trials of military personnel, state apologies, denunciations of a Nobel laureate, and MINUGUA's departure—the focus of the next chapters may seem like a sideshow. If the big divisions that seem to mark the war—State versus People; Right versus Left; Ladino versus Indian—are like posts in the sense of something fixed or stuck in the ground, the next chapters take up the other meaning of "post": "what moves across a doorway or passage point." While rejecting the abhorrent hierarchizing of evolution, this may mimic the Chicago Fair's "opportunity for the scientific mind" to descend the spiral to address the intensely local and personal experiences of everyday, unfamous people's assumptions of identity. Without getting too conspiratorial, although many postwar Guatemalans do, I'll say these local, personal experiences were central to the army's counterinsurgency plans.

Ronell's "aberrant structures of technological promise raised by the horror or freak show" saturate the "theory of memory" I proposed for Final

At the fair. Photograph by Netta van Vliet. Used with kind permission.

Girls and Boys in chapter 3. In turn, "the profound complicity with the supernatural . . . the concept of 'mind reading' . . . [and] noncontact hermeneutic stunts" she associates with the sideshow occasion both horror at being acted on and hope for acting on—or mobilizing—others. Carnival is etymologically linked to incarnation or embodiment and to carnage. The next chapters pull back the curtain on what seem to be separate figures of myth and legend, the Two-Faced Indian and the Duplicitous State.

But here, at the book's midway, ladies and gentlemen . . . I can reveal that they are conjoined! Only here can you see the monstrous spawn, the Frankenstein-like creature produced from, by, of, through, and beyond the war. Fresh from the lab, where our scientists work night and day, it's an awesome sight! Don't worry, we've got it lashed in tightly, but you never know, it might be hungry!

Chapter Five

ANTHROPOLOGIST DISCOVERS
LEGENDARY TWO-FACED INDIAN

> The subject is here "beheaded," "lost in the crowd," yet
> the transsubjective mechanism which regulates the
> process (games . . . carnivals) is clearly of a symbolic
> nature: it can be unearthed by means of the act of
> interpretation. Slavoj Žižek

> What happens in critique to fascination, where danger
> and promise are imbricated? Ackbar Abbas

> The military did so well here! They knew so much about
> the local culture. Simone Remijnse

David Stoll presents Menchú Tum as a freak, a duplicitous entity magically circumnavigating the globe to act on unsuspecting gringos. But once she speaks singularly, for the Maya as victims rather than the "Latin American left and its foreign supporters," he reckons her redeemed and can get behind her cause. Similarly, CEH Commissioner Otilia Lux Cotí claimed to speak for a unitary Mayan identity caught "between two armies. . . . Maya people were killed by both the left and the right, but both were ladino." These singular identities, Maya, ladino, left, right, exert a strong attraction on many people and are certainly linguistically easier to manipulate even as these acts of interpretation seem to relegate indigenous people to the margins or sideshow of the main events.

At the same time, doubleness, duplicity, and multiplicity are modes through which many people are grappling with identification, and this chapter explores the midway between identity and identi-ties. I trace a series of relations among indigenous people and between them and the Mayan movement, the revolution, the Church, the State, and big ideas like Progress, laying stories alongside each other like the booths and tents of a carnival (careful tho', it's easy to trip on the posts and tumplines that hold such structures up). Folks sometimes emphatically claim, for themselves or others, one of these identities, as at a sideshow where one may become transfixed by a particular act or ride. (I well remember falling in love with The Centrifuge, despite my mother's warnings, until the sixth consecutive ride brought up a nice cotton candy–corndog–caramel corn mix.) At other times we seem a bit "lost in the crowd" as the dazzling si(gh)tes begin to blur and converge.

Mimicking the experience of circulating through a small-town fair, we'll cross paths several times with the same people and let their enthusiasms ("you gotta see this!") guide us. But the contortions, condensations, and usurpings that Avital Ronell associates with freak shows and vaudeville may be oddly contagious. *Are* these the same people? Especially if the field-worker, like the traveling fair, returns year after year, yet writes about a ghostly ethnographic present? Is it possible to stage the entertaining "un-representable presentation . . . of 'mind reading,' unconscious transmission, noncontact hermeneutic stunts" (1989:366) that engage us in these limi-nal times and spaces? What about the similarly hard to pin down embodi/meants of and postwar confusions among victim, perpetrator, state, people, left, right, Maya, indigenous, ladino, and the difficulties of distinguishing *engaño* from knowing very well?

We visit carnivals to be amused, distracted. We scoff, disbelieving. We know F is for fake and for freak but also for fascination. In this sideshow monstrous and simultaneously normalizing figures like Two-Faced Indians appear, as does the carnivalesque centaur-state, theorized by the Guatema-lan political scientist Carlos Figueroa Ibarra (1991, see also Jonas 2000) as both rational and bestial, coldly efficient and radically excessive. As with the Indian Giver whose X arises from traversing and exchange, I explore move-ment through the strange mix of old and new, here and there, distraction and fascination, rationality and bamboozlement. We'll ponder the creepy and violent conjugation of disparate things, old awful stereotypes, and ex-periences that blast the known world. But first, try a sample of what we have in store . . .

Coming attractions!

Dr. Hector Nuilá, formerly an ORPA commander and in 2006 the general secretary of the URNG political party (and a ladino) said that the culture of clandestinity has been a big problem for the party: "It's a way of life. Many former combatants have a hard time projecting, speaking, making them-selves known. And there is still a lot of fear." I asked if this might be why people like Lux Cotí could say there were no Maya in the guerrilla. "The in-digenous have always been two-faced," he said. "This has always been true, from way back. They have always had to hide as a way to survive. They would go to church so no one suspected they didn't believe and then go to the mountains and pray to their gods. They are very good at keeping secrets." Then he told a thrill-packed story about narrow escapes as a guerrilla that ended with a tale of how an indigenous sympathizer would keep the very best liquor hidden away under the carved wooden figure of Maximon[1] till he could pass it on to the guerrillas for their fiestas. "You know," he said, "we never had any security problems among the indigenous people. Among the ladinos, yes, but never with the indigenous."

The *alcalde indígena* of Joyabaj complains about ladinos in the area who called him an *indio*. He is not one of those, he said, because "those were people who lived here a long time ago . . . naked, without schooling. Now there are schools in all the hamlets. There are only *naturales* here." I asked if there were any Maya in the town. "Like in a museum?" he asked. "Here there aren't any of those, like from before." He paused. "But there is an organization in Guatemala City. People who have their degrees. . . . Wait! No. There is a Grupo Maya here. . . . They talk about how we can all be united, how to come together. Yes, they meet upstairs at the pharmacy. What they say is very interesting! When I leave here [retire from being mayor] I'm going to become a Maya."

A Guatemalan sociologist went to run a *taller* (workshop) with Maya-Ixil women in northern El Quiché and told me about her utter surprise at finding that all of them identified most strongly as *ex-combatientes*. The identity categories she assumed she'd find—woman, Maya, poor, *campesina* (peasant), or returned refugee seemed nowhere near as salient as their sense of self as members of the formerly armed revolutionary movement. They told her how they had decided, some when they were only twelve years old, to sacrifice everything for the revolution, to take off their traditional clothes and don *verde olivo* (olive green). "They said, 'We are still revolutionaries, but now in our *colores* [*traje*]. The struggle is political now, as everyone knows.' But," she went on, "they are also very angry, they feel *engañado*, *abandonado*. They were willing to die for the revolution and what do they have to show for it? They want recognition but the URNG is not doing anything."

Since around 1994, several hundred people have been killed and wounded by lynching, especially in the highlands. MINUGUA (2001) registered 337 cases between September 1996 and December 2000. Suspected thieves, rapists, Japanese tourists taken for devil worshipers, and the perennially haunting gringa *robaniños* (child-snatchers) have all fallen victim. Attempts to understand these acts of excessive violence often swerve between explaining them as essentially indigenous, an age-old expression of Mayan culture, or as being carried out by state-backed provocateurs manipulating highland people. For example, two years before the peace treaty was signed, June Weinstock, a North American woman, was beaten and left for dead in a Maya-Q'eqchi village because she was accused of kidnapping a child to extract and sell its organs (A. Adams 1999, Kadetsky 1994). A number of commentators placed the attack in the context of the deployment of the MINUGUA peacekeepers—that it was planned and incited by the Guatemalan state to frighten off foreign human rights observers. The presence of road workers in the crowd and the slowness of police and army to respond suggested the state's sinister role. The army claimed it did not intervene to stop the attack because it was afraid of being held responsible.

For his doctoral dissertation the Mayan anthropologist Alberto Esquit is interviewing indigenous people who have decided to work within the Guatemalan state. As we sat and talked in a Guatemala City café near the Congress, he drew up a list of the words they have deployed as they reckon with their experiences:

engaño	duplicitous
decepcionado	deceived
abandonado	abandoned
demogogía	demagoguery (defined as a leader who stirs people up through emotion or prejudice rather than reason)
defraudado	fraudulent or a cheat
distractor	distracting
espejismos	mirage or illusion (also reference to getting nothing for something—as in beads and mirrors for the island of Manhattan)
manipulación	manipulation
prestado	to be lent (as to someone else's scheme)
ignorante	ignorant
ingenuo	naïve
tragado	swallowed up
comprado	bought off
mezquinidad	stingy, wretched, or mean
el estado es la escuela de hipocresía	the state is the school for hypocrisy

Fermín Gómez is a Mayan priest who participated in processing the peace through COPMAGUA's sacred areas commission. He was recently invited to perform a Mayan ceremony in Alta Verapaz to gauge the response of the

Tzuultaq'a (earth deity) to a planned mining venture. He reported back that the deity felt just fine about it, to the relief of the mining company that sponsored the visit.

> Ladies and Gentlemen, Step Right up to See
> A Figure of Myth and Legend, Acquired through Courageous Travels
> To Faraway Lands! Get Your Tickets and
> Come See the Two-Faced Indian!

Just as carnivals return with new attractions and old favorites, I'd like to return to an embellished version of the story I told earlier about the Two-Faced Indian I "found" in Patzulá, an outlying hamlet of Joyabaj. Just a year after the CEH report came out, he led the services connected to the Vatican's Jubilee Year by lashing together biblical martyrdoms and the genocide of the Mayan people. I felt rather surprised when he used the term "Maya" because it's usually associated with urban-based, white-collar indigenous activists.

As I did some deep hanging out (i.e., sleeping in the school), I learned that the Guatemalan Mayan Language Academy (ALMG), an autonomous state agency run by indigenous people, was providing the village with culturally sensitive curricular materials in both Spanish and Maya-K'iche'. The representatives of the central state who trekked out to the hamlet on their motorcycles to check up on things were more and more likely to be Maya and mostly but not only men from various new or upgraded governmental entities. Some were from specifically indigenous-focused dependencies like the Indigenous Development Fund (FODIGUA) or the Bilingual Education Directorate (DIGEBI). Doña Miguela, whose husband had been forced to participate in the Xeabaj massacre, had served many of these people in her *comedor* (eatery), leading her to chastise her children for never truly learning Maya-K'iche'. "Now you can get a job just for speaking the *dialecto!*" she said, amazed.

For many people active in the popular movement the end of the war—its intent—was simply to possess some means of subsistence or perhaps a little more than that, aka progress. In the idiom of liberation theology that the catechist and Esperanza León would understand, it entails a "preferential option for the poor," not an acceptance of the status quo. An indigenous participant in a Catholic Action training said, "Before this course I used to thank God for rich people, who gave us jobs on the coast. Now I thank God for poor people who are responsible for creating the wealth of the country" (Remijnse 2001:80). Now the idea of progress is an Ideological State Apparatus if there ever was one and is often tied to schooling and particular forms of work, dress, habitat, and culture. As the *alcalde indígena* suggested, a change in knowledge could mean the assumption of a new identity (from *indio* to *natural*). For many ladinos and indigenous people progress means transforming or assimilating to modern life, leaving rural traditional lifeways behind (in fact, modernization is practically synonymous with it), becoming "more than an Indian," as Charles Hale explores (2006). But as Doña Miguela discovered, changes in the milieu now mean one's own *dialecto* can access a government paycheck. Assumptions about progress or improvement complexly lash in to unpredictable nodes regarding possession and identification and can give the same person several faces.

In 2000, all four of the official teachers in Patzulá's public school were local K'iche' speakers, several had been involved in Mayan revitalization efforts for many years, and several were studying intercultural education through a National University extension program taught by Mayan activists I knew from my earlier work in Guatemala City. The program is partly sponsored by the United States Agency for International Development (USAID). Leaving the Jubilee service, I ran into Domingo González, the president of Patzulá's Improvement Committee, who had just returned from a seminar on Mayan rights in Guatemala City, also funded by the Guatemalan government and USAID.

While the village of Patzulá (and González, a corn farmer who sometimes migrates to pick coffee) seems very out of the way, it is connected through multiple ties with the state. The state, in turn, is represented by González when he returns to the hamlet. He frequently visits the departmental and national capital seeking support for education, road building, and other projects. At the seminar on Mayan educational rights, González met Demetrio Cojtí Cuxil, one of the founders of the ALMG and then–vice minister of education in the Portillo/Ríos Montt government. González said, "They were gathering people from all over the country, the twenty-three languages all had representatives: Garífuna, Xinka, all were there. There were three days of discussion. Those Kaqchiqueles, from Chimaltenango and Comalapa, they are really *adelantado*/advanced, there was the *viceministro* who gave a talk. His name is Cojtí, he gave the opening talk. He's a doctor! We don't have any doctors, lawyers, engineers here. We need to do a lot more work on education among the K'iche's so our children can learn and come back, like they do there. Cojtí started his speech speaking perfect Kaqchiquel, it was very smooth. Then he went right into Spanish—he has accomplished so much, but he hasn't lost his language! You'd never know he's a doctor! He was very humble."[2] Cojtí's duality—he is Maya and a doctor, Kaqchiquel and vice minister—strongly impressed the Improvement Committee president.

González told me that the catechist who spoke of martyrdom was the driving force behind finally getting a road built to the hamlet, organizing both state funding and community labor crews. "We built it with *puro pulmón!*" pure lungpower, the sweat of our brow. The road in turn made it much easier to get goods in and out, greatly aiding Esperanza León, who had opened a little snack stand in her house by the school, and for state officials and anthropologists to get in. The catechist had also organized the community-controlled bilingual school and had served several terms as a minor elected official in the town of Joyabaj, where he maintains a small house and sometimes works construction jobs.

Several nights later, after a long day devoted to Catholic Action Jubilee activities, I sat around León's fire with her children (Juan had not yet left for the United States) and the catechist and his family. That's when he took me aside and told me he had been the hamlet's Civil Patrol leader. "I have two faces," he said. "One I show to the army, the other I show to my people."[3] While I have used the term "two-faced" as an example of both a widely held assumption and an anguished assumed identity, please remember that little do I know. The catechist spoke to me in Spanish because I do not understand Maya-K'iche'. There are surely densities of meaning behind his remark of which I am not cognizant (I alluded to these in chapter 1). Here at the center of the book, his comment is both a crux for my thinking but also a puzzle, a navel that stems toward aspects of indigenous life to which I am not privy.

Perhaps he is expressing the paradoxes of *conciencia* as McAllister describes them. If it is the basic feature of a human to be able to differentiate good from bad and to be able to act on that knowledge, state counterinsurgency and revolutionary defeat seem to cut knowing from doing, introducing a gap at the core of the human. Judith Zur, also working in southern Quiché, reads this gap or doubleness through ethnicity, that is, when indigenous Civil Patrol leaders (*jefes*) took advantage of the absolute power the army loaned them to kill, rape, and steal, they took on ladino faces in the townspeople's eyes. Zur writes, "The assumption of a ladino identity gives access to a different view of humanity which categorizes Indians as a sub-human species. . . . Such artificially constructed dichotomies resulted in the *jefes* switching from camaraderie and affection to violent abuse and punishment. . . . [The patrol leader is caught in] the oscillation between his role as an adjunct to the ladino military and the 'off-stage' world of the Indian (where he may have to answer for his behaviour in the former)" (1998: 108–09).

As in urban legends such as *Candyman* (Turner 1993), when the catechist calls himself two-faced it's a story of taking some agency in an impossible situation. The state may think it makes him do what it wants, but he knows he has another face. As we trope through Latour's Janus, to see with other eyes, these examples of the "indigenous ready-made," by stereotyping them as basically duplicitous, might be displaced by the "indigenous-in-action." Not unlike the killers of *Scream*, made by the horror film genre, or clandestinity generated by counterinsurgency, what may first appear as an essence is actually rendered, a product of state, or trans-static powers traversing the indigenous highlands.

The catechist in Patzulá seems to suggest his real face pointed toward the people. But is some of his effectiveness in organizing the hamlet to improve education and commerce due to his other face, the one he points to large, powerful institutions like the church and the state? And his real face — which people does it point to? Are they indigenous, even if, like some patrollers, they act ladino? If so, are they the Maya as victims that Lux Cotí claims to speak for? Are they the apolitical "sanctioned Maya" working inside rather than challenging the state that Jennifer Schirmer describes as an assumption of counterinsurgency hermeneutics (1998:115–17)? Patzulá, like neighboring Chorraxaj, was hit hard by counterinsurgency violence, suggesting the people there were seen as dangerous by the military state defending a race/class system enjoyed by rich criollos and ladinos. If they were organizing for their rights as peasants and workers, however, some indigenous people (similar to Stoll's argument), see them as dupes of a ladino project.

You Won't Believe Your Eyes with These Next Creatures!
They Come Down from the Mountains!
They Hide Deep in the Jungle!
Sometimes They Look Just Like You and Me!
Now's Your Chance to Match Your Wits against the Hermeneutic Stunts
of Our Amazing Shapeshifters!!

Sitting in Doña Miguela's kitchen recuperating from a bout of stomach trouble, I told her a story about liquid insides I'd heard from a similarly afflicted priest who had accompanied internal refugees in the 1990s. She responded:

Our priest was killed here, you know. It was so bad then, so bad, in the time of the guerrilla. The *militares* are *malo, malo*" (bad). But the people were *malo* too. Here, in the *aldeas*, the hamlets, they would *engañar*. They would tell the army that someone was a guerrilla when they were not. It was just for *pleitos* (disagreements) or to get their *terrenito* (little bit of land). And the army would kill them, torture them. A lot of people died then, especially in the hamlets, in the mountain.

They say the guerrilla were up there. One time they came through, people said they were coming through. I was afraid, but I looked out the window, they were all *naturales!* Every one was *natural!* They came down another time in a truck and another time too when they took away the son of the *alcalde*,[4] and his mother too. But they left her out on the road. We don't know what happened to the boy. He is still missing. From then until today. One time, I remember, when the *patojos* (boys) came down, they were *puro patojos*—just little boys. Oh, it made me so sad to see them! They were so young and covered, just covered in mud! They were sick and *so* hungry! They asked me for just a little food. It was so sad. They were tired and dirty. I gave them food. They were starving. The army gave them nothing, nothing! They had no training!" [It was only at this point in the story that I realized she was talking about soldiers and not guerrilla.]

Some had been in only a couple of months, another for a year, but they hadn't been trained. They didn't know anything. Boys! From here! They were poor, and so polite! The next day they came for some tortillas and said they had to go already. They had barely rested, and they were being taken away. Then I heard there was a bomb on the road to Zacualpa, and they were all dead. All of them! *Ay dios!* I was so sad! They brought the truck back here, just down the street to clean it up, and I remember it was full of blood. Covered with blood.

In the 1980s on posters, banners, and billboards in areas where the army had "removed the water from the fish," that is, separated the people from the guerrilla, the army emphasized its unity with the people through slogans in Spanish like

PUEBLO Y EJERCITO UNIDO JAMAS SERÁ VENCIDO

PEOPLE AND ARMY UNITED WILL NEVER BE DEFEATED

which I found rather mysterious given the high rates of illiteracy and Mayan-language monolingualism. Is Doña Miguela's horror and pity the kind of unity they mean? Or is she seeing the army as two-faced, its command structure opposed to the boys eating her tortillas? When the army kills people wrongly accused of being guerrillas it is bad but also *engañado*. In one case, when it thought it made the catechist work for them, the army couldn't see his second face. In the other, as bad people tricked it into acting for them, they didn't see how they were being used for very local ends. In these stories, local people like Doña Miguela, not the army, are in the know. But in a nightmare scenario, they may know very well but cannot act on that knowledge.

Civil Patrol station at entrance to army-controlled "model village." "Welcome to the urban center of New Saraxoch, an antisubversive community, discipline and organization." July 1986. Author photograph.

The army may seem ingenuous assuming anyone would buy their banners proclaiming,

PUEBLO Y EJERCITO JUNTOS RECONSTRUYE LO QUE OTROS DESTRUYERON
PEOPLE AND ARMY TOGETHER REBUILD WHAT OTHERS DESTROYED

but it also knows things (Schirmer 1998). A long-term researcher at AVANCSO still marvels at the *hermenéutica militar*, the in-depth army knowledge of what was going on at the village level. People who worked with the CEH talk about how they pieced together the history of the war from *testimonios* and recently released guerrilla and army documents and say it was striking to realize how in the know the army was. "It was staggering," said one North American woman. "Years and years after the fact we're still trying to catch up to what the army knew about guerrilla tactics and popular mobilization." Simone Remijnse suggests how this great and powerful hermeneutic became self-fulfilling: "Civil patrol indoctrination and military propaganda . . . told them over and over again that, if you behaved well, went about your work and did nothing wrong, you had nothing to fear. If you actually became a military target and got killed, you must have been doing something wrong, like belonging to the guerrilla. Getting killed proved someone's guilt" (2002:199). They must have been involved in *babosadas*.

Not long after Myrna Mack was murdered, one of her colleagues told me, cryptically, that he wondered if she were more "involved" than he'd been aware of. In the late 1990s the Mack Foundation commissioned a biography of Myrna from a Spanish journalist with many years of experience in Guatemala. The biographer interviewed many of her friends and coworkers and wrote a narrative nonfiction account of her life and death, taking a bit of poetic license. However, the family did not approve the final version. It remains unpublished, and the author's friends say he was terribly *decepcionado* (disillusioned) by the experience. Was it rejected because he relied too heavily on Edgar Gutiérrez's version of events when Edgar had *decepcionado* so many by joining the FRG government? Or was it because it mixed fact and conjecture too promiscuously? Or was it because he concluded that Myrna had been a member of one of the guerrilla organizations? While some say he got the organization wrong, others insist she was never formally a member, and saying so seems to blame the victim, while others wonder if the two-faced logic, admitting a clandestine life in addition to her research activities, unnerved family and friends. Or maybe she had no clandestine life. It's all rumors. I don't know.

What is creepy, however, is that in the *hermenéutica militar* (counter-insurgency hermeneutic) of her death, the army as "intellectual author" is revealed to know her with terrible intimacy. They surveilled her, listened to her phone calls,[5] read her mail, followed her research carefully, and watched her child at play, and they knew her friends, lover, family, and all the networks in which she was a node. They knew what she hoped for and dreamed of, perhaps as well as or even better than her closest friends. But does the fact that she was murdered prove she was involved?

A fledgling research association like AVANCSO seems more like an out-of-the-way town like Joyabaj than a dangerous power center. Marginal places like Joyabaj and its hamlets are often depicted, as in James Scott's wide-ranging study *Seeing Like a State*, as sites that have yet to be mapped, miniaturized, fixed, understood. They are outside state control, grasped more through myth and stereotype than through accurate information, full of often contradictory figures and resistant to state rationality. People don't have last names, taxes are irregularly collected, and native guides are few and untrustworthy. Scott balks at romanticizing but suggests these are spaces outside full state control (sites of possible resistance) that nonetheless, one day, will be penetrated by that state.

Explanations of both the brutality and governmentality of army actions in the city (intervening in the private spheres of church, family, school), and in the highlands (from massacring, selective killing, rounding up displaced people and ensconcing them in modernist planned model villages to the massive investing in infrastructure projects, especially roads)[6] rely on the model of a state penetrating zones formerly closed to it, fixing its too-mobile subjects. But it can also seem as if the military and the state are as intimate with the indigenous highlands as they were with Myrna, so that now we anthropologists and local activists working to understand indigenous identity, community histories, and even the effects of newer processes like the Mayan movement, may be staggering, years after the fact trying to catch up to what they seem to already know. We stumble in attempting to create a usable counter-counterinsurgency hermeneutic. For example, it wasn't until my second stay in Joyabaj that I finally figured out whom to really talk to about the Grupo Maya mentioned by the *alcalde indígena*. I found out later that the FRG had gotten there first, identified Natalia Godoy as an up-and-coming leader, and invited her to run for office on their ticket—she declined, although she found it rather thrilling to be asked.

This is an Oz-like hermeneutic stunt, the state seeming all-knowing and all-powerful, an inexorable *nom du père*. But what about that other booth we've already peeked in on, where the two-faced state provides schooling, trains health promoters, imports priests and nuns who transform religious experience over great swaths of the countryside, transports local authorities to workshops on Mayan education, and pays for Mayan language academicians to visit faraway villages? Encouraging development, progress, and improvement, it seems to promote shape shifting as *indios* assume new identities as *naturales*, campesinos (peasants) become *profesionales*, traditional authorities (*chuch kajaw*) become *catequistas*, and some of each become revolutionaries, who in turn may become other things, like Maya.[7] Does the state knowingly operate under the sign of the Virgen de Tránsito, our patron saint of mobility and transformation? As much as our main attraction, the Two-Faced Indian, "it" seems subject to contortions, condensations, and usurpings.

Alfonso García is a Xoye who criticizes the more traditional people (*costumbristas*) for refusing to send their children to school, thus denying them any chance for economic advancement. He sees the real indigenous consigning their kids to a life of (non)subsistence farming and the horrible migration to labor on the coast enacted in the *Baile de la Culebra*. For him, possessing culture, authentic indigeneity, is linked to dispossession of one's labor and of the means to obtain a more comfortable, modern life. But Alfonso is also connected to the Grupo Maya and is struggling to hold on to the language and culture. He says he is often asked by his more assimilated cousins, "Why would you want to talk that way? Be that way? It's so backwards!" They tease him relentlessly about repossessing his identity, and he says, "Now I don't like to be with them. I'm learning more about the conquest, what happened to us, how we are losing our values. It's important to try to bring them back, to recuperate our morals. I am studying a lot, it's good."

At other times, however, he says he doesn't really believe in the Mayan stuff: "We have lost all that. What people are doing and saying, it's lost, it's not true, they don't really feel those things in their hearts." When we talk about identity issues, his pronouns float around—sometimes the indigenous are us and sometimes them. While he farms a little land, he has worked as a government-trained health promoter much of his life, which is how he missed the Xeabaj massacre, and now receives a somewhat precarious pension from the state. Alfonso is a catechist in the Catholic Church, where he strongly resisted attempts to introduce hybrid Mayan practices into the mass. "They have their place," he said, "but not in the church!" His children are mostly trained as elementary school teachers, and his daughters, unlike their mother, do not usually wear *traje*. "It's too expensive," he said. "Do you know how much it costs? To buy a *corte* [skirt]? Even to make a *huipil* [blouse]? I invested in education instead. We can't afford both." Alfonso, like many of the organized Mayas, is proud of the continuing tradition of the *bailes* and *cofradías*. "A friend of mine from Chajul pointed this out to me," he said. "Joyabaj has culture, the *cofrades* are strong. In Zacualpa they don't have this anymore. They have lost it." But one day we walked past a man and his young children hoeing their cornfield, and he said, "They are traditionalists, and I really feel sorry for them, how hard they have to work. It hurts me to see it."

In Joyabaj those who perform the *bailes* and older rituals or who have been initiated in sacred roles like *aj q'ij* or *chuch kajaw*, aka daykeepers, diviners, or as healers are known as *costumbristas*, or traditionalists. Most speak little Spanish and showed little interest in being interviewed by me (and I'm kind of shy around them). Many people in Joyabaj and throughout the highlands sided with the army against the popular movement. This means they are implicated in the murder and displacement of many of the indigenous people, like León and the folks in the CPR that Mack worked with, who were engaged in or were suspected of being engaged in struggles for the possession of land and labor rights. In some cases the very conservatism that retains allegedly authentic culture also supported their collaboration with genocide. Remijnse said, "The military did so well here! They knew so much about the local culture and the conflicts, because the local military commissioners were from here and told them all about people's fears, their organization. They went around telling the *costumbristas* that the Catholic Action people had first tried to take away their religion and *then* they were going to try to take away their land. And it worked. Some of the strongest

Civil Patrols were in the towns where the *costumbre* was strongest" (pers. comm.; see also Le Bot 1995).

As I mentioned above, Catholic Action was appropriated from its anti-Communist origins to become a powerful tool in local challenges to traditional authorities, both village elders and *contratistas*. As a somewhat Weberian movement, it offered the allure of progress to people like Alfonso's parents and, as those promises were stymied in various ways, became more radical, linking to liberation theology and in the 1970s to the popular and even revolutionary movement.

A Kaqchiquel man in his late fifties, now active in the urban Mayan movement, told me he was raised in Catholic Action but was curious about *costumbre*. However, his family insisted it was the devil's work. It was evil, and he should stay away. Frightened, he did, until his late twenties. A Mayan activist with the ALMG in the capital now repents of his Catholic Action work: "I went with my father to help stamp out the other practices. I knew both sides—the traditional and the Catholic, so I was very good at finding the traces of idolatry. Now that I see the importance of our culture I am so sorry for what I did. We were the worst destroyers of our own culture." He is now dedicated to salvaging and repossessing what he once worked so hard to root out. This is like the two-faced catechist, who has returned to wearing traje and who builds roads and works with the Mayan movement in the bilingual school and within the church by adding his own take on the prepared lessons. They are all struggling to possess material, spiritual, and cultural goods while simultaneously being good people.

In Chupol, McAllister says, the improvements rendered by Catholic Action developmentalists made them popular with everyone, *costumbristas* included, and in the K'iche' town of Momostenango Barbara Tedlock found dialectical ways that *costumbristas* confronted the challenges of Catholic Action. Garrett Cook, working in the same area as Tedlock, however, emphasizes the enormous sadness and confusion engendered when members of Catholic Action attacked people's way of life as pagan or as the devil's work—often targeting their own parents or grandparents and shaking deeply held understandings of age and familial propriety. Many traditionalists laid their loss in social prestige and economic standing at the door of Catholic Action, losses and fears the army, as Remijnse says, played on expertly. Perhaps more discombobulating was the way in which the dangerous work and the sacrifices that *costumbristas* make in order to maintain balance in the world were transformed into witchcraft. Their good deeds became evil in others' eyes. Against their wills the milieu changed around them, and they suddenly had two faces.

Some traditionalists before and during the war regarded their neighbors as two-faced, possessed by strange assumptions about good, evil, and the common wealth and assuming strange new identities as teetotalers and maximizing individualists. Identi-ties to nonlocal actors, purity movements, and uncommon ideas like liberation theology threatened once-shared tra-ditions and communi-ties. The local organization and economic and social power hierarchies that have maintained the dances, understandings of time, illness, and healing through which many people possess themselves seemed in danger.

Of course, traditional people are not isolated from national and trans-national networks. Some of the *costumbristas* and their forebears, like men all over the highlands, were involved in militias and earlier civil wars. In the 1950s these ties sometimes lashed them into the right-wing National Lib-eration Movement (MLN). This was the party that backed Colonel Castillo Armas in deposing President Arbenz and later became known as the death-squad party.[8] Unlike Joyabaj, which was mostly represented by ladinos in its dealings with the national political economy, neighboring San Bartolo is almost entirely K'iche', so it was always indigenous men who mediated be-tween state and community, the plantations and the *mozos* (their neighbors and kin). Matilde González describes how, in the mid-twentieth century, *los meros jefes del pueblo* (the real ones in charge) began to accumulate wealth as *contratistas* (labor contractors) and *enganchadores* (people who offer short-term loans as hooks, *enganches*, to be paid with labor on the coast). This wealth and these translocal ties, in turn, allowed them to buy or just take with im-punity land and to set up shops, thus accruing more wealth and power. Their comfortable positions were threatened by the efforts of local catechists to find ways to evade going to the coast, through, for example, improving local production and setting up credit and consumption cooperatives rather than relying on the usurious interest rates offered as *enganche*. To protect their interests, San Bartolo's leaders activated their ties to the army, becoming military commissioners and later Civil Patrol commanders, using that power to ruthlessly kill and expropriate during the war. They have maintained a brutal lockdown deep into the postwar and now have been "democratically" legitimated by winning in the mayoral elections. During and after the war they consistently identified NGOs, the CEH, Catholic priests, or anyone else who might question their power as "those from outside," "strangers," the very terms they deployed along with Pavlovian "mechanisms of horror" to describe the guerrilla. González says that although they are indigenous, the K'iche' leaders of San Bartolo assumed "ladino conceptions" that "los indios son para servir y obedecer, son para hacer trabajo gratis [Indians exist to serve and obey, they exist to perform labor for free]" (2002:343).

On the other hand, some ladinos assumed what we might call indigenous conceptions—that progress would mean equal rights and access to resources for all Guatemalans. Remijnse says that although indigenous and ladino relations in Joyabaj were often fraught, in the 1950s members of both ethnicities joined coalitions that supported either Arbenz's land reforms or the MLN—i.e., it was not a ladino versus indigenous divide. She says people remember "poor indigenous villagers were being manipulated and exploited by smart *caciques* like Rogélio and Próspero Ogáldez. . . . [The latter] paid the *sajorines* [priest de costumbre] to help him win the elections . . . to do their ceremonies so he would win" (2002:74–75). But the relation between *costumbristas* and the MLN was complex, lashing together networks, advancing interests, and translating borrowed forces. For example, links to ladinos controlling the Joyabaj municipality *did* benefit indigenous supporters of the MLN. Just as some villages, like Patzulá, became almost completely identified with Catholic Action and later the Christian Democrat political party (DC)—which in the late 1960s ran the first indigenous candidate, a man from Xeabaj, for Joyabaj mayor—other villages, like Xecnup, developed reputations as all MLN. Engagement in Catholic Action and national political parties crossed ethnic lines, connecting indigenous and ladino people through complex ties of interest, conviction, hope, fear, and long-term family and village histories.

Someone like Esperanza León is clearly indigenous—she wears hand-loomed indigenous clothing, speaks Maya-K'iche' almost exclusively, and is dependent on her little plot of corn (and now Juan's remittances) to eat. Yet her embrace of Catholic Action may appear to other indigenous people as a betrayal. To them she actually has another face—that of a modernizer threatening their millennial lifeworlds. Maury Hutcheson says that in nearby Xococ, Rabinal, also renowned for the violence carried out by its Civil Patrols, the conservatives

saw the guerrillas as unclean foreigners, *universitarios* who came to deceive them. They were particularly scandalized by the way the guerrillas valorized the image of liberated, pants-wearing women soldiers and otherwise advanced anti-traditional, egalitarian models of social organization and authority. Under the influence of the military they soon came to denounce the guerrillas as "demons who live inside the mountain," and to cloak their bloody, counter-insurgency operations with religious symbolism, "converting their massacres into human sacrifices destined to appease the *antepasados* and the spirits aggravated by the 'dirty war,' as they termed it, of the guerrillas, against the identity of the indigenous people." (2003:42)

"Under the influence of the military," parts of this horror-soaked narrative may have been articulated *après coup*, after the violence, but some people also reacted to what they saw as a threat by siding wholeheartedly with the army.

Another form of assumed identity—conversion to Protestantism—has occurred for at least one hundred years. It exploded, however, in the midst of the violence and during the first postwar. At the time, some dismissed this assumption of identity, like much conversion, as inauthentic, purely utilitarian. As head of state during the worst massacres, General Ríos Montt's vaunted Evangelical identity joined with on-the-ground experiences of Catholics being massacred while Protestants survived, suggesting that conversion was a sound survival strategy. (Yet in the Chupol area some of the biggest massacres were of Evangelicals, "who believed God would protect them from the military" [McAllister 2003:117].) Mind reading is more a sideshow stunt than stable hermeneutic, so it is hard to know if or why Evangelicals sided wholeheartedly with the state, but it certainly looked like betrayal to the radicalized Catholics, who often felt they were risking their lives for the progress of all. Doubling the *"costumbre* is evil" discourse of some members of Catholic Action, some Evangelicals denounced Catholics as devils and Communists. I've heard that the army encouraged this identification by dressing the Judas-figure, which is burned in some religious festivals, as a guerrilla. In this counterinsurgent but also multicausal transformation of the milieu, Catholic activists who had felt themselves to be (w)holy found themselves divided; seen as two-faced by some of their neighbors. Perhaps all these faces contributed to Joyabaj's renown for the ferocity of its Civil Patrols. The Xoye "are different . . . *fuerte, enojados, bravos*, strong, angry, out of control" said the priest from Zacualpa. The civil patrollers of Joyabaj carried out a number of massacres both within the Joyabaj municipality and elsewhere. Already divided communities now carry the blood memories of violent acts carried out against each other, but often both sides felt justified in their actions because they understood they were struggling against dispossession.

While in Zacualpa exhumations of the clandestine cemeteries resulting from these actions began in 1988, it took a landslide in August 1999 to force Joyabaj to face its past, albeit reluctantly. The landslide occurred only a couple of days after a lynching, so it took more than a week for word to be sent to state officials about the newly exposed mass grave. Remijnse emphasizes people's fear of stirring up trouble, of bringing back problems (2002:277). That fear, combined with the extensive paperwork involved, resulted in the official exhumation being postponed until January 2000. At that time a member of the Catholic Church's forensic anthropology team said, "There was little moral or practical support from the Joyabatecos." One of the few people who did help received threats and dropped out. Remijnse says that because no one came forward to tell where the bodies were, she was told that the team never uncovered the largest pit, "in which many more bodies were supposedly buried" (280). Not until July 2001 were the remains reburied in Joyabaj, and to this day there have been no other follow-ups. However, exhumations are occurring in the hamlets.

Manuel Hernández is from the southern hamlet of Los Llanos. He has been to the United States three times, and his English is pretty good. He spent one long, cold winter on an isolated sheep farm with a gringo, which helped his English a lot. He has enough savings from his time there that when his pickup truck was stolen in Guatemala City he was able to replace it without much difficulty. In 2006, making small talk while he taxied me around, I brought up the fiesta, a topic guaranteed to animate Xoye, and we spoke about the Baile de la Culebra and the death of the contractor. He suddenly said, "My father was killed. Sometime in 1982, '83. I was little. But he was murdered in the time of the war. The military killed him. It was very hard, very hard. I was too little to help much, and my mother had to be both mother and father. We all had to work. But two years ago we did an exhumation. We organized it, to find my father. There are a lot of holes (*fosos*) around here. They'll have to do a lot more." Because he is fluent in Spanish and K'iche', Hernández went around with the exhumation team, helping make lists of people who had lost family members. "Lots of people needed help," he said, "and there were *lots* of papers (*expedientes*)! Some people asked, 'Why are you doing this? What do you want?' Those responsible (*los hechores*), they were afraid. They were watching, watching us, all the time. But they aren't in control anymore. So they are afraid. They know we can take them in now if we want. But I am not going to seek justice. I have my father back and that's what really matters. If not, it's like a wound." I asked why he had decided not to seek justice. "There's no need," he answered. "They aren't so powerful anymore. I have my father, my life. My children know where their grandfather is. We lived in fear for so long. I remember as a child I was so afraid, all the time. With my mother, hiding in our house. But now they know that same fear. It hangs over them. Maybe other people will take them to be tried, but I know God will pay the *hechores*. Perhaps it is not for us to decide. Now, at least, they are afraid."

Faced with a similar choice, the people of Chupol, McAllister suggests, are confronted by a dilemma: Where do you turn to seek justice for those who are responsible? She was told, "People say we have the right to demand (*reclamar*). But who are we going to ask for our demands? Not the government, that's no good. Instead, we must demand things from God" (2003:359). In seeking redress from the state one risks being condemned for the past, being told you deserved it, you should have known better. Hernández seems content with the thought that *los hechores* are feeling afraid. McAllister says, however, that in Chupol, those who ask for more than that are transformed into "warring subjects [who] threaten their neighbor's ability to seek recourse with God. State violence, therefore, has been internalized as a division in the body of good people" (2003:359). Even as an exhumation closes one wound it may open another, dividing even tiny communities, making them two-faced.

Behind This Curtain, Ladies and Gentlemen,
We Have a Very Exotic Treat for You, a Real Maya *Bruja*!
Yes, a Mountain Witch with Secret Powers Beyond Your Wildest Dreams!
You Never Know What Juju She'll Do!

One of the people in the Joyabaj Grupo Maya mentioned by the *alcalde indígena* is Natalia Godoy. She was described by several people as the founder of the group and as a Mayan priestess. When I met her for the first time in July 2000 she was in her store on the main plaza, preparing the Indigenous Queen contest for the annual fair[9] and attending to the young ladina woman who had been chosen Queen of Sports.[10] Godoy was younger than I expected, pregnant, and a bit wary of us at first. She was very busy attending to her customers and what seemed to be a constant stream of people "seeing about something."

Godoy became a Maya in Costa Rica. She got involved with a group of Guatemalans there who had formed the Maya League and were studying esoteric literature, music, and social change. They were also connected to ORPA, Efraín Bámaca's group. During that time she began to suffer several of the illnesses that call for training as a diviner.[11] She says that a Dutch woman working for a European Union NGO helped her travel back and forth to Guatemala to apprentice herself to a daykeeper in Momostenango, Totonicapán. She was initiated and in the mid-1990s returned to Joyabaj.

Godoy and her young husband, who is K'iche' and was working as a peddler in Costa Rica when they met, lived with her parents until they could get their feet on the ground. She seems well respected and is involved in a number of projects to support Mayan cultural survival. But she is chafing at the gender attitudes of local indigenous leaders, including the *alcalde indígena*. She is also frustrated with her parents, who want her to concentrate on having more children and who constantly rib her husband about who "wears the pants" in their relationship. She has worked with the Rigoberta Menchú Foundation and with COPMAGUA, although she complains about the way the men there treated the women: "Ooh! I was so mad at what happened there!! They came and told us what to do and we just kicked the men out—we really got *brava* [bold, angry]! A meeting was called to form the committee for the women's forum. But they already had the list of women they wanted, who were all very young, very inexperienced, no training, *muy sumisas* [very pliant]. We said, 'Where did you get these names?' And they said, 'Please, stop making problems. The foreigners are going to come, and we just need to get the list to get the project going.' We refused. They invited me for other meetings but I couldn't go, and I pulled away after that." For awhile she was also working on a pan-Quiché project sponsored by USAID to increase voter turnout in indigenous villages. At some point the organizers just stopped coming around, and she didn't know why. Later she heard there were two sets of books being kept and that USAID had defunded the project.

Now she helps support her family with the store and works on a variety of local issues. She said, "The Maya Committee, we are facing a lot of obstacles. In a lot of ways I think it's because I'm a woman. I wonder why there are so many problems. They say I'm a *bruja* [a witch], that I'm not from here, that I'm a *manipulador* and just want to make money. I don't want anything to do with that—how could they think that?" Her parents are originally from another town, so although her family has lived in Joyabaj for decades and she dresses and identifies as Xoye she is seen as an outsider. Godoy's (b)identification as a Mayan and a woman is in turn complicated by her business success and the envy it seems to cause. Since I met her eight years ago, she and her husband have expanded their stores and other business dealings into several other towns.

Marcelo Arenas, a Xoye, has worked as a labor contractor in Joyabaj for a number of years and intermediates between the workers and the *finca* overseers on the South Coast. Arenas insists he is constantly agitating for better treatment, fairer wages, and an end to discrimination against indigenous workers. As in the *baile* in which indigenous men wear masks of Spaniards when they play the doomed (and revived) *contratista*, historically labor contractors have been "whiter," ladinos who are literate and Spanish speaking.

But as *indios* assumed the identity of *naturales*, as speakers of *dialecto* became bi- or trilingual and literate, as cooperatives, local credit associations, NGO- and state-support for community development began to take effect, some "browner" people moved into these positions. This *tránsito* accelerated with the violence in the early 1980s as indigenous people came down from the mountains and many ladinos fled to urban areas.

Andrés Gutiérrez is one of these newer indigenous contractors and also an Evangelical pastor. One day Liz Oglesby witnessed his labor recruitment rally for the Santa Ana sugar mill. With the permission of the mayor they set up a big flatbed truck right in the middle of Joyabaj with a huge speaker system and a live band. They had really powerful microphones, and the band was very good. Oglesby described the event as half Evangelical service and half a labor drive, and it completely drowned out the candidate for major who was speaking nearby. About five hundred people gathered to hear his message that just as the kingdom of heaven is open to both Catholics and Evangelicals so is the mill.[12] "Because the owners will be judged by God they will have to treat you right. The contract conditions are good, the wages and the food. You know me, and I know the family, and I know they will take care of you!" promised Gutiérrez, as his *caporales* (helpers) went through the crowd doubling people over and signing them up.

Gutiérrez has an impressive new house near the center of town that has verses from the Bible embedded in the exterior walls. Other K'iche' labor contractors also seem to be doing well. Some have diversified into such lucrative businesses in downtown Joyabaj as hotels, restaurants, cantinas, and pharmacies, and tool around in late-model SUVs. Some have expanded their traditional role of providing an *enganche* into loaning people money to pay *coyotes* (guides) to take them to the United States. Their pay from the volcano-like Herreras and others is miraculously increased by the interest they earn on these loans, 10 percent compounded monthly, and from foreclosing on people's land when they don't make it to the United States or when the new immigrant doesn't send money back. One such wealthy Xoye contractor, despite speaking little Spanish and being unable to read or write, ran for mayor on the FRG ticket. He lost but has served as a *concejal* (counselor) in the town hall. These men remind me of the contradictory trajectory of Fermín Gómez, who is a respected *aj q'ij*, or Mayan priest, has worked within the state for Mayan rights with COPMAGUA, and has served the interests of transnational capital by giving both an authentically indigenous and a supernatural thumbs-up to mining companies hoping to legitimate their exploitation of Guatemala's natural resources.

Arenas is a contractor, but to all appearances he's not well off, living in a humble house on the edge of town. If he is engaged in loan sharking, it seems to be on a very small scale. He has studied the peace accords and is angry at the state and the owners, who he thinks are not fulfilling the obligations they signed on for. He is becoming increasingly interested in his Mayan heritage. While he, Alfonso García, Natalia Godoy, and other members of the Grupo Maya maintain relations with the *cofradías* that organize the traditional *bailes*, they are not members and are not invited to perform. Instead, they tend to sponsor events like the *convite*, a masked dance associated in other towns with ladinos, but also with the merchant class. (The costumes are drawn from global popular culture and are quite expensive to rent. It was in a *convite* that Maury Hutcheson saw the Star Trek Borg, the very ones who insist that resistance is futile.)

I found out later that Arenas was not just saying he struggles for worker's interests because Oglesby and I asked about labor conditions. He is in fact two-faced, both an agent for the plantations and the local representative of the National Indigenous and Campesino Committee (CONIC), an implacable foe of the unjust power structure. Founded after a split in the CUC, in the past ten years CONIC has assumed the struggles for land reform, collective bargaining, and implementation of the peace treaty and against CAFTA and mining concessions to transnational companies (Velásquez Nimatuj 2005). These activities have led to multiple assumptions of identity: a CONIC activist told the sociologist Ligia González that he is struggling as a campesino but still thinking as a *jornalero*, meaning that as a CONIC activist he was conscious of his rights as a peasant, those who produce the wealth of the country, but he still assumed the identity of a dependent day laborer, afraid of the *finquero* (boss) and acting humble. González said that as she accompanied CONIC it was "amazing to see how people develop, how they change over time. Now this same guy says he wants to be a *vocero* [spokesperson] although he says the idea makes him panic." These are all struggles for possession and against the dispossessions of capitalist globalization. Several CONIC activists have been killed, and a number have received death threats.

In preparation for a large CONIC meeting in Joyabaj, Arenas went to a diviner to choose the most auspicious day for the event and hired a local *aj q'ij* (spiritual guide) to perform an opening ceremony. Working with the *aj q'ij* is new for him, and he said he felt a bit uncomfortable because he really didn't know what to do. But in general it went well, and he will definitely do it again. Like many people in CONIC, he increasingly identifies as Maya, and the possession of cultural rights is taking a more central place in their struggles for equity. Some ladino allies with whom CONIC has recently cut ties wonder if it is becoming too central. "They have essentialized their strategic essentialism," said a sympathetic but frustrated ladino observer.[13]

The doubleness or fluxion of assuming the Mayan identification—possessing it can mean dispossession and backwardness or progress and development—stems in part from the changing milieu, itself the site and stake of struggle. In the postwar period, possession of an immaterial thing, identification, has been increasingly lashed together with possession of more material goods: having enough food to eat, medicine, a more comfortable house, a few animals, a school uniform, a book or two. This, of course, was the end goal of movements for radical political change.

Humanoid Underground Dwellers! Masked Ninja-Like Warriors!
The Ever-Popular Rambo! The Spy Who (Wanted to) Love Me!
Only in the *Convite* Dance at Our Fiesta Do Creatures from Fantasy
and Reality Parade Together for Your Delight!

At the national level many Mayan cultural rights activists disavow their relation to the guerrilla. "Under the influence of the military" this is, in some ways, an assumed identity for activists in the wake of the scorched-earth violence. Especially in the first postwar (1985–96) those struggling for cultural rights or for any political space at all had to strongly disidentify with the guerrilla in order to survive. Calling oneself a Maya was meant to differentiate oneself from the *populares*. Many Maya, in the sense of urban activists, *had* come through the guerrilla movement and strategically essentialized when it seemed expedient to hide that face. As time goes by some are increasingly coming out, like the activist who told me, five years after I'd met him and in talking for the first time about this past, that in the guerrilla he was like Rambo.

Others who were involved, however, have strong critiques of the revolutionary movement as exclusionary, racist, and brutally violent (Bastos and Camus 2003, n.d.). In a "you're either with us or against us" phase the guerrillas did order people to kill their neighbors and even their own family members if they were not sufficiently supportive of the cause. McAllister says, "Despite their legitimation as revolutionary justice, these executions, Chupolenses note, could be motivated by behaviors ranging from being an actual military commissioner . . . to refusing to join the guerilla . . . [to] not understanding what was going on in the community and thus making an indiscreet public remark, or complaining about the rigors of organized existence." Even one of the main organizers admitted that the "*ajusticimientos* [executions] had gotten out of control, telling me the story of a man . . . who had to be restrained from murdering his own wife when she uttered a disparaging comment about the insurgent struggle" (2002:273). Some also remember that there were few indigenous commanders and that the people who did try to form an indigenous-led armed front were killed by other guerrillas. An army cassette played during months or years of reeducation reiterated to indigenous people that "they [ladino revolutionaries] provided the ideas, you provided the bodies." People might reiterate these ideas as their own because they've been doubled over, but they are also sincere—in part because the army *was* in the know. In turn, sometimes people on the ground were not.

Clandestinity is counter-counterinsurgency. It is also part of an articulatory practice, joining people in networks, sometimes without their even knowing it. As a response to violence and state terror, the vital importance of keeping secrets can make particular deaths—of spies (*orejas*), people who gave up names (*delataron*), those without the proper consciousness—seem to be "for life." Whether we think the war began in 1963, 1954, or far earlier, highland people had long known that to conceal a political agenda was the same as defending it (McAllister 2003:46). Thus, clandestinity is a means and an end. But it can also turn identi-ties into chains that pull one into the abyss, dragged by the weight of falling comrades. As such, it also disarticulates. It can divide those in the know from those who aren't, sowing suspicion, undermining trust. It reinforces verticalism and military forms of discipline as life and death practices, supplanting more drawn-out discussions, critical questioning, and the consensus-oriented interactions of political and social organizing (not that the Catholic Church or age-, ethnic-, and gender-segregated communities are not vertical). Clandestinity insinuates itself into already-raced and -gendered assumptions about who is educated and who naturally functions as the head, the hand, or the heart. When attacked, (b)identifications like catechist and CUC member, researcher and guerrilla contact, above- and underground get flattened into one, cutting connections held together by the two faces.

When the decision was made to fold the CUC and its unarmed political projects into the military structure of the EGP, many people didn't even know they were in the guerrillas. This is less because the organizations were trying to trick them into doing something against their will than because the milieu changed, and quickly. There was a sudden acceleration as church-based development projects, claims for land through the legal system, a family's desire to save a son from the army's forced recruitment, and non-violent protests—all ends and means of people like the Menchús and others who co-laborated with CUC —assumed another identity: enemy of the state, a state that responded with deadly force. Connections forged through earthquake relief work, Catholic Action seminars, and trade were cut off, people went underground, information stopped flowing, contacts were lost. This disarticulation was externally imposed as people were killed or disappeared and internally developed as mechanisms were created on the fly to try to save people and networks.[14]

"Risk culture" assumes that the people should have known. The state's brutality should have been calculable based on statistical tables establishing the regularity of certain events and calculations of probabilities (Ewald 1991). This assumes, however, that nothing new ever happens, and the end of war is always the same. Yet most accounts emphasize the absolute irregularity of the state's response, the improbable way it blasted the known world, changed time, ripped up the fabric of certainty. In turn, have we reckoned the state when we make it the main event at the fair? Is that fair to my claim that one is not enough, that instead we might interpret the means and ends of war as carnival-like, conjoining carnage and incarnation — of, by, from, and through?

Stoll may be right when he questions the stakes in, as he says, "dichotomizing participants into victims and victimizers. On one side is the army and its local allies, on the other hapless victims. Conveniently for the guerrillas, they remain at the margin. . . . Failing to ask . . . questions protects the left's assumptions from scrutiny" (1999:61). How do we scrutinize the "left's assumptions" yet, like the state's, Mayan, ladino, or any other assumptions, keep them under the sign of the Virgin of Asunción (de Tránsito)? Especially in the postwar, are these simultaneously fixed (a post), as some people remain wholeheartedly engaged, and yet also mobile (what moves across), as some assume new identi-ties that may look back and claim they were duped?

While accounting for 3 percent of the abuses examined in the CEH report, the guerrilla did kill and massacre in ways that are remembered and that resonate in comments like those made by Otilia Lux Cotí. Like the state but without its resources, the left was certainly not one. Not only was it composed of a number of organizations — some were never armed and there were guerrilla groups that never joined the Revolutionary Unity — but disagreements about strategy, fault, and whether and how to continue the struggle gave rise to massive splits, including one I didn't know about but that affected me in faraway Boston. It has also apologized, agreed to *asumir responsabilidad*, and tried to "exorcise its demons" (Hernández Pico 2005: 85–90).

On the one hand, Stoll and Lux Cotí remind us to be circumspect in questioning assumptions. On the other, it is incumbent upon us to remember genocide and an army partly in the know as we try to reckon with these histories. The vast majority of indigenous people and many of the ladinos who wholeheartedly supported the guerilla were murdered, died from exposure and starvation, or went into an exile they have not returned from.[15] They are not here to co-memorate with us. Too, habits of clandestinity die hard and should keep us humble before we make any assumption of being in the know. Even within families, many postwar children do not know of their parents' involvement. One effect has been that many younger Mayan adepts, especially those who matured in the later 1990s and have no personal memory of the war, have assumed (Three and One) the more culturalist identity, leading to increasing reification of a split between Maya and the popular sectors. This, in turn, has led to countercritiques that the Maya are all elites and urban professionals who are out of touch with the true experience of rural indigenous life, which consists of poverty, racism, and sometimes revolutionary consciousness.

These struggles and debates are essential components of the postwar-in-action as people argue and reckon, try to settle rewards and penalties, and measure possibilities for the future. At the Mayan Studies Conference where Lux Cotí denounced both the left and the right for being ladino and for killing Maya, she was answered by Juan Tinay, an indigenous man and leader of CONIC, who assumed a different identification. He said, "We are suffering constant attacks, from the ladinos and from the Maya. They try to discredit our efforts, they say we're manipulated. We are organized because of hunger, pain, exclusion, oppression at the hands of the state and powerful sectors. Brother Mayans, make this struggle your own! Our divisions are terrible! Some Maya do not invite certain people to their meetings because they say, 'They're not Maya, they're *popular*.' But . . . the Maya are not at the margin of the class war!"

When she told me the story of peeking out her window at the insurgents coming into Joyabaj, Doña Miguela seemed surprised that the guerrilla were all *naturales*, indigenous people, who came down from the mountain. But in the early days the revolutionary movement had a lot of support among both ladinos and indigenous people in Joyabaj. Reminjse says guerrilla visits to Joyabaj were frequent beginning in 1979, and a lot of political work went on in the more northern hamlets, like Patzulá [2002:92–95]. In 1978 Felipe Natareno, a partly indigenous Xoye on the Christian Democrat (DC) ticket, was elected mayor with strong progressive ladino support, displacing (as happened across the increasingly organized highlands) the decade-plus rule of the right-wing MLN and its Joyabaj representatives, the ladino Ogáldez family. The inauguration was joyous. Natareno was carried on the shoulders of his indigenous supporters, as the *alcalde indígena* traditionally was (Remijnse 2000:89). Natareno was open about his progressive program, and people now remember he had links to the not-yet-clandestine CUC. He says that when he started to receive death threats he was protected by EGP body-guards. But neighboring DC mayors began to be murdered, and when Father Villanueva was killed in July 1980 Natareno fled to the capital.

As the diocese shut down and many catechists left town, the municipal government and schools began to falter, and Alianza, a national NGO working since the earthquake on development issues, pulled out of Joyabaj. In addition to the fear engendered by murder, exile, army occupation, and the military's aerial bombardment of the area, people remember two actions that weakened revolutionary support, especially among the ladinos. One was the kidnapping of the fifteen-year-old-boy Fredy Ogáldez and the other was the murder of a well-liked ladino pharmacist. Twenty years later, however, there is some uncertainty about these events. Some people wonder if Ogáldez was kidnapped as revenge for his father's actions as mayor, if there really was a ransom note, or if, maybe, he wanted to join the guerrilla, and this was a spectacular way to shame his family for its strong military ties. ("We don't know what happened to that boy. He is still missing. From then until today.") Some people also wonder now if it really was the guerrilla who killed the pharmacist — maybe it was army people dressed up. They did that a lot in those days, people say, trying to divide people from the guerrilla.[16]

In Joyabaj, many of those who now identify publicly with the Grupo Maya were involved in the mass movements of the 1970s. In the late 1990s, when Natareno returned to Joyabaj, he became involved in the town's cultural revitalization efforts and is also a sponsor of the Baile de la Culebra. When he decided to run for mayor again it was with the URNG, and many Maya, including Natalia Godoy, threw themselves wholeheartedly into the campaigns. They have twice come in a strong second. Godoy says people didn't have a big problem with Natareno's left politics. As with many returnees, they understand that he left to save his life. But some still resent that, having fled, he didn't live through the worst of the violence or the horrors of the mop-up, especially civil patrolling.

A problem among many ladinos, however, is Natareno's association by ethnicity with the only other indigenous elected mayor, Juan Toj Solis, who won in 1990 on the DC ticket. Toj Solis was run out of office two years later on corruption charges, including selling off indigenous communal land. While several ladino mayors have been charged with corruption, at least two of whom were almost lynched, Godoy says many ladinos remember the *indígena* as the *engañador*, the thief and a cheat. Toj Solis has recently returned to public life, after spending a year in prison, and tried to join the Grupo Maya. He has been currying favor with the *alcalde indígena* and is seeking, according to Godoy, to wrest control of the fiesta's queen contest and other high profile events. "He says he's changed," she said. "He has been saved, now he's in the Evangelical church. He says he's not the same man he was before. But mostly he wants in on the *multicultural*. He's seen what we've done, what we've accomplished, how the people respect us. But he is only using the Maya, he's an *engañador*, the same as before."

Godoy is extremely enthusiastic about Natareno and his political platform. She campaigned very actively for him and the URNG, traveling all over the municipality. She worked closely with resettled former combatants in many of the hamlets and says she felt energized by these interactions but troubled by their attitudes toward the URNG: "They talk about deception, *desconsuelo* [grief], that they were *engañado*. They say, 'We didn't get anything from it.' They say, 'We gave our time, our youths, our money, our lives. We sacrificed and what do we have to show for it? We aren't even getting the reparations, none of the goods.'" Much of their discontent was directed toward the leadership. Gaspar Ilom / Rodrigo Asturias was sidelined at the culmination of treaty negotiations by the kidnapping for ransom of an elderly woman from one of the country's richest families. He and the EGP's Comandante Rolando Morán / Ricardo Ramírez have since passed away. Pablo Monsanto/Jorge Soto of the Fuerzas Armadas Rebeldes (Rebel Armed Forces, or FAR) has thrown in his lot with a party that also represents military genociders, a move seen as a major betrayal by the rank and file. He is rumored to have said he was tired of associating with losers. But the ex-combatants also feel *engañado* by the judicial system and the other democratic state agencies: "There is no one, nothing, taking care of us," they said to Godoy.

State and UN officials as well as URNG commanders concur that the demobilization was the least successful part of the peace processing. Differences in postwar lives reflect long-standing class and ethnic hierarchies. People from wealthier ladino and indigenous families had more resources to draw on in exile and had more to come home to after the accords were signed. But even for those with a material base, return is often terribly discombobulating. The child has grown, the dream has gone. Old school friends are doing well, often seemingly oblivious to the genocide that made their success possible, and former revolutionaries face bourgeois conundrums like having families to support on patchy resumés. The disorientation is often profound, and for those already dispossessed it's even harder. Many villagers, indigenous and ladino, lost not only years of schooling and job training that could be transferred to civilian life, but parts of their bodies and often their families, their houses, their land, and their livestock. Combatants who reported to demobilization centers in early 1997 were given some household goods and a little start-up money, but it didn't go far. If people accepted the amnesties offered in the early 1980s or were captured before the peace accords and survived they were usually classified as refugees, not combatants. They were allowed to have only one face. Only those under arms at the time of the accords received the goods and, perhaps more important, judging from the Ixil women mentioned above, the recognition of their status as agents in the war.

These sentiments have recently been sharpened by extremely emotional debates over who deserves and who will have access to state resources through the Programa Nacional de Resarcimiento (National Reparations Program, PNR). Its indigenous coordinator, Rosalina Tuyuc, was the founder of CONAVIGUA as an aboveground human rights group during the first postwar, and she served several terms in the Congress. After the accords, it became more generally known that the widows' group, like many of the organizations that arose from the violence, had ties to the revolution. Recently, however, Tuyuc has shocked many of her former companions by denying these ties, calling the guerrilla *engañadores*, and refusing to give goods and funds to former combatants. As one observer of the struggles over the PNR noted, "It's dangerous to have two faces. One can always turn on the other."[17]

I was unable to interview Tuyuc and can't do a mind-reading hermeneutic stunt to explain her shift in attitude. However, her stance was a major topic of conversation in 2006. A K'iche' man who has worked closely with her read her reactions as dating to an election early in the postwar when she thought she would be a vice presidential candidate but was passed over: "It's personal. She's very angry. It's about particular people in the organization, and that's justified. But I think she's also stopped seeing that the left and its ideas, analyses, possibilities are not the same as the people. They are limited and trying or not to do work. Pedro Ceto, Gaspar Ilom, Rolando Morán, whoever they are, they are not 'the left.'" Others were less understanding. A ladino ally on the reparations project said, "Rosalina is sick. Emotionally sick. You can't reason with her. It's been entering into this aspect of victims, victimhood. She's been there too long. It's been too much for her." Some vouched for her utter honesty and transparency. "With Rosalina it's 100 percent, guaranteed," said one Mayan activist. Others saw her as *comprado*, bought off, just trying to secure the money for her organization, her town, her family. "She was in the state too long. It's hard to swim in the muck without becoming dirty yourself. There's no vaccine against that," said a ladino URNG activist.

In Joyabaj Natalia Godoy had followed the issue closely. "It's horrible!" she said. "The PNR is a *vergüenza*—a total and terrible shame. They are only trying to get money for their own groups, their own people. It's terrible. They just keep us divided." I said, "And who is laughing?" She replied, "That's the worst! There's so much need, so much hope invested, people really trusted it! *Que verqüenza!*" So I told her a joke that was circulating in the capital. Two men are on the beach catching crabs. One of them has a bucket with a very secure lid so the crabs won't get out, but the other one's bucket is open. "Aren't you worried your crabs will escape?" asks the first man. The other replies, calmly, "Oh no, these are Guatemalan crabs. Whenever one tries to climb up the other ones pull it down." Godoy could barely stop laughing but admitted it was a painful joke.

On another of my visits Godoy told me she was heartened that more ex-combatants "are around, they are involved, doing more things, trying to find a way, creating their little businesses. But a lot of them really don't believe in the revolution anymore. I try to say if we could organize more, do the work with the bases like we used to do, there's a lot we could accomplish. Look at Bolivia, with what's his name? [Evo Morales]. He has taken over the energy and that is amazing! It's a huge step! And [Hugo] Chávez, there are lots of things that can be done."

Godoy has her own frustrations with the URNG. She first ran into trouble in Costa Rica when, unbeknownst to her, she was approached by a Guatemalan spy, a cute guy who had begun attending her university classes and was hanging around a lot. She was called into the office of the director, Dr. Nuilá, and warned to be careful with the man. Soon after, she said, ORPA pulled some strings with the Costa Rican foreign service and had the spy returned to Guatemala. However, when she started to date the man who is now her husband she lost the URNG's confidence completely. From one day to the next. Apparently, although he's Maya-K'iche', he dressed in the cowboy style popular in the western highlands, and that style looked military to her bosses. She was abruptly told one morning by the same Nuilá who claimed to have "never had any security problems among the indigenous people," that the locks had been changed, the computer codes reprogrammed, and her services were no long necessary. "At first I was very angry. How dare they question my loyalty after everything—after what I had sacrificed and abandoned? But I'm still true to the ideas, to the organizing." She was in luck because a local NGO, catching the quincentennial wave, was seeking to hire someone indigenous, and she got a new job right away. "It also paid three times as much" she said with great satisfaction.

Natalia Godoy seems to transit among identifications, a position that leads some to call her a *manipuladora*. One identity is her own, true self as opposed to the gender stereotype those around her are trying to impose. Another is her role as a Mayan activist and her expression of that, not through traditional dances, but through the *convite*, which is more identified with a class than with an ethnic position, and through the local queen contest, a complex expression of class, gender, and ethnicity. Finally, there is her conviction that possessing government power through the URNG political party (rather than the FRG, which wooed her) expresses her indigenous identity, while other Xoye and Maya saw the revolution as a threat to indigeneity. But now many of them are working together to create a first-rate fiesta.

> Do Aliens Walk among Us? Could You Sight One
> If It Were Right Next to You? Test Your Skill at Detection,
> Ladies and Gentlemen, Girls and Boys.
> Who Knows? Maybe We're All a Little Alien?

Late one afternoon in June 2006, I was walking through the outskirts of a majority Maya-Kaqchiquel town which is quite *adelantado* (advanced). The sky darkened, a rainy season downpour commenced, and the friend I was with yelled, "I have family near here, let's go!" In the back room of a nearby compound we found a man named Rigoberto and his two children nestled close against the dark and damp on a mattress laid on the floor. They were watching *Jurassic Park III* on television. As I walked in, Rigoberto said, "I know you, you're the Queen of the Lizards." I'd been IDed as this once before, twenty-one years ago to be exact, on my first trip to the Ixil area of northern Quiché, when a group of children connected my name to the alien invader from an early eighties television show called *V*. The television Diana looked human but was really a lizard with dastardly plans for humankind. I'd written about the incident to explore modernity and tradition and had presented it in Guatemala. Rigoberto couldn't remember where he had heard me give the talk, but the gringa as alien stuck in his head. As the children, rapt, watched giant reptiles menace humans on the tube, we talked. "The revolution came late to where I was," he said. "We were waiting for arms that never came." Later he said, "Things are bad now. I talk to my friends, and we realize we are looking back with nostalgia, with longing for when our war was against the state. It was clear who the enemy was. I'm only alive now because I knew my enemy well. We are still at war—but now it is a war against violence and you never know where to fight or who to fight against. Against delinquency? It's very different. Who is the enemy?"

Like modernity and tradition, state and people, Maya and ladino, I am imbricated in what I write about. Like the people I've described I also traverse the countryside with (at least) two faces. Like them, I wonder, who is the enemy? *Costumbrista* patrollers? Boys "from here," hungry and covered in mud? Leftists trying to figure out, on the fly, how to stay clandestine, get their hands on weapons, and accurately calculate risk and maybe a little less concerned with indigenous versus ladino casualties? The state? The people who deceived it? The people who represent it as Mayan activists or mayoral candidates? How does one fight the war between good and evil?

I have purposely made this midway chapter a bit confusing. Rather than pull a noncontact hermeneutic stunt and impose clear analytical categorizations I've tried to give a sense of what it feels like to talk to people in Joyabaj, its hamlets, and much of Guatemala. While I've carefully considered which sideshow attraction to lay next to the other, I wanted to share the sense of sensual overload, of blur and confusion, that I experience there—and that is mentioned in so much writing on postwar Guatemala but too often smoothed away. The past hovers close to the present, people's pronouns slip and slide. Sometimes it's fun; other times we shudder with horror or *vergüenza* (shame). Seeing like a state, one might think marginal places like Joyabaj were a mess, but that's not because the state is absent. Oh no, it's in these places. And, like rubber and glue, seeing from in the state, like Alberto Esquit's interlocutors, *it* is a mess, full of *engaño*, *espejismos*, manipulation, and ignorance.

This chapter's title is a carney-like attempt to lure you to read it (hey, it worked for Stoll!). But it's a con. No more than Columbus discovered America do anthropologists find two-faced people in untouched hinterlands. The very ideas of static highlands or duplicity as a "basic feature" are, instead, *produced* by movements—of colonial capitalism, ideas of progress, armies, Mayan revitalization, anthropology. The Two-Faced Indian was always already there, a figure of myth and legend, produced by the traversals of the state and transstate actors through labor regimes, counterinsurgency protocols, and epistemic fixes—the very same flows that brought me, the Lizard Queen, to Joyabaj.

In the *Tzul* dances indigenous men dress up like white people to play roles now held by brown men. Guerrillas are *naturales*, but the army is *puros patojos*. The left is ideas, analyses, possibilities, which are not the same as the people. Yet Rosalina Tuyuc and others are angry at specific individuals and distance themselves from the left. Others are also angry but instead want to draw closer, demanding recognition for being ex-combatants. In 1978 the popular movement was the elected mayor and controlled a bit of the state. In 2000 the same state accused of genocide against the Mayan people starts to looks pretty Maya, humble and *desenvuelta* but also most impressive, when Demetrio Cojtí appears onstage at a conference or when indigenous people representing the ALMG show up on a motorcycle. The state apologizes for its errors, but the army can still roll into town anytime; recently it opened fire on peaceful protesters. The state was the enemy, but now it's not so clear.

The Two-Faced Indian may be produced by these processes, but it is also an assumed identity, inhabited, painfully, by people I've met. People try to be good but often sense they've been *engañado* and have, perhaps unwittingly, deceived others and caused pain. The state, the church, the left, development, the army, among other apparently stable identities, are also understood to be two-faced, bamboozling, desirable, deceptive, and dangerous. A play of masks, a theater, they move about the countryside like a terrifying and alluring circus, often ventriloquizing their demands and promises through local people with identi-ties to them. They are in-human — out there and in here. Could the something extra in these duplicitous states be related to a double bind, to embodi/meant? That identities, like ideas or analyses, must be simultaneously embodied in the flesh (*carne*), yet also transcend the individual body? Carne-vale, farewell to flesh.

LOOK OUT! STEP RIGHT UP! PARANOIA AND OTHER ENTERTAINMEANTS

Pay no attention to the man behind the curtain!
The great and powerful Oz

Maybe I should start with the world that has made
conspiracy theory not only possible (and popular) but
ever present, unavoidable, pervasive, compulsive, fun,
frightening, and fascinating often to the point of a
paranoid-mystical urgency. . . . The networked world of
system and power . . . coupled with the suspicion that
someone is hiding the REAL behind the curtain. The
burgeoning new world order of starkly divided camps
where haves and have-nots have become, more simply
and efficiently and finally, winners and losers. This
couples with a desire for an Other order of a true US and
THEM coming from someplace outside our control. . . .
The sure knowledge (and experience) that everything is
interconnected and merging—a seduction, a dreaming,
a moving toward and within—coupled with the guilty
pang, the moment of terror when something whispers
in our ear that the inter-connectedness is all controlled
by a dark and monolithic Other and we are in it, no
exit. Kathleen Stewart

I'm rubber. You're glue. What you say to me bounces back
and sticks on you. Schoolyard taunt

In an episode of his 1990s television show *TVNation* Michael Moore visited
the leaders of the then-dreaded Michigan Militia, the most notorious of
a burgeoning national movement of right-wing, racist, anti-immigrant,
gun and Bible toting, mostly male reactionaries. Moore accompanied several Militia men to a small local carnival, where they rode the Tilt-a-Whirl,
tried their hand at the games of skill, and sampled the midway treats. When
Moore asked them about their lives, they told what are now familiar stories

of being laid off from good union jobs despite their hard work and loyalty to the company, and the slow loss, first of benefits, then of their homes, and finally of their wives and children. While not the language they use, the American Dream transforms into an *engaño*, in which their "expectations of modernity" are a con. Like Neo's first excursion with Morpheus, the layoffs allowed them a glimpse at a system that treated them like Coppertops®, batteries whose energies could be consumed until they were no longer needed. Unlike Neo, who initially resists but then links with the black man and his multicultural crewe, the men in Michigan organized a homoracial and -social militia.

Moore suggests these are the lumpen whose very real grief and loss have been articulated to a racialized nationalist project. They could be just as strongly lashed in to a more progressive network if lefties would get off their duffs and overcome their distaste for "white trash" and its "bad, sublime" popular culture. Perhaps deploying an art nearer to the masses, these men might see that behind their scapegoats, like people of color and liberal professors, is a bigger system that, in the name of (market) freedom, has chewed up their lives and hopes and spat them out. In the midst of the enticements of carnival Moore encourages them and us to explore "the actual forces that govern us behind what appears as reality" ("It's the economy, stupid!"). But he is also interested in the form these beliefs take, their excess.

In *Bowling for Columbine* Moore addresses another panic — this time about mass media, those "aberrant structures of technological promise raised by the horror or freak show"—the one that circulated in the wake of the school massacre in Littleton, Colorado. The insinuations of radio waves and television carrying the Goth-rock music of Marilyn Manson and other strangely gendered performers were seized on as the "transsubjective mechanism which regulated the process." What possessed them? asked a nation trying to reckon with boys opening fire, and many answered, popular culture. In this formulation the shooters assume the identities of "consuming youth" (Latham 2002). They lap up popular culture and then, perversely, devour the happy stasis of small-town white America. Like Nobel Savages these kids are two-faced: both dangerous and in danger. In turn, the boys are consumed by the media and their audiences, who find them alluring, exotic, and unsettling. Simultaneously, they are absorbed into long-standing assumptions of race, class, gender, and sexuality. Like the horror film's blurring of psycho killers and Final Girls, hybrid figures like vampires (dead yet undead) and cyborgs (machine yet organism), Latham finds, are often deployed in attempts to account for such in-human experiences. As such, "consuming youth" become avatars for the faraway and out-of-reach power of the state or capitalism and its simultaneous intimacy.

Carnivalesque tales of the Two-Faced Indian may perform similar hermeneutic stunts: ways to reckon the weird yet everyday experience of being acted on by an external force. In the *baile* men are doubled over in performances that try to represent the unrepresentable: of living as both yourself, an agent in the world, and as a debt, a tiny node in huge global networks of labor and capital exchange. Through these relations they are made in-human—a Coppertop®, an indispensable yet also expendable source of energy for those consuming networks.

Like Stoll's and Canby's description of Rigoberta Menchú as doll-like— manipulated like a puppet by the controlling left—stories of a great and powerful Oz-like state circulate like a drug in explanations of lynchings and other mass mobilizations (like descending to the coast or patrolling) that I explore in chapter 6. Evoking a sense of possession, peoples' stories parallel the painful images of inhabitation by Agent Smith from *The Matrix*. Whenever this immortal agent needs to be somewhere, it takes over some normal person's body. When the agent is "killed," it's the poor schlub's corpse left on the pavement. Carne-vale.

ACCOUNTING FOR IN-HUMAN STATES

Moore is intrigued by how a "networked world of system and power" may act on us, but he deconstructs the paranoid story that rock music possessed the boys at Columbine. "Why not bowling?" he asks, since that's what they did the morning of the shootings. But one explanation is not enough, and Moore proceeds to trace more convoluted assumptions of identity, traversing President Clinton's simultaneous bombing of Sudan in the midst of his sex scandal; homophobia and gender panic; racism; the National Rifle Association–Kmart nexus that makes guns and ammo cheap and easily available; and the military–industrial complex, which has a major outpost in Littleton and even in the home of one of the boys, whose father was career military.[1] Perhaps together and contingently they created the massacre.

The Michigan Militia and the Columbine boys are two cases of people taking up arms on a small scale, harking back to the militants in *Bamboozled* who gun down Mantan, and Sloane, who shoots Dela. Spike Lee and Michael Moore try to reckon or assess responsibility for these acts and link them, but do not reduce them, to larger-scale, more systemic violence. In chapter 5 I described some different postwar understandings of local violence. There, identification as two-faced was assumed to be a basic feature of indigeneity by some *and* assumed — taken on as an identity — by others. In chapter 6 I explore attempts to do what Moore and Lee did, trace complex, mediated, and sometimes carnivalesque connections to larger structures and their "hidden powers" and "clandestine apparatuses" (Peacock and Beltrán 2003) — like Dela's little autonomous bank. It *is* the economy, stupid, but that is not the only real face of the state. Even following President Dwight Eisenhower in pulling back the veil to reveal the military–industrial complex is not enough. Perhaps that's why attempts to understand it, "The State," are so often couched in terms of freaks, magic, du- and multi-plicity, (b)identifications. Perhaps that's why Moore supplemented his research on the Militia with carnival rides, why we might need to think our studied explanations (they're lumpen, it's neoliberalism) along with rumor, fantasy, excess, and the paranoia that lends such a frisson, an X-statis, to both the state and its others. This midway between chapters 5 and 6 divides and conjoins the Two-Faced Indian with the Duplicitous State because these identi-ties constantly intertwine.

Moore and Lee tell humor-laced but deadly serious tales about power as being overdetermined and multicausal and our grasp of it contingent and vulnerable to duping, bamboozlement, and amnesia (Moore's *Fahrenheit 9/11* references Ray Bradbury and the temperature, 451° F, at which books — print capitalism's memory — burn). Amorphous as it may seem, we are in a life-and-death struggle to counter power's counterinsurgency. To do so, as a sideshow attraction, I'll attempt some Jell-O wrestling with that Janus-faced freak: knowledge as both rational and conspiratorial, as fixing (*connaissance*) and transforming (*savoir*).

Now, some accusations of duping count and, like Stoll's, end up on the front page of the *New York Times*. Others are summarily dismissed as conspiracy theory, the loony left, unjustified paranoia, or *babosadas*,[2] accusations leveled at both Lee and Moore.[3] Perhaps similar interests were involved in revealing Menchú's "duplicity" — undermining her challenge to the system by suggesting she was paranoid in thinking the state, showing its military face, was out to get her, since the state, showing its INTA face, was happy to give her family land. Deeming something ludicrous or "conspiranoia" (West and Sanders 2003) is a powerful delegitimation device and allows the accuser to assume the identity of modern, rational, transparent, and nonduped. It is a weapon in the war of the cross and can be more powerful than silencing, which, to power's chagrin, can swerve into martyrdom.

The heroine of the horror movie *Candyman*, Helen, investigates the urban legends of Chicago's African American underclass. She herself laughs at the story and is determined to rationally explain the figure haunting Cabrini Green. She is laughed at in turn as she begins to buy the tale. Such legends constitute an emerging subcategory of folklore and circulate not only in cities, but in suburbs, exurbs, and rural areas (and now quite hastily through the Internet). Alligators in the sewers; Dobermans choking on a robber's severed finger (Brunvand 1986); fried chicken that sterilizes black men; a clothing line popular with African Americans that is owned by the Ku Klux Klan so that black consumption profits white supremacy (Coombe 1997, Turner 1993);[4] stolen kidneys; "AIDS clubs"; Satanists passing as tourists; detonation charges in place on 9/11 so the World Trade towers would fall after the CIA-trained hijackers hit them; a small group of monotheistic men in dark suits meeting regularly to plot world-changing events and . . . well, you can Google "conspiracy theory" for a whole lot more.

Activists and anthropologists tend to rebuke the laughers, those who would dismiss urban and rural legends as ludicrous, even as many of us would be hard-pressed to believe all the versions mentioned above. We tend to argue that, while couched in mythic language, these are situated knowledges, subaltern ways of knowing, legitimate articulations of "power revealed and concealed," working "in unpredictable and capricious ways" (West and Sanders 2003:7). Like Stewart, who describes the "suspicion that someone is hiding the REAL behind the curtain" (1999:13), West and Sanders call these "occult cosmologies:" "systems of belief in a world animated by secret, mysterious, and/or unseen powers [suggesting] . . . that reality is anything but 'transparent' . . . that power operates in two separate yet related realms, one visible, the other invisible; between these two realms, however, there exist causal links, meaning that invisible powers sometimes produce visible outcomes" (2003:6).[5] Similarly, Ranajit Guha (1983) sees rumor as an important modality of peasant insurrection, and Patricia Turner analyzes the truths about racism and poverty embedded in urban legends. George Marcus calls it "paranoia within reason"—an outgrowth of living in the modern world: "a time of saturation of descriptions, diagnoses, and analyses of social change . . . in which there [are] a number of equally comprehensive and plausible, yet apparently mutually exclusive, conceptions of the same events" (1999:4–5).

It's taken a mountain of Freedom of Information Act requests, but the terror at the existence and extent of the Counter Intelligence Program, or COINTELPRO, and related U.S. government surveillance, infiltration, rape, and murder of U.S. and global activists of various hues—from Fred Hampton to Orlando Letelier and Roni Moffit[6]—has been proven to be well founded rather than the easy superstitions of (how does one put this?) the less educated. In fact, it is historically grounded rather than baseless paranoia or proof of guilt to fear National Security Agency wiretaps and subpoenas of library records. Just as examining statistical data and coldly calculating risk, African American and Puerto Rican mothers are in the know when they teach their sons and daughters that there's something strange in the neighborhood — who you gonna call when 911 is both shield from and source of danger? While often inchoate or freakish, conspiracy theories are also, often, right on.

In the plot of *Candyman* and stories of gringa *robaniños* / child-snatchers, monstrous figures threaten wee ones. These are popular horror film scenarios, but Guatemala really is one of the largest per capita exporters of children for adoption. Too, the statistical mean (as in average) for life expectancy for those who remain can be mean (as in cruel). The REMHI and CEH reports make it clear that it was hardly paranoid for members of the Guatemalan left to believe that people were out to get them. It may actually be quite rational for a Guatemalan to circle the park three times, then get in a cab to make sure she or he is not being followed, and then use the pay phone in a bar to make a contact call, and to constantly wonder if even her or his best friends have two faces. Not for the downtrodden or the rebel is Anthony Giddens's blithe "confidence in the operation of institutions that people cannot directly monitor and control [that] is the lifeblood of modernity" (in West and Sanders 2003:11). Instead, this modern expectation is revealed as a dupe. Confidence transforms into its derivative: to be conned. And magically, through the analyses I am deploying here, the formerly gullible subaltern is transformed into the nonduped. Via something like double consciousness, they may be more in the know than anyone.

However, the "underclasses" — constantly anxious about their chickens and their children — are not the only ones constructing fabulous monsters to keep themselves on their toes. While racism, classism, sexism, and colonialism carry out the most violent and barbaric cuts on the bodies and souls of their Others, they also leave the very people we think are pulling the strings and manipulating our fears shaking in their shoes. In 1952, as plans to overthrow President Arbenz were being hatched, Richard Hofstadter wrote, "A feeling of persecution is central to the paranoid style, but whereas the clinically paranoid person perceives a world hostile and conspiratorial against him or herself, the spokesperson for the paranoid style finds it directed against a nation, a culture, a way of life whose fate affects not himself alone but millions of others. . . . His sense that his political passions are unselfish and patriotic, in fact, goes far to intensify his feeling of righteousness and his moral indignation" (in Marcus 1999:1). Moore and Lee and many others point to a special compulsion, with race as its node, within the general militarized paranoid-mysticism of the Cold War and New World Order. Like the

CEH genocide ruling, like the Smithsonian's sideshow of the evolution of "man," like Spike Lee's genealogy of minstrelsy, as the past actively impinges on the present, Moore insists on a certain primacy of racism that keeps people in power awake at night. In *Bowling for Columbine* he animates U.S. history via a storytelling bullet that links every meager move toward race equality in the United States with a spike in white people owning guns.

The fear mongering that Moore satirizes, linking raciological anxieties about swarthy foreigners with weapons of mass destruction to *Cops* chasing down black evildoers, to deadly African bees crossing your border, is a counterinsurgent "noncontact hermeneutic stunt" aimed at convincing the gullible masses of vast conspiracies out to get them. There are clearly think tanks, media cartels, PR firms, political parties, and nonhuman actants like the Fox TV slogan "Fair and Balanced" and the conservative commentator Anne Coulter's hairdo linked in what some have called "a vast right-wing conspiracy" (Brock 2002 is one who has *delatado*)[7] to produce and deploy these images. Yet those very images seem to double back to scare that very same "dark, monolithic Other," that "transsubjective agency" lurking out there. Few are immune to fear's seductive powers or resistant to the excess of the threat-response (Appadurai 2006, Robin 2004).

So, what is so simultaneously fun and frightening about the racialized Other that it exudes the exuberance of minstrelsy, bamboozlement, the terrifying charge of the Two-Faced Indian, or of the N-word and "the N-thing" that, as the comic Chris Rock jokes, terrifies not only palefaces but also blacks, and is a constant object of interest? A similar mythic creature leading the powerful to fear that throne and altar are at risk is the hydra. If you cut off its head, it grows back two more, it can shape shift and live underground for months at a time with no visible means of support and roams the world full of implacable hatred toward you. Linebaugh and Rediker suggest that many rulers use the story of the hydra, a many-headed beast born of Typhon, a tempest, and Echidna, half-woman, half-snake, as "an antithetical symbol of disorder and resistance, a powerful threat to the building of state, empire, and capitalism (2000:2). These rulers model themselves on Hercules, slayer of the Hydra, "to describe the difficulty of imposing order on increasingly global systems of labor. They variously designated dispossessed commoners, transported felons, indentured servants, religious radicals, pirates, urban labourers, soldiers, sailors, and African slaves as the numerous, everchanging heads of the monster. And the heads, though originally brought into productive combination by their Herculean rulers, soon developed among themselves new forms of cooperation against those rulers, from mutinies and strikes to riots and insurrections and revolution" (2000:3–4). (As Price [2004] suggests in *Threatening Anthropology* [a nice pun], even a small arm of the humanistic social sciences can take on hydra qualities.)

So, the poor schlubs forced to assume the identity of the N-word, Indian Giver, or two-faced anything—patroller with a face turned toward the people, Natalia Godoy as an ORPA member whose face was also turned toward a cute guy—seem to be intensely powerless: profiled by an inimical external power, their only refuge the flimsy screen of a second face. However, that moment of assumption also transforms an ordinary human into a freakish terror, so frightening that the most advanced weapons in the state's arsenal may not be enough to contain it. How could the great and powerful state be so skittish? Michael Taussig has assiduously traced the self-constituting other of the "consuming" cannibal who both desires the colonizer (for a tasty snack) and is consumed by the colonizer to fulfill their desire to be desired. "Hated and feared, objects to be despised but also of awe . . . they are . . . clearly objects of cultural creation" (1987:9) arising from a not-very-solid identity among those who seem to be in power (see also Ali 1993, Aretxaga 2000).

Kathleen Stewart describes the yearning to be nonduped embedded in conspiracy theory and its attendant desire for a clear-cut, unassumed identity: "The suspicion that someone is hiding the REAL behind the curtain . . . couples with a desire for an Other order of a true US and THEM" (1999:13). The thing is, when Dorothy's dog, Toto, pulls back the curtain, the THEM, the great and powerful Oz, is revealed as a timorous white man, not dark at all. He is a humbug—although with some tricks up his sleeve. The Guatemalan state in the 1970s was solid enough to preemptively tell the United States where exactly to put its aid when Jimmy Carter threatened to cut it off and then, basically, to get away with murder. But when we look closely, this government is not so fearsome—its soldiers were poorly trained, *puros patojos*; it has been "historically plagued by corruption, lacking in resources and without a stable or qualified civil service" (MINUGUA 2004:3). As one of their advisors later admitted, "The Army won the war but at the same time was ruined by internal corruption and personal ambitions" (Héctor Rosada in Hernández Pico 2005:35). Rather than "working very well by themselves" it took the torturing of thousands and murdering of over 250,000 people to get citizens to obey; it had no financial credit to speak of until the mid-1990s; and the excesses of counterinsurgency discredited any claim to represent rationality, modernity, or development.

Assuming the logic of fault (Ewald 1991), activists have pulled the curtain back, proving that what's really behind damage, loss, murder, and impunity are people with names, addresses, government-issued titles like colonel and president, and shaky alibis. They also show that the judicial face of the state, if pushed hard enough, may challenge the military face. Edgar Gutiérrez and others who have gone inside argue they chose to work within one part of the state to make other parts more accountable. These efforts, including court cases, apologies, monuments, and reparations, are reckonings and have led to assumptions of responsibility. There *was* a conspiracy. People in the state *did* make plans. Then they enlisted allies, raised funds, bought weapons, and carried out their plans. And then they tried to cover up with disappearances, clandestine cemeteries, displacement, murdered witnesses, forced collaboration, and memories of silence. Counternetworks have turned some of those monolithic powers into little people, silly people, greedy, barbarous and cruel[8] but nonetheless vulnerable, hiding in their houses.

As a political strategy and an act of interpretation this work of uncovering disperses an IT (no longer in the National Palace or the White House) into the individual faces of the authors of crimes. Foucault is similarly encouraging: "Perhaps the state . . . does not have this unity, this individuality, this rigorous functionality, nor, to speak frankly, this importance" (1991b:103). It's like that wonderful moment when Glinda the Good tells the Wicked Witch of the West to "fly away, you have no power here." Yet the state is also hated, feared, and an object of awe. Helen Mack, Jennifer Harbury, or Esperanza León may courageously hold it still for a moment in a courtroom or at the edge of an exhumation site, like Neo when he actually fights Agent Smith and sometimes wins. But in reel life Smith magically reintegrates himself, and in real life the "magical state" seems able to slip from its vulnerable face back into its great and powerful one. Foucault chides us for not yet cutting off the head of the king, but perhaps we already have and it's a hydra—not only Army Specialist Noél de Jesús Beteta and Colonel Julio Alpírez, but also every patroller, every soldier, every woman cooking for the men who rape her, and even every Maya showing up in a far-off hamlet to promote indigenous rights. But every collaborator is both himself or herself and the in-human Agent (Smith). Explicating the rational core of rumors is important but may not dispel their hallucinatory appeal. Dispersing the state may help us understand the complexities of the postwar-in-action but may not fully account for "the x that is in it more than it." In our Neo-like struggles to master kung fu and other self-defense techniques we need to feed optimism by unveiling the people behind the curtain, but the tripwires of our pessimism of the intellect remind us that it's a freak, a two-faced bamboozler.

entertain [ME. *entretinen* < OFr. *entretenir*, to maintain, hold together < (L. *inter*), between +*tenir* (L. *tenere*), to hold 1. to keep the interest of and give pleasure to; divert; amuse; 2. to give hospitality to; 3. to allow oneself to think about; have in mind; consider [to *entertain* an idea]

amuse [Fr. *amuser* < a (agout) at + OFr. *muser*, to stare fixedly] 1. to keep pleasantly or enjoyably occupied or interested; 2. to engage or distract the attention of; *SYN.* — **entertain** implies planned amusement or diversion.

The state seems to simultaneously hold us together and divert us: to say, "Look! Here's the main attraction!" and "Pay no attention. Move along. There's nothing happening here." Less a state than an X-stasis, it over-whelms, like Walter Benjamin's phantasmagoria of the commodity. Anti-dote? Visiting the arcade for both enjoyment and analysis. Moore visits a local fair, where he and the displaced Militia men are both entertained and allow themselves to think. The next three chapters explore the state as dis-traction and the countermilitary hermeneutic that stares fixedly, struggling to discern interests at work and to make perpetrators assume responsibility. We'll struggle with the question of how planned such amusement (and ter-ror) is, and why it's like glue—as both its accusations of two-facedness bounce back and stick to it, but as it also enter-tains, sticks stuff together. We should remember that everyday experiences of the state may be like the carnival coming to town. Blessed souls living outside totalizing institutions like prisons can mostly go about as if the state weren't there. It's easy to ignore how deeply regulated our lives are by state functioning. However, there are times when boom! it suddenly arrives (via the "Hey, you" of the police, a jury summons, being called to war) and it is all engulfing, terrifying, murderous, yet sometimes full of promise. Sideshows are also like the state in that the experience is often deathly boring. "I want to be bamboozled but I'm always disappointed," said one fairgoer (Marianne Ferme, pers. comm.). It means long lines and sharp disillusionment in the failure of its awesome promises, in discovering the banality behind the carney's pitch. But it may be the only game in town, so back we go.

Dorothy Gale has been our fellow traveler through our midway journey-ings, in part because of the sideshow frame to her tale. The Wizard, the hum-bug who sets her off on her journey and greets her when she arrives home in the end, is a carnival performer, and the Witch and the rest of the main characters are all two-faced. But more important, it is only through *travers-ing* Oz that Dorothy and the other characters assume their identity. And it only works because she's bamboozled. Dorothy could have clicked her Ruby Slippers right there in Munchkinland, but she had to believe in the ruses of the Wizard and the Witch in order for her to assume her identity and for her traversals of Oz to have their effect. So let's keep moving.

Chapter Six

HIDDEN POWERS, DUPLICITOUS STATE/S

This paradox of inadequacy and indispensability has robbed the state of its naturalness. Thomas Blom Hansen and Finn Stepputat

How to construct development alternatives where "*we are not allowed to talk, only endure*"? How to speak of democracy where power relations rest on a prolonged history of "offences" and violations of citizens' and human rights, where military indoctrination and responsibilities permeated the ideas and lifeways of those who administer the town and its projects? How to imagine processes of local development that strengthen creative freedom for women, men, children, young people and elders, if we do not understand the depth of the destruction caused by the war, not only for the victims, but also the victimizers? . . . How to measure the gulf between the discourse of decentralization, local power and democracy, without taking into account the apprenticeship in military authoritarianism experienced by every boy who one day was *grabbed for the base* and/or was forcibly integrated into the PAC and was trained to persecute an internal enemy that found refuge in his community and in the intimacy of his own family? How to transcend the discourse of "peace and development" if there is no in-depth research, no serious reflection on the damage that the counterinsurgency strategy of security and development created in ways of understanding the world, life, and relations in all those places that were so highly militarized during the conflict? Matilde González (italics indicate her direct quotes from interviews in San Bartolo Jocotenango)

The state of nature and the state of exception are nothing but two sides of a single topological process in which what was presupposed as external (the state of nature)

now reappears, as in a Möbius strip or a Leyden jar, in the inside (as state of exception), and the sovereign power is this very impossibility of distinguishing between outside and inside, nature and exception, *physis* and *nomos*. The state of exception is thus not so much a spatiotemporal suspension as a complex topological figure in which not only the exception and the rule but also the state of nature and law, outside and inside, pass through one another. It is precisely this topological zone of indistinction, which had to remain hidden from the eyes of justice, that we must try to fix under our gaze.

Giorgio Agamben

(SIDE)SHOWGIRLS OR AFFLICTIONS?

In June 1999 an editorial cartoon called "No Todas las Plagas" (Not All the Afflictions) promised a "great spectacle" with "the participation of international stars." It portrayed Guatemalan NGOs as bodacious showgirls arrayed for the viewer's pleasure. At the top of the staircase is the UN Mission (MINUGUA) followed by Peace Brigades International (PBI) and Coordinadora de Organizaciones del Pueblo Maya de Guatemala (COPMAGUA), the Mayan organization formed by the state to oversee implementation of the Peace Accord on Indigenous Identity. The curtains are festooned with the names of groups, many of them Maya, which receive funding from the Guatemalan or other state/s, represented by male dancers carrying the sign "friendly countries concerned with democratic processes."

Copies of the cartoon were circulated by COPMAGUA with the attached letter: "Friends, This publication constitutes a direct attack, on the part of conservative sectors, who are working to disrupt the development of our work. It also clearly supports the policy of taxing NGOs. Because of this we must respond, taking care to talk reasonably, not from the liver" (in anger).

Published at a time when locust and rat infestations (*plagas*) were threatening various areas of the country, the cartoon suggests that these NGOs are also noxious plagues or calamities, *disguised* as attractive people promising a good time (troping Bolívar's warning about the rhetoric of freedom hiding the "plague"). Festooning the curtains with the names of many Mayan organizations also suggests that this is a cover—that readers should take care not to be cheated or tricked by these bamboozling Indians who are hiding outside intervention. It is intriguing that the UN is the queen showgirl since

"No todas las plagas," Not all the infestations are rats and locusts.
Siglo XXI, June 13, 1999. Dick Smith. Used with kind permission.

the Guatemalan state is a member. Grupo de Apoyo Mutuo (GAM), Familiares de Detenidos y Desaparecidos de Guatemala (FAMDEGUA), and Centro de Acción Legal en Derechos Humanos (CALDH) are Guatemalan civil society organizations, and Amnesty International (AI) and PBI are international groups monitoring human rights violations,[1] but COPMAGUA was part of the state—receiving state funding, although this was mainly funneled foreign aid.

The cartoon warns that Guatemala is in danger of being dispossessed from both within and without by shifty entities hiding their nefarious intentions. It appears to encourage the state to be more two-faced. If it is supposed to penetrate the inside of the nation to bring modernity and rationality, it should also be a defensive shield to protect that nation from penetration by an *other* state, which, the cartoon implies, may sneak in under cover of an "N"GO. In this, it evokes the Möbius strip, Klein bottle, or Leyden jar, oddities that are sideshow-ready since their insides are also their outsides. A certain masculinized nationalism infuses the cartoon—as it does many critiques of the Maya, the left, gender activists, and human rights organizations — with anxieties about being opened up, acted on, mimicking horror film themes. COPMAGUA, one of the organizations targeted by the cartoon, also warns of bamboozlement: "We must respond, taking care to talk reasonably, not from the liver." They also seem to fear being acted on and through by something coming from outside (the cartoon) *and* from inside (one's liver, which makes one speak without thinking, saying things one might later regret).

To me, the cartoon suggests anxieties similar to those expressed by the Michigan Militia men, a groping consciousness of "invisible powers sometimes produc[ing] visible outcomes (West and Sanders 2003:6). This chapter explores attempts to pull back the curtain on the faces that seem to lie behind and act on the state without denying its hallucinatory quality. Alluring and terrifying, the state might also be figured as "consuming" (Latham 2002), as it extracts and devours. It is dangerous, and paranoia is not an irrational response, yet it, too, is in danger. Powerful, working like a drug on the weak minds of its people, it is simultaneously weak, subjected to other powers, including, sometimes, its own subjects.[2]

Thus the indigenous become like rubber as the two-faced stereotype bounces off, and the state is like glue in the sense that the idea that it is duplicitous sticks fast. This chapter entertains (considers and tries to hold together) various reckonings of the state as two-faced. We'll stroll through midways between politico-military (Schirmer 1998:258), political-economy, non-governmental, and inter-state and keep an eye on conspiracy theories about hidden powers, those "shadows of war" (Nordstrom 2006) that blur law and crime and are vital actors in and beyond the postwar Guatemalan state.

Engaging the counterinsurgency "zone of indistinction," Agamben calls for a fixed gaze (a/muse/meant) seeking what remains "hidden from the eyes of justice" (1998:37). The Guatemalan historian Matilde González asks how to construct alternatives, speak of democracy, and imagine processes of local development while reflecting on the damage done by the war and accounting for the depths of the military state's authoritarianism (2002:454). I do not see through "the eyes of justice," but I try to respond to the double demand of such calls — double in desiring a true US and THEM but also acknowledging mobile assumptions of identity. Harm may be done but not always with a plan. To do this, I seriously reflect on *engaño* "dela" (of, by, and through) duplicitous states. The question is, who is to *asumir responsabilidad* when incarnated bamboozlers are only one of its faces?

Discussions about whether the state is strong or weak take up a lot of activists' time (see also Sluka 2000:30), and the powerful state acting on gullible natives appears in urban and rural legends circulating through postwar Guatemala. In 1990 during the first postwar, when the patrols were *forcivoluntarias*, McAllister recounts that several men were killed in a Chupol hamlet for refusing to patrol. A survivor of the attack got help from a U.S. nun, Barbara Ford, who called in a delegation, including institutions appearing in the "Afflictions" cartoon like GAM and Witness for Peace, the government's Human Rights Ombudsman Office, and the national press.[3] Hundreds of patrollers chased them back to their cars, throwing stones and wounding twenty people. Witnesses said the army told the patrollers that members of GAM were guerrillas and should be killed. They also said that "the army also gave the patrollers a pill that 'made them drunk and their faces red'" (McAllister 2003:300). This story recalls the many rumors about drugs used by the army to turn young recruits into killing machines. How else could nice indigenous kids do what they did? The state acts on the patrols, and they, representing it, seem quite strong, unafraid of the internationalists or the press. But isn't the ombudsman also the state, cutting a not-so-dashing figure as he runs for his life?

In 1995 a man from Xecnup, Joyabaj, went to MINUGUA to denounce that after two years of harassment by the local patrol, his father and a friend had been assassinated. In January 1996 the Interior Ministry issued a warrant for the arrest of the patrollers, but the auxiliary mayor was too afraid to carry it out. When National Police were called on, they said they had no money, no vehicles to get up the mountain, and were also afraid. When MINUGUA visited they were told that they would be killed if they tried to arrest anyone, and when they complained to the military base in Santa Cruz the commander replied, "The [Military] Zone does not have jurisdiction or the competence to start an investigation into these allegations, because in Guatemala we have a perfect separation of power" (Reminjse 2002:216).

Is the postwar state relatively weak vis-à-vis the demands of its subjects, as mayors, police, the president (see below), and even the UN cede to a few armed villagers? Or is it two-faced, its "perfect separation of power" a useful ruse because one face has a plan—deploying the patrollers (and the discourse of two powers) for its own ends? Similar questions were raised in June 2002, when thousands of Ex-PAC took over the department of Peten, seizing the airport, roads, tourists, and the Mayan ruins of Tikal and demanding compensation for their service to the state. Represented by Edgar Gutiérrez, the FRG government agreed to negotiate and was immediately inundated with similar demands from Ex-PAC around the country. They continue to periodically take over highways and once even occupied downtown Guatemala City in their bid for restitution. The alacrity of the state response and the Ex-PAC alliance with the army veteran's group, the Asociación de Veteranos Militares de Guatemala (AVEMILGUA), led to suspicions that while the mobilization claimed to be antigovernment, perhaps Ríos Montt's party had produced it to cover up its use of state monies to buy votes in the upcoming elections. Thus the hundreds of thousands of primarily indigenous people turning out for the demonstrations were duped, bought off. The patrollers, in turn, are accused of duplicity—they are not really victims of the war but profit maximizers, their ranks full of people too young to have patrolled. The Ex-PAC is a movement that is not one. Composed of at least three subdivisions, many rank and file accuse their leaders of manipulating them and decry the state as duplicitous, making promises it never keeps, in part because it is two-faced—the executive promises, the judicial denies.

Around Joyabaj the Civil Patrol is remembered as barbaric, when it wasn't just corrupt, blackmailing, and demanding bribes, and it is still very powerful. A Xoye told Simone Remijnse, "When I see them in the street I never discuss anything important and I always have a smile on my face" (2001:465). But they are also remembered as keepers of order and security. After a lynching in Zacualpa in 1999 some called for their reinstatement: "That way our communities would be clean and under control," said a villager (in Remijnse 2001:467).[4]

Method or Madness?

Postwar lynchings have also been explained as the actions of state-backed provocateurs manipulating highland people, even as the excess violence challenges state legitimacy. In the spring of 2000 a tourist from Japan was beaten to death by a mob, and a Guatemalan bus driver serving as tour guide was burned alive in Todos Santos, Huehuetenango. On a video of the incident, one can see, among the many people delivering blows, an elderly indigenous woman repeatedly hitting the man with the wooden shuttle of her backstrap loom. As in the near-murder of June Weinstock on suspicion of being a baby-snatcher in an indigenous town in 1994, the state was blamed, this time for spreading rumors via public school teachers and a radio broadcast speech by the departmental governor that devil worshipers were targeting the region for proselytizing (Barrera n.d., Burrell 2000, Gutiérrez and Kobrak 2001). Here the state looks exactly like the conspiracy theorists imagine it to be: a thing of immense power, able to magically induce hundreds of men, women, and children to act, controlling them like a sideshow ventriloquist manipulates the dummy.

In another case, the manipulation seems as total but more mundane. McAllister writes that on July 8, 2000, in Xalbaquiej Chichicastenango, where a particularly brutal patrol commander dominated, "eight men, six from one family, were burnt to death while two hundred people watched and ate snack food. Later investigations revealed that the lynched men had previously informed the Commission of Historical Clarification of human rights abuses committed by the ringleaders in the lynching, former patrollers. In turn, these ringleaders had close contacts with the secretary of the municipality, then controlled by Ríos Montt's Guatemalan Republican Front [FRG], who turned out to be a former high-level army officer." The state both acts on these men and is at their mercy. Afterward President Alfonso Portillo was compelled to go to Chichicastenango to meet with the patrol leaders. He supposedly said, "'Come on, boys, you're making the party look bad,' while they told him that if the authorities tried to do anything about it 'four thousand armed people would march on Chichi'" (McAllister 2003:327).

McAllister says, "Chupolenses cannot set fire to the government, even if they might wish to" (2003:328), but throughout the highlands government officials have been lynched or have narrowly escaped their subjects' wrath. In Joyabaj in spring 2006 a lynch mob of both indigenous and ladino citizens went after the ladino FRG mayor, who fled for his life. Everyone agreed that he was intensely corrupt, roundly hated, and unable to calm concerns about people's access to clean water. However, some said the mob had lent themselves (se prestaron) to internal divisions in the town hall. A ladino Xoye said, "His own council went up into the aldeas [outlying hamlets] and told the people he was going to sell the town. The whole town! And they believed it and came down!" The mayor returned several weeks later with carloads of National Police in tow, and, because people thought he was chastened, he was allowed to resume his duties. Here, in the form of police, the state shows some strength, but its other, elected face seems rather vulnerable.

State weakness, in fact, is often used to justify lynchings as "popular justice" (Mendoza and Torres-Riva 2003). Duplicity is its basic feature since the state claims to be the law but cannot (or does not) uphold it. Since 1996 there have been a number of lynchings in Joyabaj and its hamlets, and the victims have been Guatemalan men, often indigenous, accused of robbery or even murder. McAllister says that elaq'om, K'iche' for "thief," has "wider semantic connotations than in Spanish or English" (2003:325). It encompasses both stealing and murder and is considered by many highland residents to be the worst problem they face. Circulating throughout Guatemala are stories of thieves being caught red-handed and taken to the police or justice of the peace, only to be set free, often set on revenge against those who turned to the law for help. "Chupolenses often wonder aloud if the government in fact exists to serve thieves' needs rather than their own; the government's failure to address stealing means it has in effect stolen the law, making it the head of a thieving body" (McAllister 2003:326). In Joyabaj, precisely because of the often-lamented rule of impunity, i.e., *because* the state refused to move against them, local men and women say they have to take matters into their own hands. They have tortured people to get information on other gang members and hanged one group of reputed murderers in the central square of a hamlet.

A ladino man who was born and raised in Guatemala City after his Xoye parents moved there in the 1960s brought his whole family back to Joyabaj in 2005. "The crime in the city is just too much," he said. "We can't raise our children there. The gangs charge incredible 'taxes.' We're afraid to ride the buses. But we don't worry about that here. Thieves know the Indians will lynch them so it's much more tranquil."[5] People express a mix of emotions about lynchings. After a group of supposed robbers were killed on the road to San Martín Jilotepeque in early 2006 some people expressed satisfaction, saying things had gotten more *tranquilo*. Others, horrified, thought the wrong people were killed. Some proudly view these acts, including running the mayor out of town, as defense of their sovereignty. McAllister says that when Chupolenses are asked what to do about thieves "everyone promptly answered, 'Burn them!' although most would laugh to show me they were joking" (2003:326). Rachel Seider says that Q'eqchis in Alta Verapaz told her they keep gasoline under their beds in case they are called up for a sudden lynching. I am sometimes teased by friends in Joyabaj who threaten to "get the gasoline," and like most gringas in the wake of the Weinstock *robaniños* attack, I am extremely circumspect with children.

While the recent returnee felt safer as indigenous lynch mobs take over government responsibilities of capturing, sentencing, and punishing supposed criminals, other representations of these incidents reinscribe the Two-Faced Indian as threat, endangering the state. In cartoons about the trial of the Todosanteros accused of murdering the Japanese tourist and Guatemalan guide, the Maya are as mysterious and foreign as the Asians. Their languages equally unintelligible, they staunchly resist the law's faltering implementation of rationality and order. Other commentary suggests

"Lynchings: Things remain confused." The Japanese and Todos Santos man are "speaking" gibberish. The judge says, "What?" *Prensa Libre*, May 5, 2000. Jota Ce. Used with kind permission.

that in lynchings a primeval indigenous tradition of human sacrifice makes a tiger's leap out of the past to act on modern-day Maya (like Menchú's "subversive" blood type). This idea has been reinforced for some by Mel Gibson's big budget horror film *Apocalipto* (which is used in history classes in Joyabaj's high school).

But this stereotype of the bloodthirsty Indian becomes famillionaire if the violence is simultaneously read as a product of the modern state: induced by radio and other communication systems first tried out in vaudeville; by men assuming the counterinsurgent identities of patrollers; by the radicalizing effects of free trade, which make the already devastated rural economy even more precarious; and by the frustrated assumptions of what modern states should do but in postwar neoliberalism don't (Velasquez Nimatuj 2005). An army commander refuses to *asumir* responsibility because "in Guatemala there is a "perfect separation of powers," yet two is clearly too many. Conspiratorially we ask, *Cui bono?* Who benefits from democracy looking weak, ineffective, a dupe? Jennifer Schirmer reminds us of General Gramajo's reversing of Clausewitz: "Politics must be the continuation of war" (1998:1) and warns that democracy is part of the war machine as civilians become responsible for the human rights violations and democratic failures caused by the military (262). But is one enough?

Magic or Money Making the World Go Round?

Rural legends about patrollers on drugs or possessed by ancient rites of human sacrifice are stories about what mediates between unfleshy and incarnated faces, about the magic of the state. That magic may also arise from another pair of faces: political and economic. In Argentina a popular saying attributes this magic to a deity: "God puts right at night the mess the Argentines make by day" (Naipaul 1981:124). For Venezuela Fernando Coronil argues that the petrostate appears magical through the alchemy of rent capital, amnesia, and doubleness: "Venezuela was seen as having two bodies, a political body made up of its citizens and a natural body made up of its rich subsoil. By condensing within itself the multiple powers dispersed throughout the nation's two bodies, the state appeared as a single agent endowed with the magical power to remake the nation" (1997:4).

Guatemala's political-economic magic is less potent. Mountainous, in Quiché only 10 percent of the land is arable—her "natural body's" wealth is primarily accumulated by brutally extracting agroexport products through the sinews and muscles of the population—itself composed of two bodies: criollo/mestizo and indigenous (itself two-faced).[6] Although not profitable compared to Venezuela's, Guatemala's potential mineral wealth, as Luis Solano has recently shown, is an important motor for counterinsurgency and the foci of brutal interelite competition. Like the transnational flows that have historically bound sweetness, caffeine, and power (Oglesby 2002, Wilkinson 2002), Solano says, "petroleum and mining are most appropriately understood as political networks that have defined the course of the State and of the economy" (2005:10). Marta Casaus Arzú's *Linage y Racismo* (Lineage and Racism) (1992) complements our understanding of state, economy, and one of the nation's two bodies by emphasizing racism's role, against both indigenous and mixed-race ladinos, in (re)producing Guatemala's tiny, supposedly white oligarchy. These books list names and chart kin and other connections, making them vital companions to the naming work of war monuments, REMHI, and Ricardo Falla's *Massacres in the Jungle* (1992).

The imbrication of class, kinship, and ethnicity in a primarily extractive economy has produced one of the most unequal divisions of wealth and one of the most retrograde upper castes in Latin America. Guatemala ranks 117 out of 175 countries in the UN Development Programme Human Development Index (PNUD 2005). Accustomed, magically, to practically free labor and little personal investment in infrastructure, the Guatemalan elites currently pay one of the lowest tax rates in the world—barely 8 percent of GDP. Although the peace accords mandated an increase to 12 percent by 2000, this goal remains unachieved. Susanne Jonas says the stance of the elites' public face, the Coordinating Committee of Agricultural, Commercial, Industrial and Financial Associations (CACIF), is, "We produce the wealth for Guatemala, so why should we have to pay taxes?" (2000:175). They even dismay their allies in genocide, as the military periodically rages at their refusal to pay for the army's services. "We put in the bodies, they put in the ideology — but not the cash," might express their frustrations. Allies in global finance find them similarly irritating. Not only the peace accords but also lending agreements with entities like the IMF stipulate an increase in taxes to cover human needs, yet a Guatemalan journalist recounts seeing an IMF officer literally begging the Finance Ministry to increase the tax base. "It was really pretty pathetic," he said. The Tax Administration Superintendancy (SAT), created in 1998 to cut evasion and otherwise increase revenue in compliance with the peace accords, has not "taken the bull by the horns," Hernández Pico says. No structural changes have been made to the tax system, and when a minor reform was proposed in 2001 CACIF, "business' shock troops" accused the government of "fiscal terrorism," and it immediately backed down (Hernández Pico 2005:374–76, see also Jonas 2000:167–86). SAT has not gone after the real daddy-owes and has itself been pillaged by intense corruption — at least one former director is in jail. Two-faced, accountability itself becomes a screen for stealing.

If the state represents the interests of the elites, it looks strong, making big bullies like the army and international finance into wimps, moving them practically to tears. But in the postwar it also claims to represent the people who need schools, roads, health care, and security (so the gangs don't drive them out of the city), and there it looks pretty pathetic, unable to stand up to this tiny minority of Guatemalans. Elites and elite wannabes in government positions drain the state of resources and thus of legitimacy until it looks like the anemic victim of vampire attacks, hardly a strong defender against afflictions.[7] It is so incompetent and corrupt that many progressives, the very people calling for a strong state and the end of war via compliance with the peace accords, themselves resist the means — unwilling to feed the beast of corruption with their taxes (Hernández Pico 2005:378, Matt Creelman, pers. comm.).

However, while electoral democracy may look like a dupe, a mask hiding the same old economic and military powers doing whatever they want, the fact is that the postwar is not the same as the war or the prewar. Those powers now have to struggle to win their places at the trough, working through parties, winning some votes, and making some compromises.

Of course, such elites still might be getting indigenous people to do their work for them. The Mayan anthropologist Dr. Victor Montejo recounts his experience of being convinced to run for Congress on the Gran Alianza Nacional (GANA) ticket because he admired its vice presidential candidate, Ricardo Stein, a former Jesuit and a peace accord negotiator. When they won, to his surprise, people he'd never seen before stepped in and started wrangling about who would get what ministry, what position. He realized these were "the money people, who had been behind the scenes all the time. I felt *defraudado*," he said, "although it was an important learning experience."[8] He served in the Congress but ended up switching parties.

While "the money people" seem great and powerful, a number of them have been jailed on corruption charges or, like the former president Portillo, are on the run. And here is where the figures who appear in the "Not All the Afflictions" cartoon—NGOs, human rights, Mayan organizations, and even some faces of the state—*are* pests, calamities, interfering, just as locusts do, in the smooth operations of production.

Sideshow Indians or Motors of Value?

Like any magic trick, the bedazzlement of the state and elites getting Indians to work for free is less astounding when its laborious and violent methods are revealed. Joyabaj has been tightly lashed in to these politico-economic networks for over one hundred years because it is a *finca de mozos*. While different areas have been given over to the cultivation of export monocrops—*fincas de café, banano, azúcar, algodón* (plantations of coffee, bananas, sugar, cotton), *mozo* means field hand, so literally what was grown in Joyabaj were agricultural laborers. The Herrera family owns vast tracts of land in the hot coastal lowlands and also bought up land around Joyabaj. In a repeating ritual of dispossession, in return for farming what had been their communally held land, Xoye—individuals and families—were expected to migrate to work during the harvest season. The state regulates these transactions between the two bodies of the population, rich criollos and poor indigenous and mestizos, and between the natural and political bodies through landholding, labor, vagrancy, debt, and other laws, through practices of accounting, and through police and military insistence on compliance. Matilde González has assembled a powerful and desperate description of these processes and their huge human costs to Joyabaj's neighbors, the Sanbartolos, and how they produced a certain idea of *indios* as those who work basically for free (*trabajo regalado*). One man told González, "We have to go to the coast, but often those who go just arrive there to die of fever . . . but we do it because we have to" (2002:216). These relations of production are organized through ethnicity and become consolidated (racialized) into class as "political networks that have defined the course of the State and of the economy" (Solano 2005:10).

Liz Oglesby, who first took me to Joyabaj, is exploring the changes in sugar production through the networks that articulate the South Coast and the *fincas de mozos* (2002). Over several years of visiting and interviewing she has found that almost every man older than thirteen from the northern hamlets of Joyabaj has spent time working on the coast, and so have many women. Most of them hate it and struggle to find ways to make ends meet without having to go down. González argues that this hatred was the major impetus for Catholic Action and the later, more radical organizing. In interviews with these young K'iché' men Oglesby found that after performing backbreaking labor, often continuously for over two months, they would return to Joyabaj with about one hundred dollars after paying the plantation for their food and lodging, as duly noted in the ledger books, now fully computerized (Oglesby 2002). One might compare this sum to the intake of the administrator of the Chuacorral finca south of Joyabaj, who, in the finca's heyday, sent fifteen hundred to two thousand laborers to the coast at a profit of thirty-five thousand dollars a year (Remijnse 2002:62). And this is only the locally accrued benefits. Compared to the profits of the Herreras, it's a molehill next to a volcano.

The histories of dispossession through enclosure that mandated earlier trips to the coast make the Xoye who believed that the almost-lynched mayor was going to sell "the whole town!" seem less gullible (Carmack 1995, Handy 1984, 1994, McCreery 1994, Piel 1989, Smith 1990). Precursors to the military commissioners and patrol commanders, and later actually filling these positions, *contratistas* and their helpers were deeply in the know about indebting opportunities to hook people (*enganche*) into debt through *costumbre* obligations, family rituals like marriages and funerals, domestic crises like illness, and alcohol consumption habits—often the same people owned the stores and grew and processed cane into *cuxa* (hooch). Government tax policy, the expenses of schooling—a necessity for those who increasingly needed Spanish to defend themselves against the regnant ladinos—and the infamous vagrancy laws that were overturned by the government of Juan José Arévalo around 1945, doubled people over, forcing them to work first for nothing, then for a pittance. Thus, the problem of hungry, angry Indians pouring down from the mountains, supposedly fixed by the security state, is actually produced by this political-economic organization.

As in the case of the patrols and the army, drugs are a way to reckon with being acted on by these not-always-visible national and transnational forces. Drugs are said to be in the food provided for migrant workers by the plantations to make them work harder and be more docile. Recalling urban legends in the United States that express anxiety about masculinity and powerlessness, men in Joyabaj tell stories about unknowingly imbibing substances that either erase or crazily enhance their sex drive. They warn each other of further addictions, including stories of falling into such terrible debt at the brothels near the plantations that they can never pay it off and are trapped in servitude (Oglesby 2003).[9] In turn, migrants tell horror tales about fellow workers who dope *themselves* up in order to meet quota in the cane fields but who go haywire, able to cut tons of cane for awhile but then burn out and are left to wander the plantations like semizombies.[10]

In these stories *finqueros* are inhuman in their treatment of workers and work both through and above the state and its law. They administer drugs at will and, given the ease of hiding airstrips on vast tracts of land, it is said, augment the wealth first accumulated through circulating Xoye with narco-circulation.[11] The law that is supposed to catch them itself embodies illegality: a U.S. embassy cable from Guatemala in March 1995 suggested that Colonel Julio Alpírez, CIA asset and assassin, may very well have been guilty of the murder of the U.S. citizen Michael Devine, probably to cover up army connections to drug smuggling (Weiner 1995:A6; Weiner 1996). Similarly, in May 2002 the U.S. government revoked the visas of a number of high-profile Guatemalans for suspicions of drug trafficking (Peacock and Beltrana 2003:63), and in September 2006 the former Guatemalan drug czar, Adan Castillo, was found guilty of trafficking by a U.S. court. Belying states' claims to rationality, this proof of collaboration and of the utter uselessness of interdiction does not stop money from pouring into the so-called war on drugs. Capturing a few of the powerful for mistreatment of workers, corruption, or drug running does not disperse the astounding accumulation accessed through these simultaneously legal and illegal, immoral but racially justified, secret yet obvious movements of people and substances that seem to magically produce so much surplus — for some.

But Joyabaj, true to its patron *Virgen*, is a major point of passage for other traversals, and increasingly Xoye are escaping the horrible descent to the fever-ridden coast. More and more of them, indigenous and ladino, look to the United States as a way to save up money for a home, car, business venture, or exhumation.[12] The hamlets of Joyabaj, like hamlets all over Latin America, often show a conspicuous absence of young men as they head out for "Proveedenz," "Carolina del Norte," "Eeowa," "Labamba," faraway names that families stumble to pronounce.[13] People point to houses missing one, two, even three people who have gone north or to homesteads boarded up and abandoned altogether. A teacher in a northern hamlet worries about the "abandoned children" he is supposed to teach. Their parents are in the States, and they are left with their grandparents, who are too old to really care for them. "There is a lot missing," the teacher says. "Discipline, preparation, they come to school dirty, hungry. It is hard for them to concentrate, to study. I don't know what will become of them."

In Patzulá, after serving Liz and me freshly picked peaches, a young woman who speaks no Spanish brought out pictures of her husband, who is working in Alabama (Labamba). In the first photo he looks like any of the young men in the hamlet, standing gingerly near an electric stove, unknown at home, to show he's cooking tortillas for himself. In the most recent image he's smartly dressed in hip-hop clothes, with long hair, posing near a sports car. No one was sure if the car was his. His remittance money comes sporadically. It's not clear if some of it is just not making it to Joyabaj or if he rarely sends it. In the patrilocal community, she lives with his family, although he's been gone for four years and barely knows their child. Giving a sense of how difficult such a life is, Domingo González, responsible for improving the community, says he's constantly involved in crises when these young women, who haven't seen their husbands for years, take up with other men.

Remittances are increasingly the major source of foreign currency for many Latin American countries. A young Xoye who works at the local Western Union office says at least fifty thousand dollars come through the office every week. An advertisement for Banco Metropolitano acknowledges that Guatemalans working in the United States are "making the effort to contribute to the development of their families and of Guatemala" and urges these transnational citizens to use the bank's convenient branches in California (and soon in Chicago and Florida) to send their money home. The ad's background mixes the American and Guatemalan flags with indigenous weavings. A private company but regulated by the state, Banco Metropolitano, which calls itself "Your bank with human feeling," is one of millions of spaces through which human beings, human feelings, and the expression of human labor circulate across national, state-patrolled boundaries.

An apparently marginal circuit, a sideshow to the big issues of political economy, the labor of *mozos* on the plantations and now abroad (like the Klein bottle merging inside and out) and the state, ethnic, kinship, and gender relations that make them possible are absolutely central. What would happen to the Guatemalan national economy if that young woman joined her husband beside the snazzy car, and no money was sent back? It is estimated that some ninety thousand Guatemalans go to the United States each year and contribute close to 30 percent of the gross internal product, more than the combined totals of coffee, sugar, banana, and cardamom exports. Some 86 percent of migrants are literate, and many have university degrees. "Guatemala plants the seeds and cultivates them, and another country enjoys the harvest" (INFORPRESS 2003a:2).

While banks skim some money off the top, immigration challenges well-ensconced profit-making ventures. At the same time, it may act as a safety valve, releasing energies that might otherwise be turned to transforming Guatemala. Perhaps this is one reason that political exiles returning from years or decades outside the country comment on how hard it is to organize political activism in the early twenty-first century as compared to the 1970s. They know that a big reason for the difficulty is decades of well-planned material and psychological warfare insisting that resistance is futile. But they also say that the magical-seeming power of consumerism, propped up by the state's signing of free trade agreements and empowered by remittances, curbs people's willingness to question the status quo. Some also look to state-encouraged Evangelical churches and to a few crumbs from the government, like some infrastructure or a paid position to bedazzle and distract those formerly willing to entertain critiques of structural inequality and state violence. Remittances have accelerated decades-old transformations in Joyabaj's class/ethnicity system, as the sugar plantations are forced to compete for workers, and indigenous people from the surrounding hamlets can now lay down thirty thousand dollars in cash to buy increasingly scarce land downtown; being surrounded by ravines, the land is a limited good.

In Joyabaj it's very hard to ask about the global migration process because a curious gringo is immediately tagged as la migra (U.S. immigration), out to discern how people bamboozle the state and its borders. However, the trip seems to cost three thousand dollars, a mind-boggling amount in a place where the daily wage is still only about a dollar and a half. People sell goods, even land, and turn to kin networks or people already in the United States for loans and dollars. As I've mentioned, in a new twist on the *Baile de la Culebra*'s old story, those who are in-between (inter-esse), like the labor contractors, now lend money to enable these new journeys (*tránsitos*) at interest rates that often necessitate several years' work in construction, domestic labor, slaughterhouses, or roadwork to pay it back. If they have put up land as collateral, those who don't make it endanger their families' entire subsistence structure—an acceleration in the opposite direction for many who are already in a precarious position. Gupta calls this the "Janus-face" of proletarianization: "the other side to self-assertion . . . was increasing immiserisation, marginalization, and victimization" (1998:140). The tenuous and labor-intensive efforts to possess and improve community through "bringing the state in" to build roads and support bilingual schools, or Domingo González's attendance at state- and USAID-funded Mayan workshops, along with his efforts to mediate sexual crises, must confront these growing and very local threats of dispossession.

The other afflictions associated with going north were vividly brought home in the summer of 2000 when a boat carrying over a dozen young men from a village in Huehuetenango went down off the Pacific Coast of Mexico. Collections were taken up to bring the bodies home, and the huge funeral was heavily covered in the Guatemalan press. For many people I talked to the rows of coffins evoked the mass reburials of exhumed massacre victims. The past is also present in the way parents talk about sacrificing a child for the trip, the same word they used to describe sending sons to the army for the monthly wage. But many people don't make it and are never identified or even found in the deserts of the U.S. Southwest, another parallel to the war years, during which state-perpetrated disappearances left so many with no body to mourn or not even knowing if they are dead or alive—and aren't these also state-perpetrated?

But the trip north is also an exciting adventure and, like the Guatemalan highlands were for me when I was young, a rite of passage. Most of the young men and women I talk to in Patzulá remember, as children, hiding in the mountains from army soldiers, seeing family members die, or waiting for their father or brother to return from Civil Patrol duty. Now, however, they prefer to discuss going to the United States. Of course, perhaps because they are possessed by the spirit of Bruce Lee, many thousands of Guatemalans do make it across, and where would the U.S. economy be without them? Thick descriptions of the process circulate through Joyabaj, another form of rural legend.

Late one afternoon, Liz and I sat on a family's patio while a woman, unable to walk because of an untreated infection, shucked corn with her daughter-in-law. Another daughter-in-law prepared a makeshift kiln to fire pottery, while the smallest grandchildren hid from the two gringas. There we heard a fascinating story told by Tomás, the family's third son, about a failed bamboozlement as he made his way to the United States. Only eighteen, Tomás, a wonderful storyteller, recounted in stirring detail how the *coyote* he'd paid to get him through Mexico to the U.S. border had enrolled him in a school in Chiapas in southern Mexico. There, over the course of several weeks, the would-be migrants learned how to erase the telltale signs of their Guatemalanness so they could assume a false Mexican identity. Armed with false papers, new clothes, new geographies, new family histories, and just-learned Mexican slang, they embarked on the several-day bus ride toward the northern border. He described several thrilling brushes with the law as Mexican state officials tried unsuccessfully to trip him up in long interrogations that showed a truly amazing grasp of the tiny details that differentiate Guatemalan from Mexican Maya. A belt buckle, a certain way of blowing your nose, or saying the wrong word—for example, *coche* means pig in Guatemala, but car in Mexico—could give you away to the cops and bring it all to naught. The travelers made it as far as Mazatlán, where one of Tomás's buddies slipped up and got them all caught. They spent several weeks in jail in Mexico City with people from the Americas and the Caribbean, China, and several countries in Africa, before being sent back to Guatemala. He's gearing up to go again and instilling the same desire in his younger friends, who hang on his every word like careful ethnographers and practice their Mexican accents: *Orale, chingado!*

The state splits. Which state shows its face here? The U.S. and Mexican states are intriguingly potent in Joyabaj through remittances, fantasies of wealth and risk, police and border control, through USAID as a funder of indigenous revitalization projects and educational scholarships, and, of course, in my person, able to travel risk free, unlike local youths back-tracing my steps. Is the Guatemalan state weak, unable to absorb the labor power of its people, pathetically allowing others to harvest this wealth? Or is it a brilliant ploy to get off the hook of having to provide for people, a neoliberal dream in which they eagerly privatize themselves?

Assumptions of NGOization:
Anti- or Uber-Political Machine?

Similar questions have been raised, and not only by more conservative critics like the "Afflictions" cartoonist, about the massive postwar spread of NGOs. As the war wound down and especially after 1997, NGOs were seen by many as a saving grace. They support projects similar to those of the devastated popular movement—life improvement, justice, truth, and gender and ethnic equality. They provide funding, food, and other material assistance, technical know-how, and live-in experts who may also double as witnesses in the case of human rights abuses. Money comes from states, especially the United States, Canada, the European Union, Taiwan, Japan, and, post–Hurricane Mitch, Cuba, and from religious and social change organizations. They support indigenous rights, access to potable water, police reform, women's issues, union organizing, children's labor rights, sweatshop monitoring, education, health, psychological treatment for trauma, and road building. They have provided a soft landing for returning exiles; salaries and moral support for people who risk criticizing state abuses; and transnational networking opportunities. Thanks to NGOs, Mayan leaders connect to indigenous people throughout the continent, and a few have explored even the Arctic on homestays with the Scandinavian Sami. They allow Guatemalan refugee women to visit Rwanda, a gay and lesbian rights leader to represent Guatemala at the Stonewall commemorations in New York, and AIDS activists to go to South Africa. They helped Natalia Godoy visit Momostenango so she could train as a Mayan priestess, and they have produced a prodigious number of reports and studies (Riles 2001).

Forming an NGO or attaining funding for a project (*gestionar*) entails assumptions of identity.[14] People must figure out a number of things that often go without saying: that an NGO rather than the state or your neighbors is where one goes for assistance; the kind of project particular funders find appropriate; the sort of person they find worthy of support; the language in which the petition must be made in order to be understood; the form of petitioning versus *reclamando* or *reivindicando* (to claim or demand one's due); the temporality of funding; and accounting procedures (see chapter 8). In articulating these assumptions people change. They may cynically assume a false identity conforming to funding requirements, or they may more subtly assume, that is, take them on as their real self.

In San Bartolo *los meros jefes* received military training to transform the Civil Patrol into Peace and Development Committees and took charge of the Municipal Council for Urban and Rural Development. They now administer the 8 percent of GNP that goes directly to the municipalities under neoliberal decentralization and money from the government Social Investment Fund (FIS), Solidarity Fund for Community Development (FSDC), and the National Fund for Peace (FONAPAZ). They can effortlessly talk the NGO talk of "local power," "strengthening intercommunity organization so that the participatory processes they undertake will become self-sustaining," and the "inclusion of gender in creating sectoral plans and specific projects" (González 2002:442). When representatives of donor institutions ask to meet directly with beneficiaries to "understand the degree of 'community participation,' to create 'participatory diagnostics,' or to define people's necessities and priorities' . . . the mayor who was also the PAC commander calls together *his people*, that is to say, the PAC chiefs from the hamlets, so they can arrange for their patrollers (and their wives if necessary) to assemble and thus represent a 'community that is united to work for development'" (443). Most heinously, when *los jefes* heard there were projects for widows, they called together the women whose husbands they had killed and whom they and the resident soldiers had raped continuously for years and told them they "*had to* present themselves as an organized group, but they *must not* discuss anything that had happened, that they *must ask for aid* and accept that the military commissioners were the 'spokesmen' for the group. . . . They justified their presence in the meetings [with funders] [by] saying, 'The ladies don't speak, they don't know Spanish. They can't read, they can't write, they can't do sums or balance the accounts, we will help them'" (450, emphasis indicates direct quotes).

González makes clear that people know very well the terrible crimes these men have committed and that the *jefes'* possessions are a direct result of the townspeople's own dispossession. However, the aura of the *jefes'* almost total power in the local milieu, and what they can offer to collaborators, are attractive. Some young men, already deeply enmeshed in the new debt culture the *meros jefes* have created—for example, Sanbartolos who work almost for free in the stores these leaders own in the capital city—will go even further into debt to participate in the festival *convite* dance these men sponsor as the theatrical display of their power (473–81). In San Bartolo local militarized power has assumed NGO development work. Like the *convite* and the "Afflictions" cartoon, it masks an other face.

In other *ambientes* these identifications are more difficult to assume. McAllister suggests that Chupolenses have not learned NGO-speak very well, unlike people in the Ixil region, where NGOs were already working in 1983: "Chupolenses have not learned to make claims for money or aid on the basis of their victimhood. Sometimes people would give me drafts of 'project profiles' they were sending to funders for various development schemes, and I was always surprised to notice that they did not discuss or even allude to *el ochenta* [the violence of the eighties]. Given that most money available for such projects in Guatemala is allocated with an eye to reparations for the war, I would encourage them to say that they were internally displaced peoples who had suffered through the war, but this suggestion only seemed to make them nervous" (2003:349).[15]

These are stories of the success (or not) of working *on* NGOs. The Joyabaj Grupo Maya falls somewhat between these extremes. Several members, like Godoy, have experience in office work, transnational and national connections, including me, and relative fluency in proposal-ese. They have managed to procure support for a number of cultural projects, some of which are related to the fiesta, and have had to mount a rearguard defense against other Maya like the former mayor, who wants in on the multicultural goodies. They act as intermediaries between their monolingual neighbors and groups like Habitat for Humanity, USAID-sponsored get out the vote efforts, and the forensic anthropologists who are carrying out the exhumations.[16] They also participate in national-level NGOs like COPMAGUA, but Godoy bridled when the men tried to impose submissive women as representatives because the funders were pressuring them.

Which brings me to the fears of being acted on *by* NGOs. A very careful observer of indigenous organizing summed up comments I have heard for years from both ladino and indigenous Guatemalans. He said, "It's becoming clearer to me that the image that financiers have of what the Maya is, what the Maya should be, has been imposed in very subtle ways. You see it first in people's proposals, how they present themselves, but then you start to hear it in their positions on particular issues. The Maya is victim, the Maya is passive." Domingo Hernández Ixcoy, a founder of CUC who returned from exile in the late 1990s, was more forceful. He said, "What should be political projects, plans that arise from organizing and people's needs, are more and more determined by the funding. The projects are just to spend the money, and that will always attract the wrong kind of people. Worse, they will be fighting with each other even before the money runs out. The same way the state is being run is how everything is being run now—all of the political organizations are about interests, about making money. We've been infected. The money is ruining us. This is all very carefully planned; don't think it's an accident. But it's our own fault too. There's been a lack of education [*falta de formación*]. We need to help young people have other morals, be able to resist this." A ladina who has worked with NGOs since the early 1990s was similarly suspicious: "We really see a transformation of what once were political movements into NGOs. Instead of working on larger transformations, the best people are *gestionando fondos* [managing funding]. The international cooperation has been big collaborators in this. Now the task people are concerned with is just keeping their organization going." This may be why CUC and CONIC are so staunch in their insistence that they are political movements, not NGOs (although some wonder how much is activism and how much *gestión*), and why it is such an insult to the political goals of the revolution to run together the sounds of URNG with ONG.

Even elite intellectuals well versed in the study of power/knowledge feel increasingly trapped in these logics and temporalities. A well-respected academic told a friend, "Doing the NGO consulting is bitter for me. I have to do things I don't believe in" (see also Rocha 2004). The National University, its faculty and curriculum tattered by the massive counterinsurgency attack and more recently by neoliberal funding cuts, is unable to hire new faculty or pay a living wage. Professors supplement with consulting, leaving little time for their students or research. As external funding dwindles, some private research institutions, justifiably proud of their autonomy and of undertaking risky investigations, must accept work for the government and the various limitations this entails. One disillusioned researcher said, "We are against the state until it calls us. We spent our youths trying to destroy this unjust system. Will we spend our maturity in perfecting it?" In turn, intellectual labor is becoming more like *mozos*—informal, insecure, paid by the piece rather than the hour, so the worker assumes more of the production risk.

NGOs have also played an ambivalent role in operationalizing the peace accords. The system of *comisiones paritarias* (joint commissions) brought civil society and NGOs, including indigenous and women representatives, together with the government to jointly decide on implementation. Jonas calls them "process-related gains for democracy . . . providing training and capacity-building among those who have never had such opportunities" (2000:96). Most agree that the strength of the Accord on Indigenous Rights is due to the unstinting insistence of these sectors. While once understood as an innovative way to institutionalize dialogue and negotiation, however, people are now suspicious that they were a distraction, a way to "displace, to the interior of the government, the national agenda for peace . . . marginalizing [by creating a separate structure] civil society and the international community" (Hernández Pico 2005:108). Someone who participated wholeheartedly in the very time-consuming process now (2005) says, "I'm not sure how it got decided that creating democracy and strengthening institutions would be the job of NGOs, but what it did was to create this whole parallel structure to the state, with the ASC [Civil Society Assembly], NGOs, and the 'friendly countries.' The state did not really have much to do with the accords and so now what we have is that peace was never really part of the state's project." A congressional aide said something similar in 2004: "The problem with institutionalizing the accords is they were always between two counterparts [the governing party and the URNG] and never truly state commitments. . . . There hasn't been an accumulation of forces. The civil society, the popular movement, don't confront the state, they don't push. Instead, they triangulate, working with foreign donors and then the donors are supposed to push the government."

While similar in their warnings about the hidden agendas of NGOs, these suspicions are different from those in the cartoon, which is a small piece of a very large, very long-running campaign against particular forms of outside interference in Guatemalan affairs. During the postwar, as in the war, the

Guatemalan version of Hofstadter's Cold War paranoia was constantly on the defensive about outsiders messing with their Indians and other workers. Dark warnings about dangerous strangers imbued with strange ideas like human rights were central to the penetrating education dispensed (with drugs?) to patrollers and captured refugees. Postwar airwaves, newspapers, and political debates are rife with panicked vitriol about national sovereignty in danger.

Why might otherwise opposing interests tell similar conspiracy stories about NGOs as "afflictions," "the money is ruining us . . . don't think it's an accident"? This simultaneously rubbery and sticky effect may arise because government and nongovernment work is double: they enact interests that benefit some, while being inimical to others, and are also inter-esse, what is between and therefore not fully controlled by any side. Reading development and postwar democracy—and its failures—with James Ferguson alerts us that we must entertain the possibility that such apparati "may do what it does, not at the bidding of some knowing and powerful subject who is making it all happen, but behind the backs of or against the wills of even the most powerful actors" (1994:18). On the other hand, McAllister suggests this anti-conspiratorial take "conceals an important fact: that development was always intended as an exercise of power" (2003:140), that Cold War and counterinsurgency hermeneutics *and* politics as war by other means were developed and deployed by people who have names and can assume responsibility. And yet, things certainly don't always turn out the way they plan. The anti-Communists who brought right-wing Catholic Action priests into the highlands in the 1950s produced, but certainly did not plan for, the ensuing assumptions of identities as *campesino*, union organizer, Maya, revolutionary, Nobel Savage. How to entertain in the sense of holding together, Ferguson's Foucauldian only partly fleshy apparatus with the incarnated people behind the curtain? And many of them—like those who participated wholeheartedly in the ASC but now wonder if it was an unamusing distraction—have good intentions, if unexamined assumptions. But others are cynically pursuing gain through and above the state and its law.

A PERFECT SEPARATION OF POWER OR MONSTROUS HYBRID FREAK?

As the postwar supposedly ends, many Guatemalans reckon everyday experiences of insecurity—such as escalating *delincuencia* (crime), lynchings, streets closed for an Ex-PAC demo, unpaved roads, and other unmet state responsibilities like catching criminals—by telling urban and rural legends about a calculated and excessively violent creature. This enormous, multi-part being is spread throughout the national territory, thicker at escape points, pooling wherever it senses money or blood, lurking in real and virtual spaces with thousands of ears to the ground. Always alert, it is entwined in the bowels of everyday institutions and the popular imaginary like a Guatemalan Freddy Krueger, haunting the school basement, the town hall, and people's dreamscapes. It enjoys absolute impunity, openly mocks its challengers, and sits on mountains of ill-gotten wealth, yet is insatiable, all-consuming, needing more. Its extent and true form can only be guessed at, mainly taking shape through its effects: dead bodies appearing daily, sometimes in horrific states. Some of these corpses raise suspicions—an activist nun, an indigenous rights campaigner, a judge on a sensitive case, a small businessman who threatened someone's monopoly—but most remain anonymous and accompanied by the story (why does it seem so familiar?) that they must have been involved in *babosadas*. Like any being of such extraordinary force, the perpetrator goes by many names: hidden or parallel powers, clandestine apparatuses, the state within the state, death squad government. And, like many conspiracy theories, barring the racist, sexist ones, it's true—at least some of it. The Final Girls and Boys who are turning it into a target name it Illegal Bodies and Clandestine Security Apparatuses (CIACS), and in an innovative deployment of international law proposed a Commission to Investigate them (CICIACS). The CIACS do resemble a creature from horror films' repertoire or a hydra, but they are also falling under the purview of brave social scientists and activists struggling to unmask and emasculate them, to inventory their tools so they can be used against them.

Jennifer Schirmer, in her unsettlingly titled book *The Guatemalan Military Project: A Violence Called Democracy*, says, "The Guatemalan military have crafted a unique Counterinsurgent Constitutional State . . . [in which] counterinsurgency structures are incorporated into the very heart of the State" (1998:258) via cogovernance with the civilians. She says this "gives new meaning to 'civilian oversight' as purposeful blindness to violations" (263). Like Solano and others, she argues that the state is two-faced "politico-military" and that the "private" realm of market relations is increasingly econo-military. Like some local PAC leaders accumulating through dispossession, many army officers profited handsomely from the war, joining the ranks of economic elites, no longer the oligarchy's *mozos* but defending their own interests. Hernández Pico says, "Our countries live subject to impunity and we are blackmailed by the lords of the war, today transformed into *empresarios del capital delincuencial*" (entrepreneurs of criminal capital) (2005:118). More specifically, he says that during the war

> the economic, political and military leaderships hid behind clandestine groups that sowed terror through assassination. . . . They also used the Death Squads to carry out economic kidnappings to extort members of the oligarchy and Guatemalan bourgeoisie and to allow high military officials to become unwanted stakeholders in various industrial monopolies. The most famous was the kidnapping in the 1970s of Enrique Novella, member of the prominent cement monopoly family. The military also has a history of controlling the country's imports and exports, customs, revenue service and taxes, civil aeronautics, and the ports. Through these offices they formed alliances with [many economic sectors]. . . . The war, with its military "aids" to the Army, was also a dark wellspring of illicit businesses. Another source of the "hidden powers" of the state has been narcotrafficking and all the other prohibited traffics, beginning with arms, that created the *capital delincuencial* and the organized crime it finances—with its transnational connections—allowing them to rise into the oligarchy even as it strengthens the inequality and poverty for which it was first responsible. . . . The grafting of the army to the tree of the State, with its branches of the hidden powers vigorously fed by the sap of corruption, will not be easily undone. (227–28)

Iduvina Hernández also describes the army's public and private financial resources: in addition to receiving the lion's share of ministry funding, $170 million in 2005, not including what's off-book, it owns several companies that produce or import chemicals, explosives, military vehicles, and munitions as well as pharmacies, a hospital, and a bank (Report on Guatemala 2005:6–8). Army members have also been linked to the massive cash infusions from the recent rash of concessions to forests, water, oil, and minerals granted to transnational companies as well as through *gestionando*, the export of children through international adoption. The CIACS also draw power from auto theft, bank robberies, and paid assassinations and utilize networks of spies in place since the war. In addition, the high rates of unemployment make it easy to draw in new recruits (see Camus 2005). In some areas, practices of "social cleansing" win them legitimacy from people feeling harassed by growing numbers of street children, sex workers, and assaults—between January and May 2005, thirty thousand bus robberies were reported. Many people point to the marked rise in violence against women and its *saña* (barbarity) as another sign of the CIACS' existence. As a participant in a round table discussion said about the spectacular brutality, "They are saying 'we are here'" (Foro 2005:27). Like Rigoberto, who IDed me as the Lizard Queen, activists may be looking back "with longing for when our war was against the state. It was clear who the enemy was . . . now it is a war against violence and you never know . . . who to fight against."

Rejecting the magical aura of this rumored disembodied violence, activists formally proposed the CICIACS in 2003 to create a new category of perpetrator and a new legal instrument hybridizing national justice with UN backing. The UN's technical commission concluded that such an innovation was necessary because

> behind the acts of violence perpetrated against human rights defenders, those working in the justice system, journalists and other sectors, are found groups or clandestine bodies linked with the security forces, particularly with military intelligence. . . . These groups tap phones, use official vehicles, show that they have tactical experience and an infrastructure and extensive operational capabilities that suggest they can count on the participation or at least tolerance of state agents. . . . For those who object that such an extraordinary measure is unnecessary, we emphasize that 90% of such cases brought to the district attorney are filed away without even undertaking the initial processes of investigation. (UN 2004, see also del Valle et al. 2006)

The CICIACS would enjoy a juridical personality, could institute legal proceedings, and intervene in the entire criminal process, from bringing evidence and participating in the indictment, investigation, and trial phases to proposing a system of remedies. It would have full legal access to state archives and institutions, unlike MINUGUA, but like the mission would monitor progress for the UN, which in turn would provide technical support, bring international attention to cases, and rely on CICIACS' reports when determining Guatemala's human rights rating. Like the Racketeer Influenced and Corrupt Organizations Act (RICO) legislation in the United States, the CICIACS would pay special attention to linkages and empower more wide-reaching legal responses to both the material and intellectual authors of crimes. Against right-wing cries of sovereignty violation, proponents reiterate that prosecution would occur only through existing, but, via the CICIACS, strengthened national institutions.

The legislation was signed in January 2004 by outgoing FRG Foreign Minister Edgar Gutiérrez. The human rights activist Frank la Rue, assigned to follow up for the administration of Oscar Berger, said, "Anyone who opposes the CICIACS must have some tie with organized crime." However, the claim bounces back and sticks to the Berger government, which (*doble cara*, two faces) supported the legislation in public while voting against it in Congress. And, despite support from some faces of the FRG, the party's appointees on the Constitutional Court ruled against the CICIACS legislation. After extensive rewrites, including a new name, "La Comisíon Internacional contra la Impunidad en Guatemala" (CICIG), it began operations in January 2008 with a two-year mandate.

A ladina human rights activist said, "The CICIACS process has been very educational. I've learned how many people are invested in these structures, how many people are involved. These are folks you would *never* think . . . not just elites or former military, but many people I think of as the middle class. Unexpected people, whose privileges are at stake. [An important player in the peace process] turned against it at the last moment, and at first I couldn't understand why. Then it became apparent how many people were invested— how completely the parallel powers were making not only an elite, the oligarchic form of life (this would be the more traditional view— to see the State as a cover for the elite) but I learned that a lot of the middle class is involved, that it really allows a whole set of ways of life to continue. So the question arises—what can be done? Can these powers actually be removed?" I said, "It's like bad apples." And she replied, laughing, "Yes, but if we take them away there might not be any tree!"

One is not enough because the state is both: legitimate and criminal, corrupt, murderous; rational and irrational, magical. It is for the people, our representative, and against the people, constantly assessing the risk of our rebellion, always at the ready to repress. It is a regulator, creating and maintaining standards by normalizing, and a freak show, functioning precisely through its abnormality, its awesomeness, its massive differentiation from the everyday. It simultaneously manages the mechanisms of horror and is accountable for them, "self-restraining" (Schedler, Diamond and Plattner 1999). Yet two is too many. As my friend wonders, would taking away its corrupt face leave anything at all?

The CICIG links to the political machine, struggling to turn the state's forces against its self. It's a Glinda the Good counter-counterinsurgency hermeneutic, carefully designed to disaggregate the useful (ruby slippers) from the wicked aspects of power and making the latter "fly away!" As such, it is a site to study magical powers, a collaboration to open what Bruno Latour calls "black boxes":

> If everything goes well it begins to look as if the black boxes were effortlessly gliding through space as a result of their own impetus, that they

were becoming durable by their own inner strength. In the end, if everything goes really well, it seems as if there are facts and machines spreading through minds, factories and households, slowed down only in a handful of far-flung countries and by a few dimwits. Success in building black boxes has the strange consequence of generating these UFOs; the "irreversible progress of science," the "irresistible power of technology." (1987:132)

or "the great and powerful Counterinsurgency State." But proponents of the CICIG, like Glinda's conspiracy theory that views power as perhaps not so powerful because it's a network rather than a UFO (in Spanish, OVNI, *Objeto Volando No Identificado*), can make things go not so well. They are naming names, following the money, publishing photos, unraveling interesses, turning one face against another. Activists are astute in the ways of OMNIs (Unidentified Military Objects), knowing, as Latour warns, that not all actants are equally powerful. The military may be the primary creator of magical-seeming truths:

> For centuries, they have enlisted people and interested them in their action, so much so that most of us are ready to obey them blindly and to give up our lives if required. As far as enrolling, disciplining, drilling and keeping in line are concerned, they have proved their mettle. . . . The military have been interested in unexpectedly shifting the balance of power with new resources and weapons. . . . Today no army is able to win without scientists, and only very few scientists and engineers are able to win their arguments without the army. . . . Technoscience is part of a war machine and should be studied as such. (1987:172)

What does the duplicitous state do? Many things. But maintaining counterinsurgency relations is certainly one of them. The name of the military father infuses the postwar political, governmental (and non-), and economic milieu (ambiente), creating what Mike Davis calls an *ecology* of fear (1998). In postwar Guatemala the military may be the largest of the charismatic megafauna inhabiting this ecosystem, with racism and patriarchy a significant source of its daily nutrients. But in the postwar-in-action, as Filóchofo and other Greens know, the metaphors of environment and ecology emphasize the deep imbrication of every component of a habitat. A jaguar in a cage may survive and even reproduce, but it is not a sustainable species without the density and interactions of animals, vegetables, minerals, space and time concatenated into a rain forest. One or even two are not enough, and the trans/actions are vital. The CICIG and other activists, like Marcelo Arenas, joining *aj q'ij* with CONIC, are transacting in this fear-filled ecology, just as Dorothy Gale did. They are lashing in allies, enrolling counternetworks, studying the state as a war machine, and producing reverse discourses. The soldiers, *chafas*, who smash and destroy also *chafear*, they're cheaters, useless humbugs who can be unmasked. At great personal risk these activists become contagious carriers of optimism of the will.

Yet however much she may comfort us, Glinda the Good was every inch a white girl. In the aftermath of genocide it may be a different matter for poor indigenous people to risk capture in these same sticky webs, returning us to the special compulsion, with race as its node, within the general militarized paranoid-mysticism of the New World Order and the Cold War. McAllister recalls a scuffle in Chupol between civilians and a soldier over "who gives the orders?" She remarks on the anguish surrounding the question: "Demanding things of the state will inevitably bring [people] under the state's purview" (2003:344). This is a problem because "with regard to the state Chupolenses cannot fully exercise their *conciencia* [knowing what is right and acting on it], for as bearers of rights, Chupolenses must make demands of the state, while as members of a community they must seek to evade the state's recognition. The conditions under which good people could be both things at once were destroyed by the insurgency's defeat. All attempts to act as good people vis-à-vis the state, therefore, raise the phantasm of *el ochenta* [the eighties] and the possibility of its return in the flesh" (306–07). This creates a bind: "To try to exercise their rights as bearers of *conciencia* and risk exposing themselves as subjects outside the law, or to exercise their *conciencia* strictly within the ambit of the community and risk losing their rights" (322). And, because state violence "has been internalized as a division in the body of good people" (359) throughout the highlands, organizing and demanding rights may make some people feel "well-planted [*bien sembrado*], like I couldn't be moved any longer" as one Chupolense activist said (297), while it terrifies others. These are not just the *meros jefes* and *los hechores* that Manuel Hernández said are now afraid, the way he and his family used to be. But he himself has decided not to seek justice, leaving it to God to pay them back. As Adela said about the exhumation in Joyabaj, "The people came, two gringos working so hard, sweating, in the heat, and no one would help them. No one would help! La gente tiene miedo—tiene miedo! [the people are afraid]." Even for people whose family members might be in the grave, who are passionately interested in knowing their fates and in laying their souls to rest, seeking redress from the state risks reanimating the past, tearing the thin membrane between postwar and war. Histories of collaboration transform reckoning into risk, as people are transformed not only into "warring subjects," a threat to their neighbors (359), but also are revealed: everyone has "tie[s] with organized crime."

My ladina friend who had worked very hard to create the Commission to Investigate the hidden powers said, "The state is schizophrenic and our reaction to it is as well. That is the problem. We go to it. We demand recognition of our claims and our claims are to inhibit the state. We have to turn to it to do our work. But what else can we do?" She's expressing the frustration that the state is like glue in that the stereotype bounces back and sticks—it is as duplicitous as that colonial construct the Two-Faced Indian. It is a THEM *and* an US, inadequate *and* indispensable, dangerous *and* in danger. But it's also glue because she is stuck with and to it, in intimate intercourse with monsters. Taking this psycho killer's tools can be empowering since they include "the entire idea of political legitimacy, of the difference between power and authority, the idea that 'the Law' is something that stands above the contingencies of everyday life and incarnates a certain collective justice, the crucial discourse of rights as something that once defined and authorized become unassailable and inalienable: all hinge on the perpetuated myth of the state's coherence and ability to stand 'above society' as it were" (Hansen and Stepputat 2001:15).

The state is a myth, a rumor. Like Candyman. And like him it takes life from believers. McAllister says that by addressing rights claims to the state one assumes the identity of citizen and thereby "further legitimate[s] the state's control over society (Boli 1987:19, in McAllister 2003:344). To assume (take for granted) the state as the addressee of rights claims makes us collaborators in its assumption of freakish power. Hernández Pico says its enormous attraction "has resulted in many people who took power with the best intentions of socializing it and thereby creating a new historic subject ending up themselves being 'taken by power'" (2005:15). Being taken, doubled over, is the very promise and danger of the assumptions of identity. As *Candyman*'s Helen and all Final Girls and Boys know, co-laboration risks consumption, infection, ruin. But where can you hide? The monster finds you in the closet, the basement, wherever you run—even assuming the identity of immigrant and escaping north does not remove you from the clutches of the state/s. Yet well-planted activists might emphasize that the gluey state is also in a bind. It needs our legitimation, so it targets our hearts and minds, not only our hides. The vampire's kiss is a two-way street, taking and giving power (Latham 2002, Stone 1995). The state is the *nom du père*, an obligatory passage point for both suspicions of bamboozlement on the lower, chaotic registers and as a reverb chamber for the paranoia of the powerful. It is a knot in the identi-ties of race, class, gender, colonialism, and the military.

The "Afflictions" cartoonist hopes that his warning about the plagues hiding behind the bodacious showgirls will help his readers remove the masks and thereby escape the seductions of bamboozlement. His suspicions are shared by folks who may share little else with him. Is the truth behind the curtain? Are the dancers hiding a real face? Or should we perchance look to the motion of the dance, the continual processing and rendering of the assumptions of identity, the action of the postwar? The headings in this chapter have offered the false choice of "or" (as if one were enough), but substituting them with two (weak and strong, anti and über) is not sufficient. We have to go through, Dela.

Marx says that the value of money is materialized in our effective social activity, just as, I argue, is the allure of the duplicitous state. Its effectivity is not in it but comes from mobility, from circulation that, like the vampire kiss, is ambi-valent. It is not just a one-way activity of the state on the people, or of economics or the military on the political, or of external actors on the Guatemalan state. Instead, the state-effect emerges from these multiplicities of exchanges. The x that is in the state and in the Two-Faced Indian that gives bamboozlement its charge is this constant mobility, its X-stasis. But what about reckoning, assuming responsibility?

There's a joke people tell in Guatemala: "What is the ego? It's the little Argentine that lives inside us all." (In many parts of Latin America Argentines enjoy an unfortunate reputation for having a superiority complex.) The joke mimics Durkheim's uncanny description of the self: "There is something impersonal in us because there is something social in us" (1995:447). For Feldman and for horror films this is the in-human—both not and yet most deeply in-us. Althusser, of course, calls this internal not-us, which is simultaneously the condition for our possibility, the state (1971). Perhaps we and it are always already two-faced because it is only via our subjection to and by it that we experience subjectivity at all.

So, where is the state? When we look for it, it melts away. We see only its effects, and those only as they are incarnated in human action. The state, like Hobbes's Leviathan, the King for Kantorowicz (1981), and Poole's description of "el Peru legal y el Peru real" (2004) has two bodies. One is the individual who carries out its deeds—as soldier, bureaucrat, representative, etc.—through everyday ordinary actions. The other is the body politic that transcends the flesh (carne-vale) into the larger social forms of incorporation, a sublime Thing. Margaret Mead supposedly said that those who hate their society become political scientists, those who hate themselves become psychologists, and those who hate both become anthropologists. This pivot point *midway* between the life of the individual and the life of the species has always been anthropology's turf—and the site of great ambivalence. We study and thus try to draw close to that which also simultaneously horrifies us.

The carnival, entertaining, distracting, and fascinating, is also a place we hate. It offers safe horror, but a horror nonetheless, like that of my friend who still kinesthetically recalls her encounter with the sideshow attraction of Otis the Frog Boy by—years later!—covering her mouth and recoiling. My own memories of the midway mix with nausea and shameful vomiting, screaming at the operator of the Ferris wheel to let me and my frantic little sister off (he blithely ignored us), crying children adamantly refusing to have fun, and real terror in the eyes of adults. It's a little taste of those other, dangerous horrors that surround us. A woman who worked on the CEH report said, "I have interviewed people who carried out massacres, and I have read everything I can find on why people would do those things, how training can dull you, how you fear for your own life, how you come to believe it's for a higher ideal, that the person you're killing or torturing somehow deserves it, but none of that explains what I encountered in that work. I feel I confronted something radically evil."

I have been describing the often terrifying general experience of identification as unfixed and mobile, as alien, two bodies in one, and the painful possession by a Matrix-like Agent Smith, by a volcano-like Herrera family. This is the anthropological crux (puzzle and deciding point) of the social, aka state, economy, military, in/as the individual. Slavoj Žižek describes it via Lacan's "agency of the big Other" and sees it present in two mutually exclusive modes. In one it functions as a hidden agency, pulling the strings, running the show.[17] This is good old-fashioned conspiracy theory, in which the state has two faces. It presupposes the Subject presumed to know and, Žižek says, can quiet and strengthen our attempt to make sense of the world, even as it may swerve into terrifying paranoia. It is a counter-counterinsurgency hermeneutic that sees through the workings of one form of two-faced power toward something more just. A subject presumed to know is something we can interpret; there are clandestine apparatuses, but they can be investigated. The jokey idea of a little Argentine inside us at least suggests that someone is in control! As at the carnival we play games of chance, go on rides that fling us about, and shudder in horror at the freaks, submitting to forces outside our control. While we may feel "beheaded, lost in the crowd," we are held (*tenir*) between (enter) as if by glue, by a plan. Like the Guatemalans I've been quoting I hope this conspiracy theory can strengthen efforts to ferret out and disarticulate these plans, despite the limitations that McAllister flags.

But Žižek also suggests this agency of the big Other is present in an exactly opposite way, as pure semblance, as nothing, but whose appearance is essential and must be preserved. This is how he explains the parades of East European socialism. The long lines of happy people are a spectacle for the gaze of this Other, although neither the people nor the party believe they are happy, and everyone knows that no one else believes. It is an essential appearance that rules our lives. Here the Subject is supposed *not* to know (1992: 38–41). Žižek suggests that what is monstrous, terrifying, and perversely enjoyable about this second mode is that it hints at "a traumatic shock for the symbolic universe" (1992:22) by acknowledging that there is something that lies outside of what is dreamt of in our imagining:

> The symbolic identity [of any given community] is bestowed upon it by a series of legal, religious, and other values which regulate its life; these values are literally 'fictions,' they exist nowhere, they possess no substantial ontological consistency, they are present only in the form of the symbolic rituals which enact them. . . . The point here is not the cynical insipidity that 'these are just fictions' but the fact that because of these 'fictions' thousands die in wars. . . . In other words, although such a 'fiction' effectively exists only in its real effects (the state is actual only in the real activity of its citizens, the Fatherland only in the patriotic feeling and acting of those who recognize themselves in its call), we cannot *reduce* it to these effects . . . on the contrary, these very deeds assume their ontological consistency only by way of reference to the symbolic fiction 'Fatherland.' [It] is nowhere in reality but in spite of this, we cannot explain the very 'material' reality of fights and suffering without reference to it. . . . What we forget, when we pursue our daily life, is that our human universe is nothing but an embodiment of the radically inhuman 'abstract negativity' of the abyss we experience when we face the 'night of the world.' (Žižek 1992:52–53)

Carnival, like horror films and the state, offers both domesticated versions of our submission to the underlying terrors of the world and a glimpse into the other face of implacable government counterinsurgency; the inevitability of collaboration; the obscene arbitrariness of the market.

What is the state? A site and stake of struggle (Althusser 1971). But it is also a traumatic thing, an excess exuding from people's banal everyday actions which is never reducible to that. Perhaps the sense of something radically evil just outside our grasp is also the state-effect. We gropingly acknowledge that our reliance on the consistency of some big Other is an illusion, that there is bamboozling with and without a bamboozler. Perhaps the state is the Thing Žižek describes, which "is not simply a foreign body, an intruder which disturbs the harmony of the social bond: precisely as such, the Thing is what 'holds together' the social edifice by means of guaranteeing its fantasmatic consistency. . . . Our relationship to the Thing becomes *antagonistic*: we abjure and disown the Thing, yet it exerts an irresistible attraction on us; its proximity exposes us to a mortal danger, yet it is simultaneously a source of power" (1992:123).

Sometimes we pull back the curtain and find a humbug, not the Great and Powerful Oz. But other times we err to think we are in the know. A counter-counterinsurgency hermeneutic has to figure out which face of duplicity is our antagonist and how to harness its power through the ruby slippers (those psycho killer tools) we've been wearing all along. The myth of state power, its fantasmatic consistency may arise from our effective social activity as we—Guatemalans, Mayas, ladinos, indigenous, gringos, patrollers, brujas, etc.—struggle to act despite and through our own two-facedness or schizophrenia, despite and through the stickiness and entertainment of double binds, even as we are acted on by forces outside our control. Perhaps these are our hidden powers.

COUNTERSCIENCE IN COLONIAL LABORATORIES

Do you think that everything that can be known should
be known?" "Of course," said Antar. "I don't see why not."
"All right," said Murugan, dipping his spoon in his bowl.
"I'll turn a few pages for you; but remember, it was you
who asked. It's your funeral." Amitav Ghosh

The power we feared (hoped?) was hiding behind the everydayness of life, which we suspected was a bamboozlement, stands itself revealed as two-faced. For Slavoj Žižek it may be both the big Other behind the curtain conspiratorially pulling the strings and an empty mask, pure semblance. It doubly wields the sword of Repressive State Apparatuses (the right of death, the no of the father) and the cross of Ideology (the power over life, the name of the father). In turn, the power over life splits between the life of the individual and the life of the species. And "Life itself" also appears, on the Western philosophical stage at least, as two-faced. Aristotle (via Agamben 1998) calls one face *bios*, the social life of the polis, the stroll through the midway, getting lost in the crowd. The other face is *zöe*, bare life, the body and its functioning, its health, maintenance, or meaningless death. In the next chapter I explore these multiple faces and the transactions among racial, military, and colonial milieux, the plagues and afflictions carried out in the name of life. I return to questions about knowledge raised by the CEH author confronted with "radical evil," by Žižek pondering that nothing whose appearance is essential and must be preserved, and by the characters in Amitav Ghosh's novel *The Calcutta Chromosome*—some who assume that everything that can be known should be, while others know that knowing can lead to assuming identifications that transform the whole caboodle.

INJECTION

In highland fairs, amidst the games of chance, video salons, rides, dances, food booths, and processions of the Virgen de Tránsito, one might also find a *puesto de salud* (health booth). A local health promoter or sometimes a city-bred doctor conducting his or her required social service, takes advantage of the crowds to provide information from the national public health service, usually underwritten by another state or metastate like UNICEF. The information may include, for example, verbal explanations in Spanish of vaccination campaigns, pamphlets on general health, and free posters on the life cycle of the mosquito with dire warnings of the dangers of standing water. The posters, along with aging campaign photos from elections past and soft-porn ads for soda, adorn the walls of many highland homes. Health promoters also circulate through the countryside, gamely covering mountainous miles in all sorts of weather to inoculate children and dispense information and medicine, although the outposts are often poorly supplied. Almost across the board these people are deeply committed to improving life in their communities.

Health workers have become such a distinctive sight in rural areas that any stranger arriving with a backpack on will send young children scurrying away screaming, sure they're about to be poked with a needle. For many adults, however, the injection has accrued almost magical powers. Doctors find that people reject oral medications and far prefer medicine, vitamins, and supplements administered directly into the body. Joyabaj has dozens of modest houses sporting the sign "Se ponen inyecciones" (Injections done here), and they run a brisk business. Adela, the marvelous raconteur so fascinated with the famillionairety of the exhumed mass grave, supplements her meager income this way. Matilde González traces complex interactions among people descending to the coast to *sufrir* (suffer) and encountering new diseases like malaria that resisted the ministrations of traditional healers like the *chuch ajaw*. This combined with the Catholic Action missionaries who appeared, providing often injectable drugs that *did* work and for free, while preaching against the Satanism of traditional authorities and other witches. This sometimes led to conversion from the nominally Catholic *costumbre* to the official church while "generating among the population the myth of 'the needle and the syringe'" (2002:281). People are now willing to pay to be acted on by this force coming from outside them, like the young men who dose themselves to meet quota on the sugarcane plantations.

Lashing together questions about the two faces of the state and the at least two-way activities of power, I return to embodi/meant. Chapter 6 looked at state powers incarnated in named individuals, even as a less carnal but still quite material face emerged from their circulations. The next chapter explores bamboozlement without a bamboozler and an emerging variant of the war of the cross, now carried out through the instruments of life, science, and health. Its talismans might be the microscope and the hypodermic needle rather than the cross and the accountant's pen, but likewise its practices transform entire milieux.

I segue from the sideshow to the health booth as an outpost of technoscience via the science fiction novel *The Calcutta Chromosome: A Novel of Fevers, Delirium, and Discovery*, written by the social scientist Amitav Ghosh, who also connects conspiracy and its simultaneous terror and hopes for healing (or at least interpretation) to racism and colonialism. I will explore whether Foucault's theory of a singular, yet two-faced power, what he calls biopolitics, is good to think with about duplicity and postwar Guatemala. Also good for thinking is remembering that colonialism was and is not a one-way action of the colonizer on the colonized, but a recombinant articulation, a deeply hierarchized relation of unequal players. Nonetheless, it transforms all involved. Guatemala's postwar-in-action is a moment in this ongoing relation and, like Ghosh's novel, the next chapter focuses again on what lies in between, mi-lieu. Latour squished together the term "technoscience" to emphasize the networking involved (*tekth*- to weave, build, join) in the process of discerning (*scire* — distinguish — etymologically rooted, like scissors, screen, and science, in "to cut"), of actively making sense or figuring. What laboratories do, like the windmill example, is lash or tie actants, human and nonhuman, together into networks — it is in this sense that the efforts to create the CICIACS are a lab. They translate what lies in-between them so they begin to act together.

Ghosh's book is a (La)tour de force tracing a speculative future connected to the lashings and unexpected passage points of imperial networks that made the colonies into "laboratories of modernity." As in postcolonial encounters, twentieth-century labs in the global north created transuranic elements and transgenetic animals that, like the in-human, both fit right in (us) yet "blast widely understood senses of natural limit" (Haraway 1997:56). And, like any laboratory, these are sites of hard work and of discovery, where theories and techniques are tested and new beings are created. But etymologically "laboratory" is linked both to labor and hardship and to *labi* — to slip, fall, or totter.

Genetic experiments and nanobot-like interventions are nothing new for colonized peoples. In the Americas their sinews, hearts, minds, and germ lines (remember Malinche) have been put to the service of alien invaders for five hundred years. But the bodies of the colonizers are also visited and sometimes reprogramed by microscopic invaders like genetic material and ideas, as well as infections and microbial parasites. Tropical medicine developed as counterinsurgency. "Fever and dysentery are the 'generals' that defend hot countries against our incursions and prevent us from replacing the aborigines that we have to make use of," complained Brault, a French colonial official in 1908 (in Latour 1988:141).[1] We must always expect strange alliances, unexpected consequences, and new forms of the human in these labs, which may be why freaks and sideshows were such an important effect of the colonial project.

SOCIAL SCIENCE FICTION

> Murugan said, "Not making sense is what it's all about—
> conventional sense, that is. Maybe this other team started
> with the idea that knowledge is self-contradictory; maybe they
> believed that to know something is to change it, therefore in
> knowing something, you've already changed what you think
> you know so you don't really know it at all: you only know its
> history. Maybe they thought that knowledge couldn't begin
> without acknowledging the impossibility of knowledge. See
> what I'm saying?"
>
> "I'm listening," said Antar. "For what it's worth."
>
> ". . . if it's true that to know something is to change it, then
> it follows that one way of changing something—of effecting
> a mutation, let's say—is to attempt to know it, or aspects
> of it. Right? . . . You know all about matter and antimatter,
> right? And rooms and anterooms and Christ and Antichrist
> and so on? Now, let's say there was something like science and
> counter-science." Amitav Ghosh

The borderline defining the human, and life itself, is constantly put to the test in colonial laboratories. It is hypothesized, tested, and remapped in at least two ways. One is tropically, via tropes or figures, through meaning (White 1978)—as in debates over enslavement and whether the naked creatures "discovered" in the brave new world "counted" as human. This is the work of the cross, of those immaterial beliefs that have such devastating and concrete effects. Donna Haraway suggests that the way one knows something is a technology. It may be obvious, like the advanced microscope that allows us to know that *Mixotricha paradoxa* even exists in the hindgut of a South Australian termite, or the space race that reveals Gaia, our world, able to be rethought as a dynamic, self-regulating system (1995). Or it may be more subtle, like the mental technologies of the records, ledgers, science, fictions, assumptions, NGO ideas of the Maya, and genres through which we grasp the world and then transmit it to others. Social science and science fiction are technologies struggling to understand the promises of monsters created in the violently hybridized interzones of colonized, raced, gendered, and sexualized bodies in the midst of the postwar-in-action. But the borderline defining the human in the colonial laboratory is also hypothesized, tested, and remapped troopically, through armies deploying the highest-tech weapons of their time (see Driscoll 1994). Racialized and gendered assumptions of identity emerge from the tropics via tropes and troops, as do counter-counterinsurgency hermeneutics. These are alchemical networkings, interventions in the germ line, assimilations and immune system defenses, and forms of reproduction that may exceed the Darwinian bottleneck of the (hetero) sexual.

Calcutta Chromosome is a science fiction novel about malaria. The science part is about a terrible illness with astronomical mortality rates, which is spread by mosquitoes—as discovered by Ronald Ross in Calcutta in 1898. "A virtuoso of disease" (Brody 2001:D1), the mosquito will bite almost anything and travels easily, making leaky many apparent hard-set boundaries—between human and animal, rich and poor, military and civilian, here and there. In the fiction part of the novel the mosquito (and the parasite/plasmodium it transmits) even blurs the border between now and then, connecting the late 1800s, the mid-1990s, and the very near future. The character Antar was orphaned as a boy in Egypt by a mysterious fever. The only survivor from his village, he still suffers periodic malaria relapses. In the near future of the novel he works for what used to be an NGO with the creepy name of LifeWatch, now the International Water Council, where he became involved with a coworker named Murugan who was fascinated with malaria and disappeared mysteriously in Calcutta while tracking down details of Ross's discoveries.

A COLONIAL LABORATORY

Murugan's counterstory of malaria goes something like this: Farley, a young U.S. malaria scientist turned missionary doctor journeyed to India in 1893, convinced, thanks to Pasteur, that malaria was caused by a bacteria and would soon be eradicated, so he could concentrate on the natives' souls (bios, not zöe). Once in India he learns that Laveran, a French military doctor in Algeria, is in vogue with a theory of malaria as a protozoan or animal parasite using human and mosquito bodies as home, love hotel, and sewer. Farley gains access to a lab in Calcutta and encounters another science being practiced among the Indian assistants. The illiterate cleaning woman Mangala not only has an extraordinary expertise with the sample slides and microscope, but also seems to be running a cult healing practice on the side for people suffering late-stage syphilis. Fed up with Farley's presence in the lab she makes sure he finds what he seeks, but soon afterward he mysteriously disappears, making way for Ross, a schlocky poet and soon-to-be Nobel winner owing to his discovery in that same Calcutta lab assisted by (or assisting?) Mangala.

If colonies are laboratories, they are so in a number of ways. Colonial science itself, linked as it tried to be to modernity and progress, struggled to become an obligatory passage point, and it generally succeeded. But science, obligatorily, is always apparently elsewhere than the third world. In turn, what usually goes without saying when colonies are described as laboratories of modernity is that the colonizers were the scientists and the colonized people were the mice and guinea pigs. Human subjects protocols were suspended, and one could get away with a lot, including murder.[2] But Latour also suggests that even as each element tied together becomes a conductor or transmitter, it is a multiconductor as well and an unpredictable one at that. Each object trying to become a fact is "not only collectively transmitted from one actor to the next, it is collectively *composed* by actors. This collective action then raises two more questions. To whom can the responsibility for the game be attributed? What is the object that has been passed along?" (1987:104).

The Calcutta Chromosome offers both a rather straightforward and a totally mind-boggling answer to these questions. I'll start with the first—that obviously science does not belong only to the West, and not only rich white men do science (see also Eglash 2000, Prakash 1999, Verran 2001). I start there because my surprise at being confronted with this truism is what made me realize I had to take Ghosh's science fiction as seriously as his social science.

Lunching in 2000 with a Mayan cultural rights activist, I met her husband, Jorge, who has also assumed the identity of Maya. He ran a wonderful bookstore in the highland town of Quetzaltenango. In its courtyard there was a small shrine to his older brother, who was a guerrilla fighter in ORPA—one of a handful of indigenous people to attain a command position in the revolutionary forces—and who was murdered by the army. Jorge is also a scientist who worked in labs in Guatemala and Honduras to develop a technique for spotting malaria in blood donations. In addition to his duties at the bookstore and with the Mayan political party that had recently won the mayorship, he works in the local blood bank to keep the supply secure from disease.

Having read a lot of postcolonial theory and feeling a bit self-congratulatory about my progress in unthinking Eurocentrism, I'm embarrassed to admit I was surprised to find original research going on in Guatemala, one of the "famished resourceful regions of the Third World" (Kumar 1997:36). I realized I had assumed that any work there would be what a Guatemalan friend called "maquila science," or science in the guise of export processing. Maquila science would parallel the production of knock-off Levis and cheap shoes, created in outsourced production plants where minimally paid workers put together pieces developed in the global north to make our clothes, electronics, and cartoons. In the classic Marxian sense of humans as appendages to the machine, maquila employees are seen as mindless workers, allowed no spark of creativity, much less genius, as they dutifully and prosthetically embody plans devised elsewhere (Wright 2001).

Yet here was a Maya-hacker (Nelson 1999), as comfortable with the cyborg technologies of ritual cave sacrifices to tellurian deities and the soul splitting of his *nahual* spirit as with laboratory techniques of microscopes and test tubes. Through Jorge I began to explore networks of knowledge and practice linking malaria scientists and eradication teams throughout the hemisphere—the famous malaria school in Maracai, Venezuela, and the breakthroughs made in the effort to develop a malaria vaccine on an island in the Amazon jungle by the Colombian Manuel Elkin Pattaroyo—considered a national treasure in that war-torn country, enjoying the celebrity North Americans grant only to film and reality TV stars (Robin Kirk pers. comm., Honigsbaum 2001). Not only is science happening in India, Egypt, South Korea, Guatemala, and elsewhere, but these are laboratories lashing together a wide range of actors and actants. This science may pass through the obligatory passage points of science and state with a big S and acknowledge the immense power of troops and Big Pharma (le Carré 2001a), but it's also weedy and promiscuous, going to seed (Haraway 1995:xvii).

Just a few months after I met Jorge news broke of just such a challenging alliance, as the Bombay-based company Cipla Ltd. announced the availability of its low-priced version of a patented AIDS drug cocktail for sale to countries in the global south. The patented version runs $5,000 per patient per year while Cipla's costs $350. Colonial laboratories are sites for desperately hard labor as well as slippages and totterings. As R&D in labs in India and Brazil gets tied together with Brazilian and Ugandan models for AIDS prevention, with law cases brought against pharmaceutical giants like Glaxo-SmithKline to force the sale of generics, and with NGOs like Doctors without Borders, the border war goes on. Science-fiction-in-action changes the object passed along, brings new players in who take on new responsibilities. Latour says that laboratories become "powerful enough to define reality," but "reality, as the Latin word res indicates, is what resists. What does it resist? Trials of strength" (1987:93).

TROOPS AND TROPES: TRIALS OF STRENGTH AND DELIRIOUS REALITY

Now, the Cipla tale is a rather sweet social science story of another reason, a counterscience with science fiction overtones, although India's entry in 2005 into WTO compliance is threatening this network. But, you may be asking, in the day and age of shock and awe can such a web really resist a trial of strength in the highly asymmetrical confrontation with "modern" science? In fact, Guatemalans lost their most recent trial on this terrain. In late 2004, when the Congress approved a law making generic drugs more available, the United States threatened to cut aid, refuse to renew the IMF standby agreement, exclude Guatemala from CAFTA, and freeze the free trade process in general, thus making other Central American governments into U.S. allies in pressuring Guatemala to conform, given their economies' deep dependence on such trade relations. U.S. Trade Representative Robert Zoellick made personal calls to a number of Guatemalan politicians using what was described as "not very diplomatic language" (Rodríguez P. 2004:3). The Berger government caved.[3]

Latour warns, "The layman is awed by the laboratory set-up, and rightly so. There are not many places under the sun where so many and such hard resources are gathered in such great numbers, sedimented in so many layers, capitalised on such a large scale. . . . We are left without power" (1987:93). "After all, the power of any lab is proportionate to the number of actants it can mobilise on its behalf" (1987:91), which is why modern labs have such close ties to the military.

This is where the mind-boggling aspects of Ghosh's answer to the questions of responsibility and objects come in, via the Calcutta chromosome and malaria as an awesome and unpredictable ally. Are we left without power? Of course not! Ghosh, like Latour, writes in order to change by knowing. Like the many people I've described who testify, file lawsuits, dig up bones, make films, tell jokes, all as battles in the war of the cross, as challenges to Assumption One, they insist we know the enemy and understand our ties to it. Counter-counterinsurgent hermeneutics will take us through some tropes and troops of the war machine of malarial technoscience, a site of both linking and cutting.

The big discoveries in malaria research were made primarily by military scientists. The military campaigns that undergird the colonial laboratories were waged against nonhuman actants as well as the "restless natives."[4] The human army is interested in winning and translated many interests into its counterinsurgency machine. Likewise, malaria eradication campaigns, like those of William Gorgas in Panama 1906 and Fred Soper in Brazil 1938, relied heavily on military discipline and precision. As David Akin writes, "Armies and [antimalarial drugs] have grown up together. . . . Private sector drug companies rarely initiate malaria research for the simple reason that there is little money to be made in wiping out a disease that affects the world's poorest people. But armies have an incentive to keep their soldiers healthy in the jungle" (2002:F7). But even as the armies and their laboratories are powerful, tying in allies, making us all complicit, each ally may act in multifarious ways, modifying, appropriating, ignoring, mutating, incorporating into it new elements, incorporating it into new contexts. Malaria is particularly unpredictable, in part because it is not a thing but a series of interconnections.

In fact, malaria is a fundamentally weird disease. David Turnbull calls it a "motley" (like Chartres cathedral), meaning completely heterogeneous, deeply messy (2000:162). So much so that the fictional and the scientific get pretty fuzzy in Calcutta Chromosome. As in the novel, the malaria parasite (plasmodium) does divide in two and then have sex in the gut of an anopheles mosquito, and Mangala's healing cult using malaria to cure syphilis was a real treatment.[5] Plasmodium Falciparum has a genome more like an animal than a bacteria and contains an ancient enslaved alga, making it plant-like as well. A major plot twist in Calcutta Chromosome also depends on the strange but true capacity of malaria to live dormant in a human body for years, even decades, then suddenly blossom again into desperate chills and fevers. As Antar is decoding Murugan's whereabouts he begins to feel a fever coming on, allying him, not completely willfully and quite unpredictably, to a counter-technoscience.

Malaria and troops have a long, strange relation, going head to head in trials of strength to determine who resists, who defines reality. But laboratories are also sites for slippage, just as tropes are swerves or Latourian translations. There, interests are transformed just enough to enlist allies. For Urmila, a new ally in his quest, Murugan traces a counterscience in which assistants in British military labs translate those labs themselves to other purposes. Murugan suggests that Mangala had a flair for the artisanry of microscopy but was also free of the "black boxes" of orthodoxy:

Because she actually believed that the link between the bug and the human mind was so close that once its life cycle had been figured out it would spontaneously mutate in directions that would take her work to the next step. That was what she believed, I think: that every time she reached a dead end, the way ahead was by provoking another mutation.

Pushing away her empty plate, Urmila said, "How?"

"By trying to make certain things known."

"So did she succeed?" she asked.

Murugan smiled. "I think we're going to find out." (Ghosh 1995:252)

The knowledge is transformative, and *The Calcutta Chromosome* ends with the twist of many a great science fiction book (and Hernández Pico's warning about state power): that when we humans think we're using the machines it turns out the machine is using us. We are lashed in to a logic not entirely our own, even as we assume it. Latour says, we "end up being trapped by a completely new element that is itself so strongly tied that nothing can break it up. Without exactly understanding how it all happened, people start placing transcontinental phone calls, taking photographs, having their cats and children vaccinated, and believing in phrenology" (1987:133). In Ghosh's novel a shadowy conspiracy, perhaps some of it guided by human agency, but much of it not, allows an inchoate logic to take form. The Calcutta chromosome allows for a transcendence of life and death, overcomes the heterosexual bottleneck of Darwinian reproduction, dabbles in Lamarckian hopes that acquired traits could be transmitted along, just as stories are, just as science is.

Humans make science, but not as we choose. Another reason emerges from the connections made in colonial laboratories. Such labs become powerful enough to define reality, as Latour says. If, in a given situation, "no dissenter is able to modify the shape of a new object, then that's it, it IS reality . . . the minute the contest stops, the minute I write the word 'true', a new, formidable ally suddenly appears in the winner's camp, an ally invisible until then, but behaving now as if it had been there all along: Nature who is sometimes faithful, sometimes fickle" (1987:93–94). But this reality, this Nature, of plasmodium, mosquito, troops, tropes, resistances, Mangala, is terribly fickle. We seek to change by knowing but what emerges is not something we could foretell. Is this why we feel duped?

Chapter Seven

LIFE DURING WARTIME

> The mechanisms of power are addressed to the body, to
> life, to what causes it to proliferate, to what reinforces the
> species, its stamina, its ability to dominate, or its capacity
> for being used. Michel Foucault

> The worst effects of American power are the result of the
> best-intentioned actions. As a result, the animosity in
> other parts of the world often seems unaccountable to
> the US. Ziauddin Sardar and Merryl Wyn Davies

REMOVING THE WATER FROM THE FISH,
GIVING WATER TO THE PEOPLE

"The army gives water to the people!" This slogan adorned a float at the Army
Day parade in Guatemala City in 1993. Ladino children dressed in indigenous
clothing pumped actual water amid greenery and papier-mâché structures
meant to look like a Mayan village while a smiling soldier looked on. The
float was sponsored by the S-5, army civil affairs, to highlight its community
development work. "I wonder if they realize," said Pepe Lara, my Guatemalan friend, as we watched the parade together, "that 'to give water' is slang
for killing someone?"[1]

Potable water systems and latrines are centerpieces of late twentieth-
century development and hygiene strategies, meant to improve life and
health. If "'deduction' [taking life] has tended to be no longer the major form
of power but merely one among others," as Foucault suggests (1980a:136),
then the float, traversing the streets of the city surrounded by soldiers,
works tropically and troopically as a double entendre.

According to Tom Tomorrow, when smart bombs live up to their names
they discuss Foucault's theories of power. I've also found such theories good
to think with about the many entendres in the assumptions of identity
and end/s of war. While power is as dangerous as a bomb it may swerve
off course, like a counterscience. In turn, what are the stakes in knowing
through bio/power. Is it unitary or two-faced?

Foucault suggests that power does not repress an already existing subject

Smart bombs live up to their name. Tom Tomorrow. Used with kind permission.

(two is too many) but that our experiences of subjectivity are themselves produced by power. While it may be expressed against our bodies in punishment, from Daddy spanking us to state-sanctioned capital punishment and wartime mass killings, such power is relatively weak, only "the negative and emaciated form of prohibition" (Foucault 1980a:86). Power is also exercised productively, through each and every one of us when we pick up a pencil, strive to do well in school, turn to doctors for health, desire a sex partner, or engage in political activism. I've deployed such a reading already to signal connections between apparent opposites—counterinsurgency and insurgency, clandestinity and unveiling, docile workers and armed rebels. Power subjects us to capitalism, patriarchy, racism, and homophobia, but it also subjectivizes us, makes us who we are, which is multiconductors. Working with anatomo-politics ("centered on the body as a machine: its disciplining, the optimization of its capabilities, the extortion of its forces"), the main role of biopolitics is "to ensure, sustain, and multiply life [*bios*], to put this life in order" (1980a:137–38). Health, the future of the species, the vitality of the social body—these are the sites and promises of this power.

But if power is capillary—like a bloodstream, everywhere, inside us, around us—is resistance futile? Is this a theory of one? Duccio Trombadori says, "There is no escaping the impression that Foucault, far from providing a new stimulus to demands for liberation, limits himself to describing a mechanism of pure imprisonment" (in Foucault 1991a:20). A friend whose politics I much admire echoes this attitude: "The problem with Foucault is you don't see the stakes, you don't get a sense of what is being fought for. He's a conspiracy theorist without conspirators." As real-world smart bombs wreck havoc in Afghanistan and Iraq, how does one get smart with Foucault's injunction to cut off the king's head and think of power not as concentrated in one place (the state, the Pentagon) but dispersed throughout individual bodies, including those of conspirators like CIACS, and social bodies?

Although it makes me sound like a contestant in a beauty queen contest, I like to think of myself as someone who wants to improve life, and when I try to imagine what that would look like it sounds like Foucault's theory of power—healthy and vital. But, with apologies to Public Enemy, I thought I was fighting the power—the repressive one that denies us the free and healthy lives we deserve. This is the power of death concealed in the life-giving promise of the army's float. By an act of interpretation, of getting the joke that "giving water" also means "to kill," the healthy, happy children and smiling soldier look far more sinister. So I become suspicious when "they" offer health in the form of potable water. Although seeming to help me, is it really just controlling me (only more insidiously than a cop with pepper spray)? Is it just trying to win me over through an updated version of the war of the cross, a *Matrix*-like ideological program to make me willingly acquiesce? Am I duped by this "power over life"?

In this vision "it" resembles the cat in Sam Gross's cartoon.

"I wonder if they realize," ponder many returned exiles to postwar Guatemala, that the state is being nice when it funds bilingual education, roadwork, democracy, and other improvements. Many feel that their pleas to "think!" fall on deaf(ened) ears. But given that the same assumptions may undergird opposing political strategies, is "Think!" a strong enough defense?

This chapter circulates through three nodes that coalesce these anxieties—with each node itself seemingly Janus-faced. One is my, the mouse's, and many Guatemalans' suspicious conspiracy theory and—the other face—my and Tom Tomorrow's sense that Foucauldian theory (like Ferguson's apparatus that may do what it does "behind the backs of or against the wills of even the most powerful actors") *can* help us understand risks, stakes, and what is being fought over—the ends of war. The second node is a doubleness that Foucault was well aware of: the terrifying contradictions of twentieth-century (modern) regimes that visit never-before-seen holocausts on their own populations but simultaneously "now it is over life,

"For God's sake, think! Why is he being so nice to you?"

throughout its unfolding, that power establishes its dominion" (1980a:137, 138). The third returns us to the crux of our relation to culture, aka the state, ideology, hegemony, collective consciousness, power. Foucault terms it the relation between the life of the species and the life of the individual, "omnes et singulatum" (Foucault 1981), our two faces. How can we feel like an individual, the "subject effect," while still being part of something larger—that acts on and through us, doubling us over? How, in turn, is that something to be understood? Is it only other people? Or does it include our own bodies, the environment, or even the past, and how all of these influence how we relate to ends, what we hope and struggle for? I will try to get smart with biopolitics by diffracting these tensions through not one but two wars in Guatemala. The one against people we are already familiar with. The other is against mosquitoes and *Falciparum*.

"Hey, You!"

I first encountered Foucault's order of things in 1986, recently returned from my first research trip to Guatemala and trying to account for army strategies of massacres and scorched earth aimed at taking the water—population— away from the fish—the guerrilla, combined with more life-giving policies like the Development Poles. The knowledge I had accrued in these travels was leading me to assume the identity of activist, engaging with networks connecting Guatemala with U.S. foreign policy and with local and globalized activism around antiapartheid, the nuclear freeze, Central America solidarity, and reactions to the Iran Contra scandal.[2] These movements offered new models of government that would spread the fruits of modernity—education, health, economic development, and access to resources—to improve the lives of entire populations. "Schools not bombs!" we chanted. "Money for health care, not for war, U.S. out of El Salvador!"

While I often felt overwhelmed with horror and pity at what Guatemalans were suffering, I also had a sneaking suspicion that part of the appeal of solidarity was that power relations seemed clearer there than in the United States. Guatemala seemed cleanly divided between the elite-military state and the resisting people. They seemed to have been spared the opiates of the welfare states that kept northerners blandly acquiescing. There, people had to be beaten to make them obey. Maybe they were ahead in seeing how oppressive power worked because they were behind in the biopolitical evolutionary ladder.

One day I came home to find two books on my porch: Maribel Morgan's *The Total Woman* and Michel Foucault's *Discipline and Punish*, courtship gifts from a suitor experimenting with dialectical montage.[3] Maribel was good for a laugh, but I began to read the Foucault seriously, and that helped me see, when I returned to Guatemala a few months later to study the army's model villages, that they were using every trick in the Panopticon guide to population control: every prisoner was a warden and subjectivized through schools, clinics, sports, hygiene, urban planning, and new agricultural production techniques (the *frijoles* of Ríos Montt's two-faced beans and bullets strategy). Schirmer calls it "restructuring indigenous life" (Schirmer 1998:64–80). "Se cambió el tiempo," say Sanbartolos to describe the war (González 2002). "Time changed," along with everything it connects to in Mayan cosmology: geographical and spiritual space, social relations and the connections to nonhuman beings as well as to one's own body and the fragile parts of one's soul. And the war also changed. Increasingly after 1982, with the Security and Development program, counterinsurgency began to address life, time, and connection, with the army disbursing desperately needed food aid, clothing, housing, and health care and paying minute attention to the details of the everyday, like installing traditional steam baths in the refugee reception centers. These were provided through S-5 as well as through the post-1986 civilian government ministries, Guatemalan Catholic and Protestant churches, foreign aid, and NGOs. The army, the government, and transnational actors "gave water to the people," setting up sanitation systems and latrines as part of more general development.

Now I thought I was pretty in the know, reading cutting-edge Continental theory into the Guatemalan highlands. But about ten years later I was sitting in a downtown Guatemala City café with my friend Pepe Lara.

An acquaintance of his, another journalist, stopped by our table, and I was introduced as "an anthropologist who wrote a book about Guatemala and Foucault." Shaking my hand, the man smiled broadly and said, "Oh, I *love* Foucault! You must show me this book sometime." After he left, my friend seemed uncomfortable. "That Cifuentes, he's not really my friend," he said. "I know him through the radio work, but he's with the army. He's the designer of the development poles."

Unable to interview Colonel Cifuentes, I can't prove a nefarious connection between reading Foucault and masterminding the follow-up to genocidal counterinsurgency.[4] But might this justify the suspicion that biopolitics is really a sly cover for social control? That when the army gives water to the people by attending to their desperate need, which counterinsurgency caused, it's just buying docility—or conducting propaganda to trick outside—observers?[5] Along with CIA torture manuals and their guidelines for funding assets, or Israeli Mossad handbooks used by Indonesian troops in East Timor (Aditjondro 2000), is Foucault just one more how-to book in the global diffusion of modern counterinsurgency?

I met Cifuentes toward the beginning of the second postwar as development pole strategies became more pronounced, now under the aegis of well-funded and energetic organizing to implement the peace accords. The government, goaded by the Maya and the left as well as by international experts, threw itself into infrastructure development like roads, potable water, sanitation, and schools. The health system was overhauled. Mayan organizing focused on the state to make it assume responsibility for making schooling, economic development, and the law culturally sensitive. Many progressives involved in these projects understood themselves to be pursuing the same struggle as during the war, but by other means. As a Mayan woman and returned exile said to me, "When I go into the highlands to do these human rights, democracy, and development workshops I am saying the exact same things I said in the early 1980s when I was in the guerrillas. Only now I don't have to hide. And I'm getting paid." She laughed.

In the name of health and vitality Schirmer argues that civil affairs was a sophisticated army counterinsurgency hermeneutic, including the "Sanctioned Maya prototype constructed and continually reconstituted through the military's optic" (1998:115). Hale might call this "the menace of neoliberal multiculturalism" as the "authorized Indian [who] has passed the test of modernity, substitute[s] 'proposal' for 'protest' . . . forced to operate within certain constraints both material and symbolic" (2006:220–21). "Schools, not bombs! Money for health care, not for war!" we chant. Yet like Schirmer and Hale, many analysts of colonialism describe schools, health care, science, and other ideological apparatuses as being similar to bombs in acts of conquest. They are weapons in the war of the cross. As Aimé Cesaire (1972) notes, colonized peoples now struggle *for* these very same techniques of oppression,[6] and the former colonizers seem cold and heartless when they refuse to provide them. They deny life, progress, and development to the very people who need it most.

Is life a ruse? Are we duped into collaborating with a thoroughly militarized Civic Action when we struggle for water systems and health care, especially the materially and symbolically constrained forms on the neoliberal table? Schirmer and Hale are quite alive to the complexities of postwar political work, yet, like the suspicious mouse, are intent on troubling the way counterinsurgency projects that benefit particular people may become unexamined assumptions for us all. I'd like to push the admonishment to "Think!" just a bit further. Anthropology (ludicrous, yet my tool), like the sciences of madness, health, prisons, and sex that Foucault charted, simultaneously produces objects of knowledge and subjects judged capable of knowing them. How am I to know, in the sense of *savoir* (being modified by the labor performed in order to know), the Guatemalan army and other faces of the state? They are both individually and institutionally brutal, racist, and violent, and their powers over death are important to denounce. But I also know that the army and the state are acted on, they act on us, and furthermore that they are imbued with power over life. When the postwar politico-econo-military state does provide the benefits its people demand, do we dismiss it as a curtain of benevolence hiding malevolent intent, in part because it's not as I'd choose, via a truly popular government? On the other hand, this small victory, that the state is assuming its responsibility to provide education and health, does not mean the struggle is over. Rather than a conspiracy to dupe, perhaps we can understand Cesaire, our chants, and the popular struggle for a more equitable distribution of the common wealth as what Foucault calls "'reverse' discourses," ones that demand that "legitimacy be acknowledged, often in the same vocabulary, using the same categories by which it was . . . disqualified" (Foucault 1980a:101).[7]

These link with the complex reasons, explored throughout this book, that led people, including primarily indigenous patrollers and soldiers, to participate in the civil war. They also link to how they know and reckon with the postwar. I hope they are good to think with about villagers as not only passive victims waiting for the guerrillas or the army (or me) to save them but also about the conditions of possibility for counterinsurgency and the tensions in modern power enacted through the postwar-in-action. These are the contradictions Foucault calls politics, with its two poles of development: anatomo-politics, with its attention to the individual body as a site of pain as well as vitality, and biopolitics, the species body, "linked together by a whole intermediary cluster of relations" (1980a:139). There are many "astonishments [in] a society in which political power had assigned itself the task of administering life" (1980:139). While never denying that power is brutal and dangerous, Foucault's theories of biopolitics push us through an analysis of conspirators and their duped victims, of crafty kitties and mice blind to their manipulations. I both want to know whether a particular strategy is repressive or liberatory and also question the appeal of fixed knowledges. And I continually ask about assumptions—how I think at all, especially in such either/or forms. For example, how did repression or liberation come to form the very limits of thought? How did we come to see the state as responsible for our health? What are the discursive waters that we, like little fishes (or guerrillas), swim in? And from there, rather than from an all-knowing, unchanging position outside of those relations, how do we develop biopowerful strategies? To continue elaborating on these questions and tensions I turn from a war that horrifies to one most would support: the war to eradicate malaria.

AT THE JUNCTURE OF THE BODY AND THE POPULATION: THE CAPILLARY POWER OF MALARIA

Malaria doesn't only kill, it enslaves the local population . . . malaria keeps its victims economically unproductive and is an epidemic disease that can depopulate entire areas of rich agricultural potential. We must cut the transmission chain, draining the sites of infection, overcoming the disease in those infected, and intercepting the mosquito vector so that the ill are no longer a danger for the collective. Antonio Argueta, Guatemalan journalist, *El Imparcial*, 1955

It is a human right to be healthy. With malaria the problem is not limited to often-imprecise medicine. It is fundamentally an economic-social problem that gradually undermines the economy and the human status of nations. It is a barrier to the evolutionary march of improvement and progress. Ten to fifteen percent of infant mortality is attributed to malaria. This illness consumes and eliminates a considerable portion of the human group that constitutes the future of the nations. Each and every one of us, regardless of class or caste, must

study how, through what attitudes, we can collaborate in its
elimination, even minimally, given that every man is part
of humanity and every contribution is clearly a contribution
to our own protection and survival. Werner Ovalle Lopez,
Guatemalan doctor and journalist, 1960

The CIA–United Fruit Company–MLN coup of 1954 cut short the Arbenz
government's efforts to improve the lives of poor Guatemalans through mild
land reform and ending forced labor, and by setting up a very basic safety
net of social security, health care, and workers' rights. However, in February
1955, in the midst of the counterrevolution and martial law, the Guatemalan
Health Ministry began a massive antimalaria campaign. While the previous
democratically elected governments had conducted antimalaria projects, as
had the United Fruit Company and the dictatorship of Jorge Ubico in the
1930s, this one was described as an all-out war. Malaria was the number
one health problem in nineteen of the twenty-two departments, and Guatemala was reported to have the highest morbidity and mortality rates in the
Americas (*Imparcial* 2/29/60). So just as U.S. officials were declaring Guatemala a political showcase, the malaria campaign became a different kind
of laboratory, serving as a pilot study for the World Health Organization's
(WHO) Global Malaria Eradication Programme. Begun in 1958, this was the
largest transnational public health project in history (Gladwell 2001:47).

Malaria, that motley, manifests in the infamous and overwhelming fevers
and chills that so stymied the colonial projects of the nineteenth century.
While local people develop some immunity after repeated exposures, it is
very often deadly for newcomers — one reason Africa was called the white
man's grave. The fevers are caused by a parasite, not by the *mal aires*, or bad
air, from which it gets its name. Entering the bloodstream from a mosquito
bite, the parasites migrate to the liver and replicate, forming a cyst that
bursts, sending parasites into the red blood corpuscles, where they feed on
hemoglobin; by this point thirty or forty have become trillions. The parasite also makes the red blood cells sticky, forming a plaque that clogs the
vascular system, including the capillaries of the brain. It kills through ane-
mia, organ failure from the fever (which can reach 106 degrees Fahrenheit)
or from brain swelling that leaves the organ starving for blood. Those who
survive experience a much-commented-on listlessness and malaise.[8] As the
English colonel Ronald Ross saw in India, the parasites mate and reproduce
in the sufferer's body, passing through a number of developmental stages. A
medical magic bullet is thus hard to develop, even now that the genome is
decoded. The parasites' progeny may live in the body for years, causing peri-

odic relapses, the "enslavement" Argueta describes. There are several forms of malaria plasmodium, four of which affect humans: *Plasmodium falciparum* is the most virulent and *Plasmodium vivax* the most common. They also develop immunity to the favored cures—quinine and its chemical replicants.

Malaria is a vector-transmitted disease, spread by mosquito bites from one human to another. Female mosquitoes ingest blood to fuel the production of eggs. Those that bite humans generally do so at night. Then, heavily laden, they sit on the nearest vertical surface to digest the meal. Later she will lay her eggs in nearby standing water, where they develop into larvae and then more mosquitoes. Sick people become a parasite reservoir the mosquitoes dip into, then carry out into the world. With the vector's help, a single human carrier can infect over one hundred others.[9] Mosquitoes in their various forms—eggs, larvae, adults—seem to travel easily in ships and airplanes, as do the parasites, carried inside mosquito and human bodies moving about the globe. It's all about what's in-between, as a headline reads: "Hovering where Rich and Poor Meet: The Mosquito" (McNeil 2000). There are some sixty species of *Anopheles* mosquitoes that carry malaria plasmodia. Like the parasites, mosquitoes tend to develop immunities to the insecticides used against them. However, once malaria is eradicated in an area, humans tend to lose their immunity.

Malaria has been blamed for the fall of Rome and French failure to build the Panama Canal, and it may have been as decisive to Allied victory in the Second World War as was breaking the Enigma code and the Russian and Chinese sacrifices of millions of lives. The struggle to understand and control malaria was central to the colonial project (its tropes *and* troops) and gave rise to the well-funded field of tropical medicine and its Nobel iconicizing.

Facing such a complex, mobile target, Guatemala's eradication campaign of 1955 had to respond in kind.[10] A special unit was created, the Servicio Nacional de Erradicación de la Malaria (National Service for Malaria Eradication), or SNEM, partly funded by the WHO, UNICEF, and later USAID. Curing those who harbored the plasmodium was difficult enough. First, how to identify sufferers, often in remote areas, with little public health infrastructure? Many, thankfully, recovered without benefit of medication, but they were still carriers, a "danger for the collective." Second, the diagnosis. How to link the clinic, if those suffering even made it there, to the laboratory for analysis of the *gota gruesa*, or blood sample, to ensure it was malaria? As one SNEM doctor put it, "This is the hardest and most delicate work. These are *complicadísimas* [extremely complicated] biological tests" (*Imparcial* 3/11/57). Then there's the problem of distributing the medicine and getting people to take it. Chloroquine and related drugs are notoriously unpleasant to consume because they are foul tasting and have nasty side effects. Once fevers, which run in cycles, abate, many people, thinking they will economize by saving the pills for next time, stop taking the drugs, thereby allowing the stronger, increasingly resistant *Plasmodia* to survive.

Then there's the vector or, more accurately, vectors. Even in a small country like Guatemala there are different kinds, with different habits, inhabiting various ecosystems (while they do not seem to transmit malaria, there are two species of *Anopheles* found only in Guatemala). As Dr. Carlos Gehlert-Mata, former director of SNEM said, "Malaria is very, very social. It's all about the *ambiente*." Those dedicated to the eradication of malaria must combine the skills of phlebotomy and entomology and anthropology. They must both take blood and catch mosquitoes. As a SNEM representative put it, "Just finding out the current susceptibility of the *Anopheles* is so time consuming, it's almost an overwhelming task, completely fatiguing" (*Imparcial* 2/4/57). Once the diagnosis is made, one site for attack is the standing water where eggs are laid and larvae develop. But this means anything from wetlands to limpid pools, to the small flower vases built in to graveyard mausoleums, to footprints left by cattle in damp ground. Abandoned tires are favorite breeding grounds, as are discarded soda cans.[11] This means a massive intervention in the ecosystem, as wetlands are drained, rivers dammed, lake surfaces oiled and chemically treated, houses, yards, patios, and villages scoured for offending containers. Then there is the mobile mosquito itself, notoriously hard to swat, who may light on walls, in the thatch roof of a hut, or on trees. Aerial insecticide spraying was deployed as well as house-to-house campaigns in which Dieldrin and DDT were applied directly to all inside walls, to kill the mosquito while she digests her blood meal. The post–*Silent Spring* generation (Carson 1994) may find it hard to believe, but DDT was considered a miracle in the 1940s—the very sign of modernity.

In 1955 SNEM organized brigades to fan out across the countryside to test for malaria, hunt mosquitoes, destroy breeding areas, administer quinine for free, and spray down walls. This entailed a major investment in *savoirs* (knowledges) and techniques. Vehicles, spraying equipment, medicines, and insecticides had to be bought, and personnel had to be trained in their use and surveilled in their practice. Just as a few undisciplined patients who resist taking their drugs can maintain the hardy plasmodium in their bodies, ready to spread with any passing mosquito, so careless spraying—missing some buildings, skipping a wall, diluting the solution too much—can undermine the entire effort. Given the emerging proof that mosquitoes developed resistance to DDT within seven years, SNEM was also in a race against time.

Areas had to be mapped, individuals identified, networks explored, movements analyzed, and dangers accounted for. This is where the anthropological *savoir* comes in.

Sorely lacking among the population, according to reports of the time, were education and an understanding of what was at stake, in addition to basic sanitary infrastructure. "We must raise peoples' consciousness about the kind of enemy we are confronting. They must tell us if they are sick, they must get treatment, and not become a focal point for malaria transmission, feeding mosquitoes with their damaged blood" (*Imparcial* 9/30/55). In one of the poorest countries in the hemisphere, where twenty-two languages are spoken, many people are monolingual in a Mayan language, and illiteracy rates were over 90 percent in some areas—not to mention that the program occurred in the wake of a bloody coup—some frustration was to be expected. As Dr. Epaminondas Quintana, a SNEM collaborator, explained in the national newspaper, it takes not only the work of volunteers, researchers, epidemiologists, people skilled in taking and analyzing blood samples, DDT sprayers, doctors, and public health experts, but also a human touch. He wrote, "We have to understand that in rural areas there is good reason to mistrust those who come from outside, who are often arrogant. For the campaign to work people have to understand it, and we need to be conscious of their personal issues, learn their names" (1/5/73).

Gehlert-Mata admitted some of the errors SNEM made:

We assured people that the medicine does not cause a stomachache, that it doesn't cause miscarriages, or anything, but once I took the medicine and it gave me gastritis for four days! So you are saying things that aren't true, and when it causes suffering then they won't take the full eight-day treatment. . . . Another problem is that the DDT killed everything—the bugs and roaches and then the animals, the chickens that ate them, the cats, so there were rat invasions, and they ate the crops. This was a big problem that led people to refuse the fumigations. The director before me committed an error in a community that didn't want to allow it. They came out with sticks in the street when the brigade showed up and so the other director called out the military police and put them in front of the fumigators. They beat some people up. Yes, they managed to spray, but from that day on the people turned against the system of malaria. I practically had to go house to house in that community to convince them that despite what had happened we would respect them. There's a lot you can do, based on dialogue, methods you can take. It has to be based in respect. I think we've advanced in Guatemala, in a few things.

At the global level, William Gorgas, who eradicated yellow fever from Cuba and Panama in the early 1900s, said that in order to fight malaria, you had to learn to think like a mosquito. Fred Soper, who headed the WHO Global Eradication Programme, disagreed. As Gladwell describes it, "Fighting malaria had very little to do with the intricacies of science and biology. The key was learning to think like the men he hired to go door-to-door and stream-to-stream, killing mosquitoes. His method was to apply motivation, discipline, organization, and zeal in understanding human nature" (2001:44). As a WHO official said in 1957, "It's easy to write about eradication in countries where you just need to press a button to get everything moving, but not even the best informed understand how hard it is to get even the most rudimentary projects under way in those areas where malaria causes the worst ravages. We can rely on technical promise, but we will need a fundamental reorganization of existing services" (*Imparcial* 1/20/57).

Such reorganization would require careful systematization and subjectivization (*assujetissment*). These knowledges (*connaissance*), carefully collated from around the globe[12] and trailing the glory of Nobel prizes, had to be incorporated into the most minute aspects of people's lives, activities, techniques, and selves. If people were to be saved from the scourge of malaria, these knowledges had to become *savoirs* in Foucault's sense: to "permit an alteration, a transformation, of the relationship we have with ourselves and our cultural universe: in a word, with our knowledge [*savoir*]" (1991a:37). These "alterations" are examples of the microphysics of capillary power. Defending the individual's blood meant acting through the social body's tiniest sites of flow and transfer, which in turn entails the assumptions of identity. Subindividual actants (mosquito larvae, the parasites) are thus "linked together by a whole intermediary cluster of relations" (Foucault 1980a:139) to superbodies politic like the Guatemalan state, anthropology, and WHO via the individual, who thereby becomes an "effect" of power and "the element of its articulation" (Foucault 1980b:208).

Quintana outlined these biopolitical challenges in a series of articles in 1964, around the time the U.S. Congress cut off funding to WHO. "To carry out the necessary organization in towns, villages, hamlets, even the tiniest parcels, we need courage!" he wrote. "Optimism, energy, resources, executive support and sincere cooperation from everyone in the country. We need an extraordinary energy to eliminate the thousands of elements involved, but it is precisely in this that administration—in the modern sense of 'to administer'—consists!" (*Imparcial* 1/15/64). In an article headlined "Guatemalans! If you are Patriotic, Don't be Lazy, Help Out!" he lists how citizens could help: volunteer to discover malaria cases and make sure ("even if it means grabbing them by the hair") that sufferers take the full course of medicine, and keep up enthusiasm by talking about the importance of collaborating. Priests, pastors, teachers, journalists, soldiers, mayors, business leaders, all must lend their aid. Without these steps, SNEM's entire project could fail, bringing international shame to Guatemala, decreasing worker efficiency, increasing risks for everyone of contracting malaria, in strains stronger than ever, and creating a serious obstacle to development (*Imparcial* 1/8/64).

"To administer" the project, volunteer brigades were set up in 1960 to make local people responsible for keeping track of each other. Volunteers were to identify those showing malarial symptoms, begin to treat them, and send a sample of their blood to the nearest laboratory. By special government decree, postage for the blood samples was free. According to a journalist who visited a brigade in 1964, the men and women of the Pro-Health Committee had donated land for a small office, and it contained a welter of documents, maps, statistics, graphs, and charts showing all the water sources, houses, churches, and land parcels, and tracking registration, cooperation, and notifications of malaria cases. The anonymous journalist said, "To the uninitiated in such paperwork, it was difficult to interpret. We were quite impressed with their rigor and exactitude" (*Imparcial* 1/6/64). Gehlert-Mata said,

> We created a *mística* [mystique], yes. Back then the brigades looked great, all in their khaki uniforms, they had their hard hats, their yellow masks. I have a photo album of it all.[13] We had special jeeps. We also created maps of all the malaria regions of the country with each *house* drawn in. Around one hundred maps. And this was long before there were satellites! They knew where the person lived when they took the blood sample, so if it came out positive they could be there within twenty-four hours with the medicine. There was a network of volunteers who indicated that there was a case that appeared to be malaria, a fever. I think they were trained to take blood themselves. It's really very simple—just a prick. *It was an entire social organization.* Now, of course, this was all before the problems of the internal war that we lived through. This would have been *very* dangerous in those times, for one band, or for the other band, either for the government or the insurgency, to know the whereabouts of each and every person. They had even identified the little children. When you have to take the medicine every fourteen days, when it is the preventive medicine, you have to keep track.

Gehlert-Mata was proud that under his watch malaria cases dropped precipitously and *Falciparum* was practically eliminated. This *mística* may name the special affect surrounding the state as it moves through the countryside embodied in the great-looking brigades and slipping *Matrix*-like into us as we in turn grab our neighbors by the hair to act on them. It is in-human, in-us, our assumed identity.

As glowing reports on SNEM's progress frequently pointed out, the war on malaria was opening previously difficult-to-inhabit areas to commercial production, contributing to a surge in export crops, especially cotton (see González 2002 for what this meant for *mozos*). While records of the time frequently criticize the cotton growers for not doing enough in the malaria struggle, by the mid-1960s they too "realized it was better to cooperate than be indifferent." They began to keep track of work teams coming down from the *fincas de mozos* and set up medication sites and specialists to administer chloroprimaquine to each worker upon arrival (*Imparcial* 1/6/64). Unfortunately, their massive use of DDT against cotton pests was simultaneously increasing mosquito resistance with remarkable speed.

Malaria is an imperial disease. It was brought to the Americas by the Spanish colonizers, and it takes the heaviest toll on nonlocals in tropical areas, including highland Maya descending to the tropics for work. To repeat Brault's comment from 1908, "Fever and dysentery are the 'generals' that defend hot countries against our incursions." The French, British, and U.S. race to find a cure in the late 1800s was meant to keep whites alive in their new milieu, and the de jure and later de facto enslavement of Africans and their Caribbean descendents in the fever-ridden agroexport zones was justified by their supposed immunity.[14] The creating of transportation infrastructure like canals and railroads, stationing of armies, clearing of ground to plant and harvest tropical products, all had to confront, in addition to uprisings, escapes, work slowdowns, and other human-level obstacles, the invisible microbial resistance and its effects. As Frederick Upham Adams wrote in 1914,

> The natives would not work on plantations, and most of them still have an unconquerable aversion to sustained physical toil. The reason is not far to seek. The mosquitoes . . . have so inoculated them with their virus that they have neither the ambition nor the strength to compete with workers not thus afflicted. It is entirely possible that a generation of Central American natives of the laboring class might, if forced or persuaded to conform to modern sanitary science, surprise the world by displaying none of the laziness inherent in those who now inhabit mosquito-ridden sections. (267)

The biopolitical strategies of "modern sanitary science"—hygiene, medicine, health, or Pasteurization—are aimed at life, and their goal is double.

They are concerned with the life of the individual worker's body ("the adjustment and economy of energies"), and they are also aimed at the social body ("the regulation of populations, through the far-reaching effects of its activity" [Foucault 1980a:145]). Adams foresees entire classes and subsequent generations improved by these interventions. Like sex for Foucault, malaria eradication "fitted in both categories at once, giving rise to infinitesimal surveillances, permanent controls, extremely meticulous orderings of space, indeterminate medical or psychological examinations, to an entire micro-power concerned with the body. But it gave rise as well to comprehensive measures, statistical assessments, and interventions aimed at the entire social body or at groups taken as a whole" (Foucault 1980a:145–46). Like counterinsurgency, this was not a race war or a class war, but both, simultaneously.

In 1957 an anonymous journalist compared Guatemala to the United States, where malaria had been eradicated. "Their efficiency is helped by geography, organization, and education. Guatemala will require a lot of work, considerable investment and a limitless tenacity to achieve such co-ordination and systematization" (*Imparcial* 1/11).[15] But the *savoirs* of science, technology, and human nature *did* begin to work. While in 1940 there were more than thirty thousand cases of malaria and over thirteen thousand deaths, in 1963 no autochthonous cases were registered. People now remember the incredible spirit of the SNEM teams, their *mística*, the organization, the discipline, the sense of mission—in fact, the aging veterans still meet periodically to reminisce. Clara Arenas, who grew up on a United Fruit plantation, exclaimed, "I lived that! I remember so well! They came directly to the house and they gave you the pills and they stayed. They made you take it right then and there, and they watched you swallow it. Only then would they leave." Here *brigadistas* embody Foucault's pastoral power. As state representatives, like today's backpack-wearing vaccine injectors, they crossed raging rivers, braved fever zones, fumigated in the heat, and cared for the flock, then and there, each and every one, thereby enacting the state's willingness to sacrifice for its people and not only demand sacrifice. Perhaps in response a *mística* also developed among the population. People proudly displayed the little papers that showed they'd been regularly fumigated and participated in the immense, energetic network of volunteers who aided in mapping and then carefully administering their hamlets, seeking out feverish neighbors, ensuring they took the full course of medicine, attending to all the human and environmental sites that are "a danger for the collective" (Argueta 1955). The *mística* was also assumed as a national identity, in Guatemala and globally. Just as some little pieces of paper were affixed to people's walls to show incorporation into the project, other little pieces—specifically postage stamps commemorating the project—were proudly displayed and exchanged, traversing the planet, to show Guatemala's participation in this global struggle for a general improvement of life. As Rabinow would say, risk becomes socialized as each person's health becomes the responsibility of others (1989:187). In this willingness to take responsibility they would seem to agree with Ovalle Lopez that "it is a human right to be healthy" (1960).

Biopower on the Loose?

While I've definitely skewed my description toward a Foucauldian reading, it is pretty easy to describe Guatemala's postcoup WHO-supported malaria campaign point for point as a classic case of biopower on the loose. Governmental techniques of systematization are deployed throughout the social body, and individuals are actively engaged in optimizing their health. You will also, no doubt, have noticed striking similarities between the strategies and tactics of the two wars I've been describing. As Gehlert-Mata acknowledges, SNEM's sophisticated mapping "would have been *very* dangerous . . . either for the government or the insurgency, to know the whereabouts of each and every person." (The government *did* have this information, which is why the guerrilla burned down municipal archives. As Murugan suggested, knowing things changes them. Secrecy may be the point.)

How might we think about the parallels between the two wars? While even the Guatemalan army admits that the civil war was a national tragedy it's hard to dispute that eradicating malaria would be good for the world.[16] I would say this is true even if the eradication were instigated in order to support neocolonial capitalist assaults on resistant "unproductive" lowland environments, and on "lazy natives." So, was the campaign of 1955 just a cover for the nefarious purposes of the Guatemalan military and a newly regnant United States? Does it matter that the counterrevolutionary government didn't really care about the well-being of their citizens? Or that the plantation owners didn't truly give a damn about the health of the workers outside of their ability to pick cotton? Or, given the terrifying ease with which the target of such tactics can switch from *Falciparum* and mosquito to Indian, activist, terrorist, Jew, Palestinian, black, Tutsi, Timorese, etc., should the two wars be lumped together as the same thing? Should those of us truly, authentically invested in improving the world oppose them both?

Bruno Latour, keen on disputing the indisputable, warns against any resting assured that we know what true improvement might be. Describing the Pasteurization of France, he records translations, displacements,

"The World United Against Malaria": Stamps commemorating the global eradication program. Note that Guatemala did not issue a new design but overprinted an existing stamp. From the collection of Donald Nelson. Used with kind permission.

strengthenings, and reorganizations that over time and through struggle produce a redefinition of the social: "We cannot reduce the action of the microbe to a sociological explanation, since the action of the microbe redefined not only society but also nature and the whole caboodle" (1988:38). He might call the *savoirs* of the malaria eradication campaigns of the twentieth century a "strengthening," as new subjects are formed who understand and act on the "new facts" that standing water is dangerous and that your neighbor needs to take her medicine. "This unexpected strengthening is not in itself 'reactionary,' as suggested by some authors who are used to speaking only of power and who see hygiene as a 'means of social control.' The allies of the microbe are to be found on the left as well as on the right. . . . It is often impossible to tell whether such wars serve the right or the left because the microbe, like other actors in such networks, 'renders unpredictable interests that would be too predictable without [them]'" (Latour 1988:36–37).

The genocidal counterinsurgency definitely served the right in Guatemala, although often with unexpected consequences. While many in Guatemala were and are sympathetic to the aims of the guerrillas, their modernizing nationalist grid of intelligibility sometimes excluded Maya, women, and others, many of whom, however, passed through revolutionary organizations, thereby redefining the whole caboodle. Too, pursuing the unpredictable interests in wars against microbes is not to say that the plantation owners were not viciously exploiting *mozos* who had no alternative but to work for miserable wages in fever zones, or that the military state was not brutal when it beat up villagers who didn't want to be fumigated and murdered labor organizers struggling for higher wages, improved health care, and better working conditions. Using biopolitics to think with, however (like Latour's actor-networks, horror films, Two-Faced Indians, and sideshows), pushes us to focus on *relations*, often violent, but not always, on what lies between *minifundia* (tiny highland parcels) and *latifundia* (plantations); between *fincas de mozos y fincas de algodón* and *azúcar*; and among the Guatemalan state, local and transnational capital, mosquitoes, and indigenous workers; among SNEM *brigadistas* and *Plasmodium*, doctors, entomologists, soldiers, local collaborators, and anthropologists.

The productivity of power, the very subjectivization that works through these relational networks, suggests we are not actors in the liberal autonomous sense (nonduped), but neither are we docile automatons (*engañados*). We are acting all the time—not only when taking up arms—in relations through which power always flows in more than one direction. Latour suggests that "such distinctions among types of actors matter less than the fact that they are all renegotiating what the world is made up of, who is acting in it, who matters, and who wants what. They are all creating—this is the important point—*new sources* of power and new sources of legitimacy, which are irreducible to those that hitherto coded the so-called political space. They cannot be reduced to a 'social or political explanation,' since they are renewing the political game from top to bottom with new forces" (1988:40).

I've been wagering that getting smart (like Tom Tomorrow's bombs) with Foucault's theories of power helps us resist reductions (one is not enough) and instead work through the tensions between conspiracy theory and *savoirs* that subjectivize us, between the power over death and over life, and between the life of the individual and the life of the species (rather than position ourselves only on one side, the other, or outside). Getting smart means thinking about assumptions—"that without which I cannot think at all"—and how, through that, to chart an ethical way to make the world a better place. This entails, as Foucault suggests, attending to "subjugated knowledges," "preserved possibilities," and the "grid of intelligibility" (Gordon 1980, see also Stoler 1995) that makes improvement thinkable at all. He did this in his genealogies of fearless speech, pastoral power, confession, and care of the self. I wager these preserved possibilities, like the past returning in horror films, are good to think with to genealogize biopolitics and war/s in Guatemala as Lamarckian.

LIFE AND LAMARCKIAN INTERVENTIONS
IN THE MILIEU

> Lamarckianism was the mechanism by which man's conscious
> social activities affected and effected his further physical
> evolution. . . . [it] expressed an almost pathetic yearning for
> the old belief . . . of the social worker [who] thinks that his
> efforts to help individuals are of social importance.
>
> George Stocking

Lamarck? Isn't he the one from junior high biology who says that acquired traits are passed down? The old giraffe example? If you remember, an individual giraffe stretches to reach higher leaves, lengthening its neck slightly, then passes this trait on to her young, leading, after numerous generations of stretchers, to the giraffe of today, comfortably adapted to her niche. In junior high I was taught to giggle at this ludicrous explanation and prefer the random workings of natural selection in Darwinian evolutionary theory. After Mendel it became "aberrant" to believe in Lamarck (Stocking 1982:253), and Arthur Kroeber said, "heredity by acquirement is equally a biological and historical monstrosity" (259). But it turns out there may be more to Lamarck than my bio teacher let on. In fact, Lamarckianism may provide a grid of intelligibility for hopes to improve the world *and* exist as a preserved possibility within the practices of biopolitics — an Assumption One in both left and right thinking.

Around 1800 Lamarck articulated an evolutionary theory that undermined the then-current essentialist understanding of species as timeless ideal types.[17] Instead he focused on dynamic changes in creatures that would eventually lead to more widespread changes through which new species emerged. He developed the notion of milieu from its use in Newtonian physics to conceptualize an active relationship between an organism and its environment. He posited that when the body is faced with changing circumstances, its needs change. Attempting to fulfill these needs leads it to change how it acts, to transform its habits. By exercising different parts of the body — muscles, fluids, parts of the brain — those organs themselves change. It is a little unclear how this occurs, whether through fluids, electricity, or a *sentiment intérieur*, which Michael Ruse translates as "life force" (1999:7). These changes would then be passed down to succeeding generations. It was believed that germ cells (egg and sperm) were produced from the whole body, including the brain, which is why the changes in such organs would be heritable (Ruse 1999:153, also Jordanova 1984).

Lamarckianism is a behavioral and ecological theory of biological evolution. Rabinow says that "life was the central concept in Lamarck's system [but] he vigorously sought to strip the notion of any metaphysical or religious residues. Life was physical; matter was passive, life active" (1989:135). Lamarck's notion of milieu (in-between) is a mode of thinking about interactions among the natural environment, social elements, and individual humans. It insists on a relational system. Stocking says, "Lamarckianism helped to explain the evolution of races and the mental evolution of man in terms which gave what we would now call 'culture' a crucially determining role. It helped to explain and to validate the cultural progress of mankind in biological terms, at the same time that it freed man from the conservative implications of biological evolutionism" (1982:256). By "conservative" he seems to mean that in traditional Darwinism the past determines the future, everything comes down to that bottleneck where egg and sperm meet, and then there's no escape from the genetic map laid down.

Stocking describes Lamarckianism as influencing August Comte, Herbert Spencer, Booker T. Washington (via the "uplift of the race"), the colonial sense of "the white man's burden," many socialist projects emphasizing cooperation rather than competition, and some of Franz Boas's thinking. When Frederick Adams, a United Fruit Company apologist, writes in 1914 of a generation of Central American natives surprising the world with their vitality, once they are subjectivized by modern sanitation, he is a Lamarckian. But, as I was taught in school, Lamarckianism is now *so* over. The growing popularity of Darwinist theories was reinforced by the rediscovery of Mendelian genetics in the early 1900s. Mendel's work with pea plants provided the random genetic mutations that scientifically explained "the descent of man," and August Weismann claimed to prove the continuity of germ plasm and its inability to acquire and pass on characteristics. This combined assault ensured the extinction of the increasingly unfit Lamarckian paradigm. A school of neo-Lamarckians emerged post-Weismann to argue that "the acquired characteristics they had in mind were . . . subtle, slow, internal, adaptive changes of the organism to the environment" (Stepan 1991:69). But the blows delivered by Weismann, Boas, Kroeber, and others undermined the Lamarckian position so much that by the late 1910s in the United States and Britain it was practically a curse to accuse someone of holding such ideas. No one could plausibly argue that the net results of an individual's life had any effect upon germ plasm, especially not past the first generation.

Lamarckians were also weakened by their apparent obfuscation of the fundamental difference between race as a biological determinant and the new object of enquiry: culture. A mark of modern, progressive Euro-American cultural anthropology became the steadfastness of its refusal of Lamarck and embrace of Darwin. And not only anthropology defines itself this way. Think of the bumper wars carried out in U.S. parking lots with the little Darwin fish-with-legs challenging the Christian symbol, as well as continuing battles over the teaching of evolution in U.S. schools.[18]

In the hands of modern antiracists like Stephen Jay Gould, Darwinism, despite its implication in murderous eugenics campaigns and sterilization abuses, is a powerful weapon. But Stocking says it was not easy to give up Lamarck's theories, which legitimized "in *biological* terms the causal efficacy of *social* processes" (1982:243). Nonetheless, by the 1930s the antibiological tendencies in behavioral science were completely disseminated, and Lamarck was finally done for, except for the pathetic yearnings of some backward-looking social workers (268) who, like Latour's vestigial "dimwits," refused the diffusion of this black box of Truth.

However, Nancy Leys Stepan suggests that Lamarckianism retained aficionados in Latin America well past the mid-twentieth century. Latin American neo-Lamarckians defined themselves as humane and sensible against Anglo-Saxon "practicality, materiality, and extremity" (1991:19) and championed the theory's progressive possibilities against social Darwinism's insistence that poverty, criminality, and other forms of so-called degeneration were genetically determined and racially fixed. Lamarckianism was linked to hopes for modernity and progress through state intervention in sanitation (giving water to the people), hygiene, family and reproductive health, and exercise. Here they mean sports and recreation,[19] but Stocking calls exercise the Lamarckian law: a change in circumstances creates a change in needs creates a change in exercise and action that leads to a change in the organism. The doctors, activists, and state officials involved in Lamarckian eugenics linked "general hygiene, anti-alcohol campaigns, sports education, a minimum-wage law, and a reduction in the cost of living" (1991:100) to improving the miserable conditions of their nation's citizens. Doctors and public health workers allied with the state gave Lamarckian theories a major role in struggles for the common good against both internal and external enemies. In postcolonial Latin America external aggression takes the form of military, political, and economic intervention, but it also attacks through aesthetico-scientific criteria. Euro-American Social Darwinism blamed Latin American "backwardness" on the degeneracy caused by mixed unions or "miscegenation" (Young 1995). "As evidence that 'halfbreeds' could not produce a high civilization, anthropologists pointed to Latin Americans who, they claimed, were now 'paying for their racial liberality' . . . the 'promiscuous' crossings . . . had produced a degenerate, unstable people incapable of progressive development" (Stepan 1991:45).

Latin American Lamarckianism responded to these racist dismissals by emphasizing nurture rather than nature and the importance of a collective antidote. It functioned as a *savoir* among socialist, anarchist, and feminist groups throughout the continent, even if it was often hidden or unconscious (Stepan 1991:83, 95). But like Darwinism, Lamarckianism could be made an ally of racism, and it also legitimated fascist policies in the Southern Cone in the 1930s and 1940s.[20] Similarly, in tracing the "French modern" Rabinow finds deep-seated and long-lasting Lamarckianism appealing to both socialists and the soldiers engaged in pacifying colonial subjects (1989:137–50). The deployment and alliance of Lamarckianism with a particular valence— left, right, racist, antiracist, insurgent, counterinsurgent—depended on its milieu, how it was exercised there, on what lay between it and the various actors struggling over its meaning, and over the strength it offered in particular moments. Its valence also depended on its work as a *savoir*, changing and subjectivizing those who "knew" it via the assumptions of identity. Lamarckianism contends that the collective body should manage life. It legitimates interventions that improve social conditions and strengthen both individual and social bodies. It thus functions as a grid of intelligibility enabling the power over both life and death.

In 1931 a British reviewer critiqued Brazilian eugenics for being "more sociological than biological" (in Stepan 1991:64). This was exactly the appeal and the terror of Lamarckianism, according to Stocking: it was the last theoretical link between the biological and the social (1982:265).

But was it the last? Malaria eradication campaigns seem resolutely Lamarckian: they intervene to safeguard collective health and must pay attention to the milieu and its range of actors, social and biological, from *Plasmodium* to standing water, from suspicious townspeople to global funding agencies, from screened houses to general prosperity (Humphreys 2001). In 1976 the *History of Sexuality* is published, linking bio to politics. In 2000 the progressive biologist Richard Lewontin declares himself decidedly non-Lamarckian: "There is no credible evidence that acquired characteristics can be inherited or that the process of gene mutation will produce enough of just the right variants at just the right moments to allow species to survive changing environments without natural selection. *But* the claim that the environment of an organism is causally independent of the organism, and that changes in the environment are autonomous and independent of changes in the species itself, is clearly wrong. It is bad biology" (48, emphasis added).

By "environment" he seems to mean something very close to milieu or even to what the Maya understand as *tiempo*: "The space defined by the activities of the organism itself" (Lewontin 2000:53). Like SNEM *brigadistas*, like this famous biologist, like a French historian, like Guatemalan army counterinsurgency theorists, as I exercise my self as a modern anthropologist I have to deal with the mysterious relation between the life of the individual and the life of the species, the power over death and life—in other words, with biopolitics and with Lamarck. In this milieu I am subjectivized, *produced* by certain often-unacknowledged *savoirs*, aka assumptions, including reverse discourses and preserved possibilities.

Remarks on Lamarck

> The theme of social war articulated in biopower provides the overarching principle that subsumes both *la lutte des races* and *la lutte des classes.* Ann Stoler

In the early 1980s, in four regions of Guatemala, including the Joyabaj/ Zacualpa area, the Guatemalan state carried out genocide against the Mayan people (CEH). Even if that state had also tried to eradicate malaria or later installed potable water systems in these areas, was it only acting nice because, for its real face, to give water means to kill? As the CEH commissioner Otilia Lux Cotí once argued, was it really a race war—about *bios* and not politics? Think! But to do so, perhaps we should ask what is assumed to be the *genos* (race, species, kind, origin) under attack? Is race an already existing solid identification with a presumed biological component? Yet the war targeted primarily ladinos in the 1960s and both ladinos and indigenous people in the 1970s and 1980s, when it was primarily carried out by indigenous people. Or perhaps something like subversion began to take on biological characteristics in the mind of the military state, making it racist, but not along a fundamental divide between ladinos and indigenous—which returns us to the creepy raciology of joking about Rigoberta Menchú's blood type being URNG-positive.

In turn, despite the Guatemalan state's profound legitimation crisis, riddled with impunity and rife with corruption, abuse, and deadly force, it plays the legitimizing neo-Lamarckian role of intervening in social life, responsible (despite neoliberal pressures) for health, food, education, sports, development work, and general improvements in the individual and collective body. Enfolded here is a promise of future improvement because this work is tied not only to politics or culture but also to type and to descent.

Perhaps these policies, which appear to be in favor of life, bring so much death because the state is two-faced. Not unlike the catechist, it shows one face to implacable external actors and another to its people. If developing the national body politic is understood to depend on free trade, direct foreign investment, loans, and credit ratings—for example, if a minimum wage law conflicts with attracting global capital through promises of cheap labor—then perhaps subversion and instability are seen as a threat to the life of the whole.[21] Racism, Foucault argues, should be understood as the constant war against threats to the health and happiness of the body politic, and it promises a common good. "It establishes a *positive* relation between the right to kill and the assurance of life. It posits that 'the more you kill . . . the more you will live'" (Stoler 1995:84). Perhaps that premise was yet another way that people were convinced to participate in counterinsurgency. In part they were forced, through the violence of scorched earth and mass murder. But they were also convinced through a *mística*—the contradictory pastoral policies of a state acting through them to give water to the people and to eradicate malaria—that allowed them to think they were acting for the common good. These assumptions, these preserved possibilities, are the refolded surfaces that join state biopower with lived experience in the postwar-in-action.

Re: Marx on Lamarck

Revolutionary discourse may also draw on neo-Lamarckian raciology, biopolitically promising a common good and joining the life and death of the individual to the life of the nation and the species. Like Lamarckians more generally, the Guatemalan left, Maya and ladino, refuses to view misery and poverty as genetically determined and foresees a healthy vital future body as an effect of struggle (a surprising number of URNG cadre and commanders were doctors and health promoters). In fact, the guerrilla struggle seems transfused with a grammar of race in Foucault's sense, which provided the moral authority to defend the social body. This is not racism as unthinking abjection of a phenotypically marked body. It is a grammar of folding and vacillating differentiations, a discursive tactic which can map on to social classes and nations, as well as races, and that legitimates killing via the assurance of life. Influenced by uneven development and dependency theory (Amin 1974, Cardoso and Faletto 1979, Gunder Frank 1967), it challenges capitalist assumptions of national development once internal differences are assimilated.[22] Instead, relations of dependency—the north's all-consuming accumulation by dispossession—are seen to hemorrhage off the vital components necessary for integral development. These theories powerfully undergird revolutionary organizing by showing that the body politic will not naturally mature and that poverty is not the result of some inherent weakness like degeneracy based on interbreeding or an "unconquerable aversion to sustained physical toil." Instead, such supposed laziness is the result of mosquitoes and diseases of poverty as well as of alienation and the resistance it engenders. "Backwardness" is caused by Guatemala's unnatural insertion into the world system of unequal exchange. This relation can be changed through struggle, by exercise, which in turn transforms the whole caboodle. The revolutionary conviction that it's about class and the global divide, not race, offers a very powerful cultural and political promise in response to genocide. And, like state politics, it may have an other face—the *mística* of Lamarckian eugenics.

Re-Marking the Maya

The Mayan movement also refuses to accept that "backwardness" is inborn, and as such may fold in strands of neo-Lamarckian thinking. The robust and eloquent denunciations of neocolonialism and continuing racism in Guatemala are undergirded by horror at their effects on the Mayan body politic and its future. Mayan activists struggle against the loss of potential as children work grinding hours on the plantations, are denied education in their language, and are forced to amputate a part of themselves by wearing nontraditional clothes in order to attend schools. Language valorization, the right to culturally sensitive education, and freedom from violence are about improving individual bodies and lives in the moment, but the larger goal, often clearly stated, is to revitalize a larger entity, the Pueblo Maya. Much of the discourse around the Quincentennial focused on five hundred years of survival with the implied corollary that with struggle this body politic would survive, healthy and happy, for many more rounds of the Mayan calendar.

So, was malaria eradication a good war and the civil war a bad one? And was the thirty-six-year conflict a race war or a class war? Like the state, and the Two-Faced Indian, the answer is: both, neither, and "dela"—by, through, and beyond. The war was and is *raciological*, racism being not "an *effect* but a *tactic* in the internal fission of society into binary oppositions, a means of creating 'biologized' internal enemies against whom society must defend itself" (Stoler 1995:59). Racism, like Lamarckian eugenics, is not just the assignment of hierarchical value to a range of phenotypic expressions (hair, skin color, nose shape, etc.) but a grid of intelligibility which is not necessarily about any particular group of people, but a more generalized and extraordinarily productive division within a body politic.

Now, as you've probably noticed, I don't really think that Lamarck is over, even if, in this day and age, no one would ever admit to holding such "aberrant" views. Lamarckianism, which I think infuses biopolitics, may undergird and animate the tensions with which I began this chapter: How do I get smart with power? How do I understand the discourses that act like the water we swim in, that go without saying in my deepest, most authentic desires for a better world and my sense of responsibility to actively intervene to make it so? How do I know that without which I would not be able to think at all, about, say, how to bring *bios*—life—together with the political, in an active productive relation? Answering these questions entails the assumption of identity.

UBTHE*

> In what way are those fundamental experiences of madness,
> suffering, death, crime, desire, individuality connected, even
> if we are not aware of it, with knowledge and power? I am sure
> I'll never get the answer; but that does not mean that we don't
> have to ask the question. Michel Foucault

The Lamarckian milieu is a transformist conception that brings space and society together and is constantly changing. There is no fixed center, no graphic whole. It is a space of processes with nothing preordained (Rabinow 1989:128–29). This suggests both Latour's description of the constant redefinition of "nature and the whole caboodle" and even more so Foucault's notion of *savoir* that, in the very practice of knowing something, produces the knower and the known. It also recalls Luxemburg, Žižek, and Menchú Tum's terribly contingent "appropriate moments," and the world of horror and the sideshow experience of state functioning—where one knows very well that victims and perpetrator or state and people are profoundly different but at the same time we contemplate mutations and slidings whereby one begins to look a lot like the other. It's a lot like the postwar-in-action, full of transient, mobile assumptions of identi/ties.

The Guatemalan army "won" the war but by making the country into a pariah, destroying the economy, and becoming riddled with corruption. Now they are sharing power with the very people they would have killed a few years ago, and some of them are going to jail for their victory. Always in-action rather than ready-made, the war/s continue on multiple fronts, their meanings constantly remade, co-memorated.

SNEM lost the war on malaria. Increased resistance in both mosquito and *Plasmodium*, the DDT ban, lowered human immunity, and lack of medicine led cases to rise again in the 1970s, and now they may be as high as ever. But no one really knows. The brigades and volunteer networks were mostly disbanded under health guidelines drawn up to implement IMF support for the new civilian government in 1986. When I checked at the Pan American Health Office in 2002, the latest malaria statistics available were from the mid-1990s.[23]

Globalized neoliberal reforms have increasingly privatized risk, making it each person's individual responsibility to stay healthy and fit (Hale 2006,[24] Peterson and Bunton 1997, Rose 1990, Verdugo Urrejola 2007). The careful if creepy attentions of biopolitical power—the infinitesimal surveillances, permanent controls, statistical assessments, and interventions aimed at the entire social body—seem to give way to the cynical graffiti warning from Pat Cadigan's cyberpunk novel *Synners*: "UBthe*" or You Be the asterisk/ass to risk. Subjectivization has made you free, and now you're free to take care of yourself. As Thomas Osborne argues, patients must become entrepreneurs of their own health (1997:186). The cat is no longer pulling the car, both the suspicious and the naïve mouse are uninsured, and it's darn scary.

Juan Tinay said, "Who has bled with the people? . . . We are risking our lives in a full on struggle." His organization, CONIC, was on the front lines in spring 2005, when highway blockades shut down the entire nation to protest CAFTA, ecologically destructive mining concessions and especially the water pollution they engender, and the slow pace of land reform and other improvements promised in the peace accords. Likewise, I and millions of others have been spending time recently clashing with police at antiglobalization protests because the WTO, CAFTA, and the Group of 8 (G8) are dismantling the world's social welfare systems and environmental protections. As when I chanted, "Money for health care, not for war," I am still fighting "for" biopower.

But even in the neoliberal milieu, U and B are precisely what is at stake, they are what biopower is all about. It is exercise or struggle that pulls power left or right. Milieu, remember, means what is in-between. But as with all productive power—via assumptions of identity, *savoirs*, subjectivization, the moving internal frontier between individual and social bodies, between death and life, and the constantly changing whole caboodle—these directions are often unpredictable, veering off course. There are many questions left to be asked (and more will be raised in the conclusion!) and preserved possibilities to be explored, as we seek to understand and influence the control panel of smart bombs, deploying our bloody, capillary power. We're all conspirators in biopolitics; we are all co-laborators now. But amidst all the risk we can be vitally unpredictable.

HOW DO YOU GET SOMEONE
TO GIVE YOU HER PURSE?

Warning: This prose unveils a con. Proceed at own risk.

As a colonial plague that malformed the third world into
narrowly specialized primary product exporters, the
Dutch disease should be renamed the third-world or neo-
colonial disease. Fernando Coronil

Nine Queens is an excellent cinematic example of a certain
River Plate tradition of paranoid narratives, of which
Borges is just one example. A society looks normal on the
surface but is run by corrupt secret societies and secret
deals, with a conspiratorial atmosphere that leads you to
ask who is real and who is just playing a role.
Richard Peña

NO MATTER HOW PARANOID I GET,
I JUST CAN'T KEEP UP

Approaching the end of the book I return to milieu and what's in-between
money, health, and war. But first a number of leading questions: Why are
disease and contagion metaphors so prevalent in discussions of financial
issues (as are sexual double entendres)? Why are the end results of the global
economy so mean (cruel) when their means appear so neutral and transparent? Why are those systematizations and subjectivizations—the knowledges (*connaissance*) carefully collated from around the globe and trailing the
glory of Nobel prizes—that went into malaria eradication so similar to the
painstakingly devised methods of accounting, auditing, and other checkups
on economic health? And why, given the painstakingness, are we so often
left feeling duped, that we invested our money and got left holding a worthless IOU, often couched in terms suggesting being sexually acted on? UB*
indeed.

The Argentine film *Nine Queens* (2000) explores risk and confidence and
points to an illness in the social body, one that puts the lives of the nation's
inhabitants at risk. Being a postrevolutionary caper film, it doesn't prescribe

an antidote; it just pulls a good twist at the end. There's an x in it, but no Rx. Yet it may help us answer those leading questions.

One of the film's two protagonists, Juan, is a not-very-good con artist whose ass is at risk when he flubs an easy switcheroo in a Buenos Aires convenience store. Marcos, the other protagonist, has been casing the joint himself and smoothly comes to the rescue by assuming the identity of a cop. A dance of suspicion ensues. Marcos has lost his partner and is looking for a replacement, especially when a very big deal goes down concerning the titular "nine queens," a set of stamps. But it has to be someone who can get the job done. Juan is unsure at first. He's a small-timer, just trying to get some money together to help his father. He's also a little unsure of Marcos's methods, which literally include taking money from little old ladies. But maybe he can learn a trick or two from the older artful dodger. To convince Marcos that he's trustworthy and can handle the deal, on the spur of the moment Juan bets he can get a random woman to willingly hand over her purse in less than two minutes. He succeeds, to Marcos's disbelief: "That wasn't planned? That was improvised?"

A few minutes later Juan says, "You would have taken the purse, wouldn't you?" Marcos is aghast and outraged. He's a con artist, not a robber. "You think I'm a thief," he says. "I don't kill people. I don't use a piece. Anyone can do that. Do you want to see thieves?" He takes Juan into the street and gives him new eyes, like Nada in *They Live* or Rigoberta Menchú Tum when her consciousness was born. Marcos's con man p.o.v. allows him to pierce the veil of the everyday, and, as he points out two men on a motorbike, another talking on a cell phone, a group of women on a street corner, all plotting a grab, suddenly we see the whole world through his nonduped eyes, and it changes into one of constant risk and loss. "Mind your ass," he says, "because they're there and they'll always be. They are there, but you can't see them. That's what it's all about: they are there, but they are not there. So mind your briefcase, your windows, your car, your savings. They're spitters, breakers, skin workers, blind fronts, hoisters, hooks, stalls, night raiders, mustard chuckers, fences, operators, swindlers."[1] Is it paranoid or just common sense to think they're out to get you? Is it stupid not to assume you need to get yours? What are the limits of paranoia within reason?

STAMPS AND WARRANTS

The nine queens is a set of rare stamps, and a buddy of Marcos's has a master forgery of it. A famously rapacious collector, the Spaniard Esteban Vidal Gandolfi, is in town, but just for one day. He is being deported because of some holding that has gone wrong, so he won't be able to do a full authentication. Juan's moral qualms are assuaged by learning that their mark is worth far more than they'll take from him and, as a thief himself, hardly an innocent victim, and he decides he wants in. The game is on, with many a twist and double cross as the two men race around Buenos Aires calling in every chit and energizing their networks near and far, from deeply estranged family members to completely contingent ties, like the expert Gandolfi brings in to authenticate the fake—but after doing so he corners the conners and asks for a cut. They go through many scrapes and near misses, including one that destroys the fake, leading them to substitute it with the real thing, which means investing all their own money. They cajole, promise, and verge on the threatening to line up all the multiconductors necessary for the momentary con to occur, but these are not dominators, they wield no sword.[2] Like the woman who, believing she's trapped in the elevator and can't climb out while holding her purse, hands it willingly to Juan; in every case their allies join because they seem to want to, because they believe they have an interest in the proceedings.

At one point it seems all is lost. The deal has been brokered, but Gandolfi makes one last demand. The exchange of stamps for the check must traverse Marcos's sister Valeria, who has a respectable job as a concierge in the hotel where the con is going down. She hates Marcos and his shifty lifestyle, and she's enraged at him for stealing an inheritance from her and their little brother. It is clear what the buyer expects from her. Marcos is pimping his sister.

The word "pimp" probably comes from the French *pimper*, to allure. A pimp is a medium between the sex worker and her or his customer. The Hughes brothers' documentary *American Pimp* explores his beguiling powers. These may sometimes include threatening or harming the people, mostly women, who work for him, but most of the men whom the Hugheses interview, like Marcos in *Nine Queens*, sharply delineate their craft from two-bit robbers, who simply take what they want. Such differentiation could be simple delusion and self-justification, but it returns us to the questions: Is one enough? Is pimping, duping, lashing in, the war of the cross, isomorphic with—the self-same as—forcing, repressing, dominating? The ends may be similar (someone who didn't earn it ends up with the purse) but, as the perpetrators keep insisting, the means are different, and that makes all the difference.

How *do* you make someone give you her purse? *American Pimp* is Haraway-esque in that neither the practitioners nor the filmmakers offer one answer. Instead, a series of translations emerges, among sets of interests, desires, fantasies, investments, hopes of improvement, the aura of the expert, and deeply embedded relations of inequality structured around gender, race, ethnicity, class, and sexuality. Sex work seems to take the exchange of women as an assumption (it goes without saying), even, sometimes, to the women themselves. The allure of assuming the identity of sex worker (or wife, "*i.e.,* of prostitution both public and private" [Marx and Engels 1988:57]) may rest on very deep-seated relations. The traffic in women (Rubin 1975), aka the social pact based on the Law of the (White) Father (*nom du père*), means that "enduring and viable identity is thus purchased through subjection to and subjectivization by the patronym" (Butler 1993:153). Or it may be less a lure than a cold demand. Depending on your class position, what is the answer when you look in the mirror in the morning and ask, "What can I sell today?" (Berman 1998:16). Such identifications traverse the three forms of assumption—for many women, and some men, it's taken for granted that you pretty much have only two choices: virgin/whore. You may take one on or have it assumed for you as a false identity, but, as Latour might suggest, without exactly understanding how it all happened, you may begin to believe it yourself.

In *American Pimp* several of the men express laughing disbelief that their early offers to pimp women were accepted, that they, mostly poor African American men, were able to "make (them) believe." Freud was not the first to suggest a purse as a double entendre for portions of a woman's anatomy. What induces women to give it to them? What makes the pimp such an alluring node in the multiple exchanges bolstering the traffic in women, often across the color line? Several of the men historicize their actions via the post–Civil War U.S. race/sex milieu, where the labor options for black men were terribly limited and doubly con/strained by white stereotyping. Sex work was a survival mechanism for both African American women and men, a way to get white men to give them their wallets. As Alarcón asks of Malinche, what choices do (x)-slaves have (1989)? While forcing someone is considered *outré*, is it immoral if they, johns or women, willingly give it to you?[3]

In *Nine Queens* Marcos says that most people would be con artists if they had the balls. He's suggesting that everyone wants to receive the non-Indian gift, to get something for nothing, to be excused from the circulations of reciprocity.

But might we also query, as Marcos asks Juan, "That wasn't planned? That was improvised?" Is duplicity always calculated? Is there someone with balls pulling the strings? What if, like the two-faced catechist or Doña Miguela's husband marched through the night to a massacre site, you can't help yourself? What if duplicity—like living clandestinely, like Elmyr's first fake, like speaking for all poor Guatemalans, like Natalia, a Maya taken for a witch, like the names of indigenous people, slaves, or women, like Dela's TV show, like much of the co-laboration in the labor-atories of the postwar-in-action, like the pimps themselves, who feel denied any other path—is produced by the conditions of existence, by attempts to survive and even thrive? Yet, in turn, what of the allure (the *pimper*), the beguilement, the desire, the Xtra in duplicity? Are these experiences the same as simply being forced to do something? Marcos, in a huff, insists he is not a thief.

The pimp expresses laughing surprise at pulling one over and getting something for nothing. Why might the donor get—or even expect—so little in return? What might change this assumption of identity—willingly giving up the purse—into the realization that it's a con? Why are some trans-actions entered into compliantly every day? What, in turn, happens so that on some other day that same action produces, instead, the uncanny realiza-tion that one has been duped? When, suddenly, the assumptions about how the world really works are revealed as gullibility? One is usually aware that she has been robbed and feels righteous anger at such an experience. Why does it take a *nacer de conciencia*, a new assumption of identity, to realize one has been *engañado*? The reaction may be shame, self-splitting, dumb-foundedness, but sometimes it translates into political action. The Indian, the woman, the investor, or the debtor may tremble, laugh, even cry out and then may ask for the gift back, insert snakes in the *contratista*'s shirt, head for the hills, and come down from the mountains. It may be the end (what is desired or hoped for) of war but also the commencing of new struggles.

The trick with reckoning is keeping an eye simultaneously on the con-tractor and his shaman, on the local schlub and the larger Agent (or is that Structure?), *and* on what's in-between, how they connect, aka race, gender, class, and other assumptions.

In their efforts to traffic the stamps Juan and Marcos alluringly manage to make everyone believe, and all the exchanges, including that of Valeria, are made. The duped Gandolfi is escorted out of the hotel by the police, leaving Juan and Marcos with his check. But in a final twist of fate, when Juan and Marcos arrive at the bank to cash it, they encounter an angry mob banging on the doors. The bank is closed. Its reserves are gone. When Marcos catches the eye of someone he knows inside he is told, "We were all royally screwed. We found out this morning. They held as long as possible but when the going got rough they sold all the assets and took off." "Who?" asks Marcos. "The Board, all eleven. They took 135 million. The Central Bank did know but they only took part today." Then, looking at the check in Marcos's hand, the banker laughs and says, "You'll have to shove it up your ass, Marquitos."

Juan wanders away in a daze. The check is, like an Elmyr painting, worth so much yet worth so little. Its warrant has been withdrawn.

Because of this scene *Nine Queens* has been called prophetic, released as it was just before Argentina's entire economy crashed. Almost from day to night the country went from being the poster child for the miraculously improving effects of neoliberal orthodoxy to being broke. In December 2001, after twenty billion dollars had fled the country, bank deposits were frozen, and public outcry caused President Fernando de la Rúa to resign. By then Argentines realized they'd been duped by the whole caboodle and wanted everyone out: "Que se vayan todos!" was the chant. One of the several presidents who held power over the next few weeks declared "the biggest sovereign default in history, on public debt of $80 billion" (*The Economist* 2004:3). More than half of all Argentines dropped below the national poverty line, and, as in Brazil only a few years earlier, the crisis was feared to be contagious, threatening all of South America. While international lenders like the IMF expressed rage and horror that their confidence in Argentina had been so rudely repaid (and are supposed to use their sticks on countries in such straits) the fact that Argentina held some 15 percent of the IMF's loans made the fund believe it had to bail it out. A cash infusion seemed necessary to save the hemorrhaging patient, so it gave Argentina its purse.

BAD APPLES IN A GOOD BARREL OR A BAD BARREL THAT CORRUPTS EVERYTHING IT TOUCHES?

Fabian Bielinsky, the director of *Nine Queens*, said, "The idea of sudden wealth has always been incorporated into the psychology of the Argentine, but during the 1990's it reached obscene levels and reached into the highest spheres of politics and government. We were forced to be witnesses to impunity and corruption, indifference to the common welfare and absolute frivolity, so of course a movie like *Nine Queens* reflects that state of affairs" (in Rohter 2002: B25). Here is a familiar story of duplicity: as in Guatemala, corrupt, two-faced officials abuse public trust for private gain. Like ex-President Portillo, former Argentine president Carlos Menem is hiding from investigations of corruption. Their stealing convincingly explains the collapse of the economy. "Everybody Out" was the demand of the *cacerolazos*, the Argentine protests, because every politician was seen as corrupt. The beguilement had evaporated, all were exposed as complicit in duping the populace. Things changed, and Argentines, like Indians, wanted their gifts back.

But is the problem really some bad apples, people who couldn't resist the allure of taking the people's purse? They weren't using a piece, after all. Is it their fault, as the *cacerolazos* or CICIACS activists would maintain? "Oh no," say those charged with corruption, taking refuge in the risk-based "insurance regime" of responsibility (Ewald 1991). The duped themselves are to blame. They just needed to watch their ass, their briefcase, their windows, their savings a little better. (It is a democracy, after all!) And it's not like this hadn't happened before. When UB* you are responsible to not get fooled again. In other words, as George W. Bush once tried, unsuccessfully, to say, "Fool me once shame on you, fool me twice shame on me." Is it true that if the Argentines or the IMF weren't so stupid and gullible they would never have lost so much?

Like Bielinsky, I have actually been fooling you, reader (and if you haven't seen the film, please stop reading!). The bank collapse was not the final twist of the film. Juan, appearing in a daze or perhaps in laughing disbelief, walks into what looks like the backstage at a theater. Sitting at a table, gambling at cards, are all of the film's characters — now out of role (à la *Wizard of Oz*): the forger, the stamp expert, Gandolfi, and Valeria, Marcos's sister, who, it appears, has been trafficking with Juan. One of them hands Juan a bag filled with money — Marcos's stake to buy the supposedly real stamps — that Juan in turn gives to Valeria with a kiss. It is her stake in the swindled inheritance. Marcos has been the mark all along. The nonduped erred, and the ruse was just to get what Valeria had coming to her, if only Marcos had not been so unkind to his kin. The only victim was the perpetrator. As in the case of the Calcutta Chromosome, a different reason from what we assumed had been at work. It turns out that Juan and his band of tricksters played something like the role of Lacan and Žižek's "agency of the big Other," pulling the strings, running the show. While it's a little creepy to find that we, the audience, have also been duped, it's actually a happy, almost reassuring ending. Justice is served.

But what if there's another face? What if all the corrupt ones *se vayan* (get out) and you're still "royally screwed"? The flesh-and-blood plantation owner Herrera may come to Joyabaj to dedicate some development project now and then. But there is another Herrera, working through his barely conceptualizable volcano nature, magically inducing people, through intimate and mostly invisible networks, to descend to the coast, to give him their purse and labor, to risk malaria and thiamine injections. Certainly, if there is anything that feels like a very big Other hiding behind the everyday world of work, school, church, family, or electoral politics — yet also dominating the horizon like a volcano — it is finance. Depending on one's class position money may be a consuming anxiety, but the larger economy seems to so undergird our assumptions, ideology, and habits that it is like air — we only notice it when it's missing or noticeably rancid. We are fish swimming in its water. One tries to get and do a job, fulfill domestic tasks, pay the doctor, maybe bank some savings, and pay some attention to politics. But underneath this world is another that both fits right into late twentieth-century capitalist culture and that, from day to night, can blast every assumption. As happened in Argentina in 2001, during the 1998 Asian contagion, in the United States in 1929, and currently to employees of and investors in Long-Term Capital Management, Enron, WorldCom, Amaranth, Bear Stearns, etc., this other world can turn people's entire life's accrued value into a worthless IOU, strip them of their home, their car, their pension, if they were lucky enough to have one, and there's not a damn thing they can do about it. Finance's effects are like Marcos's thieves—there, but you don't see them. And yet, they are also not like them. As Rigoberto said, it's an unclear enemy. Who exactly is the *elaq'om* (thief) you might lynch to make things more tranquil? Can you ever be wary enough to escape this big a con?

In Argentina the postcrash has been very much in action, as intense struggles are joined to reckon with the pragmatics of survival as well as with more existential questions—what is the etiology of the crisis? And therefore what medicine should be used to heal it? Rather than look to something essential, like Argentines' get-rich-quick psychology (bad apples), many people are attending to the barrel.

It's certainly not new to suggest that economic disasters like Argentina's are not solely the result of factors inside the nation, like egoism or even corruption, but are instead effects of being doubled over by a force coming from outside—the trans/actions of global capitalism. This plague may act in the name of freedom—freedom of the market—or of development, improvement, even life itself. But scholars, like the guerrillas who ran for the hills, like the *cacerolazos* and *piqueteros* (the unquiet unemployed), and like the global networks of fair trade activists, are questioning whether lashing in to imperial globalization will strengthen and improve a country's economy or leave it diseased, weak, easily bent over.[4]

June Nash writes, "Where enormous wealth and power differences exist within a country, neoliberal practices exacerbate economic and social inequalities that make the play of the market a game between life and death. When those nations *pretend to be* players in global capital arenas they can be destroyed by sudden changes in their investment ratings. Those losses are frequently shifted to the poorest producers in the nations" (2001:87, emphasis added). Fernando Coronil, too, links the feverish cycles of boom and bust to the colonial and postcolonial production of "nature exporting societies."

When similar internal specialization and external dependence happened to a first world country—for example, when the Netherlands expanded into North Sea gas development and subsequently eroded its manufacturing base—it was called the Dutch disease. Coronil says, however, it "constitutes an epidemic in the monocrop economies of the third world. . . . [it] should be renamed the third-world or neo-colonial disease" (1997:7).

As David Harvey argues, however, it is not only the third world's ass that is at risk:

> Stock promotions, ponzi schemes, structured asset destruction through inflation, asset-stripping through mergers and acquisitions,[5] and the promotion of levels of debt incumbency that reduces whole populations, even in the advanced capitalist countries, to debt peonage, to say nothing of corporate fraud and dispossession of assets (the raiding of pension funds and their decimation by stock and corporate collapses) by credit and stock manipulations—all of these are central features of what contemporary capitalism is about. The collapse of Enron dispossessed many of their livelihoods and their pension rights. But above all we have to look at the speculative raiding carried out by hedge funds and other major institutions of finance capital as the cutting edge of accumulation by dispossession in recent times." (Harvey 2003:147)

Perhaps we are all tracing the steps of the *Baile de la Culebra* now.

The final chapter addresses finance and accounting, their various means, contingent ends, and allure (*pimper*). This means entertaining the role of media as that which lies in-between, like a pimp, like the state, and that simultaneously beckons and betrays. It means reckoning with post, simultaneously a fixed point and that which moves across it as in the postwar or postage—conveying a message, sending out an SOS. Governments issue stamps marked with their names to prove that a duty has been paid. That mark, the name, allows things to which those small pieces of paper are affixed to move, trans-acting between nations and net-working people. Malaria stamps were issued to represent a nation-state's commitment to life, and they circulated globally, more mobile than monies carrying those same nation's names. Stamped, that name warrants enough value for the letter to leave one's hand, exit the country, and arrive in someone else's hands, somewhere else. Once there, a little girl might save it in a book. The book becomes endowed with something Xtra, a whiff of the exotic, of an elsewhere that has found its way into her home. Years later a representation of that stamp may travel again, indeed, in this very book. In the film *Nine Queens* stamps circulate not on letters but in a different economy, endowed with similarly mysterious value—whether or not they're fake. A postage stamp was originally a sign of a debt discharged, yet in these very traversals, like the carnival or fair, it remains charged with an unaccountable energy (perhaps because it's un/fair?).

The German word *stellan* roots *darstellan* (to represent) and also to stamp or mark, as in imprinting a form against a material—a seal in wax, for example. This is also a form of assuming identification, how one (person or paper) takes on a value, comes to matter, is able to circulate. There are people who have no more brains than you do, Scarecrow, but they have one thing you haven't got—a diploma, a seal of approval, a name that confers identity. Where does a name acquire such value? Is it a *nom du père* or a nonduped err? To stamp (are we surprised?) has two meanings. It can also mean to strike down on forcibly. To beat, crush, pulverize, *chafar*. How do you get someone to give you her purse? What if she says no?

Chapter Eight

ACCOUNTING FOR THE POSTWAR, BALANCING THE BOOK/S

finance n. < OFr wealth, revenue < *finer* to end, settle accounts

Es la hora de cobrar facturas. It is time for an accounting. Otilia Lux Cotí

It is futile to try to make the universe add up. But I guess we must go on anyhow. Philip K. Dick

There can be no "end" to the desire for political freedom because that would mean the end of historical transformation and redistribution. And there can be no closure to theoretical speculations on the meaning of freedom because that would demand the death of political aspiration and the erasure of the conceptual imagination. Homi Bhabha

RECKONING THE POSSIBILITIES FOR THE FUTURE

There is an implicit promise in that doubling over movement that so caught my eye in the *Baile de la Culebra*—a man is doubled over so his back can be used as a table, so that his debt can be inscribed in a little book. While it is an imprinting, a mark of five hundred years of politico-econo-military exchanges stamped into postwar lifeways, the promise arises from that technique, so deeply embedded that it constitutes "the modern fact" (Poovey 1998), of double-entry bookkeeping. Beside the debit column runs a corresponding line of credit, and the two will at some point reach zero and balance each other out. There can be an accounting. You can close the book.

The allure (*pimper*) of reckoning is double: both the Assumption One of secure knowledge, the everyday fact, and the more transcendent hope that there will be a settlement of rewards or penalties for any action. Reckoning suggests that history is not just one damn thing after another but that action is meaningful, directed toward a future. It undergirds our yearning that, as Stocking said, "efforts to help individuals are of social importance" (1982:255). It suggests there is a rule of law and some hope of justice in a final judgment. While few expect a catharsis that simply expunges the past, reckoning the postwar raises hope that the gains and losses will approach a more even balance, that the disjuncture between winning and losing can be adjusted through accounting, memorials, legal rulings, truth commissions, reparations, government representation, curricular reforms, and the rooting out of corrupt officials and human rights violators from the webs of state power and from one's neighborhood (despite suspicions of a rotten barrel).

The dictionary's first definition of reckon is "to count," and in war's after/math it is clearly incumbent on us to do the sum, to tally war's effects—hundreds of massacres and villages destroyed, hundreds of thousands dead—and to divvy up responsibility—93 percent of the violence perpetrated by the military state, 3 percent by the guerrillas (CEH 1999, Grandin 2000c). The many consuming struggles I have recounted here—Esperanza León's dogged walking about the countryside, Jennifer Harbury's hunger strikes, Helen Mack's legal tenacity, Filóchofo's interventions into the *ambiente*, CONIC's full-on struggle, attempts to create the CICIACS, the exhumations that Manuel Hernández and Esperanza León have organized—are all battles against impunity and for ac*count*ability, even if it's left to God to balance the books. But Mary Poovey describes a vexing doubleness in the numeric fact, which she calls inherently ambiguous and epistemologically peculiar: "Numbers seem both essential and insufficient" (1998:xi). Apparently noninterpretive, they lead to systematic claims. In her explorations of the bookkeeping how-to guides published on the eve of European colonialism she finds duplicity at the very heart of the numeric fact and of the balance promised by accounting: "In the late sixteenth century . . . number still carried the pejorative connotations associated with necromancy. . . . Instead of gaining prestige from numbers, double-entry bookkeeping helped confer cultural authority on numbers. It did so by means of the balance, which depended . . . on a wholly fictitious number—the number imported not to refer to a transaction but simply to rectify the books. For late sixteenth-century readers the balance conjured up both the scales of justice and the symmetry of God's world" (1998:54).

And this conjuring may distract us from how two-faced assumptions about numbers are, although the Spanish *contar* means both to count and to tell. Counting offers the soothing objectivity of the facts, ma'am, just the facts. But then why is it that one death is a tragedy, but two hundred thousand are just a statistic? One counts, but it is insufficient. It is telling—context, milieu, identi-ties—that makes that one (death) count. It is connections that articulate us, love that makes that life grievable. Writing this, I recall the face of Myrna Mack's daughter, Lucrecia Hernández Mack, at the state's apology ceremony. I hear her say how she misses her mother, and, sitting here at my desk re-counting this story, I start to cry. I cannot help myself. I miss Myrna too. I grieve her death, and I also struggle to reckon with her loss, in part through this book. Yet she is one of so many. Can we count *and* tell their tragedies? Can we make systematic claims, be in the know? Can the losses be accounted for in all senses—audit, narration, and religico-cosmopolitical judgment?

Once again, in seeking the crux I find a puzzle, and even the basic terms I try to use in co-memoration (like "fact") seem two-faced. Which brings me back to that little ledger book in the Baile de la Culebra. It seems perfectly transparent and neutral. Anyone sent in to check the figures would probably find no cooking the books, no fraud, no bamboozlement. Yet it's a double-cross. Somehow, mysteriously, for individuals as well as for nations like Argentina and Guatemala, the debt grows much faster than the credit. No matter how many injections the young *mozos* take to keep up, no matter how many tons of cane they cut, they never seem to reach that magic balancing point, that zero their Mayan ancestors so famously discovered.

Strongly lashed networks acted on the Berger government to make it apologize for the assassination of Myrna Mack Chang and to pay indemnization, where "indemnify" means to repay or compensate for a loss, to redeem or make good. But even as it is paid, the debt it is meant to cancel has grown. Grown not just in the sense of what could possibly compensate for the gaping hole left in Myrna Mack's social networks, her undeveloped potential, and the loss of the intellectual and political contributions she might have made. But as her ideas are exercised, her work articulated, cited, drawn on, and lashed together into new configurations—and not just analytically but through lives and activities inspired by it and sustained through the networks, like AVANCSO, that she generated—it transforms the whole caboodle, retroactively multiplying the effects of her loss.

How is the worth or value of a life to be adjudicated? How is what might have been to be foretold—especially for the thousands of children killed? What if the milieu had changed? What if the revolution had triumphed and really transformed the conditions of poverty and racism? How might one calculate the potential value, the accomplishments and contributions of a healthy, well-nourished, educated, dignified, and hopeful person? Or, to think like a Lamarckian, of their children and grandchildren? This is an X, an unknown in our equation. It is as mysterious as the question of how these entries can be balanced, these accounts settled. There is an X in them that is more than them. Ewald suggests it may emanate from the dual status of suffering as it is caught between assumptions of fault and of insurance: "The risk-treatment of injury works through a dualization of the lived and the indemnified . . . the irreparable and . . . a contractually agreed tariff" (1991:204), enacted through struggles between a judge who may try to match the full extent of an injury and the expert "who assigns a person's insurantial identity, allocates a placement in a table of categories where the individual is 'objectively' located" (205). Balancing these two forms may be less an effect of addition and subtraction than of the topological calculations that allow us to envision Klein bottles and Leyden jars. Or perhaps it necessitates completely new forms of accounting.

In 2009 war may be over (if we want it), but what I've been articulating here is not really an end, any more than Bhabha sees an end to the desire for political freedom. While I've certainly been trying, my attempts to be in the know, to fix Guatemala's postwar, quickly swerve into a fixion, an unbalanced book—more the x in an unsolved algebraic equation than a neat summing up. In this conclusion I tease out some of the assumptions of accounting and suggest the power of "audit culture" in the postwar-in-action. I explore tensions between notions of *finer* as to end or settle accounts, especially regarding finance as wealth or revenue, and the suspicion that something escapes audit's promise of arithmetical balance, transparent communication, economic efficiency, and good practice (Strathern 2000a:1). I'll briefly explore several current struggles in Guatemala over the two faces of dispossession that evoke the double character of accounting—the deeply mundane that fits right in and the cosmopolitical that blasts open the assumptions of our lifeworlds. The following is only one way this account could finish up but (just this once!) it will have to be enough.

HUMAN SUBJECTS AND AUDIT SOCIETY

"Audit society" (Power 1997) is a concept for theorizing an emerging form of governmentality that promotes the values of responsibility, openness about outcomes, and widening of access. Marilyn Strathern says, "Audit regimes accompany a specific epoch in Western international affairs, a period when governance has become reconfigured through a veritable army of 'moral fieldworkers' (NGOs) . . . and when transparency of operation is everywhere endorsed as the outward sign of integrity. . . . The apparently neutral 'market' provides a ubiquitous platform of individual interest and national politics alike, while 'management' is heard everywhere as an idiom of regulation and organization" (2000a:2). It is marked by a rhetoric of "helping (monitoring) people help (monitor) themselves" (4).

The IMF, like its Bretton Woods sister the World Bank—both part of the

UN family, is an important global carrier of the audit culture, sending teams on missions to audit, or create an overall picture of, national economies, quite like UN missions such as MINUGUA. Richard Harper describes the rituals of these missions, which transform speechless, or raw, numbers into ones with a voice, into the numbers that count. Audit is a complex amalgam of suspicion and confidence. Its basic assumption is conspiracy. Always fearful of duplicity, it assumes the need to check and recheck. Yet it functions through trust—invested in the specific mechanisms and the overarching system of audit itself and in the expert. In what IMF staff call "the facts of life," they acknowledge their dependence on specific people in the offices of countries being audited who "have the rank to sanction the relevant interpretations and associated numbers. These people provide the stamp of approval" (2000:23). Harper, a participant/observer, shows the complex play of doubt and confidence in the "social process of agreeing and determining the facts in question" (30) between these national representatives and the international team, and how numbers are subjected to trials of strength— assessments and sanctionings that allow them to be used in analytical tasks. He argues that creating useable information is a "moral transformation." The numbers themselves move from a doubtful, assumed identity to an Assumption Three, aka a credible fact. It is "social agreement" that warrants simultaneously the number and the individuals and institutions who produce it. In turn, "though the raw material of those processes may be wholly mundane, agreeing to count them may make them seem sacred" (2000:51). These "sacred numbers"—with that something Xtra—allow the Fund to "bet on the future," to make policy that will affect every life in the country and to which many, though not all, will acquiesce.

While the Fund missionaries and their collaborators may look like what the Comaroffs call "technicians of the arcane" (2003:297), Harper insists that "such grasping towards the future is not a kind of magic. It is undertaken on the basis of materials which can be demonstrated to be 'reasonable,' 'warranted,' 'accurate,' and 'objective:' in a phrase, that have been audited. . . . Missions get themselves into a position where making predictions is a reasonable thing to do. . . . This is a practical, 'real world,' hands-on skill" (2000:24–25). These facts, combining credibility and creditworthiness, are what make people credulous, willing to give the IMF their purse.

Always suspicious, always checking, the Fund itself raises suspicions, and it figures in global conspiracy theories, assumed to be a front for the real face of rapacious capitalist interests. David Harvey connects it to the "Wall Street–Treasury–IMF complex," whose primary task is to "protect the main centres of capital accumulation against devaluation (2003:185). Richard Peet calls the IMF, World Bank, and WTO an "unholy trinity" (2004) that gives free rein to the profit-maximizing interests of huge transnational corporations. It is tempting to dismiss Harper's descriptions of the intense labor, sleepless nights, calculations, econometrics, and social skills that produce the carefully elaborated spreadsheets as simply elaborate performances by actors who, as powerful as they are, are still kind of pathetic dupes, given the strong evidence of the interestedness and in-credibility of these "objective predictions."

I tend to side with the many activists involved in the "50 Years Is Enough" campaigns against the World Bank and the IMF (and with my little buddy the suspicious mouse) who question the means and ends of these activities. I assume that the economists (like David Stoll) are sincere in their efforts to create an accurate representation by drawing on their mountains of expertise so that interventions will be effective. But I also think they are duped by their undergirding assumptions—for instance, that the balance of payments is the end all and be all of development or that they've counted what really counts. Perhaps, like the *contratista*'s notebook or former U.S. Defense Secretary Rumsfeld warranting Guatemala's military policies as transparent, the accounts look balanced precisely because of what is off-book—like Joyabaj's history as a *finca de mozos*, like the paramilitarization of political violence and organized crime, or like the outright stealing of land and the murders of peasant and labor organizers. As Gyan Prakash (1999:13) puts it, "Rational routines of governance double as alien despotism."[1] The books record only one of the two faces of accumulation by dispossession—the economic, rule-bound one, apparently based on simple and consensual transactions. In this way the IMF's audits are tools of the crafty kitty: a weapon in the war of the cross, producing Herzfeld's "bureaucratic indifference," whereby the state and market evade accountability through the very procedures designed to bring them to account (1992, also Strathern 2000a:5). Given the confessions by the IMF and the World Bank that their policies have exacerbated financial meltdowns around the world, it seems more like the double entendre of "oversight" as interested blindness (Schirmer 1998:263) than authentic duping when these actants claim their means are fair even as their ends are so mean (as in cruel) (see Perkins's *Confessions of an Economic Hitman* 2004).[2]

However, neither my suspicions nor my careful analyses excuse me from the make-believe of the same audit culture that lends credibility to the Fund. As Strathern (2000), Maurer (2005), Riles (2001), and others have noted, anthropology—whether in the mundane banality of our everyday institutional lives or in our real cosmopolitical existence of research, fieldwork, and thinking deep thoughts—is interpenetrated through and through by audit culture and its rituals of verification (Power 1997).[3] We have to justify ourselves and prove our moral worth by accounting for time and money spent, engage in student and peer review — monitoring others to monitor themselves — argue passionately over professional ethics and for responsibility, and produce and use any number of appraisal documents, including the all-important human subjects protocol. And, just like the IMF, we check and recheck data, confer with local experts, and attempt to cook raw information to give it a voice in the hopes of creating accurate representations that will result in improving conditions, or at least warrant our assumed identities as experts. Strathern calls audit "an agent of a non-human kind" (2000a:5). Perhaps it's the authority that issues, to the Scarecrow's rapture, diplomas in thinkology.

Adding to my discomfort at once again being doubled over, Strathern also suggests that a central feature of audit is making procedures visible. And what else is this book's very end or aim? Isn't this the point of investigating the assumptions of identity and tracing audit as an undergirding form of reckoning in postwar Guatemala? Once again, I err in believing that my most sincere internal interests and passions are truly and only my own. Yet, paraphrasing the science fixionist Philip K. Dick, my hopes of being in the know may be futile, but we must go on anyhow. Below I explore duplicity and the rendering of accounts through the MINUGUA departure and struggles over the financing (money and settling) of the Ex-PAC demands and the National Reparations Program (PNR). Poovey calls such bookkeeping an "intermediary between empirical events and the theoretical system that constitutes the site of general knowledge" (1998:77). I'll explore what lies between and beyond the auditor and auditee, a relation Strathern sees as overdetermined by "third parties, which are at once the reason for and lie outside the loop through which . . . adherence to standards" or ethics is demonstrated (2000b:292). She sees this third party taking at least two forms: it can be the state or those "who need protection from the individual who acts with his or her own ends in mind" (2000b:293). Strathern, like a horror film fan, suggests that these two may seem quite separate, but the manifold products of people's interactions and the creative power of social relations make these "human subjects" quite slippery. The state is both auditor, of the ALMG, for example, and auditee of the IMF. Yet it also seeks protection from both internal and external actants who call it to account. As I explored in chapter 6, victims petition the state for protection from former civil patrollers — who have themselves submitted invoices to the state and are waiting for their checks (both verification and payment) — or from the hidden powers of CIACS, even as these may be faces of that same state. These same people also turn to the state to warrant their own accounts via the PNR, thereby becoming its auditees, as they turn to the UN to protect them by auditing the state. They also struggle for credibility so they can monitor the state monitoring itself.

NATIONALIZING AUDIT CULTURE:
HELPING THEM HELP THEMSELVES I

MINUGUA

> While MINUGUA will leave a huge void, what little has been gained up to now with the Peace Accords has been due more than anything to fierce and prolonged social pressure.
> INFORPRESS

MINUGUA was charged with monitoring the final two years of peace treaty negotiations and the implementation of the accords. Having regional offices throughout the country, they investigated many forms of human rights violations, from racial discrimination[4] to massacres and lynchings (over forty-five hundred cases in all), and produced nine important reports on peace processing. Some, primarily right-wing, Guatemalans protested that MINUGUA constituted an affliction (*plaga*), a breach in national sovereignty, yet the popular movement and many ordinary citizens felt it performed an essential service of checking (both supervising and restraining) that increased their sense of security. Concerns over insecurity moved the UN to extend its mandate an extra year,[5] but after slowly shutting down the outlying offices and training sixty National Transitional Volunteers, among other efforts to generate a "culture of verification," in October 2004 it warranted that the peace process "had matured" and on December 31, 2004, officially closed, although full wrapping up extended into mid-2005. The day before, the mission chief, Tom Koenigs, had released a flock of pigeons at the ceremony marking the eighth anniversary of the peace accords. President Oscar Berger was on vacation and unable to attend.

In their final report, MINUGUA offered a general accounting of their auditee, the state, and its relation to the peace accords, the "third party" needing protecting. It frequently deployed the discourse of two faces, suggesting that the state's progress involved more rhetoric than reality: that it consistently refused to put its or anyone else's money where its mouth is and evaded its responsibilities, substituting dialogue for action (3). While acknowledging that the accords remain a major source of ideas and inspiration, the report detailed the problems remaining: regarding the rights of indigenous people, "progress in this area has been more formal than substantive" (6), and "many key land-related legal reforms have not been carried out. . . . International donors provided major assistance for pilot projects in this area but official promises to enact enabling legislation have repeatedly proven hollow" (8). Even the major accomplishments of the CEH have stagnated as "Guatemala has largely had truth without justice and this has fostered bitterness and impeded national reconciliation" (5). There has been an "absence of national ownership, necessitating assistance and pressure [aka audit] from the international community" (4).[6]

The policies proposed to transform rhetoric into results are interpenetrated with the promises of accounting and beguile with the promise of resolving two faces into one. An external auditor should become internal as "Guatemalan national actors [become] stronger motors of the process" (4); the state becomes nation as "Victims' organizations, the Government and the Congress work . . . in a spirit of unity and transparency to overcome" delays in implementing reparations (10); and elite and popular combine through "sacrifices and solidarity, particularly from those in the upper echelons of society, who need to look beyond their narrow interests to those of the nation as a whole" (11). The nonhuman actant of the audit, including "more standard forms of international cooperation" and continued monitoring (11), is a central player in this process.

Guatemalans have worked to nationalize MINUGUA's verification functions through networks like CICIACS, now CICIG, the UN Human Rights office, and the Human Rights Ombuds Office (PDH),[7] all of which are engaged in trials of strength with outsized competitors. Ambivalence surrounded MINUGUA's departure. "The Accords have been in a coma," said a journalist. "With MINUGUA gone they will get even less attention." Some were frightened that the check or restraint it placed on violence, especially against activists, would be gone, and the clandestine forces would act as if they've received a blank check. However, while not as celebratory as the right, some activists thought the exit was an important step toward self-sufficiency. There was a sense that MINUGUA fostered dependency and produced its own "parallel powers," atrophying national political capacities. These concerns were also couched in an audit idiom—that Guatemala ought to be mature enough to monitor itself.

The new year brought a new government and cause for hope, as MINUGUA's imminent end seemed to motivate a more national accountability. In February, President Berger "relaunched" the peace process by creating the National Peace Accord Commission (CNAP), charged with working out the legal framework for implementation, reanimating the process stymied by the failed Consulta Popular of 1999. Draft versions of the new laws were presented at the eighth anniversary rituals. Berger also named the Mayan anthropologist Victor Montejo as peace secretary and reenergized the PNR by naming the leader of CONAVIGUA, Rosalina Tuyuc, to head it while promising three billion quetzales. Thanks to a great deal of effort and struggle, reparation has become an assumption, a taken-for-granted aspect of the postwar, as the state assumes responsibility for it, although not without checks, reversals (and bounced checks). Postwar actuarial puzzles over assigning value, redeeming (making good) loss and labor, and defining the categories of gift, debt, wage, and duty—and the audit procedures adequate to each—continue to transform this end of the postwar, coalescing most intensely in the cases of the Ex-PAC, the PNR, and transnational finance.

Waging War and Paying the Price

> History is reduced to "memory," oppression to "victimhood," the latter to be redressed less by empowering *social* reform than by the payment of *financial* reparations. The productive tensions, in modern life and thought, between subject and society, member and congregation, citizen and nation, are reduced to a dialogue of customers and contracts, consumers and rights, clients and therapists. Stakeholders, all, in a vast impersonal order of exchange. Small wonder, then, that the millennium, in neoliberal guise, tends to be radically privatized; hence the planetary popularity of . . . technicians of the arcane who "see" into the future. Small wonder, too, that we should be witnessing the widespread pursuit of new forms of moral accountability. Jean Comaroff and John Comaroff

R/e/valuating the Civil Patrol

Earlier I explored the more individual impact of the Civil Patrols and suggested the horrors people face living between being victim and victimizer, observer and participant, being acted on and acting. The audacious mobilization of the Ex-PAC in Peten in 2002, when they basically took over the entire department, including the airport and the Mayan ruins of Tikal, taking tourists hostage, pushed these issues into national consciousness, with accounting in its multiple senses very much at the crux. First, it has been hard to count the Exes. The first payout, of three contemplated, in March 2003 went to 250,000 men—the official number submitted by the army to MINUGUA when it was trying to downplay its total mobilization of the countryside. Soon, however, the number jumped to 500,000, and by early 2005 the organized patrollers claimed between 800,000 and 1.3 million (REMHI reported 900,000 mobilized in 1983). Perhaps of most interest to the politicians was the claim that one in four potential voters were Ex-PAC. Of most concern was the fact that they far outnumber the civil and military security forces combined.

At least as contested as to whom the "economic recognition" will go is how much and in what form. The first promise, brokered in July 2002 by Edgar Gutiérrez, was for $660.00 (Q5,241.00) per patroller in cash to be supplemented by development projects and monuments to the victims in some six hundred communities. When legal and financial objections were raised, the government, now under Berger, began to offer instead housing and farming supplies, some hoes, hens, and hogs. Both of the government's Janus faces (turned inward and outward) have been slapped for their inability to account for either the source or the destination of these resources. Under Portillo, the country's standing in the international financial markets was jeopardized by suspicions that the so-called Peace Bond offerings, supposed to fulfill government obligations under the accords, would be used instead to reward victimizers and "fund projects that could make [the FRG] the first administration to win re-election" (Silver 2003).[8] The government offering the bonds seemed a bit unclear on the peace they would finance. The proposal for $700 million in Eurobonds did not mention the PAC, claiming the money would finance "attention to the population in a state of poverty . . . affected by the armed conflict," but the president of the National Bank said it would pay debts to contractors, indemnify retired military, and use the rest to shield resources (NotiCen 2002). The Constitutional Court froze payments because it is unconstitutional to offer government payment in the absence of available funds. In turn, activists were enraged that the sums in question (Q1.48 billion) rivaled the entire 2004 budget for health (Q1.69 billion). This stalled the financing process, leading the Berger government to organize a sort of Civilian Conservation Corps, paying Ex-PAC to plant trees (probably not the environmentalism Filóchofo has in mind!). The PAC will "give water to the people" through a trust fund called Forests and Water for Harmony Guategreen (Bosques y Agua para la Concordia Guateverde), administered by the Agriculture Ministry.

In Joyabaj, Doña Miguela's husband has received some money but hasn't planted anything. She's incensed because he spent it on another woman instead of helping their youngest son get to the United States. Another Xoye friend, who votes URNG, has not been paid but has heard that others from his squad have. "It's all political," he says, "who gets it and who does not. It's planned. That's why the FRG won the mayor here, they were promised a second payment if they voted for him. The same thing will happen for the next election, just wait and see." And they did.

Yet the thorniest problem of the Ex-PAC may be accounting in the sense of explanation—as attempts to reckon with collaboration. The PAC were named self-defense patrols by the military that created them, but claims that patrollers were not acted on by the military state have become increasingly feeble, although some commentators continue to insist that the service was a gift *prestado* (bestowed) by a people on the state, or a *deber*, a duty, even a service owed. But the patrollers are calling the state two-faced by saying *it* owes *them*. And they are doing so in two ways.

Some articulate their demands in the discourse of rule-bound transactions between employer and worker, claiming they only want back wages for unpaid labor. Turning the tables, like the doubled over but rebellious dancers in the *baile*, they are pointing to the debit side in their own double-entry notebooks and asking for a balancing out. Others, by using the language of indemnization and reparation, which carries a sense of compensation for a loss, translate their experience into something horror film–like, where the rules were broken and they were victims of "force, fraud, oppression, looting." Their own acts of victimization, the 12 percent of wartime abuses the CEH laid at their door, become proof of their own victimhood. Congressman Efraín Asij Chile, a former patroller, said, "I have friends who still carry bullets in their bodies and no one has given them reparations. It is an injustice that they have to jump through so many hoops just to get the money they deserve" (in del Cid 2004). Others emphasize the long-term consequences and sacrifice entailed by the years of patrolling. What is a just accounting for a bullet in the flesh, for a family member killed when forced to fight the guerrilla or because they refused to patrol, or for the thousands of hours that could have gone into productive projects or children's schooling (many boys patrolled from age twelve or even younger)?

Human rights activists denounce that patrol members have already been remunerated because they stole land, food, livestock, and tools from their victims. In the public charges and countercharges unleashed by the emergence of the Ex-PAC, the extent to which new rural economic formations are the effect of accumulation by dispossession, and the experience of watching your children starve while your neighbor and former patrol leader enjoys the generativity of your animals and fields were more widely discussed. But victims' rights groups also acknowledge the slipperiness of these identities. Jorge Morales, coordinator of Organizations for Reparations for the Pueblo Maya del Valle, said, "We refuse to call the PAC and the paramilitary forces 'victims.' But if an individual was tortured or forced to participate in the violence, either on the side of the state or that of the guerrilla, this person is considered a victim and eligible for reparations" (in INFORPRESS 2003a:9). Others insist that as members of families and communities affected by the violence, former patrollers will receive compensation under the PNR and should come out of the Ex-PAC cold and fully assume this identification. In January 2005 the PNR said that patrollers were individually petitioning the government to acknowledge them as victims. Mario Polanco, a leader of GAM, said, "The economic crisis is so fierce that it is pressuring people to hope for a *double acknowledgement* from the state" (Guoz 2005:5, emphasis added).

Can we acknowledge the double state these men inhabit? Can we account for acting and being acted on, for simultaneously embodying that entity whose interests sometimes lash in to your own (giving access to a desired woman or field, settling old debts) but also grievously hurt you, making you two-faced, both victim and victimizer? What about the argument of the Guatemalan anthropologist Ricardo Sáenz Tejada that the Ex-PAC are a successful, primarily indigenous social movement that shares many members with CONIC and other peasant organizing? "The ex PAC act with certain autonomy from the FRG and have produced important political realignments . . . they succeeded in having their demands assumed by the majority of the presidential candidates [in the 2003 elections] and have forced the new government to maintain the commitment to pay" (2004:144–45). They translate varied interests and multiconduct, "reminding Guatemalans of the unfinished business of the war . . . that reconciliation will only come with knowing and reckoning with [*conocer y reconocer*] their role in this history, the suffering and abuses they experienced and rejecting the generalization that they are all human rights violators. They call for justice, that those responsible for war crimes be tried and punished and those innocent be absolved, but [most of all] that this be known" (147).

National Reparations

Fondly do we hope, fervently do we pray, that this mighty scourge of war may speedily pass away. Yet if God wills that it continue until all the wealth piled by the bond-man's two hundred and fifty years of unrequited toil shall be sunk, and until every drop of blood drawn with the lash, shall be paid by another drawn with the sword . . . 'the judgments of the Lord are true and righteous altogether." Abraham Lincoln, Second Inaugural Address, 1865

There have been demands for reparations, for an accounting of the war's losses and some settlement to offset them, from at least the beginning of the postwar.[9] Sometimes these are couched in pragmatics. Without some economic parity the country will not advance, so financial support for victims—already the most excluded from development, being rural, Maya, poor, and/or women—makes good economic sense. While rarely acknowledged as war reparations, international donors have financed Social Investment Funds in Guatemala and elsewhere, targeting exactly these populations since the late 1980s. More cosmopolitically, reparations have also been demanded as a duty, an obligation of the state to acknowledge its actions and make amends. They are not a gift or a calculated investment, but a morally binding responsibility. Someone who worked on the CEH put it this way: "No one really thinks that if you do certain things it will be over. The state, the elites claim we are living in the past and they want to move on, but if you sit down to coffee with any of them no one believes that paying $10,000 for someone who was disappeared will make up for that loss, for what has happened to the *lives* of the people around that person. . . . It's not the same as an accounting, the financial is only a small part of it. It's much more than that."

But to achieve "just" the financial part has taken years of intensive labor, of accounting in both the senses of storytelling and counting, greatly bolstered by the statistics in the CEH and MINUGUA reports. It was Edgar Gutiérrez in the Portillo government who finally made it happen, and even those who felt duped by his decision to work with the FRG admit he made an important contribution. The PNR's opening ceremony was held in July 2003 and attended by many Maya. Although its director was named at the last minute and without much consultation, the government promised $9.5 million over eleven years for direct payments, material and technical support, and mental health programs. Problems quickly surfaced, however, as only Q16 million of the first Q70 million budgeted were disbursed, and the handover to the Berger government was confusing, especially for those tallied in the original ledger but who were then told they had to reregister.

With Rosalina Tuyuc in charge, Mayan, and nationally known for founding CONAVIGUA and for her years in Congress, the program was reinjected with credibility. In January 2005, when I visited the bustling Sexta Avenida office staffed almost entirely by Maya, they were planning the May openings of the first two of nineteen planned regional offices, busy creating radio and print ads to publicize the program, and developing audit procedures and compiling lists of beneficiaries.[10] To the surprise of those counting, 70 percent of their cases did not appear in either of the truth commission reports.

While some suggest this shows cynical manipulation—"victims" *engañando* the program now that there's something to be gained—Tuyuc suggested instead that only now is the postwar beginning: "Many people did not have the heart to denounce what had happened, because from 1997 to 1999 there was so much fear, and as one might expect in a country that is at war, the people could not gather the courage or confidence to speak of what had happened. They said 200,000 dead and 40,000 disappeared. But it looks like we'll have to add more" (in *Prensa Libre* 12/27/04:6). Similarly, forensic anthropologists have added seven hundred more mass graves to the six hundred already documented by the CEH.

As with the Ex-PAC, arithmetic (addition) is only one counting challenge. War crimes were committed not only against individuals but, as genocide, against the collective of the Mayan people—a multiplicity that is more than the sum of its parts. Tuyuc has also struggled to make a particular number count—that of Mayan women raped during the war (the CEH says that 89 percent of sexual violations were directed at indigenous women)—and to *contar*, or contextualize, the special horror of this statistic in the milieu of attempts to wipe out a people. She argues that it is a double violence: the rape of Mayan women is a collective crime both because of their special role among a threatened population and because the state policy of rape victimized both survivor and perpetrator. "Perhaps the most damaging legacy from the armed conflict comes from crimes that the civil population was forced to commit. The CEH identified hundreds of cases in which 'civilians were forced by the army to rape women.' The CEH concluded that the state used these strategies as a method of social degradation" (Tuyuc, in INFORPRESS 2002:2). Thus, reparations activists have demanded collective indemnizations for the Maya, including land rights; communal ownership of sacred places; locally controlled autonomous development projects; legal changes that support bilingual education, make racism a criminal offense, and define the rape of Mayan women as a crime against humanity; and massive investment in education and health across the board, with full scholarships for war orphans (see Dill 2005).

Neither Tuyuc nor other activists have claimed the one-to-one payback that Abraham Lincoln feared might be required to balance the blood shed and the labor stolen from enslaved Africans and their descendents (who still struggle for reparations), but she has suggested that the postwar will be lengthy, perhaps as long as the war itself. These claims, like those of some of the Ex-PAC, are made to the two faces of counterinsurgent capital accumulation: both the rule-bound contractual one ensconced in the contractor's notebook and the fearsome, violent, and magically excessive one of murder, rape, and dispossession.

Like the FRG, the Berger government has been most adamant in denying the second face, with the exception of the Interamerican Human Rights Court (CIDH)-mandated reparations for the massacre of 1982 in Plan de Sánchez, Baja Verapaz. This ruling in 2004 was historic for the number of victims (268), for the mention of ethnic cleansing, and for its charging the state with moral damages, specifically, not allowing burials according to Mayan custom. Reparations must include "giving water to the people" with a potable water project, sewers, and health clinic as well as a road network, bilingual teachers, and individual payments of Q175,000 to each victim and next of kin (Brown 2005). Fernando López of CALDH, who is representing the community in the national legal case, said, "Countries have preferred to pay up, to make public speeches of apology, and to construct plazas and monuments to the victims instead of confronting the military officials who committed crimes" (in Brown 2005:13). He and many other activists insist that the end (*finer*) of the war is both financial and cosmopolitical. Like some Ex-PAC, they call for justice and acknowledgment, reckoning as *conocer y reconocer*.

But even the "pay up" remains limited. Despite the CEH findings, the state has refused to provide compensation for genocide, even as the PNR has already registered a quarter of a million victims. They have also reneged on their funding promises, first claiming that FRG corruption left their coffers empty, then that international audit procedures — complex calculations of external debt vis-à-vis the bond market, and current government spending determining disbursement rates — had tied their hands.[11] And, perhaps unsurprisingly, the state has justified withholding funds due to the charges of two-facedness — corruption, lack of transparency, interestedness, and political manipulation — lodged against the PNR, and due to the ugly and very public internal struggles that have caused so much pain and "*vergüenza*," as Natalia Godoy said.

"The state has not assumed its responsibilities," Tuyuc denounced at the eighth anniversary of the accords; it apparently prefers postwar inaction. And that state definitely looks two-faced. As MINUGUA critiqued, it promises but doesn't deliver; it apologizes, but the apologies are mere rhetoric so long as it won't even settle financially, much less address the "much more" of structural transformation and bringing perpetrators to justice. It is also *de doble cara* because it's in-between, showing one face to transnational capital and another to its people. Or perhaps it is only one face. Twelve days after

Tuyuc laid claim on behalf of the people, Berger proclaimed that the government needed to establish law and order: "We have to protect investors," he said, and later that day troops opened fire on Mayan villagers and CONIC members protesting the Glamis mining company, killing one man and injuring dozens.

NATIONALIZING AUDIT CULTURE:
HELPING THEM HELP THEMSELVES II

Money

Circumscribing the need for reform to the domestic, the "internal adjustment" demanded now by neoliberal wisdom promises to make the nation modern by wrenching it from the fantasy world conjured up by the magical petrostate and bringing it to the transparent world of the rational free market. Fernando Coronil

It's not an emergency anymore. Now we're just another third world country. Guatemalan activist

The exit of MINUGUA coincides with and has contributed to another exodus from Guatemala, one the state uses as an excuse for inaction. Not only the UN but most donor nations and NGOs are slashing aid and turning their largesse on parts of the world with more pressing problems; from 1996 to 2003, $1.7 billion was spent on Guatemala's peace process, but 2004 saw the lowest levels of aid in a decade. This reversal stems in part from concerns about accounting. With MINUGUA gone, some funders, like many Guatemalans, feel less secure being in the country. But it's also part of the assumptions of audit—of the balance and development that undergird Coronil's "neoliberal wisdom." The war and endemic poverty represent a sort of deficit column in an imaginary international ledger, but the generosity of funders has stacked up credit on the other side. While investment and loans will continue, there's a postwar sense of having balanced out, and now Guatemala can go it alone. "We've graduated," says a government planning officer; the peace process "has matured," says MINUGUA's head, and now Guatemala is ready to be wrenched from the fantasy world of the magical peace processing state and brought into the transparent realm of the rational free market (Coronil 1997:12). "Surprisingly," according to the *Financial Times*, "Guatemalan debt is regarded as a relatively safe bet. Because it was shut out of the capital markets during its civil war, from 1960 to 1996, its debt load is among the lowest in Latin America" (Silver 2003). Off-book are other numbers: that inequalities in land tenure have sharply increased since 1979, the date of the last census, with 3 percent of the fincas occupying 65 percent of the arable land and the combined holdings of the largest 879 landowners comprising 22 percent of all land, equal to that held by the 119,000 smallest holders. The size of small farms decreased from an average of 11.1 manzanas (a manzana is about 1.7 acres) to 6.4, but in some highland, majority Maya areas they average only 0.7 to 3 manzanas. Meanwhile, the minimum wage has decreased 13 percent from 1990 to 2000, whereas to keep up with inflation it needed to increase 140 percent simply to cover basic needs (AVANCSO 1999, 2000). Also mostly off-book have been the famine and mass unemployment unleashed by the 2001–03 coffee crisis, as global overproduction sent prices down to 1950s levels, plantation owners left beans to rot on the trees since they couldn't make back the cost of harvesting, and tens of thousands of *mozos* were consigned to starvation with no work, often owed years of back pay, and with little official attention to their welfare (Velásquez Nimatuj 2005).

As they were about MINUGUA's departure, many Guatemalans are of two minds about the decrease in aid. The ambivalence I described in chapter 6 mixes with the half-relieved, half-despairing sentiment that Guatemala is no longer a special postwar case, but just another third world country. For many this post-postwar is disillusioning, even terrifying, as projects very carefully tended for over a decade, people's livelihoods, and a certain independence from local and often corrupt and violent inter-esses are now in jeopardy. Money that supports research into and directly ameliorates the conditions of those most affected by the war is disappearing, and many of the identities assumed through this intense co-labor-ation—bilingual teacher, woman's advocate, Mayan activist, legal expert, representative to international fora, environmentalist, human rights monitor, intellectual—are being thrown back into the desultory politics of survival, as people juggle several jobs to make ends meet or, as the treasurer of Joyabaj's Grupo Maya did, head north. It's harder to make believe that resistance is not futile.

But others see the decrease in aid as a blessing in disguise since aid can be as much an Indian gift as the loans that expect something, plus interest, in return. An analysis by *INFORPRESS Centroamericana* in 2004 explored its two faces, asking, Is aid "altruistic or does it respond to commercial interests? Does it strengthen or atrophy a country? Is it a medicine or a drug?" (García 2004a). I've already noted the fears that dependency on the means of external funding threatens possession by its ends. My friend the former guerrilla jokes that she's doing the same things she used to do, but now she's getting paid. However, does this make her two-faced, as the source of the money demands an accounting, while she, like the Patzulá patroller, must also settle accounts with her people? International cooperation is shot through with audit culture and its temporality. NGOs may be a carrier, but audit far more subtly doubles people over. Just like anthropologists, when Guatemalan organizations plug in, it can virally transform not only the content of their work but also its rhythms, molding long-term goals to fit the external demand of assessment periods and fiscal years and necessitating long hours invested in accounting rather than actually doing. What was once a minor, personal frustration—finding it difficult to hook up with Guatemalan friends in midsummer because their annual reports are due—I now see as a symptom of something larger. Like Natalia Godoy's frustration with COPMAGUA's failure of democracy in choosing women's committee members; like knowing the workshop preferences of K'aqla' s membership because organizers had to systematize and submit that information; like the way an original goal is torqued to fit the funder's guidelines and time lines, which are determined in turn by the funders' accountability to their funders;[12] like the transformation of means, i.e., getting the financing, into ends; these are all signs of people's imbrication in these new surveillance technologies. They point toward increasing subjection to the assumptions of audit culture.

But these identi-ties to transnational networks are also a Latourian marshalling of forces that can translate a range of interests to make certain numbers count and thereby make a cause more powerful. Powerful enough to create new facts and transform the whole kit and caboodle. A petard is an explosive device meant to force an opening, and that's exactly what the multiply networked Guatemalan NGOs have done—cracking the wall of impunity and insisting on accountability. But there's always the risk of being hoisted on this same device. If the supportive funds cannot be accounted for and credibility is withdrawn, the entire network can collapse, as happened with COPMAGUA and the USAID-funded get-out-the-vote campaign that mysteriously stopped appearing in Joyabaj.[13] Dependency also means that even when everything is accounted for the funder may just get tired or, hoping for a better return, simply move on—not unlike a maquila owner.

But the links of a network mean the same audit petard can hoist different actants. Guatemalans are calling donors to account and asking what that $1.7 billion has bought? Thanks to transparency and those "sacred numbers," critics can unveil a "double agenda" with the façade of peace hiding accommodation to the neoliberal system. They can demonstrate how aid and loans were directed far less toward ameliorating poverty and suffering (only 11 percent went to NGOs) than toward enacting the standard structural adjustments of enforcing macroeconomic stability, strengthening the financial sector, and opening the economy. For example, in 2002, 30 percent of the $200 million in loans and donations went to the finance and insurance sector, of which 70 *percent* was disbursed while other areas saw only 0–7 percent actual disbursement.

Investment aid posing as a gift is under investigation. It has been recalculated instead as the down payment on a long-term debt, as historic reparations. The activist Mario Godínez said, "The U.S. and Europe have not even begun to pay all the money they owe to this country" (in García 2004b:6).[14] Voicing precisely this argument, in September 2004, 3000 Maya-Achí took over the Chixoy dam in northeast Guatemala, demanding that the government, the World Bank, and the Inter-American Development Bank acknowledge the oppression and looting that occurred when they invested there in the late 1970s. As Rosa Luxemburg might have foretold, one face of the dam is a sound investment: the loans have been paid back in full, and it now generates some 60 percent of the country's electricity. But its other face is the massacre in 1982 of 450 people who refused to leave their ancestral village of Río Negro.[15] "For the local communities . . . this imposed 'development' project was a horrendous, global crime; massacres, community destruction, robbery of animals and tools, survivors fleeing into the mountains, further death by hunger and disease in the mountains, no real compensation, and certainly no reparations or justice since that time" (Russell 2004:1). In February 2005 a petition was submitted to the CIDH to establish the liability of the banks and their other faces: the governments who fund them and sit on their boards of directors. While activists on this campaign are suffering threats and intimidation, the World Bank is suddenly willing to fund poverty-alleviation projects in the area, what organizers are calling "an indirect way of offering reparations" (Botello 2005:8).

Without intending to *pimper* activism in Guatemala, to sell you on its allure, I think it offers a challenge to the Comaroffs' somewhat dismal diagnosis of a millennial moment in which history is evacuated and victimhood is to be redressed solely by the payment of financial reparations. It's much more than that. I've been outlining precisely the in-between of "the productive tensions, in modern life and thought, between subject and society, citizen and nation" *and* "customers and contracts, consumers and rights" (2003:297). These are like the inter-esses or what lies between Coronil's two bodies of the nation: the political, made up of citizens, and the natural, made up of the rich subsoil (1997). In Guatemala contests over mining and the role of rural land-based production are heating up, in the milieu of a more collective Mayan relation to the natural body, which is, in turn, lashed in to other networks which enjoy increased legal support via International Labor Organization (ILO) conventions, CIDH rulings, the peace accords, and national laws.

BALANCING ZERO-SUM AND THE X THAT IS IN IT THAT'S MUCH MORE THAN THAT

Fact either means evidences or it means anything which exists. The fact, the thing as it is without any relation to anything else, is a matter of no importance or concern whatever: its relation to what it evinces, the fact viewed as evidence, is alone important. G. Robertson (1838)

Asking if international aid for peace processing is a medicine or a poison and denouncing it as two-faced—counterinsurgency, not repair, neoliberal restructuring, not therapeutic support—suggests another first-rate word or double entendre: pharmakon, simultaneously poison and medicine—reminding us that "or" is often a false binary, too static for the ways identity comes *through* assumption, healing *through* terror. Questions about transnational capital flows echo my quandaries in the last chapter about the Guatemalan state's two wars because the meshings between war and finance are at least as tight as those Latour describes between war and science. (Perhaps the name of this father is Daddy Warbucks, and Paul Wolfowitz's move to the World Bank, following unconvicted war criminal Robert McNamara's similar trajectory, and General Colin Powell's employment with a Silicon Valley venture capital firm are just its most recent public expressions.) In chapter 7 I suggested that violent counterinsurgency and the eradication of malaria both carry the undergirding assumptions (*nom du père*) of biopolitics. The biopolitical, in turn, is both singular and two-faced—the right of death and power over life—and may carry its own unspoken assumptions of Lamarckian eugenics. Similarly, I think that postwar struggles over reparations and finance assume, or operate in the milieu of, audit culture that is also two-faced. It promises both the simple settlement of a zero-sum or balance and something more: redemption, making good, the moral, even sacred qualities of number that Harper finds in that apparently most secular space, the IMF mission. This is so, Poovey suggests, because via the intermediary of double entry, virtue came to lodge in balance and order, and the idea of system itself came to carry moral connotations (1998:xvi–xvii). Counter-counterinsurgency hermeneutics, also trying to lay a moral claim, have to keep their eyes on the individual "spitters, fences, operators, and swindlers" that Marcos from *Nine Queens* warned about and on this other Agent, acting, perhaps, through us.

As I have argued throughout, one is not enough. Foreign investment in Guatemala certainly has many nefarious results, some premeditated, some unexpected, but aid is not only counterinsurgency—like Marcos protesting, "You think I'm a thief. I don't kill people." Such an analysis does not account for its multiple effects, including giving water, funding workshops that enable embodi/meant, creating unpredictable connections, verifying human and indigenous rights, and producing many of the facts I cite here, from the CEH, MINUGUA, AVANCSO, etc.[16] Nor can it account for how those effects may be articulated to other projects. No more does reducing the war of the cross to the war of the sword—and dismissing anyone who invests in the former as a dupe—let me off the hook of being duped myself. Little did I know! But that doesn't let me off the hook either—the hook of the *nacer de conciencia*, when, through the exercise of knowing something, partly thanks to financing, I am no longer the person I was.

But if one is not enough, two is too many. Financial aid is never fully separate from immorality and violence. World Bank experts did not pull the triggers at Rio Negro—like Agent Smith, their interests acted through others, mostly indigenous soldiers. But that massacre was deeply imbricated in making the Chixoy dam a good investment. Financial missions, like religious ones, are linked to the sword as they struggle to re-form their human subjects. That's because the very transformability that makes conversion thinkable simultaneously lodges the fear of duplicity deep in its procedures, giving rise to the need to check and recheck and to produce systems of creditworthiness and credibility, aka our very own audit culture. And the laboratory for this modernity? The Spanish Inquisition, with its infinitesimal agonies, shocking and awe-ful intimacies, and excesses of violence (Silverblatt 2004). It honed accounting procedures. It produced both warranted experts and, being as deeply interpenetrated by colonialism as it was, the Two-Faced Indian. If virtue is in the system, so are violence and injustice.

And so is duplicity. Fear of it is the goad for accounting, but duping is also its form. Just as *Bamboozled* opens with an invocation of 1492, so Mary Poovey finds deception at the inception of double-entry bookkeeping in the manual *De Computis et Scripturis* (1494). Here, balance, reaching zero, depends on a "wholly fictitious number—the number imported not to refer to a transaction but simply to rectify the books" (1998:54), which makes the zero balance a "matter of formal precision, not referential accuracy" (55). Also in the system, generated by its interrelations (as in the case of the Inquisition), is the Assumption Three of subjectivization. Poovey shows how fictitious personifications like Stock, Money, Profit, and Loss were produced by the bookkeeping system and in turn "created writing positions that caused anyone who wrote in the books to subordinate personality (and status) to rules" (56). Just like the modern make-believe of the IMF audit that simultaneously warrants numbers and the individuals and institutions producing them, the "fictions" of Money and Balance that might have undermined the book's display of honesty did not do so because "preserving the precision of the system required anyone who wrote in the books to act as if these fictions were true, and in so doing, to help make them so. . . . [In turn,] the priority given to writing to rule created writing positions," (58–59) thereby subjecting humans to and by the system.

In more mundane terms the duplicity inherent in such subjectivization allowed merchants to really become what they claimed to be: the ledger displayed the very honesty and creditworthiness necessary to receive the credit that would actually make them solvent (64). These were self-actualizing fictions. But they were not only a false face directed toward an external auditor. In the sixteenth-century how-to manual *A Briefe Instruction and Maner How to Keepe Bookes of Accompts after the Order of Debitor and Creditor* John Mellis describes the dangerousness of juggling money-to-hand and money-at-work (in action) and the risk and unpredictability of trade, a form of betting on the future, so that "a company's public books constituted the only place where a merchant could even *seem* to be in control" (59), including to himself. Like the other preserved possibilities I have traced in this book, which act on the future out of the past, Poovey argues that double-entry-engrained "attempts to gather theory- and value-free data are marked by the very theoretical assumptions they seem to leave behind" and that number and "all systematic knowledge systems require something like a leap of faith" (xix).[17] There is something in them more than them. In addition to the leap, this Xtra is the other face of *contar*, the telling. Poovey shows how changes in European organization of space, family relations, and writing in the fifteenth century influenced the control of information, valorized number, and thereby constituted some things as excessive — especially narrative details that became increasingly connected to women and sexuality (35, 61). (Just the facts, ma'am.)

The other extra, hidden by the zero of the double-entry balance, is the whole point of trade: profit. When the accountant enters the pertinent information about each transaction twice, once as a credit and once again as a debit, he is not simply adding because expenditures and receipts almost never actually equal each other. The goal is to get more than you paid for. In addition to the problems connected with accounting for the variable of time, as profits are realized in the future, not at the time of investment, this Xtra makes the accountant supplement the records of actual transactions with numbers lacking a referent in the company's business (43 & 54): "Fluctuations [not balance] in prices, production, and demand were the source of the profit that made commerce worth pursuing in the first place" (62). Just as Feldman finds the in-human (what is in us) in what seems least us (the horrifying inhuman), it is the economy-in-action, the Xtra of circulation and of Xploitation, that simultaneously undergirds and exceeds the balancing acts of this accounting system.

Perhaps this is why Lacan said that Marx invented the symptom. According to Žižek, this is "a certain fissure, an asymmetry, a certain 'pathological' imbalance which belies the universalism of the bourgeois 'right and duties.' This imbalance, far from announcing the 'imperfect realization' of these universal principles — that is, an insufficiency to be abolished by further development — functions as their constitutive moment; the 'symptom' is, strictly speaking, a particular element which subverts its own universal foundation. . . . The procedure of 'criticism of ideology' . . . consists in detecting a point of breakdown *heterogeneous* to a given ideological field and at the same time *necessary* for that field to achieve its closure, its accomplished form" (1989:21). The actions of unveiling the make-believe — revealing the second face hiding behind the first (financial assistance is really counterinsurgency) and uncovering the lie or what is heterogeneous to the field (the balance of bookkeeping is really about hiding profits) — are vitally important. But they are not always enough. There are cons(piracies) and bamboozlements where someone pulls the strings and takes your purse, land, animals, even your life. Following the money we can find *cui bono*, who benefits at someone else's expense, who tipped the scales of justice for their own gain. It is both a moral and a therapeutic endeavor to call them to account, find fault, fight back, resist dispossession, make them *asumir responsabilidad*. And this endeavor is moral, even as we work through the same institutions, networks, and assumptions that enabled the duplicity in the first place: because by that very articulation they may be transformed.

But then there are the fakes, the breakdowns that are constitutive — like Elmyr's forgeries, the ones no one seems to want to know about. Or like, say, freedom. In this universal notion, comprising freedom of speech, consciousness, assembly, and religion, I do most sincerely believe. However, as Marx pointed out, it is "a specific freedom (that of the worker to sell freely his [*sic*] own labour on the market) which subverts this universal notion. . . . By selling his labour 'freely,' the worker *loses* his freedom — the real content of this free act of sale is the worker's enslavement to capital. . . . [P]recisely this paradoxical freedom, the form of its opposite . . . closes the circle of 'bourgeois freedom'" (in Žižek 1989:22). The same goes for "fair, equivalent exchange," which, under capitalist production, creates a "new, paradoxical type of commodity: the labour force." Their exploitation is not a simple violation of free trade, to be improved by better accounting procedures and increased transparency. The problem will not be eradicated by cleaning the system of corrupt labor contractors, bought-off government inspectors, and sleazy maquila operators, although this would help. Instead, it is "*internal* to equivalent exchange" (1989:22). In other words, it's a dupe, but an indispensable one—that produces us as we know (*savoir*) it, as we assume the identifications it makes possible. Žižek says, "The 'quantitative' development itself, the universalization of the production of commodities, brings about a new 'quality,' the emergence of a new commodity representing the internal negation of the universal principle of equivalent exchange of commodities: in other words, *it brings about the symptom*" (1989:22–23). This is the Xtra of the assumption of identity. But it's also why, even in these dark days, resistance is not futile. It may be as inevitable as duplicity.

Marx, like the Maya-Achí survivors of the Rio Negro massacre, Rosalina Tuyuc, the plaintiffs of the PNR, the workers grown on the *finca de mozos*, and some of the Ex-PAC, is exploding the very idea of balance. This is because the system itself, through circulation, networking, traversals, and crossings, is generative. It produces both contradictions and new identi/ties (Assumptions One, Two, and Three). So Marx may still be caught in audit culture, if one of its central features is making procedures visible, as he reveals the absolutely mundane yet world-blasting emergence of a new historical subject: the proletariat.

I am similarly produced as a worker/Coppertop, as a subject of audit, and via the procedures that Brian Rotman argues create what he calls the algebraic- and xeno-subjects. Audit subject that I am, I will follow him in making such beings visible because I want to add them to our sideshow attractions of transuranic elements, transgenetic organisms, Psycho Killer/Final Girls, ludicrous anthropologists, Two-Faced Indians, and duplicitous states: aka all those qualitatively different identifications produced by the massification of connections (media, inter-esses, what's in-between) of racist patriarchal capitalism's colonial milieu. To do so, I'll elaborate a bit more on that assumption of accounting, the zero balance, which is both fraudulent and alluring. It seems to be the end of the audit but may really be a beginning, generating new, unexpected human subjects and nonhuman actants. It will close this book but unsettle its accounts.

Ground Zero

> In the meta-paintings of Vermeer and Velásquez there occurs
> . . . the internal depicted figure of the looker. By offering
> an internalised image of the perspectival subject such a
> figure neither embraces such a subject nor takes any part in
> signifying its absence; rather the figure is a sign which stands
> in the code at a place between the two: by challenging, on
> the one hand, the idea of literality, of a clear-cut distinction
> between prior reality and a subsequent figurative depiction of
> that reality, without, on the other hand, in any way suggest-
> ing how such an idea might be denied or shown to be illusory.
> Brian Rotman

Brian Rotman describes a constitutive dependency and wild excessiveness in the concept of zero. While apparently quite mundane in our everyday worlds of audit culture, zero tolerance, ground zero, zero sum, and Patient Zero, early modern Europeans, unlike their contemporaries in the Indus valley, Arabia, al-Andalus, and the Americas, resisted it tooth and nail, and, Rotman argues, some of their horror is retained to this day. That horror emerged, in part, from its introduction via the principle of zero balance in bookkeeping, which attended the "disruption and moral disintegration inherent in capitalism's threat to commoditise social reality, its capacity to nihilise fellow feeling and reduce human beings to acquisitive wolves fixated on money and power" (1987:78). He reads Shakespeare's *King Lear* (1605) as a treatise on zero, an ominous warning and a promise of violent explosion emerging from Lear's arithmetizing of social relations and from the force, threat and "horror of *ex nihil*, of that which issues from nothing" (85).[18] Lear's youngest daughter, Cordelia, embodies, in contrast, "love in *action*, in kinship, in context, in use, in obligation, in mutual responsibility. . . . Such love is *produced*, and has meaning only *in situ*, in the context of its production" (80). This is the milieu of the Indian gift, a term coined by the arithmetizing occupiers of the Americas to denigrate that very world and to justify getting something for nothing.[19]

Rotman argues that horror also arises from "the peculiar, enigmatic, and profoundly abstract challenge that zero presented, as a *sign* . . . whose connection to 'nothing,' the void, the place where no thing is, makes it the site of a systematic ambiguity between the absence of 'things' and the absence of signs" (1987:2). And some of that horror stems from zero's two faces—as both "a sign inside the number system and as a meta-sign, a sign-about-signs outside it. . . . [Zero serves] as the site of an ambiguity between an empty character . . . and a character for emptiness, a symbol that signifies nothing" (13). Perhaps this is a preserved possibility encoded in "horror's special F/X." What is genocide if not the total reduction of something to nothing? Are the stutterings, the difficulties in accounting for it, not only the result of mundane, even pragmatic, fears that it might return, but also the human reaction to the religico-cosmopolitical cracks that genocide opens: this very void, this systematic ambiguity, this scorched-earth annihilation of existence itself?

Yet Rotman says that zero also contains a "trace of subjectivity, pointed to but absent." By representing "the starting point of a process it indicates the virtual presence of the *counting subject* at the place where that subject begins the whole activity of traversing what will become a sequence of counted positions" (13). Zero, the apparent end of an accounting process—like reckoning the postwar—is also the beginning. It is a quantitative development that brings about a new quality. Like the postwar-in-action, it actively subjectivizes, as with CONAVIGUA, CONIC, AVANCSO, the Mayan movements, and any number of other networks formed from the very traversings of the war and the horrors of genocide. And they in turn produce counting subjects, both figuring up loss and how to indemnify (make it good) and insisting that they count.

Rotman also links zero to the assumptions of identity through its role in transforming visualization technologies like the vanishing point, which, he says, also plays a dual role: it is a definite location within a real physical scene, but also infinitely far away and thus unoccupiable by any person, which gives it a metalinguistic relation to the signs in the painting "since its function is to organise them into a coherent unified image." Prototype for the slippery identities in horror film, the vanishing point "mediates between two different subjectivities . . . offer[ing] the spectator the possibility of momentarily becoming, via a thought experiment, the artist" (19).

The milieu of transition from Roman to Hindu numerals and iconic to perspectival representation also facilitated the shift to imaginary money, which, unlike coin, had no material referent in gold or silver. This new money was essential, along with the occupation of the Americas and the African slave trade, in transforming mercantilism into capitalism. Paralleling Poovey's work on the rise of the "induction problem" in Europe (how can we be in the know?), Rotman traces how these changes reversed the movement "from object to sign. The signs of the system become creative and autonomous" (28). This gave rise to a meta- or algebraic subject who, by mirroring the relation between a variable and a number, can "signify the absence of the counting subject, the displacement of the one-who-counts from an actual to a virtual presence" (32). This milieu generates both the punctum in painting, as in Vermeer and Velázquez, which posits "the necessary absence of any externally situated, perspectival seeing" (40), and paper money, with its own "ambiguous duality, its ability to appeal to the anterior existence of gold at the same time it deconstructs, via its capacity to *manufacture* money, the very possibility of this anteriority" (53). Early promissory notes were like today's checks. They were written to an individual with a name and had to be turned over and endorsed, retaining a link to a person. Bank notes, by contrast, are promises to "a de-personalised anonymous *bearer* . . . a *variable* subject, a subject in meta-lingual relation to any particular named and dated individual" (48–49), and they caused a scandal when they were introduced. Now they're old news. We've assumed this identity.

The latest transformation of these vexed relations among number, knowledge, vision, and money is a financial version of the category-blasting and simultaneously mundane transbeings: what Rotman calls xenomoney, aka offshore currency or Eurodollars.[20] Xenomoney emerges from long-term processes of turning money into a good, itself "bought and sold through the medium of money. As both object and medium, thing and token, both a commodity and a sign for a commodity, money is a dualistic and self-reflexive sign" (92). Xenomoney, through the development of financial derivative markets, allowed debt to be "spread, split up, swapped, syndicated, traded and reassigned. . . . 'We are all joined together in one long chain of credit; but we can't examine the balance sheet of every link, and we never know who the ultimate borrower is,' is how one Eurobanker has described it" (90). By 1984, close to Rotman's publication, it was already a multibillion-dollar-a-day market. More currently, Edward LiPuma and Benjamin Lee (2004) put the numbers in the trillions. But no one really knows. So much of it is off the book.

Part of the allure and power of these new forms of speculative capital is that they are two-faced: simultaneously insurance and speculation. LiPuma and Lee detail how the size of the market creates extraordinary leverage so that a trader's hedge, or attempt to manage the risk of a price rising or falling in the future, is simultaneously a wager placed on those changes, but a wager so large—ten million dollars is considered a small trade—that it can actually create the change it is foretelling. In the Asian contagion of 1997 currency markets actively depressed the Thai baht by 30 percent, leading to financial chaos, massive unemployment, and IMF-imposed constitutional reforms that forced Thailand to adapt to global flows of transnational capital (2004:26). The Argentine crisis was similarly generated. LiPuma and Lee warn that this circulation is increasingly disconnected from production and consumption in any particular nation—the Thais did not change their habits from one day to the next but their economy crashed nonetheless—or even to politically negotiated contracts like IMF and World Bank loans. In fact, the examining of their virtual presence, constant mutation, and light-speed effects generates a nostalgia for white men negotiating over red ink to be worked off by brown men cutting sugarcane and brown women posing for tourists; or for the U.S. trade secretary's heavy-handed tactics in pressuring Guatemala to refuse generic drugs. Creepy as such negotiations are, at least there's a gesture toward human interaction, like the uncanny but oddly reassuring little Argentine inside us—at least someone's in control! But "exchange rate volatility seems to materialize out of thin air. The economic power that this violence confers on speculative capital in no way depends on popular awareness, let alone political consent; rather, the power is so abstracted and transverse that those in its path mostly intuit the existence of the derivatives market" (LiPuma and Lee 2004:28). Not so in the know, we academics are just now developing theories of audit culture, yet the whole concept of balance and order may be not only a con but also passé.

Derivatives, supposed to insure against volatility, actually cause it to increase. The politico-econo-military system of export production *produces* a racialized *mozo* threatening to take up arms and come down from the mountain. Counterinsurgency *induces* the clandestinity and the Two-Faced Indian it supposedly seeks to unveil. The balance, order, transparency, and efficiency promised by audit are only one face of a system perhaps better served by chaos and increasing risk that can be leveraged into profit for some (Joxe 2002, Arrighi and Silver 1999), while U (and me) B*, we are the ass to risk. In the *baile* the workers organize to take out the powerful *contratista* who doubles them over, but there is another, barely intuited power behind him— the outsider shaman, the *Maxe necio*. Under the sign of financial derivatives and the globalization of risk, the conspiracy theorist's Big Other of the state or World Bank looks less like a bulldog and more like someone's poodle. There's a bigger, scarier Other on the block.

Rotman's designation of this new money form as xeno (strange, foreign) highlights similar geographically external impingements on sovereignty and development to those denounced as afflictions by the cartoonist or decried by anti-IMF activists, or those half-relieved that MINUGUA is gone so they can create their own monitoring capabilities. Even more chillingly, LiPuma and Lee see derivatives producing new, viral networks that subsume the relations among citizens, installing in their place "forms of connectivity in which no common project exists or can even be imagined" (188). In turn, they suggest, we are duped by the very thing we struggle for and think is in opposition to this enemy: democracy. As LiPuma and Lee say, "The open, externally exposed, market-oriented democratic state is the preferred form of governance of speculative circulatory capital. What the participants of the derivatives market desire is fully transparent financial structures within states even as their activities remain invisible and unsupervised. . . . the capitalist culture of the circulation of derivatives is a power that seems answerable to no other power" (2004:188–89). William Robinson makes a similar point about U.S.-backed wars in Central America: they were not just against revolutionary movements, but also meant to depose the old oligarchs and to orchestrate the rise of a "New Right with allegiance to the transnational neoliberal economy" (2004:14).

Although LiPuma, Lee, and Robinson base their analyses on materials which can be demonstrated to be reasonable and warranted, these are dark conspiracy theories indeed: less pharmakon than full-on horror film scenarios. If we are to reckon a postwar we must take them with deadly seriousness. But even as these analyses may be no more magical than an IMF audit, they conjure old images of gullible natives duped by democracy, getting involved in *babosadas*. They also echo rumors of baby-snatchers or dangerous fried chicken, similar graspings toward meaning in a world increasingly inundated with too much information and not enough significance. The frisson or allure of all such stories reminds us to take a little care—even as our intellectually pessimistic allies do the important work of unveiling the monstrous freaks that double us over—to remember that one face (derivatives always get what they want) is never enough. There is more.

Marx was hardly sanguine at the bloody birthing of a world historical new subject, the proletariat. He called it "the unreason of reason itself" (in Žižek 1989:23). It's an aspect of the Xtra, why the universe will never add up, and precisely why he had to go on anyhow. Perhaps the Two-Faced Indian and the other assumed identities traced here—even as they are the products of almost unaccountable violence and horror—can spark similar hope? Rotman is also not sanguine about the dangers of xenomoney and certainly doesn't think there's a way to escape it. But he seems to find a bit of hope in its very freakishness, its temporal strangeness. He calls it scandalous, actually, because "it is a sign which creates itself out of the future" (96). Like the war, derivatives have changed time, and this has led some to fear that xenomoney will collapse the world system because it simultaneously carries debt from the past and brings vertiginous and anarchic volatility from the future (1987:96). However, Rotman links it to a notion of "xenotext" via Derridean *différance* in ways that signal many of the terrors and promises faced in reckoning with postwar Guatemala: "Paper-texts point backwards: they offer to deliver that which has been deposited, something buried in a vault in the past. Their value stems from the promise of this redemption, the possibility of retrieving at least in principle some original full self-affirming 'meaning.' The xenotext offers no redemption . . . no delivery of some precious, proto-signifying specie. What was a past meaning, waiting intact and whole to be claimed, independent of the act of retrieving it, is displaced by a de-mythologised future significance, fractured, open and inherently plural" (102). There is no end.

Zero Patience

The filmmaker John Grayson also plays with time in his musical science-fiction romantic comedy AIDS agitprop co-memoration called *Zero Patience* (1994). In the film, a debt is carried over from the colonial past into the present in the form of Sir Richard Burton, the Victorian explorer, sexologist, and translator of the *Kama Sutra* and *Arabian Nights*. An encounter with the Fountain of Youth has kept him alive, and now he is in charge of dioramas at the Toronto Museum of Natural History. The opening musical number invokes Scheherazade and doubles the power of her life-saving storytelling. The song suggests that, like her life, if the tales — of a person, of a virus, of a culture of blame, of the persistence of hope — are told right (*contar*, articulated, *contado*, made to count), other lives might also be saved.

Grayson then turns to Burton, a pompous expert, secure in his "culture of knowledge." He exults in his first song: "Let's all be empiricists, victors of the mind, rulers of the stupid, leaders of the blind." Burton is intent on creating a "Hall of Contagion" that will center on Patient Zero, a "promiscuous" French Canadian flight attendant blamed for bringing AIDS to North America. In the meantime,[21] he stumbles on a network of people, men and women, black, brown, and white, all impacted by AIDS and articulated through grief and mourning and through "love in *action*, in kinship, in context, in use, in obligation, in mutual responsibility." Among them is the increasingly material ghost of Patient Zero himself, who has been trapped in a limbo of guilt because he believes himself responsible for the suffering caused by AIDS. Thus conjured, Zero agrees to participate in his own stereotypification in Burton's upscale freak show. However, like any good two-faced native, he demands a return gift — that Burton help him disappear. Burton and Zero begin to play detective, tracking down the studies that first implicated Patient Zero; exploring the bigotry, racism, and panic that replaced complex and contradictory knowledges with facile scapegoating (see Farmer 2006, Treichler 1999); and exposing the corporate interests that keep people in the dark. And, overcoming their pride and prejudice, they start to fall in love.[22]

Burton's articulatory reciprocity with Zero and with the networks of AIDS activists, Big Pharma, researchers, and others transforms "the vision of a pacified world achieved through the scientific arrangement of society and the domination of nature . . . crowned in a museum" and opens it out onto different possible futures, although ones gained through terrible loss. With members of Aids Coalition to Unleash Power (ACT-UP), Burton and Zero subvert the Hall of Contagion to tell different stories of survival and the agential engagements of people who suffer but are not passive victims. Connections to the scapegoat Patient Zero lead Burton to assume a new identi-tie-in-action of Zero Patience for the forms of structural violence and profit making that undergird the AIDS crisis. He gains new knowledges and comrades but loses his lover. Absolved through the new stories they have told together, Zero is able to dissolve, to finally rest in peace. Through this silly, moving film Grayson reminds us that focusing only on the horror or poison of zero may be the con in Pharmakon, whose other face may be healing and generative; a starting point for new forms of accountability or relations that transcend audit completely.

Chapter Nine

THE ENDS

What grief displays . . . is the thrall in which our relations with others hold us. . . . Let's face it. We're undone
by each other. And if we're not, we're missing something.
Judith Butler

¿DÓNDE ESTÁ EL FUTURO? WHERE IS
THE FUTURE OF THE POSTWAR?

What makes someone believe? What makes them run for the hills—either
to escape fake Martians or to take up arms? What sort of "practical, 'real
world,' hands-on skill" convinces someone that "making predictions [say,
starting a cooperative, joining a student group, studying displaced people,
taking over an embassy, deciding to give someone your purse, or withholding a loan] is a reasonable thing to do," a "warranted" understanding of the
present that "enables determination of the future" (Harper 2000:24–25)?
An actuary, tallying up risk versus assured payoff, might be puzzled by the
accounting procedures that lead someone to bet on the future, to go on anyhow even knowing they will suffer terrible pain and probably die. This auditor might assume such a person was bamboozled, a gullible rube, or just bad
at math.

Perhaps that's because certain numbers don't count for this actuary: the
ones about land tenure, animals stolen, infant mortality, death as a tragedy,
not collateral damage; or because he or she has trouble evaluating collective holdings; or is perhaps too focused on balancing things out, reaching a
zero. Maybe the actuary understands only the counting sense of *contar* and
not the telling, aka, the *articulating*—of simultaneously making sense and
making connections and by so doing transforming those who are so linked
and maybe the whole caboodle.

I've suggested that articulation produces something more than the sum
of its parts. The doubled-over experience of living simultaneously as victim,
killer, and Final Girl, as oneself and as the state via a constant traversing of
the three forms of assumption, produces the X in us that is more than us.
And perhaps this very experience of more is what warrants the hope for

something better and mobilizes actions aimed at development and progress. Whether or not one knowingly subscribes to Lamarckian principles, they seem preserved in the popular and revolutionary willingness to exercise and even sacrifice oneself for improvement in the future, for succeeding generations (and also, among those who served in the army, defending the Fatherland). No more can that cramped accountant whose emerald visor reduces everything to the monochrome green of a dollar see this rainbow potential in the world than the rational choice theorist, consumed with balancing investment with payoff, can understand risking altruism or the similarly limited evolutionary psychologist grasp the "fitness" of the female orgasm.

But this reading assumes that this imaginary auditor is a dupe, thereby warranting me as that figure of myth and legend, the nonduped. But I err in so many ways, including perhaps by thinking that I'm outside a capitalist logic. For I too operate on the profit motive, hoping my contributions and investments will not only balance out but will improve—and not only my individual life, but also those of others. I'm banking on Xtra, that more will come out than I put in. That's the unsettling puzzle at the crux of finance (and of sexuality): its productivity, generativity, surplus, interest. The carney's promise "Double your money!" doubles me over.

My *nacer de conciencia*, getting in the know about the U.S. role in the coup against President Arbenz in 1954, revealed my true identity: I was a gringa, a collaborator. Like one of the *Tz'ul* dancers, I was transformed. So was Guatemala, as it became a laboratory of modernity, a *plan piloto* for intervention and biopolitics whose findings are currently deployed in twenty-first-century Iraq.[1] I began this book with an epigraph from a button I bought near the Marine Corps' Camp Lejeune, where my father was once stationed: "In the battle between good and evil we are winning." I got it at a gas station in a row of strip joints, check-cashing outlets, and pawnshops on the way to the beach. Across the road the wire fences that divide the base from the civilian world were festooned with bed sheets adorned with Magic Marker messages sending someone off with love or welcoming them home. Are those welcomed and those welcoming victims, dupes, perpetrators? What about me: just passing through, thinking I'm in the know with my gas-efficient Honda and the "No War in Iraq," "No Blood for Oil," "Healthcare For All" bumper stickers? Don't I also think that when I demand money for health care, not for war, I'm also in a battle between good and evil? Perhaps we're all caught in a horror film scenario as collaborators and also victims in the Guatemalanization of the United States and by extension the planet: "This is what is happening in our country. We have to watch this so we don't forget."

But the realization that it's like glue and we are stuck, tied in, can't tie us up. We can't settle for postwar inaction. The global stakes are too great. This book is an account of how Guatemalans in different ways and through widespread networks, including anthropologists, media, IMF funding, mosquitoes, freak shows, books, and traditional dances, among other unexpected allies, have generated the postwar-in-action, forcing openings, calling to account. I've tried to show how the social spaces that comprise the cross and even the sword are sites and stakes of struggle. It was, after all, young military officers who started the URNG, and in the United States there are many young soldiers and their families who are risking everything (far more than I) to oppose the U.S. war in Iraq. Like Guatemala, these are laboratories, sites of enormous, deadly power and also labile, slippery. Learning from Guatemala means working under the sign of Our Lady of Assumptions, a woman on the move. It means the enjoy/meant of the *bailes* in which masked dancers enact rituals of rebellion against labor contractors, both enduring and burlesquing the culture of audit. It means remembering, when we get too serious about being in the know, that "the disruptive jesting of the players continually subverts attempts at explanation" (Hutcheson 2003:77) and that the nonduped err. But we go on anyhow.

Judith Butler suggests that grief and mourning are transformative in ways that cannot be charted: "One mourns when one accepts that by the loss one undergoes one will be changed, possibly forever. . . . Something takes hold of you: where does it come from? What sense does it make? What claims us at such moments, such that we are not the masters of ourselves? To what are we tied?" (2004:21). This senti/meant of loss is a doubling over. It mimics the effects of collaborating, recalling the realization that you've been duped, acted on by a force coming from outside. Yet this force is one that is so close as to be almost isomorphic with the very assumption of a self. As such, it cannot easily be exorcised. We may not be able to disentangle what seems to possess us from the us, giving rise to the simultaneously creepy and X-static sense of living beside oneself, becoming dela, having two faces. Horror, passion, grief, rage, fear, hope, and laughter all "tear us from ourselves, bind us to others, transport us, undo us, implicate us in lives that are not our own, irreversibly, if not fatally" (25). Our "primary sociality" (28) produces these emotions and induces us to pay strict attention to interests, to who benefits and who suffers. We follow the money and focus on what's in-between, the milieu, the identi-ties.

Acknowledging the fact that we are articulated, bound together (that what makes a fact is "its relation to what it evinces") may actually make resistance inevitable rather than futile. So, in the spirit of Gramsci's optimism of the will I suggest taking a page from Lamarck and the suspicious mouse.

Instead of exorcising, our best bet for survival may be exercising, in the sense of praxis. Think! then put it in-action.

Rotman says that xenomoney, faced with the loss of gold's intrinsic presence, is obliged to manufacture a signified, a value, from the possibilities of its own future. Perhaps in this sense we have become xeno-subjects. Like Myrna Mack, her research team, and the refugees they worked with who ask, "Where is the future?" we are obliged to DIY, "Do it (y)ourself." The master rule may be that you never master the rules. The fix (healing) we long for may be a fixion. But we can still make believe. Strengthened by our identi-ties we don't have to "Surrender, Dorothy!" We can go on singing. We can bet on the future.

PREFACE

1 The Guatemalan journalist Luis Solano says the phrase was borrowed from fascist Spain. Often appearing as graffiti in the 1970s and early 1980s, it incited book burning, attacks on those deemed intellectuals, and murder. It was closely associated with the right wing party that overthrew President Jacobo Arbenz in 1954, the National Liberation Movement (MLN).

2 The percentage of Guatemalans who are identified or identify themselves as indigenous ranges from 40 to 80 percent of the population, depending on who is counting. This identity is marked culturally, through language (over twenty indigenous languages are spoken in Guatemala), dress (often hand-loomed and distinctive for each town), worldview, employment (stereotypically peasant farmers, retaining a close identification with the land and corn production), and class status (statistically indigenous people are overrepresented among the poorest of the poor) as well as through explicit self-making enunciated in political claims (for example, a person might speak only Spanish, wear Western clothing, make their living as a lawyer, drive a fancy car, and practice Evangelical Christianity and simultaneously claim indigenous identity and agitate for indigenous rights). It is also lived raciologically through assumed phenotypic marks that often translate into discriminatory practices (a person may not identify as indigenous but still suffer racism). The word "Maya," originally attached to pre-Columbian peoples by foreign scholars, has been taken up by cultural revitalization activists to name modern-day indigenous people. Because the term "Maya" is associated with a specific political project with roots in particular locales, not all indigenous people identify with it. However, through struggle, it has become the politically correct word for nonindigenous people to use, although its deployment may mask complex assumptions of identity, which I will explore throughout. Nonindigenous Guatemalans may also be called ladinos, mestizos, criollos, or other terms. "Gringo" is a disrespectful term for someone from North America or Europe.

3 Col. Carlos Castillo Armas replaced him, beginning a long succession of mostly unelected military leaders. The coup in Guatemala was a laboratory, a testing ground for many modern propaganda techniques, including recordings of airplanes broadcast to make it seem like the invading force was much larger than it was. It was also a two-faced affair: one public, the government's anti-Communist interests; the other private, the United Fruit Company's economic projects.

4 The dirty wars of Latin America turned "disappear" into a subjectless transitive verb, meaning an unnamed agent wipes away all signs of another human's existence, removing them physically from their home, school, or work to someplace from whence they seldom, if ever, reappear, even as a corpse. There is no

official record of them anywhere, and family members and colleagues do not know if they remain alive in some secret detention center or if their bodies are hidden in clandestine cemeteries or were dumped into the sea. This special pain of not knowing is what makes the Catholic Church call disappearance one of the "mechanisms of horror" (REMHI, vol. 2).

5 "Resistance is futile, You will be assimilated," is the refrain of the colonizing Borg of *Star Trek: Next Generation*. Maury Hutcheson found actual Borg (or people dressed like them) in the *convite* masquerade in Rabinal, Baja Verapaz. Hutcheson describes the *convite* as a type of folk dance, performed during highland festivals, whose "semiotic domain [is] the contemporary, globalized flow of media imagery" (2003:4).

6 While Guatemala certainly exists under the shadows of war (Nordstrom 2006), in many ways it is a success when compared with sites where treaties have been signed but war is much further from ending.

7 As I discuss later, many Guatemalans take quite seriously the existence of non-human actants, including the forces of envy (*envidia*), evil eye (*mal de ojo*), witchcraft, retributive illness, or entities like the one that is said to have left the flayed body of a much-hated former Civil Patrol commander in a Joyabaj roadway.

8 I first explored war refugees in 1985 as part of a team assembled by Beatriz Manz, then studied the Guatemalan military government's refugee resettlement projects, known as Development Poles, in 1986; in 1987 I worked as a journalist stringer and in 1988 as a development consultant, all in all spending about twenty months in Guatemala and Mexico. Entering graduate school in 1989, I spent another eighteen months in Guatemala, including summer fieldwork and the year of dissertation research. After Guatemalans signed a peace accord in December 1996 and after a financially imposed exile of my own I returned to fieldwork in Guatemala in 1998, having made only two short visits since 1993. This book is based on yearly trips since then. My early work was quite peripatetic, encompassing much of the indigenous highland areas where state violence was most extreme, while my dissertation research focused solely on the capital city. For this book I traversed city and highlands, working in several areas, with special focus on the municipality of Joyabaj, where I have returned every year since 1999. Unless otherwise indicated, all quotations are from author interviews, all translations from the Spanish are mine, and all English definitions are from Webster's (1980).

9 Troubling assumptions of cause and effect inhere in the language of insurgency and counterinsurgency: that the insurgent seems to arise out of nowhere, forcing the otherwise passive, blameless state to counterattack. The opposite may be more accurate when, after years or centuries of enduring violence, robbery, labor extraction, and displacement—what David Harvey (2003) calls accumulation by dispossession—people counterattack, taking up arms against this sea of troubles.

10 The *Recuperación de la memoria histórica*/Recuperation of Historical Memory (REMHI) was the first large-scale systematic postwar effort to reckon with what had happened. Carried out by the Catholic Church, although not all dioceses participated and non-Catholics are generally underrepresented, it resulted in a four-

volume report. Two days after the public presentation the supervising bishop, Juan Gerardi, was murdered by members of the army.

11 "Work," at least, for the Guatemalans. I feel a lot of shame about the Mexicans who helped us.

12 Aka, "also known as," mimics wanted posters that list the assumed identities of criminal suspects. I use it throughout to play with the insecurity of meaning, especially when identification is on the line.

13 Although one of the most important transformations in postwar Guatemala, as elsewhere, this form of conversion was not the focus of my research (see Adams 1999, 2001, Garrard-Burnett 1998, Stoll 1988, 1990). Similar to the assumed identities I address, it is experienced as a deeply embodied possession, with Jesus coming into one's heart, and is often analyzed by nonbelievers as an Assumption Two (a false identity). Converts and those who study them struggle to show it's rational and true, an Assumption Three.

14 I borrow this slash-play from Slavoj Žižek to emphasize the semiosis of experience. I want to resist a mind/body split with the flesh enjoying or suffering while the mind makes meaning on its own, and to not assume or let it go without saying that the body or knowledge or pleasure have only one obvious meaning.

15 Similarly, W. E. B. Du Bois warns of "three temptations" that dog the souls of black folk who seek to know the world and know themselves, and these are Hate, Despair, and Doubt (1989:152).

16 I remember my own shock when indigenous war widows made jokes, some of them strikingly obscene. This does not mean that their horror and pain are insincere. Charles Hale also appreciatively describes the singular *humor chapín* and its *chingaderos* (Guatemalan humor and ribbing) (2006).

17 Hypertextually, I would urge readers to transform into viewers and, if you haven't already, learn to see these sublime, bad films: *Buffy the Vampire Slayer*, *They Live*, *The Matrix*, *Candyman*, *Scream*, *F for Fake*, *Bamboozled*, *Bowling for Columbine*, *American Pimp*, *Nueve Reinas/Nine Queens*, and *Zero Patience*; and read that so-called low genre of science fiction, like *Calcutta Chromosome* and *Synners*. I'll also be revealing my age, race, nation, and class via references to *Star Trek*, Jane Austen, and Monty Python.

18 I think he was referencing the movie version of Lee as lithe and powerful, rather than his mysterious early death. While I doubt it showed in Joyabaj, Juan's comment mimicked the plot of the strangest movie I've ever seen, *Crazy Safari* (courtesy Rob Latham). This Hong Kong–made film takes the premise of the apartheid-era South African film *The Gods Must Be Crazy*, in which a Coke bottle falling from an airplane changes the life of a member of the Ju/hoansi people of the Kalahari. It even uses the same actors—the star is credited, I'm sorry to say, as Xao the Bushman, and Jamie Uys, the creator of *Gods*, appears as a crazed Afrikaans diamond thief. In *Crazy Safari*, however, a Chinese hopping vampire falls from a plane and has to be rescued by a Chinese priest and the vampire's human descendant. Much hilarity ensues as the vampire saves the Ju/hoansi from rapacious whites and is adopted by the tribe and as the Chinese visitors struggle to adapt to life in the Kalahari. But the whites return with their own magical monster, an African blue zombie, and even the vampire cannot defend

his new friends. At the last minute, when it appears all hope is lost, the priest magically imbues Xao with the spirit of Bruce Lee, and he becomes a kung fu whirlwind, handily defeating their enemies.

It's fun to recount these silly images or the surprise evoked when the anthropologist finds Senegalese villagers well versed in Bollywood cinema (Deborah Heath, personal communication) or is enthusiastically urged by a video rental proprietor in rural Uganda to watch a soft-core, chicks-in-prison film (Peter Redfield, personal communication). It's hard to account for the transnational and traversing effects of their circulations around the globe, so they are often relegated to fieldwork anecdotes rather than regarded as sites of analysis. Although this *is* a footnote, I do try to make these in-between forms of media central to this book (Askew and Wilk 2002, Devereaux and Hillman 1995, Shohat and Stam 1994).

ONE UNDER THE SIGN OF THE VIRGEN DE TRÁNSITO

1 In Joyabaj over six hundred people died, fifty-five thousand were seriously wounded, and over 95 percent of the buildings were destroyed (Remijnse 2002:83).

2 In a similar death-defying performance in Momostenango, Garrett Cook says, "The animal impersonators in the Monkeys Dance are possessed by animal spirits at a shrine before the performance. This renders them fearless when they do their tricks on the tightrope sixty feet above the pavement in the plaza" (2000:82).

3 She cuts an amazing figure as she moves around town, traveling from the *cofrade*'s home, where she has resided for the year, through the streets to the church and then on to her new residence. While the wooden image is rather small, she is ensconced in a massive frame that is a dialectical montagist's dream: covered in peacock feathers, whirligigs, lithographs of other sacred beings, and clocks. While the entire *municipio* (township) of Joyabaj celebrates the Virgin, her image is maintained by an indigenous *cofradía*. Translated as "fraternity" or "brotherhood" (although women are deeply involved in all their practices, especially the work of the fiesta), membership includes responsibility for maintaining an icon, paying for the fiesta (including food, musicians, new clothes, and accoutrements for the virgin or saint), or sponsoring one of the dances. Often termed *costumbristas* (traditionalists), they consider themselves Catholic but are often seen as pagans by those converted to Catholic Action, a purifying movement. Ladinos in Joyabaj, about 15 percent of the population and mainly living in the municipal center and southern, temperate hamlets, have their own Catholic *comunidades*. Catholic Action includes both indigenous people and ladinos, and both resist the Mayanist project to incorporate more *costumbre* into the Mass, although it was supported by one of the local priests. Racism is certainly strong in Joyabaj, but far from absolute—many other interests and divisions traverse this community. Thanks to Liz Oglesby (and Arturo Taracena) for drawing my attention to the importance of mobility and thus of the Virgin.

4 The Guatemalan historian Matilde González, who worked in nearby San Bar-

tolomé Jocotenango, emphasizes the importance of this book, a modernized version of the forced-labor era's *libreto de jornaleros* carried by indigenous laborers to prove they'd worked the required 100 to 150 days a year on the coffee plantations. At home in the highlands, it records the *borracheras adelantadas* (drinking binges on credit) in which people lose awareness of the exact amount of their debt (2002:174) and once down on the coast its power only grows. "Among all the punishments applied by the authorities on the *finca* (plantation) the annulling or non-notation of a day's work was the one that most affected the workers and was the one that caused the most violent reactions. Designed as a measure to 'discipline' crew-members who did not fulfill the required tasks, the *caporales* often applied it arbitrarily so they could take the payment for the day and to increase their quota of power. This measure put the workers in their hands, they depended on them to write down, or not, in the records of each day" (254). In the 1930s Ruth Bunzel said, "The finca constantly affects their lives. It is at their doors like a multiple Circe, waiting to draw men to their destruction" (1981:42 in McAllister 2003:217). Circe, the enchantress who transformed men into swine, might be a fitting companion for the Virgin of Assumption.

5 A traditional, usually handmade blouse that is distinctive for every highland town.

6 While the student/worker uprisings in Paris and the anti–Vietnam War mobilizations and Summer of Love in the United States are perhaps the best-known examples, we might see related effervescence in Mexico City, Japan, China in the Cultural Revolution, and elsewhere.

7 Guha argues that both colonial power and left nationalist historians tend to dismiss peasant insurgency as unconscious, not fully formed, and spontaneous. He counters that the political-economic relation between the peasant and the colonial triumvirate of landlord, moneylender, and state official "was so fortified by the power of those who had the most to benefit from it and their determination, backed by the resources of a ruling culture, to punish the least infringement, that [the peasant] risked all by trying to subvert or destroy it by rebellion. . . . There was nothing spontaneous about all this in the sense of being unthinking and wanting in deliberation. The peasant obviously knew what he [*sic*] was doing when he rose in revolt" (1983:8–9).

8 And these "*same old* stories . . . told (compulsively) again and afresh and . . . differently gratifying and terrifying each time" (Bhabha 1994:77) are reanimated for the current U.S. war, as in the *New York Times* headline: "In Iraq, the Insurgency has Two Faces, Secular and Jihad, but One Common Goal" (Oppel 2004:A6).

9 Grandin (2000a) analyzes the complex relations between indigenous leaders in Quetzaltenango and the National Liberation Movement (MLN), the anti-Communist party that helped overthrow Jacobo Arbenz. Remijnse says the MLN was also a force in Joyabaj, where "the only group of indigenous leaders that came close to [success in] local party politics was the one backing the right wing political parties of the ladinos. . . . these indigenous pro-MLN villages were places where the civil patrols were first set up. They were also among the most aggressive" (2001:459).

10 The apparent ineffectiveness of the massive global demonstration of February

15, 2003, against the Iraq war—the largest in planetary history—has made many people fear that resistance *is* futile. *Cui bono?*

11 This "different time" has been a long time coming. In 1848, some folks were already railing at how personal worth was being depleted into exchange value, and in place of the numberless indefeasible chartered freedoms, that single unconscionable freedom, Free Trade, had been set up. Brian Rotman places it earlier, reading the tragedy of *King Lear* as enunciating the horrors of reducing humans to exchangeable commodities (1987, see chapter 8). Lévi-Strauss places women's exchangeability at the dawn of in-human culture (1969, Rubin 1975).

12 Information is always a vital part of war ("loose lips sink ships") both vis-à-vis the opponent and between those directing war and those fighting it. Secrets, encryption, strategic revelations, refusal to gather specific forms of information (say, Iraqi casualties), cover-ups, and the old standby of plausible deniability are all sites and stakes of struggle over hearts, minds, and bodies. If those challenging state power dissimulate and dupe, state powers also rely on disinformation and psychological operations (PSYOPS). The autopsy by the CIA agent Nicholas Cullanther of the Arbenz coup confesses that agency tactics included "rumors, anonymous letters, telegrams and phone calls in addition to visible symbols," and he cites these helpful hints from the agency's manual: "It is preferable to make the phone calls in the early morning, between 1:00 and 4:00 am when a man's psychological resistance is usually at its lowest level. Symbolic violence might include a casket or a noose in front of the house of someone you want to threaten, painting threats on the wall, sending a fake bomb in the mail" (in CEH 1:105). Given all this simulation and dissimulation postwar questions always arise: What did you know? When did you know it? Should you have known, even if you claim you didn't?

13 Many who supported the U.S. war on Iraq now claim they would never have done so if they'd known then what they know now, with former CIA director George Tenet one of the more recent to make the case for having been used and duped.

14 See above, preface, note 4.

15 Most of these terms were in Spanish, but I also had some translation assistance.

16 The Civil Patrols were a counterinsurgency strategy designed to untie community bonds. They also gave the state another face—one that lets it off the hook for violations through the plausible deniability of all parastate actors, paramilitaries, death squads, privatization of functions like prison management or "rendition," and subcontracting more generally (Sluka 2000). Transnational corporations like Exxon (Sawyer 2004) and Union Carbide (Fortun 2001) also try to get away with murder through similar two-faced tactics but can be thwarted by activists who are paying attention to what lies between.

17 One hundred eighty-three people appear, kidnapped between August 1983 and March 1985. One hundred of them were killed, a fate marked by codes like "he is with Pancho," apparently referencing being with an imaginary friend. The military at first claimed it was a simple fake. Then, after a week of investigating, it claimed it could not be military because they always use letterhead (Reminjse 2002:255).

18 Fear of this strategy created a two-faced reaction to those victims who did escape—had they made it out on their own or were they now double-crossers? To
those raised in peacetime the suspicions of the Guatemalan left look overdone,
almost psychotic (in fact, in Michael Moore's *Fahrenheit 911* we laugh at the ludi-
crousness of infiltrating the cookie-eating peaceniks in Fresno). However, decades of suffering the devastation of a single informer made it quite rational to
cultivate distrust, compartmentalization, and secret keeping so deeply assimilated that the body itself would not let one speak, among other security measures.

19 Victor Montejo (1993b) has elegantly critiqued Anglo anthropologists' obsession
with exotic Mayan beliefs (see also Castañeda 1996). Like all the stereotypes I
address in this book, this is fraught terrain, scored by inequality *and* a sacred
ground for anthropology, which has earned its daily bread from contextualizing such apparently exotic beliefs. Understandings of the world that do not jibe
with secular enlightenment (Eurocentric) worldviews are too often deployed as
signs of backwardness and proof of the need for intervention from those more
advanced. In struggles over identification, however, it is precisely these fragile
connections to tradition that can legitimate struggles over shared rights (Clifford 1988).

20 Cook glosses *delicado* as the sensitivity and danger associated with contact with
the supernatural, which also mediates rain, drought, interpersonal relations
among families and communities, and the unwanted attention of earthly authorities.

21 These include *criollo*, *gente decente* (decent people), *blancos* (whites), or elite, who
in turn are differentiated from the *cachimbiros*, *gente común*, *gentuza*, *shumo*,
chusma (commoners or more colloquially "trash"), etc. (Adams and Bastos 2003,
González Ponciano 1991, 1995, 2005, Hale 2006). Ladino or mestizo, as the other
to indigenous, is "inherently relational, context-sensitive, and thus blurry and
unstable" (de la Cadena 1996:117).

22 This is basic Saussurean linguistics, but it still creeps me out!

23 The quote is from a letter of August 5, 1829. Its critique of duplicity, in the political pursuit of aligning the two faces, echoes Frederick Douglass's Independence Day speech of 1852: "What to the American slave is your Fourth of July? I
answer, a day that reveals to him, more than all other days in the year, the gross
injustice and cruelty to which he is the constant victim. To him, your celebration
is a sham, your boasted liberty, an unholy license; your national greatness, swelling vanity; your sounds of rejoicing are empty and heartless; your denunciations
of tyrants, brass-fronted impudence; your shouts of liberty and equality, hollow
mockery; your prayers and hymns, your sermons and thanksgivings, with all
your religious parades and solemnity, are to him mere bombast, fraud, deception, impiety, and hypocrisy—a thin veil to cover up crimes which would disgrace a nation of savages. There is not a nation on the earth guilty of practices
more shocking and bloody, than are the people of these United States, at this
very hour" (in Foner 2004:10).

In November 2004 *Parade* magazine reported, "After more than a year in Iraq,
the U.S. Army has officially renamed 17 of its bases around Baghdad to sound,

well, a lot less warlike. Camp Victory is still there, but gone is Camp Steel Dragon, replaced with the gentler moniker of Camp Honor. Also gone: Headhunter, Banzai, Warhorse and Gunslinger. They now sport the titles of Independence, Justice, Freedom and Solidarity" (Winik:21). Thanks to Paula Worby.

24 Unlike Joyabaj, where the *Culebra* is performed in August, Momostenango holds the *Tzulab* dance during Holy Week. In that version, Cook found three sets of doubles connected to the *contratista* figure: the Twins of the *Popol Wuj*, who also die and are reborn; the double Christ figure and its alter, San Simon [aka Maximon], a sort of Judas who is necessary to Christ's divinity; and the two "Dandies" or ladinos who are hornswoggled repeatedly in this version of the dance. Cook's fascinating reading (which I cannot do justice to here) gives a much denser trajectory to the resurrection of *xoye contratista*, a theme often associated with snakes, reborn as they shed their skins.

25 And it is understood as such by its targets, as in U.S. white supremacist Websites that target Franz Boas (Baker 2004).

26 Marx similarly cautions against seeing capital as a thing when it is really a relation, and "not a simple relation, but a process; in whose various moments it is always capital" (1973: 258). Thanks to Mark Driscoll.

27 New information technologies have made this easier, leading the U.S. government to enact the Identity Theft and Assumption Deterrence Act (Mihm 2004:44).

28 And, of course, charge for them? It costs over $160,000 for the bachelor's degree issued by the private U.S. university that pays my salary.

INTERTEXT ONE

1 This is the desire in Diderot's story of *les bijoux indiscrét* — the jeweled ring that forces one's lover's lips to speak the truth of their being (and sex) (Foucault 1980), and the fantasy of transparent communication through telepathy or the Vulcan mind-meld.

2 For example, it's what helps you decide if something is objective reporting or Faux News, aka propaganda.

3 Maurer goes on: "The metapragmatics of accounting never necessarily mirror nor mythologize something else, some other level of reality behind or before accounting. Rather, they assume an identity with the very form of knowledge intrinsic to reflexive anthropological reason, a form that is based on nested hierarchies of abstraction and an inevitable partiality of perspective through which perspective, as an organizing rubric for anthropological knowledge, reveals itself in its own failure" (2002b:4). The lion tamer is from a Monty Python skit about a job counselor informing a rather dweebish man that tests show he is perfectly suited to accountancy. "But I already am an accountant," he cries. "It's dull, dull, dull, it's so deadly dull and tedious!" Instead, he says, he wants to be a lion tamer (he already has the hat). This takes the counselor aback, but as they talk he realizes that the accountant has mixed up lions with an anteater. "I could tame one of those. They look pretty tame to start with!" Informed of his mistake, the ac-

countant goes meekly back to his job, as the counselor turns to the camera and says, "It's sad, isn't it, but this is what accountancy does to people."

4 Rather than *chafarote*, it is rooted in the Guatemalanism *chafear*, whose roots are obscure. Thanks to Luis Solano for translation aid, always above and beyond the call of duty.

5 This list draws on a range of sources and is far from exhaustive; Baudrillard 1983, 1987; Bourdieu 1977, 1987; Du Bois 1989; Durkheim 1995; Foucault 1979, 1980a 1980b; Gramsci 1989; Hardt and Negri 2000; Lacan 1977; Laclau and Mouffe 1985; Latour 1987; Marx 1977.

6 It is June 2004 as I write this in the morning, read in the afternoon, and hunt for cinematic examples in the evening. A *Harry Potter* and a *Spiderman* have opened—stories about one's true identity also being false, thrust upon them, full of surprises rather than familiar. As the rewriting of this text streams into other summers, the multiplex continues to support my theoretical insights with cinematic examples like Anakin Skywalker assuming his foretold identity as Darth, and Sing of *Kung Fu Hustle* becoming the master of the Flying Buddhist Palm (which had at first seemed nothing but a cruel con).

7 These might be the opposite of the green-tinted glasses that Dorothy and her friends must wear in the literary version of the Emerald City. L. Frank Baum was probably satirizing the fantasy world of "greenbacks," or paper money, with no connection to gold (see chapter 8). What gives precious metal its (sacred) value if not a consensual hallucination?

8 These films all smuggle pretty critical readings into our heads, but they can't seem to get how deeply both race and gender assumptions are implicated in the very structures they question. Buffy is balm for feminist viewers (and the TV show pioneered cool attitudes toward sexuality) but needs a severe color adjustment. *They Live* and *The Matrix* at least acknowledge that nonwhites are often far more clued in than their Caucasian saviors (and Keanu Reeves/Neo is not quite white), but their gender politics are seriously messy.

9 Zora Neale Hurston beautifully describes the three senses of assumption and the way our true identities seem to come from outside us: "I was glad when somebody told me, 'You may go and collect Negro folklore.' In a way it would not be a new experience for me. When I pitched headforemost into the world I landed in the crib of negroism. From the earliest rocking of my cradle, I had known about the capers Brer Rabbit is apt to cut and what the Squinch Owl says from the house top. But it was fitting me like a tight chemise. I couldn't see it for wearing it. It was only when I was off in college, away from my native surroundings, that I could see myself like somebody else and stand off and look at my garment. Then I had to have the spy-glass of Anthropology to look through at that" (1990:1).

TWO THE POSTWAR MILIEU

1 Is Greenwich Mean Time mean as in average, or mean as in cruel?

2 The title of this section is adapted from Stone 1995.

3 They were also apparently disgruntled by the disparities, made obvious by their

training at U.S. installations, between their own government's attentions to their health and well-being and the gringos'.

4 Thinking war and postwar between the U.S. and Guatemala, *Brown vs. Board of Education* was also decided in 1954, part of the United States' own continuing post-[Civil]war (Foner and Kennedy 2004). On the aftermath of 1954, see Adams (1970), Grandin (2004), Gleijeses (1991), Handy (1994), and Wilkinson (2002).

5 Post is both something fixed, stuck in the ground, and what moves across it, a doorway or passage point where someone is stationed. "Postage" as mail comes from riders posted at intervals to carry information.

6 Greg Grandin says that in 1982 "everything changed." The army "decimated the social base and military structure of the guerrillas [making] . . . the struggle no longer a progressive, historically inevitable fight for a more socially just nation. . . . It became a rearguard defense of human rights and a fight for the reestablishment of the rule of law" (2000c:405).

7 Hector Gramajo was defense minister in the first postwar, from 1985 to 1991, and later ran for president. He was indicted in absentia by the United States for war crimes and in 2004 died when he was attacked by bees—unexpected allies, indeed.

8 Rather than go into greater detail here I direct readers to Bastos and Camus (1991, 1995, 2003) and Cojti Cuxil (1990, 1994), among others.

9 Similarly, the root of "end" is *andeis/antyos*, meaning lying ahead or facing.

10 Like Lancaster, Kulick, and others, I am wary of assuming that Euro-American identity models like gay or lesbian move about the globe, liberating as they go. However, the *lesbigay* movement has lashed in a number of Guatemalans to a rights machine (in Latour's sense) which has created several queer-friendly NGOs in Guatemala City, provides safe sex training, and protests police murders of queer sex workers.

11 The questions were grouped as follows: 1. "Nation and Social Rights; The Guatemalan nation is recognized as multiethnic, multilingual, and pluricultural; indigenous languages will be official, just as Spanish is; the spirituality of indigenous people is recognized as are their particular forms of social organization: 2. Legislative Branch; a commission to supervise State intelligence organs will be created to stop any abuses of power and to guarantee respect for citizen's rights and liberties; opportunities to express opinions on legislation before the Congress approves it will be available 3.Executive Branch; the participation of all social sectors in making local decisions on public policy and community development through the Development Councils; the new role of the army will be to patrol and maintain the country's borders, it will no longer be in the streets; the National Civil Police will be responsible for internal security and will respect human rights: 4. Judicial Branch; new judicial training will be implemented so that judges and magistrates will be professionalized and will impart justice quickly and fully; access to the justice system will be free and in the indigenous languages of each respective region; justice will be the same for all and corruption and impunity will not be tolerated." Each section was color coded on a different piece of paper with a box to be marked yes or no at the bottom. Thanks to Netta van Vliet for the sample.

12 In 2001 three army officers were found guilty of Gerardi's murder; they were later released on appeal (Hernández Pico 2005).

13 In July 1998 former army spokesman Colonel Otto Noack was jailed and downgraded in rank for suggesting that the army should apologize for the atrocities committed during the war (Remijnse 2002:254).

14 During the campaign, Berger expressed his interests in Menchú quite nakedly: "Rigoberta with her *corte* [traditional skirt] and dignity selling the country, a tourist destination for the world, promoting foreign investment, especially in the areas she knows, she'll have to accept my invitation, she will be part of my team because she will be an ambassador with all the qualifications and power to sell the country touristically" (*La Hora* July 28). Thanks to Luis Solano for this cite. Larue's and Menchú Tum's companions in the popular movement have expressed dismay that as of September 2006 neither had resigned, given the Berger government's violent reprisals against activists, its deeply neoliberal bent, and its increasing abandonment of the peace accords.

15 A resonant date: the Chilean Ariel Dorfman says, "I have been through this before. During the past 28 years, Sept. 11 has been a date of mourning, for me and millions of others, since that day in 1973 when death irrevocably entered our lives and changed us forever. . . . [As] in the United States today, terror descended from the sky to destroy the symbols of national identity, the Palace of the Presidents in Santiago, the icons of financial and military power in New York and Washington" (2001).

16 This event is crucial in Ríos Montt's two-faced political trajectory and his complex relation to legitimacy. While a military officer he ran for president in a democratic election representing a progressive party and was denied what was apparently a rightful victory. Later taking power in a coup against a clearly corrupt and violent military leader, he oversaw army campaigns that are now identified as genocidal and was himself deposed by force in 1983 because of such excesses. In the mid-1990s he returned to electoral politics.

17 Departments are geographic administrative areas, like states in the United States.

18 In June 1982 Ríos Montt said, "Naturally, if a subversive operation exists in which the Indians are involved with the guerrillas, the Indians are also going to die. However, the army's philosophy is not to kill the Indians, but to win them back, to help them" (CEH V.III:324).

19 Concerned that their presence might endanger people, academics in the north boycotted research in Guatemala. Most exiles went to Mexico, Canada, or Europe because the United States turned down all but .03 percent of asylum cases from Guatemala. This denied anything wrong was going on there, and it limited access to direct testimony.

20 Opus Dei is now more familiar to U.S. audiences thanks to *The Da Vinci Code*, another popular book and film about interpellation and the assumptions of identity.

21 Such commemoration was made possible by and in turn helped make possible other organizing and other vital public actions, like the massive five-day May Day march in 1992 staged by the reorganized Campesino Unity Committee

(CUC); more than ten thousand people, mostly indigenous, participated (Velásquez Nimatuj 2005:113–18).

22 Thus the move to sidestep this mobile aspect of the law through offshore military tribunals, suspension of habeas corpus, secret evidence, "ghost detainees," and "rendering."

23 "In July of 1992, Santiago [an ORPA combatant who escaped from the army's prison] saw [Guatemalan army colonel] Alpírez bending over Everardo's torture table. That same month, Alpírez received $44,000 from the CIA" (Harbury 2000:326).

24 Guatemalan army officials confirmed to Jennifer Schirmer that drug use among troops was a problem and that officers were deeply implicated in drug trafficking (1998:272), an aspect of the *Cuerpos Ilegales y Aparatos Clandestinos* (CIAC; Illegal organizations and clandestine apparati) addressed in chapter 6.

25 As I type this in May 2004 the Supreme Court–selected commander in chief has also just apologized for the prisoner abuses at Abu Ghraib prison. While knowledge of the abuses existed for months in the Taguba and Red Cross reports, it took a particular lashing together of a number of elements, including photographs, testimony, and publicity, to make them facts. Who, knowing anything about U.S. policy in Latin America, was surprised at the abuses? And yet they are now real in a different way.

26 Once elected, Portillo even admitted what everyone already knows, that he, like every politician, lied on the campaign trail. "If one said what they were really going to do as president, they'd never win because a candidate is a salesman of dreams" (Rodríguez 2002:1). Thanks to Luis Solano and Paula Worby for this quote.

27 In July 2003, as part of the intimidation campaign to get his name on the ballot, the FRG staged mass demonstrations in Guatemala City, bussing in people from all over the country, including Joyabaj. Rather than target the Palace and the Congress, they went straight to the business centers and blocked off the wealthy neighborhoods of Zone 15. Horrified as many felt at their thuggery, it was striking to see white men in business suits running away from kids with stones and to hear the laments of high society types who couldn't get to their club dates.

28 Describing the "deeply social process" of an IMF country audit (see also chapter 8), Richard Harper describes the central ritual role of people like Edgar with "the rank to sanction the relevant interpretations and associated numbers. These people provide the stamp of approval. A Fund mission must seek these out . . . [their] accounts of policy [a]re . . . vital to the mission's ability to comprehend the situation" (2000:24). Gutiérrez has parlayed this identi/tie into a well-funded NGO from which he continues to articulate analyses of the conjuncture.

INTERTEXT TWO

1 "Cut" can mean change in direction as well as to pass through or across, to traverse. It is also linked to "discern," which means to separate in order to perceive something (and shares the same roots as scissors, screen, and science).

2 When the REMHI project began, fear restrained most Xoye from participating. The anonymous letters that several people sent did not fit the criteria for data

collection, so their stories were not included. Some forty people did give testimony, but only fragments of it made it into the report. The priest who had risked a great deal in organizing the area's response said ruefully, "My memory of Joyabaj seems to be much bigger than the memory REMHI has of Joyabaj." Remijnse says, "People thought the report would tell it all . . . they hoped that the perpetrators would be caught, financial compensation would be paid, or that things would change from then onwards. But nothing changed. Expectations had risen but could not be met" (2002:268–69).

3 The filmmakers attempt to enhance the veracity of the play by cutting the children's performances of torture and massacre with interviews and talking heads. Perhaps they hoped to make the film more legitimate and more bearable, as it is very painful to watch. I found, however, that this detracted from the play by breaking the suture, but I don't know which works best in "coping with what took place."

THREE HORROR'S SPECIAL EFFECTS

1 Netta van Vliet, the anthropologist here, was my (always invaluable) research assistant. She came running to see me the next morning and said, "You know that horror film stuff you're working on? I didn't buy it at all, but listen what happened last night!"

2 I don't mean to dismiss how terrifying it is to grow up in the United States, to be a person of color under the violent signs of racial profiling, how fear stalks every woman who walks alone, or even how uncertain the world feels for "traditional villains" like white men, increasingly less able to fulfill family and class obligations, much less the terrifying global effects of the U.S. government's new first-strike doctrine. While horror films may seem a bit more fantasmatic in a U.S. multiplex, there is plenty of horror on Elm and Main streets (Edmundsun 1997, Heller 1987).

3 In 1998 a friend who was working for MINUGUA contacted me about a puzzling case she and her colleagues had encountered in an indigenous village. A murder had been reported and after driving and hiking for hours to reach the remote hamlet they easily confirmed that a man had been killed. But, Agatha Christie-like, everyone in town claimed responsibility — the person was a witch, and they were defending themselves. My friend wondered if MINUGUA was being duped. "You're an anthropologist, so tell me," she said. "Could they really *believe* this?"

4 Why something is popular, why we like it, is not easy to discern. As reception studies have encountered, it is often difficult to articulate our enjoy/meant, as it seems to occur elsewhere than in our verbal mind. I have not conducted systematic audience research but, to suggest their popularity, draw on practical knowledge of the ubiquity of these films and the large numbers in the audiences when I attend. Even the most media savvy have a hard time articulating what exactly happens in the darkness of the theater-"it was cool!" "great," "scary," or "good effects." "Wanna see another one?"

5 But as Johnson and Stam describe in the case of progressive Brazilian filmmakers in the 1960s, their attempts to make a popular film — one that takes peoples'

daily realities of poverty, exclusion, and underdevelopment as its major theme and makes the masses, as opposed to a bourgeois individual, its protagonist— were not very popular. No one wanted to see them (1988). There are many great horror films that function as popular in Stuart Hall's sense, but the popular can also be a site of stalwart conservatism and right wing, even fascist tendencies. For every *Candyman* or *Night of the Living Dead*, in which racism is clearly shown to be the downfall of those who would otherwise survive the zombies, there are hundreds, perhaps thousands, of awful films that gruesomely punish women, queers, African Americans, etc.

6 The mind–body hierarchy organizes a range of social topographies. Labor is more valued if it's intellectual, not manual, and those people who have historically been relegated to body labor—African Americans under U.S. slavery, indigenous people in Latin America's plantation system, women in childbirth, etc.—have been devalued, not only in their earning power, but in how much they matter as humans.

7 The motto of the CUC (Campesino Unity Committee), "*Cabeza clara, puño combativo, corazón solidario*" (head clear, fist raised, heart solidary), also underlines the importance of embodied resistance.

8 These films directly engage the viewer's body. They are not metaphorical or implicit but physically excessive and viscerally manipulative. They are forcibly ecstatic, jerking the viewer out of stillness or stasis, whether we want to go or not (see Hawkins 2002, Paul 1994, Shaviro 1993). A contemporary review of the horror film *Doctor X* (1932) says, "Take the girl friend and by the middle of the first reel she'll have both arms around your neck and holding on for dear life. And you'll be giggling hysterically, too, trying to convince her you are not scared to death" (in Berenstein 2002:137). Of course, camp could also describe most modern horror and open us to a queer reading (Halberstam 1995, see also Todd Haynes's *Poison*).

9 In Joyabaj, which is a pretty small town—census figures range from four thousand to ten thousand inhabitants in the municipal center and thirty-four thousand to fifty-three thousand in the outlying areas (Remijnse 2002:43)—I have counted seven video salons that are open about twenty hours a day from Friday morning to Sunday afternoon, showing a range of schlock horror, action adventure, and martial arts films. Judging from my frequent viewing in these often very crowded little rooms, which get quite steamy during rainy season downpours, and from discussions with the entrepreneurs who run them, the films that work best seem to be the ones in which victim and victimizer merge. It would take another chapter to analyze the increasing popularity of kung fu and action adventure, but they usually contain several scenes that provide incredibly voluptuous and drawn-out contemplation of the hero's body in pain. They also borrow many of the special F/X developed in horror films to depict bodies that splatter.

10 Remijnse says that some ladinos accepted the military out of a sense that "only communists and *naturales*" were killed, as an older ladina told her, or because they felt their way of life was threatened, or from "fear of an Indian majority literally pouring down from the mountains, demanding their rights and intent

on killing every ladino in sight" (2002:162). However, many ladinos resisted the army in various ways, including refusing to patrol. The Xeabaj massacre was a turning point, "opening their eyes to what the military were capable of doing" (154).

11 I am able to be in the know about this (d)evaluation of my carefully articulated arguments only because the women are already part of "audit culture" (Strathern 2000, chapter 8), having to systematically evaluate each funded project.

12 DVDs seem a bit more Freudian in that they are often quite different from their original version.

13 Zur says the widows she worked with have difficulty accessing their memories owing to the drastic alterations of awareness imposed by the violence. It was "without precedence and there was no way of thinking about it while in the middle of it. Mental processes function in relation to something that happened previously, that has been felt, seen, or heard; without this the usual mechanisms of perception and memory (such as association) do not work and chaos results. The K'iche' express the idea that wisdom is based on knowledge and memory (and intelligence and feelings) in just one word: *na'ooj*. People feel that their *na'ooj* was rendered worthless by the events of *la violencia*; they speak of losing their *na'ooj*" (1998:161). "Once memories are triggered, women are sometimes possessed by them. They seem to return momentarily to the world they are trying to evoke instead of re-creating it in the present. Their eyes turn inward and they are back in the hostile climate of *la violencia*. Women's anguish, as they wrestle with deep memories or painful or guilt-provoking events, is conveyed more by tone of voice than the content of their speech. Sometimes women find no language adequate to describe the atrocities they survived although it is clear they remember something in some form" (168).

14 The new name of the school is a perfect Assumption Two. After years of protest the U.S. Congress finally voted to close it. But the same day they opened the new Western Hemisphere Institute for Security Cooperation in the same buildings, with the same teachers and instruction manuals.

15 The term "indio" comes from Columbus's mistaken geography and was forcibly applied to a wide range of pre-Columbian peoples in the Americas. The Guatemalan historian Severo Martínez Pelaez suggests that the postcolonial Indian is a colonial creation, produced via the host of ingeniously varied Spanish mechanisms installed to extract labor from the bodies of native peoples (1990). Their forced labor was not abolished until halfway through the twentieth century, and in many cases the state still does not treat the murder of an indigenous person as a serious crime. Ladinization, or dropping indigenous identity markers like clothing and language, has been one way people try to escape this assumed identity. A revolutionary restructuring of the political economy of the nation has been another. As I explore more thoroughly in the next chapters, becoming Maya, a nominal, political, cultural, and often economic transformation, is another strategy.

16 A number of towns and villages have organized exhumations of clandestine cemeteries, but no one in Joyabaj had been willing to do so until the unexpected ally of the landslide. Since then CONAVIGUA has helped organize a number of

digs in surrounding hamlets. However, there is such high demand for forensic anthropology teams that they are backlogged several years.

17 I would link the films to bricollaged folktales and traditional dances like the *Baile de la Culebra*, which also address oppression, haunting, bodily disaggregation, possession, and dispossession. Clover's specialty is medieval Scandinavian literature, and she sees multiple connections between her "serious" work and horror films: the predictability supplies not boredom but communion, and their highly ritualized, formulaic character is like folklore. Adela, when not overwhelmed with work, is an amazing storyteller and especially loves telling gruesome stories about the ghosts and monsters inhabiting the surrounding mountains—especially the *duendes*, or sprites, who grab *gringas* who venture up there!

INTERTEXT THREE

1 Iraq—Halliburton—Cheney—Unocal—Rice-Karzai-CIA—Bush—Saudis—Carlyle Group—Iraq.

2 The other commissioners were Christian Tomuschat, a German and a representative of the United Nations, and Alfredo Balsells Tojo, a ladino man. The two Guatemalans were chosen in consultation with the government and guerrilla and approved by members of the civil society.

3 Driscoll (2009) charts the (d)evolution of Kipling's "white man's burden" as it is deployed for the New Millennium Great Game.

4 The title of a documentary about Brazil by Orson Welles.

FOUR INDIAN GIVER OR NOBEL SAVAGE?

This chapter owes a special debt to conversations with Mark Driscoll.

1 Thanks to Donald Nelson for responding to this, and to Marjorie Agosín, Elizabeth Ferry, Adan Quan, and Ted Swedenburg for other examples. Until recently this was the version supplied to the world on Wikipedia.

2 Other skirmishes in a larger battle include Alan Sokal's "exposé" of "higher superstitions"; the list of academics with questionable patriotism compiled in 2001 by the American Council of Trustees and Alumni (ACTA), founded by Lynne Cheney, Vice President Dick Cheney's wife, and Senator Joseph Lieberman; the paid ads in college newspapers in 2004 calling on students to turn in their professors if they are "using the classroom as a political soapbox. This is a Violation of your Academic Rights"—both local and national numbers were included to be used in these denunciations; and the tens of thousands of hate e-mails, including death threats, generated through right-wing websites and directed at professors like Nick de Genova, Joseph Mossad and others at Columbia, Juan Coles at the University of Michigan, Cathy Lutz and Elyse Crystal at UNC-Chapel Hill, Ward Churchill at the University of Colorado, Wahneema Lubiano, Mark Anthony Neal, Karla Holloway, and others at Duke University, among many others.

3 Just as we academics launch into our careful arguments about memory and trauma, the differences among testimonial, autobiography, and social science, or between collective and individual truths (Beverly 1993, Coutin and Hirsch 1998,

Gugelberger 1996, Randall 1985), we are brought up short by the tears of betrayal and the demand to know, "But did she lie?" I feel stymied, unable to fit my answer into the double trouble of either/or, caught in the crosshairs of Lynne Cheney and the *American Enterprise* journal, who accuse us of immorality for not knowing the difference between fact and fiction, truth and lie. To which I respond with more obfuscating discourse about double entendres and assumptions. We can practically hear the exasperated lawman insist, "Just the facts, ma'am, just the facts." We ma'ams, of course, tend to "skirt" the issues, burdening historical truths with sentimental, even hysterical, flourishes. On the he said / she said divide, the Menchú scandal broke during President Clinton's impeachment hearings.

4   The notion of revolting peasants is a double entendre from *The Wizard of Id*. The King is brought a flea-bitten rebel and told, "The peasants are revolting." He replies, holding his nose, "They sure are!" I want to keep in play the tricky convergence of accounts that Mayan peasants are revolting (rising up) and Stoll's story that they are revolting (unpleasant) as they sue each other for land, beat each other up, and try to ensorcell their neighbors.

5   John Beverly is aware of the urge to treat Rigoberta Menchú as "tu." We often call her by her first name as if she were a friend or, in the double entendre of such informality, a subaltern. Like Beverly, I want to be her friend, for her to be "our Rigoberta," for us to be *compañeras*, joined in the same political movement (Beverly 1996:267–68). While not her friend, I have translated for her in that strange intimacy of speaking with and for.

6   Like Stoll, a political activist, unlike him, a woman; like me, a woman, unlike me, a Maya; like gringos, a border crosser, unlike us, forced into exile. As David Turnbull says, "It is having the capacity for movement that enables local knowledge to constitute part of a knowable system" (2000:20).

7   The Ixil are a Maya ethnolinguistic group in the north of Quiché province. Although the Menchú family are K'iche', they lived on the edge of the Ixil region, one of the areas hardest hit by the counterinsurgency and one of the four cases in the CEH's genocide ruling.

8   There are a number of such inconsistencies in Stoll's text and lots of assumptions about who counts as a reliable witness and what "certain" remarks mean. Critiquing him at this level, however, is the easiest way to resist Stoll's text and retain our own assumptions.

9   Clearly, much of the attention given to Stoll's charges in the U.S. academy is owing to the fact that Menchú Tum is "canon" fodder here in the legitimation wars over reading lists and curricula, another terrain through which identity detours (Pratt 2001).

10 This parallels Said (1978) and Coronil's (1996) critique of the self-making of "Occidentalism." The "us" Stoll assumes, and I follow him here, is mainly but not only United States, Caucasian, privileged, and benevolently liberal. Menchú Tum's "us," to whom she is thereby accountable, is multiple. She has different effects in Europe, Asia, South Africa, and Ecuador and on different constituencies within these geographies. Many gringas are also Latinas, Chicanas, African Americans, or part of other diasporas. Like Menchú Tum, they live in relation to many elements that modify their identities.

11 Grandin notes that Stoll may be worked on (and may work on his "sentimental readers") by a similar technology. The "attempt to discredit Menchú and by extension the revolutionary left is really boilerplate. Take out the specifics, and it could be Edmund Burke talking about the French Revolution or Todd Gitlin talking about the New Left" (pers. comm.).

12 Stoll is clearly having a blast in his heated debates with Menchú Tum's supporters, who also enjoy the debate. Circulating through journals and professional meetings, these interlocutions mimic the structure of the smutty joke from which the woman in question is excluded. When I asked her about Stoll at her home in July 1999 Menchú was much more interested in talking about the CEH report, the Bishop Gerardi murder case, and her foundation's work around peace treaty implementation, citizen participation, and their court case against soldiers who massacred returned refugees in Xamán. She also spoke of her difficult pregnancy and the death of her child the year before. Rather than mime her eloquence here, I urge readers to explore her books and interviews.

13 Judith Butler says, "Foucault challenges us to make fun of ourselves in our search for truth, in the relentless pursuit of the essence of our selves . . . it appears that desire makes us into strangely fictive beings. And the laugh of recognition appears to be the occasion of insight" (1987:238).

14 See also Hulme 1992 and Taussig 1987. In his genealogy of wild men and women Hayden White touches on many of the understandings that frame Menchú Tum, including the question of speech. For the Greeks, the barbarian could not speak Greek and was thus denied political life and true humanity. They twinned the uncanniness of the articulate (*desenvuelta*) with slyness—wild people trick the shepherd, befuddle the gamekeeper. "It was the oppressed, exploited, alienated, or repressed part of humanity that kept on reappearing in the imagination of Western man—as the Wild Man . . . always as a criticism of whatever security and peace of mind one group of men in society had purchased at the cost of the suffering of another" (1978:180). White writes that the Wild Man of the Christian Middle Ages distilled anxieties about three securities: sex (family), sustenance (political economic institutions), and salvation (church) (165–67). As a supposedly Marxist guerrilla practicing liberation theology, Menchú Tum clearly stirs anxiety about the capitalist system and the traditional church, and there are dozens of jokes that situate her as White's Wild Woman, "supposed to be surpassingly ugly . . . [but] supposed to be obsessed by a desire for ordinary [ladino] men" (167).

15 State-sanctioned extrajudicial murders occur in the United States as well, and naming is also a counterstrategy here. Reading the names of people killed by members of the Los Angeles Police Department since 1990 took over half an hour during a protest of police brutality in August 2000 (thanks to Mark Driscoll, a participant-observer).

16 Not surprisingly, gender remains a fundamental divide, as men choose from the 260-day annual count and women from the 20-day month count (Warren 1998:157, 241). The slipperiness of these practices means that "names used in revitalization circles—where Raxche', Nik'te', and Ixkem displace Demetrio, María Juana, and Nora—may or may not be known in one's home community (Warren

1998:xxi). The citing of a series of works by Mayan intellectuals who have subsequently changed their names leads to the kind of bibliographic somersaults we used to encounter only with women authors taking or dropping their husband's name. As Erika Nelson reminds me, an important part of decolonization is renaming schools, streets, cities, and countries, and in a similar spirit, several of the reparations agreements in Guatemala stipulate naming places after the army's victims.

17 One of the more exciting, yet discombobulating aspects of the postwar-in-action, with people entering public life and the return of thousands of exiles, is finding out the real names of people I've "known" for some twenty years.

18 In Guatemala I have found no equivalents for the food metaphors used in the United States to try to shame ethnic "sellouts" by suggesting they have one color on the outside but are white on the inside: "apple" for Native Americans, "Oreo" for African Americans, "banana" or "Twinkie" for Asian Americans, but the idea here seems the same.

19 As anthropologists we are methodologically assumed to be able to tell, through participant observation, when our interviewees are trying to dupe us. In his letter to the *Chronicle* Haley vacillates between acknowledging the "easy seduction of scholars by certain themes and symbols" and insisting that Menchú Tum's book is "no substitute for rigorous ethnography" (1999:B12). Between rigor and seduction, Orin Starn (1991) and Carol Smith (1996) remind us that we do often miss things, even big things, like revolutions.

20 Žižek uses the roundabouts of Austen's *Pride and Prejudice* as the example. The failure of Darcy's and Elizabeth's first encounter is the precondition of the final outcome. What if the "first encounter of the future lovers was a success—that Elizabeth had accepted Darcy's first proposal. What would happen? Instead of being bound together in true love they would become a vulgar everyday couple, a liaison of an arrogant, rich man and a pretentious, empty-minded young girl" (1989:63). He also cites Elster on "states that are essentially by-products, that is, states that could be produced only as non-intended, as the side-effect of our activity: as soon as we aim directly at them, as soon as our activity is directly motivated by them, our procedure becomes self-defeating." If, in the U.S. jury system "the jurors become aware that the judicial effects of their work are rather null and that the real point of it is its effect on their own civic spirit—its educational value—*this educational effect is spoilt*" (1989:83).

21 Thanks to Bill Maurer, whose work charts similar terrain (1997 and Collier et al. 1995).

INTERTEXT FOUR

1 Although the U.S. "one-drop rule" of race identity (a very particular *nom du père*) seems to clash with the *mestizaje* or race mixing/improvement ideologies in Latin America, the tools of U.S. critical race studies are quite useful south of the border (see Arenas Bianchi 1999, Hale 2006, Velasquez Nimatuj 2005). Forming a conjunction between Spike Lee and Guatemala does not just acknowledge my sources or mark me as a transaction point, but also tries to crosscut and bam-

boozle that apparent border between North and South America. *Abya Yala*, an indigenous term for the Américas, is not one entity, but neither is it two.

2 Both Lee and Michael Moore (see next intertext) critique and use media, delinking its more abhorrent images to lash them into different stories like antiracism, class analysis, and their abiding faith in the common sense of the average person to do the right thing. For their troubles they are accused of crafting propaganda and attempting to manipulate the populace. As John Carpenter asks in *They Live*, are the fears of the powerful that the masses are duped actually fears that they can actually see quite clearly?

3 Similarly, women and children of specific races and classes have long been assumed to be especially prone to suggestion, hysteria, and outside influence, leading to the development of elaborate codes to protect their vulnerable sensibilities.

4 Are these miniature versions of capitalism, the great casino (Strange 1998)?

FIVE ANTHROPOLOGIST DISCOVERS
LEGENDARY TWO-FACED INDIAN

Portions of this chapter are reprinted by permission from *Anthropology in the Margins of the State*, edited by Veena Das and Deborah Poole. Copyright © 2004 by the School for Advanced Research, Santa Fe, New Mexico.

1 San Simón, aka Maximon, is a saint figure, patron to drunks and sex workers, and sometimes associated with harmful magicks; he requires alcohol and cigarettes, which he miraculously drinks and smokes, to hear petitions. In some places he is barely anthropomorphic; in others he explicitly doubles the white(r) *patrón*, boss, plantation owner.

2 Cojtí has written extensively on Mayan identity in relation to the state. A flashpoint for ethnic-national identifications during the Quincentennial period, he was frequently labeled with the familiar stereotype "uppity," that is, not humble enough. During an interview I conducted in 1993 with a ladino state official, he got up from behind his desk and started strutting around his office with his chest puffed out to explain to me how arrogant he thought Cojtí was—an uncanny bit of minstrelsy.

3 Despite having very circumscribed choices—the army often gave a list of names of people who had to be killed or even a quota of alleged subversives to be captured—the men who became patrol leaders could influence a village's experience. In Chupol, McAllister says that some "are happy to admit that they maintained contact with the EGP while they led the patrols" (2003:291), while another spent the time of violence in the army base serving as a "privileged informant on his home region," then became a ruthless patrol leader (292). Simone Remijnse describes diverse patrol experiences, many leaders looking the other way when confronted by either guerrilla activity or nonconformist patrollers. In Joyabaj proper one leader joined his squad in holing up to drink before performing a cursory stroll through town once they were inebriated enough to miss anything that might force them to intervene. Xecnup, known for being conservative, and MLN split in January 1981 when a group disagreed with the choice of patrol

leader. The dissidents took refuge in Chorraxaj, which borders Patzulá and is known as a Catholic Action, DC village. The Xecnup patrol followed them and killed everyone it could find, both refugees and those giving them shelter. Again, in March 1982 they killed at least fifty men, women, and children in Chorraxaj, carrying out their tasks "like fanatics," according to survivors. The flayed body of the Xecnup patrol leader was found in 1994. Chorraxaj was the site of a third massacre in April 1983, when five hundred patrollers from surrounding villages attacked with sticks and machetes, followed by the military, which took prisoners down to the square of Joyabaj. Some of them were hacked to pieces (*hicieron picadito*) in broad daylight, while others were held prisoner and one by one handed over to patrollers to kill. The patrols of Chorraxaj, however, were themselves led by a very violent man who was close to Leonel Ogáldez and who forced the majority of unwilling patrollers to do terrible things, including participating in massacres that killed at least one hundred people (Remijnse 2002:143–58).

4 Remijnse says that on October 1, 1981, the guerrillas kidnapped Fredy Ogáldez—the youngest of four brothers and son and nephew of former MLN mayors Próspero and Rogelio Ogáldez—who was never heard from again. Newspapers at the time reported a one-hundred-thousand-quetzal ransom demand. His brother Leonel became the infamous commander of the Joyabaj Civil Patrol, while another brother is a dedicated health promoter.

5 A joke told in Guatemala goes, "When you tell a joke on the phone in Guatemala, three people laugh." Perhaps gringos should laugh carefully, given the current threats to our privacy and other rights, but here's a similar joke that Erika Nelson told me: "What number do you call to get the National Security Administration?" "Any number you want."

6 *Fuertes Caminos* (strong roads) was the name of one army-run development project that involved U.S. National Guard units in areas where the guerrilla were once strong (Adams, n.d.). Roads were built through forced labor under General Ubico in the 1930s, as is well remembered throughout the highlands (González 2002). They facilitate the arrival of troops in isolated areas and profoundly transform rural space (Stepputat 2001). The K'iche' word for road, *B'e*, condenses many ideas surrounding morality, one's life course, and relations among past, present, and future. It also forms part of the word for leader or go-between (*c'amal b'e*), as in a marriage broker, who makes two people into one (Cook 2000, McAllister 2003).

7 Encouraging development and progress has other effects as well. As Akhil Gupta says, "Development discourse . . . not only has served to subject the Third World to Western control through a phalanx of institutions and treaties but has also created the 'underdeveloped' as a subject and 'underdevelopment' as a form of identity in the postcolonial world" (1998:11).

8 Greg Grandin shows how in Quetzaltenango the more modern, merchant K'iche's joined the MLN (2000a).

9 A sort of beauty contest, the selection of local queens is closely followed and hotly contested and tends to be ethnically segregated in highland towns. In the 1970s, anger at the shoddy treatment of indigenous contestants compared with ladinas helped spark mainstream indigenous organizing.

10 A few days later the ladina woman's brother shot and killed an indigenous man who was also a resettled guerrilla. The family claimed it was an accident, and no charges were filed.

11 Tedlock (1992) describes these. In chapter 3 I told the story of a man who is suffering severe depression and anxiety attacks. He attributes his problems to the continuing effects of the war. His wife, however, scoffs (but told me not to tell him). She said, "It's because he's a Mayan man. Do you know what that means?" "I'm not sure," I said. I knew he had been involved in the Grupo Maya and was very frustrated with Alfonso's resistance to Mayanizing the Catholic services. "No, it's not the Mayan Movement," she said. "He has to *asumir* his Mayan identity. He's getting a call."

12 This softer line on rivals' heavenly potential has also been noted by Abigail Adams (pers. comm.) and is a major about-face from the positions held during the early postwar. Similarly, McAllister says, "The expressions of deep mutual antagonism between members of different religions, however, belie the frequency with which Chupolenses shift between their supposedly contradictory and exclusive options" (2003:117).

13 He was referencing Gayatri Spivak, the postcolonial critic who has argued that an ahistorical "essential" identity, untouched by colonial violence and ideology or by the world-transforming effects of commodity capitalism, cannot exist, but that strategically claiming such a thing may enable important political work in certain contexts (1988a).

14 In 1978 and 1979 the still-incipient movement that would become the URNG drew on the experiences of survivors of the original FAR campaigns, the aid of Cuban advisors, and close study of other experiences of regime change. McAllister shows the influence of Vietnamese theorists like Vo Nguyen Giap and says that in the 1960s FAR commander César Montes was invited to observe the Tet Offensive (2003:183–84). While not wanting to appear an apologist, I do note that theory is different from practice, that the Guatemalan milieu was different from that of Cuba or Nicaragua, in part because of the indigenous population and the raciological state formation, and that as hard as both leaders and organization members tried, it is hard to be in the know. Too, the counterinsurgents studied similar cases; for example, Benedicto Lucas García, the brother of Romeo, the de facto ruler in 1978–82, served with the French in Algeria. (Like the refrain "like a movie," the Gillo Pontecorvo film *Battle of Algiers* was screened for White House and Pentagon audiences involved in the battle of Iraq.)

15 A ladino in Joyabaj explained the effects of the war on the town's residents to Remijnse: "They were like frozen people . . . [they] had learned a lot, they had learned to shut their mouth and not to protest, they had learned not to talk and not to ask, they had learned to obey when you were called for patrol duty. . . . The ones who did stand up [to] the military are the ones that are now in the graves behind the convent" (2002:284).

16 This version figures in a case against military and state officials brought by the Rigoberta Menchú Foundation (Remijnse 2000:108–15).

17 Velásquez Nimatuj (2005 chapter 3) describes a similar painful experience of two

faces turning on each other, even as each sees its position as necessary in the war between good and evil.

INTERTEXT FIVE

1 Jeffrey Sluka writes, "The arms or 'security' industry is the largest industry in the world, and a multibillion dollar international repression trade flourishes" (2000:8, see also Nordstrom 2006). *Tough Guise*, by the Media Education Foundation (2002), also addresses Columbine to explore the complex construction of violent guys through the face of toughness they are encouraged to assume.

2 If those who make them don't end up dead. RIP Gary Webb, the exceptional investigative reporter who, having been dismissed at first as a conspiratorial crackpot (paralleling questions about his supposed suicide), has been consistently absolved by history.

3 On this very day, August 21, 2006, a columnist in the *New York Times* called Spike Lee two-faced: "There are two Spike Lees. One is an artist capable of directing exceptional films, the other a public personality who suffers from flare-ups of foot-in-mouth disease and a fondness for conspiracy theories" (Kulish:A20), referring to *When the Levees Broke*.

4 In *Bamboozled*, Lee has the Mantan show break for ads for Tommy Hiln**ger clothes in which a smiling white man dances with black folks, then counts up all the money they've given him.

5 One might wonder why this collection emerged simultaneously with others addressing the same topic, like Comaroff and Comaroff (1999, 2001), Marcus (1999), and Meyer and Pels (2003).

6 Hampton was a Black Panther killed in his bed in 1969 by the Chicago police with support from the FBI's COINTELPRO. A car bomb killed former Chilean ambassador Letelier and the U.S. activist Moffit in Washington, D.C. in September 1976. While in 2000 the CIA admitted collaborating with President Augusto Pinochet of Chile in the Letelier and Moffit murders, it had originally, while headed by George H. W. Bush, planted rumors that were published in *Newsweek* and elsewhere that the hit was a "revolutionary murder" carried out by the left to create martyrs. The resonance with the "revolutionary suicide" Stoll claims occurred in the Spanish embassy fire must be accidental.

7 Hillary Rodham Clinton's denunciation of same was jeered as conspiracy theory until confirmed by one of its human actants, David Brock, in *Blinded by the Right*, which shows that making people who believed in a conspiracy look ludicrous was an important tool.

8 In David Lean's *Lawrence of Arabia*, Lawrence first uses these words to describe the Arabs, but like rubber and glue they are later turned back on him to describe the colonizers.

SIX HIDDEN POWERS, DUPLICITOUS STATE/S

1 Guatemalanizing the United States, in June 2005 George W. Bush denounced Amnesty International's critiques of "impunity and accountability deficit" in

U.S. prison camps as "absurd" and denounced the organization as composed of people who "hate America" (Alvarez 2005:A5).

2 See Bayart (1991) on state power and the "politics of the belly," which Hansen and Stepputat describe as both "a practical politics of feeding populations and a symbolics of power around metaphors of eating and digestion" (2001:19).

3 Sister Ford was killed on May 5, 2001, in a robbery whose modus operandi smacked of hidden powers.

4 Kobrak (1997) notes similar ambivalence in Aguacatan, where patrols were loathed but people were loath to give them up because, under threat of army punishment, forms of communal labor and solidarity were revived. In January 2005 South Coast Ex-PAC asked to reorganize in order to fight *delincuencia*—for a salary of Q500/month. However, the National Council of Ex-Members of the PAC said they did not want to patrol—that was the responsibility of the state.

5 When I asked if they had been victimized, he said no, but he heard about it all the time. Many hear via the mass circulation tabloids, which run lurid, graphically illustrated stories about daily body counts, lynchings, monstrous births, crimes of passion, highland witchcraft, cannibalism, and ensorcelling. Like carnivals and horror film, they are disdained by the middle and upper classes yet read avidly by the "popular." There are plenty of true horror stories, but the frisson of rumor uprooted this family, leaving their teenage daughter despairing at Joyabaj's limited dating opportunities.

6 Much has rightly been made of the racism that undergirds this production system—as González mentioned, even indigenous *jefes* assume that *indios* are those who work for free—and that clearly contributed to the genocide. However, the brutality of the exploitation of dispossessed ladinos and the counterinsurgency violence against them in the 1960s should not be underestimated. At that time the practice of disposing of victims in the Montagua river gave rise to the slang *dar agua* (to kill) and to this horrific joke: "In Europe Colonel Arana's German hosts, thinking they could impress this tropical man with the force of their winter, took him to the banks of the frozen Rhine. 'Big deal,' said Arana. 'You've got rivers that freeze. In Guatemala we have rivers that coagulate.'"

7 For more information on the impressive corruption among government officials and their cronies, see INFORPRESS, Hernández Pico 2005, Robles Montayo 2002, and Transparency International 2004. Coronil's anatomy and physiology of corruption in Venezuela (what he calls "the devil's excrement") is a brilliant tracing of similar networks (1997 chapter 8). It's hard to throw stones while living in a glass house with Halliburton, Tom DeLay, Jack Abramoff, et al.

8 Of the thirteen ministries in the Berger GANA government, representatives of the private sector headed nine; of eleven secretariats they had six; and of eleven commissions they controlled eight.

9 Oglesby suggests the *finqueros* are in the know about gender, showing films like *Rambo* to encourage workers to link machismo to increased production (2003).

10 One of the substances said to have this effect is injectable thiamine, adding the high-tech edge of performance-enhancing drugs to devil contracts and history as sorcery (Taussig 1980, 1987).

11 Rumors also suggest Joyabaj is a drug transshipment point, something increas-

ingly true of the whole country: one can obtain pot, cocaine, and heroine with absolute ease in Guatemala City and most tourist areas. Global overproduction has led to increasing payment in kind, flooding urban neighborhoods like Primero de Julio with drugs and transforming family, labor, and political networks (Camus 2005).

12 Few Xoye have inserted into the global economy through the nontraditional exports that have so profoundly impacted neighboring Chimaltenango (Dary Fuentes 1991, Fischer 2001, Goldin n.d.).

13 The state, struggling to keep up (and lagging behind national banking interests), is opening new consulates in many of these places to better serve these citizens.

14 This discussion is especially indebted to talks with Santiago Bastos, Matt Creelman, and members of AVANCSO. The growing ambivalence among many Guatemalans toward the effects of NGOs and development more generally resonates with critiques like Dagnino, Alvarez, and Escobar 1998, Escobar 1995, Ferguson 1990, 1999, Gupta 1998, Moore 2005, among many others.

15 She also suggests that their limited response to the CEH, despite the high level of organization in the town, was an effect of their not being accustomed to divulging their stories or giving testimony, "which describes the acts of violence one has witnessed or experienced without much political or historical context" (39, 349).

16 Because of such skills and her family's cash flow, Natalia is able to mediate in other ways as well. For example, she helped Esperanza avoid Western Union surcharges by arranging for Juan's remittances to be deposited directly into her bank account.

17 For capitalists, this hidden agency is the market, for Hegel it is the cunning of reason, for anti-Semites it is the Jewish conspiracy, etc. While in Oz it seems to be the Wizard, the effect of everyone getting what they want is ambivalent. It is made possible by his demand that Dorothy bring him the Wicked Witch's broomstick but also in spite of it. He thought he was just getting rid of her. He never expected her to succeed and probably never imagined that the *process* of getting it would, by being lived, fulfill her and her companions' desires for a heart, a brain, the nerve, a home. Yet the conspiratorial agent, the transsubjective mechanism (the demand that fairy-tales have happy endings), does seem to regulate the process, precisely through such detours.

INTERTEXT SIX

1 Charlie Piot tells me that Ghana's Kwame Nkrumah suggested raising a monument to the mosquito precisely for this reason, that it saved West Africa from some of the worst ravages of settler colonization.

2 Today, some countries in the global South have a thriving and largely unsupervised industry that provides subjects for drug trials to global pharmaceutical companies (Le Carré 2001a, b, Shah 2002, Sunder Rajan 2005).

3 Why so much pressure? Apparently for fear that Guatemala would set a bad example for the rest of Latin America. While Guatemala is the largest *maquila* drug

producer in Central America, medicine prices there are among the highest — unlike Nicaragua and Honduras, where the governments limit price increases. The United States here updates its two-faced relation with the United Fruit Company by playing public face for the private interests of Big Pharma, a relation the *New York Times* described succinctly as CAFTA passed the U.S. Senate in July 2005: "Drug Lobby Got a Victory in Trade Pact Vote": "Drug industry courtiers, who represent what is arguably Washington's biggest and wealthiest lobby, appear to have succeeded in the Central American Free Trade Agreement. The agreement would extend the monopolies of drug makers and, critics say, lead to higher drug prices for the mostly impoverished people of the six Latin American countries it covers" (Saul 2005:B1).

4 In June 2002 war and malaria became lashed together again when four soldiers returned to North Carolina from service in Afghanistan and, in separate instances, brutally murdered their wives (several also suicided). One woman was stabbed seventy-one times. All of the men had been taking Larium (mefloquine) as a prophylactic against malaria, and that has been shown to cause severe neuropsychiatric disorders, including manic behavior, acute psychosis with delusions, and aggressive mood swings, making the drug a suspect in the violence. An official army report later cleared the drug of suspicion, just in time for it to be administered to the two hundred thousand plus soldiers deployed in Iraq. But in 2004 it was again linked to the alarming suicide rate among those very soldiers, which is apparently three times higher than in any other historic conflict. Little mention is made of military training itself as a lethal drug (Lutz and Elliston 2002), although that is suggested by the rumors of Guatemalan soldiers being under the influence as they carried out massacres. We might also question the way soldiers' willingness to die has made them excellent guinea pigs in military laboratories, where untested drug combos are routinely used in their bodies.

5 Julius Wagner-Juaregg won a Nobel Prize for discovering it. While discontinued as a treatment once penicillin came into use, uncannily, Henry Heimlich, of the Heimlich maneuver, recently raised a ruckus by employing malaria therapy to treat AIDS — in Chinese bodies, not Euro-American ones (McNeil 2003:D1).

SEVEN LIFE DURING WARTIME

1 This usage traces to the 1960s, when death squads dumped bodies into the Motagua river (the one that coagulates). It also grimly presages current U.S. torture practices like waterboarding.

2 Foucault was especially interested in Iran and visited the country several times.

3 Mark Driscoll also suggested the title for this chapter.

4 According to an anthropologist who has interviewed him, "He knows a lot about the indigenous stuff. Army strategy was divided among either killing them all, ladinizing them, you know, assimilating them, or taking their culture into account. He was the spokesman for the latter. He said, in fact, that he was often distrusted within the army because he had these subversive ideas that they had to know their enemy." See also Schirmer (1998) and Cifuentes (1982). Greg

Grandin pointed me to his book on "modern history and ethnicity in Guatemala" (Cifuentes 1998).

5 The Development Poles, like their predecessors—strategic hamlets created by the British during the Boer War and used by the United States in Vietnam, or the Potemkin villages under Stalin—were often open to the public and the subject of glossy reports. I was easily able to acquire the Development Poles PR book after showing my passport at the Guatemala City army base. Full of photos (see page 43), quotes from the Mayan sacred book *Popol Wuj*, and paeans to the soldiers who saved Guatemala from Communism, it reflects enormous pride in the resettlement areas, especially the provision of potable water (Government of Guatemala 1985).

6 Which reminds me of Monty Python's *Life of Brian*, set during the Roman Empire, when an underground anti-imperialist declaims, "What have the Romans ever done for us?" and his companions mumble, "Well, there are the sewers." Sputtering with anger he acknowledges this, "OK, besides the sewers, what have the Romans done for us?" "Well, there are the roads," says another, and on it goes.

7 "We must make allowance for the complex and unstable process whereby discourse can be both an instrument and an effect of power, but also a hindrance, a stumbling block, a point of resistance and a starting point for an opposing strategy. Discourse transmits and produces power; it reinforces it, but also undermines and exposes it, renders it fragile and makes it possible to thwart it. . . . There is not, on the one side, a discourse of power, and opposite it, another discourse that runs counter to it. Discourses are tactical elements or blocks operating in the field of force relations; there can exist different and even contradictory discourses within the same strategy; they can, on the contrary, circulate without changing their form from one strategy to another, opposing strategy" (1980:101–02).

8 In the nineteenth century, caricaturists poked fun at people from the malarial Carolinas as "gaunt . . . with their 'careworn expression and languid mien'" (Honigsbaum 2001:264, see also Humphreys 2001).

9 This calculation is based on the notion of basic reproduction number, or BRN, the number of additional infections that an originally infected person will generate under ideal conditions. By comparison, the highly contagious measles carrier tends to a BRN of twelve to fourteen, while AIDS transmission may have a BRN of only one (Spielman and D'Antonio 2001:96).

10 As had earlier malaria fighters, like John Smith in the United States, who created mosquito brigades in the early 1900s, and Fred Soper in Brazil (1938) and Sardinia (1947). According to U.S. sources, Italy saw the first civilian DDT use, but a counterscience suggests that this really occurred in Venezuela, administered by the Maracai Malaria Institute (an event commemorated by a huge statue of a mosquito).

11 "Did you know we're responsible for all the old tires in Guatemala?" asked the doctor in charge of malaria eradication in Guatemala during a group interview. Her colleague, in charge of dengue, looked shocked. "What? That too?" "Yes, the

new law says it's our responsibility." "As if we don't have enough to do," said the other doctor, who was dealing with a dengue outbreak (July 2002).

12 In his charming *Conquest of the Tropics* (1914) Frederick Adams splices action-adventure with a United Fruit Company puff piece and succinctly describes global biopolitics and the relations between *connaissance* and *savoir*: "It was impossible to call on American experts on tropical sanitation, for . . . there [were] none. We knew nothing about the tropics at our gates, commercially, medically, or otherwise. The cultured people of Central America knew nothing about the sanitary problems of their lowlands, for the good and ample reason that they did not deem them a fit place to live, and they kept as far away from them as possible. . . . Scientists and physicians with experience in Java, India, the tropical sections of Africa, responded to the call to assist American enterprise in this pioneer industrial invasion of the tropics. It was this paucity of our knowledge concerning tropical diseases which impelled the United Fruit Company to suggest and later give substantial financial assistance to the founding of a department in Tulane University for the exclusive study and investigation of maladies specific to the coastal regions of the Caribbean, and much of the advancement since accomplished has been due to the discoveries made and the remedies applied by those sent out by this university" (268).

13 In 2002, to celebrate the fiftieth anniversary of the Pan-American Health Organization, the Banco de Café, in upscale Zone 9, sponsored a photo exhibit featuring portraits of the SNEM brigades standing proudly with their fumigating equipment or spraying down walls.

14 Malaria deeply impacted the social, labor, and national politics around black, indigenous, and white(r) bodies in Guatemala. The United Fruit Company, opening jungle areas to banana production in the early 1900s, brought hundreds of Jamaicans and African Americans — thought to be immune — to work there as well as importing indigenous laborers from the highlands. Adams wrote, the worker's "life had to be protected and his energy conserved, and the men who employed [them] were faced with the responsibility of doing this" (268). "Relentless war was declared on the mosquito. The use of copper wire gauze had already been made, but one of the first steps was to insure that all houses used by employees *not immune* to mosquito bites should be screened, and, in some cases, double screened. Petroleum was used unsparingly in stagnant pools and slow-running streams. Large sums were expended in drainage and in all of the proved expedients for eliminating tropical menaces to health" (272, emphasis added).

15 His tone recalls that of Domingo González after his return from the ALMG conference, comparing the allegedly backward K'iche' to the seemingly more advanced Kaqchiquel.

16 In May 2004 a group called the Copenhagen Consensus convened to review the status of global development and set priorities regarding how improvement could best be attained with limited resources (fifty billion dollars was the working budget). They ranked malaria eradication as number four on the list of most pressing problems measured by ratio of social benefit to cost (*The Economist* June 5, 2004:63).

17 Although George Stocking says that "the Lamarckian assumption had been part of the baggage of European thought for 2,000 years" (1982:235).

18 My native state of Ohio legalized the teaching of creationism in 2002. In a study made in February 2005, close to one-third of U.S. high school biology teachers polled said they are afraid to mention evolution in their classes, even when it is included in the curriculum. It makes me wonder if the bumper sticker is right when it says, "When evolution is outlawed, only outlaws will evolve."

19 I've addressed elsewhere (1999) how the apparently odd combination of Culture and Sports in the ministerial portfolios of many countries suggests a lurking Lamarckianism.

20 Stepan says it also informed competing notions of negative (sterilization or killing the "unfit") versus positive eugenics. "It is tempting to think of the meliorism of Lamarckian biology as an inherent feature; since the effects of social reform were expected to be inherited, a negative eugenics of reproduction may have seemed unnecessary. . . . [Yet] a neo-Lamarckian eugenist could equally well argue that the accumulated effects of damaging environments had created a tainted heredity that no amount of social reforms could improve quickly" (Stepan 1991:111). Similarly, Stocking says, "To those of us whose thinking has been molded by the conventional wisdom of the modern social sciences, the very word *race* calls up a distasteful image of deep-seated hereditary biological forces fundamentally antithetical to those of 'culture' and 'environment.' . . . [But] hereditarians and environmentalists had more in common than one might think . . . eugenicists tended to assume the physical inheritance of quite complex mental characteristics that we understand today in cultural terms. But to the extent that they were Lamarckians environmentally oriented writers exhibited the same tendency to confuse social and physical heredity, and to assume the physical inheritance of complex cultural characteristics . . . one could be at one and the same time racialist and egalitarian" (1982:250–51). See the threat mongering of Samuel Huntington's *Who Are We?* (2004), in which he insists it's the Anglo-Protestant creed, not Anglo-Protestant people per se, that he values. It is Mexican culture (*mañana* attitudes and lethargy in learning English) that endangers the United States.

21 An infamous Citicorps memo from 1994 demanded that if Mexico wanted to preserve financial stability undergirded by international confidence the Zapatista rebels in Chiapas should be liquidated.

22 Hale (1994a) and Saldaña-Portillo (2003) explore the assumptions of national development and modernization that may undergird these praxes as much as their Other—the IMF-backed nation-state. Saldaña-Portillo focuses especially on the masculinism and heteronormativity embedded in both these Janus faces.

23 In Venezuela in 2002 I found that those in charge of malaria eradication could call up the numbers of infections from the previous day as well as computerized notes on local state responses.

24 Hale emphasizes that this individual can also be a collective, like the Maya, creating unexpected allies between indigenous activists and global neoliberalism (2006).

1 According to Larry Rohter, this "scene so unnerved Argentine audiences that the film has become a cultural phenomenon, dissected and analyzed countless times in newspapers and on radio and television" (2002:B25). The director, Fabian Bielinsky, said, "Every one of the scams you see in the movie is taken from real life, with the exception of the Nine Queens" (B25). I am quoting from the English subtitles. The film's translator was not named in the DVD version.

2 At one point Marcos tries to get a gun off a fellow con man, who looks horrified and wounded at the suggestion, like Marcos before him. "I am not a criminal!" he says.

3 The Hughes brothers do not interview any of the women who work for the pimps. Many find sex work shameful and extraordinarily dangerous. Women and men are vulnerable not only to physical attack and STDs, but also to the police, the "thin blue line" that is supposed to protect citizens but is often the source of danger. However, in burgeoning journalistic, literary, and ethnographic production, others express quite pragmatic relations to this job. Some feel they are even duping the johns—who stupidly spend all that money. Sex work advocates point out that the hourly wage is far higher than minimum, offsetting some of the dangers of the work, and despite the antisex backlash of the 1990s, organizing to protect the bodies and purses of workers valiantly continues (see *Live Nude Girls Unite!*).

4 See Amin 1974, 1985, 1997; Harvey 2003, 2005; Hoogvelt 1997; Payer 1974; Rahnema 1997; Sardar and Davies 2002; URNG 1988.

5 This is what the lovely date in *American Psycho* understands when she asks the snazzily dressed protagonist what he does. What he actually said was, "Murders and executions."

EIGHT ACCOUNTING FOR THE POSTWAR, BALANCING THE BOOK/S

1 The auditable ledger doubles as "prestidigitation, double-shuffling, honey-fugling, hornswoggling and skulduggery," as William Z. Ripley tried to warn President Calvin Coolidge in 1928 (Evans 2005:14).

2 Thanks to Mark Driscoll for the citation.

3 Strathern says, "Audit does not just impinge upon the academic's conditions of work but also interpenetrates it, and in the same way as the 'external' mechanisms by which products are valued are also internalized. . . . more and more individuals and organizations are coming to think of themselves as subjects of audit" (2000b:280–81).

4 A former guerrilla who had chosen a ladino *nom de guerre*, but who was becoming Maya through his work with COPMAGUA, registered a complaint with MINUGUA when the state refused to put a name from the *Popol Wuj* on his daughter's birth certificate, telling him only Christian names were allowed.

5 In December 2004, fifteen to twenty bodies a day were appearing on the capital's streets, many with signs of torture. Activist groups were drawing attention to the large numbers of women killed and often horrifyingly mutilated—at least

five hundred in 2004 alone—drawing comparisons to the *niñas extraviadas* (lost girls) of Ciudad Juarez, Mexico (although in January 2005 the government cut the number of police officers assigned to "femicide" by 75 percent).

6   Strathern's audit idiom of transparency, efficiency, good practice, regulation, and organization (2000a:1–2) interpenetrates the report (and the World Bank's covenant with Guatemala), as in the summing up: "Through its verification, good offices, technical cooperation and public information, MINUGUA has made countless contributions, helping over the years to remind Guatemalans of the commitments they have made and to keep the country on the path of peace" (10). Pointing this out is no more a critique of MINUGUA than it is of my own anthropological project, as I assume the very same intentions and methods, though make *far* more modest contributions.

7   The latter is the only existing national institution that could "assume full responsibility" for human rights monitoring (MINUGUA 2004:1), and the UN has invested financial and human resources to prepare it for taking the reins. But while a minimum budget of Q140,000 to 300,000 was judged necessary, its allotment for 2005 was only Q15,000.

8   The article also notes that "in just one example, 80m Quetzales (more than $10m) disappeared from the Interior Ministry last year."

9   Thanks to Corey Robin for the citation to this subsection's epigraph. The text is engraved on the wall of the Lincoln Memorial on the Washington Mall, which served as the backdrop for Martin Luther King's "I Have a Dream" speech in August 1963.

10 The how-to directions include: 1. approach victim; 2. fill in forms; 3. verify; 4. systematize data and qualifications and add analysis; 5. compile lists. They suggest several things: a suspicion of duplicity, to be averted by checking and rechecking; the possibility of the auditors themselves being audited, with a focus on transparency and "purifying" the lists; and a larger faith in audit culture's monitoring regimes. On the pamphlet explaining the program to potential beneficiaries there is a warning: "Reparations are free. Don't allow yourself to be duped by people who charge or say they represent the PNR" (*No se deje engañar por personas que cobren . . .*).

11 As Erika Nelson reminds me, the same excuses have been deployed in New Orleans to explain the shocking neglect of the survivors of Hurricane Katrina.

12 However, this strategy can have various unpredictable outcomes. In San Bartolo, despite the power of *los meros jefes*, the "fake" widows' group that they created became a multiconductor as the women lashed in church networks to create their own garden project. With enormous effort and at great risk they "learned they could support each other, that they were capable of working in a group and to take charge . . . although just a little bit [*en pequeñito*] it was an alternative form of working and relating" (González 2002:453).

13 Santiago Bastos and Manuela Camus (2003) recount in detail the complex processes that brought COPMAGUA low. Many faces simultaneously made up the coordination, all of them engaged in struggle, networking, translation, doubtless some heavy-handed politicking, and perhaps some graft. However, the well-intentioned funders, apparently hoping to support the most authentic Maya,

had trouble acknowledging this multiplicity and ended up reconciling it into a single account of Two-Faced Indians: COPMAGUA was accused of corruption and of being a Mayan front for the URNG, which led to a funding cut and the virtual disintegration of the organization.

14 In June 2005 Godínez received death threats for his resistance to World Bank–supported mining.

15 Another Two-Faced Indian was produced by this massacre. One of its orphans, Dominga, was adopted by a couple in Iowa and raised as Denese, fully assuming the identity of midwestern American teenager. Only when she was grown, married, and the mother of two children did she, with the help of a U.S. cousin, put together her nightmares with stories coming out of Guatemala to realize that she had another identity. *Discovering Dominga*, a documentary about her experiences, shows the wrenching process of moving through the three assumptions as she struggles to be Denese *and* Dominga, speaking no Spanish or Maya-Achí, but connecting to her surviving kin and assuming the role of plaintiff in the case brought against the military. There is no shortcut through the painful detours of her life.

16 *And* the facts I'm trying to make you believe, since I collaborate, accepting (begging for?) similar funding for my own research.

17 For Poovey, this duplicity is what makes the "modern fact" so "epistemologically peculiar." It seems to simply describe, to transparently grasp what is in the world. It appears untheorized and thus disinterested, a position Boyle championed with his "modest witness" (see also Haraway 1997). But "only when particulars are interpreted *as evidence* did they seem valuable enough to collect, because only then did they acquire meaning or even, I contend, identity as facts" (9). Disinterestedness comes from actively omitting the in-between of inter-esse.

18 In the play Lear wants to lay down the heavy weight of his crown's responsibilities and pass on his holdings to his three daughters, Regan, Goneril, and Cordelia. He asks them to tell him how much they love him and will divide his kingdom according to this amount. The oldest two happily exaggerate and get their pieces, while Cordelia is horror struck at the idea that love could be tallied. When asked, "What can you say to draw a third more opulent than your sisters? Speak." She can only reply, "Nothing." "Nothing will come out of nothing," Lear rages, and thus the tragedy is set in motion in which almost all the main characters perish—come to naught (see also Maurer 2005:115–21).

19 I'm not saying that Indian Givers who demand reciprocity and reckoning, like Rigoberta Menchú Tum, Esperanza León, Helen Mack, Jennifer Harbury, et al., are mere anachronisms, traces of a premodern time, due to be wrenched from their fantasy realm into the rational world of the free market. They are more *of* this world-in-action than most of us and are surviving, unlike Cordelia, perhaps because they are more willing to defy the *non du père* than she was.

20 In the early 1970s a perfect storm of floating rates of exchange, an inconvertible world currency (when the dollar went off the gold standard it became a "tautological void with no intrinsic internal value" [89]), the growth of offshore money in the Euromarkets, and the emergence of secondary markets in financial futures/options contracts generated this phenomenon (Rotman 1987:88).

21 And we recall the "meanness" of the conspiratorial stories about the epidemic that targeted not only gay men generally but Haitians, Africans, intravenous drug users, sex workers, and others considered outside orthoculture.

22 Which leads to a hilarious musical number in which the two men, one representing *scientia sexualis* and the other *ars erotica* rehearse the scholarly debates over anal eroticism via that very orifice.

NINE THE ENDS

1 Most specifically through the U.S. Marines' "Small Wars" manual, derived "from 20th century interventions in Central America" (Gordon 2003:A17) and the U.S. Army/Marine Counterinsurgency Field Manual (Petraeus 2007).

Abbas, Ackbar. 1999. "Dialectic of Deception." *Public Culture* 11(2): 347–64.

Adams, Abigail. 1997. "Organ Harvesters and Harbury: Transnational Narratives of Impunity and Accountability in Postwar Guatemala." *Mesoamerica*.

———. 1998. "Word, Work, and Worship: Engendering Evangelical Culture in Highland Guatemala and the United States." Ph.D. diss. Anthropology Department, University of Virginia.

———. 1999. "Gringas, Ghouls, and Guatemala: The 1994 Attacks on North American Women Accused of Body Organ Trafficking." *Journal of Latin American Anthropology* 4(1): 112–33.

———. 2000. "El género y la tradición de entrar en trance en las culturas mayas" [Gender and the trance tradition in Maya culture]. *Memorias del Segundo Congreso Internacional sobre El Pop Wuj*, Quetzaltenango, Guatemala.

———. 2001. "'Making One Our Word': Evangelical Q'eqchi' Mayans in Highland Guatemala." In *Holy Saints and Fiery Preachers: The Anthropology of Protestantism in Mexico and Central America*, ed. James W. Dow and Alan R. Sandstrom. Westport, Conn.: Praeger Press.

Adams, Frederick Upham. 1914. *Conquest of the Tropics: The Story of the Creative Enterprises Conducted by the United Fruit Company*. Garden City, N.Y.: Doubleday, Page.

Adams, Richard. 1970. *Crucifixion by Power*. Austin: University of Texas Press.

Adams, Richard, and Santiago Bastos. 2003. *Las relaciones étnicas en Guatemala, 1944–2000*. Antigua, Guatemala: CIRMA.

Aditjondro, George J. 2000. "Ninjas, Nanggalas, Monuments, and Mossad Manuals." In *Death Squad: The Anthropology of State Terror*, ed. Jeffrey A. Sluka. Philadelphia: University of Pennsylvania Press.

Agamben, Giorgio. 1998. *Homo Sacer: Sovereign Power and Bare Life*. Trans. Daniel Heller-Roazen. Stanford, Calif.: Stanford University Press.

Akin, David. 2002. "Worse than the Disease? As Investigators Debate Its Role in a Series of Military Killings, Anti-Malaria Drug Mefloquine Carries a Long, Strange History." *Globe and Mail*. Sept. 14: F7.

Alarcón, Norma. 1989. "Traddutora, Traditora: A Paradigmatic Figure of Chicana Feminism." *Cultural Critique*. Fall.

Aldana, Carlos, Juan Quiñónez Schwank, and Demetrio Cojtí. 1996. *Los acuerdos de paz: Efectos, lecciones y perspectivas*. Debate 34. Guatemala City: FLACSO.

Ali, S. Mahmud. 1993. *The Fearful State: Power, People, and the Internal War in South Asia*. London: Zed Books.

Alianza contra la impunidad. 2001. *Efectos de la impunidad en Guatemala: Análisis comparativo, casos Xamán, Carpio y Tululche*. Guatemala City: Servicios San Antonio.

Althusser, Louis. 1971. "Ideological State Apparatuses (Notes Towards an Investigation)." In *Lenin and Philosophy and Other Essays*. New York: Monthly Review Press.

Alvarez, Francisca. 1996. "Las Mujeres Mayas Etnocidas." *El Periódico Domingo*. Nov. 24.

Alvarez, Lizette. 2005. "Rights Group Defends Chastising of U.S." *New York Times*. June 4:A5.

America's Watch. 1986. *Civil Patrols in Guatemala*. New York: America's Watch Committee.

Amin, Samir. 1974. *Accumulation on a World Scale: A Critique of the Theory of Underdevelopment*. Vol. 1. Trans. Brian Pearce. New York: Monthly Review Press.

———. 1985. *Delinking: Towards a Polycentric World*. Trans. Michael Wolfers. London: Zed Books.

Amnesty International. 2002a. *Guatemala's Lethal Legacy: Past Impunity and Renewed Human Rights Violations*. London: International Secretariat.

———. 2002b. "The Civil Defence Patrols Re-emerge" [Internet] Sept. 4. http://web.amnesty.org/aidoc/aidoc_pdf.nsf/index/AMR340532002ENGLISH/$file/AM3405302.pdf.

Andersen, Nicolas. 1983. *Guatemala, Escuela revolucionaria de nuevos hombres*. Mexico City: Editorial Nuestro Tiempo.

Antze, Paul, and Michael Lambeck, eds. 1996. *Tense Past: Cultural Essays in Trauma and Memory*. New York: Routledge.

Appadurai, Arjun. 2006. *Fear of Small Numbers: An Essay on the Geography of Anger*. Durham, N.C.: Duke University Press.

Arenas Bianchi, Clara, Charles R. Hale, and Gustavo Palma Murga, eds. 1999. *¿Racismo en Guatemala? Abriendo el Debate sobre un tema tabú*. Guatemala City: AVANCSO.

Aretxaga, Begoña. 2000. "A Fictional Reality: Paramilitary Death Squads and the Construction of State Terror in Spain." In *Death Squad: The Anthropology of State Terror*, ed. Jeffrey A. Sluka. Philadelphia: University of Pennsylvania Press.

Argueta, Antonio. 1955. "Malaria o Paludismo, Uno de los Grandes Peligros: El azote número uno del pueblo guatemalteco." *El Imparcial*, June 16.

Arias, Arturo, ed. 2001. *The Rigoberta Menchú Controversy*. Minneapolis: University of Minnesota Press.

Armon, Jeremie, Rachel Sieder, Richard Wilson, Gustavo Palma Murga, and Tania Palencia. 1998. *Guatemala 1983–1997: ¿Hacía dónde va la transición?* Debate 38. Guatemala City: FLACSO.

Arrighi, Giovanni, and Beverly J. Silver, eds. 1999. *Chaos and Governance in the Modern World System*. Minneapolis: University of Minnesota Press.

Asad, Talal, ed. 1973. *Anthropology and the Colonial Encounter*. London: Ithaca Press.

Associated Press. 2004. "Guatemala Officials Apologize for Killing." *South Florida Sun-Sentinel*. May 4. http://www.sun-sentinel.com/news/local/caribbean/la-fg.

AVANCSO. 1992. *Dónde está el futuro? Procesos de reintegración en comunidades de retornados*. Guatemala City: AVANCSO.

———. 1999. *Por los caminos de la sobrevivencia campesina I*. Guatemala City: AVANCSO.

———. 2000. *Por los caminos de la sobrevivencia campesina II*. Guatemala City: AVANCSO.

Aznárez, Juan Jesús. 1999. "'Los que me atacan humillan a las víctimas': Entrevista Rigoberta Menchú, Líder Indígena Guatemalteca y premio Nobel de la Paz." *El País* (Spain). January 30.

Baker, Lee. 2004. "Contextualizing Du Bois: White Supremacy and the Anti-Racist Research of Franz Boas." April 8, Lecture, Georgetown College.

Bakhtin, Mikhail. 1984. *Rabelais and His World*. Bloomington: Indiana University Press.

Barrera Nuñez, Oscar. n.d. "Informe sobre las relaciones interétnicas en Todos Santos Cuchumatán." Reporte para CIRMA.

Bastos, Santiago, and Manuela Camus. 1993. *Quebrando el Silencio: Organizaciones del Pueblo Maya y sus Demandas (1986–1992)*. Guatemala City: FLACSO.

———. 1995. *Abriendo Caminos: Las Organizaciones Mayas desde el Nobel hasta el Acuerdo de Derechos Indígenas*. Guatemala City: FLACSO.

———. 2003. *Entre el mecapal y el cielo: Desarrollo del movimiento Maya en Guatemala*. Guatemala City: FLACSO and Cholsamaj.

———. n.d. "La difícil complementariedad: Relaciones entre el movimiento maya y el revolucionario (1980–2000)." Unpublished manuscript.

Baudrillard, Jean. 1983. *Simulations*. Trans. Paul Foss, Paul Patton and Philip Beitchman. New York: Semiotext(e).

———. 1987. *The Ecstasy of Communication*. Trans. Bernard and Caroline Schutze. Ed. Sylvere Lotringer. New York: Semiotext(e).

Bayart, J. F. 1991. "Finishing with the Idea of the Third World: The Concept of Political Trajectory." In *Rethinking Third World Politics*, ed. James Manor. London: Orient Longman.

Benjamin, Walter. 1969. *Illuminations*, ed. Hannah Arendt. Trans. Harry Zonh. New York: Schocken Books.

———. 2001. *The Arcades Project*. Cambridge, Mass.: Harvard University Press.

Berenstein, Rhona. 2002. "Horror for Sale: The Marketing and Reception of Classic Horror Cinema." In *Horror: The Film Reader*, ed. Mark Jancovich. London: Routledge.

Berman, Marshall. 1998. "Unchained Melody." *The Nation*. May 11: 11–16.

Beverly, John. 1993. *Against Literature*. Minneapolis: University of Minnesota Press.

———. 1996. "The Real Thing." In *The Real Thing: Testimonial Discourse and Latin America*, ed. Georg M. Gugelberger. Durham, N.C.: Duke University Press.

Bhabha, Homi K. 1994. *The Location of Culture*. London: Routledge.

———. 2004. "Foreword." In Robert Young, *White Mythologies: Writing History and the West*. 2d ed. London: Routledge.

Binford, Leigh. 1999. "Hegemony in the Interior of the Salvadoran Revolution: The ERP in Northern Morazán." *Journal of Latin American Anthropology* 4(1): 2–45.

Boone, James A. 1999. *Verging on Extra-vagance: Anthropology, History, Religion, Literature, Arts . . . Showbiz*. Princeton: Princeton University Press.

Borneman, John. 1997. *Settling Accounts: Violence, Justice, and Accountability in Post-Socialist Europe*. Princeton: Princeton University Press.

Botello, Rebeca. 2005. "The Chixoy Dam Case: Petitioning for Reparations." INFORPRESS, Feb. 25.

Bourdieu, Pierre. 1977. *Outline of a Theory of Practice*. Trans. Richard Nice. Cambridge: Cambridge University Press.

———. 1987. *Distinction: A Social Critique of the Judgment of Taste*. Cambridge, Mass.: Harvard University Press.

Bouvard, Marguerite Guzman. 1994. *Revolutionizing Motherhood: The Mothers of the Plaza de Mayo*. Wilmington, Del.: Scholarly Resources.

Boyarin, J., ed. 1994. *Remapping Memory: The Politics of Timespace*. Minneapolis: University of Minnesota Press.

Bricker, Victoria Reifler. 1973. *Ritual Humor in Highland Chiapas*. Austin: University of Texas Press.

Brintnall, Douglas. 1979. *Revolt Against the Dead: The Modernization of a Mayan Community in the Highlands of Guatemala*. New York: Gordon and Breach.

Brock, David. 2002. *Blinded by the Right: The Conscience of an Ex-Conservative*. New York: Crown Press.

Broder, John M. 1999. "Clinton Offers His Apologies to Guatemala." *New York Times*, March 11: A1.

Brody, Jane E. 2001. "More Than Just a Nuisance, a Virtuoso of Disease: Epidemiologists Say the Spread of a Variety of Mosquito-borne Viruses Is Just a Matter of Time." *New York Times*, Aug. 7: D1, D8.

Brown, Aisha. 2005. "Justice Served? Commemoration and Reparations in Plan de Sánchez." *Report on Guatemala* 26(3) Fall.

Brown, Wendy. 1995. *States of Injury: Power and Freedom in Late Modernity*. Princeton: Princeton University Press.

Brunvand, Jan Harold. 1986. *The Choking Doberman and Other Urban Legends*. New York: Norton.

Bunster-Burotto, Ximena. 1986. "Surviving Beyond Fear: Women and Torture in Latin America." In *Women and Change in Latin America*, ed. June Nash and Helen Safa. South Hadley, Mass.: Bergin and Garvey.

Bunzel, Ruth. 1952. *Chichicastenango, a Guatemalan Village*. Locust Valley, N.Y.: J. J. Augustin.

Burrell, Jennifer. 2000. "Update: The Aftermath of Lynching in Todos Santos." *Report on Guatemala* 21(4) Winter: 12–14.

Burt, Jo-Marie, and Fred Rosen. 1999. "Truth-Telling and Memory in Postwar Guatemala: An Interview with Rigoberta Menchú." *NACLA Report on the Americas* 32(5) March/April: 6–10.

Butler, Judith. 1987. *Subjects of Desire: Hegelian Reflections in Twentieth-Century France*. New York: Columbia University Press.

———. 1993. *Bodies that Matter: On the Discursive Limits of "Sex."* London: Routledge.

———. 1997. *The Psychic Life of Power: Theories in Subjection*. Stanford, Calif.: Stanford University Press.

———. 2004. *Precarious Life*. London: Verso Press.

Cadigan, Pat. 1991. *Synners*. New York: Bantam Books.

CALDH (Centro para Acción Legal en Derechos Humanos/Human Rights Legal Action Center). 2000. *Justicia y reconciliación: Pasos prácticos para un futuro con paz*. Guatemala City: CALDH.

Camus, Manuela. 2005. *La colonia Primero de Julio y la "clase media emergente."* Guatemala City: FLACSO.

Canby, Peter. 1999. "The Truth About Rigoberta Menchú." *New York Review of Books*, April 8, 28–33.

Cardoso, Fernando Henrique, and Enzo Faletto. 1979. *Dependency and Development in Latin America.* Trans. Marjory Mattingly Urquidi. Berkeley: University of California Press.

Carmack, Robert M. 1988. *Harvest of Violence: The Mayan Indians and the Guatemalan Crisis.* Norman: University of Oklahoma Press.

———. 1995. *Rebels of Highland Guatemala.* Norman: University of Oklahoma Press.

Carroll, Noël. 2002. "Why Horror?" In *Horror: The Film Reader*, ed. Mark Jancovich. London: Routledge.

Carson, Rachel. 1994 (1962). *Silent Spring.* Boston: Houghton Mifflin.

Casaus Arzú, Marta. 1992. *Guatemala: Linaje y Racismo.* Costa Rica: FLACSO.

———. 1998. *La metamorfosis del racismo en Guatemala.* Guatemala City: Cholsamaj.

Castañeda, Quetzil. 1996. *In the Museum of Mayan Culture: Touring Chichén Itzá.* Minneapolis: University of Minnesota Press.

Castel, Robert. 1991. "From Dangerousness to Risk." In *The Foucault Effect: Studies in Governmentality*, ed. Graham Burchell, Colin Gordon, and Peter Miller. Chicago: University of Chicago Press.

Castells, Manuel. 1989. *The Informational City: Information Technology, Economic Restructuring, and the Urban-Regional Process.* Oxford: Basil Blackwell.

CEH (Comisión de Esclarecimiento Histórico/United Nations Commission of Historical Clarification). 1999. *Guatemala: Memory of Silence, Tz'inil Na'tab'al.* 12 vols. Guatemala City: United Nations.

CEIDEC. 1988. *Guatemala Polos de Desarrollo: El Caso de la desestrucción de las comunidades indígenas.* Vol. 2. Mexico City: CEIDEC.

Cesaire, Aimé. 1972. *Discourse on Colonialism.* New York: Monthly Review Press.

Chirix García, Emma Delfina. 2003. *Alas y Raíces: Afectividad de las mujeres mayas/ Rik'in ruxik' y ruxe'il: ronojel kajowab'al ri mayab'taq izoqi'.* Guatemala City: Grupo de Mujeres Mayas Kaqla.

Chronicle of Higher Education. 1999. "Footnotes," March 12.

Cifuentes, Juan Fernando. 1982. "Operación Ixil." *Revista Militar* 27 (Sept./Dec.): 25–72.

———. 1998. *Historia moderna de la etnicidad en Guatemala, la vision hegemónica: Rebeliones y otros incidentes indígenas en el siglo XX.* Guatemala City: Universidad Rafael Landívar.

Clendinnen, Inga. 1987. *Ambivalent Conquests: Maya and Spaniard in Yucatan, 1517–1570.* Cambridge: Cambridge University Press.

———. 1991. *Aztecs: An Interpretation.* Cambridge: Cambridge University Press.

Clifford, James. 1986. *Writing Culture.* Berkeley: University of California Press.

———. 1988. *The Predicament of Culture: Twentieth-Century Ethnography, Literature, and Art.* Cambridge, Mass.: Harvard University Press.

Clover, Carol. 1992. *Men, Women, and Chainsaws: Gender in the Modern Horror Film.* Princeton: Princeton University Press.

Cojti Cuxil, Demetrio, aka Waqi' Q'anil. 1990. *Configuración del pensamiento político del Pueblo Maya.* Part. 1. Quetzaltenango, Guatemala: AEMG.

———. 1994. *Políticas para la reivindicación de los Mayas de hoy (Fundamento de los Derechos Específicos del Pueblo Maya).* 2 vols. Guatemala City: Cholsamaj.

———. 1995. *Ub'anik Ri Una'ooj Uchomab'aal Ri Maya' Tinamit: Configuración del pensamiento político del Pueblo Maya.* Part 2. Guatemala City: Cholsamaj.

Collier, Jane Fishburne, Bill Maurer, and Liliana Suarez-Navaz. 1995. "Sanctioned Identities: Legal Constructions of 'Modern' Personhood." *Identities: Global Studies in Culture and Power* 2(1).

Comaroff, Jean, and John L. Comaroff. 1999. "Occult Economies and the Violence of Abstraction: Notes from the South African Postcolony." *American Ethnologist* 26(2): 279–303.

———. 2003. "Transparent Fictions: or, The Conspiracies of a Liberal Imagination: An Afterword." In *Transparency and Conspiracy: Ethnographies of Suspicion in the New World Order*, ed. Harry G. West and Todd Sanders. Durham, N.C.: Duke University Press.

Comaroff, Jean, and John L. Comaroff, eds. 2001. *Millennial Capitalism and the Culture of Neoliberalism.* Durham, N.C.: Duke University Press.

COMG (Guatemalan Council of Mayan Organizations). 1995. "Análisis evaluativo sobre el Acuerdo de Paz: Identidad y derechos de los Pueblos Indígenas." *B'oko'*, April.

Cook, Garrett W. 2000. *Renewing the Maya World: Expressive Culture in a Highland Town.* Austin: University of Texas Press.

Coombe, Rosemary. 1997. "The Demonic Place of the 'Not There': Trademark Rumors in the Postindustrial Imagination." In *Culture, Power, Place: Explorations in Critical Anthropology*, eds. Akhil Gupta and James Ferguson. Durham, N.C.: Duke University Press.

COPMAGUA (Coordination of Organizations of the Pueblo Maya of Guatemala). 1995. *Acuerdo Sobre Identidad y Derechos de los Pueblos Indígenas.* Guatemala City: Cholsamaj.

Coronil, Fernando. 1996. "Beyond Occidentalism: Toward Nonimperial Geohistorical Categories." *Cultural Anthropology* 11(1).

———. 1997. *The Magical State: Nature, Money, and Modernity in Venezuela.* Chicago: University of Chicago Press.

Coutin, Susan Bibler, and Susan F. Hirsch. 1998. "Naming Resistance: Ethnographers, Dissidents, and States." *Anthropological Quarterly* 71(1): 1–17.

Crónica. 1993. "El libro que desató un escándolo." April 30.

Cullather, Nick. 1999. *Secret History: The CIA's Classified Account of its Operations in Guatemala, 1952–1954.* Stanford, Calif.: Stanford University Press.

Dagnino, Evelina, Sonia E. Alvarez, and Arturo Escobar, eds. 1998. *Cultures of Politics/ Politics of Cultures: Re-Visioning Latin American Social Movements.* Boulder: Westview.

Dary Fuentes, Claudia. 1991. *Mujeres tradicionales y nuevos cultivos.* Guatemala City: FLACSO.

Davis, Mike. 1998. *Ecology of Fear: Los Angeles and the Imagination of Disaster*. New York: Vintage Books.

Dean, Cornelia. 2005. "Evolution Takes a Back Seat in U.S. Classes." *New York Times*, Feb. 1:D1, D6.

de Gregori, Carlos. 1989. *¿Qué difícil es ser Dios? Ideología y violencia política en Sendero Luminoso*. Lima: El Zorro de Abajo Ediciones.

de la Cadena, Marisol. 1996. "The Political Tensions of Representations and Misrepresentations: Intellectuals and *Mestizas* in Cuzco (1919–1990)." *Journal of Latin American Anthropology* 2(1).

del Cid, Marvin. 2004. "Patrulleros y diputados, Pac a la fuerza." *Prensa Libre*, Aug. 29.

Delgado Pop, Amanda, Juana Batzibal Tujal, María Luisa Curruchich Gómez, Virginia Ajxup Pelicó, Lucía Willis Paau, Luisa Anaité Galeotti Moraga, Amanda Pop Bol, and Emma Defina Chirix García. 2000. *Identidades: Rostros sin máscaras (Reflexiones sobre cosmovisión, género, y etnicidad)*. Guatemala City: Oxfam-Australia.

del Valle, Ruth, Claudia Samayoa, Ana Gladis Ollas, Erenia Vanegas and María Martín. 2006. *El terror se expande: Análisis de ataques contra defensores y defensoras de Derechos Humanos durante el año 2005*. Guatemala City: Movimiento Nacional por los Derechos Humanos.

Dill, Kathleen. 2005. "Guatemala's 'Transitionless' Transition Towards Democracy." NISGUA website, http://www.nisgua.org/articles/guatemala.htm.

Doane, Mary Ann. 1991. *Femmes Fatales: Feminism, Film Theory, Psychoanalysis*. New York: Routledge.

Dorfman, Ariel. 2001. "America Looks at Itself Through Humanity's Mirror." *Los Angeles Times*, September 21.

Dosal, Paul J. 1993. *Doing Business with the Dictators: A Political History of United Fruit in Guatemala 1899–1944*. Wilmington, Del.: Scholarly Resources Books.

Driscoll, Mark. 1994. "Bring the Tropes Home!" *Journal of Urban and Popular Culture*. Summer.

———. 2000. "Erotic Empire, Grotesque Empire." Ph.D. diss., Department of East Asian Studies, Cornell University.

———. 2003. "Ideology vs. Immanence, or Why *The Matrix* is Better than Hardt and Negri's Empire." *Gendai Shisô*, Dec.

———. 2009. "White Dude's Burden." *Cultural Studies*, in press.

———. n.d. "Fluidarity Forever." Manuscript.

Du Bois, W. E. B. 1989 (1903). *The Souls of Black Folk*. New York: Bantam Books.

Durkheim, Emile. 1995. *The Elementary Forms of Religious Life*. Trans. Karen E. Fields. New York: Simon and Schuster.

The Economist. 2004. "Putting the World to Rights: Special Report Copenhagen Consensus." June 5: 63–65.

———. 2004. "Becoming a Serious Country." Special Section "The Long Road Back, a Survey of Argentina." June 5: 1–12.

Edmundson, Mark. 1997. *Nightmare on Main Street: Angels, Sadomasochism, and the Culture of Gothic*. Cambridge, Mass.: Harvard University Press.

Eglash, Ron. 1999. *African Fractals: Modern Computing and Indigenous Design*. New Jersey: Rutgers University Press.

Escobar, Arturo. 1995. *Encountering Development: The Making and Unmaking of the Third World*. Princeton: Princeton University Press.

Esquit, Edgar. 2002. *Otros poderes, nuevos desafíos: Relaciones interétnicas en Tecpán y su entorno departamental*. Guatemala City: Instituto de Estudios Interétnicos.

Evans, Harold. 2005. "Follow the Money." *New York Times Book Review*, March 13: 14–15.

Evans Prichard, E. E. 1937. *Witchcraft, Oracles and Magic among the Azande of the Anglo-Egyptian Sudan*. Oxford: Clarendon Press.

Ewald, François. 1991. "Insurance and Risk." In *The Foucault Effect: Studies in Governmentality*, ed. Graham Burchell, Colin Gordon, and Peter Miller. Chicago: University of Chicago Press.

Falla, Ricardo. 1980. *Quiché Rebelde: Estudio de un movimiento de conversión religiosa, rebelde a las creencias tradicionales, en San Antonio Ilotenango, Quiché (1948–1970)*. Guatemala City: Editorial Universitaria.

———. 1984. "We Charge Genocide." In *Guatemala: Tyranny on Trial, Testimony of the Permanent People's Tribunal*, ed. Susanne Jonas, Ed McCaughan, and Elizabeth Sutherland Martínez. San Francisco: Synthesis Publications.

———. 1988. "Struggle for Survival in the Mountains: Hunger and Other Privations Inflicted on Internal Refugees from the Central Highlands." In *Harvest of Violence: The Mayan Indians and the Guatemalan Crisis*, ed. Robert Carmack. Norman: University of Oklahoma Press.

———. 1992. *Masacres de la Selva: Ixcán, Guatemala, 1975–1982*. Guatemala City: Editorial Universitaria.

Farmer, Paul. 2006. *AIDS and Accusation: Haiti and the Geography of Blame*. Berkeley: University of California Press.

Feldman, Allan. 1995. "Afterword." In *Fieldwork Under Fire: Contemporary Studies of Violence and Survival*, ed. Carolyn Nordstrom and Antonius C. G. M. Robben. Berkeley: University of California Press.

Ferguson, James. 1994. *The Anti-Politics Machine: 'Development,' Depoliticization and Bureaucratic Power in Lesotho*. Cambridge: Cambridge University Press.

———. 1999. *Expectations of Modernity: Myths and Meanings of Urban Life on the Zambian Copperbelt*. Berkeley: University of California Press.

Fernández, Nelson. 2004. "Pago a ex patrulleros: Más conveniente que convincente." *INFORPRESS* 27:8–9.

Figueroa Ibarra, Carlos. 1991. *El recurso del miedo: Ensayo sobre el Estado y el terror en Guatemala*. San Jose, Costa Rica: Editorial Universitaria Centroamericana.

Filóchofo. 1999. *La otra historia (de los mayas al informe de la "comisión de la verdad")*. Guatemala City: HIVOS/Arte, Color, y Texto.

Fischer, Edward F. 2001. *Cultural Logics and Global Economies: Maya Identity in Thought and Practice*. Austin: University of Texas Press.

Fischer, Edward F., and R. McKenna Brown, eds. 1996. *Maya Cultural Activism in Guatemala*. Austin: University of Texas Press.

Flores, Carlos Y. 2004. "Indigenous Video, Development and Shared Anthropology: A Collaborative Experiment with Maya-Q'eqchi' Filmmakers in Post-War Guatemala." *Visual Anthropology Review*. 20(1): 31–44.

Foner, Eric. 2004. "True Patriotism: What to the Slave Is the Fourth of July?" *The Nation*, July 19/26: 10.

Foner, Eric, and Randall Kennedy, eds. 2004. "*Brown* at 50." *The Nation*, May 3: 15–50.

Foro Ecuménico por la Paz y la Reconciliación. 2005. *Guatemala: El dilema ético de la violencia*. July, Litografía Nawaj Wuj.

Fortun, Kim. 2001. *Advocacy after Bhopal: Environmentalism, Disaster, New Global Orders*. Chicago: University of Chicago Press.

Foucault, Michel. 1979. *Discipline and Punish: The Birth of the Prison*. New York: Vintage Books.

———. 1980a. *History of Sexuality Volume I, An Introduction*. Trans. Robert Hurley. New York: Vintage Books.

———. 1980b. *Power/Knowledge: Selected Interviews and Other Writings 1972–1977*, ed. Colin Gordon. New York: Pantheon.

———. 1981. "Omnes et Singulatim: Towards a Criticism of 'Political Reason.'" *The Tanner Lectures on Human Values*. Vol. 2, ed. Sterling M. McMurrin. Salt Lake City: University of Utah Press.

———. 1991a. *Remarks on Marx: Conversations with Duccio Trombadori*. Trans. R. James Goldstein and James Cascaito. New York: Semiotext(e).

———. 1991b. "Governmentality." In *The Foucault Effect: Studies in Governmentality*, ed. Graham Burchell, Colin Gordon, and Peter Miller. Chicago: University of Chicago Press.

Franco, Jean. 1999. *Critical Passions: Selected Essays*, eds. Mary Louise Pratt and Kathleen Newman. Durham, N.C.: Duke University Press.

Freud, Sigmund. 1963. *Jokes and Their Relation to the Unconscious*. Trans. James Strachey. New York: W. W. Norton.

Fundación Myrna Mack. 2000. *Myrna: Décimo aniversario del asesinato de Myrna Mack*. Guatemala City.

Fuss, Diana. 1995. *Identification Papers*. New York: Routledge.

Fussell, Paul. 1983. *Class: A Guide through the American Status System*. New York: Simon and Schuster.

García, Eduardo. 2004a. "Cooperación internacional, ¿medicina o droga?" *INFORPRESS*, June 4:8–9.

———. 2004b. "Cooperación internacional, ¿medicina o droga?—II." *INFORPRESS*, June 11:5–6.

———. 2004c. "Cooperación internacional, ¿medicina o droga?—III." *INFORPRESS*, July 2:6–7.

García Escober, Carlos Rene. 1998. www.uweb.ucsb.edu/~jce2/cescobar.htm.

Garrard-Burnett, Virginia. 1998. *Protestantism in Guatemala: Living in the New Jerusalem*. Austin: University of Texas Press.

Geertz, Clifford. 1980. *Negara: The Theater State of Nineteenth-Century Bali*. Princeton: Princeton University Press.

Ghosh, Amitav. 1994. *In an Antique Land*. New York: Vintage Books.

———. 1995. *The Calcutta Chromosome: A Novel of Fevers, Delirium, and Discovery*. New York: Avon Books.

Gladwell, Malcolm. 2001. "Annals of Public Health: The Mosquito Killer." *New Yorker*, July 2: 42–51.

Gleijeses, Piero. 1991. *Shattered Hope*. Princeton: Princeton University Press.

González, Matilde. 2002. *Se Cambió el Tiempo: Conflicto y poder en territorio K'iche' 1880–1996*. Guatemala City: AVANCSO.

González Ponciano, Jorge Ramón. 1991. "Guatemala, la civilización y el progreso: Notas sobre Indigenismo, Racismo e Identidad Nacional 1821–1954." In *Anuario: Instituto Chiapaneco de Cultura*. Tuxtla Gutierrez, Mexico: Dept. de Patrimonio Cultura e Investigación.

———. 1997. "'Esas Sangres No Están Limpias' El Racismo, el Estado y la Nación en Guatemala (1944–1997)." Anuario Separata, San Cristóbal las Casas, Mexico: Centro de Estudios Superiores de México y Centroamérica.

———. 2005. "De la patria del criollo a la patria del shumo." Ph.D. diss. Anthropology Department, University of Texas, Austin.

Gordillo, Gastón R. 2004. *Landscapes of Devils: Tensions of Place and Memory in the Argentinean Chaco*. Durham, N.C.: Duke University Press.

Gordon, Michael R. 2003. "Leathernecks Plan to Use Velvet Glove More than Iron Fist in Dealing with Iraqis." *New York Times*, Dec. 12:A17.

Government of Guatemala. 1985. *Polos de desarrollo y servicios: Filosofía desarrollista, Historiografía institucional*. Guatemala City: Editorial del Ejército (Army Press).

Gramajo, Hector. 1995. *De la guerra . . . a la guerra*. Guatemala City: Fondo de Cultura Editorial.

Gramsci, Antonio. 1989. *Selections from the Prison Notebooks*, eds. and trans. Quintin Hoare and Geoffrey Nowell Smith. New York: International Publishers.

Grandin, Greg. 1995. "Taking Sides: Resistance and Its Representation in New Guatemalan Scholarship." *Radical History Review* 63:189–99.

———. 1998. "He Said, She Said." *Anthropology Newsletter*, American Anthropology Association.

———. 2000a. *The Blood of Guatemala: A History of Race and Nation*. Durham, N.C.: Duke University Press.

———. 2000b. "No Victory for Dictators." *New York Times*, March 7.

———. 2000c. "Chronicles of a Guatemalan Genocide Foretold: Violence, Trauma, and the Limits of Historical Inquiry." *Nepantla: Views from the South* 1(2) 391–412.

———. 2004. *The Last Colonial Massacre: Latin America in the Cold War*. Chicago: University of Chicago Press.

———. 2006. *Empire's Workshop: Latin America, the United States, and the Rise of the New Imperialism*. New York: Metropolitan Books.

Grandin, Greg, and Francisco Goldman. 1999. "The Attack on Rigoberta Menchú." *The Nation*, February 8.

Green, Linda. 1995. "Living in a State of Fear." In *Fieldwork Under Fire: Contemporary Studies of Violence and Survival*, ed. Carolyn Nordstrom and Antonius C. G. M. Robben. Berkeley: University of California Press.

———. 1999. *Fear as a Way of Life: Mayan Widows in Rural Guatemala*. New York: Columbia University Press.

Grupo de Mujeres Mayas Kaqla. 2004. *La palabra y el sentir de las mujeres mayas de kaqla*. Guatemala City: Cholsamaj.

————. 2006. *La internalización de la opresión: Una propuesta metodológica*. Guatemala City: Cholsamaj.

Gugelberger, Georg M. 1996. *The Real Thing: Testimonial Discourse and Latin America*. Durham, N.C.: Duke University Press.

Guha, Ranajit. 1983. *Elementary Aspects of Peasant Insurgency in Colonial India*. Delhi: Oxford University Press.

————. 1988. "The Prose of Counterinsurgency." In *Selected Subaltern Studies*, ed. Ranajit Guha and Gayatri Chakravorty Spivak. Oxford: Oxford University Press.

Gunder Frank, Andre. 1970. *Latin America: Underdevelopment or Revolution: Essays on the Development of Underdevelopment and the Immediate Enemy*. New York: Monthly Review Press.

Gunder Frank, Andre, and Barry K. Gills, eds. 1993. *The World System: Five Hundred Years or Five Thousand?* London: Routledge.

Gupta, Akhil. 1998. *Postcolonial Developments: Agriculture in the Making of Modern India*. Durham, N.C.: Duke University Press.

Gutiérrez, Marta Estela, and Paul Hans Kobrak. 2001. *Los linchamientos pos conflicto y violencia colectiva en Huehuetenango Guatemala*. Guatemala City: CEDFOG (Centro de Estudios y Documentación de la Frontera Occidental de Guatemala).

Guoz, Abner. 2005. "Ex patrulleros se acercan al PNR para pedir resarcimiento." *El Periódico*, Jan. 7:5.

Halberstam, Judith. 1995. *Skin Shows: Gothic Horror and the Technology of Monsters*. Durham, N.C.: Duke University Press.

Hale, Charles R. 1994a. *Resistance and Contradiction: Miskitu Indians and the Nicaraguan State, 1894–1987*. Stanford, Calif.: Stanford University Press.

————. 1994b. "Between Che Guevara and the Pachamama: Mestizos, Indians and Identity Politics in the Anti-Quincentenary Campaign." *Critique of Anthropology* 14(1): 9–39.

————. 1996. "*Mestizaje*, Hybridity, and the Cultural Politics of Difference in Post-Revolutionary Central America." *Journal of Latin American Anthropology* 2(1).

————. 1997. "Consciousness, Violence and the Politics of Memory in Guatemala." *Current Anthropology* 38(5).

————. 2006. *Más Que un Indio/ More Than an Indian: Racial Ambivalence and Neoliberal Multiculturalism in Guatemala*. Santa Fe: School of American Research.

Haley, Brian D. 1999. Letter to the Editor. *Chronicle of Higher Education*. February 12.

Hall, Stuart. 1992. "What Is This 'Black' in Black Popular Culture?" In *Black Popular Culture*, ed. Gina Dent. Seattle: Bay Press.

————. 1996. "When Was 'the Post-Colonial?' Thinking at the Limit." In *The Post-Colonial Question: Common Skies, Divided Horizons*. London: Routledge.

Handy, Jim. 1984. *Gift of the Devil: A History of Guatemala*. Boston: South End Press.

————. 1994. *Revolution in the Countryside: Rural Conflict and Agrarian Reform in Guatemala, 1944–54*. Chapel Hill: University of North Carolina Press.

Hansen, Thomas, and Finn Stepputat. 2001. "Introduction." In *States of Imagination: Ethnographic Explorations of the Postcolonial State*. Durham, N.C.: Duke University Press.

Haraway, Donna J. 1991. "A Manifesto for Cyborgs." In *Simians, Cyborgs, and Women: The Reinvention of Nature*. New York: Routledge.

———. 1995. "Cyborgs and Symbionts: Living Together in the New World Order." In *The Cyborg Handbook*, ed. Chris Hables Gray, with Heidi J. Figueroa-Sarriera and Steven Mentor. New York: Routledge.

———. 1997. *Modest Witness@Second Millennium.FemaleMan© Meets OncoMouse™: Feminism and Technoscience*. New York: Routledge.

Harbury, Jennifer. 1994. *Bridge of Courage: Life Stories of the Guatemalan Compañeros and Compañeras*. Monroe, Maine: Common Courage Press.

———. 2000. *Searching for Everardo: A Story of Love, War, and the CIA in Guatemala*. New York: Warner Books.

Hardt, Michael, and Antonio Negri. 2000. *Empire*. Cambridge, Mass.: Harvard University Press.

Harper, Richard. 2000. "The Social Organization of the IMF's Mission Work: An Examination of International Auditing." In *Audit Cultures: Anthropological Studies in Accountability, Ethics, and the Academy*, ed. Marilyn Strathern. London: Routledge.

Harvey, David. 2003. *The New Imperialism*. Oxford: Oxford University Press.

———. 2005. *A Brief History of Neoliberalism*. Oxford: Oxford University Press.

Hawkins, Joan. 2002. "Sleaze Mania, Euro-Trash, and High Art." In *Horror: The Film Reader*, ed. Mark Jancovich. London: Routledge.

Heller, Terry. 1987. *The Delights of Terror: An Aesthetics of the Tale of Terror*. Urbana: University of Illinois Press.

Hendrickson, Carol. 1995. *Weaving Identities: Construction of Dress and Self in a Highland Guatemala Town*. Austin: University of Texas Press.

Hernández Pico, Juan. 2005. *Terminar la guerra, traicionar la paz: Guatemala en las dos presidencias de la paz: Arzú y Portillo (1996–2004)*. Guatemala City: Editorial de Ciencias Sociales, FLACSO.

Hersh, Seymour M. 2004. *Chain of Command: The Road from 9/11 to Abu Ghraib*. New York: HarperCollins.

Herzfeld, Michael. 1992. *The Social Production of Indifference: Exploring the Symbolic Roots of Western Bureaucracy*. Chicago: University of Chicago Press.

Hess, David J. 1995. "On Low-Tech Cyborgs." In *The Cyborg Handbook*, ed. Chris Hables Gray, with Heidi J. Figueroa-Sarriera and Steven Mentor. New York: Routledge.

Hill, Robert. 1992. *Colonial Cakchiquels: Highland Maya Adaptation to Spanish Rule 1600–1700*. Fort Worth: Harcourt Brace Jovanovich.

Hill, Tami R. 2000. "Indigenous Cultural Survival in Postwar Guatemala: Historical Truth, Memory, Identity and the Role of the Exhumation Process." MA thesis, University of Oregon.

Hinton, Alexander Laban. 2005. *Why Did They Kill? Cambodia in the Shadow of Genocide*. Berkeley: University of California Press.

Hinton, Alexander Laban, ed. 2002. *Annihilating Difference: The Anthropology of Genocide*. Berkeley: University of California Press.

Hofstadter, Richard. 1965. *The Paranoid Style in American Politics and Other Essays*. Cambridge, Mass.: Harvard University Press.

Hollander, Nancy Caro. 1997. *Love in a Time of Hate: Liberation Psychology in Latin America*. New Brunswick, N.J.: Rutgers University Press.

Honigsbaum, Mark. 2001. *The Fever Trail: In Search of the Cure for Malaria*. New York: Farrar, Straus, and Giroux.

Hoogvelt, Ankie. 1997. *Globalization and the Postcolonial World: The New Political Economy of Development*. Baltimore: Johns Hopkins University Press.

hooks, bell. 1984. *Feminist Theory: From Margin to Center*. Boston: South End Press.

———. 1992. "Madonna." In *Black Looks: Race and Representation*. Boston: South End Press.

Hulme, Peter. 1992 (1986). *Colonial Encounters: Europe and the Native Caribbean 1492–1797*. London: Routledge.

Humphreys, Margaret. 2001. *Malaria: Poverty, Race and Public Health in the United States*. Baltimore: Johns Hopkins University Press.

Huntington, Samuel. 2004. *Who Are We?: The Challenges to America's National Identity*. New York: Simon and Schuster.

Hurston, Zora Neale. 1990 (1935). *Mules and Men*. New York: Harper and Row.

Hutcheson, Maury. 2003. "Cultural Memory and the Dance-Dramas of Guatemala: History, Performance, and Identity among the Achi Maya of Rabinal." Ph.D. diss., Department of Anthropology, State University of New York at Buffalo.

INFORPRESS Central America Report. 2002. "Reparations Closer to Reality." Nov. 29: 1–2.

INFORPRESS Centroamericana. 1996. *Compendio del Proceso de Paz II: Análisis, cronologías, documentos, acuerdos*. Guatemala City: INFORPRESS.

———. 2003a. "Ex PAC, retorna lenguaje de guerra." April 4:8–9.

———. 2003b. "Remesas familiares rescatan país de recesión." May 23:1–3.

IOB / Intelligence Oversight Board. 1996. Report on the Guatemala Review. Anthony S. Harrington and Chairman General Lew Allen, Jr. USAF (Ret.) Ann Z. Caracristi, Harold W. Pote.

Irigaray, Luce. 1985 (1977). *This Sex Which Is Not One*. Trans. Catherine Porter. Ithaca: Cornell University Press.

Irwin, William, ed. 2002. *The Matrix and Philosophy: Welcome to the Desert of the Real*. Chicago: Open Court.

Jackson, John L. 2006. *Real Black: Adventures in Racial Sincerity*. Chicago: University of Chicago Press.

Jameson, Fredric. 1981. *The Political Unconscious: Narrative as a Socially Symbolic Act*. Ithaca: Cornell University Press.

Jancovich, Mark, ed. 2002. *Horror: The Film Reader*. London: Routledge.

Jaramillo, Velia. 2004. "CICIACS abre la puerta a la justicia internacional." *INFORPRESS*, no. 1544, Jan. 23.

Jay, Alice. 1993. *Persecution by Proxy: The Civil Patrols in Guatemala*. New York: Robert F. Kennedy Memorial Center for Human Rights.

Johnson, Randall, and Robert Stam, eds. 1988 (1969). *Brazilian Cinema*. Austin: University of Texas Press.

Jonas, Susanne. 2000. *Of Centaurs and Doves: Guatemala's Peace Process*. Boulder: Westview Press.

Jordanova, L. 1984. *Lamarck*. New York: Oxford University Press.

Joxe, Alain. 2002. *Empire of Disorder*, ed. Sylvére Lotringer, trans. Ames Hodges. Los Angeles: Semiotext(e).

Kadetsky, Elizabeth. 1994. "Guatemala Inflamed: Accused of Stealing or Murdering Babies, American Women Are Attacked by Hysterical Mobs." *Village Voice*, May 31.

Kantorowicz, Ernst H. 1981 (1957). *The King's Two Bodies: A Study in Mediaeval Political Theology*. Princeton: Princeton University Press.

Kick, Russ. 2001. *You Are Being Lied To: The Disinformation Guide to Media Distortion, Historical Whitewashes and Cultural Myths*. New York: Disinformation Company, Ltd.

Kinzer, Stephen, and Stephen Schlesinger. 1983. *Bitter Fruit*. New York: Doubleday Books.

Kipnis, Laura. 1993. *Ecstasy Unlimited: On Sex, Capital, Gender, and Aesthetics*. Minneapolis: University of Minnesota Press.

Kobrak, Paul Hans. 1997. "Village Troubles: The Civil Patrols in Aguacatán, Guatemala." Ph.D. diss., Department of Sociology, University of Michigan.

Körner, Peter, Gero Maass, Thomas Siebold, and Rainer Tetzlaff. 1984. *The IMF and the Debt Crisis: A Guide to the Third World's Dilemma*. Trans. Paul Knight. London: Zed Books.

Kulish, Nicholas. 2006. "Spike Lee Films the New Orleans Disaster His Way." *New York Times*. August 21:A20.

Kumar, Amitava. 1997. "The Calcutta Chromosome." *The Nation*, Sept. 27, 265(9): 36.

Kyrou, Ado. 1963. *Le Surrealisme au Cinema*. Paris: Le Terrain Vague.

Lacan, Jacques. 1977. *Ecrits: A Selection*. Trans. Alan Sheridan. New York: W. W. Norton.

Laclau, Ernesto, and Chantal Mouffe. 1985. *Hegemony and Socialist Strategy: Towards a Radical Democratic Politics*. London: Verso.

Laclau, Ernesto. 2004. *The Denigration of the Masses*. New York: Verso.

La Hora. 1990. Editorial. August 11.

———. 2003. "Berger hace llamado a activistas DDHH a integrar su gobierno." July 28.

Latham, Rob. 2002. *Consuming Youth: Vampires, Cyborgs and the Culture of Consumption*. Chicago: University of Chicago Press.

Latour, Bruno. 1987. *Science in Action: How to Follow Scientists and Engineers through Society*. Cambridge, Mass.: Harvard University Press.

———. 1988. *The Pasteurization of France*. Trans. Alan Sheridan and John Law. Cambridge, Mass.: Harvard University Press.

———. 2002. *War of the Worlds: What About Peace?* ed. John Resche, trans. Charlotte Bigg. Chicago: Prickly Paradigm Press.

Le Bot, Yvon. 1995. *La guerra en tierras mayas: Comunidad, violencia y modernidad en Guatemala (1970–1992)*. Mexico City: Fondo de Cultura Económica.

le Carré, John. 2001a. "Big Pharma: In Place of Nations." *The Nation*, April 9, 11–13.

———. 2001b. *The Constant Gardener*. New York: Simon and Schuster.

Levenson-Estrada, Deborah. 1994. *Trade Unionists Against Terror: Guatemala City, 1954–1985*. Chapel Hill: University of North Carolina Press.

Lévi-Strauss, Claude. 1969. *Elementary Structures of Kinship*. Boston: Beacon Press.

Lewontin, Richard. 2000. *The Triple Helix: Gene, Organism, and Environment*. Cambridge, Mass.: Harvard University Press.

Leys, Ruth. 2000. *Trauma: A Genealogy*. Chicago: University of Chicago Press.

Linder, R. Ruth. 1999. Letter to the Editor. *Chronicle of Higher Education*. February 12.

Linebaugh, Peter, and Marcus Rediker. 2000. *The Many-Headed Hydra: Sailors, Slaves, Commoners, and the Hidden History of the Revolutionary Atlantic*. Boston: Beacon Press.

LiPuma, Edward, and Benjamin Lee. 2004. *Financial Derivatives and the Globalization of Risk*. Durham, N.C.: Duke University Press.

Loucky, James, and Marilyn M. Moors. 2000. *The Maya Diaspora: Guatemalan Roots, New American Lives*. Philadelphia: Temple University Press.

Lutz, Catherine, and Jon Elliston. 2002. "Domestic Terror." *The Nation*, Oct. 14:18–20.

Maldonado, Oscar. 2007. *So That All Shall Know / Para que todos lo sepan: Photographs by Daniel Hernández-Salazar*. Austin: University of Texas Press.

Malinowski, Bronislaw. 1961 (1922). *Argonauts of the Western Pacific*. New York: Dutton.

Mamdani, Mahmood. 1996. *Citizen and Subject: Contemporary Africa and the Legacy of Colonialism*. Princeton: Princeton University Press.

———. 2001. *When Victims Become Killers: Colonialism, Nativism, and the Genocide in Rwanda*. Princeton: Princeton University Press.

Manz, Beatriz. 1988. *Refugees of a Hidden War: Aftermath of Counterinsurgency in Guatemala*. Albany: SUNY Press.

———. 2004. *Paradise in Ashes: A Guatemalan Journey of Courage, Terror, and Hope*. Berkeley: University of California Press.

Manz, Beatriz, Elizabeth Oglesby, and José García Noval. 1999. *De la memoria a la reconstrucción histórica*. Guatemala City: AVANCSO.

Marcus, George, ed. 1999. *Paranoia within Reason: A Casebook on Conspiracy as Explanation*. Chicago: University of Chicago Press.

Martín-Baró, Ignacio. 1989. "La institucionalización de la guerra." Paper presented at the XXII Congreso Internacional de Psicología, Buenos Aires.

Martínez Pelaez, Severo. 1985. *Motines de Indios: La violencia colonial en Centroamérica*. Puebla: Universidad Autónoma de Puebla.

———. 1990 (1970). *La Patria del Criollo: Ensayo de interpretación de la realidad colonial Guatemalteca*. Mexico City: Ediciones en Marcha.

Marx, Karl. 1977. *Capital*. Vol. 1. Trans. Ben Fowkes. New York: Vintage Books.

———. 1988 (1848). *Manifesto of the Communist Party*. Beijing: Foreign Languages Press.

———. 1993. *Grundrisse: Foundations of the Critique of Political Economy (Rough Draft)*. Trans. Martin Nicolaus. New York: Penguin Books with *New Left Review*.

Maurer, Bill M. 1997. *Recharting the Caribbean: Land, Law and Citizenship in the British Virgin Islands*. Ann Arbor: University of Michigan Press.

———. 2002a. "Repressed Futures: Financial Derivatives' Theological Unconscious." *Economy and Society* 31(1): 15–36.

———. 2002b. "Anthropological and Accounting Knowledge in Islamic Banking and

Finance: Rethinking Critical Accounts." *Journal of the Royal Anthropological Institute* (formerly *Man*), 8(4): 645–67.

———. 2005. *Mutual Life Limited: Islamic Banking, Alternative Currencies, Lateral Reason*. Princeton: Princeton University Press.

McAllister, Carlota. 2003. "Good People: Revolution, Community and Conciencia in a Maya-K'iche' Village in Guatemala." Ph.D. diss., Department of Anthropology, Johns Hopkins University.

McCreery, David. 1994. *Rural Guatemala. 1760–1940*. Stanford, Calif.: Stanford University Press.

McNeil, Donald G. 2000. "Hovering Where Rich and Poor Meet, the Mosquito." *New York Times*, C1–3.

———. 2003. "Malarial Treatment for Chinese AIDS Patients Prompts Inquiry in US." *New York Times*, March 4:D1.

Menchú Tum, Rigoberta. 1983. *I, Rigoberta Menchú: An Indian Woman in Guatemala*. Introduction by Elisabeth Burgos-Debray. Trans. Ann Wright. New York: Verso.

———. 1985. *Me llamo Rigoberta Menchú y así me nació la conciencia*, ed. Elisabeth Burgos-Debray. Mexico City: Siglo Veintiuno Editores.

———. 1993. "Introduction." *Guatemalan Women Speak*, ed. Margaret Hooks. Washington: EPICA.

———. 1998. *Crossing Borders*. London: Verso.

Mendoza, Carlos, and Edelberto Torres-Rivas, eds. 2003. *Linchamientos: ¿barbarie o "justicia popular"?* Guatemala City: Editorial de Ciencias Sociales.

Metcalf, Peter. 2002. *They Lie, We Lie: Getting on with Anthropology*. London: Routledge.

Meyer, Birgit, and Peter Pels. 2003. *Magic and Modernity: Interfaces of Revelation and Concealment*. Stanford, Calif.: Stanford University Press.

Mihm, Stephen. 2004. "Dumpster-Diving for Your Identity." *New York Times Magazine*, 42.

MINUGUA (U.N. Verification Mission). 2004. "Ninth and Final Report on Fulfillment of the Peace Accords in Guatemala." UN Publishing.

Montejo, Victor. 1987. *Testimony: Death of a Guatemalan Village*. Willimantic, Conn.: Curbstone Press.

———. 1993a. "The Dynamics of Cultural Resistance and Transformations: The Case of Guatemalan-Mayan Refugees in Mexico." Ph.D. diss., University of Connecticut.

———. 1993b. "In the Name of the Pot, the Sun, the Broken Spear, the Rock, the Stick, the Idol, Ad Infinitum and Ad Nauseam: An Exposé of Anglo Anthropologists' Obsessions with the Invention of Mayan Gods." *Red Pencil Review: A Journal of Native American Studies* 9(1):12–16.

———. 1999. *Voices from Exile: Violence and Survival in Modern Maya History*. Norman: University of Oklahoma Press.

Moore, Donald S. 2005. *Suffering for Territory: Race, Place, and Power in Zimbabwe*. Durham, N.C.: Duke University Press.

Moraga, Cherrie. 1983. *Loving in the War Years: Lo que Nunca Pasó por sus Labios*. Boston: South End Press.

Morales, Mario Roberto. 1992. "Editorial." *Prensa Libre*, December 15.

Murray, Timothy. 1993. *Like a Film: Ideological Fantasy on Screen, Cinema, and Canvas.* London: Routledge.

NACLA (North American Congress on Latin America). 1974. *Guatemala.* Berkeley, Calif.: NACLA.

Naipaul, V. S. 1981. *The Return of Eva Perón.* New York: Vintage.

Nash, June C. 2001. *Mayan Visions: The Quest for Autonomy in an Age of Globalization.* New York: Routledge.

Nelson, Diane M. 1999. *A Finger in the Wound: Body Politics in Quincentennial Guatemala.* Berkeley: University of California Press.

———. 2001a. "Stumped Identities: Body Image, Bodies Politic, and the *Mujer Maya* as Prosthetic." *Cultural Anthropology* 16(3) August: 303–13.

———. 2001b. "Phantom Limbs and Invisible Hands: Bodies, Prosthetics, and Late Capitalist Identities." Introduction to special issue, *Cultural Anthropology* 16(3) August: 314–53.

———. 2002. "Relating to Terror: Gender, Anthropology, Law, and Some September Elevenths." *Duke Journal of Gender Law and Policy* 9:101–18.

———. 2003. " 'The More You Kill, the More You Will Live': The Maya, 'Race,' and the Biopolitical Economy of Peace in Guatemala." In *Race, Nature, and the Politics of Difference*, ed. Donald Moore. Durham, N.C.: Duke University Press.

Nordstrom, Carolyn. 2006. *Shadows of War: Violence, Power, and International Profiteering in the Twenty-First Century.* Berkeley: University of California Press.

NotiCen. 2002. "Seeking the Secrets of Guatemala's Mystery Bonds." Latin American Data Base: Latin American Institute. Sept. 26.

NSA (National Security Archives). 1999. "Diario Militar." www.gwu.edu/~nsarchiv/latin_america/guatemala.html.

Oglesby, Elizabeth. 1995. "Myrna Mack." In *Fieldwork Under Fire: Contemporary Studies of Violence and Survival*, ed. Carolyn Nordstrom and Antonius C. G. M. Robben. Berkeley: University of California Press.

———. 2002. "Politics at Work: Elites, Labor and Agrarian Modernization in Guatemala, 1980–2000." Ph.D. diss., Department of Geography, University of California-Berkeley.

———. 2003. "Machos, Machetes and Migrants: Masculinities and the Dialectics of Labor Control in Guatemala." Paper presented at the SSRC Workshop "Translocal Flows, Migrations, Borders and Diasporas in the Americas." Santo Domingo, June 26–28.

———. 2004. "Historical Memory and the Limits of Peace Education: Examining Guatemala's 'Memory of Silence' and the Politics of Curriculum Design." Paper presented at the Carnegie Council on Ethics and International Affairs, New York.

Oppel, Richard A., Jr. 2004. "In Iraq, the Insurgency Has Two Faces, Secular and Jihad, but One Common Goal." *New York Times*, Dec. 19:A6.

Orr, Jackie. 2005. *Panic Diaries: Performing Terror in the Age of Technoscience.* Durham, N.C.: Duke University Press.

Osborne, Thomas. 1997. "Of Health and Statecraft." In *Foucault, Health and Medicine*, ed. Alan Peterson and Robin Bunton. London: Routledge.

Otzoy, Irma. 1996. "Maya Clothing and Identity." In *Maya Cultural Activism in Guate-*

mala, ed. Edward F. Fischer and R. McKenna Brown. Austin: University of Texas Press.

Ovalle Lopez, Werner. 1960. "Del día mundial de la salud: La erradicación del paludismo un reto al mundo." *El Imparcial*, April 8.

Parry, Jonathan. 1986. "*The Gift*, The Indian Gift and the 'Indian Gift.'" *Man* 21(3).

Paul, Benjamin, and William Demarest. 1988. "The Operation of a Death Squad in San Pedro." In *Harvest of Violence: The Mayan Indians and the Guatemalan Crisis*, ed. Robert Carmack. Norman: University of Oklahoma Press.

Paul, William. 1994. *Laughing, Screaming: Modern Horror and Comedy*. New York: Columbia University Press.

Payer, Cheryl. 1974. *The Debt Trap: The International Monetary Fund and the Third World*. New York: Monthly Review Press.

Payeras, Mario. 1997. *Los Pueblos Indígenas y la Revolución Guatemalteca: Ensayos Etnicos*. Guatemala City: Luna y Sol.

Peacock, Susan C., and Adriana Beltrán. 2003. *Hidden Powers in Post-Conflict Guatemala: Illegal Armed Groups and the Forces behind Them*. Washington: WOLA.

Peet, Richard. 2004. *Unholy Trinity: The IMF, World Bank and WTO*. New York: Zed Books.

Perkins, John. 2004. *Confessions of an Economic Hit Man*. San Francisco: Berrett-Koehler.

Peterson, Alan, and Robin Bunton, eds. 1997. *Foucault, Health and Medicine*. London: Routledge.

Petraeus, David. 2007. *U.S. Army/Marine Counterinsurgency Field Manual*. U.S. Army.

Peyser, Andrea. 2002. "Shameful Art Attack." *New York Post*, Sept. 18.

———. 2002. "Sick 9/11 Art Yanked." *New York Post*, Sept. 19.

Piel, Jean. 1989. *Sajcabajá: Muerte y resurrección de un pueblo de Guatemala 1500–1970*. Mexico City: Centre d'Etudes Mexicaines et Centroamericaines.

PNUD (UN Development Program). 2005. *Diversidad étnico-cultural: La ciudadanía en un estado plural. Informe nacional de desarrollo humano*. Guatemala City: UN Publishing.

Poole, Deborah. 2004. "Between Threat and Guarantee: Justice and Community in the Margins of the Peruvian State." In *Anthropology in the Margins of the State*, ed. Veena Das and Deborah Poole. Santa Fe: School of American Research.

Poovey, Mary. 1998. *A History of the Modern Fact: Problems of Knowledge in the Sciences of Wealth and Society*. Chicago: University of Chicago Press.

Power, Michael. 1997. *The Audit Society: Rituals of Verification*. Oxford: Oxford University Press.

Prakash, Gyan. 1999. *Another Reason: Science and the Imagination of Modern India*. Princeton: Princeton University Press.

Pratt, Mary Louise. 2001. "*I, Rigoberta Menchú* and the "Culture Wars." In *The Rigoberta Menchú Controversy*, ed. Arturo Arias. Minneapolis: University of Minnesota Press.

Price, David H. 2004. *Threatening Anthropology: McCarthyism and the FBI's Surveillance of Activist Anthropologists*. Durham, N.C.: Duke University Press.

Quintana, Epaminondas. 1964. "Guatemalense, si eres patriota no seas indolente, dá tu ayuda." *Imparcial*, Jan. 8.

Rabinow, Paul. 1989. *French Modern: Norms and Forms of the Social Environment*. Chicago: University of Chicago Press.

———. 1999. *French DNA: Trouble in Purgatory*. Chicago: University of Chicago Press.

Rahnema, Majid, with Victoria Bawtree. 1997. *The Post-Development Reader*. London: Zed Books.

Rajiva, Lila. 2005. *The Language of Empire: Abu Ghraib and the American Media*. New York: Monthly Review Press.

Randall, Margaret. 1985. *Testimonios: A Guide to Oral History*. Toronto: Participatory Research Group.

Reed, Thomas F., and Karen Brandow. 1996. *The Sky Never Changes: Testimonies from the Guatemalan Labor Movement*. Ithaca: Cornell University Press.

REMHI (Recuperation of Historic Memory Project). 1998. *Guatemala: Nunca Más*. 4 vols. Guatemala City: ODHA (Human Rights Office of the Archbishop of Guatemala).

Remijnse, Simone. 2001. "Remembering Civil Patrols in Joyabaj, Guatemala." *Bulletin of Latin American Research* 20(4): 454–69.

———. 2002. *Memories of Violence: Civil Patrols and the Legacy of Conflict in Joyabaj, Guatemala*. Amsterdam: Rozenberg.

Report on Guatemala. 2005. "Power, Impunity, and Wealth in the Military: Interview with Iduvina Hernández." *Report on Guatemala* 26(3): 6–8.

Revista de Critica Cultural. 2002. *Lo Popular: Pueblo, Masa, Gente, Multitud*. June, no. 24.

Ricks, Thomas E. 2006. *Fiasco: The American Military Adventure in Iraq*. New York: Penguin Press.

Riles, Annelise. 2001. *The Network Inside Out*. Ann Arbor: University of Michigan Press.

Robin, Corey. 2001. "Closet-Case Studies: The Rumors that Mohamed Atta Was–Well, You Know–Are Part of a Long American Tradition." *New York Times Magazine*, Dec. 16: 23–24.

———. 2004. *Fear: The History of a Political Idea*. Oxford: Oxford University Press.

Robinson, William I. 2004. "The New Right and the End of National Liberation." *NACLA Report on the Americas* 37(6): 14–20.

Robles Montayo, Rodolfo. 2002. *El 'poder oculto.'* Guatemala City: Myrna Mack Foundation.

Rocha, José Luis. 2004. "Se alquilan burócratas: La rentable industria de las consultorías." *Envío*, Dec., 25–30.

Rodríguez, Luisa. 2002. "Políticos califican de mentiroso a Portillo." *Prensa Libre*, May 6.

Rodríguez P., Martín. 2004. "EEUU molesto por genérico." *Prensa Libre*, Dec. 27:3.

Rohter, Larry. 1998. "Nobel Winner Finds Her Story Challenged." *New York Times*, Dec. 15:A1.

———. 2002. "Unseen Yet Seen, a World of Evil." *New York Times*, April 7: B25.

Ronell, Avital. 1989. *The Telephone Book: Technology, Schizophrenia, Electric Speech*. Lincoln: University of Nebraska Press.

Rosales O., Edgar Gabriel. 1999. "Ex Guerrillero se confiesa: delaté a compañeros del PGT." *Siglo Veintiuno*, Aug. 13.

Rose, Jacqueline. 1996. *States of Fantasy*. Oxford: Clarendon Press.

Rose, Nicholas. 1990. *Governing the Soul: The Shaping of the Private Self*. London: Routledge.

Rotman, Brian. 1987. *Signifying Nothing: The Semiotics of Zero*. Stanford, Calif.: Stanford University Press.

Rubin, Gayle. 1975. "The Traffic in Women: Notes on the Political Economy of Sex." In *Toward an Anthropology of Women*, ed. Rayna R. Reiter. New York: Monthly Review Press.

Ruse, Michael. 1999. *The Darwinian Revolution: Science Red in Tooth and Claw*. Chicago: University of Chicago Press.

Russell, Grahame. 2004. "Chixoy Dam Massacre Survivors versus Global Impunity." Sept. 13. info@rightsaction.org.

Sáenz de Tejada, Ricardo. 2004. *¿Victimas o vencedores? Una aproximación al movimiento de los ex-PAC*. Guatemala City: FLACSO.

Said, Edward W. 1978. *Orientalism*. New York: Vintage.

Saldaña-Portillo, María Josefina. 2003. *The Revolutionary Imagination in the Americas and the Age of Development*. Durham, N.C.: Duke University Press.

Sam Colop, Enrique. 1991. *Jub'aqtun Omay Kuchum K'aslemal, Cinco siglos de encubrimiento*. Guatemala City: CECMA.

———. 1996. "The Discourse of Concealment and 1992." In *Maya Cultural Activism in Guatemala*, ed. Edward F. Fischer and R. McKenna Brown. Austin: University of Texas Press.

Sanford, Victoria. 2001. "'It Fills My Heart with Sadness': Testimony, Memory, and the Healing of Fragmented Communities." Paper presented at the School of American Research, March.

———. 2003. *Buried Secrets: Truth and Human Rights in Guatemala*. New York: Palgrave Macmillan.

Sardar, Siauddin, and Merryl Wyn Davies. 2002. *Why Do People Hate America?* Cambridge: Icon Books.

Saqb'ichil-COPMAGUA. 2000. *Resumen de las acciones políticas y organizativas de las Comisiones Nacionales Permanentes*. Guatemala City: Departamento de Documentación y Sistematización Saqb'ichil-COPMAGUA.

Saul, Stephanie. 2005. "Drug Lobby Got a Victory in Trade Pact Vote." *New York Times*, July 2:B1, B13.

Sawyer, Suzana. 2004. *Crude Chronicles: Indigenous Politics, Multinational Oil, and Neoliberalism in Ecuador*. Durham, N.C.: Duke University Press.

Scarry, Elaine. 1985. *The Body in Pain: The Making and Unmaking of the World*. Oxford: Oxford University Press.

Schacter, D., ed. 1995. *Memory Distortion: How Minds, Brains and Societies Reconstruct the Past*. Cambridge, Mass.: Harvard University Press.

Schedler, Andreas, Larry Diamond, and Marc F. Plattner. 1999. *The Self-Restraining State: Power and Accountability in New Democracies*. Boulder: Lynne Reiner Press.

Schirmer, Jennifer. 1998. *The Guatemalan Military Project: A Violence Called Democracy*. Philadelphia: University of Pennsylvania Press.

Schmitt, Eric. 2005. "Rebels Said to Have Pool of Bomb-Rigged Cars." *New York Times*, May 5:A11.

Schwartz, Hillel. 1996. *The Culture of the Copy: Striking Likenesses, Unreasonable Facsimiles*. New York: Zone Books.

Scott, James C. 1987. *Weapons of the Weak: Everyday Forms of Peasant Resistance*. New Haven: Yale University Press.

———. 1998. *Seeing Like a State: How Certain Schemes to Improve the Human Condition Have Failed*. New Haven: Yale University Press.

Seider, Rachel, ed. 1998. *Guatemala after the Peace Accords*. London: Institute of Latin American Studies.

Shah, Sonia. 2002. "Globalizing Clinical Research: Big Pharma Tries Out First World Drugs on Unsuspecting Third World Patients." *The Nation*, July 1: 23–28.

Shaviro, Steven. 1993. *The Cinematic Body*. Minneapolis: University of Minnesota Press.

Silver, Sara. 2003. "Guatemalan 'Peace Bond' Causes Alarm." *Financial Times*, Jan. 8.

Silverblatt, Irene. 2004. *Modern Inquisitions: Peru and the Colonial Origins of the Civilized World*. Durham, N.C.: Duke University Press.

Silverman, Kaja. 1983. *The Subject of Semiotics*. New York: Oxford University Press.

Sluka, Jeffrey A. 2000. *Death Squad: The Anthropology of State Terror*. Philadelphia: University of Pennsylvania Press.

Smith, Carol A. 1990. *Guatemalan Indians and the State: 1540 to 1988*. Austin: University of Texas Press.

———. 1996. "Myths, Intellectuals, and Race/Class/Gender Distinctions in the Formation of Latin American Nations." *Journal of Latin American Anthropology* 2(1).

———. n.d. "Marxists on Class and Culture in Guatemala." Paper presented at LASA, Los Angeles, 1992.

Smith, James. 2005. "Sociedad civil cuestiona nueva estrategia del Banco Mundial." *INFORPRESS*, June 3: 8–9.

Solano, Luis. 2005. *Guatemala, petróleo y minería en las entrañas del poder*. Guatemala City: INFORPRESS.

Sommer, Doris. 1996. "No Secrets." In *The Real Thing: Testimonial Discourse and Latin America*, ed. Georg M. Gugelberger. Durham, N.C.: Duke University Press.

Spence, Jack, David R. Dye, Paula Worby, Carmen Rosa de León-Escribano, George Vickers, and Mike Lanchin. 1998. *Promise and Reality: Implementation of the Guatemalan Peace Accords*. Cambridge, Mass.: Hemisphere Initiatives.

Spielman, Andrew, and Michael D'Antonio. 2001. *Mosquito: The Story of Man's Deadliest Foe*. New York: Hyperion.

Spivak, Gayatri. 1988a. "Can the Subaltern Speak?" In *Marxism and the Interpretation of Culture*, ed. Cary Nelson and Lawrence Grossberg. Urbana: University of Illinois Press.

———. 1988b. *In Other Worlds: Essays in Cultural Politics*. New York: Routledge.

Starn, Orin. 1991. "Missing the Revolution: Anthropologists and the War in Peru." *Cultural Anthropology* 6(1) Feb.:63–91.

———. 1999. *Nightwatch: The Politics of Protest in the Andes*. Durham, N.C.: Duke University Press.

———. 2004. *Ishi's Brain: In Search of America's Last "Wild" Indian*. New York: Norton.

Stepan, Nancy Leys. 1991. *"The Hour of Eugenics": Race, Gender, and Nation in Latin America*. Ithaca: Cornell University Press.

Stepputat, Finn. 2001. "Urbanizing the Countryside: Armed Conflict, State Formation, and the Politics of Place in Contemporary Guatemala." In *States of Imagination: Ethnographic Explorations of the Postcolonial State*, eds. Thomas Hansen and Finn Stepputat. Durham, N.C.: Duke University Press.

Stewart, Kathleen. 1999. "Conspiracy Theory's Worlds." In *Paranoia Within Reason: A Casebook on Conspiracy as Explanation*, ed. George E. Marcus. Chicago: University of Chicago Press.

Stocking, George. 1982 (1968). *Race, Culture, and Evolution: Essays in the History of Anthropology*. Chicago: University of Chicago Press.

Stoler, Ann. 1995. *Race and the Education of Desire: Foucault's* History of Sexuality *and the Colonial Order of Things*. Durham, N.C.: Duke University Press.

Stoll, David. 1988. "Evangelicals, Guerrillas, and the Army: The Ixil Triangle under Ríos Montt." In *Harvest of Violence: The Mayan Indians and the Guatemalan Crisis*, ed. Robert Carmack. Norman: University of Oklahoma Press.

———. 1990. *Is Latin America Turning Protestant? The Politics of Evangelical Growth*. Berkeley: University of California Press.

———. 1993. *Between Two Armies in the Ixil Towns of Guatemala*. New York: Columbia University Press.

———. 1999a. *Rigoberta Menchú and the Story of All Poor Guatemalans*. Boulder: Westview Press.

———. 1999b. Letter to the Editor. *Lingua Franca*, Oct. 9: 7.

Stoltz Chinchilla, Norma, ed. 1998. *Nuestras utopías: Mujeres guatemaltecas del siglo XX*. Guatemala City: Tierra Viva, Agrupación de Mujeres.

Stone, Allucquere Rosanne. 1995. *The War of Desire and Technology at the Close of the Mechanical Age*. Cambridge, Mass.: MIT Press.

Strange, Susan. 1998. *Mad Money: When Markets Outgrow Governments*. Ann Arbor: University of Michigan Press.

Strathern, Marilyn, ed. 2000. *Audit Cultures: Anthropological Studies in Accountability, Ethics, and the Academy*. London: Routledge.

Sunder Rajan, Kaushik. 2005. "Subjects of Speculation: Emergent Life Sciences and Market Logics in the United States and India." *American Anthropologist* 107(1): 19–30.

Taracena Arriola, Arturo, ed. 2002. *Etnicidad, Estado y nación en Guatemala, 1808–1944*. Vol. 1, Colección ¿Porqué estamos como estamos? Antigua, Guatemala: CIRMA.

———. 2003. *Etnicidad, Estado y nación en Guatemala, 1944–2000*. Vol. 2, Colección ¿Porqué estamos como estamos? Antigua, Guatemala: CIRMA.

Taussig, Michael. 1980. *The Devil and Commodity Fetishism in South America*. Chapel Hill: University of North Carolina Press.

———. 1987. *Shamanism, Colonialism, and the Wild Man: A Study in Terror and Healing*. Chicago: University of Chicago Press.

———. 1992. *The Nervous System*. New York: Routledge.

———. 1997. *The Magic of the State*. New York: Routledge.

———. 1999. *Defacement: Public Secrecy and the Labor of the Negative*. Stanford, Calif.: Stanford University Press.

Taylor, Clark. 1998. *Return of Guatemala's Refugees: Reweaving the Torn*. Philadelphia: Temple University Press.

Tedlock, Barbara. 1992. *Time and the Highland Maya*. Albuquerque: University of New Mexico Press.

Tedlock, Dennis. 1993. *Breath on the Mirror: Mythic Voices and Visions of the Living Maya*. San Francisco: Harper.

Tenet, George, and Bill Harlow. 2007. *At the Center of the Storm: My Years at the CIA*. New York: HarperCollins.

Thompson, Ginger. 2005. "U.S. to Lift Ban on Military Aid to Guatemala." *New York Times*, March 25.

Transparency International. 2004. *Global Corruption Report 2004: Special Focus: Political Corruption*. London: Pluto Press.

Treichler, Paula A. 1999. *How to Have Theory in an Epidemic: Cultural Chronicles of AIDS*. Durham, N.C.: Duke University Press.

Trinh T., Minh-ha. 1986. "She, the Inappropriated Other." *Discourse* 8.

———. 1989. *Woman, Native, Other: Writing Postcoloniality and Feminism*. Bloomington: Indiana University Press.

Trouillot, Michel-Rolph. 1991. "Anthropology and the Savage Slot: The Poetics and Politics of Otherness." In *Recapturing Anthropology*, ed. R. G. Fox. Santa Fe: School of American Research.

Turnbull, David. 2000. *Masons, Tricksters, and Cartographers*. Amsterdam: Harwood Academic.

Turner, Patricia. 1993. *I Heard It Through the Grapevine: Rumor in African-American Culture*. Berkeley: University of California Press.

Tylor, Edward B. 1871. *Primitive Culture*. London: J. Murray.

UN (United Nations). 2004. "Acuerdo entre las Naciones Unidas y el Gobierno de Guatemala relativo al establecimiento de una Comisión de Investigación de los Cuerpos Ilegales y Aparatos Clandestinos de Seguridad." UN Publishing.

URNG. 1988. *El pensamiento político de la URNG: Selección de textos Febrero 1982–Febrero 1988*. Guatemala City: URNG.

Valenzuela, Luisa. 1983. *The Lizard's Tail*. New York: Farrar, Straus, Giroux.

Van Natta Jr., Don, and Elaine Sciolino. 2005. "Police Debate if London Plotters Were Suicide Bombers, or Dupes." *New York Times*, July 27:A1, A6.

Velásquez, Leidy. 2004a. "Nueva incertidumbre ante pago de ex patrulleros." *INFORPRESS*, Oct. 15: 4.

———. 2004b. "El círculo vicioso de los ex PAC." *INFORPRESS*, Nov. 12: 4.

Velásquez Nimatuj, Irma Alicia. 2005. "Pueblos Indígenas, estado y lucha por tierra." Ph.D. diss., Anthropology Department, University of Texas, Austin.

Verdugo Urrejola, Juan Carlos. 2007. "La política y reforma del sector salud en Guatemala 1986–2000: Del estado desperfecto al mercado imperfecto." In *En el umbral: Explorando Guatemala en el inicio del siglo veintiuno*, ed. Clara Arenas Bianchi. Guatemala City: AVANCSO.

Verran, Helen. 2001. *Science and an African Logic*. Chicago: University of Chicago Press.

Virilio, Paul, and Sylvére Lotringer. 1983. *Pure War*. Trans. Mark Polizzotti. New York: Semiotext(e).

Vogt, Evan Z. 1990 (1970). *The Zinacantecos of Mexico: A Modern Maya Way of Life*. Fort Worth: Harcourt Brace Jovanovich.

Warren, Kay. 1978. *The Symbolism of Subordination: Indian Identity in a Guatemalan Town*. Austin: University of Texas Press.

———. 1993. "Interpreting *La Violencia* in Guatemala: Shapes of Mayan Silence and Resistance." In *The Violence Within: Cultural and Political Opposition in Divided Nations*, ed. Kay Warren. Boulder: Westview Press.

———. 1998. *Indigenous Movements and Their Critics: Pan-Maya Activism in Guatemala*. Princeton: Princeton University Press.

———. 1999. "Decir verdades: Tomando en serio a David Stoll y al exposé sobre Rigoberta Menchú." *Debate Feminista* 20.

———. 2000. "Death Squads and Wider Complicities." In *Death Squad, the Anthropology of State Terror*, ed. J. Sluka. Philadelphia: University of Pennsylvania Press.

———. 2002. "Voting Against Indigenous Rights in Guatemala: Lessons from the 1999 Referendum." In *Indigenous Movements, Self-Representation, and the State in Latin America*, eds. Jean Jackson and Kay Warren. Austin: University of Texas Press.

Warren, Kay, and Jean Jackson, eds. 2002. *Indigenous Movements, Self-Representation, and the State in Latin America*. Austin: University of Texas Press.

Watanabe, John. 1999. Letter to the Editor. *Chronicle of Higher Education*, Feb. 12.

Webster's. 1980. *New World Dictionary of the American Language*. Second College Edition, ed. David B. Gutalnik. New York: Simon and Schuster.

Weiner, Tim. 1995. "A Guatemalan Colonel and a C.I.A. Connection." *New York Times*, March 26:A6.

———. 1996. "Records Tie C.I.A. Informer to Two Guatemala Killings." *New York Times*, May 7.

———. 1997. "The Spy Agency's Many Mean Ways to Loosen Cold-War Tongues." *New York Times*, Feb. 9:C7.

Weismantel, Mary. 2001. *Cholas and Pishtacos: Stories of Race and Sex in the Andes*. Chicago: University of Chicago Press.

West, Harry G., and Todd Sanders, eds. 2003. *Transparency and Conspiracy: Ethnographies of Suspicion in the New World Order*. Durham, N.C.: Duke University Press.

Whetstone, Trevor. 1999. "A Fraud Lurks in Academia." *Miami Student* (Oxford, Ohio), March 30.

White, Hayden. 1978. *Tropics of Discourse: Essays in Cultural Criticism*. Baltimore: Johns Hopkins University Press.

Wilford, John Noble. 2001. "DNA Shows Malaria Helped Topple Rome." *New York Times*, Feb. 20: D1, D4.

Wilkinson, Daniel. 2002. *Silence on the Mountain: Stories of Terror, Betrayal, and Forgetting in Guatemala*. Boston: Houghton Mifflin.

Williams, Brackette F. 1991. *Stains on My Name, War in My Veins: Guyana and the Politics of Cultural Survival*. Durham, N.C.: Duke University Press.

Williams, Linda. 2002. "Learning to Scream." *Horror: The Film Reader*, ed. Mark Jancovich. London: Routledge.

Williams, Raymond. 1977. *Marxism and Literature*. Oxford: Oxford University Press.

Williams-Forson, Psyche. 2006. *Building Houses Out of Chicken Legs: Black Women, Food, and Power*. Chapel Hill: University of North Carolina Press.

Wilson, Richard. 1995. *Maya Resurgence in Guatemala: Q'eqchi' Experience*. Norman: University of Oklahoma Press.

Wilson, Robin. 1999. "A Multicultural Icon under Fire: Many Professors Will Stick by a Book Whose Veracity Is Now Doubted." *Chronicle of Higher Education*, Jan. 15: A14–A16.

Winik, Lyric Wallwork. 2004. "What's In a Name?" *Parade Magazine*, Nov. 28: 21.

Worby, Paula. 2002a. "Changes and Opportunities Wrought by Exile and Repatriation: New Identities among Guatemalan Refugee Women." In *Ethnic Conflict: Religion, Identity, and Politics*, ed. S. A. Giannakos. Athens: Ohio University Press.

———. 2002b. *Los refugiados retornados guatemaltecos y el acceso a la tierra: Resultados, lecciones y perspectivas*. Guatemala City: AVANCSO.

Wright, Melissa. 2001. "Desire and the Prosthetics of Supervision: A Case of Maquiladora Flexibility." *Cultural Anthropology* 16(3): 354–73.

Yezer, Carolyn. 2007. "Anxious Citizens: Insecurity, Apocalypse and War Memories in Peru's Andes." Ph.D. diss., Department of Cultural Anthropology, Duke University.

Young, Robert J. C. 1995. *Colonial Desire: Hybridity in Theory, Culture, and Race*. London: Routledge.

Zilberg, Elana. 2007. "Gangster in Guerrilla Face: A Transnational Mirror of Production between the USA and El Salvador." *Anthropological Theory* 3(7): 37–57.

Žižek, Slavoj. 1989. *The Sublime Object of Ideology*. London: Verso.

———. 1992. *Enjoy Your Symptom! Jacques Lacan in Hollywood and Out*. New York: Routledge.

Zur, Judith. 1998. *Violent Memories: Mayan War Widows in Guatemala*. Boulder: Westview Press.

FILMS CITED

American Pimp. 1999. Allen Hughes and Albert Hughes, dirs. MGM/UA Studio.

Bamboozled. 2000. Spike Lee, dir. New Line Home Entertainment.

Bowling for Columbine. 2002. Michael Moore, dir. Metro Goldwyn Mayer.

Buffy the Vampire Slayer (film). 2001. Fran Rubel Kuzui, dir. Twentieth Century Fox.

Buffy the Vampire Slayer (television series, seven seasons). 2003. Joss Whedon, dir. 20th Century Fox Entertainment.

Candyman. 2004. Bernard Rose, dir. TriStar Pictures and Polygram Filmed Entertainment.

Crazy Safari. 1991. Billy Chan Wui Ngai, dir. Hong Kong Samico Films.

Death Squadrons: The French School. 2003. Marie-Monique Robin, dir. First Run / Icarus Films.

Dirty Secrets: Jennifer, Everardo and the CIA in Guatemala. 1998. Patrica Goudvis, dir. New Day Films.

Discovering Dominga. 2002. Patricia Flynn, dir. Jaguar House Films, University of California Center for Media and Independent Learning.

F for Fake. 2005. Orson Welles, dir. Janus Films, Home Vision Entertainment.

Fahrenheit 911. 2004. Michael Moore, dir. Lions Gate Films, IFC.

Fahrenhype 911. 2004. Alan Peterson, dir. Trinity Home Entertainment.

Forbidden Planet. 1999. Fred Wilcox, dir. Metro Goldwyn Mayer.

The Gods Must Be Crazy. 1986. Jamie Uys, dir. Columbia TriStar Home Entertainment.

Hidden in Plain Sight. 2002. John Smihula, dir. Raven's Call Production.

Lawrence of Arabia. 1962. David Lean, dir. Columbia Pictures.

Life of Brian. 1999. Terry Jones, dir. Monty Python, Paragon Entertainment.

Live Nude Girls Unite! 2001. Julia Query, dir. First Run/Icarus Films.

Matrix. 1999. Warchowski brothers, dir. Warner Brothers.

No hay cosa oculta que no venga a descubrirse: La tragedia de Santa María Tzejá/There Is Nothing Hidden That Will Not Be Uncovered. 1999. Guatemala City: Comunicarte/ Arte y Comunicación.

Nueve Reinas / Nine Queens. 2000. Fabian Bielinksy, dir. Argentina: Patagonik Film Group.

Poison. 1999. Todd Haynes, dir. Fox Lorber Home Video.

Semblanza de una profeta/Portrait of a Prophet. 1999. Guatemala City: Comunicarte/ Arte y Comunicación.

They Live. 2003. John Carpenter, dir. Universal Studios.

Tough Guise. 2002 (1999). Sut Jhally, dir. Media Education Foundation.

Undercover Brother. 2002. Malcolm D. Lee, dir. Universal Pictures.

Videodrome. 1983. David Cronenberg, dir. Universal Studios.

Wizard of Oz. 1939. Victor Fleming, dir. Metro-Goldwyn-Mayer Pictures.

Page numbers in italics refer to illustrations.

Argueta, Antonio, 259
Aristotle, 242
army. *See* military
Army Day parade, 79–80, *81*
art, 115–18
articulation, 45–46, 54, 61, 322–23
ASC (Civil Society Assembly), 229, 230
Asij Chile, Efraín, 301
assumptions of identity: in anthropology, 27–28; Christianity and, 34; cons and, 284; duplicity, relation to, 27; experts and, 124; ex-stasis of, 148; in films, 35–38; fraud and investment and, 118; gender and ethnicity, 183; of government, 42–43; as gringa or gringo, 22, 136, 147; interpellation, 35, 47, 67; jokes and, 138; ladinization, 341n15; ladino, 170; Lamarckianism and, 274; as Maya, 175–78, 182–86, 189, 327n2, 348n11; Menchú Tum and, 128, 133–35; milieu and, 56; NGOs and, 226; pleasure and, 24, 28; of political actor, 60; against power, 10; racists stereotypes and, 140–41; as revolutionary, 166; stamps and, 289; subjectivization and, xvi–xvii; for survival, 29; suspicion and, 27; three modes of, 32, 131; traversing and, 151; unstable selves and, 141–43; zero and, 316. *See also* identification
Asturias, Rodrigo (aka Gaspar Ilom), 141, 191
audiences, 111
audit: aid, decrease in, 306–10; auditor as duped, 322–23; balance concept, 310–14, 318; corruption charges and, 48–49; as culture, 293–96; Ex-PAC and, 299–302; human subjects and, 296–97; Maurer on, 52; MINUGUA and, 297–99; reparations and, 302–6; 357n10; social processes of, 338n28. *See also* accounting; corruption
Austen, Jane, 345n20
authenticity, xvii, 134, 158
authentification, 28
AVANCSO (Association for the Advancement of Social Science in Guatemala), 55, 65–66, 174
AVEMILGUA (Asociación de Veteranos Militares de Guatemala), 213

babosada (foolish things): collective action as, 9; counterinsurgency discourse of, 57–58, 62, 173, 231; rebellion as, 8
"backwardness," 277
Baile de la Culebra (Dance of the Snake), 4; animal impersonators in, 330n2; description of, 2–3; doubling over in, 3, 8, 123, 199, 290; identi-ties and, 9–10; La Malinche and, 158; ledger book, 292; as *Tz'ul*, 24, 31; during war, 13
Baile de Palo, 1–2, *2*
bailes and Maya identity, 176
Bakhtin, Mikhail, xxx
balance, 310–14, 318
Balsells Tojo, Alfredo, 342n2
Bámaca Velásquez, Efraín (aka Everardo), 63–66, 141
Bamboozled (film), 156–61, 199–200, 349n4
Banco Metropolitano, 222
Bastos, Santiago, 357n13
Bataille, Georges, 86, 99
Beans and Bullets (Frijoles y Fusiles), 23, 42, 256
Benjamin, Walter, xvii, 91, 116, 206
Berger, Oscar, 52–53, 54, 233–34, 297, 298–99, 300, 337n14
Bernstein, Eduard, 152
Beverly, John, 343n5
Bhabha, Homi, 68, 139, 148–49, 290
Bielinksy, Fabian, 285, 356n1
biopolitics: Foucault's theory of power and, 244, 252–59; Larmarckianism and, 271, 278; war against malaria and, 259–70
blood: horror and, 39, 82, 172; in horror films, 74, 83, 89, 113; in Mack murder, 87; malaria and, 247, 260–65; one drop rule, 345n1; river of, 97, 350n6,

guerrillas: executions by, 186–87, 188; indigenous relations, 179–80; Lamarckianism and, 276–77; Mayan, disidentification with, 186; responsibility of, 291; Stoll on, 132, 134; unknowing involvement in, 187–88. *See also* EGP; FAR; ORPA; popular movement; URNG

Guha, Ranajit, 201, 331n7

Gupta, Akhil, 10–11, 54, 223, 347n7

Gutiérrez, Andrés, 184

Gutiérrez, Edgar: CICG and, 233; decision of, to work in government, 70, 205; description of, 69; Ex-PAC and, 213, 300; NGOs and, 151, 338n28; reparations and, 303

Hale, Charles, 257–58, 329n16, 355n22, 355n24

Haley, Brian D., 135, 345n19

Hall, Stuart, 91, 340n5

Halloween (film), 105, 110

Hampton, Fred, 201, 349n6

Hansen, Thomas Blom, 208, 350n2

Haraway, Donna, xix, 1, 30, 129, 130, 245

Harbury, Jennifer, 63–66, 121

Harper, Richard, 294–95, 310, 338n28

Harvey, David, 4, 5, 288, 294, 328n9

Hawkins, Joan, 94

health promoters, 242–43

Hegel, G. W. F., 67

Heimlich, Henry, 352n5

Hernández, Iduvina, 232

Hernández, Manuel, 181, 236

Hernández Ixcoy, Domingo, 20–21, 228

Hernández Mack, Lucrecia, 291–92

Hernández Pico, Juan, 231–32, 237

Hernández-Salazar, Daniel, 77

heroes and heroines, 105–6, 109–10

Herrera, Julio, 12, 286

Herzfeld, Michael, 295

HIJOS (sons and daughters), 79

hijos de la guerra (children of the war), 16

"history" vs. memory, 108

Hofstadter, Richard, 202

hooks, bell, 29

Horowitz, David, 128

horror, mechanisms of: embodimeant and, 95; horror films and, 80, 85, 103, 105; REMHI report on, xxii, *xxii*, 87

horror films: anthropology and, 87–89, 114; appeal of, 90–91, 104, 113; boundary transgressions and subject formation in, 102–6; as comemoration, 80–85; elite reactions to, 90; embodimeant and, 94–95, 98–100, 340n8; enjoymeant and, 339n4; Final Girl figure in, 105–6, 107, 111; fluidity of identity and, 109–14; folklore and, 342n17; in Joyabaj, 89, 95; Joyabaj video salons and, 340n9; memory vs. history and, 106–8; monsters and, 202; popular culture and, 91–93; possession and, 24; sequels to, xxiv; on Sexta Avenida, 89; in United States, 339n2. *See also under specific titles*

Hughes, Albert, 282–83, 356n3

Hughes, Allen, 282–83, 356n3

Human Rights Ombuds Office (PDH), 298, 357n7

Huntington, Samuel, 355n20

Hurston, Zora Neale, 335n9

Hutcheson, Maury, 25, 179, 185, 328n5

I, Rigoberta Menchú (Menchú Tum), 126–27, 146. *See also* Menchú Tum, Stoll's allegations against

identification: as assumption, 32; horror and fluidity of, 109–14; as indigenous, 19; linguistic divisions and, 22–23; as Maya, 107–8; in Mayan cosmologies, 19; power inequalities, 55–56. *See also* assumptions of identity

identi-ties: clandestinity and, 187; counterinsurgency and, 68; definition of, 9; to nonlocal forces, 178; state-related, 71; to transnational networks, 308

ideological state apparatuses (ISAs), 42

ladinos (*continued*)
179, 333n21; military, acceptance of, 340n10; as nonindigenous, 22. *See also* race and ethnicity
Lamarck, Jean-Baptiste de Monet de, 271
Lamarckianism, 271–78, 323, 355n17, 355n20
land reform, 6, 260
land tenure inequalities, 307
Langer, Marie, 27
language, 22–23, 168, 169
Lanuza Martínez, Rafael, 81
Lara, Pepe, 252, 256–57
Lares Ciprian, Tomás, 15
Larium (mefloquine), 352n4
LaRue, Frank, 233, 337n14
Latham, Rob, 198
Latour, Bruno, 46–47, 54, 234–35, 244, 247–51, 268–69, 270, 278
Lawrence of Arabia (film), 349n8
Lee, Benjamin, 317–19
Lee, Bruce, xxxi, 30, 224, 329n18
Lee, Spike, 156–61, 199–200, 202–3, 345n1, 349nn3–4
lesbigay movement, 336n10
Letelier, Orlando, 201, 349n6
Lévi-Strauss, Claude, 87, 138, 332n11
Lewontin, Richard, 274–75
liberation theology, 57, 126, 344n14
libreto de jornaleros, 331n4
Life of Brian (film), 353n6
Ligas Campesinas (Peasant Leagues), 57
Lincoln, Abraham, 302, 357n9
Linder, R. Ruth, 139
Linebaugh, Peter, 203
linkages of power, 62–63
LiPuma, Edward, 317–19
Lizard Queen, 194, 195–96
Lopez, Aníbal, 79
López, Fernando, 305
Lucas García, Romeo, 23, 348n14
Lux Cotí, Otilia, 123, 149, 164, 165, 188–89, 275, 290
Luxemburg, Rosa, 4, 42, 152
lynchings, 15, 166–67, 213–16, *216*

Mack, Helen, 62–63, *63*, 65–66, 121
Mack, Myrna: apology over, 53, 55, 291–92; assassination of, 55, 61, 66, 87; background of, 56–57; biography of, 173–74; body of, meanings of, 61–62; commemoration of, 71, *72*, 76; court cases, 65, 66–67; *Dónde Está el Futuro?*, 58–59; Menchú Tum on, 54
Madonna, 29
Madre Selva (Mother Jungle), 45
malaria: basic reproduction number (BRN) and, 353n9; biopolitics and, 249–51; in Calcutta Chromosome, 246; Copenhagen Consensus and, 354n16; Lamarckianism and, 274; psychosis from drugs for, 352n4; SNEM and war against, 259–70, 278–79, 353n11, 354n13; stamps, *269*, 288; as therapy, 352n5; in United States, 353n10
Malcolm X, 158
mal de ojo ("evil eye"), 20
Malinche, La, 158, 283
Malinowski, Bronislaw, 25
Manz, Beatriz, 82–83, 328n8
"maquila science," 248
Marcus, George, 201
Martín-Baró, Ignacio, xix
Martínez Pelaez, Severo, 11, 341n15
Marx, Karl, 27, 238, 313–14, 319
masquerades, 25
Matrix (film), xix, 36, 199, 335n8. *See also* Agent Smith; Neo
Maurer, Bill, 33, 52, 334n1
Maxe, 3, *4*
Maximon, aka San Simón, 346n1
Maya: anthropologists' obsession with exotic beliefs of, 333n19; as assumption of identity, 175–78, 182–86, 189, 327n2, 348n11; cosmologies of, 19; guerilla, disidentification with, 186; indigenous rights movement and, 21–22; naming and, 140–41, 344n16; NGOs and, 228; past and identity of, 107–8; religion of, 167–68, 182; repa-

model villages, 143, *173*. *See also* Development Poles

modernity: expectations of, 198, 202; laboratories of, 244, 247, 311, 323; Lamarckianism and, 273; modernization and, 169; torture and, 34

Moffit, Roni, 201, 349n6

Molina, Diego, 11

Momostenango, 20, 25, 158

money: exchange rates, 318, 358n20; imaginary, 316–17; value of, 238; xenomoney, 317, 319, 325. *See also* accounting; audit

Monsanto, Pablo (aka Jorge Soto), 191

monsters, 203–4

Montejo, Victor, 140, 219, 299, 333n19

Monty Python, 125, 334n1, 353n6

monuments. *See* co-memoration and memorializing

Moore, Michael, 197–200, 202–3, 206, 346n2

Morales, Jorge, 301–2

Morán, Rolando (aka Ricardo Ramírez), 191

mosquitoes, 246, 278–79, 351n1

Motagua River, 352n1

Mouffe, Chantal, 45–46

movies. *See* films

Myrna Mack Foundation, 62

name of the father. See *nom du père*

naming: activism and, 5–6; of disappeared, 15–16, *17*; politics of, 139–41, 344n15, 345n16, 345n17; racist restrictions on, 356n4

na'ooj, 341n13

Nash, June, 287

Natareno, Felip, 189–91

National Cathedral, 76

National Palace, Guatemala City, 75–76

National University, 228–29

naturales, 166, 172

Nelson, Erika, 345n16, 357n11

Neo, xix, 198, 205. See also *Matrix* (film)

networking, 46, 62, 244, 308

New York City, 86

New York Times, 126, 349n3

NGOs (nongovernmental organizations), 209–11, *210*, 225–30, 308–9

Nicaragua, 58

9/11/01, 86

Nine Queens (*Nueve Reinas*) (film), 280–85, 288, 356nn1–2

Nixon, Richard, 8

Noack, Otto, 337n13

Nobel Prize, 44–45, 76, 127, 137

Nobel savage, 198

No hay cosa oculta que no venga a descubrirse (There is Nothing Hidden that Will Not Be Discovered) (play and film), 82–83, 339n3

nom du père (name of the father): accounting and, 49; definition of, xxvii; duping and, 155; as nonduped err, 153; as patronymic, 140; pimping and, 283; state and, 175, 237

noms de guerre, 141

nonduped: cons and, 281; erring, xxvii, 149–55, 286; Stoll's politics of, 135–36, 145

non du père (no of the father), 9, 49

Noriega, Cándido, 15

"No Todas las Plagas" (Not All the Afflictions) cartoon, 209–11, *210*

Novella, Enrique, 232

Nuilá, Hector, xvi, 165–66, 193

Nunca Más (Never Again): Gerardi and, 77; REMHI report, xxii, *xxii*, 50, *51*, 67, 77, *78*

Ogáldez, Fredy, 190, 347n4

Ogáldez, Leonel, 15

Ogáldez, Rogélio and Próspero, 179, 347n4

Oglesby, Elizabeth, 66, 121, 220, 350n9

Oliva Carrera, Juan Guillermo, 65

Opus Dei, 62, 337n20

Organizations the Pueblo Maya del Valle, 301–2

ORPA (Revolutionary Organization of the People in Arms), 64, 141, 165, 182, 193, 247, 338n23

DIANE M. NELSON is associate professor of cultural
anthropology at Duke University.

LIBRARY OF CONGRESS
CATALOGING-IN-PUBLICATION DATA

Nelson, Diane M., 1963–
Reckoning : the ends of war in Guatemala / Diane M. Nelson.
p. cm.
Includes bibliographical references and index.
ISBN 978-0-8223-4341-7 (cloth : alk. paper)
ISBN 978-0-8223-4324-0 (pbk. : alk. paper)
1. Guatemala — History — Civil War, 1960–1996 — Peace.
2. Guatemala — History — 1985–
3. Guatemala — Politics and government — 1985–
I. Title.
F1466.7.N45 2009
972.8105'3 — dc22
2008055246

Nelson Chapter 6 Questions:

1. On page 217 Nelson states "The imbrication of class, kinship and ethnicity in a primarily extractive economy has produced one of the most unequal divisions of wealth and one of the most retrograde upper castes in Latin America." Explain the unequal divisions of wealth. How do the elite feel about their taxes? (217-219)

2. The people of Joyabaj go to the coast to work. Why is their work considered *trabajo regalado*? (219-220)

3. How are drugs used with the workers? What else are the *finqueros* guilty of? (220-221)

4. "Guatemala plants the seeds and cultivates them, and another country enjoys the harvest." (223) How has migration affected Guatemalans and their economy? What are the struggles the immigrants face in their journey north? (223-225)

5. How have NGO's helped the Guatemalan people?(225-226) In the story told on pages 226-227 how did *los jefes* ask for aid?

6. Nelson discusses "the fears of being acted on *by* NGOs"(228) and also "the hidden agendas of NGOs" (229) what does she mean by this? (228-230)

7. On page 232 how does the military get money and what are the army's public and private financial resources?